ISBN: 9781313513395

Published by:
HardPress Publishing
8345 NW 66TH ST #2561
MIAMI FL 33166-2626

Email: info@hardpress.net
Web: http://www.hardpress.net

CORNELL
UNIVERSITY
LIBRARY

BOUGHT WITH THE INCOME
OF THE SAGE ENDOWMENT
FUND GIVEN IN 1891 BY
HENRY WILLIAMS SAGE

DATE DUE

OCT 3 1963 K P			
JUN 1 4 1965			
FEB 28 1974 S			
OCT 26 1974 S			
GAYLORD			PRINTED IN U.S.A.

Cornell University Library
HB171 .W63

The common sense of political economy, i

3 1924 030 395 606

olin

THE
COMMON SENSE OF POLITICAL ECONOMY

MACMILLAN AND CO., Limited
LONDON · BOMBAY · CALCUTTA
MELBOURNE

THE MACMILLAN COMPANY
NEW YORK · BOSTON · CHICAGO
ATLANTA · SAN FRANCISCO

THE MACMILLAN CO. OF CANADA, Ltd.
TORONTO

THE COMMON SENSE

OF

POLITICAL ECONOMY

INCLUDING A STUDY OF
THE HUMAN BASIS OF ECONOMIC LAW

BY

PHILIP H. WICKSTEED, M.A.

> L'analyse économique proprement dite ne me semble pas devoir finalement être conçue ni cultivée, soit dogmatiquement, soit historiquement, à part de l'ensemble de l'analyse sociologique, soit statique, soit dynamique.—AUGUSTE COMTE.

MACMILLAN AND CO., LIMITED
ST. MARTIN'S STREET, LONDON
1910

A242103

TIBI

CONJUNX ADJUTRIX

NECNON ET ALIIS QUIBUSDAM

URBI FORSITAN ET ORBI PAENE IGNOTIS

TIBI SALTEM ET MIHI

FAMILIARISSIMIS.

LIBRUM HUNC QUALEMCUNQUE

DEDI DEDICAVI

PREFACE

THIS book is intended primarily as a popular but systematic exposition of the "marginal" theory of Economics. The Introduction will make it clear that the author makes no claim to originality or priority with respect to anything that it contains. It is not a history; and the question it is concerned with is not who first made any given application of the "marginal" theory to Economics, but what are the main applications of that theory inevitably demanded by the facts. The general absence of references or acknowledgments, therefore, must not in any case be regarded as an implied claim on the author's part to a special property in the argument or illustration in question.

But whereas this general explanation will, I hope, clear me from the charge of ingratitude, or worse, with reference to the great masters and the published works on Economics, it cannot absolve me from the duty of registering some few of the personal obligations under which I have from time to time been laid during the many years over which the direct and indirect preparations for this work have extended.

To Mr. Graham Wallas, to Mr. H. H. Cunynghame, and to several members of my own family, I owe criticisms or suggestions which they may well have forgotten, but which have been of decisive importance to the development of my own thought. To very many friends, of whom I will only mention Mr. H. T. Gerrans of Worcester College, Oxford, Professor Kuenen of Leiden, Mr. James Rigg of the Royal Mint, Mr. H. R. Beeton of the Stock Exchange, and Mr. S. H. Davies of York, I owe help and information ungrudgingly given on special points. To Professor Foxwell I am grateful for encouragement and support that have never failed since I first began the study of Political Economy, and to Professor Steffen of Gothenburg I owe a like debt of almost as long standing. To Professor Lees Smith I have to offer my very special thanks for his kindness in reading the manuscript of the First Book and giving me valuable suggestions about it. I need hardly add that not one of these gentlemen is either directly or indirectly responsible for any arguments or conclusions contained in this work.

Other obligations, not less deeply felt, I am, for one cause or another, precluded at present from expressly acknowledging.

CONTENTS

	PAGE
INTRODUCTION	1

BOOK I
SYSTEMATIC AND CONSTRUCTIVE

CHAPTER I

INTRODUCTORY: ADMINISTRATION OF RESOURCES AND CHOICE BETWEEN ALTERNATIVES. PRICE AND THE RELATIVE SCALE 13

CHAPTER II

MARGINS. DIMINISHING PSYCHIC RETURNS . . . 37

CHAPTER III

ECONOMICAL ADMINISTRATION AND ITS DIFFICULTIES . . 95

CHAPTER IV

MONEY AND EXCHANGE 126

CHAPTER V

BUSINESS AND THE ECONOMIC NEXUS 158

CHAPTER VI

MARKETS 212

CHAPTER VII

MARKETS (*continued*). INTEREST, TOOLS, LAND . . . 266

CHAPTER VIII

MARKETS (*continued*). EARNINGS 315

CHAPTER IX

DISTRIBUTION. COST OF PRODUCTION 358

BOOK II
EXCURSIVE AND CRITICAL

CHAPTER I

MARGINS AND THEIR DIAGRAMMATIC REPRESENTATION . . 401

CHAPTER II

ON THE DIAGRAMMATIC METHOD OF REPRESENTING AREAS OF SATISFACTION AND MARGINAL SIGNIFICANCES . . 439

CHAPTER III

ON THE NATURE OF CURVES OF TOTAL SATISFACTION . . 474

CHAPTER IV

BUYER AND SELLER. DEMAND AND SUPPLY . . . 493

CHAPTER V

THE THEORY OF "INCREASING AND DIMINISHING RETURNS" . 527

CHAPTER VI

The Diagrammatic Exposition of the Law of Rent and its Implications 550

CHAPTER VII

Banking. Bills. Currency 575

BOOK III

ANALYTICAL AND PRACTICAL

CHAPTER I

Samples of Analysis 627

CHAPTER II

Some further Analyses 660

CHAPTER III

Conclusion 696

THE COMMON SENSE OF POLITICAL ECONOMY

Ein jeder lebt's, nicht vielen ist's bekannt.—GOETHE.

We are all doing it ; very few of us understand what we are doing.

INTRODUCTION

In the ordinary course of our lives we constantly consider how our time, our energy, or our money shall be spent. That is to say, we decide between alternative applications of our resources of every kind, and endeavour to administer them to the best advantage in securing the accomplishment of our purposes or the humouring of our inclinations. It is the purpose of this book to evolve a consistent system of Political Economy from a careful study and analysis of the principles on which we actually conduct this current administration of resources.

I assume no previous acquaintance on the part of the reader with works on Political Economy, and rely on no hypotheses except such as the common experience of life suggests and explains. But since the system evolved from them will differ in some important particulars from traditional doctrine it will be suitable at the outset to render some account of the relation in which it stands to current or recent economic theory.

On the 1st of June 1860, William Stanley Jevons wrote to his brother, Herbert:

> In the last few months I have fortunately struck out what I have no doubt is *the true Theory of Economy*, so thorough-going and consistent, that I cannot now read other books on the subject without indignation.

Some eight weeks later he spoke of his theory as destined to " re-establish the science on a sensible basis"; and at last, in 1871, he embodied it in his *Theory of Political Economy*. Now Jevons's great discovery, like so many others, was nothing but a discovery of the obvious; for it was the discovery that whereas human wants are sometimes capable of complete satisfaction, and sometimes of gradual assuagement, in any case the relative urgency with which they demand further gratification is affected by the extent to which they have already been satisfied. So that a slice of bread and butter is not of the same significance in comparison with other things—the pleasure of smoking a pipe of tobacco, or of going out to look at a sunset, for example—if one has had nothing to eat for several hours, and if he has just enjoyed a hearty meal.

Walras in Switzerland, Menger in Austria, and Jevons in England, were all of them, without knowledge of each other's work, erecting a theory of value upon this obvious but strangely neglected principle, which bases economic thought on the broad experiences of daily life and the psychology of choice between alternatives. All the most noteworthy advances in the theory of Political Economy that have since been made are the inevitable developments of this single principle.

This principle furnishes the clue to all the most intricate problems of the abstract theory of Political Economy; and I believe that the reconstruction contemplated by Jevons has been carried to a far more advanced point than is generally realised even by those who are themselves accomplishing it. Adhesion to the traditional terminology, methods of arrangement, and classification, has disguised the revolution that has taken place. The new temple, so to speak, has been built up behind the old walls, and the old shell has been so piously preserved and respected that the very builders have often supposed themselves to be merely repairing and strengthening the ancient works and are hardly aware of the extent to which they have raised an independent edifice. I shall try to shew in this book that the time has come for a frank recognition of these facts.

My book therefore has two distinct but connected aims. It attempts to start with the reader from the very beginning, and to place a clue in his hands which will lead him, directly and inevitably, from the facts and observations of his own daily experience to an intimate comprehension of the machinery of the commercial and industrial world. And secondly, it attempts (implicitly in the First Book, more explicitly in the Second) to convince professed students of Political Economy that any special or unusual features in the system thus constructed are not to be regarded as daring innovations or as heresies, but are already strictly involved, and often explicitly recognised, in the best economic thought and teaching of recent years.

It may be convenient here to indicate in advance the main features of the construction thus attempted.

It will easily be shown that the principle laid down by Jevons is not exclusively applicable to industrial or commercial affairs, but runs as a universal and vital force through the administration of all our resources. It follows that the general principles which regulate our conduct in business are identical with those which regulate our deliberations, our selections between alternatives, and our decisions, in all other branches of life. And this is why we not only may, but must, take our ordinary experiences as the starting point for approaching economic problems. We must regard industrial and commercial life, not as a separate and detached region of activity, but as an organic part of our whole personal and social life; and we shall find the clue to the conduct of men in their commercial relations, not in the first instance amongst those characteristics wherein our pursuit of industrial objects differs from our pursuit of pleasure or of learning, or our efforts for some political and social ideal, but rather amongst those underlying principles of conduct and selection wherein they all resemble each other; for only so can we find the organic place of industry in our conception of life as a whole.

Having made our preliminary study of the psychology of choice, or the principles which regulate our selection between alternatives, we shall proceed to the special application of these principles to the commercial and industrial life, and to the characteristic phenomena which it manifests. It is not surprising that our definition of the area of the industrial and commercial or economic life should demand some revision when approached from this point of view. If earlier generations of investigators were chiefly intent on sharply defining Political Economy as a separate and self-contained area, and if our present tendency is to regard it as an integral part of the general life of society; if former generations were anxious to emphasise, and even hypothetically to magnify, the difference between the economic life and all that lay outside it, and if we, on the other hand, are intent on rediscovering in every branch of commercial and industrial life the identical motives and principles with which we are familiar elsewhere, it is not surprising that the old definitions of the economic life itself should prove unsatisfactory to us.

Accordingly, I shall try to shew that it is time frankly and decisively to abandon all attempts to rule out this or that "motive" from the consideration of the Economist, or indeed to attempt to establish any distinction whatever between the ultimate motives by which a man is actuated in business and those by which he is actuated in his domestic or public life. Economic *relations* constitute a complex machine by which we seek to accomplish our purposes, whatever they may be. They do not in any direct or conclusive sense either dictate our *purposes* or supply our *motives*. We shall therefore have to consider what constitutes an economic relation rather than what constitutes an economic motive. And this does away at a stroke with the hypothetically simplified psychology of the Economic Man which figured so largely in the older books of Political Economy, and which recent writers take so much trouble to evade or qualify. We are not to begin by imagining man to be actuated by only a few simple motives, but we are to take him as we find him, and are to examine the nature of those relations into which he enters, under the stress of all his complicated impulses and desires—whether selfish or unselfish, material or spiritual,—in order to accomplish indirectly through the action of others what he cannot accomplish directly through his own.

We shall find that the economic relations constitute a machinery by which men devote their energies to the immediate accomplishment of each other's purposes in order to secure the ultimate accomplishment of their own, irrespective of what those purposes of their own may be, and therefore irrespective of the egoistic or altruistic nature of the motives which dictate them and which stimulate efforts to accomplish them. And the things and doings with which economic investigation is concerned will therefore be found to include everything which enters into the circle of exchange —that is to say, everything with which men can supply each other, or which men can do for each other, in what we may call an impersonal capacity; or, in other words, the things a man can give to or do for another independently of any personal and individualised sympathy with him or with his motives or reasons.

A full realisation of this, while bringing home to our minds the fundamental importance and the wide area of these relations, will at the same time convince us of the impossibility of permanently isolating them in practical life from the non-economic relations into which they perpetually play.

When our conception of the nature of economic facts and relations has become clear, we shall see without difficulty that the market, in the widest sense of the term, is their field of action, and that market prices are their most characteristic expression and outcome. The individual, in administering his resources, regards market prices as phenomena which confront him independently of his own action, and which impose upon him the conditions under which he must make his selections between alternatives. But when he has arrived at a thorough comprehension of the principles of his own conduct, as he stands confronted by market prices, he will find that those market prices are themselves constituted by other people's acting precisely on the principles on which he acts; so that he is in fact himself, by his own action, contributing towards the formation of those very market prices which appear to be externally dictated to him. Because other people are doing exactly what he is doing a phenomenon arises, as the resultant of the sum of their individual actions, which presents itself to each one of them, severally, as an alien system imposed from without.

For the complete establishment of the theory of the market we shall be driven again to search for resemblances where stress has previously been laid on differences. The buyer and the seller have usually been opposed to one another, and the interplay of their rival interests has been regarded as the source of the phenomena of the market. But we shall try to go below this. The obvious and universally recognised fact that the same man may be a buyer under one set of circumstances, or a seller under another, and that even in the same market a man who would buy if prices were low may sell if prices are high, will lead us to a decisive simplification of the theory of markets, based on the consideration of buyers and sellers as a homogeneous group arranged and graduated on a single principle. But the explanation and elaboration of this conception cannot be anticipated here.

Our theory of markets once complete, all the rest is straightforward; but again it must be by attending to resemblances rather than to differences that we advance to the solution of the problems of "distribution." Wages, rent, interest, profits, etc., will be found to resolve themselves into mere questions of special markets, so that, strictly speaking, there is no more room for a separate theory of rent or a separate theory of wages than there is for a separate theory of the price of boots or a separate theory of the fees of a classical coach. If we mean by theory a system of general truths dealing with generalised facts, as distinct from the isolated factors and influences proper to some concrete phenomenon or group, then there can be no theory of rent, interest, or wages; there can be but one theory of distribution, and that the theory of the market.

We may attempt to develop this thought a little further. A man decides that a certain book and a certain article of clothing are each worth a guinea to him, but no more. If he can get either of them for that sum, or for anything less, he will purchase it; if not, not. This man has established an equality between the book and the article of clothing, and it is on such equalities or inequalities that he bases his whole administration of resources. Equality implies that the equal things have been reduced to a common measure. They are balanced against each other, therefore, by considering them as homogeneous magnitudes. In what sense are they such, and how are we to arrive at their common measure? Obviously not by dwelling on the specific nature of the services which the one article renders in clothing the body, and the other in clothing, feeding, or otherwise gratifying the mind, but by dwelling on the fact that both alike satisfy certain wants, or minister in a defined degree to the vital necessities and impulses of the purchaser. In this sense they may be regarded as substitutes for each other. A man cannot (conveniently or adequately) clothe himself in a book, or educate himself on a coat, and therefore there is a sense in which the coat and book cannot be regarded as substitutes for each other. But he may please himself with either, and, given a certain general state of his supplies and tastes, it may well be that a set of flannels of given quality and a certain specified book would equally gratify his tastes and desires at the moment; so that, from the point of view of his general vitality, they might be regarded as equivalent. Each would be equally pleasing and would be felt equally to enrich his life. The marginal theory of the administration of resources, as developed in this book, will shew that it is by contemplating commodities and services under their aspect of equivalents or substitutes (that is to say, by concentrating our attention on that point of view from which the services they render are like, not on that from which they are unlike) that we shall be able to constitute the theory of the market.

In like manner, in dealing with the particular markets of the productive factors or agents, we shall find that it is not by considering the special services that land renders to production, and the special conditions under which it renders them, or by considering the same problem with reference to labour or capital, that we shall worm out the secrets of the process of " distribution," but by considering that aspect under which all of these, and any other factors of production there may be, resemble each other. An addition or withdrawal of a small amount of any one factor of production, the others remaining constant, will produce a certain defined effect on the output; and, given certain supplies and conditions, this effect might often be counteracted by the addition or withdrawal of a small amount of some other factor. Thus under given conditions a small withdrawal of land might be compensated by a small addition of labour, so that the product might remain the same. When we have realised this we may reduce land, labour, and other productive agents to common terms and regard them as substitutes for each other, much as we did the book and the flannels; and thus, by fixing our attention on the identity rather than the diversities in the services rendered by the several factors of production, we may reduce them to a common measure and so solve the problem of distribution.

In all this there is nothing revolutionary or startling, but it will be found that a connected and systematic exposition of these truths will call into question much that still holds its place in text-books of Political Economy. It will be sufficient here to indicate, without any attempt to justify or elaborate, some of the main conclusions that will be reached.

We shall have to abandon the favourite diagrammatic method by which prices, whether market or normal, are indicated by the intersection of a curve of demand and a curve of supply, or a curve of demand and a curve of cost of production. We shall call for a revision of the whole theory of increasing and diminishing returns as usually expounded, and this will be seen to involve either the abandonment or the restatement of much ingenious theory that has been based on the supposed phenomena presented by industries subject to the law of diminishing returns.

In close connection with the subject just mentioned, we shall have to note that certain general truths, of universal application, which were first observed and formulated in relation to land, have been mistaken for specific characteristics of that particular factor of production. This has produced a perfect spawn of errors, misconceptions, and misnomers, which will long continue to infest economic thought. I have tried to indicate with perfect precision the specific source of these errors.

And finally, the general principles of our investigation will involve (less directly, but not less inevitably) an abandonment of the so-called Quantity Law in the study of finance, and some readjustment, at least, in the usual statement of the nature of foreign trade and the phenomena of bill-broking.

All this controversial matter has been as far as possible avoided in the First Book of this treatise, which aims at simple and direct construction, with the minimum of polemical reference to current terminology or theory. And it is my hope that, whatever may be the verdict passed by experts on the Second Book, the First may be found to have some independent value, which may be acknowledged even by those who dispute the legitimacy of the inferences subsequently drawn from the principles it expounds.

Finally, in a brief Third Book I have endeavoured to shew

that the principles elaborated in the first two Books will furnish the student of political and social reform with something like an instrument of precision, by which he may be able to analyse both the familiar phenomena of public life and the various movements and suggestions which are put forward with a view to social amelioration. This last Book aims at no more than suggestion and illustration, and makes no claim to systematic completeness, even in outline.

BOOK I

SYSTEMATIC AND CONSTRUCTIVE

ΚΑΛΛΙΚΛΗΣ. περὶ σιτία σὺ λέγεις καὶ ποτὰ καὶ ἰατροὺς καὶ φλυαρίας. . . . ποῖα ὑποδήματα φλυαρεῖς ἔχων; . . . ὡς ἀεὶ ταὐτὰ λέγεις, ὦ Σώκρατες.   PLATO.

CALLICLES. How you keep on, Socrates, harping on the same old string about food and drink and doctors and sandals and such-like trivialities!

CHAPTER I

INTRODUCTORY: ADMINISTRATION OF RESOURCES AND CHOICE BETWEEN ALTERNATIVES. PRICE AND THE RELATIVE SCALE

SUMMARY.—*This work is a study of the organisation of industry and commerce in its bearing upon social problems and upon human life. The derivation and the current use of the terms "Economy," "Political Economy," and "Economics" suggest that we should approach the problems of the industrial administration of resources from the field of domestic and personal administration to which we all have access. Every purchase being a virtual selection and involving a choice between alternatives is made in obedience to impulses and is guided by principles which are equally applicable to other acts of selection and choice. To understand them we must study the psychology of choice. The price of a thing is an indication of the range of alternatives open to the purchaser, and is a special case of "terms on which alternatives are offered to us." We are constantly weighing apparently heterogeneous objects of desire against each other and selecting between them according to the terms on which we can secure them. All these things that we balance against and compare with each other, whether they can be had for money or not, may ideally be arranged on a scale of relative significance in our minds.*

"Economy" etymologically means the regulating or managing of a household, that is to say, the administration of the household affairs and resources. It describes a branch of activity. In current language "economy" means the administration of any kind of resources (time, thought, or money, for instance) in such a

<small>Ideas of economy, waste, and worth.</small>

way as to secure their maximum efficiency for the purpose contemplated. It is administration with a minimum of waste. It describes not a branch but a characteristic of administrative activity. If we go on to analyse our conception of "waste," we find it to be expenditure upon objects in excess of their worth, or loss and destruction of resources by mere thoughtlessness or negligence. And finally when we say that a thing is not "worth" what we expend upon it or devote to it, we mean that there is some alternative application of the resources in question, either actually or prospectively open to us, by which a more worthy, more extended, more important, or in general terms a more desired or more desirable object could have been accomplished by the outlay. All successful administration, then, consists in the purposeful selection between alternative applications of resources; and the ultimate value or significance of such success depends on the nature of the objects at which the administrator aims.

If we engraft the current meaning of the word "economy" (the avoiding of waste) upon its etymological meaning (the administration of a household), we shall arrive at "the administration of the affairs and resources of a household in such a manner as to avoid waste and secure efficiency" as our conception of "Economy." "Political" Economy would, by analogy, indicate the administration, in the like manner, of the affairs and resources of a State, regarded as an extended household or community, and regulated by a central authority; and the study of Political Economy would be the study of the principles on which the resources of a community should be so regulated and administered as to secure the communal ends without waste.

Political Economy.

Now since the idea of "worth" enters, as the regulating and dominating principle, into every act of administration, and since it is our ends or objects that determine the relative worth, or worthiness, of this or that achieved result, it follows that the ultimate ideals of any individual, household, or community—the nature of the ends it seeks and desires—must give the tone and character to its "economy," and must be the soul and inspiration of its administrative system. We should therefore expect Political Economy in the first place either

Means and ends. Deliberate and spontaneous organisation.

to assume or to inculcate certain ends as proper for the State to pursue, and in the second place to consider how the central authority can best direct the State resources to their accomplishment. But both these expectations are disappointed when we look into books on Political Economy. The tendencies of modern thought and the conditions of modern life have combined to sever the consideration of the administration of resources from the discussion of the ultimate ends it has in view; and it has therefore become usual to treat Political Economy as concerned with increasing the communal means rather than securing the communal ends; and though there has recently been some reaction against this tendency it is still dominant. And again the deliberate direction of communal resources to communal ends, by a central authority, now occupies only a small place in treatises of Political Economy. It is true that the science still embraces the study of taxation, including all the fiscal arrangements of the State or the municipality, whether made with a view to raising a revenue or to the advantageous regulation of commerce; but in modern times it has become obvious to the reflective mind that the rhythm and articulation of societies depend more upon spontaneous adjustments in which each individual contemplates but a very small portion of the consequences, antecedents, and implications of his actions, and less upon deliberate regulations laid down with a view to their effect on the whole community, than was supposed by earlier thinkers. And even where we are considering the deliberate and collective administration of communal resources, as in questions of taxation, public finance, and fiscal arrangements, it is obvious that we cannot hope to understand either the direct result or the indirect reactions of systematic regulations unless we have carefully studied the spontaneous organisation of individual efforts upon which these regulations will react and with which they will combine, and the spontaneous relations which establish themselves under any or every system of regulations, and which are based upon the permanent ' characteristics of human nature. ' Political Economy " then, or the administration of resources of a society, must at any rate include and imply a study of the way in which members of that society will spontaneously administer their own resources and the relations into which they will spontaneously enter with each other.

In modern European society it may be questioned how far the ties of religion, of family, of feudal patronage and cliency, of civic, national, and imperialistic sentiment, are individually or collectively effective as organising powers; but it can hardly be questioned that relations of a business or commercial nature take a larger place in proportion to all these other forces than they did in ancient or medieval times. And the growing sense that the spontaneous relations into which men enter with each other in the administration of their resources are largely or even predominantly of the nature of business or commerce is reflected in the fact that Political Economy has come to concern itself more and more largely, and sometimes exclusively, with the principles on which all kinds of commercial and industrial enterprises and relations tend to regulate themselves. And indeed this tendency has gone so far that it has often been expressly laid down that Political Economy, strictly speaking, is only concerned with business relations, subject to whatever minimum of external control is regarded as inevitable. The reaction between these permanent tendencies to spontaneous organisation amongst individuals, and the deliberate regulations which trade unions, associations of employers, municipal or national assemblies, or contracting parties of any kind, may see fit to impose, has sometimes been isolated as the subject of Applied Political Economy. Thus, by an intelligible and instructive series of modifications, Political Economy has come to be generally understood as concerning itself mainly, if not exclusively, with industrial relations. It considers the forces and principles that determine market prices, rate of interest, foreign exchanges and so forth, in communities the individual members of which are free to organise themselves spontaneously in pursuit of their industrial interests.

Business relations as an organic force.

The more general term "Economics" (corresponding to "Ethics," "Politics," or "Physics") has recently found increasing acceptance. It is probably felt that etymologically the term "Political Economy" has little relation to the study it now describes, and that the connotation it has recently acquired is too

Economics the general science of administration of resources.

narrow to suit our present ideas, so that a more neutral term is preferred. "Economics," then, may be taken to include the study of the general principles of administration of resources, whether of an individual, a household, a business, or a State; including the examination of the ways in which waste arises in all such administration.

The object of this book is, indeed, to elucidate the problems of "Political Economy" in the narrower and modern sense; that is to say, to bring the reader to a comprehension of the mechanism and spontaneous organisation of industrial and commercial life; but at the same time it is the author's firm conviction that this comprehension can be best achieved by a thorough preliminary study of "Economics" in their widest scope; that is to say, a study of the principles of administration of resources and selection between alternatives, conceived without any formal or conventional limitations. Therefore we shall not exclude from our studies the consideration of ends and of those general purposes and impulses which determine the drift and flow of our energies. The movement can hardly be studied intelligently if we have taken vows at the outset never to think of the motive. The motive that inspires the study of Political Economy is almost invariably social, and the field of observation that lies nearest to each one of us is necessarily personal. The study of the problems of industry, then, must be based on personal Economics and must be inspired by social ideals; and even if we exclude direct consideration of the latter from some parts of our investigation it will still be for their bearings upon them that we value our results.

Relation of study of personal and industrial Economics to social ideals.

We shall seek our point of departure, then, in the regions with which we are most familiar, and shall endeavour there to find the clue to the general principles of administration, and so far our study will be personal; but it is by the bearing of these principles, when discovered, upon the social and communal weal that we shall justify our studies to the social instincts which prompt them. Thus personal and domestic administration will at first be our chosen field of observation, and our chief collecting ground of examples. We shall then proceed to the elucidation of the general principles on which men spontaneously administer their resources and conduct their business. And in the bearing of this conduct in business upon the general welfare of the community we shall find the justification of our desire to understand its inmost workings. Following these indications, then, let us begin our investigations at the point they suggest, and let us take the administration of the affairs of a household as our starting-point.

As we oftener think of women than of men as administering the affairs of a household, and as we oftener say of a woman than of a man that she is "economical," we may naturally draw our first illustrations mainly from the doings of housewives; and this will have the great advantage of keeping us upon ground with which we are all broadly familiar and with which all of us, man, woman, and child, are closely concerned. As bankers, manufacturers, dealers, or mechanics, we may have some inside knowledge of one or another order of industrial facts, but these special fields of experience give us no common ground. In the administration of the affairs of a household the matriarchal type of civilisation is indeed dominant, but every member of every family is more or less closely participant and more or less keenly interested in it. It furnishes us with a common ground, the exploration of which demands no special or technical information, and from which we may therefore conveniently start on a general investigation. Many of us are, severally and by training, more familiar with some other region of the economic world, but collectively and spontaneously we are most closely intimate with this. Starting then with the investigation of the management of household affairs, we will begin by taking for granted without examination the purchasing power of money and the existence of market or current prices, as facts which the housewife has to deal with; and on this basis we will observe and analyse the principles on which she administers the household resources. I shall then try to shew that these principles are identical in that part of her administration in which money is employed and that part in which it is not; and further, that they are identical with the principles that regulate the conduct of life in general, and the administration of all resources whatsoever.

From the vantage ground thus gained we will then go back upon the phenomena we had at first taken for

Method of study.

granted, and I shall hope to shew that the principles we shall then have formulated will themselves enable us to explain the meaning and those functions of money and the constitution of those market prices which at first we took for granted. We shall then be in a position to go on to the direct treatment of the ordinary categories of Political Economy.

Our position may be restated thus. We will begin with that part of our economic world which we ourselves immediately control, or which is generally accessible to observation from the inside, about which we are constantly thinking, and in which we are all concerned, namely, the expenditure of our personal and domestic resources. This we may reasonably hope to be able to understand and analyse. But it is conditioned on every side by facts that we are not conscious of controlling, that we do not understand, and that cannot be generally got at from the inside (such as market prices), and instruments which we generally take for granted (such as money and the mechanism of exchange). We may hope, however, that a careful examination of what we ourselves or those with whom we are most intimately associated are consciously doing may throw light upon the great movements, institutions, and combinations which seem to be the result of the unconscious, or half-conscious, aggregate of doings that we vaguely conceive of as due to the "community."

Beginning our study of the administration of domestic resources, then, we note that in marketing, shopping, giving orders to tradesmen and so forth, the mother of a family is administering her pecuniary resources and trying to make the money go as far as possible; *Administration of money and of stores.* and when her purchases have been brought home she still has the kindred task, sometimes a delicate and difficult one, of so distributing them amongst the various claimants (whose wants they may be very far from completely satisfying) as to make them tell to the utmost. In marketing she is constantly compelled to buy less of this or that than she would like, because her whole resources are inadequate to the satisfaction of every desire, and the thoughtless indulgence of one would involve disproportionate neglect of others. At home she is compelled to give one child less than she would wish of something he wants, because the whole stock is inadequate to meet all the claims she would like to admit, and too liberal indulgence of one child's desires would involve disproportionate neglect of another's. Her doings in the market-place and her doings at home are therefore parts of one continuous process of administration of resources, guided by the same fundamental principle; and it is the home problem that dominates the market problem and gives it its ultimate meaning. The problem of the limitations which she must face at home in concrete detail is the same problem of which she is conscious, in a more collective form, in the market.

This task of home administration is not of uniform difficulty. Materfamilias will not mind who gets hold of the bread though she will exercise a general watchfulness against its being wasted, but when she has begun her first purchases of new potatoes for the year, she will be very careful to keep the dish under her own direct control and not let one of the children determine, at his own discretion, what is his proper share; for if she did there would be disproportionate gratification and disproportionate privation. " I am as the centre of the circle to which all parts of the circumference bear a like relation. But thou art not such," she says in effect to each child in turn. She may let the milk-jug pass freely round, and her vigilance will only take note of mugs full, but she will keep the cream-jug in her own immediate vicinity, and however nobly she tilts it on some occasions, there will be others on which she measures and estimates its contents by drops. But in all cases, whether she is spending money, helping the potatoes, pouring out the cream, or exercising a more general vigilance over the bread and milk, she is engaged in the same problem of the administration of resources and she is guided by the same principle. She is trying to make everything go as far as it will, or, in other words, serve the most important purpose that it can. She will consider that she has been successful if, in the end, no want which she has left unsatisfied appears, in her deliberate judgment, to have really been more important than some other want to which she attended in place of it. Otherwise there has been waste somewhere, for money, milk, potatoes, or attention have been applied to one purpose when they might better have been applied to another. Note that "attention" is included amongst the things that have to be administered and that are often wasted. The art of life includes the art of effectively and economically distributing our vital resources of every kind, and domestic administration is a branch of this art in which it is possible to pay too dear in money for the saving of time, or too dear in time for the saving of money, or too dear in thought and energy for saving in bread, potatoes, or cream. Whatever the nature of the alternatives before us, the question of the terms on which they are offered is always relevant. If we secure this, how much of that must we pay for it, or what shall we sacrifice to it? And is it worth it? What alternatives shall we forgo? And what would be their value to us?

In the market this problem presents itself in terms of money prices. Let us work this out in detail, and try to gain a more accurate and intimate knowledge of the considerations that connect themselves with this phenomenon of "price." It is sufficiently obvious that when a woman goes into the market uncertain whether she will or will not buy new potatoes, or chickens, the price at which she finds that she can get them may determine her either way; and if she buys at all, the price may determine whether she buys a larger or a smaller quantity. For the price is the first and most obvious indication of the nature of the alternatives that she is forgoing, if she makes a contemplated purchase. But it is almost equally obvious that not only the price of these particular things, but the price of a number of other things also will affect the problem. If good sound old potatoes are to be had at a low price the marketer will be less likely to pay a high price for new ones, because there is a good alternative to be had on good terms. If there is a good prospect of damsons at a reasonable figure presently, the immediate purchase of greengages for jam may seem less desirable than if there is not. If the housewife is thinking of doing honour to a small party of neighbours by providing a couple of chickens for their entertainment at supper, it is possible that she could treat them with adequate respect, though not with distinction, by substituting a few pounds of cod. And in that case not only the price of chickens but the price of

Price as an index of alternatives.

cod will tend to affect her choice. To say this, of course, is merely to say that we do not know the actual alternatives represented by the price of any one commodity until we know the price of certain other commodities also. Under such circumstances as we have supposed, the price of 6s. for a pair of chickens means different things if cod is to be had at 6d. a pound, and if it is only to be had at 10d. In one case it would mean that the lower compliment of say six pounds of cod, as against the higher compliment of the chickens, would save 3s.; in the other, that it would only save 1s.; and it may be worth sacrificing a little distinction in the entertainment for all the possibilities opened out by 3s., though not for those opened out by 1s. This, however, is only what mathematicians call a first approximation. If the entertaining housekeeper suspects that one or more of her guests will know the price of cod and chickens as well as she does, a complication is introduced; for cod will be still less of a compliment at 6d. than at 10d. a pound, and the 3s. in the one case will then be secured at a greater sacrifice than the 1s. in the other; and this consideration may or may not turn the scale.

But on what does the significance of the saving (at whatever sacrifice made) depend? Probably upon the price of things that have no obvious connection with either chicken or cod. A father and mother may have ambitions with respect to the education or accomplishments of their children, and may be willing considerably to curtail their expenditure on other things in order to gratify them. Such parents may be willing to incur the twofold reproach of being mean and being stuck up, by entertaining their guests less sumptuously than custom demands, and at the same time getting French or violin lessons for their children. In such a case the question whether to buy new or old potatoes, or whether to entertain friends with chicken or cod, or neither, may be affected by the terms on which French or music lessons of a satisfactory quality can be secured. If they are half a guinea a lesson the terms on which the alternatives between a better education and a more elaborate table are offered determine the choice in the table's favour; but if, owing to any combination of circumstances, it chances that instruction of adequate quality can be got for 5s. an hour, the price (or terms on which the alternatives are offered) having changed, the more elaborate education has the preference given to it, because more of it is now to be had for a given sacrifice of other things.

Moreover, new inventions, or the opening of new routes of commerce, are constantly bringing new alternatives within the range of possible selection, and the price which would have been cheerfully paid for some commodity when only the old range of alternatives was open is grudged in the presence of the fresh ones. It is said that the invention of the lady's bicycle materially affected the trade in low-priced pianos. Many young women, it seems, would have saved up for a piano before this invention was made. That is to say, they would have regarded the possession of a piano as a more eligible alternative than the indulgence of the thousand small wants they would have had to ignore in order to raise the money, or than the acquisition of any other possession, or the realisation of any other purpose that the money when raised would have secured. But now there is a newly opened alternative which they prefer to any of those that were open to them before, including the possession of the piano itself, which is accordingly beaten off the field. And it should of course be noted that for this effect to follow there is no necessity for any exact correspondence of price between the piano and the bicycle. It may be a case of weighing not a piano against a bicycle, but a piano against a bicycle plus sundry other things; and the collective group that includes the bicycle might offer a more eligible alternative than the piano, though the piano would outweigh any other alternative group from which the bicycle was excluded. And so it might conceivably happen that the introduction of the bicycle, while interfering with the sale of cheap pianos, might promote that of literature or even of fruit and vegetables; for these things might now be able to enter into a victorious alliance with the bicycle and defeat the hitherto triumphant piano that had excluded them.

We may further illustrate the general thesis to which we are leading up by supposing that the members of a family have been deeply affected by the news of an Indian famine. Now although it is said that the alternatives relinquished in order to meet fresh appeals to philanthropic sympathies are generally themselves philanthropic—that is to say, that the subscriptions given to meet a special appeal are largely withdrawn from the support of existing charities—yet this is certainly not always or altogether the case; and our housekeeper's purchases of chickens may certainly be affected not only by the price of cod, or by the price of French or music lessons or of pianos or bicycles, but also by the fact that there is a famine in India and that machinery by which she and her family can help to alleviate it has been brought to her door.

It is sufficiently obvious, further, that alternatives often present themselves in the form, " Shall I have this to-day and go without that to-morrow, or shall I have that to-morrow and go without this to-day?" In fact we can assign no definite limit to the remoteness in time of the realisation of one purpose which may come into competition with the instant or imminent realisation of another. We may deny ourselves many satisfactions day by day and week by week, because we are saving up for a piano, for the education of our children, for retirement from business in old age, for the amassing of a fortune, for general provision against contingencies more or less vaguely conceived, or for insurance against evils definite in their nature but uncertain in their incidence. To the wide range of alternatives, already examined, that compete with some definite purchase at a particular stall in the market-place, we may therefore add the further alternative of not spending the money at present either on that or on anything else, but saving something out of the housekeeping allowance for undefined future contingencies, or for the realisation of hopes regarding the definite but remote (and therefore necessarily uncertain) future.

Still further, if the housewife is herself a bread-winner, in the usual acceptation of the term, or if she is conscious of having any influence upon the general scheme of her husband's life, there may be present in her mind a yet further possible alternative to some special expenditure; for she may consider the advisability of ceasing, in future, to spend money in this and in certain other ways to which she is accustomed, but, instead of spending it on anything else, or saving it, simply not earning it at all, and devoting the time and energy so released to public work, or to the cultivation of private tastes, or to acts of neighbourly service, or finding compensation merely in relief from a strain which has become painful.

Thus, through widening circles of remoter and fainter influence, everything that changes the value or significance of any possible application of energies and resources, or that changes the terms on which any alternative whatever is offered, may affect the purchase of any single article at a market stall. Primarily it will be affected by its own price, secondarily by the price of the things that are most readily thought of as substitutes for it, and more remotely by the whole range of alternatives open to the individual, or the group, by whom, or for whom, the purchase is to be made.

But the reference just made to "relief from a strain" may warn us that we have not even yet reached a sufficient generality in our survey, and that we must mount to a point which will still further extend our outlook. We have spoken hitherto as if we were habitually choosing between different objects of positive desire, and as though the privation involved in securing one thing were simply going without another. But balking an impulse or starving a desire may involve not only the sacrifice of the thing desired, but the encountering of a positive pain. In this and in other ways we may be called upon at any time to consider, not which of two satisfactions we would rather forgo, but which of two pains or miseries we would rather escape, or whether we will endure this pain in order to secure that object of desire or in order to avert a given loss. And here again all will depend upon the "price" or terms on which the alternatives are offered. A pair of pinching or ill-fitting shoes furnishes a familiar example. Are we to go on wearing them and suffering, or are we to put them aside, give them away, or sell them for what they will fetch, and buy a new pair? If we determine to go on wearing them, we are practically earning a certain sum of money (or, if you like, purchasing certain things which we should have had to go without had we bought the new pair of boots) at the "price" of a certain sum of physical suffering, with all its secondary

Securing the desired and evading the undesired experiences.

products of lowered vitality, irritability of temper, and so forth. Most ways of earning a living involve, possibly during a part of most days or every day, and almost certainly from time to time, effort or endurance which is positively, perhaps acutely, painful. So that in surveying the alternatives between which we have to choose in the ordinary course of life and business (whether in reference to earning or spending our income), we must not only compare different and heterogeneous objects of desire, but also different and heterogeneous forms of suffering, or objects of terror or aversion, which may be regarded as negative quantities on the scale of satisfaction. In the ordinary conduct of our lives we not only compare positive satisfactions amongst themselves, considering which we prefer, and negative satisfactions amongst themselves, considering which we are most anxious to avoid, but we also deliberate whether we will accept such and such a positive satisfaction on condition of having to take a negative one with it, or escape such and such a negative satisfaction on condition of forfeiting a positive one at the same time. Indeed, a moment's reflection will make us aware how very large a part of our resources is directed not so much to securing things we want as to averting things to which we object. And, in truth, moralists have such a long list of proscribed pleasures that the avoidance of a pain is often (and perhaps legitimately enough) represented as a more creditable motive than the securing of a pleasure. It is supposed to be to a man's credit if he eats, not because he enjoys it, but because he desires to avoid the faintness, inefficiency, and positive pain which would come upon him if he did not. Cato is praised by Lucan for having reduced his expenditure on clothing to the point demanded for protection against the weather; and many of us are so far Stoics that we would gladly reduce our tailor's bill more nearly to the modest dimensions sanctioned by Cato's standard, and spend the surplus on books or holidays, if we did not find that the dress which is adequate for protection against the weather is quite inadequate for protection against domestic criticism, to which we are equally sensitive. In this case we sacrifice positive pleasures in order to escape pains, and we are told that it would be disreputable to do otherwise. But we are not all or always of Cato's mood. If some people spend money on dress in order to avoid both suffering and inflicting mental pain, others do so in order to secure the positive satisfactions incidental to beautifying their own appearance and exciting the admiration, the approval, or the envy of others. Moreover, the two sets of incentives may combine, or the one may be the alleged while the other is the secretly effective motive.

Thus, in order to arrive at any adequate conception of the nature of the alternatives between which we are constantly choosing we must realise (a) that a large part of our energies and resources is habitually directed not towards getting what we want, but towards escaping what we do not want; (b) that we balance positive and negative satisfactions against each other[1] just as we balance positive against positive, and negative against negative satisfactions; (c) that positive and negative satisfactions may blend or even coincide (as when we secure sympathy that we value by the same act which averts criticism which we dread); and (d) that the principle of price obtains throughout the whole range of negative as of positive satisfactions. Whether we are willing to incur this kind of pain in order to secure that kind of pleasure depends on the terms on which they are offered. How much of the pain and how much of the pleasure may I expect? I may be glad to endure a day's sea-sickness for the sake of a fortnight's enjoyment, but may decline a day's enjoyment at the cost of a week's sea-sickness.

Insensibly we have passed from the confined conception of price as so much money, to the generalised conception of price as representing the terms on which anything we want may be had or anything we shun avoided. Current phraseology recognises this wider application of the language of the market and of pecuniary expenditure. "Spend," "afford," "waste," "worth," "price," are terms universally applicable to all kinds of material and immaterial resources and objects of desire or aversion, whether milk, money, time, pain, or vital energies. "It is not worth the money," our housekeeper may say when she determines not to buy a cabbage; "I cannot afford the time," when she

<small>Generalised conception of price.</small>

[1] Cf. pages 414 *sqq*.

explains why she has not weeded a flower-bed; "It is not worth making a fuss about," when she refrains from emphasising a slight deviation from the path of duty on the part of a maid. And note, at this point, that the implication in some or all of these instances is that the object in question would have justified the expenditure of a certain amount of money, time, and moral energy respectively, and the incurring of a certain amount of discomfort, but not so much as they would have taken. That is to say, that they are all worth having or doing, but not worth having or doing at the price. We habitually talk of a man gaining some object "at the price of his honour"; or say to some one who contemplates an action which would alienate his friends, "Oh yes! Of course you can do it, if you choose to pay the price." "Price," then, in the narrower sense of "the money for which a material thing, a service, or a privilege can be obtained," is simply a special case of "price" in the wider sense of "the terms on which alternatives are offered to us"; and to consider whether a thing is worth the price that is asked for it, is to consider whether the possession of it is more to be desired than anything we can have instead of it, and whether it will compensate us for everything we must take along with it. Selection between alternatives, then, is the most generalised form under which we can contemplate the ordinary acts of administration of resources, whether in the market-place, the home, or elsewhere; and, obviously, price or the terms on which the alternatives are offered (how much of this against how much of that?) must often be a determining consideration in our choice between them.

It would be a very great mistake to suppose that the influence of the terms on which alternatives are offered to us is confined to cases where our choice is deliberate; and a still greater mistake to confine it to cases in which that choice is rational. A great part of our conduct is impulsive and a great part unreflecting; and when we reflect our choice is often irrational. In all these cases, however, the principle of price is active.

<small>Price as affecting impulsive or irrational determinations.</small>

Habit or impulse perpetually determines our selection between alternatives without any reflection on our part at all; and the terms on which alternatives are offered us may change within wide limits without affecting us. But if they are altered beyond a certain point the habit will be broken or the unconscious impulse checked, and we shall enter a stage of conscious choice. The power of habit or impulse to resist the intrusion of deliberate choice is quantitatively defined, and may be overcome on certain terms. Thus the impulse to rescue a drowning man and the dread of taking a high dive may balance themselves without reflection within certain limits, but when those limits are transgressed a deliberate choice may be made. The principle is at work on the unconscious area, and emerges into consciousness when it crosses the boundary. A man of given temperament and accomplishments, who without a moment's hesitation would take a header of 5 feet to help a drowning stranger, might be conscious of a conflict of two forces in him, though hardly of a deliberate choice, as he took off from a height of 8 feet, might nerve himself with an effort to a 10-foot throw, might refrain, though with some measure of self-contempt, if the height were 12 feet, and without any self-reproach at all if it were 20 feet. But the same man might unhesitatingly take off from 12 feet to save his friend, or from 20 feet, with a sense of desperation, but with no fear or consciousness of an open alternative, to the rescue of his wife or child; though even in this case it would not occur to him to take off from 40 feet, and at some height short of this he might go through a rapid estimate of the relative chances of a desperate plunge or a race for other means of rescue, and into this estimate his own instinctive fears might or might not, according to his temperament, enter as a recognised or unrecognised weight.

Or again, when our selection between positive and negative satisfactions is wholly irrational, and the price required (even according to our own standards, apart from any ideal scale of values) is vastly less than the worth of what is offered, the principle of price is still active. The terms on which the rejected alternative is offered are already favourable, if judged by any rational standard, and yet we persist in our rejection. But if the terms are made more favourable still, we shall accept them. For example, we lie awake (or what we call awake next morning) half the night consciously suffering from cold, when without even getting out of bed we could reach a blanket or a rug which would secure comfortable sleep for the rest of the night. We cannot say that we deliberately prefer the discomfort we have encountered to the discomfort we have escaped. Perhaps the psychological analysis is that we prefer each second of the discomfort of cold, as it comes, to the discomfort that would accrue during that second if we secured peace for the rest of the night. At any rate our choice is irrational, yet the principle of price is at work all the same; for there is a degree of chill discomfort which, if reached, will break the spell and induce us to put on the extra blanket. Or for months, perhaps years, we have suffered our conscience to be periodically troubled, and our general vitality sensibly lowered, because we know that we ought to pay a certain call, write a certain letter, or even post-card, or return a book to a friend, who, for all we know, may be suffering more or less seriously for want of it and wondering what has become of it. An hour's or a minute's exertion of a kind we are constantly making for trivial objects, and which we do not find particularly painful, would relieve us of this burden, and yet, apparently under some spell of impotence, we continue to bear it. Nothing could be more supremely irrational (to say nothing of its morality), and yet here too the quantitative law of "price" is at work. There is a degree of depression, self-reproach, or sudden panic, which will induce us to break the spell that has prevented our writing the post-card or sending the book back. If the terms on which we can hug our indolence or aversion become too hard we shall at last cast it from us. There are people who will endure long-protracted agonies of toothache sooner than face an extraction which they know perfectly well would be comparatively easy to bear; or who are restrained from indulging their taste for foreign travel by terror of sea-sickness, though they know that it is a weak and foolish shrinking, and that what they are losing is, in their own deliberate judgment, worth much more than the price they shrink from paying. Their conduct is admittedly irrational; but though they refuse to pay a given price for something that far exceeds it in value, yet if the offer be raised still higher they will at last consent to pay. If the present and prospective pain from toothache, or the degree of prospective enjoyment from travel, reaches a certain point, they will at last face an hour in the dentist's chair, or a night and a day on the deep. When the terms on which the alternatives are offered are such as not only to enlist their deliberate reason, but also to overcome their instinctive and morbidly absorbing terror, they will face the thing they dread, though they would have done so on no lower terms. Our irrational shrinkings then, as well as our rational preferences, " have their price." And as irrational aversion or dread does not supersede the principle of price, so neither does irrational attraction or fancy. The phenomenon of enamourment is not special to one relation in life; and if it is sometimes a better guide than reason it certainly is not always reasonable. Yet the man who has "fallen in love" with a house, a horse, a book, or a scheme of business or pleasure, while he may resent the suggestions of his reason that a given price is too high, will nevertheless be daunted when it rises beyond a certain point; and that point affords an accurate gauge of his " infatuation " regarded as a quantity.[1]

Thus the principle of price, or terms on which the alternatives are offered, which decides the housewife to make this or that purchase at the stall, may be traced through the whole range of our irrational as well as our rational, of our impulsive as well as our deliberate and even of our unconscious as well as our conscious selection between alternatives.

And finally, if the principle of price extends to cases in which there is an open alternative but no deliberate estimate, it may also be traced where there is a deliberate estimate though there is no open alternative; for where there is no possibility of selection we nevertheless determine in our thought the terms which would sway our selection this way or that if there were a choice. " I would rather have lost £20," a man may say when he has forgotten a promise that it must seem heartless not to have kept; or " I would give half my possessions if I could believe it," when he is told something that he would willingly accept as a fact, but cannot. Such utterances may not be very serious or

[1] Cf. page 118.

accurate estimates, but their very form shews that there is nothing inherently absurd in the idea that a painful impression, of given gravity, on the mind of a friend would be worth removing at £20, but not at £25; or that some definite relief to my mind might be worth the sacrifice of half, but not of three-quarters, of my fortune; though neither of the alternatives is actually open to me upon these or perhaps upon any other terms.

We have thus arrived at the conclusion that all the heterogeneous impulses and objects of desire or aversion which appeal to any individual, whether material or spiritual, personal or communal, present or future, actual or ideal, may all be regarded as comparable with each other; for we are, as a matter of fact, constantly comparing them, weighing them against each other, and deciding which is the heaviest. And the question, "How much of this must I forgo to obtain so much of that?" is always relevant. If we are considering, for example, whether to live in the country or in the town, such different things as friendship and fresh air or fresh eggs may come into competition and comparison with each other. Shall I "bury myself in the country," where I shall see little of my dearest friends, but may hope for fresh eggs for breakfast, and fresh air all the day? Or shall I stay where I am, and continue to enjoy the society of my friends? I start at once thinking "how much of the society of my friends must I expect to sacrifice? Will any of them come and see me? Shall I occasionally be able to go and see some of them?" The satisfactions and benefits I anticipate from a country life will compensate me for the loss of some of their society, but not for the loss of all of it. The price may be too high. In such a case as this the terms on which the alternatives are offered are matter of more or less vague surmise and conjecture, but the apparent dissimilarity of the several satisfactions themselves does not prevent the comparison, nor does it prevent the quantitative element from affecting my decision. Using the term price then in its widest extension, we may say that all the objects of repulsion or attraction which divide my energies and resources amongst them are linked to each other by a system of ideal prices or terms of

Scales of preference.

equivalence. We may conceive of a general "scale of preferences" or "relative scale of estimates" on which all objects of desire or pursuit (positive or negative) find their place, and which registers the terms on which they would be accepted as equivalents or preferred one to the other.

Presumably no man's scale, however, is completely consistent. That is to say, if I would choose A rather than B and would choose B rather than C, it does not follow (as it ought to do) that *a fortiori* I should choose A rather than C. A man might be willing to give a shilling for a knife because he thought it cheap, and might refuse to give a shilling for a certain pamphlet because he thought it dear, and yet if he had been offered the direct choice between the pamphlet and the knife as a present he might have chosen the pamphlet. That is to say, he would prefer the knife to a shilling and would prefer a shilling to the pamphlet, and yet he would prefer the pamphlet to the knife. Or a man who is going abroad may employ half a day in finding where he can get best change for his money, with the result of getting half a crown's worth more of foreign coin for his £30 than he could have got at the tourist office without any trouble; and he may be quite pleased with his achievement. But the same man would scornfully refuse to sell half a day of his time for 2s. 6d., and will lose all his self-gratulation on the favourable exchange that he has got if it occurs to him to think of it as 2s. 6d. earnings for half a day's work. That is to say, at one and the same time he is willing and unwilling to accept 2s. 6d. as an adequate compensation for half a day's work, according to the light in which it happens to present itself to him. Or when he has arrived at the station the exact book that would suit him to read on his journey occurs to his mind, and he knows where he can get it for 1s. There is just time to go for it, but it will cost 2s. 6d. in cab fares, and it does not even occur to him to be so extravagant as to incur 250 per cent incidental expenses in transacting this little piece of business. Yet if the book had been brought out at 3s. 6d. and had been on the stall he would have bought it with much satisfaction.

The obscure impulses and associations which affect our choice, and interpose themselves between the realities with which we are dealing and our estimate of them, yield in an erratic and irregular manner to the light of reason, lingering here when they have retreated there; and thus inconsistencies of every kind are introduced into our scale. But the greater the range of that scale that is present to our minds at one and the same time, and the more precise our mental estimates, the fewer will be our inconsistencies. The man of alert intelligence and sound judgment will reduce them to a minimum, and the wider and more consistent the range of our consciously realised alternatives is, the more economical will the administration of our resources become.

A man's actual scale of preferences then may depart to any extent and for any reason from the ideal of wisdom, and may be full of inconsistencies and vacillations. But such as it is, it connects the various objects of his desire by a system of prices, and his successive acts of choice, whether purchases or other selections, are constantly revealing fragments of it, as he determines that at this price he will take this instead of that, aud on these terms he will select this alternative and reject the other.

But here it may naturally occur to us to ask why we are so seldom conscious of this ever-present fact of selection between alternatives, particularly in our money purchases. Why even in the simplest and most obvious cases do we comparatively seldom think of definite alternatives when asking ourselves whether we will or will not buy such and such an article? There are indeed many instances, if we look for them, in which we do this. Many young women, and some young men, living alone aud on narrow resources, habitually realise that literature, lectures, concerts, and theatres are in direct competition with each other, and that if they buy a coveted book they cannot go to the concert, and they also realise every day that it is the penny or twopence by which their expenditure on dinner each day of the week falls short of satisfying their appetite which enables them to make a selection between these competing satisfactions at all, and that secures them in the enjoyment of one of them every week or fortnight. The people living on or below the line of positive want in York had no difficulty in telling a sympathetic inquirer that every

Unconscious estimates, comparisons, and selections.

pair of boots bought " came out of the food." If any person living at or near the edge of his income is touched by a charitable appeal, he habitually sets about thinking what he can go without in order to respond to it; and there are periods in most people's lives at which they deliberately revise their expenditure and attempt to realise and select between the main alternatives it embraces. But most people would have some difficulty, if challenged, in giving any large number of consciously realised concrete examples of selection between definite alternatives. A girl is conscious of choosing between a number of hats in a shop, but she may hardly be conscious of choosing between a hat and something else. She never gets a hat, she will tell you, unless " she has to," and then there is no choice in the matter. In fact (like the poet) " she does but buy because she must." And when she " has to " buy a hat she leaves the one she would like best unpurchased, because she " cannot afford " it, and gets the " best she can afford." She has no schedule in her mind of the things she would have to go without if she bought the more expensive hat, and she has made no calculation that to go without them would be worse than putting up with the inferior hat. And even when a man is tempted to incur some considerable expense which he knows he " cannot afford," he does not generally realise exactly what the consequences of buying it will be, but has a vague sense of future inconvenience, privations, and possibly regrets. Afterwards, indeed, he may say from time to time, " I can't afford to get a new greatcoat just yet, after such an expensive holiday," and so on; but more often he will only be vaguely conscious of things being tighter, and of a temporary modification in his general ideas of what he " can afford "; and the pressure will perhaps as often act unconsciously as consciously in his selection of the things that he must now go without. But to say all this is merely to say that our scale of preferences often asserts itself automatically. Life would be impossible if we were always in the state of mind professed by the lady who said she liked " to get up every morning feeling that everything was an open question." We are not obliged to be constantly considering alternatives, because in a fairly well regulated mind the suggestion of any particular item of expenditure does not as a rule arise until it is approximately in its proper turn and place for gratification. The vague sense of restraint, which subdues and suppresses it, is really the unanalysed consciousness of the higher place on the scale of preferences of certain other unspecified items which will one by one assert themselves in due time and place. That is to say, if we are moderately wise we pretty generally act without reflection in the manner which reflection would have dictated. But these unconscious and automatic processes are far from being infallible, and one of the qualities most conducive to effective expenditure is an alertness to changed conditions, which reopens every question that has been materially affected by the change, while abstaining from fruitless and fidgeting reconsiderations for which there is either no ground, or ground insufficient to justify the requisite expenditure of thought and energy.

By a man's "scale of preferences" or "relative scale," then, we must henceforth understand the whole register of the terms on which (wisely or foolishly, consistently or inconsistently, deliberately, impulsively or by inertia, to his future satisfaction or to his future regret) he will, if he gets the chance, accept or reject this or that alternative. And by saying, for example, that a bunch of radishes stands higher than a red herring on his scale of preferences, or that an honorary degree stands lower than a baronetcy, we shall simply mean that he would at this moment, if he had the choice, take the radishes in preference to the herring, and receive the title rather than the degree. This conception of a "scale of preferences" will underlie all our future investigations. It is quite fundamental, and the whole purpose of this introductory chapter has been to explain and to illustrate it.

CHAPTER II

MARGINS. DIMINISHING PSYCHIC RETURNS

SUMMARY.—*The significance of any given addition to our supply of a commodity or other object of desire declines as the supply increases. Its significance for any given supply is called its marginal significance. This marginal significance therefore rises or falls as the supply itself is contracted or expanded, and the margin drawn back or advanced. If there is a market price for any commodity, we supply ourselves with it till its marginal significance sinks to its market price; and seeing that all the early increments of supply have a higher value than that at the margin, though all are bought at the market price, it follows that the satisfactions we secure are worth more than the price we pay for them. Only at the margin is there a coincidence between the thing gained and the price paid for it. In more general terms, if we can exchange things for each other or choose between them, on certain terms, then we can increase our supply of the more valued thing at the expense of the other, thereby lowering the marginal significance of one and raising that of the other, till their significance coincides with the terms on which they are obtainable as alternatives. When this point is reached there is equilibrium; and successful administration of resources consists in establishing and maintaining such equilibrium. In making these exchanges or selections we are guided by the anticipated or estimated values of the things with which we are dealing, and if we make mistakes and fail to secure the marginal coincidence between what we have got and the terms on which we got it, the price we mistakenly paid does not affect the value of the thing for which we paid it. The scale on which all objects of desire are arranged and graded in a man's mind, spoken of in the last chapter, must be thought of as a scale of marginal values.*

The present chapter will be devoted to the further examination of the conception of the "relative scale," and to the introduction, in connection with it, of a second great principle which combines with that of price to control the distribution of our resources.

We have seen that the skilful marketer has a portion of her scale of preferences definitely and even minutely present in her consciousness as she enters the market. She knows with considerable nicety the terms on which this or that alternative purchase is preferable, and the immensely complex system of combinations which can be commanded by the money she has to spend is fairly well under her ken. She may therefore come out of the market-place having done something like the best that was possible with her money. But in order for this result to represent the most effective administration of her resources in general for all the purposes of her life, other opportunities than those of the market in which she actually stood must also have been present in her mind with adequate preciseness; for her total expenditure in the market-place is not rigidly fixed in advance. It is related to her expenditure on other things (furniture, clothes, education, literature, holidays, etc.), and should be kept in close and continuous connection with it. And just as her expenditure on provisions is affected by the price of all these other things, so likewise her expenditure on them is affected by the price of provisions. The price of one or many of the commodities in the market may be considerably different from what she expected. If she finds that she can fill her basket for less than she expected she may feel at liberty to buy something else that she would not otherwise have allowed herself; and if prices are so high that the money she had meant to spend will make too poor a provision she must cast about for some saving elsewhere to enable her to spend a little more in the market-place. So when she learns the prices at the stalls, she may find she " can get that scarf for Bob after

Recapitulation.

all," or, on the contrary, that with things at such prices, she "must put off binding *Grimm's Fairy Tales* a little longer." The ideal marketer therefore will have in her mind, as she enters the market, a perfectly clear and precise realisation of that portion of her scale of preferences which is immediately concerned, while those portions of it which are adjacent and bear most directly and closely upon it will be within easy reach; and the whole range will be subconsciously present in what pyschologists call "the fringe." So much for recapitulation.

We may now go on to the next great step in advance in our analysis of the scale of preferences or relative estimates. We have noted incidentally more than once that the question may arise not only, for example, whether to buy any new potatoes at all, but also how many to buy. Suppose the usual consumption of potatoes in a family is about 4 lbs. a day (2 stone a week), and sound old potatoes are about $\frac{1}{2}$d. the lb. If new potatoes are 2d. the housewife may determine to buy 2 lbs. that week, for a treat, reckoning that they will go once round on Sunday, the second dish to be of old potatoes as usual, or if that takes too much trouble the second dish to be dispensed with. If they are $1\frac{1}{2}$d. a lb. she may buy 4 lbs. and have all new potatoes on Sunday, or one dish on Sunday and one on some other day in the week; or she may buy enough for the birthday dinner of one of the children. But when new potatoes come down to a penny she will buy no more old potatoes at all. It is not likely that she will buy new potatoes to the extent of 4 lbs. a day, as she did the old. They are still too expensive a form of food for that. She will perhaps buy 3 lbs. a day for 3d. (instead of 4 lbs. for 2d. as before), and this will involve some readjustment of expenditure on other articles of food, and perhaps in other branches of expenditure as well. But without following out these complex reactions we may at once grasp the fact to which we must now apply our closest attention, that the place which a pound of new potatoes takes on the marketer's scale of preferences is not fixed. For if at 2d. she buys 2 lbs. but not 3 lbs., this shews that she prefers the second pound per week to 2d., but prefers 2d. to the third pound

Declining significance of successive increments. Second helps never so good as first.

per week; and therefore a third pound stands lower than a second on her scale of preferences. If at 1½d. she buys 4 lbs. but not 5 lbs., it shews that she prefers the fourth pound to 1½d., but prefers 1½d. to the fifth pound—that is to say, that the fourth pound stands above and the fifth pound stands below 1½d. on her scale of preferences. If at 1d. she buys, say, 21 lbs. but not 22 lbs., it shews that she prefers the twenty-first pound to 1d., but prefers 1d. to the twenty-second pound. There is, of course, nothing inconsistent, anomalous, or mysterious in this. Each successive pound takes a lower place on the scale of preferences than the one before it, because the want to which it ministers is less urgent. "Second helps are never as good as first," said a child, with a deep sigh, when she had finished her second plate of jam-roll. The pudding may be the same, but the child is different; for to the second help comes a child who has already had a first help—that is to say, an organism which can no longer enter into the same reactions with jam-roll as before. In order to say what place on the relative scale a unit of any commodity occupies in comparison with a unit of any other, we must know the how-many-eth unit (per day, week, or year) of each commodity we are talking about; or, in other words, we must know how much of each commodity we are to suppose is already possessed when we talk of the place which an additional unit will take on a man's relative scale. If I have no supply of water and have seven loaves of bread to last me for a week, a pint of water will certainly occupy a higher place on my relative scale than a loaf of bread, but if I can already command twenty gallons of water for the week and have only one loaf of bread, another loaf will stand higher on my relative scale than a pint of water.

Hence the extreme importance of what is known as the doctrine of margins. We shall constantly find ourselves considering marginal services, marginal consumption, marginal significance, marginal expenditure, marginal values, marginal increments, and so on. Marginal considerations are considerations which concern a slight increase or diminution of the stock of anything which we possess or are considering; the marginal service rendered to us by any commodity is that service which we should have

Margins.

to forgo if the supply of the commodity in question were slightly contracted; our marginal desire for more of anything is measured by the significance of a slight increment added at the margin of our present store. And the importance of this service, or the urgency of this desire, depends, as we have seen, on the quantity we already possess. If we possess, or have just consumed, so much of a thing that our desire for more is languid, then additions at the margin have little value to us; but if we possess or have consumed so little that we are keenly desirous of more, then marginal additions have a high value to us. And when we say of anything that we "would not take any more at a gift," it means that its marginal value to us has been reduced to zero. Thus by increasing our supply of anything we reduce its marginal significance and lower the place of an extra unit on our scale of preferences; and suitable additions to our supply will bring it down to any value you please. Thus, whatever the price of any commodity that the housewife finds in the market may be, so long as its marginal significance to her is higher than that price, she will buy; but the very act of putting herself in possession of an increased stock reduces its marginal significance, and the more she buys the lower it becomes. The amount that brings it into coincidence with the market price is the amount she will buy.

In our example we have supposed that when she finds new potatoes at 2d. per lb., the first and the second pound for the week come higher on her relative scale than 2d., but the third lower. So she buys 2 lbs., but no more, and this brings the marginal value into coincidence with the price. A fortnight afterwards she finds new potatoes at $1\frac{1}{2}$d. If she only bought 2 lbs. now, the marginal value of a pound, though less than 2d., would be more than $1\frac{1}{2}$d., which is now the price she would have to pay for it; and she would therefore be refusing a good bargain in not buying more; and so too with a fourth pound; but a fifth pound would be worth less than $1\frac{1}{2}$d., and she would make a bad bargain in buying it. By getting 4 lbs., then, she brings the lowered marginal significance of her supplies into coincidence with the present price. And when the potatoes come down to 1d., by increasing her purchases to

Marginal significance brought into coincidence with market price.

21 lbs. she again brings down the marginal significance of the commodity into coincidence with the still further lowered price. Of course, her mind does not travel continuously over all the pounds from the fifth to the twenty-first, realising their gradual decline in significance until the margin that coincides with the new price is reached. It is only in the neighbourhood of the critical point that she consciously considers the question, but nevertheless the principle is at work all along the line. Its action brings her without consideration down to the point at which she has to consider.

In hundreds and thousands of suburban homes the question is asked every day, "How much milk shall we take in to-day, ma'am?" or "How much bread?" and the housewife knows without consideration that if she ordered one loaf of bread and one pint of milk, the marginal significance of bread and milk would be higher than their price, and if she said six loaves and five quarts of milk, the marginal loaf and pint would not be worth their price. Such orders, therefore, never enter into her head. But she deliberates, perhaps, whether she will want three loaves of bread or four, or three loaves and a twist, or three white loaves and a half-loaf of brown, and whether she shall take three quarts of milk or a pint more or less. Thus, whatever the terms on which alternatives are offered to us may be, we detect in conscious action at the margin of consideration the principles which are unconsciously at work in the whole distribution of our resources. When potatoes were at 2d. the marketer perfectly realised that a first or second pound were each of them worth more than 2d. When the price was $1\frac{1}{2}$d. (if all other conditions remained the same) the first and second pound would still be worth more than 2d. each, but the marketer is scarcely conscious of this fact, she is conscious only that a fourth pound is worth more to her than $1\frac{1}{2}$d. and a fifth pound less. By the time they have come down to 1d. she has ceased to realise that a first and second pound are still each of them worth more than 2d., and a third and fourth still each of them worth more than $1\frac{1}{2}$d., nor has she ever at any time reflected that all between the fifth and twenty-first are worth more than 1d. each, which is what she gives for them, though she is still conscious that a twenty-first is just worth or just more than worth 1d., and a twenty-second just not worth it.

But the facts which she has ceased to consider, or which she never considered at all, are facts none the less; and it follows rigidly from all these considerations that whenever a considerable amount of any commodity is purchased at a given price, and some, but not so much, of that same commodity would have been purchased had the price been higher, then the purchaser gets for, say, 1d. a pound something for which he would have been willing to pay 2d. a pound had there been no alternative except to go without it. If he had been confined to these two alternatives of paying 2d. a pound or going without he would have divided up the commodity into two portions, with respect to one of which he would have embraced the former alternative of giving 2d. a pound for it, and with regard to the other the latter alternative of going without it. As things are, he gets the whole of the commodity at such a price that the least significant or marginal increment (the portion which he would go without if the price rose a little) is worth the price; and consequently all the other increments are worth more. What he gets, therefore, taken in bulk, is worth more than he pays for it.

<small>Surplus value of what we get over value of what we pay for it.</small>

Note, however, that it is more accurate to speak of the marginal significance of "the service rendered by the commodity" than of that of "the commodity" itself, because when the housewife, after consideration, has determined to get a fourth pound of new potatoes, thinking that it will be just worth $1\frac{1}{2}$d. (the third having been worth more than $1\frac{1}{2}$d.), that fourth pound is not earmarked as worth less than the rest, but is indistinguishable from the other three. But it remains true that 2 lbs. would have accomplished certain purposes or rendered certain services, and that 3 lbs. will render those services and certain additional services also, which additional services are still worth more than $1\frac{1}{2}$d.; and further, that 4 lbs. will render the whole of the services rendered by 3 lbs., and certain additional services as well, and this last set of additional services are just worth $1\frac{1}{2}$d. While we cannot individualise and earmark the fourth pound, therefore, or say that it performs a less valued service than the third, we can distinguish between the services rendered by 3 lbs. and the extra services rendered by 4. These extra services are what we call the marginal services of a pound; and these marginal services will vary as 4, 10, or 50 lbs. is the margin at which we take them.

To familiarise the reader with the idea of declining marginal significance as successive increments to a commodity accrue, and of the surplus value which we obtain over and above the price we pay in the case of all commodities of which we purchase considerable quantities, it will be well to take a somewhat elaborate and artificial example and to work it out in detail. We will suppose that a housekeeper, for her ordinary household, buys 7 lbs. of tea a month at 2s. The fact that she buys 7 lbs. shews that the difference between the service rendered by 6 lbs. a month and that rendered by 7 lbs. is estimated by her as worth at least 2s., otherwise she would not buy a seventh pound. And the fact that she buys no more than 7 lbs. shews than an eighth pound would be worth less than 2s. to her. But if we ask her to direct her mind to the higher values of an initial supply of which she does not usually think, and to tell us what the difference between having no tea at all and having 1 lb. of tea a month would represent to her, we may imagine that, on careful reflection, she might tell us (the figures are of course purely hypothetical, and in that sense arbitrary) that it would be 23s. The difference between 1 lb. and 2 lbs. a month she might estimate at 17s.; the extra satisfactions conferred by a third pound at 12s., and so on to 8s. for a fourth, 5s. for a fifth, and 3s. for a sixth pound. But if the difference between no tea and a pound of tea a month is worth 23s., and the difference between 1 lb. and 2 lbs. is worth 17s., the total difference between no tea and 2 lbs. a month is 23s. + 17s. or 40s; so that if the alternative were offered the housekeeper of having no tea or a 2-lb. packet per month, she would pay 40s. for the 2 lbs. sooner than go without it. Again, we have seen that she estimates the difference between 2 lbs. and 3 lbs. at 12s. If her option therefore were to have no tea, or a packet of 3 lbs. per month, sooner than go without she would pay 52s. for the 3 lbs. Proceeding in the same way we see that the difference to her between having no tea at all and 4 lbs. a

Illustration from supply of tea.

month is represented by 60s., and the difference between no tea and 6 lbs. a month by 68s., and since we know that the last pound is worth at least 2s. to her the difference between no tea and 7 lbs. a month appears to be at least 70s. a month. Now, as a matter of fact, the tea being 2s. a pound, she gets her 7 lbs. of tea for 14s. a month. Thus she gets for 14s. that for which she would have paid at least 70s. sooner than go without it.[1]

This result, though it may seem rather startling, is in reality no more than the analytical restatement of the sufficiently obvious and familiar fact that a well-to-do person who has considerable supplies of most of the articles of his current consumption could support a small deduction without feeling it much, whereas if his supplies were reduced by three-quarters all round he would very distinctly feel any further small deductions from the residue. At his present margin small economies and adjustments do not cut into the quick, whereas at a margin further back they would; yet he pays no more for that proportion of his supplies that keeps him from starvation or from the feebleness of inanition than he does for that proportion which ministers to his comfort or perhaps his superfluity.

These considerations will throw much light on the distinction which the older economists drew between "value in use" and "value in exchange," a distinction which we should express under the terms "total significance" and "marginal significance." The total significance (value in use) of any commodity which we consume may be represented by the sum of money which we should require as an equivalent for entirely surrendering it, while the marginal significance (value in exchange) of a unit is represented by the sum of money for which we would consent to have our supply curtailed by one unit; and we have seen that if our supply consists, for example, of 10 units, its total significance (value in use of the whole) will be greater, and may be enormously greater, than ten times the significance of the marginal unit (value in exchange, or market value, of the whole). The example of the tea will make it very clear that as the "value in use" of our supply,

Pecuniary evaluation of the surplus. Total significance and marginal significance.

[1] For a more closely accurate treatment of this subject see Book II. Chap. II.

taken as a whole, increases, its "value in exchange" per unit (coinciding with its marginal value) declines. The value in use reaches its maximum when we have as much as we want and the marginal value has become zero.

Now since it is the marginal values that we are always considering, our minds are always engaged in appraising the least valued part of the commodity or service in question. One of the favourite examples of the distinction between "value in use" and "value in exchange" in the older books was the air we breathe, which obviously has an extremely high value in use, though under ordinary circumstances it has no value in exchange; the reason being that, since we all have as much of it as we want, its marginal significance has sunk to zero, though its total significance remains greater than can be measured in money. And accordingly, whenever the supply is for any reason curtailed, and can be increased or diminished by suitable appliances, air acquires a marginal significance, and may have an exchange value. If a mine-owner wished to improve his system of ventilation and asked for tenders or estimates, the engineer might put different systems before him, the more expensive ones providing for a larger volume of air to pass through the workings per minute, and the cheaper ones for less. In weighing them the owner would estimate, in each case, the additional advantages of the increased supply of air, and would consider whether they were worth the increased cost. He would therefore be considering with some precision the marginal value of air at several alternative margins. But no owner of deep mines would ever consider whether the mines ought to be ventilated at all or not. That is to say, he would never consider the most important part of the question, but would take it for granted. It would not be the total but the marginal value of the supply of air in the workings that would engage his thoughts.

Margin note: Why attention is concentrated on marginal significance.

Again, it is impossible to make any pecuniary estimate of the total value, or value in use, of our food collectively, but we are constantly considering its marginal value. We have already[1] spoken of young men and women living on

---
[1] Page 34.

TABLE I.

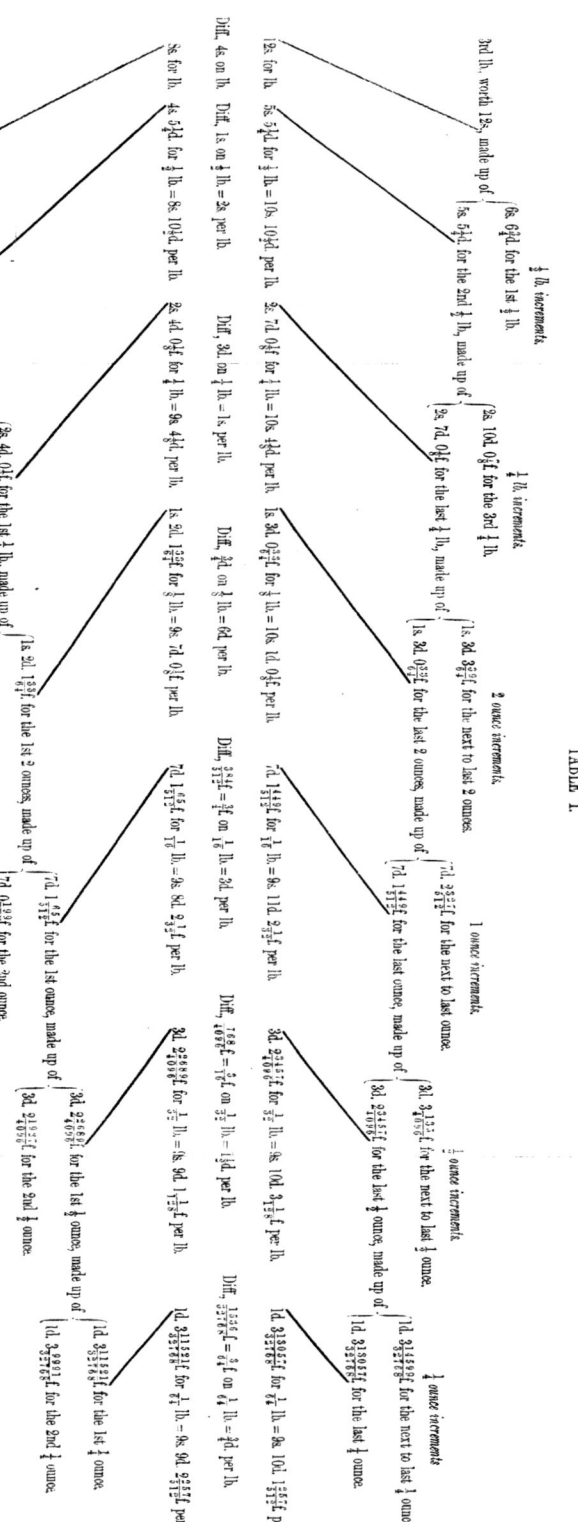

narrow means, who never consider whether they shall go without food altogether, and not often whether they shall go without a meal, but in whose minds an almost daily debate arises as to whether to spend an extra penny on a piece of cheese, or whatever it may be, at their midday meal. They are perpetually considering the marginal 1d. or ½d. per diem spent on food, though they seldom consider the remoter units which are higher up on the scale and are secured without deliberation.

It is obvious, then, that whereas the successive units of our supply of any commodity occupy different positions on our scale of preferences, it is only the units close to the margin of actual or contemplated possession that engage our close attention. Thus the scale of equivalence to which we give particular consideration is that of the marginal units of our supplies. Henceforth, therefore, whenever we speak without special qualification of the place which a unit of any commodity occupies on our scale of preferences we must always be taken to mean the marginal unit; and we must remember that as the marginal significance of anything declines owing to the supply increasing, the volume of the total satisfaction derived from it grows.[1] *(Relative scales of marginal significance.)*

We must now proceed to a closer examination of the nature of marginal units, marginal increments, and marginal significances. And in particular it will be necessary to justify the practice of speaking of the marginal significance of a commodity, at such and such a point, as measured indifferently by the value of a small increment or the value of a small decrement. *(Why marginal increments and decrements may be treated as equal.)* This practice is constantly and rightly followed in books on Economics, but since our whole theory rests on the fact that each successive increment renders less important services than the last, and that each successive decrement involves more serious privations than the last, it seems unwarrantable to assign an exactly equivalent value to the two successive increments that come one just before and the other just after a given point. The explanation and justification of this apparently illegitimate practice must now be given; and the

[1] Cf., however, pages 423 *sqq.*

reader will find it convenient to read it with the table that faces page 47 open before him. The beginner may perhaps find the investigation on which we are now entering (and which extends to page 71) of an unusually severe character. It is of the nature of grammar, and a complete mastery of it is necessary for an accurate and scholarly pursuit of the study; but as it is sometimes best when studying a new language to try, at a very early stage, to read it as best one can, and then to take up the grammatical details at the points at which the want of them is felt, so if the reader loses interest in the following argument or loses hold of it, he may find some help in reading further on, beyond page 71, to see what it is all leading up to and how it is underpropping and defining the ideas which we must assume in all our future investigations.

It is obvious that the reasons which make a second pound of tea of less value than a first, and a third of less value than a second, will also make the first half-pound more valuable than the second half-pound, and so forth. The consumption of any pound or other specified quantity of tea will naturally begin at a higher rate of significance than it ends at, and the decline will be continuous. The process by which we combined the more valued first pound (23s.) and the less valued second pound (17s.) into a total of two pounds at a value of 40s. may be reversed, and the total of 17s. for the second pound may be resolved into the significance of a more valued first half and a less valued second half pound. If the purchaser were at liberty to buy in half-pounds, therefore, he would be willing to pay more than half 17s. for the first half of the second pound, sooner than go without it, but if he had this he would value the second half-pound at less than half the 17s.; and so throughout.

Continuity of decline in marginal significance.

Further, we have supposed that while each additional pound has a lower significance (measured by the successive declines from 23s. to 17s., from 17s. to 12s., from 12s. to 8s., and so on), each successive decline in value is less marked than the one before it (the declines being by steps of 6s., 5s., 4s., etc., respectively); so if we were to go by half a pound at a time we should expect

Special law of decline in our selected illustration.

in like manner a regular decline in the significance of each half-pound, following a similar law. If, then, we ask our housekeeper for estimates of the significance not of successive pounds but of successive half-pounds, we shall expect her to give us a new series of hypothetical prices, consistent with the previous data as to the significance of successive pounds. Thus, if we ask her to start on the supposition that she has 2 lbs. of tea per month, and to go into closer details than the estimate of 12s. for the third pound and 8s. for the fourth which she has already given us, we may imagine her estimating the significance of the four half-pounds, taken severally. If she were to say, 6s. 6d. for the fifth half-pound, 5s. 6d. for the sixth, 4s. 6d. for the seventh, and 3s. 6d. for the eighth, this would give results fairly consistent with her original statement. Each successive half-pound would in this case decrease in significance, as compared with the one before it, at a uniform rate of one shilling. But we have already noticed that this is not the exact law followed by the original estimates. The decline from 23s. to 17s., and from 17s. to 12s., etc., is not uniform. It follows a law of decreasing rapidity. The difference may be made clear by tables. The original estimate may be set out thus:—

	Values of Successive Lbs., Declining.	Steps by which Values Decline, themselves Declining.	Rate at which Decline Decreases, Uniform.
1st	23s.		
		6s.	
2nd	17s.		1s.
		5s.	
3rd	12s.		1s.
		4s.	
4th	8s.		1s.
		3s.	
5th	5s.		1s.
		2s.	
6th	3s.		

Whereas if the four successive half-pounds are estimated as we have supposed, we should have—

E

Values, Declining.	Steps of Decline, Uniform.
6s. 6d.	
	1s.
5s. 6d.	
	1s.
4s. 6d.	
	1s.
3s. 6d.	

If, however, the estimates had not been 6s. 6d. but 6s. 6¾d. for the fifth half-pound, not 5s. 6d. but 5s. 5¼d. for the sixth, 4s. 5¼d. for the seventh, and 3s. 6¾d. for the eighth, we should have had—

Values, Declining.	Steps by which Values Decline, themselves Declining.	Rate at which Decline Decreases, Uniform.
6s. 6¾d.		
	1s. 1½d.	
5s. 5¼d.		1½d.
	1s.	
4s. 5¼d.		1½d.
	10½d.	
3s. 6¾d.		

in perfect consistency with the law manifested by the original estimates for successive pounds.

At this point the reader may feel that an outrage is being offered to his common sense in asking him to suppose that estimates of such accuracy can be given. This is perfectly true; but the outrage that has now been discovered and resented was committed when the original estimates of 23s., 17s., etc., were offered for acceptance. For, concealed under the round numbers there lay a law which implied, or at least suggested, that they were accurate not only to the nearest farthing, but absolutely This is a manifest impossibility; but if we carefully examine how and why it is impossible, we shall get a good deal o

Meaning and limits of accuracy in estimates.

incidental enlightenment, and shall then be able to pursue our investigations on this impossible hypothesis without peril.

Why, then, is this accuracy unthinkable? To begin with, any such estimates as we supposed ourselves to obtain originally would not really be based entirely on a true sense of the significance of the several increments, but would be partly determined by sums of money on which the mind easily rests, and with which it is accustomed to deal. One can imagine, for instance, a housekeeper saying, under certain circumstances, that she would give 8s. for a pound of tea but "not a penny more," and even actually refusing to give 8s. 1d.; but it is not easy to imagine her fixing on 7s. 9½d. as the exact sum past which she would not go, and refusing to pay 7s. 10½d. And again, whether she fixed on 8s. or 7s. 9½d., our housekeeper's declaration, that she would not give a penny or that she would not give a farthing more, would probably be nothing but a desperate determination to take her stand somewhere. She knows, let us say, that 7s. would be a good bargain and that 9s. would be more than the thing is worth. But she also knows that you can go from 7s. to 9s. by steps of a farthing each, and that unless she makes a stand she may be drawn on, always thinking that a single farthing is not worth fighting about, till she becomes conscious that she has gone too far; like the man who complained that he never knew when he had had enough to drink, though he knew when he had not had enough and when he had had too much. So, without pretending that she can really hit the exact value to a farthing, she (more prudent than the toper) pulls up somewhere and refuses to be worried any more. So she says, "I'll give you 7s. 9½d. Take it or leave it."

Therefore, when she mentions an outside price, she may, in the first place, be influenced by associations or habits, so that the price named is not based entirely on a deliberate estimate of the significance of the tea; and, in the next place, she is not in any case giving a perfectly precise and immovable estimate, for she cannot draw a definite line. There are prices which she is quite sure the thing would be worth, and prices which she is quite sure it would not be worth, but the transition from one to the other is gradual. The two are separated

Values, Declining.	Steps of Decline, Uniform.
6s. 6d.	
	1s.
5s. 6d.	
	1s.
4s. 6d.	
	1s.
3s. 6d.	

If, however, the estimates had not been 6s. 6d. but 6s. 6¾d. for the fifth half-pound, not 5s. 6d. but 5s. 5¼d. for the sixth, 4s. 5¼d. for the seventh, and 3s. 6¾d. for the eighth, we should have had—

Values, Declining.	Steps by which Values Decline, themselves Declining.	Rate at which Decline Decreases, Uniform.
6s. 6¾d.		
	1s. 1½d.	
5s. 5¼d.		1½d.
	1s.	
4s. 5¼d.		1½d.
	10½d.	
3s. 6¾d.		

in perfect consistency with the law manifested by the original estimates for successive pounds.

At this point the reader may feel that an outrage is being offered to his common sense in asking him to suppose that estimates of such accuracy can be given. This is *Meaning and limits of accuracy in estimates.* perfectly true; but the outrage that has now been discovered and resented was committed when the original estimates of 23s., 17s., etc., were offered for acceptance. For, concealed under the round numbers there lay a law which implied, or at least suggested, that they were accurate not only to the nearest farthing, but absolutely This is a manifest impossibility; but if we carefully examine how and why it is impossible, we shall get a good deal o incidental enlightenment, and shall then be able to pursue our investigations on this impossible hypothesis without peril.

Why, then, is this accuracy unthinkable? To begin with, any such estimates as we supposed ourselves to obtain originally would not really be based entirely on a true sense of the significance of the several increments, but would be partly determined by sums of money on which the mind easily rests, and with which it is accustomed to deal. One can imagine, for instance, a housekeeper saying, under certain circumstances, that she would give 8s. for a pound of tea but " not a penny more," and even actually refusing to give 8s. 1d.; but it is not easy to imagine her fixing on 7s. $9\frac{1}{2}$d. as the exact sum past which she would not go, and refusing to pay 7s. $10\frac{1}{2}$d. And again, whether she fixed on 8s. or 7s. $9\frac{1}{2}$d., our housekeeper's declaration, that she would not give a penny or that she would not give a farthing more, would probably be nothing but a desperate determination to take her stand somewhere. She knows, let us say, that 7s. would be a good bargain and that 9s. would be more than the thing is worth. But she also knows that you can go from 7s. to 9s. by steps of a farthing each, and that unless she makes a stand she may be drawn on, always thinking that a single farthing is not worth fighting about, till she becomes conscious that she has gone too far; like the man who complained that he never knew when he had had enough to drink, though he knew when he had not had enough and when he had had too much. So, without pretending that she can really hit the exact value to a farthing, she (more prudent than the toper) pulls up somewhere and refuses to be worried any more. So she says, " I'll give you 7s. $9\frac{1}{2}$d. Take it or leave it."

Therefore, when she mentions an outside price, she may, in the first place, be influenced by associations or habits, so that the price named is not based entirely on a deliberate estimate of the significance of the tea; and, in the next place, she is not in any case giving a perfectly precise and immovable estimate, for she cannot draw a definite line. There are prices which she is quite sure the thing would be worth, and prices which she is quite sure it would not be worth, but the transition from one to the other is gradual. The two are separated by a band rather than by a line, and even this band shades off, so that you cannot exactly determine its limits. There is an indefinite penumbra, as well as an umbra.

Thus, if we said that the original estimates were reliable to a shilling, we should mean that the housewife would certainly, without hesitation, give 22s. for the first pound, and that she would not entertain the idea of giving 24s. for it; and that would mean, *a fortiori*, that she would not give 23s. for 15 oz. of tea, for the difference between 15 and 16 oz. is greater than that between 23s. and 24s. To suppose such an approach to accuracy is not manifestly absurd. But to say that the estimate is accurate to a farthing would be to say that the housewife would give 23s. for a pound of tea, but not for a quantity that fell short of a pound by one sixty-ninth of an ounce. This does strike us as manifestly absurd. But we can give no definite answer to the question, "At what point between a shilling and a farthing does the hypothesis of accuracy become ridiculous?" Clearly one person might realise an indefinitely closer approximation than another, and we may therefore theoretically assume any degree of accuracy that we like. Even if we boldly make the absurd assumption of accuracy to a farthing, or to indefinitely smaller fractions of a penny yet, we shall merely be endowing our purchaser, for theoretical purposes, with normal powers raised to an abnormal degree of keenness. If we do this with our eyes open, the extreme supposition of estimates accurate down to an indefinitely minute fraction of a farthing or of an ounce, while illustrating the principles we are investigating in their inmost recesses, will not in any way mislead us.

Let us assume, then, that our data are reliable within any given degree of accuracy that we may find necessary to demand as we proceed, and that the law which they reveal applies consistently and uniformly, throughout the region which we are to submit to special investigation.[1]

<small>Assumption of ideally accurate data.</small>

We may now proceed to set forth the details of the table

---

[1] On the nature of this assumption of a regular and easily discernible law, see Book II. pages 464 *sqq.* The values dealt with in the text may be obtained by integration from the function $\frac{x^2}{2} - 7x + \frac{79}{3}$.

facing page 47, which may be carried out as far as we like. We have already broken up 12s., the significance of the third pound, into 6s. 6¾d., the significance of its first, and 5s. 5¼d., the significance of its second half; and have dealt with 8s., the significance of the fourth pound, in the same way. Carrying the process still further we shall find that 5s. 5¼d., the significance of the last half-pound that completes 3 lbs., may be taken as made up of 2s. 10d. plus ⅞ farthing for its first quarter, and 2s. 7d. plus ⅛ farthing for its second, and in like manner the 4s. 5¼d. of the next half-pound as made up of 2s. 4d. plus ⅛ farthing for the first quarter and 2s. 1d. plus ⅞ farthing for the second. The reader can test the consistency of these figures and those that follow by taking out the successive differences and satisfying himself that they follow the law of regular and equal decline that we have supposed to characterise the whole series, as implied in the original estimates. The top and bottom rows of this table (neglecting for the present the central row) set forth the estimated values of the four successive half-pounds, quarter-pounds, and smaller fractions of a pound down to the four successive quarter-ounces, that lie two and two on each side of 3 lbs.; and the reader may satisfy himself by examination that the law of the series is complied with in every case. Thus the four half-ounce increments two and two on each side of 3 lbs. run—

Values.	Difference.	Decline in Differences.
3d. $3\frac{135}{4096}$f.		
	$\frac{774}{4096}$f.	
3d. $2\frac{3457}{4096}$f.		$\frac{6}{4096}$f.
	$\frac{768}{4096}$f.	
3d. $2\frac{2689}{4096}$f.		$\frac{6}{4096}$f.
	$\frac{762}{4096}$f.	
3d. $2\frac{1927}{4096}$f.		

We are assuming an impossible degree of accuracy and precision throughout, but we must now distinguish between the different sets of distinctions we are drawing. Even when we are dealing with quarter-ounces, it requires no stretch of imagination to suppose that the quantities themselves are appreciable. A quarter-ounce of tea is not a negligible thing. With the aid of an infusor it can be made to give two cups of tea. Even with tea at 2s. a pound, a careful housekeeper considers it more or less carefully when filling her teapot, and adds or withholds it by a conscious estimate. On the supposition of its being added in the neighbourhood of the third pound it would be worth more than $1\frac{3}{4}$d. to our housekeeper. So far, then, we are dealing with easily appreciable magnitudes. But when we come to consider not the values themselves but the differences between them as the quarter-ounces succeed each other we are on very different ground. The table of approximations facing page 63 may help the reader to appreciate this. If our estimates are reliable to the nearest eighth of a penny, but not to finer fractions, it will be seen that there will be no appreciable difference in value between each of the four quarter-ounces, two and two, before and after the third pound. And even in the half-ounce increments there will be no appreciable difference in value between the last two increments before, or between the first two after, the third pound. What is the meaning, then, of the register of an appreciable difference between the second and the third half-ounce? The complete table and the general law of the series shew the difference between the second and third half-ounces to be less than that between the first and the second, and yet the table of approximations sets forth the smaller difference as appreciable and the greater as inappreciable. What is the sense of that?

To answer this question we must touch on a principle of which there are many familiar illustrations: the principle, namely, that very small differences do not consciously affect us severally, but exercise a cumulative effect which emerges into consciousness at a certain point. It is probably a common experience for a man looking at the seconds hand of his watch to think at first that the watch has stopped. It requires several seconds, during which he is conscious of the passing of time but not conscious of the moving of the hand, before the cumulative effect of the successive small movements makes itself felt. Thus the sense of declining value might be subconscious for two small units, and then might make its cumulative effect felt all at once in the transition to the third. To a mind capable of no finer discriminations than eighths of a penny, the difference between the values of the successive half or quarter ounces would be too small to make itself felt at every step. It would only be if we took units as large as an ounce that each of them would be sure to contain at least one such critical point at which the effect would become conscious.

We have now distinguished between sensitiveness to the importance of an addition or subtraction of a quarter-ounce of tea, and sensitiveness to the *difference* of importance between successive additions or subtractions, and have seen that it needs a much finer sense to be regularly and continuously conscious of the latter than of the former. ^{and become imperceptible at an earlier stage.} The difference between the significance of the two quarter-ounces that lie on either side of the 3-lb. line is less than a one-hundred-and-fifty-sixth of the significance of either of them. But it will be remembered that the law revealed in our original data implies that there is not only a decline in the significance of successive units, but that the decline itself is not uniform. In order that this characteristic should reveal itself as a regular phenomenon to a mind only capable of consciously appreciating eighths of a penny, we should need to give still larger room for cumulative effects; and a consultation of the table of approximations will shew that the action of this law is not traceable in any units smaller than a quarter of a pound. The quarter-pounds give—

2s. 10¼d.	3¼d.	
2s. 7d.		¼d.
2s. 4d.	3d.	¼d.
2s. 1¼d.	2¾d.	

[TABLE

but the 2-oz. increments give—

1s. 3⅞d.	⁶⁄₈d.
1s. 3⅛d.	⁶⁄₈d.
1s. 2⅜d.	⁶⁄₈d.
1s. 1⅝d.	

If the reader will now turn back to page 47 and recall the problem that led us into the present investigation, he will perceive that the impossibilities involved in our supposition of minute accuracy strengthen our case instead of weakening it. We noted that whereas our general theory requires us to believe that for any given margin the last unit before will have a higher significance than the next unit after, it is nevertheless customary to ignore the difference in value and to speak of the units on each side of the given point as having precisely the same significance. And we now see that for any degree of accuracy and sensitiveness, however impossibly fine, with which we choose to endow our observer, this proceeding is absolutely justified if the units in question are taken small enough. We can always take increments so large that the *significance* of the addition or subtraction of each one of them can be distinctly felt and estimated, but at the same time so small that the *difference* between the significance of two of them taken in succession cannot be separately estimated, and therefore not only may be, but must be, ignored.

<small>Answer to problem set on p. 47.</small>

To sum up. There are limits to the fineness of discrimination of which any mind is capable. Even the trained astronomer is not supposed to be able to distinguish the passage of time more accurately than to tenths of a second. But in his case the thing to be measured flows uniformly and continuously; whereas in the case of the tea our objective measurements cannot be supposed to present any such uniformity and continuity. The quality of different spoonfuls of tea is not uniform, still less is that of individual leaves. The vibrations of the nerves may themselves be supposed to respond, not continuously but cumulatively, to minute changes of external stimulus; and the surrounding conditions change not only from month to month but from second to second, so that even the most closely registering mind would not have a series of uniform and continuous phenomena to register.

We cannot, then, make our estimates indefinitely fine, and to whatever degree of fineness they actually attain, we shall be able to take increments, each of which has a definite significance, and two of which taken in succession may be treated as having the same significance.

This completes our justification of the practice of treating the marginal decrement and the marginal increment as identical in value, on the supposition that they are sufficiently small; and the reader who feels that he has reached the limit of his present capacity for following this kind of investigation may provisionally pass on to page 71. But the most perfect and satisfying part of the theory still remains to be expounded, and the reader's grasp of the subject will not be finally confirmed until he has mastered it.

The conception of "rate" on which the exposition we are now to enter upon depends is very familiar in its elementary applications. 3s. 9d. a yard is the same rate as $1\frac{1}{4}$d. an inch, 3s. a yard the same as 1d. an inch, and 2s. 3d. a yard as $\frac{3}{4}$d. an inch. *Conception of "rate," and its application to the tea illustration.*

```
        3s. 9d. a yard is 1¼d. an inch.
        3s.         "     1d.        "
        2s. 9d.     "     ¾d.        "
```

So if I give 3s. for a yard I shall be paying a higher sum, but a lower rate, than if I pay $1\frac{1}{4}$d. for an inch, but both a higher sum and a higher rate than if I pay $\frac{3}{4}$d. for an inch. And if I take the difference between a yard at 3s. 9d. and a yard at 3s. I shall be dealing with a larger sum than if I take the difference between an inch at $1\frac{1}{4}$d. and an inch at $\frac{3}{4}$d., but the sum, though larger in itself, will be smaller in proportion to the quantities compared, or, in other words, will represent a smaller difference in rate. Now let us look carefully at the three lines of entries in the central row of Table I. The last half of the third pound is worth 5s. $5\frac{1}{4}$d., which is both a lower sum and a lower rate than 12s. a pound; whereas 4s. 5¼d. for the first half of the fourth pound is a lower sum but a higher rate than 8s. a pound, for it is a rate of 8s. 10½d. per pound. Thus in comparing 12s. with 8s. we shall expect to find not only a greater difference, but a greater difference of rate, than between 5s. 5¼d. and 4s. 5¼d. And so we do; for the difference of rate in the one case is 4s. (half the lower and a third of the higher rate), and the difference in the other case is only 2s. (less than a fifth of the higher and less than a fourth of the lower rate). The difference between the half-pounds, then, is not only less than that between the pounds, but less than half of it, because it is a difference between half-pounds more like each other than the pounds were. In like manner, if we had taken the first half of the third pound and the second half of the fourth, we should have had the rates—

1st ½ lb.	.	.	6s. 6¾d. per ½ lb.	= 13s. 1½d. per lb.
Difference	.	.	3s.	„	= 6s. „
4th ½ lb.	.	.	3s. 6¾d.	„	= 7s. 1½d. „

where the difference between the half-pounds (3s.) would have been less indeed than the difference between the pounds (4s.), but more than half of it, because it would have been a difference between half-pounds less like each other than the pounds.

So the total difference of 4s. in value between the third and the fourth pounds may, if we like, be analysed into a difference of 3s. between the extreme half-pounds and a difference of 1s. between the mean half-pounds; and returning now to the difference between the inner or mean half-pounds that lie on each side of the 3-lb. point we may again analyse each of them into the extreme or most unlike and the mean or most like quarters. Taking the inner quarters we shall find them to be worth 2s. 7d. + one-eighth of a farthing, and 2s. 4d. + one-eighth of a farthing, respectively; the difference being 3d., or less than one-tenth of the higher and less than one-ninth of the lower amount. And the difference between the rates (10s. 4⅛d. and 9s. 4⅛d.) is only 1s. The table continues the successive halvings of the quantities considered till they are only a quarter of an ounce each, and at every step it rejects the more unlike outside halves and retains the more like inside halves of the pair last considered, thus narrowing down the increments, so that the difference between them not only goes on growing smaller, because the values themselves are smaller, but also becomes a smaller and smaller proportion of those smaller values themselves, because the latter are being made more and more like each other by the successive rejections of the most unlike portions of each pair. We see that the difference between the successive two-ounce increments, valued respectively at 1s. 3d. $0\frac{33}{64}$f. and 1s. 2d. $1\frac{33}{64}$f. is only $\frac{3}{4}$d., which is less than $\frac{1}{19}$ of the lower and less than $\frac{1}{20}$ of the higher term of comparison; and at the end of the table we find the difference between the two successive quarter-ounces on either side of the 3-lb. margin to be only $\frac{3}{64}$f., which is less than $\frac{1}{156}$ of the lower and less than $\frac{1}{157}$ of the higher. As we compare smaller and smaller increments on each side of the 3-lb. margin we see that the significance of the higher one falls both absolutely as a quantity and relatively as a rate, because it is taken closer and closer up to the less significant end of the third pound,[1] whereas the significance of the lower one falls absolutely as a quantity, but rises relatively as a rate, because it is taken closer and closer up to the more significant end of the fourth pound. Thus the upper and lower rate are constantly approximating to each other, and the difference between them is constantly becoming a smaller and smaller fraction of either. The falling series (read for convenience to the nearest $\frac{1}{8}$d. on the top line of the central row of Table II.) runs, as we pass from the pound to the half and quarter pound, etc.—

12s.   10s. $10\frac{1}{2}$d.   10s. $4\frac{1}{8}$d.   10s. 1d.   9s. $11\frac{1}{2}$d.   9s. $10\frac{3}{4}$d.   9s. $10\frac{5}{8}$d.

whereas the corresponding rising series (read on the lowest line) is—

8s.   8s. $10\frac{1}{2}$d.   9s. $4\frac{1}{8}$d.   9s. 7d.   9s. $8\frac{1}{2}$d.   9s. $9\frac{1}{4}$d.   9s. $9\frac{5}{8}$d.

The difference between each successive pair (read on the central line of either Table I. or Table II.) declines in accordance with a regular law, each difference being one half of the last. Thus by continuing the process we could make the difference as small as we pleased, though we could never make it nothing; and so we can bring the upper and the lower rate as near to

---

[1] Many readers may find it helpful to anticipate at this point the study of the tea curve in Book II. Chap. II.

each other as we please, though we can never make them identical. All this, together with the suggestion of the next step in our advance, will be made clearer by the inspection of the accompanying diagram.

The reader will probably have no difficulty in perceiving, as a general truth, that if two quantities approach each other indefinitely and can be brought as nearly as we please to identity but cannot be made identical, and if the one is always falling and the other always rising, they must both be falling and rising towards a certain fixed point that always lies between them. Thus the falling series, 3, $2\frac{1}{2}$, $2\frac{1}{4}$, $2\frac{1}{8}$, and the rising series, 1, $1\frac{1}{2}$, $1\frac{3}{4}$, $1\frac{7}{8}$, are falling and rising respectively towards 2. No member of either series will ever reach it, but the successive members approach it more and more nearly, and can be made to approach it as nearly as we please. If we fixed upon any quantity other than 2, ever so little larger or smaller, it would follow that either the descending quantity or the ascending quantity could pass it, by getting nearer than it to 2; for either can be made to get as near to 2 as we like, and we might like to get it nearer than this other quantity.

The idea of a limit.

The law by which, and the rate at which, the descending and the ascending series respectively approach this common point need not be identical. Thus the descending series, 7, $7 \times \frac{2}{3}$, $7 \times \frac{4}{7}$, $7 \times \frac{8}{15}$, and the ascending series, 3, $3\frac{1}{4}$, $3\frac{3}{8}$, $3\frac{7}{16}$, will both be found to be approaching by different laws the limit of $3\frac{1}{2}$. If they are taken two and two, 7 and 3, $7 \times \frac{2}{3}$ and $3\frac{1}{4}$, etc., the quantity $3\frac{1}{2}$ will be found always to lie between the two members of each pair. Both members may be made to approach this quantity as nearly as we please, and neither can ever be made to reach it by continuing the processes by which the series are formed.

The reader will now have no difficulty in perceiving that between the steadily descending series of rates, 12s., 10s. $10\frac{1}{2}$d., ..., and the steadily ascending series of rates, 8s., 8s. $10\frac{1}{2}$d., ..., which can be made to approach each other as nearly as we please, but can never be made identical, there must lie some rate that never changes and is the limit of both; but if he is not a mathematician he will have to take it on trust that that rate is 9s. 10d.

Idea of a limiting rate.

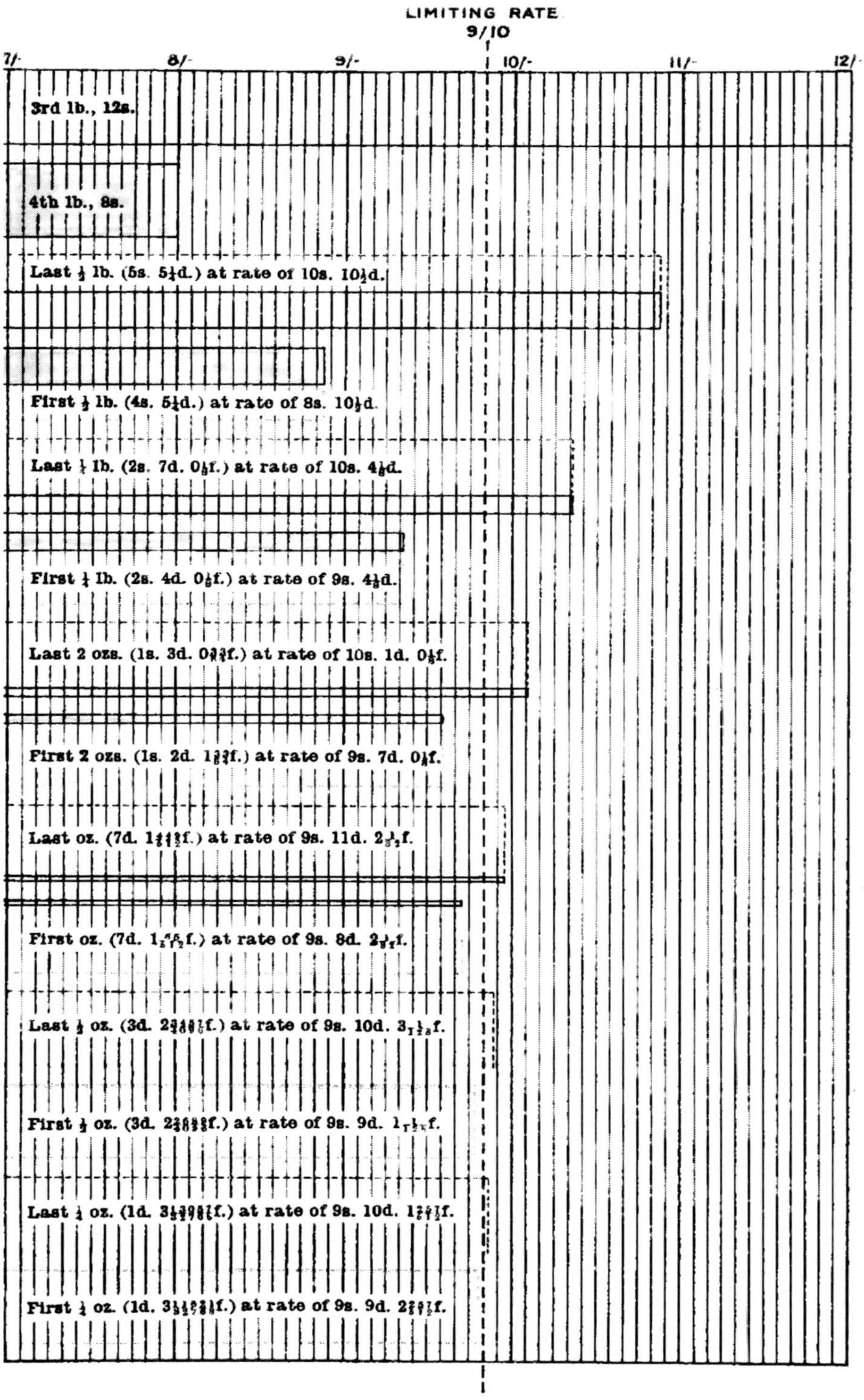

LIMITING RATE
9/10

| 7/- | 8/- | 9/- | 10/- | 11/- | 12/- |

3rd lb., 12s.

4th lb., 8s.

Last ½ lb. (5s. 5¼d.) at rate of 10s. 10½d.

First ½ lb. (4s. 5¼d.) at rate of 8s. 10½d.

Last ¼ lb. (2s. 7d. 0½f.) at rate of 10s. 4⅛d.

First ¼ lb. (2s. 4d. 0½f.) at rate of 9s. 4⅛d.

Last 2 ozs. (1s. 3d. 0⅔¾f.) at rate of 10s. 1d. 0½f.

First 2 ozs. (1s. 2d. 1⅔¾f.) at rate of 9s. 7d. 0¼f.

Last oz. (7d. 1⅞⅔f.) at rate of 9s. 11d. 2$_{3\frac{1}{2}}$f.

First oz. (7d. 1$_{5\frac{5}{12}}$f.) at rate of 9s. 8d. 2$_{7\frac{1}{4}}$f.

Last ½ oz. (3d. 2⅜⅘⅝f.) at rate of 9s. 10d. 3$_{1\frac{1}{28}}$f.

First ½ oz. (3d. 2⅜⅘⅝f.) at rate of 9s. 9d. 1$_{T}$$_\frac{1}{x}$f.

Last ¼ oz. (1d. 3½⅔⅞⅝f.) at rate of 9s. 10d. 1⅞⅞¼f.

First ¼ oz. (1d. 3½⅞⅔¼f.) at rate of 9s. 9d. 2⅞⅞½f.

DIAGRAM TO ILLUSTRATE TABLE I.

rest eighth of a pe not by the internal consistency of the entries in this table.

nts.

b.

lb., made up of *e increments.*

xt to last $\frac{1}{2}$ ounce. *$\frac{1}{4}$-ounce increments.*

st $\frac{1}{2}$ ounce, made up of { $1\frac{7}{8}$d. for the next to last $\frac{1}{4}$ ounce. / $1\frac{7}{8}$d. for the last $\frac{1}{4}$ ounce. }

more closely 10s. y 9s. $10\frac{3}{4}$d. per lb. $1\frac{7}{8}$d. on $\frac{1}{64}$ lb., more closely 9s. $10\frac{3}{8}$d. per lb.

b. 1s. p $1\frac{1}{2}$d. per lb. Diff., less than $\frac{1}{8}$d. on $\frac{1}{64}$ lb. $\frac{3}{4}$d. per lb.

more closely 9s. 4 y 9s. $9\frac{1}{4}$d. per lb. $1\frac{7}{8}$d. on $\frac{1}{64}$ lb., more closely 9s. $9\frac{5}{8}$d. per lb.

1st $\frac{1}{2}$ ounce, made up of { $1\frac{7}{8}$d. for the 1st $\frac{1}{4}$ ounce. / $1\frac{7}{8}$d. for the 2nd $\frac{1}{4}$ ounce. }

2nd $\frac{1}{2}$ ounce.

$\frac{1}{2}$ lb., made up of

d $\frac{1}{2}$ lb.

up of $\begin{cases} \text{2s. } 9\frac{3}{4}\text{d., made up of } \begin{cases} \text{1s. } 5\frac{29}{32}\text{d., made up of } \begin{cases} 9\frac{57}{256}\text{d., made up of } \begin{cases} 4\frac{1393}{2048}\text{d.} \\ 4\frac{1111}{2048}\text{d.} \end{cases} \\ 8\frac{175}{256}\text{d.} \end{cases} \\ \text{1s. } 3\frac{27}{32}\text{d.} \end{cases} \\ \text{2s. } 2\frac{1}{4}\text{d.} \end{cases}$

4th unit (4s. 3d.), made up of

A.

Rates.	Values of marginal units, and fractions of A at margin of 4.			Rates.
8s. 0d.	8s. 0d.	1	5s. 0d.	5s. 0d.
7s. $1\frac{1}{2}$d.	3s. $6\frac{3}{4}$d.	$\frac{1}{2}$	2s. $9\frac{3}{4}$d.	5s. $7\frac{1}{2}$d.
6s. $8\frac{5}{8}$d.	1s. $8\frac{5}{32}$d.	$\frac{1}{4}$	1s. $5\frac{29}{32}$d.	5s. $11\frac{5}{8}$d.
6s. $6\frac{9}{32}$d.	$9\frac{201}{256}$d.	$\frac{1}{8}$	$9\frac{57}{256}$d.	6s. $1\frac{25}{32}$d.
6s. $5\frac{17}{128}$d.	$4\frac{1681}{2048}$d.	$\frac{1}{16}$	$4\frac{1393}{2048}$d.	6s. $2\frac{113}{128}$d.

6s. 4d.
Limiting rate.

B.

7s.
6s.
6s.
6s.
5s.

We saw on page 56 that whatever we suppose to be the smallest quantity that the mind can register we can always fix upon two successive increments so large that the mind can appreciate the significance of each of them, but so small that it cannot appreciate the difference of significance between the two. But now let us suppose that there is a series of phenomena, obeying the law we are examining, so regular that there is no unit, however small, which would make it discontinuous—that is to say, which would reduce it to jumps. The passage of time may be taken as such a continuous phenomenon. And let us further suppose that there is a mind of such quality that no fraction, however minute, is small enough to escape being registered by it. This is what would be meant by supposing that our law worked with absolute accuracy. Let us make this supposition therefore. It would follow that our Table I. could be carried out as far as we chose, and the point would never be realised at which the differences between the successive units or the law of the decline in the successive differences would become too small to note. What should we then have? We should have a series of descending values beginning with 12s. and going down the series 10s. $10\frac{1}{2}$d., etc., always approaching nearer to 9s. 10d. as we halved the unit; and a series of ascending values 8s., 8s. $10\frac{1}{2}$d., etc., also always approaching nearer to 9s. 10d. as we halved the unit, but never reaching it. And if we took a sum ever so little higher than 9s. 10d. the falling series would at last get below it, or if we took a sum ever so little lower than 9s. 10d. the rising series would at least get above it. The sum of 9s. 10d., then, is absolutely fixed, and it represents a rate which is the limit alike of the significance of the third pound as you come down to its less significant end, and of the fourth pound as you come up to its more significant end. You may think of it equally well as the end of the third pound or as the beginning of the fourth. If, then, I say that 9s. 10d. a pound is the theoretical marginal value of tea, at the margin of three pounds, I mean that it is theoretically never quite true that either the last increment before or the next increment after the three-pound margin is valued at the rate of 9s. 10d., but that the rate of 9s. 10d. always lies theoretically between the values of these two increments, and the smaller they are the smaller, proportionally, is the theoretical error involved in saying that either or both of them is identical with it.

We may now epitomise our results. When we speak of the value of the marginal unit (at any given margin) we shall often mean the amount at which the last pound, or whatever it may be, is valued as a whole by the possessor, and shall not mean to imply that the next pound would be valued at the same amount. Sometimes we shall be thinking of the next pound to be obtained and shall call that the marginal pound without meaning to imply that the last pound possessed is not valued at a perceptibly greater amount. Which of these two pounds (each of which touches the actual margin with its lower or its upper limit) we mean, will depend upon the matter in hand at the moment, and the context will prevent any ambiguity. But sometimes the term "marginal value of a unit" is to be understood as applying at the same time both to the last and to the next unit; and in this case the implication will be that the units are large enough to be distinctly felt and valued, but so small that the difference of value between the two successive units is not felt. And this will always be a legitimate supposition. And lastly, we shall sometimes speak not of the marginal value of a unit of the commodity, but of the marginal value of the commodity per unit. And that expression would apply either to the actual rate of significance per unit of the increments just described, or to the theoretically limiting rate, the nature of which we have been examining. The implication in this last case would be that even though, however small the units we take, the last before the margin should always be valued at a little more and the next one after the margin at a little less than this rate, yet either can be brought as near to it as we please, and that it will always lie between them. It represents the point at the margin itself which the upper unit always touches at its lower end, stretching up from it, and the lower unit touches at its upper end, stretching down from it.

Marginal significance defined.

If we had taken any other margin, such as 5 lbs. or any other original set of estimates, we should have reached different, but always analogous results, and should have arrived at the same conclusions as to the legitimacy of speaking of marginal values, and as to the exact meaning of assigning such and such a marginal value to any commodity at any given margin. On our original data the marginal value of tea to this particular purchaser would be 19s. 10d. at the margin of 1 lb., 14s. 4d. at 2 lbs., 9s. 10d. at 3 lbs., 6s. 4d. at 4 lbs., 3s. 10d. at 5 lbs., and 2s. 4d. at 6 lbs. Marginal values intermediate to these will, of course, be reached at intermediate points. The marginal value of 17s. approximately corresponds to 1·49 lbs.; that of 7s. 6d. to 3·63 lbs.; that of 5s. to 4·48 lbs. The reader is supposed, if not a mathematician, to take it on trust that these special values are implicit in the original data, but he is supposed to understand, as the result of our investigations, that the original data, or any other similar group, necessarily imply the theoretical existence of definite marginal values, continuously declining, though they do not necessarily give us the means of determining them.[1] The estimates may be varied in any way we please, but so long as we suppose, in every case, a declining (though not necessarily a regularly declining) significance in value as successive increments are secured, we shall always be able to attach a precise significance to the conception of marginal value and shall always find it declining as the stream of supply broadens.

In some of our future examples we shall directly compare the marginal significances of two different commodities with each other without using money as a medium of comparison. The transition to this method may be made clearer and safer by certain considerations for which we are now sufficiently prepared. Let us suppose that there is some commodity other than tea, for a first unit of which our tea-consumer would be willing to give 17s. 9d., for a second unit 12s. 3d., for a third 7s. 9d., and for a fourth 4s. 3d., for a fifth unit 1s. 9d., for a sixth 3d. The table presents these estimates:— *Comparison between marginal significances of two commodities.*

1st.	2nd.	3rd.	4th.	5th.	6th.
17s. 9d.	12s. 3d.	7s. 9d.	4s. 3d.	1s. 9d.	3d.

[1] See Book II. Chap. II., especially pages 464 *sqq.*

This series, as the accompanying table shews, follows a law similar to that we have assumed as regulating the significance of tea.[1]

Values of Successive Units, Declining.	Steps by which Values Decline, themselves Declining.	Rate at which Decline Decreases, Uniform.
17s. 9d.		
	5s. 6d.	
12s. 3d.		1s.
	4s. 6d.	
7s. 9d.		1s.
	3s. 6d.	
4s. 3d.		1s.
	2s. 6d.	
1s. 9d.		1s.
	1s. 6d.	
3d.		

But it does not begin so high, and it threatens rapidly to reach zero—that is to say, the point at which another unit would not be taken at a gift. One might suppose, for instance, that it was important to a man to be at a neighbouring place, some fourteen miles distant, once a month, so that he would post there if necessary. A second and a third visit per month might have considerable but declining significance to him. A fourth visit might be just worth making if he had to pay first-class railway fare, a fifth not worth third-class fare, a sixth a matter of practical indifference, and a seventh perhaps a nuisance. In such a case half or quarter units might be interpreted as bimonthly visits, etc. Or an approximation to the hypothetical figures might be furnished by a suitably selected unit of some kind of fruit which has been medically prescribed to one member of a family, and is much desired for (or by) other important or importunate members of it, but any great abundance of which is regarded as a danger to the health of the nursery or the morals of the kitchen. It will be best, however, not to dwell on any imaginative realisations, which might easily become more of a burden than a support, and to speak not of

[1] The corresponding formula is $\dfrac{x^2}{2} - \dfrac{13x}{2} + \dfrac{125}{6}$.

tea and journeys to Crankstead, or of tea and apples, but simply of commodity A and commodity B.

Now the same methods which we applied (asking the reader to take them on trust) to ascertaining marginal values of tea, which has now become our commodity A, if applied to the data of commodity B would yield the following marginal values at the end of each unit :—14s. 10d. at a margin of 1, 9s. 10d. at a margin of 2, 5s. 10d. at a margin of 3, 2s. 10d. at a margin of 4. It will be convenient here to tabulate the estimates of the successive units of A and B which were given us, and also of the marginal values they imply.

Values of Units

	1st.	2nd.	3rd.	4th.	5th.	6th.
A	23s.	17s.	12s.	8s.	5s.	3s.
B	17s. 9d.	12s. 3d.	7s. 9d.	4s. 3d.	1s. 9d.	3d.

Marginal Significances

	At Margin of			
	1st Unit.	2nd Unit.	3rd Unit.	4th Unit.
A	19s. 10d.	14s. 4d.	9s. 10d.	6s. 4d.
B	14s. 10d.	9s. 10d.	5s. 10d.	2s. 10d.

It will be noted that if the individual who forms these estimates has a supply of 3 units of commodity A and 2 units of commodity B per month (or other unit of time), the marginal significance of each of them will be at the rate of 9s. 10d. per unit. This means, in rigid theory, that any addition to either of them, however small, is valued by him at something less than the rate of 9s. 10d.; and any subtraction, however small, would be felt

Meaning of equilibrium, and principle of selection between alternatives or of distribution of resources so as to secure it.

F

at the rate of something more than 9s. 10d. So that he would be the loser by curtailing his consumption of either by ever so small a fraction of a unit, in exchange for increasing his supply of the other by the same fraction. But if we are not speaking of an absolute theoretical margin, but of actual estimates, we shall mean that small increments or decrements of either commodity would alike be estimated, in this region, at the rate of 9s. 10d. a unit, so that it would be a matter of indifference to the possessor whether his supplies remained as they are, or a very small fraction of a unit were taken away from his supply of one of the commodities, and a like amount added to his supply of the other. In either of these cases we should say that if the terms on which the choice between the two commodities is offered him are terms of par—that is to say, if he can get any unit or portion of a unit of either of them by sacrificing the same quantity of the other,—he will have no interest in making any change, and his supplies therefore are in a state of equilibrium. Hence we may sometimes say that if a man's supplies are in equilibrium (at current prices) he would lose by making any change, and sometimes that a small change of one commodity for the other, on the terms open to him, would be a matter of indifference. It will depend upon whether we are considering quantities large enough to embrace a sensible rise or fall of significance within their several boundaries. Equilibrium does *not* exist if the possessor knows that he would gain by exchanging, on the terms open to him, a portion, however small, of either of the commodities for the corresponding portion of the other.

Thus, if the man had five units of A and 2 of B we should have—

	Value of last Unit Possessed.	Value of next Unit to be Acquired.
A	5s.	3s.
B	12s. 3d.	7s. 9d.

And there will be an obvious advantage in giving a unit of

A (5s.) for an extra unit of B (7s. 9d.). The man would then have 4 units of A and 3 of B, and we should have—

	Value of last Unit Possessed.	Value of next Unit to be Acquired.
A	8s.	5s.
B	7s. 9d.	4s. 3d.

And it would no longer be to his advantage to exchange either a unit of A (8s.) for a unit of B (4s. 3d.), or a unit of B (7s. 9d.) for a unit of A (5s.). In the first case he would lose a value of 3s. 9d., and in the second a value of 2s. 9d. We see, then, that it might be possible in a loose way to speak of equilibrium if the possessor had no opportunity of exchanging smaller quantities than a pound; but we can also see that the equilibrium is not perfect or symmetrical, for, in the first place, an exchange in the direction of A for B would be more undesirable than one in the direction of B for A; and, in the second place, if we look at our table of marginal values, we shall see that the marginal value of A to the possessor of 4 units is 6s. 4d., whereas that of B to the same possessor, if his supply is 3 units, is only 5s. 10d. This indicates that he would be the gainer by exchanging a little of B, which he values at not perceptibly more than the rate of 5s. 10d., for a little more of A, which he values at not perceptibly less than the rate of 6s. 4d. Let us, therefore, look further into the matter. A double table (facing p. 70), on the principle of Table I., sets forth the fractional values of A round about the margin of four of the units, and of B round about the margin of three. The reader may test the consistency of these data, but will otherwise take them on trust, as before. The 8s. at which the fourth unit of A is estimated is made up of 4s. $5\frac{1}{4}$d. for the first half and 3s. $6\frac{3}{4}$d. for the second; and the 5s. at which the fifth pound is estimated is made up of 2s. $9\frac{3}{4}$d. for the first half-pound and 2s. $2\frac{1}{4}$d. for the second. If the man possesses 4 units of A, therefore the significance of the last half-unit he possesses will be 3s. $6\frac{3}{4}$d., and the significance of the next half-unit he would acquire 2s. 9¾d. Similarly, the 7s. 9d. at which the third unit of commodity B is estimated will be found to be made up of 4s. 4½d. for the first half-unit and 3s. 4½d. for the second; and the 4s. 3d. at which the fourth unit is estimated, of 2s. 6d. for the first, and 1s. 9d. for the second. Taking the margin, therefore, at 3 units, the last half-unit possessed will be estimated at 3s. 4½d., and the next half-unit to be acquired at 2s. 6d.; and we shall have—

	Last Half-Unit Possessed.	Next Half-Unit to be Acquired.
A	3s. 6¾d.	2s. 9¾d.
B	3s. 4½d.	2s. 6d.

There is still no advantage to be obtained by exchanging a half-unit of A (3s. 6¾d.) for a half-unit of B (2s. 6d.), or a half-unit of B (3s. 4½d.) for a half-unit of A (2s. 9¾d.), the loss in one case being 1s. 0¾d. and in the other 6¾d., in each case much less than half the loss on exchanging a unit.

If we take ¼ of a unit we shall have—

	Last Quarter-Unit Possessed.	Next Quarter-Unit to be Acquired.
A	1s. 8$\frac{5}{32}$d.	1s. 5$\frac{29}{32}$d.
B	1s. 6$\frac{27}{32}$d.	1s. 4$\frac{7}{32}$d.

and still there is no advantage in exchange either way. But if we try ⅛ of a unit we shall have—

	Last Eighth-Unit Possessed.	Next Eighth-Unit to be Acquired.
A	9$\frac{201}{256}$d.	9$\frac{57}{256}$d.
B	9$\frac{21}{256}$d.	8$\frac{109}{256}$d.

DIAGRAM TO ILLUSTRATE TABLE III.

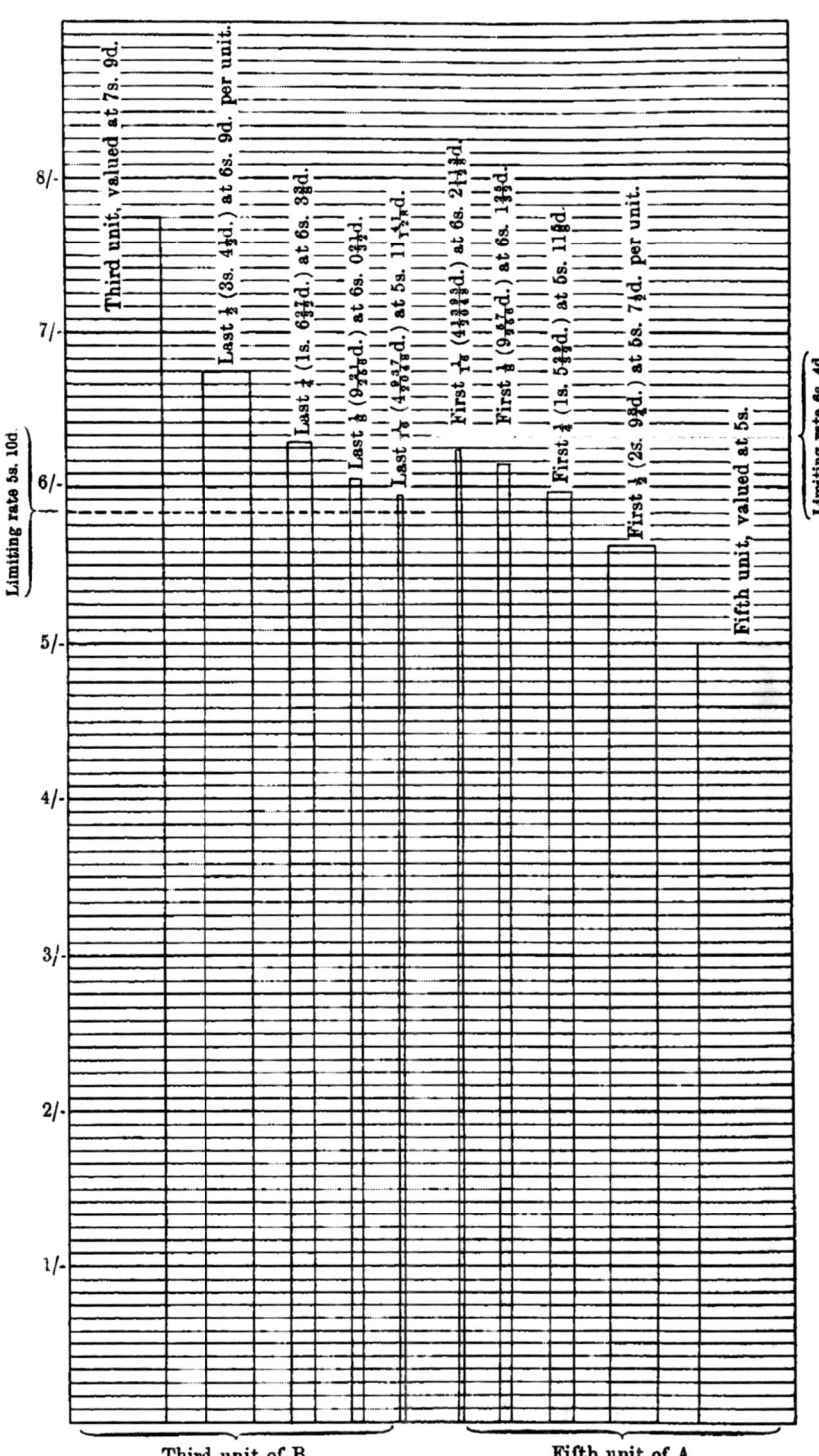

and we see that there will be an advantage of $\frac{36}{256}$d. or $\frac{9}{64}$d. in exchanging this increment of B for A.

But if we had only taken $\frac{1}{16}$ of a unit we should have had—

Last Sixteenth-Unit Possessed.	Next Sixteenth-Unit to be Acquired.
$4\frac{1681}{2048}$d.	$4\frac{1393}{2048}$d.
$4\frac{937}{2048}$d.	$4\frac{601}{2048}$d.

and the advantage in the exchange would have been $\frac{456}{2048}$d. or $\frac{57}{256}$d., which is more than $\frac{1}{5}$d., whereas $\frac{9}{64}$d. (the advantage in exchanging $\frac{1}{8}$ of a unit) is less than $\frac{1}{7}$d. Thus we see that though there would be a gain in substituting $4\frac{1}{8}$ of A and $2\frac{7}{8}$ of B for 4 of A and 3 of B, there would be a greater advantage in substituting $4\frac{1}{16}$ A and $2\frac{15}{16}$ B. There is nothing surprising in this. We have often seen that it would be better to make a certain bargain than not, but that it would be better still to make one half of it without the other half. Thus, if the man has 4 of A and 3 of B, it will be better to bargain for an exchange of $\frac{1}{8}$ unit of B for $\frac{1}{8}$ unit of A than to stay as he is; but if he can make half the exchange instead of the whole, it will be better yet.

A part of the investigation upon which we have been engaged may be illustrated by the accompanying diagram, which displays the position of the man who possesses four units of A at a marginal significance of 6s. 4d. and three units of B at a marginal significance of 5s. 10d. It shews how (since the fifth unit of A begins at the same marginal significance as that at which the fourth unit ends, and since this is higher than the marginal significance of the actual supply of B) it follows that even if there is no advantage in exchanging a unit or half a unit of B for A, yet as smaller fractions of the unit are taken, and their values in both cases approach the marginal significances, the time must come when a small fraction of A will be worth more than the corresponding small fraction of B.

But we have not reached a state of equilibrium. All the positions we have hitherto examined leave one of the

TABLE I.

For any given command of the two commodities at par, therefore, there is an ideally perfect distribution which gives equilibrium. If the man's resources are otherwise distributed he is holding something with a lower marginal significance than that of something else that he might have instead of it; and each step he takes to rectify this will raise the marginal significance of the commodity that stands lowest, and lower the significance of the one that stands highest, till the point of equilibrium is reached.

Note, finally, that we have for convenience supposed ourselves to be able to exchange, or otherwise choose between, the two commodities at par, that is unit for unit. If our units are arbitrary we may take the customary unit for A and then fix the unit of B at that quantity (whatever it is) that is offered us as an alternative to it. If we use the customary units for both, then the rates of exchange between them may vary to any extent. But the principle is exactly the same. If the terms on which we may choose between A and B are two units of A to one unit of B, instead of one of A to one of B, then, of course, equilibrium will be reached not when the marginal significance of A, reckoned as a rate per unit, is equal to that of B, but when it is half equal to it, or equal to half of it.

The reader who has followed the investigations with any degree of closeness up to this point will find nothing new in the examples to which we shall now proceed; but if anything remains obscure, tangled, or unstable in his conceptions, these new examples may give him some better power of realising exactly what we have been talking about and may throw back some light upon the ground we have already traversed.

We are still investigating the conception of marginal adjustment and the relation of marginal to total values; and as we have seen [1] that in ordinary life we seldom or never consider total values with any definiteness, or marginal values except in the close neighbourhood of the actual or contemplated margin of our supply, it will still be necessary to make large claims on the reader's imagination. Suppose, then, that in a besieged city, or under

Illustration of bread and water.

---

[1] Pages 45 *sqq.*

some merely imaginary circumstances of captivity, or what not, I had the option given me between a quart of water or a (half-quartern) loaf of bread per diem, for a week. If I were wise I should choose the water, for I should certainly have a better chance of surviving, and in any case should die with less suffering, on the water alone than on the bread alone. But if the ratio of a quart of water and a loaf of bread (each to count as a unit) were established, as terms on which I might choose between bread and water, and I were then allowed seven such units for the week, each to be taken in bread or water at my option, the problem of adjustment would become a nice one. I might ultimately choose a pint of water (half a unit) and half a loaf (another half-unit) a day. That would be $3\frac{1}{2}$ quarts and $3\frac{1}{2}$ loaves for the week. What would this mean? It would not, as we have seen, mean that I attach the same value to a pint of water and to a half-loaf in the abstract, or under all conditions; for if I had no provision of either, I should prefer the pint of water. On the other hand, if I had 7 pints of water and 3 loaves for the week, I should, it appears, prefer another half-loaf to another pint of water. The relative values of a pint of water and a half-loaf of bread therefore depend on the supply of each that I already have; and if, being free to subdivide as much as I choose, I arrive at the balance we have supposed, it means that if I had 7 pints and 7 half-loaves for the week I would not exchange the smallest amount of bread for water, or of water for bread, at the rate of a pint of water to the half-loaf. That is to say, the values of bread and water at the actual margins exactly coincide with the terms on which the alternatives between them are offered me. But though they correspond thus at the margins the significance of water rises more rapidly as we depart from the margin than that of bread does. It would be a matter of practical indifference to me whether I lost a very minute amount of water or a very minute amount of bread in the proportion of a quart to the loaf, or a pint to the half-loaf, but it would not be a matter of indifference to me whether I had lost a large part of my supply of water or a large part of my supply of bread in that same proportion. The marginal value of the unit of bread and of the unit of water, then, are the same; but the total value of the water is higher than that of the bread, and the value of any considerable fraction of the water is higher than that of the corresponding fraction of bread. Thus, if my allowance were diminished I should economise more in bread than in water, and if it were reduced very low I should take it all in water. And note also that if the allowance were much increased I should take out most of the increase in water too, for the significance of water not only rises more rapidly than that of bread as we recede towards the first increments, but also, after a time, declines less rapidly as we advance. A loaf a day would be about as much as I should want to eat; but I should always be glad of more water, until I had enough to wash comfortably or even to bathe in. The significance of a pint of water, then, begins at a higher point than that of a loaf of bread. It declines rapidly at first, but after a time very slowly. Whereas the value of a loaf of bread begins lower than that of a pint of water and falls more slowly at first, but after a time declines rapidly, almost abruptly.

We have now seen that if the terms on which bread and water are offered me are a pint to a half-loaf, then, whatever my allowance may be, I shall so distribute it as to bring the marginal significance of bread and water into correspondence with these terms. But what if the terms themselves are changed? What if a pint is to be the equivalent, not of a half-loaf, but a whole one? That is to say, let us suppose that I have now the covenanted right to draw seven pints and three and a half loaves per week, but I may if I like sacrifice a pint for a loaf, or a loaf for a pint, so that if I took it all out in bread I should now have ten and a half loaves a week, and if I took it all out in water, ten and a half pints (five and a quarter quarts). There will no longer be equilibrium at 7 pints and $3\frac{1}{2}$ loaves, for at this margin, as we have seen, it is only just not worth while to buy bread for water at the rate of a pint for half a loaf. Obviously, therefore, it is well worth while to buy it at the rate of a pint for a whole loaf. Only for a small exchange, however; for as I increase my allowance of bread it becomes (perhaps rapidly) less significant to me, and as I decrease my supply of water it becomes more significant to me. So I shall perhaps go no further than exchanging one pint of water for one loaf, and the balance will be struck at six pints of water and four and a half loaves of bread.

If, on the other hand, the terms were changed the other way, and a pint of water would exchange with a quarter of a loaf of bread, so that my whole income would realise 21 pints or $5\frac{1}{4}$ loaves, I should again alter the distribution of 7 pints and $3\frac{1}{2}$ loaves, but now in the opposite sense; for by sacrificing a quarter of a loaf I could now get a whole extra pint, and seeing that, at these margins, water is only just not worth bread at the rate of a pint for the half-loaf, I shall be glad to secure it at the rate of a pint for the quarter-loaf. But as my supply of water increases, its marginal significance declines, and as my supply of bread is contracted, its marginal significance rises; so that after a slight shifting we should reach a point at which I no longer wish to increase my supply of water at the expense of my supply of bread, even on these improved terms. Perhaps I should not go much further than sacrificing half a loaf of bread to secure two pints more of water, and I might strike the balance at 9 pints and 3 loaves a week.

Thus the proportions in which I devote my resources to either of two alternatives, my tastes remaining the same, depend both upon the terms upon which the alternatives are offered and on the amount of my resources. A change in either of these conditions will affect the distribution.

Next let us imagine a peasant who grows his own foodstuffs and also sells some of his produce. He can get 7s. a cwt. for potatoes and 14s. a cwt. for meal (meal, we will suppose, being the form in which he sells or consumes his grain); and these being the prices, he determines to keep 12 cwt. of potatoes and 10 cwt. of grain for his own use. He might have raised the same sum of money by selling less potatoes and more grain, or *vice versa*, and if he had sold more of one he would have held more of the other. In choosing, therefore, as he does, he shews that 12 cwt. of potatoes and 10 cwt. of meal are more valued by him than either 13 cwt. of potatoes and $9\frac{1}{2}$ cwt. of meal, or 11 cwt. of potatoes and $10\frac{1}{2}$ cwt. of meal; for each of these alternatives is open to him, and he embraces neither. We see,

Illustration of peasant's potatoes and meal.

then, that he will not forgo half a cwt. of meal for a cwt. of potatoes, nor a cwt. of potatoes for half a cwt. of meal. Now we will suppose that the price of meal and cereals remains constant, but that after our peasant has struck the balance and laid up his provisions for the year the price of potatoes rises from 7s. to 7s. 3d. We will ignore the difference between the buying and selling prices, and will suppose that he can buy back a cwt. of meal on exactly the same terms on which he could have kept it. Now we saw that at the margins of 10 cwt. and 12 cwt. he would neither give a cwt. of potatoes for half a cwt. of meal, nor half a cwt. of meal for a cwt. of potatoes, but it does not follow that he will not give a cwt. of potatoes for half a cwt. of meal plus 3d. The change in the terms may just induce him to make the exchange. Let us suppose that this is so. An advance of 3d., but nothing less, would just induce him to sell a cwt. of potatoes. We might therefore be inclined to say that in that case, since 3d. represents the difference in value to him between a cwt. of potatoes and half a cwt. of meal, it would follow that if potatoes fell to 6s. 9d. instead of rising to 7s. 3d. he would sell a half-cwt. of meal for 7s., buy 1 cwt. of potatoes for 6s. 9d., and secure 3d., which represents the difference between his estimate of the two. But this is a rash inference; for it may be that starting with 12 cwt. of potatoes and 10 cwt. of grain he would find the exchange of half a cwt. of grain for a cwt. of potatoes either more or less distasteful than a change the other way. He requires the premium of 3d. to make him change the potatoes for the grain, but it is possible that he would change the grain for the potatoes for a premium of $2\frac{1}{2}$d., or that he would not do it for less than $3\frac{1}{4}$d. As in the case of the bread and the water, one of the commodities may rise in significance more rapidly than the other as we recede from the margin, or fall less rapidly as we advance beyond it. But, however this may be, if 3d. just, and only just, induces him to sell 1 cwt. of potatoes, it would require a higher premium to make him sell 2 cwt., for the change from 12 and 10 to 10 and 11 would constitute more than twice the disturbance of the change from 12 and 10 to 11 and $10\frac{1}{2}$.

These examples shew how the original terms on which alternatives are offered to us, or any change in those terms that occurs after we have reached equilibrium, affect or modify our choice. But if free to choose, then whatever the terms may be we can always so distribute or redistribute our resources as to bring the marginal significance of our several commodities into coincidence with them and so reach a true equilibrium; and by doing so we always maximise the desired result.

The art of successful administration consists in so distributing our resources that the marginal significance of all the things we secure corresponds to the terms on which we can get them. These terms may be considered as registering the price we must pay in the sacrifice of any one commodity or satisfaction for the acquisition of any other. Thus they are all connected by a system of external equivalences according to which they may be had in exchange for each other. This we may call the system of their "prices" (in the large sense), measured in each other. And they are all connected by a system of internal equivalences according to which each of them is worth, at the margin, so much of each of the others. This we may call the system of their "worths," measured in each other. Successful administration of resources brings these two systems into coincidence. It can always do so, for every change of administration modifies the system of worths; it can always be modified in the direction of conformity to the system of prices until it coincides with it; and every such modification increases the volume of desired results, till the coincidence brings it to its maximum.

But we must carry all this further, and must generalise our results. It is not only such things as bread, water, plums, and potatoes that change their marginal value according to the breadth of the supply. I value an extra hour's leisure in the day, or an extra half or quarter day to my week-end, more or less according to the amount of daily leisure or the amplitude of the week-end I already enjoy. If I am considering whether I will take a piece of work for which I shall be paid at the rate of 10s. an hour, then (if we neglect the consideration of any irksomeness or any pleasure that the work itself may give me, and look upon the hour simply as subtracted from other occupations) it is easy to see that if I have abundant leisure and am severely straitened for cash, I shall be likely

Extension and generalisation of principle, and further illustrations.

to accept the offer, and if repeated offers come to me I shall go on accepting them. But each successive half-sovereign a week becomes less important, as I am better provided with cash, and each successive hour withdrawn from other occupations involves a greater sacrifice as my reserve of leisure contracts. At last I shall reach the point at which the sacrifice of another hour, at the raised margin, will just compensate the acquisition of another half-sovereign at the lowered margin.

Suppose I can command as much work as I like at 10s. an hour, and I choose to make 250 working days in the year, and to work 6 hours a day, so that I have an income of £750 a year, and suppose I do not care to increase it by £125, at the cost of an extra hour's work per diem. Leisure and money. Perhaps I should be willing to work an extra hour a day if I could thereby raise my income by £250. Suppose, however, that I can command as much work as I like at £1 an hour. If I still work 6 hours a day for 250 days, my income will be £1500 a year. It is possible that I may care to make it £1750 by working an extra hour. It is more likely that I may prefer shorter hours or longer holidays. I might choose to earn only £1000, working 4 hours a day for 250 days, or 5 hours a day for 200. Or it might chance, by a mere coincidence, that I went on working just at the same rate of 6 hours a day for 250 days. That is to say, 10s. at the margin of an income of £750 may have more significance to me than £1 at the margin of an income of £1500, or it may have less, or it may, by a coincidence, have exactly the same. In the first case I should work shorter hours for the higher fee, in the second case I should work longer hours, and in the third case just the same number. But in any case either 10s. or £1 will have more significance at the margin of an income of £750 than at that of an income of £1500.

Similar problems arise apart from money or exchange. The administration of limited resources of space between different claimants is a problem with which every middle-class London householder is acutely familiar. Administration of space. "Can I spare room for it?" or "Is it worth the room it takes?" is often a determining consideration in his selection between alternative possessions. When he gets into the country a man may meet in a pleasanter form the same problem of the administration of space. Can he both have a tennis-court and grow his own vegetables? And if not, which does he prefer? Or if, in any case, he has not room for the tennis-court, how much shall he let his cabbages and lettuces intrude upon his grass plot? Or how shall he settle the rival claims of gooseberry-bushes and rose-trees? The marginal adjustment in such matters may become a problem so delicate that the mind thinks in inches.

Or a young man has made his arrangements to get up at a given hour, to take 30 minutes to dress, 30 minutes for breakfast and the paper, and 30 minutes to walk down to his office or lecture; but when he is called, a new claimant on the time he has so carefully distributed appears, in the shape of the luxury of staying where he is. He remembers hearing that it is bad for the constitution to get up suddenly, and he lies dreamily in bed cutting minutes off one after another of the three assignees of his time, till two-thirds of his resources are exhausted, and he springs out of bed to dress in 10 minutes, to breakfast in 5, and to run down in a quarter of an hour to keep his appointment. The significance of minutes in bed has encroached upon all the others, and by its pressure has revealed the fact that as you cut into them the significance of the minutes assigned to dressing, breakfast, and locomotion, rises unequally. There was a marginal balance at 30 minutes each, but the minutes taken off the time for getting to his appointment rise in significance more rapidly than those assigned to his toilet, and these again more rapidly than those assigned to his breakfast, and when at last these marginal significances, still equal to each other, rise to equality with the now declining value of guilty and uneasy moments in bed, the margins stand, as we have seen, at 5, 10, and 15 minutes. The thirtieth breakfast minute and the thirtieth minute for walking had the same estimated significance, but as you recede the walking minutes rise in value so rapidly that you must go back to the fifth breakfast minute in order to find one as valuable as the fifteenth walking minute.

With time it is natural to associate work, for work involves effort extending over time, and industrial enterprise as a whole may be regarded as aiming at the economical distribution of human effort. At the present stage of our inquiry a hint will be sufficient. We may think of Robinson Crusoe withdrawing a little work in one direction and turning it in another, in order to bring the marginal significance of his products into correspondence with the terms in effort on which nature offers the alternatives to him. Or we may think of our indolent young man, when he has fairly begun his day, carefully considering what expenditure of labour will pay best in the examination for which he is preparing, visited at certain moments by compunction as to the sordidness of this view, and genuinely allured (by the fascination of some subject) into the pursuit of knowledge for her own sake; or fraudulently persuading himself, in another mood, that he has a soul above mere utilitarian considerations, that knowledge of the world is better than University distinction, and that his acquaintance with the modern drama or with the points of dogs or horses is in more urgent need of marginal increments than his knowledge of the niceties of the syntax of a dead language. He too is, wisely or foolishly, administering his resources and endeavouring to bring marginal values into a proper balance with the terms on which alternatives are offered.

and effort.

Thus the same law holds in intellectual, moral, or spiritual as in material matters. Cæsar tells how when surprised by the Nervii he had barely time to harangue his soldiers, obviously implying that the harangue was shorter than usual. He felt that a few moments, even at such a crisis, were well devoted to words of exhortation to his troops; but their value declined at the margin, and the price in delaying the onslaught rapidly rose; so the moment was soon reached when the time could be better spent than in prolonging a moving discourse. In a story of South America, after the war, we are told of a planter who, when warned by his wife in the middle of his prayers that the enemy was at the gate, concluded his devotions with a few brief and earnest petitions, and then set about defending himself. Had he been a formalist those final petitions would never have been uttered at all; but under the circumstances the impulse to prayer, though sincere and

Illustrations: oratorical appeal, defence and attack, courtesy and devotions.

urgent, became rapidly less imperative and exacting relatively to the urgency of taking steps for defence, as the successive moments passed. The most pious biographers of Alfred the Great praise him for "charging like a boar" at the Battle of Ashdown while his brother was still engaged in prayer; and an entirely devout and sincere person may find himself in the dilemma of having either to curtail (or omit) family prayers or to hurry a guest over his breakfast and perhaps run him uncomfortably close for his train. If he shortens, but does not omit, the prayers, it shews that he attaches declining significance to his devotions as minute is added to minute. And in this we shall see nothing ludicrous, as soon as we give up the cant of the absolute in a world in which all things are relative.

We have now abundantly established and illustrated the fact that we administer all our resources, whether of money, space, time, attention, or whatever it may be, upon the same principles.[1] Our preferences and selections as between two or more alternatives are regulated in every case by the terms on which the alternatives are offered and the supply of the desired things or experiences which we command.

We now know exactly what the marketer is doing, and see that her conduct in the market is regulated by just the same universal principles that regulate her choice between all the alternatives of life. She finds certain prices ruling in the market, and her task is so to regulate her purchases that the last penny spent on beef, apples, potatoes, etc., shall in each case bring equal value, so that a penny withdrawn from any one and expended on any other would be doing a less valued service than it now does. If the prices changed she would get more of one, less of another, none at all of a third, of the things that she buys at present prices, and she would get a little of a fourth that at present prices she does not buy; and in this way she would restore the balance between the marginal efficiencies of the last pennies spent on the several articles. The change in the amounts of every article purchased will be related to the changes in price, but will not be simply proportional to them. A small decline of price in one case will induce a large increase of purchases, and in another a slight one or none at all.

[1] As promised, or indicated, on pages 3, 18, 36.

The whole process of marginal adjustment, with the occasional consideration of an "initial" unit (that is to say, the first introduction of "some" as distinct from the modification to "some more" or "some less" of a commodity), is well epitomised and illustrated by the housekeeper who lives in the country, but deals with one of the great London Stores, and who is making out her list. She has a fairly close idea of the extent and distribution of her purchases before she looks at the price list. As she examines the different prices, in making up her order, she half consciously introduces slight modifications, putting down a little more of this and a little less of the other than she had intended, as the prices modify and define her antecedent conception of the terms on which the alternatives would be offered. When she has made up her list and cast up her total, she probably finds that it is too high—that is to say, that to spend so much on the Stores list for the month or the quarter would involve disproportionate pinching in some other spending department. And so she proceeds to revise the list, considering what she can reduce or strike out. The original order was what mathematicians call a first approximation, and now that she is considering what reductions can be made, a closer inspection of marginal values has to be instituted. Some items are struck out altogether. Perhaps they were originally inserted rather in hope than in confidence that they would remain on the effective list. They were "accepted," but only with a faint chance of being "hung." The "icing sugar," for example, that had been inserted with a view to a contemplated birthday cake, goes out bodily, and the order for candied fruits is reduced. Nutmegs (though they have been alleged as an article of consumption not likely to be affected by price) may be taken as exemplifying a kind of commodity that comes under severe review on occasions such as we are now considering; for, as the process of snipping and paring goes on, the small difference in the total reduction of the account which would be effected by the exclusion of the nutmegs altogether may become a determining consideration. During the whole process of this reduction by minuter inspection of the scale of marginal preferences, the housewife will be aware of the alternative in the background of effecting the necessary

Illustration of the Stores list.

G

economies in some other field of expenditure, closely or remotely connected with this. And the yet further question of how much thought and time it is worth while to give, in the hope of making yet further reductions, is meanwhile settling itself under the pressure, high one day and low another, of the competing claims of other duties and pleasures, the resentment or irritation of weariness, or the sudden protest of a roused consciousness that she is in danger of bartering life for halfpennyworths of rice and sugar.

This example will explain why I have occasionally used the cumbrous phrase " the quantity we possess or contemplate ourselves as possessing." It is clear that the marginal increments or decrements we consider are very often taken not at the margin of our actual possessions, but at the margin of the quantity which we have provisionally determined to acquire, or which, for any other reason, we contemplate ourselves as possessing, and take as the basis of our calculations.

The great principle of the declining significance of successive increments of valued possessions, acquisitions, or indulgences, has now been sufficiently illustrated; but before we can safely go on to the next main point we must say a few words in answer to objections that are frequently urged against the doctrine we have been expounding, and must also make certain explanations. It will be convenient to use the technical term " origin " as a contrast to " margin," meaning by the " origin " the point at which supplies of anything begin, and by the " margin " the point which they have reached, actually or in contemplation. Thus when we have a small supply of anything the margin will be near the origin, and when we have a large supply it will be remote from it. Now it is not safe to assert that the significance of any commodity declines for successive increments, unless we add the qualification " after a certain point." It may be that near to the origin the significance does not fall, but rises. We are all familiar with the fact that it is often easier to go without a thing altogether than to have a taste of it and then stop; and many people would prefer no supply at all to a very small supply of something they value.

<small>Declining significance can only be asserted "after a certain point."</small>

On the principle that " second helps are never as good as

first," if two slices of pudding given to two children made two first helps they would perform a more important domestic function than if they had both gone to one child and made a first and second help. But if there is only very little altogether, it may be that if divided into two portions it would have teased and stimulated two palates and gratified none. Here the "after a certain point" principle comes in. When single portions to two children would have to be very small, a double portion to one child might be more effective, the second increment in this case being of more value than the first. If the two children are given a share each it will be a wasteful act of administration as far as its direct purpose goes, to be justified, if at all, only by some moral or emotional reaction which the "sharing" itself may be supposed to secure—probably, after all, fostering a certain veiled materialism by over-emphasising such things. A rough system of turn and turn about is probably better husbandry both ethically and materially. This example, in illustrating the "up to a certain point" principle, incidentally indicates the reactions between material and moral problems and considerations, and the general wholesomeness of ethics that are firmly based on sound material administration;[1] but our main point is to shew that when dealing with small quantities "second helps" may often be better, not worse, than first, and a first and second better than two firsts; so that in any general statement of the doctrine of declining significance with advancing margins the saving clause "after a certain point" must always be inserted or understood.

Illustration of first and second helps.

But even with this qualification the principle is assailed by objections, many of which have already been met by anticipation, but some of which it will be well to consider expressly. It is said, for instance, that though the principle holds for gross material things, each one of which soon produces satiety, yet it does not hold for intellectual or æsthetic satisfactions, nor even for the general command of commodities and services, represented by money. The more a man knows, it is said, the more he wants to know; the more he reads, the more he wants to read; the more music he hears, the more he wants to hear; and very

Objections to the principle met. The case of money.

[1] Cf. Book II. pages 423-434.

often the more money he has, the more he wants to increase his stock. We will begin with the alleged case of money. It may be true of many men, though it is not true of all, that the more money they get, the keener they are on getting more; but we ought surely to have learnt by this time to be on our guard against vague and indefinite forms of statement concerning matters which are essentially quantitative. The man who has an enormous income may be even keener on "making money" than he was when he was struggling upwards on 30s. a week; but he is not keener on making an extra 1s. a week than he was. He has now no gauge in his mind sensitive enough to feel an addition of £2 : 10s. to his annual income; and if you ask him to work an extra hour a week, or to incur any appreciable sacrifice, or to put his brains about in any way, in order to secure so trifling a result, he will laugh you to scorn. If you want him to do anything in order to get more money, you must change the terms. There is no such thing as the marginal significance of "money" any more than of "wheat" or of "leisure," unless both the margin and the unit are stated; and the marginal significance of any specified unit, whether it be 1d., 1s., £1, or £100, has notably declined to this man as his income has risen from 30s. a week to £100,000 a year.

As to the other objections, which refer to intellectual, æsthetic, and other non-material satisfactions, we may note that here again there is a tacit neglect of a principle which must always be assumed when any two sets of conditions are isolated for comparison—the principle, namely, that they must really be isolated; that is to say, that all attendant and modifying circumstances must be supposed to be the same in both cases. Now, if all the circumstances, including the man's own tastes and capacities for enjoyment, remain the same, then it is as true of concerts as it is of potatoes, that, after a certain point, the greater his supply, the lower will be a man's relative estimate of the additional services which a further increment will render. If he only has the opportunity of hearing a concert once a month, he may decline an invitation to meet an old friend whom he has not seen for long, and is not likely to see for long again, if the invitation falls on the evening of

The case of non-material satisfactions.

the concert. Or if he determines to forgo the music, it may be with a distinct consciousness that he is making a serious sacrifice on the altar of friendship. If the same man, with the same tastes and capacities, is hearing a concert every week, he would forgo one with less hesitation and to meet the claims of a lower grade of friendship; and if he is hearing music four days a week he might consider not whether he would sacrifice a single musical evening in order to spend the time with his friend, but how many evenings he could sacrifice before the increasing marginal significance of musical evenings as they become less numerous, and the decreasing marginal significance of evenings with his friend as they become more numerous, reach a balance.

What is really in people's minds when they say that the more music a man hears the more he wants to hear, is that the man himself will develop fresh faculties and form fresh tastes by cultivation. By going to a concert once a month he may gain such increased knowledge of musical works, and such heightened critical and appreciative powers, that he is now as keen for a second concert in the course of every month as he originally was for a single one. But this is because he is a different man—that is to say, the personal tastes, capacities, and opportunities which affect his whole scale of relative estimates have changed, but it still remains true that, his scale of preferences being what it now is, the significance of a third concert a month is less than that of a second. *Reactions on the organism.*

The power of appreciating pictures furnishes another good instance. A man who at the beginning of a tour in Italy finds that, in looking at frescoes, the point of diminishing returns is soon reached, and that the value of zero is touched in from a half to three-quarters of an hour, probably finds his powers of enjoyment increasing till his zest remains high hour after hour; but it is still only a matter of time, though now of much more time, before he becomes jaded and requires a period of rest and recovery. Now this reaction of a man's experiences or volitions upon his character and tastes is a matter of extreme importance, and a careful study of it is necessary to a complete understanding of our whole subject; and accordingly I shall invite the reader in another part of this work[1] to go into the question at some length and with some minuteness. But what has already been said will probably be enough to enable him to go forward without misgiving to such applications as will be required for the progress of our main argument.

Taking it as granted, then, that there exists what may be called a law of "diminishing psychic returns," in accordance with which successive increments of any commodity (after a certain point) will render services of decreasing significance to the person who consumes or commands them, let us summarise the results so far obtained in this chapter. To do so will be to repeat in other words the programme laid down on page 80. Given the system of ruling prices, or terms on which alternatives are offered to us, the art of marketing or other expenditure of money is so to regulate the quantities purchased, that the marginal significance of 1d., 1s., or other smallest unit distinguishable in the case in hand, shall secure services of equal value to whatever branch of expenditure it may be devoted. So long as the marginal significances of services rendered by the various commodities do not coincide with their prices, increased satisfactions can be gained by transferring expenditure from the article which has the lower to the article which has the higher marginal significance. And by an extension of terms, which is something more than a metaphor, though something less than a naked statement of fact, we may think of any man who is making a choice between alternatives as going to the great market of nature or of society, ascertaining the terms on which he can make alternative applications of his resources, external or personal, material or spiritual, of money, capacity, influence, and so forth—ascertaining, that is, what are the "prices" that rule in the market of life,—and making his choice accordingly, always adopting the more eligible alternative and so reducing its significance, and neglecting the less eligible and so raising its significance, till their relative importance coincides with the terms on which they can be substituted for each other.

The unity of principle that dominates all administration of resources will become still clearer if we follow up the

Restatement of general principle.

[1] See Book II. pages 420 *sqq.*

process that Materfamilias begins in the market-place into the domain of household administration proper. When she has brought home her provisions for the day or week, she is still engaged on the same problem of adjusting marginal significances, in accordance with the law of diminishing psychic returns. The members of the family are not all treated on the same terms. For all kinds of reasons one member of the household will receive differential treatment in one respect, and one in another. It will be regarded as more important that such an one should have a fairly large supply of certain things than that others should have any supply at all. But when a certain amount has been already assigned to the favoured recipient, the marginal significance of further increments for him sinks, till an initial allowance to some one else (though not entering into competition with the initial allowance to him) asserts itself as a rival to his further increments. With this may be compared the case given on page 72 of the initial increments of water being of higher significance than those of bread, and bread becoming an effectively rival claimant at a given point.

The market and the home.

The analogy between home administration and marketing becomes yet more striking when we take a single article that has many different applications. Milk furnishes a good example. In the usual routine, milk may be wanted for the baby, for the other children, for a pudding, for tea or coffee, and for the cat. If the supply is at all short, one would be disposed to say that the baby's wants will be completely satisfied before any others are attended to at all; but even this is not true without qualification. There are circumstances under which, while the baby's bottle is being filled, one might quite well hear the remark, "Just save a drop for so-and-so's tea"; and as the proportion of milk to water is, within certain limits, an open question, and as bulk as well as nutritive quality has a certain significance in the economy of the nursery, it is not really so true as one would at first think, that the baby's wants, to the point of absolute fulfilment, have under all circumstances an unquestioned precedence over all others. And what is not absolutely true of the baby is probably not

Illustration of milk.

even approximately true of the other children. They will often go short of what they would like, and of what they would get if milk could be had for nothing. The amount that is to be put aside for other purposes will be more or less carefully considered in determining how much they are to have collectively, and this amount again will be distributed among them individually with more or less care. Even the cat is not dependent on mere superfluity, and her saucer will often be partially or wholly filled with milk that would have been valued in the children's mugs; though if there is any pressure on the supply and if the other demands have to be arrested at a relatively high marginal significance, her wants may be either neglected or very scantily met, sometimes grudgingly, sometimes with an extra allowance of friendship and sympathy, but still scantily. Milk is administered at home, then, exactly as money is administered in the market-place. The principle in both cases is to bring the marginal significance of small units into equilibrium, at whatever point they are applied; and if a thimbleful of milk has been applied at any one point when it would have met a more important want if applied at another, there has been a failure in the administration of resources, and the administratrix will recognise it by saying, " I wish I had thought of that, and I would have saved a drop of milk for it."

This brings us to another turning-point in our investigation. Mistakes of administration occur, and a mistake is a mistake. The fact that it need not have been made does not avert its natural consequence. Potatoes run short at table, and there is more cabbage than any one wants to eat. This is the result of miscalculation, and it thwarts expectations. Had a true forecast been formed it would have been easy to pull or buy a cabbage less, and take in or draw from the store another pennyworth of potatoes, and in that case cabbage and potatoes would have run out together, presumably at marginal values approximately corresponding to the prices paid for them. But the fact that we might have had potatoes that we should have valued more instead of the remaining supply of cabbage does not in itself give any value to that remaining supply. This is a very obvious and elementary truth, but if we realise it

Errors of administration and unforeseen contingencies,

in all its bearings it will strike at the root of all those " cost of production " theories of value which keep such an obstinate hold on economic thought and are responsible for such endless confusion. The value of what you have got is not affected by the value of what you have relinquished or forgone in order to get it. But the measure of the advantages you are willing to forgo in order to get a thing is determined by the value that you expect it to have when you have got it. If you make a mistake you must bear the loss. You have the thing you bought, not the price you paid for it; and the thing is worth its own value, not the value of something else that you might have got instead of it but did not.

Let us examine this principle further. We have seen, in comparing the different applications of milk in an ordinary middle-class family, that if the administration is ideally carried out, the significances of the last small increments of milk are equal in all its ordinary applications. The first thimbleful of milk given to the baby is immensely more significant than the first thimbleful given to the children or reserved for afternoon tea; but if the last thimbleful given to the cat does not perform as important a service as the last thimbleful given to the children, there would have been a gain in giving her a little less and them a little more; and there has therefore been a failure in administration. The cost of giving more to one applicant is giving less to another, and good administration consists in avoiding any application which costs more than it is worth. But as well as balancing all the uses of milk, at the margin, one against the other, the housekeeper has to balance them all, collectively, against every other alternative expenditure of the money she paid for milk, and this opens up another source of possible mistake. In taking in the milk for the day or half-day the housewife considers, consciously or unconsciously, what the significance of the last thimblefuls applied to all the varied purposes, when properly balanced, will be. The answer to the question, " How much milk shall we take to-day, ma'am ? " depends on a rapid survey of the programme of the day. If milk is 4d. a quart, the aim is to take in such an amount that the last half-pint shall be just worth 1d.; that is to say, the last thimblefuls in

[marginal note: and consequent failures of coincidence between price and marginal significance.]

every application, brought into equilibrium of marginal significance with each other, should collectively be worth just as much as anything else on which the 1d. might be spent. But unforeseen contingencies may arise. There may be a great ink-spill, and milk may be wanted to take out the stain while fresh. A little sapling, laden with many associations, may arrive, to grow in the garden or yard, and some one may have read that milk comforts and revives the roots of trees that have felt a journey. The dog may have eaten phosphorous poison, and some one may know that the proper remedy is to drench him with milk. And these sudden and unexpected claims have not been anticipated or provided for. It may really be the case (especially if you live in the country) that more milk cannot, without great difficulty, be got for some hours; or if you live in the town, it does not occur to you (owing to mental inertia) that there is any way of getting more milk except the customary one of waiting till the milkman comes round again. And so a new set of claimants on the day's supply of milk, of which there was no thought when the milk was taken in, has been introduced. In the case of the poisoned dog, it might well be that even the baby would be put on short allowance for a certain period, or driven to some substitute, in the hope of saving the life of an inmate of the house, whose loss would be long and sincerely mourned. Now it may be perfectly understood that there are always such risks, but it is bad economy to provide for a risk as though it were a certainty, and therefore when such a contingency occurs it will set up an urgent demand for which it would not have been reasonable to make provision. It must therefore be met out of the general stock, and all the other uses will be trenched upon. The last thimblefuls will still be kept in equilibrium, but each will meet a more clamorous demand than usual, the lower or less clamorous demands not being met at all; and if the dog has been poisoned, probably the cat will get nothing, even her initial and most urgent claim not being able to compete for a place amongst the higher demands that alone can be satisfied now.

The marginal significance of the last half-pint of milk will be raised above what was contemplated when it was purchased, and it will not be in equilibrium with the marginal pennyworths of other things. Another pint or quart, as the case may be, would have had to be bought to bring down its marginal significance to 2d. a pint; and it would have been bought had the state of things which has actually come about been anticipated. _{Price paid does not affect significance.} Note the principle, then (obvious indeed in itself and of enormous range of application, but often deeply disguised), that the marginal significance at which a commodity is actually consumed depends upon the urgency and extent of the claims that have to be met and adjusted and the quantity of it at command, and is not affected by the price that was actually given for it. The sacrifice that would be involved in forfeiting a little of our store, and the advantage that would accrue by increasing it a little, depend on how great our store is and what we want it for, not on the importance or value to us of other things that we might have chosen instead of it but did not.

The reverse case to the one we have supposed may also occur. Through an ordinary miscalculation or through some unforeseen change of circumstances, such as the unexpected departure of several members of the household, or the coming on of thundery weather that threatens to turn the milk, the supply for the next few hours may become so much larger than was expected relatively to the demands made upon it, that it will be consumed at a lower marginal significance than would have justified the purchase. The cat may have as much as she chooses to lap. A member of the household, coming in hot from a walk in the sultry air, and expressing a timid desire for a glass of milk, may be treated almost as a benefactor instead of being treated as a criminal, as he was when he last made the same suggestion under less propitious circumstances. And finally, the milk that has gone sour before it is consumed may go to the making of a cake, which, though much appreciated, would not have justified the purchase of the milk to the housewife's economic mind had she known from the first what it was going to be used for. These marginal applications would not have been deliberately provided for, for their significance is too low to justify expenditure at the rate of 4d. a quart. That is to say, the money spent on the milk might have been used to meet some more urgent want.

Only it was not. So here again the price that was actually given for the milk does not determine or affect its significance. An estimate of the probable conditions was made, and such a quantity of milk was taken as would under those conditions have made its marginal significance in all cases just balance that of any other alternative purchase. But if the anticipations are falsified the coincidence will fail. By regulating the supply the marginal significance may be brought into harmony with the price. But the price that has been paid for a faultily regulated supply has no influence on its marginal significance.

Similar considerations, of course, apply to time and work. Perhaps we oftener complain of having wasted time than of having wasted money. We are bitterly conscious of having spent "more time than it was worth" on this or that trifle, and we realise only too clearly that the said trifle is not worth any more because of the precious time that has been spent on it. When our undergraduate is in the examination room, the time he has spent on a branch of the subject on which there happens to be no question avails him nothing, however pathetically anxious he may be to convince himself (and, if it might be, his examiner also) that it does. Anticipated value of information in the examination room determines the amount of time and work he bestows on a subject, but the time and work he has bestowed on it do not determine its value in the examination room. Misdirected effort, however great, secures no marks.

The reader, I repeat, may be surprised at so much insistence on so obvious a fact; but let me warn him once more that this fact, so open and obvious here, will meet him again and again, under deep and subtle disguises, in every region of economic study. He will do well to scrutinise it closely now, in order that he may recognise it whenever he meets it hereafter. If the price that we pay for an article made it marginally worth what we had paid for it—that is to say, if there were any causal connection that made the value at the margin dependent upon the price—then there would be no difficulty whatever in administering our resources; for everything would be worth what we had given for it, just because we had given it, and it would make no difference how our supplies of anything else might stand. Whereas in reality the whole art of wise expenditure consists in deliberately bringing about a coincidence between "price" and marginal significance, which by no means looks after itself, and which will fail if we buy either too little or too much of anything.

And we have seen that the price paid stands for the alternatives forgone; so that ultimately the price we pay for getting this consists in going without that (which we want) or putting up with the other (which we dislike). The principle that we are examining, then, stated in its widest form is that the value of what we have does not depend on the value of what we have relinquished or endured in order to get it. Alternatives relinquished do not affect significance of alternatives embraced. If there is a coincidence, as in a wisely conducted life there will be, it is because the value that we foresee a thing will have determines what we will encounter or forgo in order to secure it, not because what we have encountered or forgone in order to secure it affects its value. If our judgment is bad, our expectations will be falsified and the coincidence will not come about. We do not always like to face this fact, for to do so is to recognise that we have made a mistake; and accordingly we sometimes try to believe that a thing is useful or ornamental because we have given a high price for it, or valuable because we have taken trouble to get it. It is to the housekeeper's credit if she does not insist on the cabbage that no one wants being consumed with simulated relish, as if it were the potatoes that can't be had. She is tempted to exact suffering in the shape of enforced consumption to conceal the tragic failure of her attempts to secure satisfaction. But all these plans for concealing the facts do not prevent them from being facts. Efforts are regulated by anticipated values, but values are not controlled by antecedent efforts.

Note, however, that mistakes of calculation are not always irreparable. In the case of rapidly perishable articles such as fish, an over-supply cannot be made use of, because its consumption cannot be spread over a longer period than was originally contemplated without entailing rapid deterioration. And in the case of things which there is only an opportunity of buying at comparatively rare intervals, it may be difficult to remedy an under-supply. But in the case of articles the consumption of which can be spread over a longer or concentrated into a shorter period at will, and the stores of which it is always easy to replenish at any moment, there is no reason why an exact correspondence should not be maintained between the price at which we can get them and the marginal significance at which we consume them. This is no more than to say that in the case of such articles we need never go without a pennyworth that is really worth a penny to us, and need never use a pennyworth to-day when it is only worth a halfpenny, for fear of its being worth nothing at all if we keep it until to-morrow. It must be carefully noted, however, that even in these cases our wise use of the article will be regulated, not by what we actually gave for it, but by what we should have to give for more of it.

<small>Coincidence of price and significance most easily maintained if the commodity does not perish rapidly and if stores are easily renewed.</small>

There is no doubt a strong tendency in many minds to economise a stock which was bought at a high price, even if it could be replaced at a low one, and perhaps a still stronger tendency to deal prodigally with a stock purchased at a low price, although it will have to be replaced at a high one. But this secondary reaction is recognised as irrational when we deliberately consider it. We know perfectly well that true economy consists in making the best of existing conditions, irrespective of the good or ill fortune, or the wise or foolish conduct, which placed us in them. All these principles will be found presently to have their applications in the commercial and industrial as well as to the domestic world.

CHAPTER III

ECONOMICAL ADMINISTRATION AND ITS DIFFICULTIES

SUMMARY.—*The ideal coincidence between marginal significances and market prices is impeded by the difficulty of keeping all departments of expenditure in connection with each other, and by the fact that we cannot always get things in the exact quantities in which we want them. We have also to keep the balance between expenditure on things that we pay for as we use them, like food, and things that we pay for at once and use over a long period, like furniture; and if all expenditures alike have to be met out of income, the period of saving during which we are stinting ourselves in current expenditure and have not yet secured the more permanent possession for which we are saving, will be a period of privation during which we are paying without enjoying, and it will be followed by another in which we are enjoying without paying. The various systems of hire are a device to enable us to spread the period of payment over the whole period of use, and so to relieve the comparative indigence of the first period at the expense of the comparative abundance of the second. Hire also enables us to enjoy the fraction we want of commodities that cannot be divided. The premium we pay for these advantages is one of the sources of interest. The administration of our resources, which is complicated by these phenomena, is also confused by false analogies and illusions generated by custom, environment, and untrained mental habits. But, however perfectly we overcome these difficulties and errors of administration, objective and subjective, the ultimate significance of our use of our means must depend on the nature of our ends.*

Having now arrived at a clear conception of marginal significance and of the principles on which the marginal significance of desired objects may be brought into correspondence with the terms on which nature or man offers them to us, we may proceed to examine some of the difficulties which are met in carrying out these principles of administration in practice.

One of the chief of them is the difficulty of bringing our different branches and different scales of expenditure into effective relation with each other. It is comparatively easy to keep our expenditure on different articles of dress or on different articles of food properly balanced; that is to say, to administer a housekeeping allowance or a dress allowance is a comparatively easy problem, and if all the money we can command is assigned to us in allowances, earmarked for this or that general purpose, the problem of administration is simple. And even where there is no such externally imposed system of divisions, the mind is apt to run into grooves, and form certain fixed ideas as to the suitable amount to spend on books, on travelling and holidays, on housekeeping, and so forth, under cover of which very considerable differences of the marginal significance of a shilling may grow up undiscovered between two branches of expenditure. When a man is carefully considering whether it would be an extravagance to take a cab or not, a quite new light may be thrown on the problem if it occurs to him that the cab-fare will be the exact price of a volume of Ruskin or of the Temple Classics. Our expenditure has a tendency to divide itself into water-tight compartments, and the difference of density of the fluid in different compartments is sometimes very high before any effective endosmosis or exosmosis takes place.

The difficulty of interdepartmental communication,

Again, we can compare quantities of about the same magnitude with much greater accuracy than quantities of different magnitude. It may be comparatively easy to determine whether two penny satisfactions are pretty nearly equal to each other, and again to equate two shilling or two pound satisfactions with each other, but it is startling to realise that when we say that one thing is worth £1 and another only worth 1d. we are

and of comparing large and small expenditures.

asserting that the first is 240 times as great as the second. We never think of satisfactions in this quantitative manner, and the very conception of multiplying a satisfaction by 240 strikes us as absurd. But, after all, multiplication is only a form of addition, and we are constantly, with more or less accuracy, endeavouring to add up small satisfactions and weigh them against larger ones. Indeed it is only by realising that a leakage by drops, which are insensible when taken alone, will amount to a sensible volume collectively, that a rich man can have any rational motive for attending to pence and shillings at all. He cannot feel the loss of a shilling in itself. He is not aware that it will in any remotest degree affect his life or his conduct in any particular, but he knows that if he does not look after the pence and shillings a large part of his income will ooze away without his knowing how, and this introduces a habit of mind in which carelessness as to pence and shillings becomes in itself unpleasant. And though the shilling has no direct significance to him, the loss of it, by association, has. The keeping of regular accounts is recommended, and rightly so, on these grounds. It helps us to bring our expenditures in pence and our expenditures in pounds into touch with each other.

Apart from the difficulty of realising the relative significance of small and large units of expenditure, which is subjective, there is sometimes an external and objective difficulty in balancing expenditure with any fineness. We cannot always get things in the quantities which would be requisite in order to bring their marginal value into close coincidence with their price.

It is conceivable that we might want a pen full of ink with an urgency greater than that represented by a halfpenny and less than that represented by a penny, and might grudge buying a penny bottle of ink while unable to get a smaller quantity for a smaller price. It does not follow that we really could not induce a stationer to give us a halfpennyworth of ink out of his own open bottle, but in the first place it does not follow that we could, and in the next place it would in any case involve proceedings for which we should consider ourselves very inadequately compensated by the saving of a halfpenny; so that we cannot get a halfpenny-

Large units.

worth of ink instead of a pennyworth except by paying in trouble, or sense of awkwardness and humiliation, more than the halfpenny saved is worth to us. We must therefore either pay a penny or go without the ink, and if we feel the want but do not value its satisfaction at a penny, we cannot adjust our expenditure to meet it. It is an instructive fact that the lowest commercial unit of a given commodity is not uniformly fixed. Shops in a poor district, dealing with customers who can discriminate between the services of very small units, will deal in ha'porths or even farthingworths, when no such units are commercially recognised in more opulent parts of the town. In these cases, however, the commodities are physically capable of much finer subdivisions than are commercially recognised or are even psychologically recognisable; whereas there are other things which in their nature are incapable of minute subdivision. Pianos, watches, bicycles, and many articles of dress, though they can all be hired, can be neither purchased in small units nor hired on such terms as to enable us to take "another pennyworth" of chronometer or high-class piano. How, then, are we to bring their marginal services into exact harmony with the price we pay for them? It is true that all these things are more or less finely graded in quality, and may therefore, to some extent, be adjusted to our marginal wants, if a poorer thing may be regarded as performing part of the services of a better one. I may have a watch which, if I set it every morning by the town clock, will enable me roughly to apportion my day, and to keep my appointments within five minutes; and the services it thus renders may be very valuable to me. Indeed, it may be that the difference between having no watch at all and such a one as this would be greater to me than the difference between having such a watch as this and the most perfect instrument that I should be capable of handling and keeping in order. And yet it would be a very considerable extra convenience, for which I should be willing to pay proportionally, if I could rely on my watch not gaining or losing more than a minute a day; and a still greater convenience if, week in week out, I could rely on it to the second in catching my daily train. Similar remarks will be found to have a wider range than would at first sight be expected; but it remains true that no man can get an initial ha'porth of time-keeping apparatus, and compare its value with a marginal ha'porth of cheese. Say, then, that I must have no watch at all or one that costs at least 2s. 6d., or must have no piano that I would take at a gift or must spend at least £10 on one. Now it may well be that a man would be glad, if he could, to get the half use of a £10 piano for £5, whereas £10 for the full use of it is " more than he can afford "—that is to say, is not worth making the extra sacrifice for. Our example of the tea on page 49 has familiarised us with this idea. If the option were between getting a fifth half-pound of tea at 6s. 6d. or going without, it would be bought, but if it were between getting a third pound at 13s. or going without it, it would not be bought. As the marginal significance of the tea declines throughout its consumption, so the marginal significance of hours of command of a piano may be higher if we have only fourteen a week than if we have twenty-one; and consequently it might be worth giving two-thirds of £10 to get the two hours a day, but not be worth giving the whole £10 to have the three hours a day, which perhaps is as much as we want. But the purchaser has not the option of buying the two-hour-a-day control of a piano. If he buys anything he must buy the whole three-hour-a-day control that he wants (and the remaining twenty-one-hour-a-day control that he does not want, as well). Now it will not be good economy to buy a piano until the whole £10 that he will have to pay for it, if distributed over all alternative expenditures, at their margins, would collectively give a smaller satisfaction than that to be derived from the piano. But when this stage is reached if he discriminates in his mind between the marginal and initial services rendered him by the piano, the marginal ones will be worth far less than their proportion of the marginal sacrifices of other things made to secure the piano; whereas long before this point has been reached the initial gratification would have been worth much more than its proportion of them; just as the first ounces of the third pound of tea are valued at more and the last at less than the average of 9d. each, which makes the collective value of the sixteen ounces 12s. The purchaser would gladly sacrifice one-tenth of the actual use he makes of his piano for £1, retaining nine-tenths of it and paying £9, but he would not sacrifice the whole for £10, nor nine-tenths for £9, nor eight-tenths for £8. The first tenths are worth more than £1 each, though the last tenth, and perhaps the last but one, and the last but two, are worth less than £1 each. But as he has no such options of tithes at a pound each, he must take them all or none, and he takes them all for his £10 as soon as they are collectively worth it.

Thus, where large units come into competition with small ones and with each other, we are always vaguely conscious of either being in arrears or being in advance in our expenditure on the large units. If I have not a piano I am conscious of the pressure of an unsatisfied want which is slowly accumulating until it shall be of sufficient weight and volume to justify the whole expenditure. Meanwhile it is absolutely unsatisfied, whereas the wants to which smaller units minister are partially satisfied, though all the while I feel that they do not add as much to the value of life as an occasional hour of the piano would do if I could get it *pro rata parte* at a fraction of the price of complete command. And when I have got my piano I am conscious, from time to time, when my appetite for playing on an inferior instrument is temporarily sated, that I would very gladly curtail my opportunities of gratifying it, if I could thereby relieve the general pressure I feel at all the points at which small units might minister to unsated desires. Probably the impossibility of bringing these two classes of expenditure into perfect harmony goes a long way towards explaining that almost universal experience embodied in the aphorism, "A competence is a little more than a man has." Conscious of a ragged edge in our expenditure, and especially of some few things, purchasable in large units, of which we constantly feel the want, we imagine that if we had them we should be satisfied. As a matter of fact they have merely attracted to themselves our whole sense of dissatisfaction. If we got these particular articles, promontories would just at these points be substituted for bays, but the coast would be no more even than before. Certain other wants would now be realised, and new voids would begin to ache. Perhaps we should be quite conscious that our general level of well-being and satisfaction

Impossibility of keeping margins trimmed.

was raised, but the vague uneasiness caused by the uneven edge would still be there.

Another problem rises immediately out of these reflections. Some of our wants are recurrent and are met by supplies which are destroyed in the process of ministering to them. I eat to-day and I shall want to eat again to-morrow. There is no sense in talking of the "amount of bread" which will satisfy my wants, unless I specify the amount of time during which it is to satisfy them. The proper form under which to consider my provision is a stream of supply, not a stock. I am well or ill supplied with bread, not according to the amount of bread I have, but according to the amount per day, week, or other unit of time, which I command. Whereas we do not talk of the rate per day or year at which I am supplied with pianos or watches. On what principle can I compare £5 spent on bread, which for a period of twelve months supplies wants which will be as keenly felt and will as urgently demand provision at the end of that time as at the beginning, with £5 spent on a watch, which will perhaps never require supplementing or renewing?

Recurrent wants and continuous expenditure.

The difficulty is not so great as it appears. Such as it is it arises from our taking the problem the wrong way about. Single purchases, such as that of a knife, a coat, or a piano, present themselves readily to the imagination, are easily and firmly held in the mind, and are regarded as normal. Whereas continuous purchases of things which are as continuously consumed, such as food or coals, seem to have something evasive and baffling about them. We always seem to be in the same position as before. We naturally attempt, therefore, to express our expenditure on this latter class of commodities in terms of our expenditure on the former, or at least to bring it into comparison with it. But this is a mistake in method. It is the continuous expenditure that really furnishes the type to which all others must be reduced; for however permanent the piano itself may be, the use of it is as much related to time as the consumption of potatoes, and though the payment may be concentrated into a minute, the employment may extend over a lifetime. In short, the instinct of the old economists was correct when they took "consumption" as the general term for all kinds of employment, use, and enjoyment of things. It is the things we really "consume" that are typical; but unfortunately the violence to current language involved in the terminology by which all use is called consumption has greatly interfered with its effectiveness.

We shall find that the difficulties of the subject yield readily enough as soon as we understand that it is payment for those things the "using" of which covers a long time and many successive occasions that is the branch of expenditure needing special study and explanation, and which must be brought into line with normal "consumption"—that is to say, the "using up" of things dissipated or transformed by a single application. It is this latter class of obviously "consumable" goods which, as a fact, has hitherto been the chief subject of our studies; and we can now go on to bring the other class under the same principles. To begin with, the whole distinction is only a matter of degree. We think of three great spending departments, food, furniture, and clothing, as representing respectively commodities that disappear after a single application to their purposes, commodities which survive an indefinite number of usings, and the intermediate class of commodities, which can be used many times, but which we should not speak of, even loosely, as permanent. But, strictly speaking, nothing is permanent; and perhaps nothing but an explosive is "consumed" or used up instantaneously, even in a popular sense. The process of eating a mouthful of food occupies a certain amount of time, and in the case of all infusions, such as tea, there may be repeated uses of the same thing, on a down scale of excellence, just as there is in the case of clothes. The careful housewife may make her sticks of cinnamon flavour a custard, and then enter into some other confection; and she will not consider that the virtues of a bag of root ginger have been exhausted after the one use of flavouring her rhubarb jam. Thus in the matter of durability and repeated use the classes of food and clothes overlap; for a calf's foot may be used several times in making successive batches of jelly, and a pair of white kid gloves can only be used a few times, and that on a downward scale of distinction; while a white tie can hardly be used twice. From the kid gloves we may mount by as small steps as we please, through muslin

Reduction of discontinuous to terms of continuous expenditure.

trimmings and what not, to a coat or frock which may be worn for six or twelve months, and the dress-coat or velvet gown that may serve a person of retiring or economical habits for twenty years or more. When we come to furniture, the single class of lighting appliances may offer us varieties running from the Japanese lanterns that will only survive a few uses, to a great lampstand that will never need to be renewed. So, too, the estimated life of a chair may run from a few months to fifty years or more. The distinction we are dealing with, therefore, is purely relative, and as soon as we begin to examine our actual budgets we shall find that even this relative distinction does not correspond at all closely with any actual distinction in our methods of administration. Coal is a perishable article, and when we use a lump we use it up (though its consumption extends over an appreciable period of time), whereas a suit of clothes survives many successive usings; yet it may very well be that if we have suitable premises we shall buy coal for six months in one order; and, on the supposition that a suit of clothes also lasts for six months, we may be buying clothes and coals at the rate of so much the half-year, just as we are buying milk at the rate of so much per day, although each portion of coal is used up by a single application, and each article of clothing stands repeated wear. This observation may put us in the way of clearing up the whole matter. Let us suppose that a man's six months' stock of coal is six tons and that it costs £1 a ton, and further that his suit of clothes costs £5 : 5s.; that milk is 4d. per quart, and that the average amount taken in the house is a quart and a half a day. Now it will be observed that although we buy our coal and our clothes only once in six months, we consume a portion of the coal and use the clothes every day. We may be said therefore to be consuming milk at the rate of 6d. a day, using up clothes at the rate (by a very close approximation) of 7d. a day, and coal at the rate of 8d. a day. And this is obviously the proper way in which to look at the matter from the point of view of the scientific analysis of administration of resources. Everything should be reduced to a question of rate of supply. In the case of milk most householders have no choice but to purchase day by day: fresh milk cannot be stored in any ordinary sense. Coals may be bought by the scuttleful, the cwt., the ton, or the truck-load, according to convenience; but you cannot get and use up your 7d. worth of clothes day by day as you want it. The forms of purchase, then, are dictated partly by the nature of the commodity, partly by the custom of the trade, and partly by the convenience of the purchaser. But in considering the budget for the year there is no difficulty of principle whatever in bringing into exact comparison and equilibrium the supply of commodities which perish with a single use and that of commodities which are relatively permanent. The apparent difficulty disappears still more completely when we remember that "buying" is not the same thing as "paying," and that the housewife who orders, and in that sense buys, her milk day by day, or even twice a day, probably pays for it weekly or monthly, and possibly at longer intervals than in the case of her coals or many articles of dress. In all cases alike the scientific basis is "rate of supply." All else is secondary.

The same principles apply to yet more permanent articles of use. The more solid articles of furniture, some of which we have perhaps inherited from our parents or ancestors, expensive books of reference, and so forth, gradually become relatively or absolutely unserviceable, and though any one of them may have to be replaced only once in a lifetime or not even that, yet we can form a general estimate of how much to allow per year, on the general account, for maintaining and replacing these expensive and relatively permanent articles, so far as it lies in our general scheme to do it at all. In the same way, if we wish not only to maintain but to increase our stock of articles that may be expected to last all our lives and beyond, we can in like manner make regular provision for successive purchases. And since so much a year is also so much a day, we may regard ourselves as spending, say, 6d. a day on milk and 1s. a day on things that will never require replacing in our time. The desire for milk and the desire to add to our stock of durable possessions are both capable of being temporarily assuaged or gratified, but neither of them of being permanently extinguished or sated, and we minister to both so as to equate their marginal urgency with the terms which the market offers.

Now the larger any single item of expenditure is, and the

rarer and less easily calculable the occurrence or recurrence of the necessity for it, the finer and wider judgment it needs to provide for it wisely, and the more shall we need to have command of resources for a considerable period in advance in order that our administration may be truly economical. This is a point of such great importance in itself and one that throws so much light on some of the darkest places of economic science, that we must dwell on it in some detail. *Purchases provided for by sacrifices extending over a shorter period than is covered by the use of the thing purchased.* Moreover, it will not really divert us from our direct subject of investigation, which is concerned with bringing into line, for the sake of administrative comparison and balancing, of branches of expenditure which appear at first sight difficult to express on the same scale.

Let us take the case of a young woman who has 14s. a week, that is 2s. a day, or £36 : 10s. a year. She certainly cannot under ordinary circumstances afford to buy a piano, yet she might well have a cultivated taste for music, and might make one £18 piano give her pleasure for some twelve or fourteen years. If she could extend her payments for it over the whole of this period they would amount to about a penny a day, and there might be no other way of spending the penny that would equally add to her happiness. If she had in hand at the present moment the whole of the resources she will actually command during the next ten or fifteen years, and having no prospect of any addition to them, had to make them meet all her requirements for that period, she would buy a piano, and would be wise to do so. She would have 1s. 11d. a day to spend on everything else (including the occasional tuning of the piano), and would value her pennyworth of piano a day as much as any other pennyworth. But if she only receives her payments daily or weekly, then in order to buy the piano within a year she would have to save half her income, that is 1s. a day, which, of course, would involve, during that year, much more than twelve times the discomfort of saving a penny a day. Thus the total expenditure on a piano, if concentrated within a year, would involve a far heavier sacrifice than if spread over twelve years or more. By spreading the saving over two years instead of one, she can lighten not only the daily but the total sacrifice, but it would still be very heavy, and she will be without the piano during all the time of saving, so that the whole of the satisfaction she would have derived from it during that period is lost.

Let us generalise our conclusion. There will be some article or articles—a house, a suite of dining-room furniture, works of art, or what not—that will render us services over a longer period than that covered by the ordinary commodities—food, clothes, current literature, and so forth,—which we purchase currently. In order to spend economically we must have so much in hand that we can choose our own time to buy the expensive and permanent things, and can spread the corresponding sacrifice of other alternatives evenly over the whole period for which they last us. Hence the double disadvantage under which persons with small incomes labour. Not only do their means enable them to command a smaller physical total of things desired, but any large expenditure has to be provided for by sacrifices concentrated into a shorter period than that over which the services obtained will extend. And this involves a disproportionately deep trenching upon other branches of expenditure. The smaller physical total of purchases therefore suffers a further deduction in psychological efficiency; and, in order to avoid ruinous psychological waste, the poor man may often have to go without things which he could well afford to secure, were he in full command of even his small income for the year on 1st January. Had he been in that happy position, then at the end of the year he would have spent no more than he will actually have spent, but he would have spent it differently, and he would have got more out of it.

Economy of being in advance.

This principle will be found, at a later period of our investigations, to give us a partial clue to the mystery of "interest." Even wealthy men may be in a position in which it would be an advantage to them to be further in advance of their normal expenditure than they actually are, and they will be willing to pay a premium to any one who will place them in this advantageous position; but as for the poor, their lives would be on a far lower level of comfort even than they are, were there not a number of agencies at work by means of which the provident amongst them can get a little in advance, and the improvident can secure—at a heavy price, perhaps, but still at a possible one—the advances, in some form of credit, needed to enable them to meet heavy isolated expenses. Yet, in spite of everything, the sacrifice involved to a really poor family in the purchase of such an article as a pair of boots is severer than it is easy for the well-to-do to realise. It may have to be taken out of one week's food and may mean something near starvation for that week; whereas if it could have been spread over the whole period during which the boots last, the privation involved would have been comparatively light, not only day by day, but in its whole sum. Moreover, purchase in small quantities is, for many obvious reasons, expensive purchase, and cheap articles are often less worth their price than expensive ones. Yet the extreme importance to the poor man of not spending much at once may make it good husbandry to get a succession of cheap and bad articles rather than one good one. An expenditure of £2 in a single year may be so palpably heavier in its incidence than the expenditure of £1 in each of two successive years, that a man may wisely prefer to spend £1 in each of three successive years rather than £2 in one year and nothing at all in the other two. In this sense he has to be wasteful. "Economy is a luxury of the rich."

It will readily be seen from what has been said above that the hire and purchase-by-hire systems are, in principle, perfectly intelligent attempts to mitigate the secondary as distinct from the primary disadvantages of small earnings. They can, at best, only mitigate, they cannot overcome them, for the hire system sells and does not give the privilege of extending the period of payment, and of corresponding economies, over a convenient period. Moreover, if the purchase by deferred payment opens opportunities of wise expenditure to the wise, it also greatly enlarges the opportunities of foolish expenditure to the foolish. A foolish idea may fascinate for a time, but if severe and sustained self-restraint is necessary for carrying it out, it will soon correct itself. If it can be instantly realised by mortgaging the future, a new risk is created. Moreover, the effort needed to make the requisite economies and encounter the requisite privations over a short period and the sense of security in an unmortgaged

The principles underlying hire, purchase by hire, and rent. Premium paid for leave to buy in the quantities and over the period that suit us.

future may well call up reserves of energy and mental reactions which would have lain dormant and wasted had the more seductive path been followed. An exultant sense of power may be very cheaply bought by the loss of some ease and calculating self-complacency. But it remains true that judicious hiring or borrowing is often the best husbandry.

It is easy now to understand the vital part that hire plays in most of our lives. It enables us to bring into easy comparison our expenditures on the purchase of rapidly perishable things, and on the hire of relatively permanent ones. Hire is indeed the most ordinary means, especially for the relatively poor man, of reducing expenditure per ten years or per lifetime to the form of expenditure per year, per quarter, per week or per day. It brings his payings into close and convenient correspondence with his usings of commodities, and different branches of his expenditure thus become easily comparable. Perhaps the house he lives in is the most permanent thing that the average man habitually uses, yet he has no difficulty whatever in equating his expenditure on "house" with his expenditure on meat, coals, or dress, because in most cases he hires his house. Whereas the purchase of a grand piano may seriously perplex his finances for the year in which it takes place, because he does not hire but buys it.

It should be carefully noted that the problem of hire we have now been dealing with is not entirely coincident with the problem of large units, though it is closely allied with it; and we must examine the distinction between the two before we can completely understand the rationale of hiring. The woman who would be delighted to give £18 for a piano if it would only involve the withdrawal for some twelve years of 1d. a day from her other expenditure, would perhaps even under those conditions prefer to give £9 (involving the expenditure of a $\frac{1}{2}$d. a day only) for half the use of the piano; and that for the reasons that have already been explained, connected with the principle of declining marginal significance. She would still, therefore, even if the difficulty of laying down the lump sum were overcome, be under the difficulty presented by the large unit; and it would only be by some such method as combining with a friend for the joint use of the piano (which might be subject to objections of its own) that she could meet the difficulty. There are, however, other cases in which this difficulty too may be met by the system of hire. A hansom cab, for instance, may be hired for a single drive—that is to say, it may be shared between an indefinite number of persons. Thus the advantage of hire over purchase may be analysed into two elements, either or both of which may be present in any given transaction. Hire may meet the difficulty of large units, relieving a man from the necessity of choosing between going without a thing altogether or supplying himself with a commercial or natural unit of it, when what he would prefer would be to purchase half or a quarter or a hundredth of the opportunities it puts at his command for half or a quarter or a hundredth of the price. And hire (or payment by instalments) may also meet the incidental, as distinguished from the essential, disadvantages of a small income by enabling a man to pay week by week for that week's proportion of the use of an expensive thing which he does not wish to share with others, but which he cannot afford to pay for all at once in advance of his use of it. For either of these advantages it will, of course, be worth his while to pay a sum proportionate to their significance. Thus, while you are spending 6d. a day on milk and 8d. a day on coals, you may be spending at the rate of 3s. a day on house-room, trams, railway plant, etc., and of this 3s. more than half may perhaps be spent, and well spent, day by day, or quarter by quarter, not in payments for the things you are using, but in payments for the privilege of taking them in the fractions, with the partnerships, and by the instalments, which suit your convenience. This is an adjustment which we seldom analyse, but which we perhaps carry out with as much accuracy as any other adjustments of our expenditure; and it comes into distinct and conscious consideration when a man debates whether he shall buy a house instead of renting one, or shall set up a carriage or a motor instead of travelling by cab, by tram, or by rail.

Suppose I could build or buy a house for a certain price. I estimate the period during which I shall live in it at twenty years; it may be either more or less, but I consider twenty years a suitable term at which to estimate the probabilities. I divide the whole cost of the house by eighty, and so arrive at the amount per quarter which, on the estimated probabilities, the house will cost me. I add a quarterly sum for maintenance. Further, the value which the house will have when I die may not be a matter of indifference to me. I shall be glad to leave it to my heirs, and the significance to me now of leaving this sum to them when I die I estimate at a certain figure. I divide this too by eighty, and subtract the quotient from the quarterly figure I had before obtained. Thus I arrive at the net quarterly sum which the enjoyment of the house during my life, as estimated at twenty years, will cost me. How much more than this shall I be willing to pay quarterly for rent of the same or an equally eligible house, the landlord being responsible for all repairs? Let us suppose, for the sake of argument, that the pleasure of the sense of possession and security on the one hand, and the relief of knowing that I am not tied to a house on the other, just balance each other.

Why should I be willing to pay any more in the way of rent than the sum arrived at by the above process of estimate? If buying a house would not disturb other branches of my expenditure, then there is, at this stage of our inquiry, no obvious reason; for I can pay down the lump sum at once, and I can then spread the relinquishing of other alternatives over the whole twenty years, just as well as I could if I paid quarter by quarter. But if, for example, I can only anticipate resources for ten years, then if I pay the lump sum I shall have to concentrate the relinquishing of the other alternatives into a period of ten years. During that period the quarterly sum of relinquishments will be twice as high, and therefore more than twice as serious and significant as the like quarterly sum would have been quarter by quarter throughout the twenty years. It is true that at the end of the ten years I shall have done all the relinquishing and shall have none at all left to do during the remaining ten. Thus I shall be poorer for the first ten years and richer for the second ten years than if I had been able to distribute the corresponding relinquishment of other alternatives over the whole period of enjoyment of the house. But the disadvantages of the period of concentrated economy will more than balance the advantages of the second period; for to make a quarterly payment twice as great is to make it more than twice as irksome. Consequently I should be willing to pay a premium for the privilege of taking my relinquishments over a period of twenty instead of over a period of ten years.

If I can anticipate resources only for five years, the yet more severely concentrated economies will rise still further in proportion, and I shall be willing to pay a still higher premium for the privilege of distributing them over the whole twenty years; and if I could not anticipate at all, but should have to save up the money, say over a period of five years, to buy the house before I got it, then I should not only be making concentrated economies in other things for those five years, but I should also be without the house all that time, and should be paying rent for another. So that as my power of anticipating expenditure that would otherwise be extended over the whole period diminishes, I am willing to pay a higher and higher premium for the privilege of extending the period of payment quarter by quarter over the whole period of enjoyment.

This principle determines how much I shall be willing to pay for the privilege, but how much I shall actually have to pay for it in the market is quite another matter. Our example of the tea has shown that these two questions—how much I should be willing to pay, and how much I shall have to pay—are perfectly distinct, and the conditions which determine the latter we have not yet examined. But whatever the terms are, and however they are fixed, I shall in each case consider whether they are good enough for me; and if they are, I shall secure the privilege of spreading my payments over the period of enjoyment, or of paying for the fraction of an article that I use, instead of for the whole of it, and shall therefore rent a house instead of buying or building, shall take cabs or 'buses instead of setting up a carriage, and shall travel by train instead of motoring.

The problems on which we have been engaged have led us to consider special cases of balancing present privations against future immunities, and we have seen how it may often be worth while to escape proximate privations at the cost of incurring remote ones. If there is a question between paying £10 a quarter for twenty years on the one hand, or £20 a quarter for ten years and nothing for the other ten, we may consider it in this way :—Taking £10 a quarter for ten years as fixed and not open to question, I have the alternative of adding the other payment of £10 a quarter for ten years either concurrently or successively at my option; that is to say, I can escape a payment in the remote future by making a payment in the proximate future, or *vice versa*. If I choose, under these conditions, to pay in the remote rather than the proximate future, it is not, so far as the data shew, because the one is near and the other is far, but because the near payment would have to be made under less favourable conditions than the far payment, and is therefore intrinsically more irksome, for it would have to be encountered at a less favourable margin. If the choice were between £10 a quarter for twenty years, and nothing for the first ten years but £20 a quarter for the last ten, it would still be good economy to make payments of £10 at the more favourable margin and secure immunity from payments which would have to be made at a less favourable margin, though now the favourable conditions would be near and the unfavourable ones far. Thus the very same principles of prudence may make one man save money in his early married life in order to have it when he wants it more in the future, for his children's education, and may make another (or even the same) man rent a house instead of buying it, because if he defers the expenditure of the greater part of the sum he will have to pay altogether, he will pay it over a period in the future during which he can better spare it than he could spare it in the lump at present.

The advantage that I derive, then, from commanding resources in advance, in such cases as we have been considering, is not the advantage of a near as against a far, but the advantage of a greater as against a less, satisfaction; and we must carefully distinguish these cases from others in which the nearness or farness of the satisfactions or privations is the

Balancing of future and present, in view of diversity of conditions, and of contingencies.

very matter we are considering. This is not so in the case of those commodities which we habitually buy in large and use in small quantities, for in such cases ordinary prudence estimates the significance of a unit in the future just as high as that of a unit in the present. We do not, as a rule, burn coal more freely because our cellar has just been filled, or eat more potatoes because we have just got in a fresh sack; or if we do, it is only by a slight and hardly perceptible mental reaction which we clearly recognise as illusory. And if we find that we have a general sense of relief and tendency to expatiate as soon as we have drawn our quarter's salary, and a corresponding sense of contraction towards the end of the quarter, we distinctly recognise this as a sign of faulty administration and foresight. In a word, the fact of remoteness or proximity should not, and within limits does not, in itself affect our estimate of the significance of things that are really of even and continuous importance to us. But very often remoteness involves uncertainty, so that we are not prepared to estimate a possible want in the remote future on the same terms as a certain want in the present or a highly probable one in the proximate future. Indeed, whether I buy fewer potatoes at this stall in order that I may in five minutes' time buy more plums at that; or whether I spend less in the market to-day altogether that I may spend more on my holiday six months hence; or whether I spend less in the whole year to make provision for the education of my children if they live to want it, or for my old age if I ever reach it, I am always estimating future wants of more or less remoteness and uncertainty (for I shall not use even the potatoes for some hours, and events may happen that will prevent my using them at all), and am always balancing them against each other and asking at what price I care to renounce relatively certain satisfactions in order to provide for relatively uncertain ones; and I am always making smaller or larger provision for some contingency according to whether the terms are harder or easier. Though in many cases this element of uncertainty in the future is negligible, in many others it is of high importance.

Finally, in closing our preliminary investigation of the balancing of present against future satisfactions and dis-

I

satisfactions, we have to note that, in addition to the rational reasons for rating one above the other which we have examined, there is the irrational factor of mere inability to realise the future or to resist a present impulse; and there is also the rarer but by no means unknown tendency to yield to a morbid dread of future distresses, or to gloat morbidly over future satisfactions, and in either case to overestimate the future in terms of the present. But throughout the whole range of these selections between present and future, or near and far, we are always in the presence of the two principles of declining marginal / significance, and the regulating effect of the terms upon which alternatives are offered. Rational considerations, by their very nature, weigh alternatives and take them only at what they seem to be worth; and as they are taken at different margins they will appear to be worth more or less; and even the most improvident or morbidly foreboding temper will refuse terms that go beyond a certain degree of extravagance, and will be to some extent blunted in its keenness by successive gratifications or provisions. Thus, whether I am wise or foolish, as my provision for the present rises in comparison to my provision for the future, or *vice versa*, the marginal significances of the two and the terms on which I shall be ready to equate them against each other will change.

<small>Balancing of present and future as such.</small>

The principle of marginal adjustments, then, runs through all the administration of our resources. Large and small units, consumption of swiftly perishable and use of relatively permanent commodities, purchase and hire, desires and projects for the present and the future, material and spiritual needs, all come under its sway. Terms upon which alternatives are offered and declining marginal significance as supplies increase are the universal regulators of our choice between alternatives.

The rest of this chapter will be devoted to the consideration of certain mental habits which tend to waste of resources, and prevent us from realising the full measure of satisfaction that the resources at our command would enable us to secure.

In the first place we must know what we want, and must distinguish the presence of things themselves from a mere assurance or conventional indication that they are there.

CH. III ECONOMICAL ADMINISTRATION AND ITS DIFFICULTIES 115

There are people who seem hardly to reckon with any direct perceptions or experiences of their own at all. They regulate their lives, and apparently even their feelings, by symbols and indices rather than facts. They are like the Professor who compared his map with the contour of the coast-line, and then declared himself satisfied as to the "perfect correctness"—of the coast-line. They cannot tell you whether they are feeling well, or whether they are in good spirits, unless they know whether the house in which the question is asked is built on clay or gravel, and how many feet it is above the level of the sea. They do not even eat what they like or what suits them, but things that have become to them symbols of festivity, languor, or of vigour, as the case may be. The extreme and all-embracing power of this disease specially besets men who pique themselves on their practical views of life, their robust common sense, and their preference for solid facts above mere phantoms. For money, as we shall see,[1] can never be more than the means (though it may be the necessary means) to happiness, and the man who habitually thinks of things under their pecuniary aspects becomes the slave to a symbol and will often sacrifice the thing symbolised to it.

Walking among shadows.

A subtler form of this tendency to pursue symbols rather than the things they symbolise manifests itself when we regulate our conduct by the tastes and desires of the people about us rather than by our own; not from any desire to gain the credit attached to conformity of any kind (a desire which takes its place on our relative scale, like any other, and normally carries its weight), nor from any value we attach to companionship, but simply from inability to distinguish between what is generally thought desirable by others and what we desire ourselves. Almost everybody's scale of expenditure is more or less distorted from coincidence with his own wants because something has been taken on credit from his social environment. We buy useless things because they are "so cheap," or refuse to buy things the price of which we find unexpectedly high, although they are well worth the money to us. We buy the cheap thing under the sympathetic illusion caused by the sense of how much

The illusion of reflected estimates.

[1] See pages 152 sqq.

more than its price it would be worth to somebody else, and we refuse to get what we want, perhaps indeed in mere inconsiderate rage at being asked "too much," but perhaps also under the sympathetic sense of the folly and extravagance which would be involved in its purchase by somebody else. The sense of the specific wickedness of wasting bread which is, or was, so common, seems to be of this social nature. We realise that bread has high value to certain people, and though our care not to waste it does not help them, and though saving in any other direction would just as well enable us to give them bread if we wished to do so, yet the direct shock of the realised contrast between our abundance and their want is softened if we behave as if bread had a higher value to us than it really has. A generation ago the relative cheapness of coal in the north of England made the consumption of fuel an item of expenditure watched much less closely in the north than in the south, and the result was that although, in general, northern hospitality was perhaps less luxurious than southern, yet a fire in a bedroom was a much more common attention in the north than, at the same temperature, in the south. And this extended to families, both north and south, whose practice was very certainly a mere compliance with social tradition. The ultimate reason why this man did and the other did not give his guest a fire was to be found in the relative value of coal, not to him, but to his neighbours.

And our minds are confused not only by the value of things to other people, but by their potential value to ourselves under other conditions. We should not hesitate, *Reactions of association.* under given circumstances, to use 1d. worth of wood or fire-lighters to set a fire going; but we should think it very wasteful to accomplish the same end by burning half a dozen boxes of matches at once. Yet the price might actually be the same, and there might be less risk of running short of matches than of wood. Only, as matches might, under wholly different circumstances, render much more valuable services, the imagination is shocked by putting them to their best real use under the circumstances that exist. A kindred habit that interferes with the fluidity or adaptability requisite for good administration is a dependence on general experience against the facts of the particular case which ought to govern

CH. III ECONOMICAL ADMINISTRATION AND ITS DIFFICULTIES 117

our conduct. There are people to whom Arctic weather would not suggest the possibility of lighting a sitting-room fire in June, and there are others who dress their children according to the calendar (and the unreformed calendar too, for that matter) rather than according to the thermometer.

These examples of the way in which analogy and association may suggest a scale of worth that does not correspond with the actual facts naturally lead to the consideration of general alertness of mind and quickness to realise the continuous diverging of true significances from the established tradition. Our purchases and our general conduct alike are largely determined by mere inertia and tradition. Our action is often guided neither by an estimate of the future nor by a direct impulse, but by mere habit formed on past estimates and impulses. And even when we form deliberate estimates, the material on which we exercise our judgment may be supplied not by the present facts, but by a traditional feeling based on what they used to be.. Most of us have known old folk who habitually set their brains to work, and made large claims upon the good-nature of their friends, in order to get letters circuitously conveyed to their destinations. The alternatives presented themselves to them not in the terms of the actual facts of the day, but in those of a tradition based on heavy postages and extensive rights of franking. The same generation would take disproportionate trouble, indirectly involving disproportionate expense, to avoid striking matches. The imagination is almost tempted to trace their conduct back to the time when the production of fire was a difficult, rare, and sacred act, while its preservation was a common precaution, and its transference a common incident of lay life ; so that the fire-transferring spill may be dealt with familiarly, but the sacred fire-begetting match is approached with an awful reserve ! So, to take another instance, the cheapening of sugar has only recently succeeded in exorcising from the mind of the average middle-class housekeeper the tradition that jam is a luxury, though butter is a necessity. And the passion for mending instead of replacing worn-out garments, which many elderly people cherish as a virtue, and the decay of which they contemplate with grave apprehension and disapproval, is a tradition from the days when materials

[margin: Traditional estimates.]

had a relatively high and time a relatively low marginal significance; because, in the last resort, it then took more time to make the material than it does now, so that nature and art offered material on harder terms measured in time then than now.

Sometimes a false symbolic value is attached to a thing neither by social environment, nor by hypothetical conditions, nor by tradition and habit, but by the mere incontinence and irresponsibility of our own imaginations. Whether in the market-place or when looking at a shop window, and particularly perhaps when travelling in foreign countries, we are all of us more or less liable to a sort of irrational enamourment. Some object hits our fancy and strikes some emotional note to which we begin in imagination to tune our whole lives. We allow this one object, and the associations it suggests, to dominate our thought, to the exclusion of all conflicting considerations; and sometimes we deliberately reject the promptings of reason, which assure us that the Venetian lamp which we covet, and which colours all our future lives with its glow, will be an intolerable nuisance during the rest of our journey, and will be nothing but a piece of incongruous affectation when we have got it home. Such infatuations naturally break the connection between anticipation and experience which is the basis of successful administration of resources. And the pathetic attempts which we sometimes make to justify our choice *post factum*, in cases of this kind, come under that very common source of waste which arises from our trying to conceal from ourselves and others a mistake that we have made in our administration. We sometimes continue to cherish and deliberately force ourselves to use, with more or less inconvenience or even suffering, things that we should throw away as rubbish if we did not remember how much they had cost. I may keep a book because I gave a guinea for it, though it is fit for nothing but to tear up for lighting fires. Because I gave something for it I cannot make up my mind to destroy it, and consequently I add to the original waste by keeping open a constant source of annoyance and at the same time sacrificing a small but real utility.

The observant reader will perhaps have noted how nearly all these sources of erroneous and wasteful administration of

Enamourment.

personal resources have their analogues in the conduct of business, and also, very specially, in the pursuit of philanthropic schemes and social ideals; and further, that most of the distorting habits of mind which we have examined are matched by errors in the opposite direction. <small>Opposite sources of error.</small> Just as there is a kind of enamourment that leads to maladministration, so there is a kind of "inodiment" which is no less fatal to the true art of living. Some particular circumstance or adjunct or article becomes hateful to us, and we allow ourselves to believe that its presence would poison our whole life; and in our imagination it actually does so. We cannot go to a city full of beauty, because we have once seen an ugly house or an ugly sight there. We cannot go the shortest way to our daily or weekly destination, because we have conceived a prejudice against a certain street or square. We cannot take a house in the country, because, although we should only go to town once or twice a year, every day of the year we should be conscious (or think we should) that the metropolitan station which we most dislike lies at the terminus of our line. And again; the whole weight of custom and tradition may, as we have seen, be regarded from one point of view as a drag upon wise living; but from another point of view it may be regarded as a fly-wheel, storing energy to carry us over dead points. As mistakes may be made by allowing too much influence to custom, so mistakes may be made by undue suspicion of it. A vast amount of the work of the world is probably done, to the great advantage of all concerned, and to the saving of much fretting upon the higher strings of motive and efforts of will, by the mere drift and momentum of acquired habit. The thought once put into the formation of habit carries life forward with an economy of thought in future, and it goes on doing its work long after it has ceased to put forth any energy. The energy devoted to opening questions that seriously need revision is well directed; but if we direct a large amount of energy down this channel, it is drawn, at rising marginal significance, from other applications, and is devoted to the opening of questions that are less and less worth opening. It will soon come to the point at which it is wasted. The alert mind is always willing to open a question, but only on an estimate, instinctive or deliberate, of the probable advantages to be gained by doing so.

This reference to estimated probabilities will lead up to the last of these notes. It concerns an error more deeply rooted in our intellect and consequently harder to recognise (though perhaps not harder to overcome when recognised) than any of the sources of maladministration already noticed. We frame our actions in accordance with expectations, and reasonable as well as unreasonable expectations may be falsified by the event. The fact that a thing happens does not prove that it would have been wise to provide against it.[1] If a man is struck by lightning in an open plain, it does not prove that it was foolish of him to be there; and yet we not only incur disproportionate inconvenience and expense to meet some remote possibility that has fixed itself unduly upon our imagination, but if a very unlikely thing actually happens, we rebuke ourselves for imprudence for not having provided against it. Alice's White Knight always carries a beehive about him, because it would be so convenient if he happened to meet a swarm of bees. Now, if the unlikely had happened and the White Knight had met a swarm of bees, had lodged it in his hive, and brought it safely home, we should be apt to say that the event had justified him. But it is not so. The capturing of one swarm of bees is an inadequate return for the carrying of beehives by 1000 knights during 1000 days; and the action of the one knight on the one day on which the swarm of bees for his hive arrives is no more to be justified by the event than are all the other 999,999 actions. Thus if a man starts lightly equipped on a journey and has to spend a few francs in the course of his holiday on books or articles of clothing which he already has at home, and which he would probably have included in his full equipment had he made it four or five times as complete, he is not demonstrably guilty of imprudence because he did not bring the greater part of his wardrobe and his library with him. It is particularly difficult for the ordinary imagination to realise that it may be very bad policy, whether at home or abroad, to retain possession of a vast number of goods because some of them may possibly, at

The doctrine of chances.

[1] Cf. Chap. VII. page 297.

some future time, be of use. That this or that odd possession now and again comes in handy may be a very inadequate justification for making one's house a marine store of obsolete odds and ends ; and a man who clears out 1000 books from his shelves and presently finds that one or two of them would have been of some use to him had he kept them, or even that he had better replace them, has not necessarily made a mistake ; but he may find it difficult to convince the thoughtless that he has not done so. We are bound to act upon estimates of the future, and since wise as well as foolish estimates may be falsified, the mere failure of correspondence between the fore'cast and the event does not in itself shew that the forecast was an unwise one. Even on his own narrow ground of after-wisdom Epimetheus may be a fool compared with Prometheus. Note again the unity of principle between personal economy and business. All kinds of insurance are based on schemes to enable us to provide, without over-providing, for uncertain events in the future by meeting the average probability, not the extreme possibility, of the case. They open the way to enormous economies of administration. It may be wise to insure against a loss which it would be foolish to provide against in any other way. Because a man's house is burnt down it does not follow that he would have been wise to save up against the possibility of such a catastrophe ; and if it is not burnt down it does not follow that he was foolish to insure it.

Not to over-elaborate these hints, let us note in conclusion that the ideally wise man will not only think wisely, but will know how much to think and when not to think at all. We have all congratulated ourselves, at one time or another, on having acted wisely on impulse when we know that we should have acted foolishly had we reflected. And we have all made a right choice, after mature deliberation, on a matter of such small consequence that the thought bestowed on getting it right was ill spent. It would have been better to have made the wrong choice than to have spent all that energy in arriving at the right one. Further, the wise man will discipline and cultivate his imagination. An undisciplined imagination magnifies, minimises, creates, and extinguishes facts, and so distorts the proportions of things.

Wisdom in administration.

A disciplined imagination vividly realises and truly estimates real conditions which are not forced upon the senses at the moment, and saves its possessor from much unwise and from much unkind and inconsiderate conduct. The wise man will defend the hour against the minute, and, like Wordsworth's Happy Warrior, will "see what he foresaw." His scale of preferences will be not only worthy, but firm and consistent, and however much events may disappoint his hopes, attainment will seldom reverse his judgment. He will be willing to encounter pain in the future on any terms on which he would rejoice to have encountered it in the past, and will never be betrayed into paying in the present a price which he regrets having paid in the past. And, for all this, having a due sense of proportion, he will take nothing seriously that is not serious, and will therefore be neither the pedant nor the prig which characterisations of wisdom are apt to suggest. He will sometimes resemble the Vicar of Wakefield in being "tired of being wise," and when he prefers the alternative of irresponsibility he will be capable of wise self-emancipation from the chains of wisdom.

Returning from this consideration of some of the causes of unwise selection between alternatives, we may once more review the general conception of the scale of preferences, or of relative estimates, itself. At any given moment, under the circumstances that then exist, the marginal values of all manner of things are arranged *de facto* upon a scale which registers how much of this would actually be accepted as equivalent to so much of that by the individual in question, and at the moment; or if this and that group of alternatives should be presented to him, which of them he will choose. It does not follow that this scale is either wise or consistent. The man's imagination may be able to seize certain items and may be incapable of combining them, so that, according to whether alternatives are presented singly or in groups (apart from any interdependence upon each other for their efficiency), he might make different and inconsistent choices. But bewilderingly complicated and perpetually fluctuating as this scale of preferences may be, it is always there. Any alternatives, however constituted, which could conceivably be offered to the

The scale of preferences reflects the man's character and is of supreme significance.

man would find him either decisively preferring one to the other or unable to decide between them; that is to say, every conceivable alternative stands either above or below any other that you may select, or on a level with it. And the things so valued constitute the man's relative scale of preferences, the basis upon which his life is built. This scale of preferences is the register of the man's ideals, of the relative weight and value that he attaches to this or that alternative under every variety of condition. What he believes it is (that is to say, the whole system of choices which he thinks he would make under every variety of conditions) is his own idea of himself. What it actually is (that is to say, the whole system of choices which under all varieties of conditions he actually would make) is his character. It is the complex of the things he wants, and the relative intensities with which he wants them, including, under wants, the objects of impulsive as well as of conscious and deliberate pursuit; that is to say, it registers (could we get at it) the things he wants, seeks, and loves, and the relative intensities with which he wants, seeks, and loves them.

> We live by admiration, hope and love,
> And even as these are well and wisely fixed,
> In dignity of being we ascend.

If the very nature of our conscious aspirations and unconscious drifts is ignoble, no degree of sagacity and acuteness, of power, prudence, courage, or firmness, can make our lives worthy. And since a man's relative scale is the register of his admirations, loves, and hopes, it is there that the ultimate regulating principles of his life embody themselves. Hence the paramount social significance of the lives of men who, whether by expenditure of their material resources or by their selections between personal alternatives, informally proclaim a system of values more worthy than that to which traditional homage is rendered. Hence, too, the feeling, entirely justified in itself, that no one who is dealing with mere questions of administration is really touching the vital spot. The man who can make his fellows desire more worthily and wisely is doubtless performing a higher task than the one who enables them more amply to satisfy whatever desires they have. The prophet and the poet may regenerate the world without the economist, but the economist cannot regenerate it without them. Yet he, too, has his place. He may help to guide if he cannot inspire. If he can give no strength he may save strength from being wasted. It is his misery that he cannot glorify the purposes to which he ministers, but it is his triumph that he can be glorified by them. He works in faith, for he knows that his work is barren unless others greater than he are working too, but he believes that wherever they are he can serve them. If he can give sight to some blind reforming Samson he too has served.

Socially as well as personally, then, we need inspiration, for our ideals may be low. We need character and vitality, for they may be the mere reflex or echo of other people's preferences, so that their realisation brings no solid satisfaction, but merely the ghost of it. We need stability, for there is a miserable type of mind that always regrets the choice that has been made and almost automatically reverses its estimate of the relative significance of two alternatives—whether between two dishes at table, two careers in life, two purchases in the market, or two sides of a moral judgment—at the moment when the choice has become irrevocable. We need imagination if we are to form any clear anticipations of the future at all, and if our selections are not to be random guesses rather than deliberate estimates. We need courage to face sharply painful or terrible experiences, and firmness to resist the seductions or pressures of the moment, when our judgment warns us that in yielding we should be choosing the worse alternative. We need energy lest we should be slack in pursuit of the good we have discerned. But we also need the discipline of reflective prudence, and this it is that teaches us " economy."

We have now completed our preliminary investigation of the principles of personal and domestic economy. Points of great importance remain to be further explained and examined,[1] but we have already laid a sufficient foundation upon which to erect a sound theory of markets, exchange, and commercial industry in general. We shall often revert to the problems and solutions that have engaged our attention

[1] See Book II. Chaps. I. to III.

CH. III ECONOMICAL ADMINISTRATION AND ITS DIFFICULTIES 125

hitherto, but it will be by way of illustration and in order to point out the fundamental unity of principle that runs through all branches of administration of resources. Our special investigation of personal and domestic economy is for the present concluded, and we must approach the great social problems which are our goal.

CHAPTER IV

MONEY AND EXCHANGE

The Communal Relative Scale

SUMMARY.—*Advantageous exchanges can take place whenever the relative significance of any two exchangeable things is marginally different on the scales of any two men in the community; and the exchange itself tends to reduce this difference. Therefore when there is equilibrium the exchangeable things on every man's scale must occupy the same relative positions. A scale registering these positions may be regarded as the communal scale. Exchange may arise incidentally, to correct errors of individual administration of energies; but complex systems of industry, that avail themselves of the economies of division of labour, contemplate exchange from the first, as an essential part of the machinery of adaptation of means to ends. In a society so organised media of exchange and standards of value arise spontaneously, and are then regulated by law. The use of gold as a medium and a standard is dependent upon its use as a commodity. The gold prices of commodities, being an expression of their positions on the communal scale in relation to gold, may become the expression of their positions relatively to each other, and of the identity of those relative positions on all the individual scales of persons who possess them. But this identity does not extend to things that cannot be exchanged. These may occupy positions differing to any degree both amongst themselves and amongst the items of exchangeable things on the different individual scales. And so may exchangeable things of which a man possesses no stock. As the ultimate objects of desire are never amongst the things that enter into the circle of exchange (though never realisable without them), the identity of scale is always objective and external, and never vital. Possessions, actual or virtual, are indeed necessary to life, but, as they increase, their marginal significance to life declines, and the danger arises of sacrificing life to them instead of supporting it on them.*

Hitherto our examination of the administration of resources has been conducted purely from the personal or individual point of view. That is to say, though the person commanding and administering the resources has been regarded as a member of a family, a circle of friends, or a community, and has been actuated by the whole range of motives and impulses that can sway human conduct, we have examined only the principles on which he chooses, and not the instruments by which he gives effect to his choice, nor the forces which regulate the terms on which alternatives are offered to him. And specifically we have assumed the existence and efficiency of money as an instrument and of the market as an institution. Both of these are obviously social or communal in their nature; that is to say, though they owe their existence or their meaning to human choice or action, yet they seem to be beyond the control of any particular individual. To these we must now turn, making the momentous transition from personal to communal economics.[1]

To begin with money. It is obvious that when I give money and get a watch, a piano, or a hundredweight of potatoes for it, the transaction is in form an act of exchange, *Purchase is a form of exchange, but not a simple one.* and though we have hitherto treated it from one side only, it is in reality a mutual transaction that may be looked at from either of two sides. Now, since this most familiar kind of exchange is by no means the simplest, we will approach the subject by examining simpler though less familiar cases. If you look at the publication *Exchange and Mart* any week, you will find such cases as this. A man has a microscope of defined quality, and would prefer to have a typewriter, also of defined quality. It may be that he attaches no value at all to the thing he has, but the essential point is that he attaches more value to the thing

[1] Cf. page 3.

he desires, and thinks it probable that there may somewhere be a man who desires a microscope which he has not, more than a typewriter which he has. And if that is really so, and if these two people can find each other out, an exchange may be effected to the advantage of both of them, each giving the thing he values less and getting the one he values more.

The conditions, then, for a mutually satisfactory exchange of two concrete articles are that two persons, who have access to each other, should each of them possess one of the articles and prefer the other. An advantageous exchange can take place if a microscope stands higher than a typewriter on Robinson's scale, and a typewriter higher than a microscope on Jones's, whereas Jones has the microscope and Robinson has the typewriter. Such simple cases, however, occupy only a very small place in *Exchange and Mart*; and indeed it is obvious that if Jones and Robinson both preferred the microscope to the typewriter they might nevertheless be able to effect an advantageous exchange. Robinson may have a typewriter and may wish to get a microscope, but, considering the quality of the typewriter he has and of the microscope he wants, he may think it very unlikely that he will be able to find any one who possesses such a microscope and actually prefers such a typewriter to it. Nevertheless, he may hope to find one who would consider the services of the typewriter more nearly equivalent to those of a microscope than he does himself, and he may therefore announce his desire to obtain a microscope and to give a typewriter " in part payment " for it. Jones may see the announcement and may think it worth following up, and ultimately Robinson may throw in " a pair of large military hair-brushes, real ebony," and complete a bargain to the satisfaction of both parties. The microscope and the typewriter enter into this act of exchange, although the microscope stands above the typewriter on the scale of preferences of Jones and Robinson alike, only the hair-brushes more than bridge the difference for Jones, and less than bridge it for Robinson.

The conditions for advantageous exchange.

Were one or both of the articles capable of small subdivision, the intervention of a third article as a make-weight need not be contemplated. We find, for instance, in a number of *Exchange and Mart* that a gentleman wants " children's new boots," and offers in exchange for them " fine old cigars." Jones, then, who has fine old cigars, and wants children's new boots, cannot, so far as our evidence goes, be said to prefer boots to cigars in the abstract, but he prefers a pair of boots of given size and quality to a certain number (more or less closely defined in his own mind, but not revealed to the public) of his " fine old cigars," and he thinks it likely that some one else will prefer that number of the cigars to such a pair of children's boots. That is to say, Jones imagines that there may be some Robinson on whose scale of preferences old cigars stand higher with respect to new boots than they do on his own. The conditions of exchange are present, then, if Jones possesses a supply of any commodity x, and Robinson of any commodity y, provided that (relatively to x) y is higher at the margin on Jones's scale than on Robinson's. And here we need say nothing about units; for though it would be nonsense to say that y stands higher on Jones's scale than x does, unless we state the unit (or unless x and y are single concrete objects), yet it is sense to say that any arbitrarily selected small quantity of y stands higher, at the present margins, relatively to any arbitrarily selected small quantity of x, on the scale of Jones than it does on the scale of Robinson; and we need not state what the small quantities are. I cannot tell you whether butter or jam stands higher on my scale unless you tell me whether I am to have an ounce or a pound of butter as an alternative to a pot of jam; but I may be able to tell you that I estimate butter (whether an ounce or a pound) as worth more jam than my neighbour does. And note here, once for all, that if y is higher in relation to x on my scale than on yours, it follows that it is lower on your scale than on mine, and also that x is higher in relation to y on your scale than on mine, and lower on mine than on yours. So that any one of these four statements carries the other three with it.

We may now advance to the general statement, that if the marginal significance of anything (old cigars) of which I have a supply stands lower on my scale than it does on yours with reference to something else (children's boots) of which you have a supply, I shall be able to offer you terms on which an exchange can be made to our mutual satisfaction; provided, of course, that the articles are in their nature exchangeable. And as our previous investigations have made us familiar with the thought that if a man possesses a large stock of any commodity, a unit of it will take a lower place on his relative scale at the margin than if he has a smaller stock, it follows that as I increase my stock of children's new boots and diminish my stock of cigars the marginal value of boots relatively to cigars declines to me; whereas you are reducing your stock of boots and increasing your stock of cigars, and the marginal value of cigars relatively to boots is declining to you. To each of us, therefore, the significance of that which he began by estimating relatively higher has declined, and the significance of that which he began by valuing relatively lower has risen; and thus the relative marginal values approach more nearly to equality. As long, however, as any difference continues to exist the conditions for a mutually advantageous exchange will still be present; unless, indeed, I have parted with all my cigars, or you with all your boots. In that case I may still think less of cigars relatively to boots than you do, but if I have no cigars, or if you have no boots, we cannot make an exchange. A relatively low estimate on my part of something I have not got does not induce business. If I value oats less highly in comparison with barley than you do, but have not any oats to give you for your barley, my relative underestimate of oats does not result in any exchange. A man once boasted that he had been offered the whole site of Chicago for an old pair of boots, and when asked why he did not close with the offer, replied, "I didn't have the boots." The conditions, therefore, for mutually advantageous direct exchange are that two men, who have access to each other, should differ in their estimates of the marginal significances of some two commodities, *and that each should possess a supply of that commodity which he relatively underestimates.*

We must note very carefully that we have not yet discovered any principle which will regulate the precise terms on which such exchanges as we have spoken of will be effected. When investigating the principles on which a man administers his pecuniary resources we assumed the existence of market prices or rates of exchange; but in an actual investigation of the phenomena of exchange themselves we may assume no such thing. It is our goal, not our starting-point. Note, then, that the limits within which a direct exchange between two men will be mutually profitable may be wide or narrow, according as the difference of relative estimate is great or small. We have not considered what will fix the terms, within those limits, on which a bargain will actually be struck. We have only shewn that there are possibilities of bargains more or less satisfactory to both parties; and it may be as well to state at once that with reference to two individuals, taken by themselves, the problem is indeterminate. Its solution will depend on the personal qualities of the two bargainers, and the accidental features or circumstances of the special case. Indeed, if the idea of a "rate of exchange" arises at all (in the case, say, of the men with the cigars and the children's boots), it will probably be only a reflex from other and more familiar transactions. The natural thing will not be for the two bargainers to try to arrive at a "rate" of exchange between boots and cigars, and then consider how many each would like to exchange at that rate; but rather for the cigar man, for instance, to say how many cigars he will give for a batch of boots that would suit him, and for the other man to try to make him give more cigars for the same batch, or take a pair of boots less for the same number of cigars. They will haggle over amounts, not rates.

Rates, as we shall see, are a phenomenon of highly organised markets; and even where money is employed, and there is a regular market, it may be organised on such primitive principles that rates do not emerge with any distinctness. So far as a foreigner can observe, this is the case in the celebrated Bergen fish-market. A housewife asks the price for a certain batch of fish which she selects, and when she is told what it is, offers something less. The fisherman will give her all but one of the fish for the price she names, or all of them for a rather higher price. She will pay the original price if he will substitute another smaller fish for the one he has withdrawn, or the higher price if he will give her a better fish instead of one of the original set, and so on. Perhaps there is not one of all the proposed bargains that both parties would not rather accept than do no business at all; but each hopes to better a good bargain.

It is indeed the ultimate goal of this part of our inquiry to arrive at a definite conception of the forces that determine market prices or rates of exchange, but we are far from having reached it yet. We have, however, already formulated the conditions under which mutually advantageous exchange is possible.

Henceforth our thoughts will generally be directed to those items on a man's relative scale which are capable of being exchanged, and since this concentration of attention has an insidious and deadly tendency to induce a tacit assumption that there is nothing else or that nothing else much matters, it is important to fix it firmly in our minds that there are many things on our scales of preference that are not exchangeable at all. One man might be willing to sacrifice a title if he could get rid of a constitutional tendency to neuralgic headaches, and another man might be willing to contract such a tendency if it would secure him the title; but though there is a diversity in the tastes of these two men, and each possesses what he relatively undervalues, no exchange can take place. One man might be willing to hand over his knowledge of Chinese to another man in exchange for that other's knowledge of mathematics, and the other might welcome the arrangement; but the exchange cannot be made. In the latter of these supposed cases, though hardly in the former, there may have been a time when the one scholar devoted to the study of Chinese, and the other to the study of mathematics, time, money, and will-power which might have put him in possession of the knowledge he would now prefer. To each individual the alternative was open once, but the fact that each has made what he now regards as a mistake, in a different direction from that made by the other, does not enable them to rectify or cancel their errors by exchange. On the other hand, if two men who have grown produce for their own personal use find that their scales of marginal preference differ, potatoes standing relatively higher on the scale of one and cereals on that of the other, they can make an adjustment, to their mutual advantage, by exchange. In some cases it is conceivable that each of them might, had he foreseen the whole circumstances, have so conducted his own individual operations as to secure the same ultimate balance

Things that cannot be exchanged.

directly and without exchange. In that case the two men, like the students of Chinese and mathematics, made an initial mistake, but, unlike them, they are able by exchange partially or wholly to retrieve their error.

But it is not necessary to suppose that there has been any error at all. Exchange need not come in *post factum* as a corrective. It may have been contemplated from the first, as an essential link in a series of options by the exercise of which each of the two men does better for himself by producing partly with a view to his own and partly with a view to the other's wants than he could have done had he directly contemplated his own wants alone. The men may have different talents or different opportunities, and on the principle of division of labour two men between them can often do more of each of two kinds of work if one works all day at one and the other all day at the other than they could if each worked half a day at one and half a day at the other. It may be, therefore, that two men deliberately produce things on such a scale that the marginal significances to each man are out of proportion to the resources which he has devoted to their marginal production; but by exchanging with each other each secures a better result from his own point of view than he could have realised had he done the best possible for himself with his own resources. And this is, of course, what actually happens in any system of industry which we can regard as successfully organised from the social point of view. It is therefore of importance to note the general conditions under which such an organisation becomes possible. My faculties and requirements may be such that, as between Chinese and mathematics, I could make more rapid relative progress in mathematics, whereas another man with whom I am in communication would make more rapid relative progress in Chinese. But it may be that I should value progress in Chinese relatively more for my purposes, and he progress in mathematics for his; yet it would be no use my studying mathematics and he Chinese, for though we should in that way have more between us of all that each of us wants, yet each of us would have what the other man wanted and we should not be able to exchange. Obviously, less of the two accomplishments in possession of the men that want them will

Production with a view to exchange.

be preferable to more in the possession of the men that do not. We should have done better, therefore, by each gaining the smaller knowledge of what he wants himself than by each gaining the greater knowledge of what the other wants. Here the alternatives between which both he and I have to choose are offered to each of us severally, and each must regulate his choice as best he may by the terms on which they are presented to him individually. No system into which exchange enters can increase our command of what each of us wants.

If, on the other hand, Jones has premises particularly suited for keeping old potatoes in prime condition, and has the kind of tastes and instincts which enable him, with certainty and without anxiety or worry, to see that the most favourable conditions for their preservation are uniformly secured, and if, moreover, while having no particular qualifications as a gardener, he has a pronounced taste for new potatoes; and if his neighbour Robinson has not his particular gifts, and has no premises which have the special advantages of his, but has all the instincts of the successful gardener, and at the same time has the good sense to prefer sound old potatoes to the earliest new ones which he himself can produce, or at any rate has no such marked preference for the latter as Jones has, it is obvious that the two men can come to some arrangement from which they will mutually derive advantage. Jones can preserve old potatoes for Robinson, and Robinson can grow new ones for Jones. Here, then, are capacities and opportunities which can be exchanged; and you and I are no longer compelled, each of us, to bring the results of his own efforts into the best harmony he can achieve with his own tastes; for by exercising the faculties which I have and you have not, I can secure the direction of your faculties which I have not to my purposes which they suit; and in this indirect manner I can distribute my transformed resources amongst the objects of my desire so as to achieve a better result than if I had applied them all directly. Each of us accomplishes his own purposes more fully by the indirect process of devoting a portion of his energies to the accomplishment of the other's purposes, on condition that he reciprocates, than we could have done by each pursuing his

[marginal note: Exchange may remedy a failure of coincidence between capacities and desires.]

own ends directly. And here of course, as everywhere, the principle of declining marginal urgency is at work. As the things that I get indirectly, by furthering some one else's purposes, increase in volume and diminish in marginal significance, and as more and more of my energies are turned to these indirect but expeditious methods of accomplishing my desires, the supply of those things which no one can do for me contracts, and their marginal urgency rises, till I have found the balance.

In a great and complex industrial society direct reciprocity of services will not be the rule. I, Robinson, may (as before) want to have my old potatoes preserved and may not have the conveniences and capacities which give me exceptional qualifications for the task; whereas you, Jones, may have what I want; but I may have no relatively superior opportunities for rendering any corresponding service to you. I may, however, know Brown, who is good at growing the new potatoes you like, but has no special taste for them; and he may want nets mending or making, to put over his fruit-trees. I may, through physical constitution, acquired skill, or any other circumstance, be relatively better qualified, or in a better position, for making or mending nets than for either growing new potatoes or preserving old ones, and so I may do netting for Brown and get new potatoes, not because I want them myself, but because I know you want them, and I can barter them with you for the old potatoes you have preserved. Here I make nets which (relatively to the trouble of making them) I do not want, and I give them to Brown for new potatoes that I do not (relatively) want either, because I know that you who want new potatoes will give old potatoes for them, to which old potatoes I do attach a value that compensates me for the work I put into the nets. Or if you know about Brown and his tastes, you may give me old potatoes for my nets, not because you want nets, but because you want new potatoes and know that Brown, who has them, will give them to you in exchange for nets. Thus each is making what some one else wants in order to get what he wants himself. Further, if it is a fruit-growing and market-gardening country, you, without knowing any specific Brown who has new

Media of exchange, and transformation at two removes.

potatoes and wants nets, and without indeed there being any such person at all, may be willing to give me old potatoes for nets because you are pretty certain of finding a Smith somewhere who has new potatoes and will give them to you on suitable terms in exchange for nets, not because he wants nets either, but because he, in his turn, will by-and-by want cherries, which he does not grow, but expects to be able to get in exchange for nets from Williams. We need not carry the illustration any further to see that any article which is well known to be valued by a large and easily accessible class of persons may be taken habitually in exchange for valued commodities, although those who take it do not want it for their own use, and it does not, on its own merits, occupy such a place on their relative scale as would justify the exchange. All that is necessary is that there should be a confident expectation of finding some one on whose relative scale it does take such a place. The derivative value that such an article will possess in the mind of a man who has no direct use for it will depend on the direct value which it is conjectured to have in the mind of some accessible though not definitely identified individual or individuals. If there is some article of very generally recognised value which actually takes its place, as directly significant, on the scales of a great number of people, it may come to be generally accepted, without any special calculation or consideration, by people who are not thinking of any use they may have for it themselves, but are aware that it occupies a sufficiently high relative place on the scales of others to recoup them for what they give in exchange for it. As soon as this custom begins to be well established it will automatically extend and confirm itself, and the commodity in question will become a "currency" or "medium of exchange," the special characteristic of a medium of exchange being that it is accepted by a man who does not want it, or does not want it as much as what he gives for it, in order that he may exchange it for something he wants more. If I have some potatoes and should prefer some cherries, and give my potatoes for some nets, which I do not want as much, because I know that some one else has the cherries and will prefer nets to them, then the nets are a "medium" by the intervention of which I can, at two removes, exchange my potatoes for the cherries, though I cannot find any one who has the cherries and will give them to me for the potatoes. Postage stamps often serve as a medium of exchange, because a large and easily accessible class of persons are constantly wanting the services that the stamps will command. Tram tickets, when issued in books, might and to a limited extent do serve as a medium of exchange in the same manner. Cook's coupons might easily pass as a medium of exchange amongst travellers on the Continent; and if the railway companies issued their dividends in the shape of claims for such and such a mileage of travelling on their lines the certificates would be readily accepted in exchange by people who had no intention of travelling themselves, if they could make sure of finding people who did want to travel and would give them valuables in exchange for the claims. It is a matter of common knowledge that cattle still perform this function of a medium of exchange in South Africa, and books tell us that furs were long used as currency by the traders on Hudson Bay, and tobacco by the planters in Virginia.

Concurrently with these developments, or perhaps in advance of them, the custom will grow up of estimating the marginal significance of things in terms of the generally accepted article even when the article does not pass from hand to hand in exchanges. There is more evidence in the Homeric poems of the valuation of female slaves, of tripods, or of gold or brass armour, in terms of so many head of cattle, than there is of any direct transfer of cattle in payment for other goods. The convenience of such a standardising of values is obvious. If everything is scheduled in terms of one selected commodity it is indefinitely easier than it would otherwise be to realise the terms on which alternatives are open to us; and if any man defines his marginal estimate of anything he possesses in terms of this standard commodity any other member of the community will at once know whether or not it stands higher on his own scale than on the other's, and therefore whether or not the conditions for a mutually advantageous exchange exist.

A medium of exchange as a standard of value.

In England the functions of a standardising commodity and of a medium of exchange are both alike performed by gold. Gold is applied to a vast number of purposes in the arts and sciences, and were it more abundant it would replace other metals in many more. Consequently a great number of easily accessible persons actually give a relatively high place to gold on their scales of preference, in virtue of its direct significance to them. It is established by custom (and, so far as that is possible, by law) as the universally accepted commodity; and at the same time it is used as the common measure in terms of which our estimates of all exchangeable things may be stated. So when we say that the marketer finds new potatoes at 2d. a pound and old potatoes at ½d. we are saying that she finds a pound of new potatoes offered in exchange for about 1·0273 grains of standard gold, and a pound of old potatoes in exchange for about ·2568 of a grain. Now she may probably possess gold which has a direct value to her. She may have a gold stopping in one of her teeth. She may wear a gold wedding-ring or a gold brooch. She may have pictures with gilt frames, or books with gilt edges, or bindings with gold lettering, and she may want more of some or many of these things. There is therefore a basis in her mind for a comparison between the marginal significance of gold and potatoes. It is no doubt highly improbable that she could herself turn a supply of gold to any of her purposes; and whenever she realises an alternative between gold and something else, for instance between a gold brooch and an umbrella, the gold is always taken in conjunction with the services of the jeweller, the dentist, or some other artist. No separate account is, generally speaking, made out and presented by these artists for the gold, and the purchaser certainly does not know to a third decimal of a grain how much gold there is in her tooth or her brooch, or what is its marginal value to her. But neither does she make a separate estimate or receive a separate account for the steel or cane in the umbrella. When she considers what a pound of new potatoes is worth, and determines that it is worth more than 1½d., but less than 2d. —*i.e.* more than ·7705 grain of standard gold, but less than 1·0273—it is not the direct significance of the gold on her own scale that she is contemplating. And the same is true of the stall-keeper who declares that he will part with his potatoes for 1·0273 grains of gold per pound, but not for ·7705. But

Gold as a commodity, a medium, and a standard.

just as, in our previous examination, the fact that there are a great number of fruit-growers on whose relative scales nets occupy a place, on their own merits, is enough to give them a secondary place on the relative scales of others, so the fact that in a great industrial community there are a number of people who accurately estimate and highly appreciate the direct services that gold can render is sufficient to define the secondary place of gold on the relative scales of others. The ordinary member of the community in forming minutely accurate estimates of the relative significance of gold and new potatoes is consciously guided not by any direct significance that gold has for him, nor for any one with whom he is dealing, but by his knowledge of its secondary place on the scale of others relatively to potatoes, neck-ties, first editions of Shelley, and all the rest. Nevertheless, our housewife is herself one of the persons whose wants determine the primary significance of gold. The bookbinder, the picture-framer, the jeweller, the dentist, and all others who use gold in making or doing things she desires, know to a nicety what substitutes can be used, and how much she and her likes will prefer so much gold in the work to so much of anything else. Thus, while the public are balancing articles with gold in them against other commodities, the experts are observing exactly how far the presence or absence of small quantities of gold in these articles affects their preferences. They know, if the consumer does not, how many potatoes they can get in return for a fraction of a grain of gold, applied to the direct satisfying of human wants; and why they know it is because they know, though the consumer does not, exactly how much gold they must apply (in gilding letters, for instance) in order to make a certain thing preferable in the consumer's mind to a stone of potatoes instead of only to six pounds. And from time to time they advertise the same article at a different price according to whether it is "gold mounted," has "gilt edges," and so forth, or not. Hereby they challenge the attention of the consumer directly to the marginal significance of gold to him in various of its applications; and in these cases the purchaser, in deciding whether to give the extra sixpence for the gilt, the extra 5s. for the mounting, or the extra £1 : 1s. for the gold in the "upper plate," is actually balancing small increments of the direct service of gold against definite amounts of other commodities. Gold, then, is merely one of the things that enter directly into a large number of individual scales of preference, which has been adopted as the common measure of all things that enter into the circle of exchange. In an ordinary way no one who buys or sells is thinking of the direct value of "gold" either to himself or others. He is thinking only of its secondary or derived value on the scales of others who, like himself, have formed no estimate of its direct significance. But, nevertheless, this secondary value of gold is closely determined and defined by its primary value, and is absolutely dependent on it. It has a definite secondary value to all and in all connections merely because it has a definite primary value to many and in some connections.

The actual function of gold in England is obviously what we have defined and illustrated as the function of a medium of exchange. It enables us, at two removes, to exchange the thing we have for the thing we want, when we cannot effect that exchange directly at one remove. I can pour my possessions or my services into the circle of exchange at one point and can draw out the services and commodities that I desire at another, though the people that I serve and supply can neither do the things I want done nor give me the things I want to possess, and though the people from whom I draw the things and the services I want have no need of anything that I possess or can do. I receive money from the one set and I pay money to the other set, making money the "medium" by the aid of which I change what I have for what I want, though no one that has what I want wants what I have keenly enough to offer me a satisfactory exchange. Thus, by teaching Greek to men who can neither make shoes nor drive an engine, I can get myself shod and carried by men who have no wish to be taught Greek. It might be a valuable exercise for any one who is "earning his living" to attempt to go through a few hours or even a few minutes of his daily life and consider all the exchangeable things which he requires as they pass, and the net-work of co-operation, extending all over the globe, by which the clothes he puts on, the food he eats, the book containing the poems or expounding the science that he is studying, or the pen, ink, and paper with which he writes a letter, a poem, or an appeal, have been placed at his service, by persons for the direct furtherance of whose purposes in life he has not exercised any one of his faculties or powers.[1] Such an attempt would help us to realise the vast system of organised co-operation between persons who have no knowledge of each other's existence, no concern in each other's affairs, and no direct power of furthering each other's purposes, by which the most ordinary processes of life are carried on. By the organisation of industrial society we can secure the co-operation of countless individuals of whom we know nothing, in directing the resources of the world towards objects in which they have no interest. And the nexus that thus unites and organises us is the business nexus—that is to say, a system of exchanges, conducted for the most part in terms of a medium that enables us to transform what we have into what we want at two removes.[2]

We are now in a position to expand the implications of certain conclusions that we have already reached. We have seen[3] that (except for friction) there is no equilibrium between any two members of an exchanging community, in respect of any two articles that they possess, unless these two articles occupy the same relative positions on the scales of the two men. And since this is true of any two articles and of any two men, it follows that it must be true of all the exchangeable articles and services and between all the members of the community in question. By an exchanging "community," in this connection, we mean a number of persons who are in such communication with each other as to know of every diversity of relative estimates that arises amongst them; so that any two of them have direct or indirect access to each other. And we now understand something of the nature of money and the manner in which it facilitates this mutual access. The money value I attach to anything is an expression of its position on my scale relatively to all other things in the circle of exchange, for all are registered in the same terms. It means that I equate it with

In a state of equilibrium things that can be exchanged must have the same relative places on the scales of all members of the community.

---
[1] Cf. pages 346 *sqq.*
[2] A further study of monetary questions will be found in Book II. Chap. VII.
[3] Page 130.

any article, service, portion, or group and combination of such, that I can command for that sum of money, that I value it more than anything I could get for a smaller sum, and less than anything that I should be willing to give a larger sum for. The relative place of any marginal unit on my scale of preferences, then, corresponds to the money value that I set upon it, and if I possess anything which I value at 1s. and which some one else, within the circle of exchange open to me, values at 1s. 6d., the conditions of exchange are present. If he has a thing which he estimates at 1s. and that I estimate at 1s. 6d., the conditions of exchange equally exist; but if we both value the article at 1s. or both value it at 1s. 6d., there is equilibrium. And if I value it at 1s. and you value it at 6d. and neither of us has it, whereas a third man, who has it, values it at 1s. 6d., the conditions are still those of equilibrium, not of exchange; for the man that values it more highly than we do already has it and will not give it us for the sums we are willing to pay. Throughout these propositions the statement that a man estimates a thing at 1s. or 1s. 6d. must be understood to mean that he is prepared actually to give that sum for it, and therefore that he possesses the sum; for if the estimate refers to merely imaginary circumstances, then of course no inferences as to the actual state of things can be deduced from it. When we say, " I value that at £100," we may only mean, " I think it would be worth £100 to some one else," or " I would give £100 for it if I had £100 to give," or (as is more likely) " I have £100 and I will not give it for this thing, but if I had £100 more I think that is what I should spend it on," or "if I had another £1000 I think I should spend £100 of it on this." In such cases, if we are speaking deliberately, our statements may have some significance and may throw light on some parts of our relative scale, but they will not affect actual exchanges and do not disturb or establish equilibria. Thus, when we supposed just now that I value a thing at 1s. and you value it at 6d., I must be supposed to have a shilling and you a sixpence which we would give for the thing; but the man who has it would not take less than 1s. 6d. for it.

Let us try to realise exactly the point we have reached. Some men eat tripe, but not beef, and others eat beef, but not tripe. Both these sets may occasionally eat bacon. It follows from the whole course of our inquiries that, in a state of equilibrium, tripe and bacon take the same relative places at the margin on the scales of all who consume them; for if they did not, then the conditions of exchange would exist and there would not be equilibrium. Their market or equilibrating prices represent the position they occupy relatively to each other on all the scales, and that position is identical for all of them. And, again, if any one does not consume them at all, it is because no portion of them is worth the market price to him. That is to say, they stand higher at the margin on the scales of all who buy them and give the market price for them than on the scales of any who do not buy them because they are not, even at the origin, worth the market price to them. In like manner bacon and beef have their uniform place relatively to each other on the scales of all those who consume them; and these places also are represented by their market prices. Thus the market prices reveal the relative marginal significances of tripe and bacon to all who consume them, and of bacon and beef to all who consume them; and so, even if there is no class of consumers who eat both tripe and beef, the places of tripe and beef on the communal scale relatively to each other are fixed, because each of them is fixed relatively to the place of bacon. In all cases, then, the market or equilibrating price of a thing represents a relative place on individual scales which is identical for all consumers.

The communal scale.

In an exchanging community, therefore, there is a perpetual tendency to establish an equilibrium. And just so far as such an equilibrium is established, the relative marginal estimates formed by all the individuals, of all the exchangeable commodities of which they severally possess a store, are identical; and the estimate of any exchangeable commodity formed by any one who does not possess any of it is relatively lower than that formed by any one who does possess it.

This proposition is a mere truism. Yet, when its scope is realised, it is so startling, and it is of such commanding importance, that I will repeat it and elaborate it yet again. We have learned that, in spite of the indefinite variety of men's tastes and wants, and general command of the means of satisfying them, there exists (ideally, and in the state of equilibrium) in any community a collective and universal scale of relative marginal significances with respect to all articles that enter freely into the circle of exchange, and that this scale is identical, so far as it is relevant, for every individual of the community.

Note the qualifications. The collective or communal scale of relative marginal significances of which we are speaking has respect to "all articles that enter freely into the circle of exchange," and for each individual the identity between his scale and the communal one extends only "so far as the latter is relevant." We will take the latter point first. By the qualification "so far as it is relevant" I mean that any man who could examine the general or communal scale in a state of equilibrium would find that it contained many entries of things which he would not care to have at all, or of which he has no store because he does not care as much for them (relatively to other things) as any of those who have them do; but all the things of which he has a supply he will find in the same relative positions on the communal scale that they occupy on his own. In our former example, for instance, the man who would not have tripe at any price will find bacon and beef occupying the same relative places on the general scale and on his particular scale, and the man who never thinks of buying beef at the current prices will find tripe and bacon occupying the same relative places on the public scale and on his own.

Its correspondence with the exchangeable items on the scale of each individual.

Of course, this ideal state of equilibrium never exists; but a sense of mutual advantage is perpetually bringing about approximations to it, by prompting both of any two men whose scales of marginal significance do not coincide, directly or indirectly to effect exchanges or readjustments until they do. The machinery by which these exchanges and readjustments are conducted, and by which equilibrium is approached, will engage our closer attention in later chapters, but it is essential at the outset that we should clearly understand the nature of the equilibrium itself.

If we return to the phenomenon of market prices we shall see that though we have not yet fully examined or explained them, their mere existence is enough to illustrate and enforce the thesis we are now examining; for whenever any article has a price in the open market every one will buy it at that price until further increments would not be worth it to them —that is to say, until it exactly balances with the marginal significance of any other thing that could be got for the same price. Thus the market tends to keep the relative marginal significance of all exchangeable or marketable things and services at the same level for all the purchasers, rich and poor, whether their purchases are large or small. In this sense, therefore, it is possible to speak of the relative marginal significance of any commodity, not to an individual, but to a community. When a state of equilibrium has been reached— that is to say, when the conditions for exchange and readjustment no longer exist—there is a uniform scale of marginal significances obtaining throughout the community; and where there is no such uniform scale, the very fact of that condition existing tends to produce exchanges and readjustments which will result in a uniform scale.

But now we must turn to the other qualification. We have seen that on every man's relative scale articles that do not "enter freely into the circle of exchange" are registered. With respect to these there is no uniform communal scale at all. Food and writing materials must theoretically occupy the same relative places on the scales of any two individuals who habitually supply themselves with both and who have access to each other; for if not, they might advantageously exchange with each other. But it does not follow that either of these things will occupy the same place relatively to the desire to escape the weariness of an extra half-hour's work at a certain margin, or the desire to be relieved from a certain intensity of hunger. To secure the same amount of food or of writing materials, one man may be willing to work when his nerves and muscles cry aloud for repose, and another man may not be willing to walk across the street or to turn a shovelful of earth. And to increase his stock of writing-paper by a certain amount, one man may be willing to stop eating when his appetite is still

The items on individual scales that are not exchangeable are not represented on the communal scale, and do not take identical positions, amongst the exchangeable items, on the several scales.

L

fierce, while the other does not and would not endure any conscious privation for it at all. Because, in dealing with weariness and hunger, we are dealing with things that cannot be shifted from man to man, for which there is no direct market of exchange, and which therefore cannot adjust themselves on individual scales to any common standard. The significance of tripe relatively to bacon is identical on the scales of all who consume both. But the significance of tripe relatively to health, happiness, and domestic affection may vary indefinitely on the scales of two members of the same community; for the man to whom it means more happiness than it does to another cannot give the other so much happiness in exchange for it—he can only give him so much bacon. When William Cobbett was a private soldier, he had once "made shift to have a halfpenny in reserve" out of his pay, with which he meant to buy a red herring in the morning. "But," he tells us, "when I pulled off my clothes at night, so hungry then as to be hardly able to endure life, I found that I had lost my halfpenny! I buried my head under the miserable sheet and rug, and cried like a child!" He was not a soft man, and yet missing an expected red herring was a matter for tears to him. At that very time he was elaborately educating himself, buying books, pens, ink, and paper out of the farthings or halfpence he saved from his pay —halfpence, therefore, which were in competition with red herrings and the like. It follows, then, from the observations we have just made on markets, that red herrings, books, pens, etc., occupied the same place relatively to each other on Cobbett's scale as they did on those of other members of the community who purchased and possessed them, and the loss of a red herring or half a quire of paper would be, relatively to other things in the circle of exchange, no more serious to him than it would be to you or me. But vitally? With reference to things that are *not* in the circle of exchange?

There is no theoretical means of constituting a comparison between the sensations and experiences of two different minds. But such theoretic differences will hardly restrain us from saying that the halfpence spent by Cobbett mattered more to him than the halfpence spent, we will not say by a millionaire, but by any man who does not encounter amongst his habitual experiences unsatisfied desires for food, so keen that the thwarted anticipation of an indulgence which a halfpenny would secure wrings tears from him. And yet the fact that one man would give 1s. for a thing, and another man would go without it sooner than give $\frac{1}{2}$d. for it, shews that the one man prefers it to any other alternative which the 1s. he spends on it would open to him, and the other man does not prefer it even to the alternatives that $\frac{1}{2}$d. would open to him. Measured by any ideal standard of the gratification conveyed by consumption, the suffering inflicted by privation or disappointment, the willingness to endure pain or to make effort, one may have the strongest reason to suspect that the man who will nearly but not quite give $\frac{1}{2}$d. for a thing wants it more than the man who will give 1s. or even a guinea for it does, only he wants all the other things which $\frac{1}{2}$d. can get still more than he wants this, whereas the other man wants another shilling's worth of anything else still less than he wants this. Nevertheless, the place which this thing occupies on the communal scale of relative marginal significances is higher in the case of the man who will give 1s. for it than in the case of the man who will not give, or will only give, $\frac{1}{2}$d. for it, and that in the ratio of twenty-four to one.

We may call the whole scale of the individual, on which are entered all things that he estimates and considers in making his selections and determinations, the vital scale or the psychological scale; and the collective scale on which only those things which enter into the circle of exchange are registered, the objective scale. *Relative significance, vital and objective.* All the items, then, that are entered upon the objective communal scale occupy identical positions *relatively to each other, but not relatively to the other items*, on the vital scale of every member of the community who possesses supplies of them. We shall speak of this as identity of "objective relative significance," thereby expressly excluding any presumption that there is also identity of "relative vital significance."

It is important to apply these considerations to the case of changing prices in a market. We have not yet examined the causes which effect these changes, but that need not prevent us from analysing the nature of their results. The considerations entered upon in the second chapter shew us that if the stock of an article should be increased and its price lowered, some of those who already bought would now buy more, and some who had not bought at all before would now begin to buy; and of these latter, some might buy a considerable quantity, and some perhaps only the smallest unit which would be commercially recognised. In this last case the marginal unit would also be the "original" or initial unit of supply; but in the case of all the new purchasers the initial demand would coincide, in its marginal significance, or place on the scale of preferences, with a unit more or less remote from the origin on the scales of those who were already possessors at the higher price; and all the marginal increments (whether initial also or not) will, as we have seen, coincide as to their objective relative significance. But what can we assert as to the vital urgency of the marginal want now gratified by the buyer of the larger quantity, compared with that of the initial or early satisfactions of the man whom the lowered price has brought into the market? Evidently we are not justified in saying that because, relatively speaking, they are all equally intense objectively they all perform equally significant vital services. Strictly speaking, no such statement could, under any circumstances, be an accurate one; for as there is no means of comparing the wants of two different minds with each other, so there could be no exact meaning in declaring that the degree of pain which one man suffers from hunger is precisely the same as that experienced by another. Nevertheless, we habitually form estimates as to the relative urgency of wants experienced by different men, and the relative intensity of the enjoyment and suffering which they experience. Philosophically we may admit that it is impossible to prove that one man suffers as much from being burnt alive as another man does from a gnat bite; but we can say that, measured by every conceivable test as to the alternatives they would accept or reject, this must be so, and we are practically troubled by no philosophic doubts on the subject. If, instead of dealing with a single individual, we are dealing with a large number, we should not strain even a philosophic doubt to the point of questioning whether collectively greater suffering would be involved by putting 100 men

Fallacy of arguing from relatively declining objective significance to relatively declining vital significance.

on the rack or by submitting 100 men to a gnat bite each. There might in one odd case be extraordinary sensitiveness, and in another extraordinary anæsthesia, but they would not be typical. Even if there were reason to suppose that the selections were not purely casual, but that a higher range of sensitiveness prevailed in one class than in the other, we should never be able to allow a metaphysical scruple or a general and vague supposition to counteract an indefinite difference in the nature of the pain inflicted.

Speaking, then, in the language of common sense, we may say that in the above instance we are justified in assuming that some at least of the men who do not begin to buy until the price is low are not in less but in greater want of the article than those who begin to buy at a higher price. The man who is willing to give an enormously high price for anything is presumably already fairly well supplied with the ordinary supports and comforts of life, or at any rate with what he himself regards as such; and we have seen that whether a man is willing to pay a given price for a given increment of anything will depend on the importance of the relinquished alternatives which that price represents. Therefore, if one man will pay high for a thing and another will not, it may no doubt be because the first man wants the thing more and is willing to make greater sacrifices for it; but it may equally well be that he wants other things, which he could get as an alternative, less, and therefore is making a smaller sacrifice. And the reason why he wants increments of other things less may be not because of any speciality of taste or requirement, but because he is already so amply supplied with them that a little more of them is hardly worth having. Their marginal increments have a low significance.

It is necessary to insist on this point for a very special reason. If the supply of any commodity is increased from x to y, and the price has fallen from u to v, some of the units of the extra supply will fall, as we have seen, to those who formerly had some and now have more, and others will fall to those who had none before and now have some. It is a strange and disturbing fact that when people expressly direct their attention to the matter, they think and speak exclusively of the latter set, but when they are applying general considerations to their conception of life, they make assertions which are justifiable only with respect to the former; that is to say, the assertions which they make, and which determine the general attitude of their minds towards social questions, are in this instance only true with respect to that portion of the subject about which they never think. It is this way :— Almost any one you speak to about what happens in consequence of an increased supply will tell you that the price falls because you " have to reach new customers," or that " people who went without the article before now get their share of it." You will find that the increased supplies taken by the old customers are almost always lost sight of. And yet when the same people are speaking of the conditions of life at large, and of the forces which direct productive effort to the supply of one commodity rather than another, they invariably speak of the increments which fetch a lower price as " less urgently needed " than those which previously fetched a higher price. Now, we have no right whatever to make this assertion, except with respect to that portion of the increased supply which goes to enlarge the share of such as were already purchasers at the higher price. The man who cannot or does not get a thing until the price comes down to 1s. may very well want it more, in any sense in which the phrase can be intelligibly used, than the man who could and did buy it at £1. To say, therefore, that the purchases induced by a falling price supply " decreasingly urgent needs " is true only of that portion of the purchases which is never in our minds when we are expressly thinking of the wants which the increased supply actually meets. It is little wonder that confusion of thought arises under such conditions, and I need make no apology to the reader for the insistence with which I have dwelt on the composite character of the collective scale, on the necessity of distinguishing between the increase in the amounts taken by the old purchasers and the shares now secured by the new ones, and between the objective coincidence of the relative scales of the individuals of a community and the unmeasured divergence of their subjective or vital significance. These fundamental distinctions must never drop into the background of our minds, and in the next chapter we shall have occasion to return explicitly to them.

CH. IV   MONEY AND EXCHANGE   151

We have been careful to note that this communal or general scale contains only those things which enter into the circle of exchange, whereas each individual scale contains all valued things, powers, and experiences, whether capable or not of being thrown into and drawn out of the circle of exchange. And this naturally leads us to inquire more closely what things do enter into the circle of exchange. Much attention has been devoted to this question by political economists, and we have already investigated cases of things that do and cases of things that do not enter into this circle; but here, as elsewhere, it is difficult to draw a sharp line. The most obviously exchangeable things are physical objects which are physically transferable: potatoes, diamonds, planks of wood, books, or spades. But there are also things, not themselves thus transferable, the legal right to exclusive command of which may be transferred. Land (carrying with it, on certain conditions, the right to exclude sunshine from a neighbouring house, or under other conditions the right to prevent the erection of a neighbouring house which shall exclude sunshine from it, and so forth) enters into the circle of exchange. Further than this, the temporary use or enjoyment of many things, such as the right to a seat in a railway carriage, or at a concert or theatre, are in the circle of exchange; and these latter uses or enjoyments involve command of a share in the services rendered by the engine-driver or the performers. The command of services, then, may likewise enter into the circle of exchange; and so may fractional shares in the property of a great railway company or a joint-stock brewery, or the right to claim from the country, as represented by its government, the sum of £2 : 10s. per annum. Any thing, service, or right may be acquired in exchange if it is capable of being transferred from one person to another, or rendered or assigned indifferently to any one of several individuals or groups. And in like manner, if an onerous obligation of any kind can be transferred from one person to another—that is to say, if Jones can make himself responsible, say, for the services which Robinson would otherwise have had to render—immunity from this obligation may become a subject of exchange. When we speak of a thing being in the circle of exchange, therefore,

What things enter the circle of exchange?

we mean that in the community concerned there are always accessible persons able to render the service, or to undertake the obligation, or transfer the right or command, or give possession of the thing, and willing to do so on terms that are precisely or approximately known, or can at any rate be ascertained.

Into this circle of exchange enter a vast number of the things which I desire, and the command of which I believe will affect my well-being; and the sign and symbol of all these is money. If a direct exchange either of commodities or of services can be arranged, the transaction is of the same general nature as if the medium of gold were employed, only it is completed in one move instead of two; and if gold is not employed as a medium, it may still be employed mentally as a common measure of comparison to facilitate the arrangement of the terms of exchange. To speak of money, then, is a convenient and short way of speaking of all the things that enter into the circle of exchange; and the difficulty in answering the question "What are they?" rises from the fact that these things, of which money gives us command, are, strictly speaking, never the ultimate objects of deliberate desire at all, and yet, on the other hand, are always essential to securing such ultimate objects. "Money," in this wider sense of the things in the circle of exchange which money commands, will secure nothing that we deliberately desire, and yet nothing that we deliberately desire can be secured without it. That is to say, there is no ultimate object of desire which itself enters into the circle of exchange and can be directly drawn thence, and there is no such ultimate object that can be secured and enjoyed without the support of things that do enter into the circle of exchange. Mere impulse may direct us this way or that without reflection, but as soon as we deliberately desire possession of any external object, it is because of the experiences or the mental states and habits which it is expected to produce or to avert. Even articles of food are desired because of the anticipated sensations which their consumption will produce or the impulse they will gratify, or because of the social pleasures with which their consumption will be associated, or because of the vigour which they will sustain, or because of

Ultimate objects of desire never enter the circle of exchange,

the suffering which they will avert; and we cannot be sure that when the time comes they will be cooked in such a way, or that we shall ourselves be in such a condition, or that our company will be such, that the anticipated pleasure will accrue. And, indeed, it may be that, instead of vigour or pleasure, torpor or pain will be the result. Or if, to our great dismay, we find it impossible to get as much food as we desire, we may be surprised to find that the evil consequences apprehended do not arise, but, on the contrary, that we are in an unusual state of efficiency and vigour. And, indeed, our habitual expressions of disappointment on the one hand, or surprised delight and self-gratulation on the other, in the possession of anything, from a necktie to a house and garden, are a sufficient proof that we habitually draw out of the circle of exchange, not the things which *will* produce, but the things that we (often erroneously) expect to produce what we want. Perhaps we recognise this fact more easily, though it is not more surely true, in cases where there is no material thing to shew as a set-off against our disappointed expectation. A journey or a concert is quite obviously undertaken or desired, not merely for the sake of going there or being there, but for the sake of experiences, opportunities, or advantages which we expect to be incidental thereto. And we may very well get what we paid for without getting what we wanted. There is therefore no single thing which we desire that can directly and certainly be got for money, because no single thing that we ultimately desire is in the circle of exchange or can be directly drawn from it.

But neither can anything we desire be got without money, or what money represents, *i.e.* without the command of exchangeable things. All the things that we so often say "cannot be had for money" we might with equal truth say cannot be had or enjoyed without it. Friendship cannot be had for money, but how often do the things that money commands enable us to form and develop our friendships! Domestic peace and happiness cannot be had for money, but Dickens's Dr. Marigold was of opinion that many a couple live peaceably and happily together in a house, who would make straight for the divorce court if they lived in a van. "Wiolence in a cart is *so*

but can never be secured without the help of things that do.

wiolent, and aggrawation in a cart is *so* aggrawating." And have we never heard of devotedly attached men and maids losing the flower of their youth because they "could not afford to marry"? In their opinion, at any rate, all those elements of domestic happiness that "cannot be had for money" were present, and only those that money could command were absent, and yet the absence of these alone prevented the full realisation of the happiness which their presence alone could not have secured. But even "waiting" requires money, if not so much as marrying does. In fact, a man can be neither a saint, nor a lover, nor a poet, unless he has comparatively recently had something to eat. The things that money commands are strictly necessary to the realisation on earth of any programme whatsoever. The range of things, then, that money can command in no case secures any of those experiences or states of consciousness which make up the whole body of ultimately desired things, and yet none of the things that we ultimately desire can be had except on the basis of the things that money can command. Hence nothing that we really want can infallibly be secured by things that can be exchanged, but neither can it under any circumstances be enjoyed without them.

It will probably be found, in the last analysis, that nothing can enter into the circle of exchange except such things as can be done for us or provided for us by people who do not care for us and for whom we do not care, as individuals. It does not by any means follow (as we shall see more fully in the next chapter) that, as a fact, they are provided or done for us by such people; but there can be nothing in their nature to prevent the possibility of its being so. And such things can never be the ultimate objects of desire; they can at best be no more than the means expected to produce or to render possible the ultimately desired experiences. Our ultimate realisation must be in ourselves and with those who care for us and for whom we care. Exchangeable things can only be more or less uncertain means towards the realisation of ends that are not in the circle of exchange.

This being so, it is obvious that in effecting an exchange we may, at the time, be thinking of nothing else than the things exchanged, but reflection, and "motive" in the deliberate sense, must always point beyond them. If the connection is very close between the command of the thing and the satisfaction of the wants to which it ministers, we are apt to overlook the difference, because we feel that in getting food, for instance, we have secured what is usually the determining factor, on which the satisfaction or thwarting of our wants depends; and so the other conditions fall into the background of our consciousness, and only appear when we ask for them. On the other hand, the money factor retreats, and as a rule does not force itself upon us, when we are thinking of the pleasures of friendship or of love, because the rarest and most specific factors which we think of as determining the situation that we desire or enjoy are not exchangeable; and the exchangeable adjuncts are not of a specific but of a general and undetermined efficacy. They could lend themselves equally well to the support of other results or combinations. Naturally, therefore, they do not occur to our imagination when we think of the conditions requisite to what we seek. But in either case the neglected factors inexorably assert themselves. Moralists have indeed done well to accustom us to the contemplation of the man with enormous command of exchangeable things seeking in vain for peace of mind or devoted affection, and the man whose command of exchangeable things is extremely small, rejoicing in these higher and non-exchangeable blessings. Nevertheless, it remains true that some command of exchangeable things is necessary for the enjoyment of the most immaterial blessings of character or experience, and this fact we perfectly well recognise in our practical conduct, however imperfectly we analyse it; for we always treat the securing of our daily bread "in the very largest sense of the term" as imperatively urgent—upon some one, if not necessarily upon ourselves.

Closer and remoter connections between things in the circle of exchange and experiences for the sake of which they are desired.

But the principle of declining marginal significance applies here too, and works in with the distinction between that which is necessary for the accomplishment of our desires and that which is itself intrinsically to be desired. These exchangeable things, which are necessary, are necessary in a diminishing degree as our stock of them increases. We must have some of the commodities and services that enter into the circle of exchange in order to live at all. Hence the extreme urgency of securing a certain supply. But we are very prone to treat this urgency as though it were inherent in the nature of the things themselves, and to regard the acquisition of money, or command of things in the circle of exchange, as characterised by a kind of intrinsic urgency. When we have gained a certain supply of these things their decreasing marginal significance makes the deflection of energy from the cultivation or enjoyment of more direct sources of satisfaction, in order yet further to increase them, extremely bad husbandry. Indeed, just as it is easy to have so many houses that we have no home, so in general there is a point at which the command of exchangeable things may cease to support and may begin to oppress, or feed upon, our store of ultimately desired experiences. And long before this point is reached the relatively feeble value, at an advancing margin, of further increments of exchangeable things, may make them worth much less than the fruition we sacrifice to get them. It is therefore well to note that the same line of investigation which has shewn us the extreme urgency of a certain supply of exchangeable things has also shewn us the futility of an indefinite increase of them. Aristotle said, long ago, that it is only the man who has no defined ends who desires the strictly indefinite accumulation of means. A tool, he says, must always be of limited dimensions.

<small>Declining significance of the growing "abundance of things a man possesses" in relation to his life.</small>

Our examination of money and of the mechanism of exchange has opened to us a vast field for consideration, for it has directed our attention to the fact that over the whole range of exchangeable things we can usually act more potently by the indirect method of pursuing or furthering the immediate purposes of others than by the direct method of pursuing our own; and it has further led us to contemplate the relation in which exchangeable things stand to the ultimate purposes of life. The remainder of this book will be devoted chiefly to the development of the former set of considerations, and we shall examine the machinery by which we get at our own purposes through a network of exchanges in which we are all doing the things that others want done, in order that we may get others to do what we ourselves want done. But insistence on the importance of this machinery would be entirely misleading if we did not think of it in connection with the wider problem that has now been indicated of the relation of the command of exchangeable things in general to the accomplishment of the real and ultimate purposes of life.

CHAPTER V

BUSINESS AND THE ECONOMIC NEXUS

SUMMARY.—*We began by assuming the purchasing power of money and the existence of market prices, and analysed the principles on which we administer our pecuniary resources in the face of these phenomena. Our analysis has shewn us that we administer our pecuniary resources on the same principles as those on which we conduct our lives generally. It has also explained the phenomena of money, which we began by taking for granted, and it already foreshadows an explanation of market prices. In the course of our investigations we have discovered no special laws of the economic life, but we have gained a clearer idea of what that life is. It consists of all that complex of relations into which we enter with other people, and lend ourselves or our resources to the furtherance of their purposes, as an indirect means of furthering our own. This life is not isolated, but it may be studied in isolation, for the economic pressures tell for what they are worth whatever other pressures they combine with, and the better we understand them, as isolated, the better we can predict their effect upon any combination of forces into which they enter. To the social reformer this is of supreme consequence, for the economic forces are persistent and need no tending. If we can harness them they will pull for us without further trouble on our part, and if we undertake to oppose or control them we must count the cost.*

We began our inquiries by examining the history of the use of the words "Economy," "Political Economy," and "Economics." We have now reached a point at which it will be well to examine the current use of a connected group of terms, and to attempt to define our relations to them. But before doing so let us take a note of the progress we have so far made. We began by studying the general laws of the administration of resources; and we reached a clear and satisfactory conception of the principle on which each individual, deliberately, blindly, or impulsively, adapts his conduct to the terms on which alternatives are offered to him by nature or by man. We saw that those principles are identical, whether we are dealing with problems of exchange (as in the expenditure of money in the market-place), or with the assigning of exchangeable things to their ultimate uses (as in the distribution of new potatoes or of milk amongst the various claimants within the household), or with the turning of personal and inalienable qualities and powers, in obedience to impulse or deliberate purpose, along the various alternative channels through which they may flow (as in expressions of temper or affection; in admonishing, encouraging, or restraining others; in self-application to tasks with a view to future power or enjoyment; in purely lyric utterances of devotional fervour; or in gratification of æsthetic appetites). Whether our housewife is apportioning the stuffing of a goose at table, or her housekeeping money in the market, or her time and attention between schemes for getting or keeping a connection for boarders and the more direct cultivation and furthering of the general tastes and interests of her life; and whether her husband is conducting family prayers, or posting up his books at the office, or weighing the advantages and disadvantages of a partial retirement from business; whether, in a word, either or both of them are pursuing their ultimate purposes in life and obeying their fundamental impulses by direct or by indirect means, they and all the people they are concerned with are alike engaged in administering resources, in developing opportunities and choosing between alternatives, under the great controlling guidance of the two principles we have been continuously illustrating throughout our investigations. From end to end of life the principle runs unchallenged that marginal significances decrease as the volume of total satisfaction swells, and that that volume should be largest when marginal values

Retrospect and stock-taking. The special domain of Political Economy. Has it any special laws?

are adjusted to the terms on which alternatives are offered.[1] Now the very widest definition of the economic life, or the range that should be covered by economic study, would not embrace the whole area that is subject to this law; for it would not be taken to extend to the administration, or distribution among varied claimants, of personal and inalienable qualities and powers that flow directly towards their ultimate purpose or expression. The widest definition of Economics would confine their scope to things that can be regarded as in some sense exchangeable, and capable of being transferred or applied according to order and agreement. No one would regard the principles upon which I balance the claims of devotion against those of friendship, or of either against the indulgence of my æsthetic appetites, as within the range of economic science. And so the first point that we have established is that, whatever our definition of Economics and the economic life may be, the laws which they exhibit and obey are not peculiar to themselves, but are laws of life in its widest extent.

Next, if we narrow our view to the consideration of exchangeable things, we may distinguish between acts of administration that directly involve exchange, and acts of administration dealing with exchangeable things, but not themselves acts of exchange. For instance, the housewife's administration of her stores amongst different claimants at home is not a series of acts of exchange, but is a series of acts relating to exchangeable things. If we pushed for the admission of such acts within the range of the general study of "Economics" our claim could hardly be refused. For what is "economy" if not the "regulating of a home or household"? But the qualification of "political," that is to say "public" or "communal," would exclude this domestic branch from the domain of "Political Economy," so that the only portion of the ground we have so far studied that would be admitted within the precincts of this science would be that portion which is concerned with exchange,—in the case of our housewife, her purchases in the market. Now here it is still more obvious that the principle of administration is identical within and without the region thus defined. The

[1] But see Book II. Chap. I.

laws of "Political Economy," so far as we have yet investigated them, are identical with those of "Economics" in the larger and inclusive sense. If Political Economy has any special laws of its own, we have yet to discover them. The expectation that such laws might exist would not have been unreasonable at the outset of our inquiry; for we found that, whereas our general principles of "marginal decline" and "terms on which alternatives are offered" gave an adequate account of domestic administration and seemed to bring us into direct contact with the ultimate facts, yet as soon as we went to the market we encountered two very imperfectly understood and analysed phenomena — the functions and efficacy of money, and the existence of market prices—which were obviously not ultimate facts, and which required further analysis and explanation. As phenomena they certainly seemed to belong to Political or Communal, as distinct from Personal or Domestic Economy. Might it not be that they had laws of their own, laws peculiar to that life of business or exchange in which they first appear? If so, these laws would be the special laws of Political Economy. But this expectation is gradually disappearing. We have already made provisional investigations into the meaning and functions of money, and they have sufficed to shew us that it is in no sense an isolated phenomenon, but that it enters naturally into a system of exchange, which is absolutely dominated, and is explained to its inmost recesses, by the principle of declining marginal significance, in conjunction with the terms on which alternatives are offered. But we have not yet made any express examination of the nature of these "terms on which alternatives are offered" or the causes that determine them. On the area more particularly assigned to Political Economy they present themselves in the shape of market or current prices—a phenomenon which it is obviously impossible to regard as ultimate, which demands explanation, and which we have not yet explained. Here, then if anywhere, we must seek the special and peculiar laws of Political Economy. But the suspicion must already be strong in our minds that we shall not find them; for in the existence of a collective or communal scale of preferences we seem already to have found, or to be on the point of finding, the clue to the explanation

M

of market prices. Much remains to be done, but we can already see that the preferences of each individual help to determine the terms or conditions under which the choice of other members of the community must be exercised. If you take the individuals of the community two and two it is clear that the marginal preferences of each determine the limits within which direct exchanges with the other can be entertained, and we must already have at least a presentiment that the collective scale is the register of the final and precise "resultant" of all these mutually determining conditions and forces.

To seize and follow up this clue will be the task of the remaining chapters of this First Book; but meanwhile we must continue our express examination of the ideas that lie behind such phrases as "economic conditions," "the economic motive," "the economic nexus or relation," "economic forces." By this examination we shall emphasise certain facts and clear away certain misconceptions which might otherwise escape our notice or entangle our inquiry. To begin with, we have seen that the broadest conception of Economics includes all dealings with exchangeable things, but does not extend beyond them. Thus when we speak of the "economic conditions" realised by any community we think of the general command of exchangeable things they enjoy, and we call these conditions good or bad, favourable or unfavourable, according to the extent and perhaps the nature of this command. And since material things are those that first occur to our minds when we think of exchanges, there is a marked tendency (sometimes conscious and deliberate, sometimes unconscious or even counter to deliberate purpose and definition) to treat "economic" as equivalent to "material" conditions. Broadly speaking, when we hear that in any community the "economic conditions" are satisfactory we think of the people as well fed, well clothed, well housed, and more vaguely as being in the enjoyment of decent and reasonable "comforts." And note that though all this depends upon the command of things that are exchangeable, it does not follow that the things are all of them actually exchanged. If a man lives largely on the potatoes he grows on his own patch, they affect, and help to constitute, the economic conditions under which he lives just as much as if he had bought them. In the use of the phrase " economic conditions," therefore, we start from a fairly intelligible basis, though it is obvious on consideration that the word in this connection can have no scientific precision. The transition from material comforts to æsthetic enjoyment, for example, is continuous and imperceptible. Clothes, crockery, counterpanes, furniture, are all valued for the comfort they afford, the pleasure they give to the eye, and the social distinctions that are attached to them. So we cannot purge our conception of the economic conditions under which a man lives from all æsthetic and kindred elements; the interpenetration is too close and intimate. And if we take a broader view and include all exchangeable things in our purview we shall have to include literature, art, education, spiritual enjoyment and edification, and much more, just so far as books, pictures, concerts, and the teachings and the ministrations of religion, come into the circle of exchange and can therefore be commanded by money. The use of the word "economic" in this connection, then, though fairly well understood, eminently convenient, and not seriously or generally misleading, is entirely without precision, and though useful in description it should be avoided in argument.

But when we pass from the phrase " economic conditions " to the phrase " the economic motive " the case becomes very different. Here we are in the presence of one of the most dangerous and indeed disastrous confusions that obstruct the progress of Economics. Many writers have thought that the Economist, as such, must not only limit his consideration to certain actions and conditions which concern exchangeable and mainly material things, but must also shut out of consideration all *motives* that are not " economic." And the economic motive is generally defined as the " desire to possess wealth." The widest definition of wealth, in this connection, would make it include all exchangeable things, but nothing else. Now since we have already seen that no ultimate object of desire can ever be the direct subject of exchange at all, we perceive at once that to regard the " economic " man (as he is often called) as actuated solely by the desire to possess wealth is to think of him as only desiring to collect tools and never desiring to do or to make anything with them. More

The economic motive.

than this, we have seen that the very law that regulates and balances one against the other a man's selections amongst exchangeable things, also regulates and balances his choice between wealth and leisure, for instance ; that is, between acquiring a larger command of exchangeable things and cultivating a finer enjoyment of those he already commands, or between command of exchangeable things and immunity from painful exertions. It is therefore impossible to examine the action of the "desire for wealth" without at the same time relating it to the desire for ease or the desire for enjoyment. And this conclusion is so inevitable that it has generally been found necessary to associate "love of ease" with "desire for wealth" under the economic motive. And yet this does not help us. A man may be just as strenuous in the pursuit of knowledge or of fame, or in his obedience to an artistic impulse, as in the pursuit of wealth. "The demands of vanity may be as imperious as those of hunger," so that all the motives and passions that actuate the human breast may either stimulate or restrain the desire to possess wealth. How, then, can we isolate that desire as a "motive"?

Yet it is not unusual expressly to exclude all altruistic motives from the field of economic study and to say, or to imply, that in his economic relations a man is purely self-regarding. We are asked then, first to recognise no other motive than "the desire to possess wealth," and then, by way of extra precaution, expressly to exclude altruistic motives. But this additional demand is not only arbitrary, but, so far from fortifying the other, it expressly contradicts it ; for a man may clearly desire wealth from altruistic motives, so that if I am to exclude altruistic motives I must insist on going behind the "desire to possess wealth" and knowing why the man desires it, so as to be able to exclude all (economically) improper motives. This is not treating the "desire to possess wealth" as itself the "motive" at all.

The truth is that the relative intensity of another man's desire to possess any exchangeable thing, regarded as a fact, apart from his reasons, undoubtedly helps to fix the terms on which possession of that thing is offered to me. If I regard it in this light all considerations of motive are irrelevant ; for I am thinking of it as a fact with which I must reckon, not as a motive which influences *him*. If, on the other hand, I look at the matter from his point of view and am interested to know how he comes to want this thing, I must be prepared to recognise all motives that are actually at work. More broadly, the collective or communal scale, on which exchangeable things only are registered, may be accepted as a fact, in which case we are only concerned with the "what" and the "how," and not at all with the "why," or we may go behind it and inquire into its genesis, in which case we must impartially recognise all the motives that actually go to forming it. We may either ignore motives altogether, or may recognise all motives that are at work, according to the aspect of the matter with which we are concerned at the moment; but in no case may we pick and choose between the motives we will and the motives we will not recognise as affecting economic conditions. There seems little sense, then, in using the term "economic motive" at all;[1] for the whole conception appears to be a false category; but the elements of truth which it is a confused attempt to systematise will presently become clear to us.

The phrase "economic relation" places us on much firmer ground; for it may be applied with perfect precision and appropriateness to a great class of relations which we have already been led to examine. We will here recapitulate and expand the conclusions we have reached with respect to them. *The economic relation.* Every man has certain purposes, impulses, and desires. They may be of a merely instinctive and elementary nature, or they may be deliberate and far-reaching; they may be self-regarding or social; they may be spiritual or material; but whatever they are it is impossible for him to give effect to them by his own unaided action upon the forces and substances of nature. No man, standing naked upon the face of the earth, can feed, clothe, or house his body, or secure an entrance for his mind into the regions of intellectual, imaginative, and emotional enjoyment; nor (suppose he has altruistic impulses) can he, thus unaided, minister to like needs or develop like possibilities in others. Neither can he accomplish these things by the direct application of his own faculties supported by all the material supplies and instruments he possesses or can possess; nor yet, except

[1] Cf., however, pages 167 *sq.*

under very special circumstances, simply by enlisting the co-operation directly inspired by sympathy with him or with his purposes. But by direct and indirect processes of exchange, by the social alchemy of which money is the symbol, the things I have and the things I can are transmuted into the things I want and the things I would. By these processes I can convert my acquaintance with the nature of different kinds of wood, and my skill in handling certain tools, or my knowledge of the higher mathematics, or my capacity for firing men's imaginations or for chastening or stimulating their religious emotions, into food and clothing, into books and pictures, into the rapid transport of my own person through distant lands, into dinners for hungry children, into May festivities for listless villagers, into the collation of Syriac manuscripts, or into any of the thousand other things that I want to have, to experience, or to get done; and all this independently of any interest in these desires of mine, or any knowledge of them, on the part of very many of the persons who assist me to accomplish them. Even when such an interest exists it may be insufficient (if unsupported by other considerations) to make my sympathisers qualify themselves for the work, and set to it for mere love of the thing to be done. Why, then, do they co-operate with me at all? Not primarily, or not solely, because they are interested in my purposes, but because they have certain purposes of their own; and just as I find that I can only secure the accomplishment of my purposes by securing their co-operation, so they find that they can only accomplish theirs by securing the co-operation of yet others, and they find that I am in a position, directly or indirectly, to place this co-operation at their disposal.

A vast range, therefore, of our relations with others enters into a system of mutual adjustment by which we further each other's purposes simply as an indirect way of furthering our own. All such relations may be fitly called "economic." The range of activity they cover is "business," and in the last chapter we have already incidentally opened our investigation into the causes that lead to it. It often happens that a man's individual faculties or possessions are not so well suited for the accomplishment of his own purposes as they are for those of another, and the great principle of division of labour, the conception of which is sufficiently widely spread to obviate the necessity of any elementary exposition, re-enforces the natural diversity of capacities and increases the economy of the indirect furtherance of many of our purposes as against their direct furtherance. The principle of division of labour would apply, as writers from Adam Smith downwards have abundantly shewn, even if all men's capacities and opportunities were identical. It gains an additional range of application and significance from the fact that they are actually so diverse. And again, the results, experienced and anticipated, of this principle of division of labour react upon the deliberate training to which men submit themselves, and enable us, by intentionally cultivating one faculty in one man and another in another, to increase still further our collective command of the things we desire. The whole life of every modern society is built upon this basis, and our activities are determined by it from the outset. If one man possesses wheat in such quantities that he finds it well to exchange some of it for potatoes, and another for like reasons is glad to change potatoes for wheat, this is not generally the result of any miscalculation, and not necessarily the result of any original and inevitable diversity of opportunities or faculties. It was deliberately contemplated and planned from the beginning, because the one man believed that the most economical way for him to increase his stock of potatoes was to grow wheat, and *vice versa*. By the system of "economic relations," then, I understand that system which enables me to throw in at some point of the circle of exchange the powers and possessions I directly command, and draw out other possessions and the command of other powers whether at the same point or at some other. And I define my relation with any other man as "economic" when I enter into it for this purpose of transmuting, either at one or at two or at more removes, what I have and can into what I want and would.

Lastly, "economic forces" or "the economic force" may suitably be used to indicate the resultant pressure of all the conditions, material and psychological, that urge men to enter into economic relations with each other. Could "motive" be used, in accordance with its etymological significance, simply as equivalent to a driving

Economic forces.

force of any kind, there need be no objection to the use, in this sense, of the phrase "economic motive." But since it easily suggests a deliberately selected end or goal and has been expressly applied, in connection with economics, to the ethical distinction between egoism and altruism, it will be far safer to avoid it altogether. I shall therefore speak of "economic relations" and "economic forces," but not of "economic motives." And by economic forces I shall mean anything and everything which tends to bring men into economic relations. Thus, the invention of machinery which tends to increase division of labour, the concentration of the industrial population, improved means of transport and communication, the credit system, the general demand for elementary and technical education, and, in a word, the whole structure, organisation, and movement of society, is perpetually opening and closing opportunities for combination and for the mutual furtherance of each other's purposes by men of differing faculty, opportunity, and desire. And these conditions determine how far and in what way the general desire of every man to accomplish his own purposes, whatever they may be, shall become an economic force, urging him to enter into relations with other men, with a view to the more effective accomplishment of his own purposes. Whether I pursue my purposes directly through the application of my own resources and capacities to their accomplishment, or indirectly by entering into an economic relation with other men, applying my resources directly to the accomplishment of their purposes and only indirectly to the accomplishment of my own, in either case my motives are identical. But the attraction which draws me towards the accomplishment of my purposes becomes an economic force whenever the state of knowledge and the organisation of life suggest my entering into an economic relation with some one else as the best means of realising my aims.

And here it may be well to note a second sense in which the term "economic conditions" is often used. Any change in men's desires or ideals, any change in their knowledge, in their power of effective combination for controlling and directing the public resources—in fact, any change in the articulation of society or

Another use of the term "economic conditions."

the purposes of man—will open up and develop some channels, and close others, by which the individual may indirectly seek the fulfilment of his purposes. And such changes are said to alter the " economic conditions " of the society in question, or specifically of this or that individual or occupation. In this sense a change in economic conditions would not mean a general rise or fall in the command of exchangeable things, but it would mean that the possession of one kind of faculty or resource put a man into a better position for the indirect fulfilment of his purposes, and the possession of another kind into a worse position than had previously been the case. No confusion arises from this double use of the phrase, but if it had not been expressly noted the reader might have observed some inconsistency between the meaning assigned to " economic conditions " earlier in this chapter [1] and the sense in which it will generally be used in the subsequent course of our investigations.

We have now, it is to be hoped, reached an adequately clear and precise conception of the meaning of " the economic relation," of " economic forces," and of " economic conditions," in this latter sense of the considerations which determine a change of flow in the economic activities. But the misconceptions and confusions that surround this subject are so obstinate, and reassert themselves so persistently, that it will be well to fortify ourselves against them; and I shall therefore endeavour in this chapter to make good certain propositions, some of which have already been provisionally established in an explicit manner, and only need elaboration and confirmation; all of which are implicitly contained in the conclusions we have reached; none of which, except perhaps the last, seem to be uniformly or adequately recognised in the current treatment of Political Economy. These propositions are :—

(a) That the economic relation is entered into at the prompting of the whole range of human purposes and impulses, and rests in no exclusive or specific way on an egoistic or self-regarding basis.

(b) That the economic forces and relations have no inherent tendency to redress social wrongs or ally themselves with any ideal system of distributive justice.

[1] Cf. page 162.

(c) That the hypothesis that the economic relations can be isolated, even if taken only as a first approximation, is too remote from the fact to be admissible, and would be useless and superfluous in any case; and that the economic relation, as well as being naturally allied to other relations in every degree of closeness, has itself a tendency to beget these other relations.

(d) That it is nevertheless both legitimate and desirable to make an isolated study of the economic relation and the economic forces, though not on the hypothesis that they actually exist or act in isolation.

(a) It is often said or implied that the housewife, for example, is actuated by a different set of motives in her economic transactions in the market and her non-economic transactions at home; but this is obviously not so. The buying potatoes and cabbages in the market and helping them at table are integral portions of the same process, and the housewife is considering the wants of her family when she is making her purchases just as much as when she is distributing them. She is herself one of the family, and her personal and particular tastes and wants are consulted more or less consciously, and carry more or less weight, according to her disposition, her powers of imagination, and her state of mind at the moment; but her purchases are effected and her distributions made with reference to one and the same set of wants. It would be transparently absurd to say that she is only thinking of herself in the market-place, and thinking chiefly of others in the home; or that her motives are entirely egoistic when she is buying the potatoes, and preponderatingly or exclusively altruistic when she is helping them. And as it will be generally admitted that she conducts her marketing in the main on business principles, it follows that the difference between what we are to consider a business transaction and what we are not so to consider is not determined by the selfishness or unselfishness, the egoism or altruism, of the inspiring motive. In like manner, when Paul of Tarsus abode with Aquila and Priscilla in Corinth and wrought with them at his craft of tent-making we shall hardly say that he was

What constitutes a business transaction?

inspired by egoistic motives. It is, indeed, likely enough that he was not inspired by any conscious desire to further the purposes (pastoral, military, or what not) of the men for whom he was making or mending tents, but it is very certain that he was impelled to practise his craft by his desire not to be a burden to the Churches, and that his economic life was to his mind absolutely integral to his evangelising mission.

And, indeed, in any complex industrial civilisation every man (unless he is subsidised, which only throws the process one step further back) must obviously be dependent for the accomplishment of his purposes on the indirect process of doing something, or allowing something, in furtherance of the purposes of others, on condition of securing from them the command of services and commodities which will directly minister to his own purposes. *Mutual dependence. Co-operation extends beyond the limits of common purpose.* The economic relation, then, or business nexus, is necessary alike for carrying on the life of the peasant and the prince, of the saint and the sinner, of the apostle and the shepherd, of the most altruistic and the most egoistic of men.

And if it be not true of any single individual, neither can we expect it to be true of any small group of individuals, whether domestic or other, that the faculties and resources which they collectively command can directly supply their collective wants or fulfil their collective purposes. The group of men who unite to propagate a set of religious doctrines or to call attention to a social or national wrong, or to secure a sanitary or dietary reform, or to preach any gospel or advertise any fad, may have in their own ranks the capacity to expound the truth they believe themselves to possess and the means and willingness to study and to write, but you may be sure that they will want "subscriptions." That is to say, they will want the means of procuring specified services from persons outside their ranks. They will wish to get persons to print or to distribute literature, or to allow them to occupy a room for a few hours in the week or to store their properties there; and the persons whose services, or the temporary use of whose possessions, they require for the accomplishment of their purpose will be persons who may be selfish or unselfish, but amongst whose purposes, good or bad, the promulgation of the particular thing in question does not take such a place as to induce them to render the services or encounter the sacrifices in question merely for love of the cause on its own merits. Even if Mr. X lends a room and Miss Y does all the clerkage for love of the cause, yet the stationery is manufactured by persons who are paid for their work and have no knowledge of the "cause," and the circulars are impartially delivered by the same postman who hands in the rival appeals of the enemy, and is himself probably unconcerned alike as to the bane and the antidote, but is intent on keeping his home together, or propagating in his leisure hours some political, social, or religious gospel of his own. Or even if the circulars themselves are printed by an enthusiastic apostle, for love, the type was founded by one of the heathen, whose co-operation in the cause was necessary, and had to be obtained for a consideration. All these profane persons have purposes of their own, which may or may not be as disinterested as those of the Society which deals with them, but which are at any rate different; and it is only if they are put in command of services which will promote their own purposes that they will be willing to render the specific services required to further the purposes of the Society. And seeing that the Society itself is only willing thus to further their purposes on condition that they further its own, there is no room for charges of selfishness on either side, but great room for satisfaction and congratulation on both. It would be ridiculous to say that the enthusiasts who give the printer an order for ten thousand copies of their most effective tract are actuated by purely "egoistic" motives, and if we choose to imagine the case that the printer, on his side, is getting weary of his trade, but keeps on in order to be able to make handsome subsidies to a certain "cause" in which he in his turn is interested, it would be equally ridiculous to say that his motives were "egoistic." Yet the relation on both sides might be purely economic. Each might enter upon it altogether in furtherance of his own purposes, and in no degree from sympathy in the other's.

Our complex system of economic relations puts us in command of the co-operation necessary to accomplish our purposes, independently of a complete coincidence between our purposes and our own faculties, and independently also of our being able to command the effective sympathy of persons possessing all the necessary faculties that we lack. A right understanding of the nature of the business or economic nexus, therefore, ought to dispel for ever the animosity with which Political Economy has often been attacked as a degrading study, and the uneasiness with which its own representatives have often defended their science against the charge. In principle the study of business relations is the study of the machinery by which men are liberated, over a large area of life, from the limitations which a failure of correspondence between their faculties and their purposes would otherwise impose upon them. The things they have and can are not the things they want and would; but by the machinery of exchange they can be transmuted into them. The economic relation, then, liberates them from the limitations imposed by the nature of their own direct resources. And this liberation comes about by the very act that brings a corresponding liberation to those with whom they deal. " It is twice bless'd. It blesseth him that gives, and him that takes." Surely the study of such a relation needs no apology, and there seems to be no room to bring against it the charge of being intrinsically sordid and degrading. The conditions under which business is actually conducted (like other conditions under which we live) may be far from ideal, but the business or economic relation, as such, does not seem to be open to the faintest suspicion of a taint, even when regarded from the loftiest æsthetic or ethical position.

And yet the ground on which this stubborn prejudice rests is obvious enough, and the example of the apostolic tent-maker has already suggested it. We have seen that although Paul was certainly not thinking of himself or of his own advantage when he was making tents in Corinth, yet neither was he necessarily or even probably thinking, in any disinterested or enthusiastic manner, of the advantage of those for whom he was working and whose wants he was immediately supplying. In his attitude towards himself and " others " at large, a man may be either selfish or unselfish without affecting the economic nature of

Each party to an economic relation enters it in furtherance of his own purposes, not those of the other.

any given relation, such as that of Paul to his customers; but as soon as he is moved by a direct and disinterested desire to further the purposes or consult the interests of those particular "others" for whom he is working at the moment, then in proportion as this desire becomes an ultimate object to him (so that he is directly fulfilling one of his own purposes in supplying these wants) the transaction on his side ceases to be purely economic. No doubt Paul took conscientious pains with his tent-making. So far as this was with a view to business it was done in obedience to an economic force. So far as it was an expression of his own personality or of his independent sympathy with his employers it was not. If you and I are conducting a transaction which on my side is purely economic, I am furthering your purposes, partly or wholly perhaps for my own sake, perhaps entirely for the sake of others, but certainly not for your sake. What makes it an economic transaction is that I am not considering you except as a link in the chain, or considering your desires except as the means by which I may gratify those of some one else—not necessarily myself. The economic relation does not exclude from my mind every one but me, it potentially includes every one but you. You it does indeed exclude, and therefore it emphasises, though it does not narrow or tighten, the limitations of the altruism of the man who enters into it; for it calls our attention to the fact that, however wide his sympathies may be, they do not urge him to any particular effort or sacrifice for the sake of the person with whom he is dealing at the moment. An economic relation may be entered upon equally well from egoistic or altruistic motives; but as long as it remains purely economic, it must remind us that no man's altruism is undiscriminating to the extent of lavishing itself upon all persons or all purposes at all times. Short of this, clearly the most altruistic person may enter into a relation with another man, the purpose of which is to further the good of those who are other than himself, and also other than the person with whom he is dealing. In that case his action is altruistic because it is inspired by a desire for the good of some one other than himself, and the relation is economic because it is entered into for the sake of some one other than his correspondent.

It is impossible at this point to refrain from anticipating the contents of our paragraph (c), and reflecting how seldom the economic motive can maintain itself in isolation; and by what insensible degrees I may pass from regarding you solely as a means to my ends into taking some measure of interest, for your sake, in what I am doing for you; but our present concern is not to shew how the economic relation allies itself with others, but to form a sharply defined conception of the nature of that economic relation itself; and to this we must return.

Distinction between egoism and non-tuism.

The distinction that we have drawn between the selfish motive, which considers me alone, and the economic motive, which may consider any one but you, is well illustrated by the case of trustees. Trustees who have no personal interest whatever in the administration of the estates to which they give time and thought will often drive harder bargains— that is to say, will more rigidly exclude all thought or consideration of the advantage of the person with whom they are dealing—in their capacity as trustees than they would do in their private capacity. Thus we see that the very reason why a man feels absolutely precluded from in any way considering the interests of the person with whom he is transacting business may be precisely the fact that his motive in doing business at all is absolutely and entirely unselfish. The reason why, in this instance, there is no room for "you" in my consideration is just because "I" am myself already excluded from my own consideration. If I counted myself I should find room for you just so far as "I" take an interest in "you," but if I do not admit myself I cannot bring in your interests as part of my own programme. The "others" for whom I act are others than you, more completely and irrevocably other than I myself should be; for though I might myself adopt as mine some of your purposes, I cannot affiliate those purposes of yours upon these "others" for whom I am acting. The transaction then becomes more rigidly "economic," just because my motive in entering upon it is altruistic.

Bursars, again (in the wide sense of representative members of a group of persons with common interests), though they have only a diffused and secondary interest in the business which they manage, have the reputation of a similar rigidity in their business dealings. And the administrators of a charitable fund, when they are distributing their charities or administering their estates, may be inclined to give easier or to exact harder terms than they would do under other conditions according to their individual conception of the nature of their trust. When they debate a special point it will generally be found that the question in their minds is whether the person with whom they are conducting business can or cannot be properly regarded as to any extent a proper subject for the exercise of the very charity which they are administering. Some of them may take the general view that charity is charity, and on the first-come-first-served principle, and actuated by the habit of mind which finds it easier to realise the specific case under consideration than the general body of claims removed by one degree from the centre of the field of vision at the moment, they may urge that it ill becomes a charitable body to drive so hard a bargain as is proposed. Whereas others, with a strict conception of the scope of the charity, and a keen sense of the imperfect manner in which the funds at command enable them to fulfil its objects, will regard themselves as differing but little from fraudulent trustees if they allow any good-natured desire to deal easily with a man to affect their bargain with him. If the question of egoism or selfishness enters here at all it probably pleads on the side of a non-economic arrangement; but in the main the doubt is not as to whether "self" or "others," but as to which "others," are to be considered.

The same principles apply to the analysis of the transactions of the housewife with which we started. When she is in the market she is actively and consciously thinking of exactly the same people and exactly the same wants which she is thinking of when she applies and distributes her purchases at home. But when she is sitting at the table she is in the presence of, and is dealing with, no other persons than those whose wants she is considering. When she is in the kitchen or the storeroom giving orders to her servants, she is in the presence of persons whose individual wants are more or less an object of direct interest to her according to circumstances and according to her disposition, and whose tastes and susceptibilities she will be wise to consider for her own sake if not for theirs. Whereas when she is in the market she is dealing with people in whose welfare she has not necessarily any direct concern, and part of whose business it is to consult her tastes and susceptibilities with sedulous care. The economic nature of the transaction therefore emphasises, though it does not impose, the limitations of her altruism. The difference between an administrative act which is also a business transaction and an administrative act which is not, is not that she is thinking of a different set of persons or is actuated by a different set of motives in one case and in the other, but that in one case she is dealing with one set of persons and considering the wants of another set, in the other she is considering the wants of the very people with whom she is at the moment dealing. She is herself one of the people for whom she is providing, yet she is probably, in the main, "unselfish" enough in her dealings in the market-place— that is to say, she is thinking chiefly of "others than herself" —but she is not thinking equally of every one that is not herself. The mere fact that a person is other than herself does not at once awake her keen interest in him, and it may well happen that the persons with whom she is dealing at the moment are amongst those of whom she is thinking little or not at all.

Both in the market-place and the home, then, her main object of consideration is a group of persons of whom she is one, and in which the stall-keepers in the market-place are not included. She is just as selfish and just as unselfish in one case as in the other. But though the members of her household are included in the group of people of whom she is thinking in the market-place, it does not follow that no one else is. You can draw no such line. We have seen that her purchases in the market may be restricted not only by the pressure of other domestic claims, but by the determination to make certain contributions to charitable or religious institutions, or by any other object whatever in which she is interested, however wide or however narrow its application, however near or however remote it may be from the centre of the domestic circle. It is by the nature of the general motives which inspire her life, the general adjustment of her resources, the general principles on which she administers one part of her husband's income, and the general trend of her influence upon the expenditure of the rest and upon his methods of earning the whole, by the pressure of her character and energy in guiding and stimulating not only his impulses, but those of his and her acquaintances, and any portion of the public to which she has direct or indirect access, by speech, by example, or by written word; above all, it is by her way of looking at things and feeling them, by her mental attitude towards life and her general sense of values, that the degree of her selfishness or unselfishness, her egoism or altruism, is to be determined; and she is actuated by selfish or unselfish, by public-spirited or private-spirited motives, by a broad or a narrow selfishness, by a stupid appetite for martyrdom or a large sense of the significance of life for herself and others, according to her character, not according to the particular act that she is performing. The reason why she does not spend more in the market-place may be because she considers others besides her family; the reason why she eats some of the new potatoes herself may be because she considers herself; the reason why she does not eat more may be because she considers others as well as herself; but probably she is not thinking at all, but feels the collective or conjunct self from which neither she nor any other individual member could be withdrawn without impoverishment to the whole collective life, and into which so much as the idea of self-sacrifice could not be introduced without destroying its vital processes. Self-sacrifice would be no less fatal than self-assertion, and altruism and egoism are alike lost in the communal sense of which she is the organ. If she has occasionally to rebuke the egoism and appeal to the altruism of the little barbarians around her, it is because their communal sense is undeveloped; and she is well aware of the danger of turning them from barbarians into prigs if she develops altruism when it is the communal sense that needs development. Her normal function is by her own unconscious communal sense unconsciously to develop theirs.

But the boundaries of this communal sense are neither stable nor rigidly fixed. Individuals or groups within the family separate themselves (more or less completely, and in few or many relations of life) from the parent stem, and arrangements with them partake of the nature of business.

The pressure of the communal sense rises and falls incessantly in the infinite variety of the relations of any community, and the formal limits of the family neither impose a barrier over which the altruistic impulses cannot pass outward, nor form a preserve into which egoistic motives can make no incursions; and wherever altruism and egoism can be rightly spoken of —that is to say, wherever there is a conscious distinction between what I do for my own sake and what I do for the sake of others—it is clear that the note of a business transaction between A and B is not that A's *ego* alone is consciously in his mind, but that, however many the *alteri* are, B is not one of them; and B, in like manner, whether he is thinking only of his own *ego* or of innumerable *alteri*, is not thinking of A.

The proposal to exclude "benevolent" or "altruistic" motives from consideration in the study of Economics is therefore wholly irrelevant and beside the mark. A man's purposes may, of course, be selfish, but however unselfish they are he requires the co-operation of others who are not interested, or who are inadequately interested in them, in order to accomplish them. We enter into business relations with others, not because our purposes are selfish, but because those with whom we deal are relatively indifferent to them, but are (like us) keenly interested in purposes of their own, to which we in our turn are relatively indifferent. "Business," then, is primarily a vast network of organisations by which any person or combination of persons can direct their resources and their powers to the accomplishment of their purposes, without the necessity of a direct relation, hard and often impossible to secure, between the objects sought and the faculties and materials directly at command.

There is surely nothing degrading or revolting to our higher sense in this fact of our mutually furthering each other's purposes because we are interested in our own. There is no taint or presumption of selfishness in the matter at all. The economic nexus indefinitely expands our freedom of combination and movement; for it enables us to form one set of groups linked by cohesion of faculties and resources, and another set of groups linked by community of purpose, without having to find the "double coincidence" which would otherwise be necessary. This economy and liberty will be equally valued by altruistic and by egoistic groups or individuals, and it would be just as true, and just as false, to say that the business motive ignores egoistic as to say that it ignores altruistic impulses. The specific characteristic of an economic relation is not its "egoism," but its "non-tuism."

It may be urged, however, that since, as a rule, "ego" and "tu" fill the whole canvas, not only to the spectator, but to the actors also; that is to say, since a man, when he is doing business, is generally only thinking of his own bargain, and how to deal with his correspondent, and not of any one else at all, the exclusion of "tu" is tantamount to the solitary survival of "ego." So that, after all, "altruism" has no place in business, and "non-tuism" is equivalent to "egoism." And, indeed, it may be true enough that, as a rule, the average man of business is not likely to be thinking of any "others" at all in the act of bargaining, but even so the term "egoism" is misapplied, for neither is he thinking of himself! He is thinking of the matter in hand, the bargain or the transaction, much as a man thinks of the next move in a game of chess or of how to unravel the construction of a sentence in the Greek text he is reading. He wants to make a good bargain or do a good piece of business, and he is directly thinking of nothing else. All manner of considerations of loyalty, of humanity, of reputation, and so forth, are no doubt present to his mind in solution, so to speak, as restraining influences; and they may easily be precipitated and emerge into consciousness at any moment of vacillation or reflection; but in making his bargain the business man is not usually thinking of these things, and when he thinks of them they act chiefly as restraints. Neither is he thinking of the ultimate purposes to which he will apply the resources that he gains. He is not thinking either of missions to the heathen or of famine funds, or of his pew rent, or of his political association. But neither is he thinking of his wife and family, nor yet of himself and the champagne suppers he may enjoy with his bachelor friends, nor of a season ticket for concerts, nor of opportunities for increasing his knowledge of Chinese or mathematics, nor of free expenditure during his next holiday on the Continent, nor of a week at Monte Carlo, nor of anything else whatever except his bargain. He is exactly in the position of a man who is playing a game of chess or cricket. He is considering nothing except his game. It would be absurd to call a man selfish for protecting his king in a game of chess, or to say that he was actuated by purely egoistic motives in so doing. It would be equally absurd to call a cricketer selfish for protecting his wicket, or to say that in making runs he was actuated by egoistic motives qualified by a secondary concern for his eleven. The fact is that he has no conscious motive whatever, and is wholly intent on the complex feat of taking the ball. If you want to know whether he is selfish or unselfish you must consider the whole organisation of his life, the place which chess-playing or cricket takes in it, and the alternatives which they open or close. At the moment the categories of egoism and altruism are irrelevant.

And yet this analogy of the game will further explain the obstinacy with which the phrase and the idea reassert themselves, that, in matters of business, a man is solely actuated by the desire for "his own advantage." It is just because we look upon two men engaged in driving a hard bargain (a very small part of the life of a man of business by the way) much as we look upon two men who are playing a game. Each is intent upon victory, that is, upon raising his score against the other's, and in this sense the man who has driven a close or a hard bargain is certainly intent on securing an advantage, and we call it "his" advantage, because he is struggling to gain it, though it may in the final instance be the advantage of a client or a ward in which he has either an indirect share only or no share at all. Once more, then, if *ego* and *tu* are engaged in any transaction, whether egoism or altruism furnishes my inspiring motive, or whether my thoughts at the moment are wholly impersonal, the economic nature of the action on my side remains undisturbed. It is only when tuism to some degree actuates my conduct that it ceases to be wholly economic. It is idle, therefore, to consider "egoism" as a characteristic mark of the economic life.

Nor is it easy to make much of the apparently more reasonable saying that the economic relation (or the economic motive) is unmoral or morally indifferent. In a certain sense, of course, this is true; and we shall have to bring out the full extent of its truth under paragraph (*b*). Any relation into which I enter for the fulfilment of my purposes may, in a sense, be called unmoral, inasmuch as it is a means and not an end. But if by unmoral we mean unaffected by moral considerations, or not subject to moral restraints, then the economic relation is no more unmoral than the relations of friendship, the relations of sex, the relations of paternity, or the family relations generally. There is no actual or conceivable community in which the economic relations are not habitually subject to the control of moral principles. There are, of course, immoral men who neglect some, or all, of the moral restraints and principles usually acknowledged; that is to say, it is possible to behave immorally in any relation of life, including the economic relations; but both law, and personal honour, and acknowledged ethical principles place restraints, more or less effective, on our conduct in the economic relation, and dictate the conditions under which we may enter it.

Is the economic relation unmoral?

It may be urged in the abstract that, since every man should be the potential object of our direct interest and benevolence, a relation which is expressly defined by the absence of any such direct interest must be in its nature unmoral, or even immoral. But this position can hardly be maintained. The limitation of our powers would prevent our taking an equally active interest in every one's affairs, even if they were all equally worthy, and it may well be that the person with whom we have entered into economic relations is one of the last whom we are bound to consider. When we are inclined to assert the unmoral, or the immoral, nature of the economic relation, we are often thinking of cases in which, for example, a man makes a fortune while he is giving starvation wages to his employees. We think it brutal callousness on his part to be in such close relations with persons whose human claims are so entirely ignored, without being stirred to active sympathy with them. That a man should be in constant relations with such pitiable people, and yet not pity them, we may rightly think shews that his heart is hardened. But we forget that the relation is quite as completely economic on the side of the employees as it is on the side of the employer. They, too, are getting their living out of a man without any direct consideration of his interests, or desire to further his purposes. And we do not blame them. We probably think that he is one of the last persons in the world that they are bound to consider. It is not because the relation is economic that we condemn the man, but because his conduct in that relation strikes us as callous. The very ground, therefore, on which we condemn the employer, but not the employee, is that the economic motive, like the animal appetites, for example, in itself neither makes us moral nor excuses us for not being so. In other words, the economic relation is unmoral only in the same sense in which family affection is unmoral. Family affection may, and often does, urge men to every kind of injustice, selfishness, and even fraud and cruelty, because it does not in itself secure the observance of those moral restraints to which it ought to be subject. To say that the economic relations, or even the economic forces, are unmoral, is in one sense perfectly true, and in another sense entirely false, and in the sense in which it is true it is in no special way characteristic.

(b) We have now seen that the taint of inherent sordidness which attaches itself in many minds to the economic relation, or even to the study of it, is derived from a faulty conception of its nature. But, on the other hand, the easy optimism that expects the economic forces, if only we give them free play, spontaneously to secure the best possible conditions of life, is equally fallacious, and even more pernicious. It is, indeed, easy to present the working of the economic forces as wholly beneficent. Have we not seen that they automatically organise a vast system of co-operation, by which men who have never seen or heard of each other, and who scarcely realise each other's existence or desires even in imagination, nevertheless support each other at every turn, and enlarge the realisation each of the other's purposes? Do they not embrace all the world in one huge mutual benefit society? That London is fed day by day, although no one sees to it, is itself a fact so stupendous as to excuse, if it does not justify, the most exultant pæans that were ever sung in honour of the *laissez-faire laissez-passer* theory of social organisation. What a testimony to the efficiency of the economic nexus is borne

The economic relation has no inherently moralising power.

by the very fact that we regard it as abnormal that any man should perish for want of any one of a thousand things, no one of which he can either make or do for himself. When we see the world, in virtue of its millions of mutual adjustments, carrying itself on from day to day, and ask, "Who sees to it all?" and receive no answer, we can well understand the religious awe and enthusiasm with which an earlier generation of economists contemplated those "economic harmonies," in virtue of which each individual, in serving himself, of necessity serves his neighbour, and by simply obeying the pressures about him, and following the path that opens before him, weaves himself into the pattern of "purposes he cannot measure."

But we must look at the picture more closely. The very process of intelligently seeking my own ends makes me further those of others? Quite so. But what are my purposes, immediate and ultimate? And what are the purposes of others which I serve, as a means of accomplishing my own? And what views have I and they as to the suitable means of accomplishing those ends? These are the questions on which the health and vigour of a community depend, and the economic forces, as such, take no count of them. Division of labour and exchange, on which the economic organisation of society is based, enlarge our means of accomplishing our ends, but they have no direct influence upon the ends themselves, and have no tendency to beget scrupulousness in the use of the means. It is idle to assume that ethically desirable results will necessarily be produced by an ethically indifferent instrument, and it is as foolish to make the economic relation an idol as it is to make it a bogey.

The world has many things that I want for myself and others, and that I can only get by some kind of exchange.

<small>Fraudulent co-operation, and co-operation in evil.</small> What, then, have I, or what can I do or make, that the world wants? Or what can I make it want, or persuade it that it wants, or make it believe that I can give it better than others can? The things I want, if measured by an ideal standard, may be good or bad for me to have or for others to give; and so with the things I give them, the desires I stimulate in them, and the means I employ to gratify them. When we draw the seductive picture of "economic harmony"

in which every one is "helping" some one else and making himself "useful" to him, we insensibly allow the idea of "help" to smuggle in with it ethical or sentimental associations that are strictly contraband. We forget that the "help" may be impartially extended to destructive and pernicious or to constructive and beneficent ends, and moreover that it may employ all sorts of means. We have only to think of the huge industries of war, of the floating of bubble companies, of the efforts of one business or firm to choke others in the birth, of the poppy culture in China and India, of the gin-palaces and distilleries at home, in order to realise how often the immediate purpose of one man or of one community is to thwart or hold in check the purpose of another, or to delude men, or to corrupt their tastes and to minister to them when corrupted.

Again, amongst the means that I control may be the vital powers of others, over which I have acquired legal or illegal power. The instances, to take a few at random, of child labour bargained for by parents and manufacturers early in the last century, the history of the slave trade and of slavery, the system known as the "white slave" traffic, with which the advanced civilisations are at last attempting to grapple, but which still recruits that industry in which the wages of shame and oppression are paid and received night by night in every great city of Europe, the exploitation of the rubber industry in the Congo State, and the like, break in with a lurid light upon the idyllic scenes of our imagination. These are amongst the ways by which and the things to which we "help" each other under the potent pressure of the economic relation. The catholicity of the economic relation extends far enough in either direction to embrace both heaven and hell, and to suggest to each that its own ends may be best served by an *ad interim* devotion to those of the other. It is strange that so many economic writers, while attempting formally to base their science on an exclusion of ethical motives, have at the same time systematically enlisted the ethical sympathies by illegitimately exploiting the associations of such phrases as "useful work," "mutual advantage," and "the common good." It is no doubt as easy to exaggerate as it is to ignore such deplorable facts as those we have just touched upon, but the point on which we must insist is that if the constructive movements in society dominate the destructive ones, or if there is any progress towards a more worthy or more desirable life in civilised communities, it must be because individual and collective ends are prevailingly harmonious and worthy; for the economic organisation of society in itself does not in any way discriminate between worthy and unworthy ends, and lends its machinery to all who have any purposes of their own and any power of furthering the purposes of others.

But even assuming that human purposes in the aggregate are wholesome and worthy to be furthered, the economic organisation of society, regarded merely as a means to an end, has certain great disadvantages that must be taken as a set-off, as far as they go, against its advantages. This brings us to the very heart of the problem of civilisation. We have seen that it is the essence of the economic organisation of effort that it tends to sever the direct connection between means and end; and since it is the end which interests us, this tends to sever our daily actions from direct connection with that to which they owe their interest. The man who pursues his immediate objects indirectly may effect great economies of effort and secure a wider command of the things he consciously wants, but he may also lose in breadth and variety of faculty. He may touch the realities of life at fewer points, and may have a less vivid sense of the significance of things and less joy in intercourse with them, than if he had pursued his objects more directly. It does not follow that the way that leads most quickly to the goal, or that leads to the most desired goal, is the pleasantest or most profitable road to travel. There is all the difference between the method and spirit of travellers who are constantly impatient to "get to their destination" and of those who taste every incident and prospect on the way, with the undersense of the goal animating and colouring the whole. The latter are, so to speak, "always there," the former are for ever hastening to "get there." This will be felt by any one who has cultivated the varied crafts involved, for example, in making a homestead on a bare heath or an almost naked bit of rock, working with his own hands and

Marginal note: Disadvantages of indirect pursuit of our ends.

contriving his own resourceful economies of material. Again, a keen satisfaction is experienced by any set of persons banded together for a common object, in bringing their faculties directly to bear upon their purpose. The artisans in a northern manufacturing district who, in vivid realisation of the significance of spiritual treasures which they hold in common, seek to give their idea a local name and habitation, and so to assert its hold upon others, will love their meeting-house if they have built it out of their savings, but they will love it yet more dearly and will take a still keener joy in raising it if the stone and timber work has been done with their own hands. A religious community in America, approximately self-supplying and self-sufficing, may lose much that we value, but it assuredly gains something by the deepened communal sense that results from the direct bearing of every effort on objects dear to every heart; and in every philanthropic or missionary enterprise those who give time and work are always felt to be nearer the centre of the movement than those who give what is well described as the "support" of money contributions. When a man directly works at his own mechanical craft for a cause which he loves, or gives professional services without charge, he is always felt to be more closely associated with the work than if he only "subscribes" to it, more closely even than if he extracts subscriptions from others by means of a benefit performance in his own particular line.

The contemplation of a whole society based on minute division of labour gives a wider scope to these and similar reflections. It may be true that too much has been said of the evils incidental to the division of labour in narrowing the direct capacities and interests of mechanical and intellectual specialists, and there has doubtless been exaggeration, and in some cases perversity, in the regrets that such considerations have provoked. Compensations even in the work itself, as well as in the enlarged opportunities of enjoyment, culture, and expansion outside it, have been neglected. But if we have little sympathy with those who declare the savage state superior to the civilised, yet any one who has watched the transition of a civilised but primitive community, in which division of labour has not been carried to a high point of elaboration, into a more advanced industrial type, must have had deep searchings of heart as to whether the gain in command of material comfort and external refinement is an adequate compensation for the loss of direct contact between a man and his environment. And in our own country we cannot trace without regret the gradual disappearance of the "notable" housewife, who could *do* and *make* such a vast number of things so excellently well. Even if we admit the plea that she can now *get* a much greater variety of things, many of them perhaps still better than those she used to make, we are but imperfectly consoled.

And if those who make are not those who use, the Nemesis that waits on bad making is less swift and certain in her stroke. The reward of good work may be snatched by False-Semblant. The art of making promises convincing threatens to supplant that of making performances sound. By the side of the fruitful art of bringing our powers and possessions to the notice of those whom they may serve rises the barren art of so working upon their imagination as to persuade them that they need what we and none but we can give them. Side by side with a wholesome and fertilising emulation in doing, rises a wasteful and desolating competition in professing to do. And at last only an expert can distinguish between the harbour light supported by a small toll on the cargoes it guides to safety, and the light displayed by the wrecker who hopes to pick stray salvage from the wealth he has taught the sea to swallow. And yet the real trouble lies even deeper than this, for some of the chief evils which we bewail in industrial society seem to rise independently of shams and frauds, and to be connected with the very fact of the narrowing of each man's power to provide for himself, and his dependence for almost all that he needs on others, which is the very nature of elaborate economic organisation. Since he gets others to do everything for him, only in consideration of his doing some one thing for others, it follows that if a change of fashion in the demands of others affects his significance to them, his one power of furthering their purposes may fail him, and leave him utterly destitute of any power to serve himself. How deeply this tells on the complication of economic problems, and even on the confusions of economic thought, will be seen with startling clearness when we come to deal with the market of services.[1]

Yet, again, our study of the collective scale has impressed upon our minds the fact that its objective unity covers an infinite variety of subjective and vital diversity of significance. But if I am interested in furthering a man's purpose, not for its own sake but as a means of furthering my own, the question to me is not how much the thing I am to do matters to the man for whom I am to do it, but how much the thing that he will do in return matters to me, or those for whom I desire it. The economic forces, then, have no tendency whatever to direct my efforts to the most vitally important ends or the supply of the most urgent individual needs. A shilling represents to me the same power of drawing on the circle of exchange, that is the same power of securing co-operation towards the accomplishment of my purposes, whether it comes from the purse of a millionaire or of a pauper; and therefore the economic forces will press me with equal power into the service of either if each offers me a shilling. When Cobbett brought his halfpenny to the stationer or the herring man he brought it to persons who had no particular concern either with his appetite or his education, and who dealt with many other people to whom a herring or a sheet of paper more or less would represent perhaps no appreciable enrichment or impoverishment of life. To the two customers A and B the vital significance of these things may differ by the whole distance between a scarce considered trifle and a matter for tears or for stern and desperate resolve. But the inducements that they offer to the stationer or the herring man to make him further their purposes are identical. Each of them offers a halfpenny, representing a certain definite power to further the purposes of the tradesman, whatever they may be. Thus Cobbett's want and the want of Sir Gorgius Midas, expressed in each case by the proffer of a halfpenny, exert exactly equal pressures upon the tradesman, as such. One is just as important as the other to him. But from any social or human point of view no limit can be assigned to the superior vital significance of the service rendered to Cobbett. It is

The market equates the wants of men objectively, not vitally.

[1] See pages 352 *sqq.*

true that to each man the herring is worth just a halfpenny. But what is a halfpenny worth to each of them? One of them cannot feel the significance of it at all, and if he gives any heed to it, does so only on general principles, because he knows that it is a representative of many halfpennies which, if not looked after, will establish leaks through which thousands of pounds will ultimately escape. To the other, for its own direct significance the halfpenny is worth prayers and tears. It stands to him for "exultations, agonies." It is the expression of a deep passion for knowledge, fighting with the profoundest impulses of his animal nature, and his turning it to the paper and ink rather than the herring is a testimony to the might of "man's unconquerable mind."

It is incredible how easily all this is forgotten, nay, how superlatively difficult it is to bear it in mind. We shall see presently how the economic organisation of industry draws all free resources and unpledged efforts towards those channels which promise the best remuneration ——that is to say, which will put us into the largest measure of undefined command of things in the circle of exchange; and seeing that remuneration is obtained by supplying some one else's wants, the wants we can get the highest remuneration for supplying are, by a gross (though natural and apparently inevitable) confusion, conceived and spoken of as the most urgent wants. What a chasm is thus concealed we can now perceive. It is, of course, true that if we are dealing with one and the same man, the thing for a marginal increment of which he will pay or sacrifice most is that which he wants most at the margin, but it is a desperate leap indeed to pass from this self-evident truth to the self-evident falsehood that if A will give more for a marginal increment of one commodity than B will give for a marginal increment of another, A is more " urgently in want " of one than B is of the other. Does the extra ruby which the agent of a millionaire thinks on the whole will improve the design of a binding for a manuscript, and for which he therefore gives £50, perform as urgent and socially important a service as 24,000 red herrings or 24,000 hap'orths of stationery applied to the wants of 24,000 Cobbetts, could you find them? One father will spend £10,000 to save the life of his child. Does it

Optimistic fallacies based on ignoring this difference.

follow that his love is ten thousand times as great as that of another father who watches his son dying when he knows that £1 spent on better food and a little change of air might save him?

The leap that would be involved in answering these questions in the affirmative is constantly made in economic arguments. The transition is so easy and so natural from the statement, "efforts will be directed to the point at which they will be best remunerated," to the statement, "efforts will go to the point at which there is the most urgent demand for them," and from this to "they will go where they are most wanted"! A whole school of cheerful optimism has been based upon the creed that if every man pursues his own interests in an enlightened manner we shall get the best of possible results, because it will be to his interest to apply his energies where they are "most useful to others." Yes, but what others? The answer is, "those who already have most of everything else that they want." This automatic action of the economic forces is at the service of every man exactly in inverse proportion to the urgency of his wants. The very fact that he is in want of everything prevents his giving much for anything, and makes his command of the economic forces light. The very fact that he has abundance of all things enables him to give largely of valued things for the gratification of the slightest impulse, for he is only checking impulses equally slight. The weight that his passing whim can throw into the economic scale is heavier than that which his neighbour can pit against it to save his life. The gospel of economic optimism, in a word, is the gospel, "to him that hath shall be given." And yet we still hear such phrases as, "if people won't pay for a thing it shews they don't want it," or "under conditions of free exchange, effort is directed to the point at which it is most useful to society." The appalling depths hidden under this litter of loose thought and language are now revealed to us. The enlightened student of political economy and of society will take care to assume nothing as to the economic forces except the constant pressure which they bring to bear upon men's action and their absolute moral and social indifference. He will see that it is our business in every instance to endeavour to yoke these forces, where we can, to social work, and to restrain them, where we can, from social devastation; never to ignore them, never to trust them without examination; and no more to take it as axiomatic that they will work for social good, if left alone, than we should take it for granted that lightning will invariably strike things that are " better felled."

The contention that whereas the economic forces are in themselves' strictly unmoral they are nevertheless necessarily beneficent in their effect, collapses when we examine it. But nevertheless it contains a certain residuum of truth, which we shall do well to consider.

A pearl of truth in the dunghill of error.

Given the whole existing conditions, there is undoubtedly a presumption that any man who voluntarily enters into any economic relation sees his advantage in doing so, and is better off than he would be if he were debarred from it, all other things remaining equal. Thus the most miserable toiler at starvation wages is presumably better off than if he were unable to obtain any employment or wages at all. And this consideration should check such too facile statements as that the moral responsibility for the condition of the most wretched workers lies with the man who employs them. If he merely ceased to employ them because the present relation was too painful to his moral and social feelings, their latter state presumably would be worse than their former; and we should see that the economic relations into which he had entered with them were beneficent in their effect so far as they went, the only trouble being that they did not go far enough. There is a truth, then, in the contention that, given the position of these pitiable persons, the possibility of economic relations spontaneously alleviates it; but when we ask the further question, how come they to be in the position in which such a relation can be acceptable to them, we see how far the economic forces are from being able spontaneously to solve the social problem.

(c) The attempt accurately to determine the nature and action of economic forces must already have impressed upon the reader's mind the fact that it is by no means necessary, or even normal, for the economic relation to exist in isolation. Other relations combine with it and intrude upon what is usually regarded

The economic relation seldom remains isolated.

as its special domain; and it makes incursions into regions of activity where we should not at first expect it. It is quite true, for example, that our housewife's main reason for entering the market-place at all, and for dealing with this man rather than with the other when she is there, is probably not to be found in any consideration of how her action will affect the stall-keepers with whom she is dealing; yet such considerations may surely be present, and may, within certain limits, be effective. In various degrees she likes or dislikes, pities, envies, or disapproves the person with whom she deals or does not deal. Because a man goes to the same place of worship that she does, or because she has been taken by the curly head or the dimpled smile of one of his children, or because his wife has just been confined, or because she knows he has recently had bad luck, or because he is good to his old mother, or because in his unofficial capacity he has shewn her some courtesy, or because she believes him to have voted straight at the last election, she takes an interest in him, and is actuated to a certain limited extent by her good-will to him, and enters upon transactions with him that she would not otherwise have found quite advantageous enough to tempt her. If she can get nearly what she wants from him, and for the same price could get exactly what she wants from a man whose religion is anathema to her, whose manners offend her, and the thought of whose ostentatious prosperity is unpleasant to her, she may deal with the man she is interested in and with whom she is in sympathy, both in order to give herself the pleasure of dealing with one she likes, and to spare herself the discomfort of dealing with one she dislikes, and also from a genuine desire to further the interests of the one man and a (perhaps unacknowledged) dislike of the thought of contributing to the other man's offensive success. When at home, on the other hand, she is by no means always considering the relative importance of the wants she satisfies on their own merits. There may well be some inmate of the house whose wants she really regards as quite trivial, but to whom she scrupulously attends because he will make himself so disagreeable if they are neglected, or because he will do something she wants him to do, or leave undone something to which she objects, if he is put into a good humour. In

o

providing for his wants she regards his feelings merely as a step towards the attaining of other ends, positive or negative, and not at all as having any significance in themselves. Her relations with him, therefore, are of the same order as if they were economic. And again, in most families there are various persons who are to some extent directly included in the communal sense of fellowship and immediate interest and benevolence, and are also to some extent regarded as a means to the end of keeping the household in working order on a certain scale and in a certain style. Such may be old domestics not quite worth their wage, or grown-up children who contribute to the household expenses, or paying guests who are also friends or relatives. In short, the more we reflect upon all these matters, the more shall we convince ourselves that the motives actuating us in our dealings with our fellows are frequently, if not generally, far from being unmixed, and that economic and non-economic relations are perpetually intertwined.

And even if we originally enter into some relation on purely economic grounds, human and non-economic relations may easily graft themselves upon it; for although the carpenter or the doctor makes a standing offer to further, in certain ways, the life purposes of indifferent and unknown persons as a means of furthering his own, yet, when he has once entered, with any one, into the relation that this service involves, he necessarily finds himself studying his wishes, and endeavouring to accomplish his purposes, and so he gradually acquires an independent interest in his well-being; and though the relation remains at its foundation economic, non-economic materials will be more or less largely built into the superstructure.

We may note that this natural tendency on the part of economic relations to ally themselves directly with humanities acts most easily in one direction. The man who gives commodities or services in return for money is called into immediate co-operation with certain specified purposes of the man who pays him, but on the other hand the man who gives money in return gives only the generalised and undifferentiated command of things and services to the man he pays, and therefore he is not made the partner of his life in any definite and specific way. The man who gives money has already made his choice of the particular way in which his purposes are to be furthered, and he calls the other into direct fellowship with himself in its execution; but the particular purposes which the other will advance by means of the money he receives are still unspecified; for the man who receives money does not declare the services or commodities he desires until he comes to deal with others to whom in his turn he pays money, and whom he calls into the direct and conscious furthering of specific purposes of his own, putting them in their turn into a position to acquire unspecified co-operation from persons unnamed. It is true, of course, that there is a human relation on both sides; but its humanities develop more naturally and more directly on the side of the man who is paid than on the side of the man who pays. This has nothing to do with the relative wealth or poverty of the two. The tailor may naturally take a direct interest in the appearance of his customer, primarily for his own credit, it may be, but secondarily because he is called upon to participate in and to further a specific purpose of his customer; but the customer is called upon to render no direct and specified service to the tailor, and at most has merely a generally benevolent or human interest in him as an individual with whom he has dealings. In the same way, the doctor, the lawyer, and, most of all, the minister of religion, is called upon to enter directly and specifically into certain branches of the lives of the people who pay him. He can see exactly where his action touches them, and can identify his individual contribution towards their well-being. This must almost inevitably superinduce upon the business aspect of the connection a disinterested concern in the welfare of those he serves. But those who pay him his fees, or contribute to his salary, while enabling him, within stated limits, to do and to get anything that he desires, are not called upon to exercise judgment, fidelity, and tact in directly forwarding specified purposes of his life. They are not participating with him in specific enterprises and achievements. They cannot identify the particular point at which they are personally and individually helping him, and so they

The humanities of our economic relation follow acts of specific more easily than of generalised furtherance of another's purpose.

feel that on his side the relation is more human than on theirs. This explains the touching circumstance that in such cases a sense of gratitude and obligation often remains when ample money payment has been made. The feeling still remains that personal and specific things have been received and nothing personal or specific has been returned; a feeling that sometimes seeks relief in presentations of things that can be specifically identified as personal and direct contributions on the part of the givers to the well-being of the receiver, or the furthering of some known and recognised purpose of his.

There are, of course, other conditions which may help to determine the free or impeded growth of personal and human relations on a basis of business. In the case of the employer and the hands in a workshop it may well be that the employer has a larger sense of social responsibility and a more direct realisation of the vital significance of what he gives to his men than they can have of what they give to him, though the one is money and the other specified service. This, however, is largely a matter of personality. The relation itself is still a direct challenge to the man employed to do faithfully a specific thing for the man employing him, whereas all that the employer does is to put the man he employs in a position to secure the unspecified co-operation not of himself, but of others, in the fulfilment of his purposes.

Thus, where there is high moral character on both sides, the employed person, whether a doctor or a factory hand, is called upon for specific services which may breed devotion to his work and to those for whom he does it; whereas the person who employs can hardly pay fees or wages devotedly, however much esteem, gratitude, or affection he may feel. What the earner of money gives, even if it remains fundamentally a means of accomplishing his own purposes, is naturally affected by a sympathetic interest in the purposes of others. What he gets is much more completely dependent on his purely economic significance, that is to say, on the significance which others attach to his services for purposes of their own. He may give with a sense of personal interest in what he is doing for another; he will get only what he is worth. And he wishes this to be so. An employer is pleased if his workmen take a disinterested pride in their work and in the credit of the firm. We are all pleased if our fishmonger or our shoemaker seems to consider our personal tastes, not only because he wishes to retain our custom, but also because he is glad to serve us. But the man who is paid does not wish to receive money from others because they are interested in his well-being or consider his life a beautiful one. He wishes to receive it because he is worth it to them—that is to say, because they are interested in purposes of their own, and need him to forward them.

Even where business transactions are of a more impersonal character, as in the wholesale markets or on the stock exchange, and where there is no permanent personal connection as there is between the employer and the employed, the picture of the business man engaged in pushing his own advantage to the utmost, without the least concern for others, and eagerly seeking to get as much and to give as little as possible, is to a great extent a fancy portrait. Opinions differ as to whether the average successful man of business is scrupulous or unscrupulous, but most men agree that he is not merely grasping. He has a certain large-hearted sense of common interest alike with his clients and his rivals, and does not desire always to push every advantage absolutely as far as it will go.

Nor must we lose sight of the fact, only too obvious and undeniable, that these human relations are not all of one kind. They may constitute a negative as well as a positive consideration. The economic relation between employer and employed is too often not supported and softened by the human relations that grow out of it, but strained and embittered by them. And if it is possible that the work I undertake for others, for the sake of furthering my own purposes, may enlist my direct interest and sympathy, it may also be that pressure of circumstances forces me into a position in which, in order to fulfil my own purposes, I lend myself to purposes of others which I regard with grave moral disapproval, as involving some kind of fraud or false pretence, or with deep social compunction, as involving misery or degradation to others; or which, at least, appear to me frivolous and unworthy, calculated rather to enervate the character and dissipate the energies than to build up sound

Attractions and repulsions.

humanity. Hence every man who lives in such a society as ours may be liable to a dismal sense of incongruity between the things for which he cares and which he seeks to realise for himself, and the things that he is doing for others and actually enabling them to realise; between the life he contemplates as an end and the life he actually furthers as a means. No man can regard himself as having solved his personal problem of life in an even approximately satisfactory manner until he has brought his business and his private life at least into such a degree of harmony that there shall be no permanent strain and conflict between the general significance and tone of the kind of life he desires to live, or at least the (much wider and more varied) kind of life which he can cheerfully contemplate other men as living, and the kind of life he is helping other men actually to live. It is obvious, therefore, that in choosing his business or profession a man is not necessarily or even probably moved by merely economic forces. He may think of his profession not only as a means of earning money but also as an occupation, not only as a means of living but as part of life; and he may be content with the prospect of a smaller income if his occupation will either be acceptable to him in itself, or will bring him incidental opportunities of directly gratifying his tastes and realising his general purposes in life.

It is impossible to exhaust the combinations of the several considerations that habitually affect our conduct, but the following rough analysis may be found useful. If we are engaged on any piece of work, there is the pain or pleasure of doing it as a mere occupation; there is further the sense of the importance or significance of the thing itself when done (which naturally reacts on the pleasure or pain of doing it); and there is the command of commodities and services of which it puts us in possession. Thus a man may be engaged in designing or executing elaborate implements of war, say torpedoes, and he may take keen delight in the problems which face him, in the experiments and tests which he applies, and in the gradual overcoming of difficulties and perfecting of processes. At the same time he may believe in the reduction of armaments, and may regard the policy which

The doing, the thing done, and the command of other things it secures.

his art subserves as a cruel infatuation. Or he may be a sincere believer in the policy of great armaments, but may be executing an order for a foreign government, because he could not persuade his own of the value of his apparatus. In either of these cases his desire that the thing he is doing should be done is a negative quantity, whereas his pleasure in doing it is positive. On the other hand, his task may be an arduous one, which does not suit his taste, and which demands excessive and exhausting effort from him, or it may be so monotonous and unintelligent as to make the greater part of his life mere drudgery; and yet he may think it exceedingly important that the work should be done. The case of a clerk in the office of some philanthropic institution with which he is in hearty sympathy may serve as an illustration. Or perhaps his work is a pleasure to him, and at the same time he thinks it important that it should be done, whether by himself or by another. A lecturer who loves his subject and enjoys the intellectual effort of expounding it and the sense of rapport between himself and his hearers, and who at the same time believes that the study he is spreading is essentially life-giving and life-raising, so that he would rejoice in the work being done, whoever did it, may serve as an illustration of this.

But all of these alike may be paid for their work; that is to say, in consideration of doing it they may be put into a position to further the general purposes of their lives, whatever they may be, to marry, to travel, to keep a luxurious table, to patronise the turf, to make a figure in the world, to buy books, to gather information, to further philanthropic or religious movements, to endow research, or to patronise art, all on the scale of their 15s. a week, or £1500 a year, as the case may be. Now, in all these cases the relation is complex and the motives are concurrent. The economic forces are reinforced or counteracted by the others, and the resultant would be different if any one of them were modified. He is in the happiest position whose work is at the same time pleasant in the doing, valued for its direct result, and indirectly helpful to all his own general purposes; or in more familiar terms, he is happiest who is paid for doing what it is a pleasure to him to do and what he desires should be done.

In such a case there is a happy coincidence between the direct accomplishment of one purpose and the indirect accomplishment of others. The very thing for which we should have been willing, if necessary, to forgo some satisfaction or incur some pain we actually secure by doing something else which is itself an independent source of satisfaction to us.

A great part of the work of many literary men and artists of every kind is, or may be, of this kind; and so may any intelligent handicraft, up to a certain point. The observation of this fact has given rise to a Utopian idea that all irksomeness might ideally be expelled from life; and some favoured individuals seem so nearly to reach this ideal as to furnish some kind of pledge of its actual possibility. But a little reflection will shew that this is inherently impossible; for if we really care for the purpose of our work, that is to say, if independently of the pleasure of doing it (which would have been secured if the effect were instantly destroyed), we also care for the effect itself, it must follow that so long as that effect is imperfectly accomplished we shall be willing to make sacrifices or to endure weariness for the sake of its further accomplishment. That is to say, no man will be content always to stop doing whatever he is engaged upon as soon as he ceases to enjoy it, except the man who has no real care that the thing should be actually done at all. And this will explain why even that man, the general tenor of whose life seems to have secured an almost perfect coincidence between his tastes and his purposes, and who enjoys every portion of his normal day to the full, will yet (unless he can hermetically seal his heart against all appeals) find that he has perpetually to break in upon the life he loves in order to meet personal or public claims which impose comparatively distasteful tasks upon him; and this because they tend to the accomplishment of more urgently needed results than those to which the daily labour of his life is ministering. He may long believe that all this is due to a series of vexatious accidents, and that presently he will be left undisturbed; but reflection will shew him that it is inherent in the conditions of human life that the man who cares for anything will often have to relinquish something else that he cares for in order to secure it, and that

The Utopia where all work is enjoyed.

while he is himself highly fortunate in finding the main supports and adornments of his life spontaneously conferred upon him simply for doing that which it is his delight to do, there yet remains a margin of unsupplied wants, or unfulfilled purposes, or neglected claims, or undeveloped opportunities, the provision for which must trench on his loved occupations, or must be met from the proceeds of excess of work that converts it into exhausting and wearying toil. No man can escape doing things he does not enjoy for their own sake, or doing more of them than he enjoys, unless he is indifferent to all the unsatisfied purposes or potential reliefs or delights, whether of himself or others, to which they might minister.

(*d*) We have now abundantly illustrated from every side the fact that the economic forces cannot be assumed to act in isolation. But it does not follow that it is impossible or illegitimate to make a separate study of them. It may be both legitimate and desirable to make an isolated study of forces that we never for a moment suppose to act in isolation, provided that the action which our isolating study reveals really comes into play and tells at its full value, though always in combination with other forces. In order to justify such an isolated study it is sufficient that the action revealed should be real. The stock example of this isolation is the tracing of the ideal course of a projectile on the supposition that the direction and force of gravitation are constant, that there is no resisting medium, and that the projectile itself is a "material particle" without extension. Not one of these hypotheses ever corresponds with the fact, and the last of them is self-contradictory; for a projectile must have extension. The second ignores a consideration which always enters into every practical application of the theory; and the first slightly falsifies the conditions under which the force of gravitation always acts; so that even if that force acted alone, which it never does, and acted on a point, which it never can, it would not make that point trace the true parabola which the theory of projectiles yields. And yet the practical study of projectiles has been incalculably assisted by the working out of this hypothetical gravitation, acting upon a body that cannot exist, in the absence of a medium which is always present. It will be

Should the economic forces be studied in isolation?

instructive to examine this example further, and in doing so we must make a careful distinction. The hypothesis that the action of gravitation is constant in direction and magnitude is positively false, and it vitiates the result; but it departs so little from the truth that the error it produces is less than the finest observation could detect or rectify; so that in a practical problem the result obtained is indistinguishable from the true result. The other two hypotheses, that the projectile has no extension, and that there is no medium, are negatively false, for they assume the absence of what is really present; but in isolating for examination those aspects of the problem which are independent of the bulk of the projectile and of the action of the medium, they guide us to an actual result, though one which never reveals itself alone, since it always occurs in combination with other results derived from other factors.

We may take this opportunity, before proceeding further, of trying to clear up certain confusions and obscurities that attach to the words "theory" and "theoretical," particularly in contrast to "practice" and "practical." Broadly, we speak of a theoretical treatment of a subject whenever the investigation proceeds by inference rather than by direct observation. This will be the case when we are dealing with generalised facts and reach general conclusions, or whenever our data or results are not open to direct observation. And this latter case may arise, because our data never actually occur in nature. For instance, our datum may be that the earth is revolving round the sun in space without being influenced by any other body. This would be a hypothesis, but not a fact, and the conclusion about the perfect elliptical orbit of the earth would not be theoretically true, because the datum is not. The conclusion would be theoretically and truly derived from the datum, but would not be theoretically true as a fact. Much confusion in the popular mind is due to the careless use of "theoretically" as equivalent to "according to the hypothesis." Or it may be that our data do occur in nature but never in isolation, whereas our treatment isolates them. Our conclusions will then be true both theoretically and practically, but their isolation will be hypothetical. If we announce the isolated result as something that will take place

What is meant by a theoretical treatment or solution. Sound theory can never be practically false.

"theoretically" but not "practically," we are using loose language; for theory, while isolating the data and the results, does not assert that they "occur" in isolation, but the contrary. It is therefore theoretically true that the isolated data would involve the isolated result, but theoretically false that the result will actually occur in isolation. There is a distinction, but not a contrast, between theory and practice. In fact it is never the case that anything is theoretically true but practically false; though a statement may be practically true but theoretically false, if it neglects quantities so small that they evade observation, though their existence can be inferred.

The theoretical method we are considering at the moment is that of hypothetical isolation. It may be illustrated by what is sometimes called in dynamics the principle of Superposition. According to this principle any force which, acting on a body, would produce a certain result, were that body at rest and were no other forces acting upon it, will actually produce its full effect (that is to say, will tell in exactly the same direction and to the same extent), whatever may be the motion of the body at the moment and however many other forces may be acting on the body at the same time or may subsequently be brought to act upon it. Thus, if a hockey ball receives an impact which would make it travel 100 feet due north in a second, if it were at rest at the moment of the blow, then whatever direction it is moving in when it receives it, or whatever impacts it receives afterwards, it will be 100 feet further north at the end of a second than it would have been had it not received this impact. For instance, if it was already travelling at the rate of 50 feet a second due west when it received it, then at the end of a second it will be both 50 feet further west and 100 feet further north than it was at the beginning. Or if a ball travelling north at 100 feet a second experienced an impact which, had it been at rest, would have sent it 50 feet south in a second, at the end of the second it will be 100 feet further north than it would have been had it not been in motion when it received the impact, and 50 feet further south than if it had not received it. In the first case it would have been 50 feet south of its original position, in the second 100 feet north of it. As a matter of fact it will

[margin: The principle of Superposition and its application to the economic relation.]

be 50 feet north of that position. Thus in every case, whether the force acts in the same direction as the motion or in the opposite direction, or at right angles to it, or at any other angle, it will produce its full effect. Similarly, if two or more forces act simultaneously, their joint effect is obtained by allowing for the full effect that each force would produce if acting separately, and then adding them all together.

There is nothing inconsistent, therefore, and nothing unpractical, in theoretically isolating the effect of a force that usually or perhaps always acts in combination with others. Note, therefore (and this is an important though apparently subtle point), that the hypothesis or supposition that a force does act alone is a very different thing indeed from the theoretical study of it in isolation. The very necessity for studying it "theoretically" may be due to the fact that it is never accessible in isolation, and our interest in it may be wholly due to its practical effect in combination with other forces. It would be false to say that "theoretically" it acts alone; but true to say that for theoretical treatment we must isolate it. We conclude, therefore, that it is open to us to consider whether there is any advantage in an isolated study of the economic forces, though the hypothesis that they always or generally act in isolation would be an absurd one. But note that the analogies adduced from physical science can be pushed no further than to the single point of a possible justification of isolated treatment. The simplicity, uniformity, and mutual independence of the forces with which dynamics deal fail us on the field of psychology.

Let us suppose, then, that, for some reason, a man desires money; that is to say, desires an increased command of services and commodities in the circle of exchange. Then if an action he is contemplating will bring him money, this fact will form a consideration, and if appreciable will tend to affect his conduct, whether the action in question is attractive, repellent, or indifferent to him on its own merits. We have admitted that the inter-relation and inter-connection of the motives that determine a man's conduct are too intricate and complex to enable us to imitate on the field of practical life the exact formulæ of mechanics; but it is safe to say that if a man wants money, then the fact that a certain open alternative will secure him money will be a consideration (though possibly a negligible one) in favour of that alternative. This is indeed merely to say that a man would rather have what he wants than not. Thus if any new order of relations between men becomes possible whereby those who enter into it can obtain a given command of things in the circle of exchange, there will be a reason for entering into those relations, which will tell for what it is worth, whether the relations themselves are attractive or repellent to the tastes, the morals, the habits, or the impulses of some or all of the members of the community affected. And any modification in those or in other existing relations will modify the forces that determine conduct in that community, whatever other forces may be present or absent. If, then, by isolating the consideration of the economic forces, we can gain any insight into the general principles on which they may be expected to influence a man's conduct, we need not be deterred from pursuing such a course by the fact that it is never safe to assume such isolation as a fact.

Closely bearing on the considerations just urged is another principle which must be expounded here. It is the principle of "Continuity." If you were to take the 1000 persons who happened to be nearest to a certain point on the earth's surface at a given moment, and then arranged them in order of height, you might rely, in general, on finding no great differences between any individual and his right-hand and left-hand neighbours. Possibly there might be an abnormally small baby at one end and a giant at the other, considerably shorter and taller, respectively, than their neighbours; but after passing the first few individuals at either end you would find the difference as you passed from one to another exceedingly small. That is to say, when you are dealing with any large number of persons you may assume that whatever reasonable standard of height you may fix, some of those who are below it will be very little below, and some of those above it very little above, so that if you had taken the standard a very little higher or lower some individuals would have been below who are now above it or some above who are now below.

The principle of Continuity and its application to the economic relation.

Now we have already examined the economic forces closely enough to realise without difficulty, that if a large number of persons are engaged in any profession, there will be some of them who, on the balance of considerations, are only just retained within that profession, and others who are only just kept out of it. So that if any of the conditions affecting this occupation are altered; if it comes to be thought either more or less dignified or honourable than it now is; if the conditions under which it is pursued are so changed as to make it either more or less easy, interesting, bracing, or agreeable to the average man, or more pleasant and so forth to some and less so to others; or if its indirect advantages (that is to say, the salary attached to it, which means its power of enabling him who pursues it to get his other purposes accomplished by so doing) are changed; then some persons who are now in it will go out, or some who are now out of it will come in, or some who would have prepared to enter it will not do so, or some who would not have prepared to enter it will. Possibly two streams, one each way, will be set in motion. This, observe, is not a speciality of the economic forces, but is common to them with all others. Thus, even if the economic forces never act in isolation, yet the psychological analogue of the law of Superposition, combined with the principle of Continuity, enables us to feel the utmost confidence that any modification in the economic conditions of life will produce its full effect. If we study these effects in isolation we shall be studying real phenomena which actually enter, though not in isolation, into practical life.

It may help to give precision to these ideas if we return to one of our former examples. The actual and potential purchasers of new potatoes in a given market may be actuated by all kinds of partialities, prejudices, and traditions, but if one man were selling at $1\frac{1}{4}$d. per pound, whereas others were selling at $1\frac{1}{2}$d., the difference in price would be felt as a reason, if not necessarily a sufficient reason, by all the marketers who noted the difference, for dealing at the cheaper stall. And if there were many of them some would already be so nearly dealing with this man in preference to some other that the $\frac{1}{4}$d. difference would determine them. Or again, if the price in the whole market passed from $1\frac{1}{2}$d. to $1\frac{1}{4}$d., though there would be many who bought just the same quantity that they would have done at the old price, yet there would be sure to be some, already just on the balance between a larger or a smaller quantity, whose purchases the fall in price would increase. Thus where large numbers are concerned we may assume a sensitiveness which we cannot assume in the case of individuals. We may be sure that the smallest appreciable cause will produce an appreciable effect. The irregularities on individual scales will compensate each other on the collective scale; and we may reckon upon any change in the economic conditions producing an effect; and, by study, we may hope to learn something of the nature of this effect, though it always combines with others. If we say that such and such an effect will actually emerge—for instance, that the price of such and such an article will rise, because of such and such a change—we assume in the first place that the force that has come into action is powerful enough to produce an appreciable effect, and in the second place that other forces will remain constant. But as a matter of fact other forces never will remain constant over any lengthened period. Hence the extreme danger and folly of concrete predictions.

But having now vindicated our right to study the economic forces in isolation, and having raised a strong presumption that such a method will throw light upon their action, we return to the question "why should we desire any particular knowledge of the action of the economic forces at all?" The answer to this question is simple and decisive. We have touched upon, though we have not explored, the various ways in which the business nexus may work for the weal or woe of the social organism. And as we can neither destroy the economic forces nor implicitly trust to their beneficence, we shall naturally wish to control and direct, to stimulate or to check their action, to open channels through which they may flow with fertilising effect, and to dam them out from regions that they might desolate. The whole range of factory legislation, the whole scheme of the Poor Law, all acts against the free sale of poisons or of fire-arms, the regulation of the liquor traffic, schemes for a scientific tariff, schemes for the compulsory levying of taxes for communal purposes, are all of them

Why should we study the economic forces?

attempts to regulate and direct, to control and supplement, or to stimulate in this direction or check in that, the action of the economic forces; and an indefinite number of movements, such as co-operation in the interests of producers, or co-operation in the interests of consumers, or schemes of profit-sharing, are attempts to educate and enlighten these forces. The housing problem, the land problem, and all the rest, perpetually deal with economic forces. Ruskin's crusade against interest contemplated a radical change in one of the most pronounced manifestations of the economic force. No one can deny the importance of the practical objects contemplated by these and innumerable other movements and activities. No one can deny the difficulties of the problems they involve. No one can deny the frequency with which results other than, or even opposite to, those contemplated rise, or are alleged to rise, out of action taken. It is clear, then, that the action of the economic forces can in many ways be controlled and modified by deliberate collective action. It is also clear that action taken for this purpose is groping and often blind; and further, that want of clear knowledge of the deeply enrooted nature and the irrevocably fixed boundaries of the facts and forces with which we are dealing causes incalculable waste of social effort and enthusiasm. Surely, then, it needs no further argument to prove that if any essential light can be thrown on the actual nature and the spontaneous action of the forces that we endeavour at every turn to direct, to check, and to control, the mind of man could scarcely be applied to a more august or urgent task than that of elucidating them.

Surely it will help us in our consideration of the problem of starvation wages if we can understand the exact nature of the influence which the economic forces spontaneously exercise in raising or depressing wages; for we shall then better know whether any measure we contemplate for raising wages will have to be carried through in opposition to them or can enlist them as allies. If we are considering whether it is moral or immoral to take interest, and whether an industrial society could or could not be carried on without it, would it not be well as a preliminary if we could gain a perfectly clear and precise conception of what interest is, how it arises, and what it does, so far as the economic forces beget and regulate it? Nor can we have any clear conception of what the housing problem is, or what are the real bearings of any proposed solution of it, until we understand exactly how and why the play of commercial forces has brought about, or contributed to bring about, the existing state of things; or why this play of forces does not spontaneously and unconsciously destroy it.

What gives their immense social significance and importance to the economic forces is that they will always look after themselves. You need not preach to a man or appeal to his imagination, you need not be perpetually reminding yourself of things which you are constantly apt to forget, in order to make him and to make yourself do those things to and for others which you know are the quickest and readiest way of getting what you want done yourself and of getting your own purposes fulfilled. Your own purposes are always with you. You have a direct and precise conception of them, so far as you have a direct and precise conception of anything. To give another man food when you think he wants it, and to keep it away from him when you think he does not, and never to forget his wants, needs a more or less sustained effort, and involves dealings with unknown quantities as to which your speculations are sure not to be accurately true, and may be disastrously false. When you are hungry and want food yourself, it needs no effort of the imagination, no sustained self-discipline, no fallible speculation, to make you aware of the fact.

<small>Importance of harnessing the economic forces to the social car.</small>

Therefore, if we can place any socially desirable work under the direct tutelage of these urgent forces, we have made sure that it will be looked after. Saint and sinner alike will desire to do the things whereby they can further their own purposes. We shall then have a driving force, the furnace of which is always at full blast, and needs none of our stoking. Practical philanthropists know this well, and they often surprise and even scandalise their supporters by insisting that their schemes should be " placed on a sound business footing " and be " made to pay." Naturally; for if I make it a part of any man's purpose, to which he is willing to sacrifice other purposes, that the housing of the people should be improved,

I do well; but if I can shew that by building better houses he can further all his other purposes instead of sacrificing any of them to it, then I have secured general and automatic support for the thing that I desire. We could not in any case afford to waste, even if it were possible to destroy, those forces whose stupendous sweep and energy bear so dominant a part in co-ordinating the efforts of men and carrying on the world from day to day. It will be necessary sometimes to oppose and check them; but what an enormous gain if we can harness them to the social car!

And, in spite of their alertness and insistence, the economic forces cannot be trusted always to find out for themselves those outlets which are incidentally beneficent. For, however bold and alert they may be in seeking passages for themselves, they can never induce those who are not directly interested in the social results we contemplate to incur any risks for their sake. Hence they may be irresponsive, timid, and perhaps blind with the blindness of indifference and lack of sympathy, in the face of many promptings and suggestions which might otherwise reveal to them that the direct road to the accomplishment of their own purposes lies along the path we would have them tread.

Scope for disinterested experiment.

There is an indefinitely large field open to those who value the social result, and have insight and courage to take the risks of making experiments. When those who care have enlisted the co-operation of those who do not, the improved order of things spreads and sustains itself. It has come within the range of the economic forces, and can enjoy the incessant and vigilant support which those forces give. There is an ever-growing number of private individuals, or of associations and organised groups, such as those constituted by the Trades Unionists or the co-operators of England, or of governing bodies that have more or less control over the lives and conduct of men, from village councils to the Imperial Parliament, that are or may be earnestly concerned with social problems for their own sake; and it is no matter of indifference whether they have, or have not, a sound knowledge of the action of the economic forces, with which, if they are wise, they will constantly seek alliance in all their reforms, and which, if they have the courage, they will not shrink from checking and controlling, on due occasion and to the due extent.

We shall enter upon an express study of the economic force, then, not because it is an evil thing which we must seek to eliminate, nor because it is a beneficent thing to which we can surrender our lives in serene confidence, but because it is a power ever active, in a world of mingled good and evil, in producing and emphasising good and evil effects; a power which we cannot destroy or lull to sleep, but which in a certain measure we can control and direct; and a power, therefore, which it is of the extremest importance for social well-being that we should understand.

And we shall study it to a great extent in isolation, because, having already elucidated on a broader psychological field the main conceptions, and established the main laws, which regulate its action, we shall now find it possible, and therefore conducive to clearness of exposition, to study the special application of these conceptions and laws to economic problems.

CHAPTER VI

MARKETS

SUMMARY.—*The market is the characteristic phenomenon of the economic life and it presents the central problem of Economics. It is the machinery by which objective equilibrium in the marginal significance of exchangeable things is secured and maintained in a catallactic society. Equilibrium exists when the commodity occupies the same place at the margin on the scales of all who possess it, and is higher at the margin on all their scales than on the scales of any one who does not possess it. The equilibrium price of any commodity is the price which if at once established would produce equilibrium without oscillations; and it is determined by the quantity of the commodity at command and the composition of the collective scale. It is the interest of each dealer to know this price, and any erroneous estimate of it he may form, while placing him under penalties, will tend to correct itself, but will have a secondary reaction on the equilibrium price itself. The law of the market is implied in the definition of equilibrium; for the market price will be determined by the place on the communal scale of the lowest of the desires for a unit that are gratified, and these will all of them be higher than any that are not gratified. Hence if there are x units of the commodity the place of the xth unit on the collective scale will determine the equilibrium price. The collective scale registers the estimates not only of the buyers but also of the sellers at reserve prices, who are equivalent to buyers at those prices. Vicarious or speculative estimates are to be reckoned in with the rest, and as long as they tend* *to regulate the consumption of the commodity they perform a valuable social service; but they often transcend this limit and become socially pernicious. There are many types of market and forms of sale, but they all conform to the same law, so far as the essential condition of free communication, and knowledge of each other's doings, is realised amongst the persons concerned; and where this is not the case men's actions are still controlled by the same fundamental laws and forces which create more or less perfect markets where the conditions are favourable. Markets in raw materials follow the same law as markets in finished articles.*

Returning from our digression on the character and importance of economic forces and relations, we approach the long-deferred examination of the constitution of markets and market prices, which presents our central problem. What we mean by the market price of an article is what a man is able to get, or is obliged to give, independently of any interest in him or his purposes on the part of his correspondent. It is a purely economic conception, and that is why we have so carefully examined the relation of economic to other considerations before proceeding to examine it. A market is the machinery by which equilibrium in the marginal significances of exchangeable things is produced, maintained, or restored. We have seen that equilibrium only exists when the relative scales of every two members of the community coincide, so far as concerns all the exchangeable commodities of which they both possess a stock. When such an equilibrium has been reached, and all the individual scales of marginal preference coincide, we may speak, in an objective sense, of the "communal scale of preferences." Each commodity occupies a definite place on that scale with reference to all other commodities, and this place may be conveniently indicated by stating the gold value of a small unit. The gold value, or equivalent in gold, we may call the equilibrium value of the commodity at the margin; that is to say, it is the gold index of the relative significance, in a state of equilibrium, of a small marginal increment of the commodity, on the scale of every one who possesses a supply of it.

Markets.

In this chapter I shall try to shew that whenever equilibrium does not exist, and the conditions for exchange are present, the persons conducting the exchanges attempt to form an intelligent estimate of the price which would produce equilibrium, and the result of that attempt fixes the actual terms on which all the exchanges in the open market are for the moment made. When (in such an open market) exchanges are made upon an erroneous estimate it tends to correct itself. The ideal equilibrium value fixes the ideal market price; the estimates formed of it constitute the actual market price at any moment; and the latter constantly tends to approach the former. In expounding this I shall at first neglect certain secondary reactions, which will, however, ultimately assert themselves and will be considered in due place and time.

The ideal equilibrating price.

An organised market is a machine for bringing people into relations with each other and so revealing and removing departures from a state of equilibrium. Its normal existence implies that there are facts and forces in action that either disturb equilibrium when it exists, or continuously initiate states and conditions of non-equilibrium that can be removed. And we already know what some at least of these facts and forces are. We are born with different capacities or different opportunities; we develop them differently; intentionally or by accident we come into different possessions; and, above all, in deliberate anticipation of the wants and desires of others we produce commodities or cultivate talents that have no direct relation to the things we ourselves want. And consequently the general level of possession, achievement, and satisfaction is maintained or raised, not by an evenly diffused process that makes things accrue at the point at which they are relatively most wanted, but by the various objects of desire being poured into the circle of exchange at certain definite points, and being thence distributed through the whole texture and tissue of society, by forces that make for equilibrium, though as a rule they never attain it. The social organism, we may say, has innumerable stomachs which digest its food and pour it into the circulating fluid at chosen points, whence it is carried all over the body. To drop metaphor, every one who takes his place in the commercial world deliberately seeks to put himself in command of certain things in relative excess of his requirements, and takes steps to secure the perpetual maintenance or recurrence of this excess; but the process of exchanging is as continuously levelling it down, so that his excess flows off as fast as it rises; and the machinery which carries off his produce to accomplish the purposes or fulfil the desires of others, and at the same time makes it indirectly minister to the continuous fulfilment of his own desires and the furtherance of his own purposes, is the machinery of the market.

It will be easiest to begin with an instance in which periodicity in Nature herself combines with elementary forms of division of labour to produce a localised supply, initiating a state of non-equilibrium. Crops of every kind give us what we want. The damson crop, the potato crop, the wheat crop, the cotton crop, are all of them periodic up-flingings of things that minister to human wants and purposes; and those into whose possession—as determined by the whole complex of historical, social, personal, and natural conditions—they primarily come are not those in whose possession they can rest in equilibrium. To their possessors, individually, when the harvest is gathered in, they are in many instances of negative marginal value; that is to say, their owners possess them in such quantities that they would not only be unable to make any direct use of the whole stock, but would be greatly encumbered and inconvenienced by it if they could not get rid of it, and would therefore be at trouble to bury, to drown, to burn, or otherwise to destroy or reduce it. But there are many others whose desire for these same things is very far from being satiated, and who are in a position in their turn directly or indirectly to gratify the unsatiated desires and further the unfulfilled purposes of the possessors. The market is the meeting ground between those who possess in relative (and possibly in absolute) excess and those who possess in relative defect. But note, once more, that if A is said to have something in relative excess which B has in relative defect, this does not mean that A has more of it or is less keenly desirous of it *relatively to B.* That may or may not be the case. What the phrase means is that the marginal significance of this thing to A *relatively to the other exchangeable things he possesses* is lower than in the case of

B. "Relative" means relatively to the other possessions or alternatives in the estimate of the same man, not relatively to the same possessions or alternatives in the estimate of another man. For instance, let us suppose that Cobbett does not lose his halfpenny but buys the herring, and before he has cooked it encounters a comparatively well-fed companion to whom a herring would nevertheless be acceptable; and suppose he finds that this other man possesses a small book which he is willing to part with for the herring. The exchange may be effected, and yet the herring may have more significance to Cobbett than to his companion, for he may be the more hungry of the two; but *relatively to the book* the herring stands lower on Cobbett's scale than on the other's, or the exchange would not be made. In like manner a peasant might have grown a crop of potatoes, the whole of which he could with great comfort consume during the year, and he might part with some of them, in exchange for clothes or tools, to a well-fed person who would take little pains to economise them, and would suffer no sensible inconvenience if his supply were slightly curtailed. In this case the peasant's marginal need of potatoes relatively to that of his customer might be high, but relatively to his own marginal need for clothes, or other things which the sum for which he sells them will purchase, its position must be lower on his scale than on that of his customer. With this caution we may return to our statement that crops occur under such conditions as to confer a relative excess of possession on certain persons; and the market is the machinery by which this local excess is levelled down.

Equilibrium is established when the marginal position of the commodity in question is identical upon the relative scales of all who have secured a supply, and higher on them all than it is on the scales of any of those who have secured no supply. What that position will be depends on the amount of the commodity that there is for distribution. For, as we have seen, the more I possess of any commodity the lower on my relative scale does it stand at the margin; so that if equilibrium amongst the consumers were established at any point on their scales and the growers still had stores in relative excess, and therefore found it to their

Equilibrium defined.

interest to effect further exchanges, this continued distribution, yet further increasing the supplies of the consumers, would lower the marginal significance of the commodity on all their scales. The more of the commodity there is to be distributed, then, the lower will be the position on the several personal scales, and therefore on the collective scale, at which equilibrium is finally reached. Thus the amount of the crop and the scale of preferences of the community are the two ultimate considerations which determine the point on the collective scale at which equilibrium will be reached, or what we call the equilibrium price or value of the commodity. Armed with this conception of the state of equilibrium as the goal of all the operations of exchange, let us return to the simple type of market with which we began our investigations, and let us once more accompany our housewife to it.

We have hitherto treated the prices the marketer finds in the market, or, in other words, the terms on which its various alternatives are offered to her, as though they were fixed by some external power, and as though all that she could do were to adjust her purchases to them. And this is, in fact, the way in which the problem presents itself in the first instance to any individual marketer. *The seller reflects the collective mind of the consumers.* It is true that we may often get things at a lower price than is at first asked, and many housewives pride themselves on their skill in bargaining; but this does not affect the fact that different prices will reign in different seasons and on different days, and the housewife herself knows perfectly well that there is a price below which she cannot get her wares. Her bargaining is, in the main, an attempt to find out what the price is rather than an attempt to change it. This price appears to the marketer to be fixed in some way by the seller, and all that she hopes to do is to get at the seller's real mind and find out what is the lowest price at which he will sell, as distinct from what he says it is. Ultimately, then, she believes that the seller fixes the price. Possibly in some instances the seller thinks so too, but, generally speaking, he is perfectly aware that the conditions of the market have determined a certain price, which he may try to conceal or evade, or of which he may even at first be ignorant, but which he cannot really change. He may think of this price in various ways, but they are all of them reducible to the question of what he can actually get. He knows that this is somehow fixed, and that he does not himself fix it. If he really insists on a certain price, and will not sell to a customer at anything less, it means a conviction on his part that he can get that price from some other customer, or that his goods are worth as much as that to him himself for his own use. If he assures a customer that he cannot possibly sell below such and such a price, and that the goods are "well worth it," we shall find on analysis that he is trying to persuade the customer that he could get this price from some one else, and that other dealers could too, and that they know they could, and will therefore not sell at less; and if he finally does sell at a lower price, it is because he knows or suspects that he could not really do any better. Thus the purchaser tries to find out what price the seller has in his mind; but the seller has got that price into his mind by trying to find out what some one or other of the customers will give, and his announcement of the price (which the individual purchaser encounters as an externally fixed condition) is really nothing more than his attempt to read the minds of the whole body of purchasers. Each individual purchaser may know his own mind better than the seller can. But if the seller understands his business he knows the collective mind better than any individual purchaser does; for he has had wider access to the whole body of purchasers, and wider experience of their wants.

We have already reached an important conclusion; for though we have not yet discovered exactly how the price which the individual customer finds in the market is fixed, yet we have learnt who ultimately fixes it—namely, the other customers, and in an infinitesimal degree this very customer herself. It is mainly what the others will give that determines what the seller asks of her, and in an infinitesimal degree it is what she will give that determines what the seller asks of the others. What the purchaser meets in the market, therefore, is but a reflection of her own mind and that of her compeers, thrown back from the mind of the seller. It is only in virtue of the obstinate illusion of the mirror that she believes the object she is contemplating to be actually, as it is in appearance, behind the fishmonger's slab, or the counter, instead of, as it really is, in front of it.

It is the collective mind of the purchasers, then, as estimated by the sellers, that determines the price proclaimed by the latter. The sellers read the collective scale, to the best of their ability, and announce their reading to the individual purchaser. If I could perfectly read your mind I should know how much tea or fruit you would buy at any price I chose to fix in my mind, and if I wanted you to buy exactly twenty-five units I should know what price to fix in order to make you do so. In like manner, if I could perfectly read the minds of all the other purchasers I should know exactly how much each of them would buy at any particular price, and what particular price I must fix in order to make the sum of all their purchases reach any given amount. When they had finished their purchases, each of them having just as much as he cared to take at that price, the marginal unit of stock would occupy the same place on all their scales; and that place would be the one that equated it to the given price. There would then be equilibrium; that is to say, since the marginal increment of the commodity would occupy the same place on every relative scale, the conditions of exchange for that commodity would no longer exist.

Let us suppose, then, that the sellers have perfect knowledge of the minds of all possible buyers and also of the whole quantity of the commodity in the market, and let us suppose that they proclaim such a price that the collective purchases it will induce amount to the exact quantity of the commodity offered for sale. Obviously, under these circumstances, when the whole stock was sold there would be equilibrium. *The machinery of the market for finding the equilibrating price.* We are therefore justified in calling this price the equilibrating price, because it, and it alone, would at once, by a single transaction between each buyer and a seller, produce a state of equilibrium. Now it is clear that some of the stock will in any case have to be sold as low as this equilibrating price, for the whole stock could not, by hypothesis, be so placed that every unit of it would have a higher significance than this price indicates. But is there any reason to expect that the whole quantity of the commodity in the market will be sold at this price? In the case of a fruit crop, for instance, the whole supply for the year may come into the market within a few weeks, days, or even hours;

and when the market opens the state of things will be such that a very extensive transfer will have to take place, broad streams flowing along one channel, and tiny dribbles filtering through another, before the general level is reached and equilibrium established. Why should not the seller make the keen purchasers pay more than the others, or make every one pay more for the comparatively eagerly desired initial supplies than for the comparatively languidly desired final ones ? Why, in fact, should not the marginal significance of the commodity, on the collective scale, be progressively lowered and the maximum price exacted at every step ? Why should the final price be anticipated from the beginning and treated as if it had already arrived ? That is to say, why should the price at which the least significant increments of the commodity will have to be sold be that at which all the rest are sold too ? Though the proclamation of the equilibrium value at the outset would obviously lead at once to equilibrium, it is evidently not the only conceivable path to that goal. Why should it be the one actually taken ? The answer to these questions involves an analysis of the machinery of the market, and an explanation of the dictum that there cannot be two prices for the same article in the same market.

To begin with, we cannot imagine that, in a free competitive market, any one will be able to get the ideal maximum price for one unit of the commodity out of that purchaser who would pay the highest price sooner than go without it. If any one seller succeeded in getting this price he would absorb the whole advantage of it, and the holder of a neighbouring stall might prefer that he himself should get a smaller advantage than that his rival should get a greater one. So he may offer the unit at something less than the maximum. Thus by playing off one seller against another the purchaser may expect to buy at that price below which no one will have to go in order to dispose of his wares; that is to say, the equilibrium price. Besides, the purchasers do not present themselves one after another in the order of the relative urgency of their needs, but some who would buy at a higher, and others who would only buy at a lower price, come into the market in a mingled stream. So that if different prices were charged to different customers

Competition.

according to their relative estimates of the significance of the commodity, those who were being charged high could get those who were being charged low to buy for them on a small commission. It would be exceedingly difficult for even a combination of sellers to defeat this move. These two possibilities, then—competition between the sellers, and dealings on commission amongst the purchasers,—will militate against the possibility of selling on different terms to different customers, or to the same customer when supplying units that take different places on his scale ; and since some of the units must obviously be sold as low as the equilibrium price it will be difficult to sell any at a higher price. So the stall-keepers will form a general estimate, based partly on actual inspection of the market, partly on a variety of sources of information and grounds of conjecture which they commanded before entering it, as to the amount, say, of some particular fruit and the most obvious substitutes for it that are in the market that day. And further, they will form an estimate, based on the experiences of previous days or years, of the equilibrium price corresponding to that amount. They will be ready to take this price sooner than lose custom, and they will not expect in a general way to get more than that for any portion of their stock.

An interesting indication that the seller is thus guided in naming the price by a series of inferences and speculations as to the ultimate facts that must determine it, is to be found in the circumstance that a seller cannot always answer the question what the price is. It often happens in small country markets that when a customer asks the price of something early in the day the stall-keeper will answer that she does not know. She feels herself unequal to forming an intelligent estimate of the amount of stock in the market, the scale of preferences of possible purchasers, and the resultant price which will ultimately reign. Possibly she is not even subconsciously aware that the price depends upon these things. But she does know perfectly well that it is not she who fixes the price. She simply proclaims it if she is in a position to do so ; and if she does not know what it is she cannot even proclaim it. The price will be determined and will be known later on in the day. At present, if known at all, it is not known to her, and she declines to speculate. It is possible that transactions may be conducted between her and her customer on this basis. The customer may take so many pounds of damsons, agreeing to pay the price, whatever it may be, when it is declared; but in such a case she cannot adjust her purchases to her requirements with any precision. All she can do is to give the minimum order, corresponding to the highest price that is at all likely to reign; and later on, when the price is known, she may make a larger or smaller addition to her order, according to circumstances, having in any case secured a certain supply even should the stock run short. Very likely, however, the limits of probable error are not such as would produce any sensible effect on her transactions. She is not conscious that the difference of a halfpenny a pound would make her buy more or less, and so she need not wait till she knows the price to a halfpenny before she makes her purchase. Her neighbour, on the contrary, to whom a halfpenny is of more consequence, will wait to give her order till she knows the exact conditions, and she herself, if it turns out that the price ultimately declared is very considerably less than she had contemplated as the lowest limit of likelihood, may regret that she did not buy more; and in the reverse case she may regret that she bought as much, may grudge having to pay, and may even try to get rid of some of her stock.

But such transactions on an uncertain basis of price, though not unknown, are exceptional. It is the function of the sellers to name a price, though here and there an individual seller may not feel equal to the task. Let us consider, then, what would happen if the sellers collectively made an error in their judgment and named something below or above the true equilibrium price. If they made it too low they obviously stand to lose. The customers that come into the market early will buy more at the lower price than they would have done at the higher, and later in the day customers who would have bought freely at the higher price find the stock gone. But the dealers will probably see in a few hours that the stock is running out too fast; and if so, they will raise the price. If, on the other hand, they fix the price too high, the early customers who would have bought, or would have bought more, at the lower figure, go away disappointed, buying nothing, or comparatively little, and they do not appear again later in the day to renew their offers, for they have already satisfied themselves with some substitute. The housekeeper who at the natural price would have taken home with her a large stock of damsons to make jam for the year will have changed her plan of campaign, and will have taken home a small supply and determined to eke out her provision for the year with apple-and-blackberry and marrow jam. Her demand therefore has been to a great extent not deferred but destroyed, so far as the market in damsons is concerned; and to find any customers at all the dealers will be obliged ultimately to sell their stock at a still lower price than they could have obtained had they fixed it in closer accordance with the facts at the outset. This result is one of the reactions which I spoke of on page 214.

We have spoken of "the sellers" collectively, but we have not really been examining the conditions of a market in which the sellers combine and act in concert. Such a market, as we shall see later on in this chapter, has features of its own. We have been thinking of a market in which the sellers act independently, however much they may be influenced by each other, and I have only meant to indicate a resultant of this independent action in speaking collectively of "the sellers." Let us see, then, by what process this resultant is arrived at, or, in other words, how individual diversities are levelled down and a general market price arrived at. Suppose at the opening of the market that some of the sellers offer damsons at a lower price than others. The market will doubtless be "imperfect" (that is to say, it will not establish complete communications between all the persons concerned), and therefore some purchasers will deal at the stalls which they usually patronise without being aware that they could get the fruit cheaper at another stall; though they may expostulate, or possibly even demand some of their money back again, if they subsequently find out that they have paid more than the true market price for that day. But the shrewd marketer who goes the round of the market and fully ascertains the alternatives open to her before choosing amongst them, will go to the cheaper stall, and as the stock runs out rapidly the seller may begin to suspect that he has put his price too low and that he will be out of stock early in the day. Or the dealer who has fixed his price too high will find himself deserted, and will fear that he will have his stock left on his hands if he does not reduce his price. So before the day is far advanced a uniform price will have settled itself in the market, probably in very fair correspondence with the actual facts. At the end of the day there should be no great stock unsold, or hastily sold at a reduction, and few customers should be disappointed by finding that damsons are no longer in the market, though they had been sold earlier in the day at prices they would gladly have paid.

But we must carry this analysis a little further. Suppose some dealers, in consideration of all the known and conjectured facts, fix 5d. a pound as the price at which the stock of damsons in the market can be sold, and others fix it at 4d. And let us suppose, first, that these latter have rightly estimated the actual facts. This means that the damsons in the market are sufficient in amount to satisfy all potential purchasers to the point of a marginal valuation of 4d. a pound. When the customers come into the market they buy by preference at the 4d. stalls and avoid the 5d. ones, and the sellers at the 4d. stalls, getting more than their natural share of the custom, see that their stock is running rapidly out and raise the price to $4\frac{1}{2}$d., still taking care to keep below the 5d. asked by their rivals, and so to retain all the custom. Now, though the whole stock in the market cannot be sold at anything above 4d., their portion of it, if the rest is withheld, can perhaps be sold at $4\frac{1}{2}$d., and presently they are sold out. The customers that now arrive in the market have no choice but to go to the 5d. stalls; but the sellers soon perceive that though they have no rivals underselling them they are not getting rid of their stock fast enough; and since a portion of the possible custom at 4d. has been destroyed (because the customers who had to buy at $4\frac{1}{2}$d. contracted their purchases and availed themselves of substitutes), it follows that in order to get rid of the whole of their stock the remaining sellers will have to come down below 4d., the price which they could originally have realised; and as soon as they become aware of this there will be a race amongst them to get down towards what is

Penalties of erroneous estimates.

now the true equilibrium price, for fear of being left in the lurch altogether. Thus the error of those who formed too high an estimate of the equilibrating price has benefited their rivals and injured themselves.

But now let us suppose that 5d. was, at the opening of the market, the natural equilibrating price. Those who named 4d. would, as before, get all the custom in the early part of the day. But, beyond this, they would induce purchases which would not have been made at all had they too struck the true equilibrating price from the first; for some who would not have bought at 5d. buy at 4d., and others who would have bought some at 5d. buy more at 4d. Now, since the stock of damsons is by hypothesis only enough to satisfy every one down to the marginal valuation of 5d., it follows that if it has satisfied some beyond this point, it will only be able to satisfy the rest to a point short of it. Later on in the day, therefore, if all the dealers have stuck to their estimates, the sellers at 4d. will be out of stock, and there will be more potential purchasers even at 5d. still left than the remaining stock can meet, for the early purchasers will have carried away more than what would be their share at the 5d. rate. When the custom is all thrown upon the 5d. sellers, therefore, they will find that they are selling out, not indeed as rapidly as the 4d. sellers did earlier in the day, but so rapidly that their stock will be exhausted before the day is out; and so they raise their price to, say, $5\frac{1}{2}$d., and in the course of the day clear out their stock at that price. The mistake of those who underestimated the true equilibrating price, at the beginning of the day, has again injured themselves and benefited their rivals. Thus, if any dealer correctly surmises that his rivals are standing out for a higher price than the state of the market justifies, he may raise his own price above it too, so long as he is careful to keep below that of his rivals, knowing that while he is getting more they will ultimately have to take less than what is now the true equilibrating price. And if any dealer correctly surmises that his rivals are selling cheaper than the state of the market requires, he will find not only that the event justifies him in standing out for what at the outset is the natural price, but also that the natural price itself is gradually rising in his favour, so that later on in the day he will be able to get still better prices than those he asked, but (owing to the conduct of his rivals) could not get, at the beginning of the day.

Thus every dealer is urged by economic considerations to endeavour to form the most accurate possible estimate of the equilibrating price, and to ask nothing above it, unless some mistake on the part of his rivals enables him to do so safely. If the sellers make no mistake they will offer and sell their whole stock at the original equilibrating price.

We have dealt in this argument with purely economic forces. But others are not excluded. Good-will and mutual interest in each other's affairs may affect the transactions between buyer and seller, and friendly communications and accommodations may take place between different sellers. Or the formation of the market price which we have traced to its economic sources may be aided by non-economic traditions; for the seller will often name a price lower than he knows he could get from an individual customer, partly perhaps with a view to future transactions with him, but partly from a genuine feeling that if he did not he would be taking unfair or unfriendly, though not illegal advantage of him.

Reactions of erroneous estimates on the equilibrating price itself. We must note, for theoretical accuracy, that if under a false impression some purchases are actually made at too high and others at too low a price, the market will close without having established a perfect equilibrium; for those whose purchases were arrested when the commodity had a high marginal significance to them, and those who by the low price were enabled to bring this marginal significance down, will be in a position to effect exchanges on mutually beneficial terms if they know of each other's existence and requirements; that is to say, if they constitute a market. And even if they met at once (before they had provided themselves with substitutes or made any other consequential modifications in their other purchases or plans) and exchanged among themselves till there was complete equilibrium, that final equilibrium would not exactly correspond with that which would have been established had the real conditions of the market been realised from the first. For those purchasers who bought at high prices, having forfeited a disproportionate amount of their resources, will be poorer, and those who had received a disproportionately large amount of the commodity will be richer, than they would otherwise have been; and therefore the terms represented by any price have a different significance to each group from what they would otherwise have had. The purchasers at a high figure are reduced towards the position of Cobbett in our former illustration, and the purchasers at the lower figure raised towards that of Crœsus, and these modifications react on the whole situation, for the collective scale of preferences is the sum of the individual scales, and if you alter the items you alter the sum. Now the mere distribution of wealth, the taking from one man's general resources and adding to those of another, essentially modifies the individual scales. Cobbetts are not bidders for fancy pug-dogs or rubies, and Crœsus is probably not a bidder for fustian cloth or tripe. If the whole income of this country were evenly distributed *per capita*, the place of diamonds on the relative scale would fall, for to buy a big diamond at present prices would mean starvation to the purchaser, and even if a man who now buys a big diamond continued to love it as much as he does now, he would not starve for it. Anything, therefore, which increases the total resources of some members of the community, and diminishes those of others, will *pro tanto* affect their estimates of the relative significance of different commodities. This will alter the elements of the communal scale of preferences, and the equilibrating price of any article will be affected, even though the tastes of the community and the total amount of the commodity remain the same.

Thus any actual transactions made in consequence of a mistake in estimating the equilibrating price at any given moment will theoretically alter the equilibrating price itself, even apart from its main effect in driving customers to the purchase of substitutes.[1] But although the consequences of mistakes may change the equilibrating price, there always exists ideally such a price at any given moment, if it can but be discovered; that is to say, there is always a price such that, if it were now recognised and proclaimed, a single set of transactions at that price would produce equilibrium. We have therefore reached a very definite conception of the

[1] Cf. Book II. Chap. III.

real or natural market price at any given moment. It is the price that corresponds to the point on the collective scale, as it actually exists at the moment, which would be reached if the rival dealers all read the minds of the purchasers correctly; that it to say, it is determined by the quantity of the commodity in the market, and the dispositions of the persons constituting the market. The price actually current in the market at any moment is determined and proclaimed in accordance with the conjectural estimates of those ultimate factors as read by the sellers.

We may now formulate the law of the market thus :—Since every desire for a unit that is gratified must stand objectively higher on the scale than any desire for a unit that is not gratified, it follows that if there are x units of the commodity in the market they will go to gratify the x desires for a unit highest on the scale. And since the price at which all the units are sold will be the same, and will be determined by the significance of the lowest desire for a unit that is gratified, it follows that the position of the xth unit on the collective scale will determine the market price. It will be readily understood, however, that the units in the collective scale taken *seriatim* will not each shew a decline that can be expressed in coin of the realm. If the supply of the English wheat market were 125,000,000 cwt., every two successive hundredweights would not shew a decline of even a farthing. Between any two prices, therefore, that the customs of the market recognise there will be many units, and we think of them all as marginal. They will represent the last units purchased by many individuals, and the lowest gratified desire for a unit on the part of each of these several purchasers will conform more closely in one case and less in another to the actual price. One will only just make up his mind to take it, and the other will be on the verge of taking a unit more, but the marginal units will occupy the same position upon all the individual scales to within the smallest sum that can be expressed in price. We may repeat this statement in several alternative forms: If there are x units of a commodity in the market they will go to the supply of the x estimates of a unit which stand highest on the relative scales of the purchasers, and will satisfy the claims of the purchasers *pari*

The law of the market.

passu down to a uniform degree of relative intensity; the point to which the supply will reach determines what that degree of relative intensity and the corresponding price shall be. Or: In order that any desire for a unit of the commodity should be gratified it must be one of the x desires that stand highest on the collective scale, and those desires that are just admitted, *i.e.* that take the lowest of these x highest places, coincide with the equilibrating price, and determine the price which will be paid for all. Or, to vary the formula once more: All the desires for a unit of the commodity which stand relatively higher on my scale than the point represented by the equilibrating price will be gratified, and none of those that stand lower will; and therefore the equilibrating price will exactly correspond with the gratified desire that stands lowest on the relative scale; all the other gratified desires will stand higher on the scale, and all desires that stand lower will fail to be gratified.

We shall now proceed to some further considerations which, while threatening to complicate our conception of the market, will in reality simplify it. Hitherto we have supposed that all the wares brought into the market are to be sold at any price that can be got, and that the minds of the sellers have been exclusively devoted to ascertaining what their goods will be worth to the customers at the various margins; except that in one instance the value that the wares might have to the seller himself was incidentally mentioned.[1] We must now go on to an express examination of this case. It may very well be that some or all of the dealers would rather not sell at all than sell below some particular price; that is to say, they have put a reserve price on their goods. There may be many reasons for this, the most obvious being that the goods have a direct and immediate use for the sellers themselves. A woman may bring her damsons to market, and may be willing to sell them if she can get a certain price for them, but may prefer keeping them for home consumption if she cannot get that price. Say that she will not sell unless she can get 5d. a pound. Another may be willing to sell at 4d., but will go no lower than that; and so forth. It might also well happen (theoretically it would be a

Sellers at a reserve price equivalent to buyers at that price.

[1] Page 218.

normal case) that just as the typical purchaser might be willing to buy plums at 6d., but would buy more at 5d. and more still at 4d., so the woman who brought her plums to market would reserve a few for her own consumption if it turned out that 5d. was the price that ruled the market, would reserve more if the price were 4d., but would sell her whole stock if she could get 6d. for them. That would simply mean that she preferred 6d. even to a single pound of damsons, but that if the choice was not between a pound of damsons and 6d., but between a pound of damsons and 5d., she would find a first and a second pound, and so on up to, say, a twenty-first pound, preferable to 5d., but 5d. preferable to a twenty-second pound; whereas if the alternative were a pound of damsons or 4d. she would prefer the twenty-eighth pound of damsons to the price in money, but would prefer the price in money to the twenty-ninth pound. In that case, if 4d. ruled in the market she would reserve 28 lbs. for her home use, if 5d. ruled she would reserve 21 lbs., and if 6d. ruled, none at all.

Now the reader will note that in making these suppositions we have simply been drawing up the position of successive pounds of plums on the relative scale of the stall-keeper, just as if she were a customer. If she prefers 6d. to a first pound of damsons, 5d. to a twenty-second, and 4d. to a twenty-ninth, the effect on the market is precisely the same as if all her plums were in possession of another seller who had no reserve price, and she herself were a potential purchaser of 28 lbs. at 4d., and of 21 lbs. at 5d., but of none at all at 6d.; and at the close of the market she will take home no plums if the ruling price is 6d., 21 lbs. if it is 5d., and 28 if it is 4d., just exactly as if she had come with the same relative scale into a market in which there was the same supply of plums, but none of them hers. It would be stretching language too far to talk of the seller at a reserved price as being a purchaser, but obviously her effect upon the market is precisely the same as if she were; and when we state the conditions that determine the market prices, in their ultimate forms of "quantity of the commodity in the market" and "relative scales of the persons constituting the market," we have already included in the latter not only the whole body of purchasers but the whole body of sellers at reserved prices.

In our first rough analysis of the market we distinguished between the buyers who know their own wants individually, and the sellers who form an estimate of the collective wants of the buyers, and also of the amount of the commodity which there is to satisfy them. But we must now substitute for this distinction between people the finer analysis that distinguishes between functions or capacities, and we shall see that the seller, whose primary function is to represent the whole body of consumers in his dealings with each individual consumer, may also himself be a consumer, and in that capacity may take his place by the side of the other consumers. This may be conveniently illustrated by taking the case of a farmer who has got in his wheat harvest and may thrash out and sell when he chooses. Let us follow him to the corn market with his specimens of wheat. If the prices that rule are low and he thinks they will rise later on, he will perhaps sell a certain amount of his stock, for he is pressed for a little ready money. But as the prices are not what he considers satisfactory, and as he expects them to improve, and as his want of ready money as distinct from his desire to maximise his total resources is a rapidly declining quantity, he will decline to sell the greater part of his stock. He may therefore have a very complete and sensitive scale of reserved prices, reserving the whole of his stock if prices are very low, and five-sixths, four-sixths, three-sixths, etc., according to a scale of rising prices. What is conceivable in the case of the plums, what seems natural in the case of the corn, may be very general in the case of livestock. Perhaps few men would take their horses, pigs, or sheep to the fair or market ready to sell them literally at any price they could get. There will, consciously or unconsciously, be some reserve price, however low, in almost every case; and if the farmer's stock is large, it is probable that he may be willing to sell a portion of it on terms which he would by no means accept for the whole.

Thus in considering markets, even of such perishable goods as damsons, or butter and eggs, much more in considering markets in general, when the nature of the goods is not specified, we must take into consideration the fact that different portions of the stock will be held back according to the prices that rule. Market price, then, depends on (1) the amount of the stock in the market, and (2) the scales of preference of all those persons who constitute the market; and this phrase includes those whom we think of as sellers as well as those whom we think of as buyers. If the farmer who goes to market with the hope of selling 1500 quarters of wheat will hold back none of his wheat at 28s., 100 quarters at 27s., 300 quarters at 26s., 700 at 25s., and his whole stock of 1500 at 24s., then he stands, with reference to his effect on the whole market, exactly as if he were two men, one of whom throws his whole 1500 quarters upon the market without reserve, and the other of whom comes to market simply as a purchaser and is willing to buy 100 quarters at 27s., 300 quarters at 26s., 700 quarters at 25s., and 1500 quarters at 24s. The whole of his 1500 quarters, then, must be regarded as being in the market, and his preferences must be included, together with those of the purchasers, in drawing up the general scale of preferences which, together with the quantity in the market, determines the equilibrating price.

Note, then, that just as buyers will take back from the market a relatively large amount of corn in preference to the money they have paid for it if prices are low, and a relatively small amount if prices are high, so, in precisely the same way, the sellers at a reserve will take back a relatively large amount of corn in preference to the money which they might have had instead of it if the prices are low, and a relatively small amount if prices are high. The seller at a reserve asserts his preference in competition with that of the purchasers just as much as the purchasers assert theirs in competition with each other. The purchaser's determination not to sell the last 100 quarters unless he can get 28s. for them, constitutes a conditional demand for 100 quarters of exactly the same nature as that of the buyer who is willing to take 100 quarters at 28s. if he cannot get them for less. The fact that the one man probably hoped that the price would be low and that he would bring a great deal of corn out of the market, leaving money instead of it, and that the other hoped that prices would be high and that he would take a great deal of money out of the market, leaving corn instead of it, simply means that each hopes to find that the things he has are high on the objective scale relatively to the things he has not. This is a circumstance important in many contexts, but not directly relevant to the fixing of the theoretical price. For this theoretical price is reached by ignoring, amongst other things, the sundry artifices by which, in accordance with their special interests, the persons constituting a market endeavour to conceal or modify the ultimate facts; which ultimate facts are the amount of stock, and the state of their own and other people's preferences.

The theoretical identity of the purchaser, and the seller with a reserved price, or rather the fact that the true analysis must distinguish between functions rather than organs, is very clearly seen in the case of a sale by auction, where the owner of the property is willing to sell a number of things if he can get satisfactory prices for them, but is not willing to sell them without reserve. The articles are all put up to sale, and the owner himself may, if he likes, appear in the crowd of bidders and assert his own scale of preferences exactly like the rest, by offering a price, though what he is actually doing is not offering to buy, but refusing to sell. The form in which this is done is usually to give the auctioneer instructions not to sell under a certain price, but the fact that this is popularly called "buying in" shews that the points of identity between holding and buying have, in this instance at least, been generally grasped. *Illustration of sale by auction.*

Returning to the country market, it may strain the reader's imagination to think of a stall-keeper who has brought damsons to the market, intending to sell, finding the ruling price so low that, instead of selling the whole, or even any part of her stock, she becomes a purchaser of more. Yet to suppose this would only mean that under some circumstances a seller might buy in all his own stock, and then further become a purchaser of the stock of others, and this supposition is by no means extravagant. A peasant who grows a little choice fruit never thinks of eating it; he will tell you that he cannot afford to eat it. Many Norwegian peasants make butter for the market, and buy margarine to eat. So a fairly well-to-do farmer's wife may sell the plums she thinks will fetch the best price, and make her winter stock of jam out of a commoner sort, gathered from her own trees or bought in the market; and if for any reason she has been widely mistaken in her expectations as to the price at which she could sell any particular fruit, she might find it best to keep and use, and even to add to, what she had originally meant to sell, and sell what she had meant to keep and use. The reverse case, which illustrates the same theory, is more easily realised. A housewife who has just gathered her own damsons and goes to a closely adjacent market with the intention of buying more, and proceeding to a jam boiling on a lordly scale, may find the prices so unexpectedly high as to induce her hastily to send home for her stock and sell the whole of it, perceiving that, at such a price, there are many available substitutes for the damsons which would come cheaper for her own winter use.

But we have already seen that the stall-keepers may refuse to sell at a certain price for other reasons than that the goods in question would be worth this reserved price to themselves for their own uses and purposes. They refuse early in the morning to sell at prices which would get rid of their whole stock in a few hours or minutes because they expect a constant flow of potential customers throughout the day. At the moment, then, they have a reserve price, not on their own account, to meet their personal wants, but in anticipation of the wants of others. At the moment these anticipations determine the place which the commodity takes on their own relative scales just as much as if they wanted it for their own use; and if this speculative holding of stocks ceased, the price would tumble down. In the case of swiftly perishable commodities that deteriorate by frequent transport, such as fresh fruit, we probably think of the wares as coming into the hands of the ultimate consumers within a few hours. In such cases we hardly realise that the attempt of the sellers to hit the equilibrating price for the whole day is really of the nature of a speculative holding back of the commodity, and keeps up the market price. It is, however, of exactly the same nature as actions that we think of at once in this light. Here, as elsewhere, it is only a question of degree. Take wheat, for example. When the farmer has harvested his crop he does not necessarily contemplate getting rid of it within a few hours,

Speculative holding essential to the constitution of a market.

or even a few days or weeks, and his attempt to gauge the mind of the purchasers might include in its scope the probable wants of eleven months hence. Speculation enters no more really into his dealings than it does into those of the stall-keeper with the stock of plums who thinks of the persons who will be in the market six hours hence, but it enters more obviously, and is more easily recognised as speculative, because it covers a longer period. The stall-keeper does not recognise her own doings as speculative, but the seller of wheat very probably does; and therefore it is more likely that speculative buying will become specialised and that the grower and the dealer will be different persons in the case of wheat than in the case of plums. Indeed we do not readily think of speculation in plums at all. If we think of an intended seller of plums becoming a purchaser because of the low price plums are fetching, we take it for granted that she wants them for her own use. It does not readily occur to us (nor to her either) that if she believes the right price to be 6d., and if a neighbouring stall-keeper is selling at 4d., it would be good business for her to buy up her neighbour's stock to sell again; and yet it would obviously be so if her estimate is correct. In the corn market, on the other hand, where speculation has reached the conscious stage, we can easily imagine a farmer taking up some of the functions of a dealer. In that case, if he came to the market to sell, but found that corn was at a considerably lower figure than he thought the facts would ultimately justify, he might buy corn instead of selling it. And of course any person who neither possessed a stock of wheat nor expected to need any great quantity for his own use might, in like manner, buy at a low figure, simply because he expected customers to be forthcoming willing to pay a higher price later on in the season.

Thus, while we think in the first instance of the purchasers as the persons who want the commodity for use, and of the seller as reflecting the minds of the purchasers who are not present at the moment, it is obvious on reflection that the parts may be reversed. The possessor of a stock of any commodity may himself be a potential consumer, and in that case his wants are registered on the collective scale of preferences; and on the other hand the function of reader of the public mind, anticipator of future wants, or speculator as to the wants of the portion of the public not present in person, may be taken by the buyer who does not possess, just as well as by the seller who possesses.

We can now restate the function of the market with a fuller insight into some of the conceptions it involves. A market is the machinery by which those on whose scales of preference any commodity is relatively high are brought into communication with those on whose scales it is relatively low, in order that exchanges may take place to mutual satisfaction until equilibrium is established. But this process will always and necessarily occupy time. The persons potentially constituting the market will not all be present at the same time, and therefore the composition of the collective scale (on which, together with the total amount of the commodity in existence, the ideal point of equilibrium depends) must be a matter of estimate and conjecture. The transactions actually conducted at any moment will be determined in relation to the anticipated possibilities of transactions at other moments. Speculation as to these future possibilities will be more or less elaborate and conscious according to the nature of the market and the length of time over which the adjustment will be likely to extend. But speculation is always present when any possessor of the commodity refuses to sell at the moment at a price which he knows he will be prepared to accept ultimately (whether an hour or eleven months hence), if satisfied that he can do no better; or if any purchaser refuses at the moment to give a price to which he knows he will ultimately be willing to rise should the alternative be to go without the commodity; or if any one buys at a price below which he would ultimately sell sooner than keep the stock for his own use. The legitimate function of such speculation is to secure the transaction of business on a broader view, and on a correcter estimate of the whole range of relevant facts, than could be arrived at without it. If no one at first has a correct conception of the facts, a series of tentative estimates, and the observation of the transactions that take place under their influence, may gradually reveal them; and if we could eliminate all error from speculative estimates and could reduce derivative preferences to

Restatement of the function of a market.

exact correspondence with the primary preferences which they represent, and on which they are based, the actual price would always correspond with the ideal price.

But as liability to error is incident to speculation by its very nature, and as it plays a really important commercial part in some markets, it is natural that certain people should specialise in taking the risks, and should receive some remuneration for it. It is in fact the principle of all insurance. Dealings in wheat and cotton "futures" furnish a good example. We will take cotton. It is often important for a manufacturer to be able to know at what price he will be able to get raw cotton some months hence, in order that he may at once take a contract to supply so much cotton cloth at such and such times with better knowledge of what his expenses will be. But it would not be convenient to him actually to buy and store the raw cotton in advance. He therefore enters into a bargain with a dealer to supply him with so much cotton of specified quality, say three months hence, at a certain price. This is ordering "future" cotton. The seller has not the goods, but he reckons on being able to get them when the time for fulfilling his bargain comes, at a price which will remunerate him for his risk and his work. If he deals on a large scale and knows his business his risk will be small, for his mistakes in over- and under-estimating the price at which he will finally have to buy will cancel each other; but the risks of his individual clients, being taken over a smaller area and with less specialised knowledge, would be considerable. They are therefore willing to avert them by paying a small commission, in the disguised form of prices slightly in excess on the average of what the actual market prices will be.

Speculative markets in "futures."

Beyond this simple and commercially useful speculation there is an immense amount of gambling in wheat and cotton "futures"; and since all anticipations are ultimately based on the place of wheat or cotton on actual scales of significance, and on the volume of the crops, and as we have seen that it may be to a dealer's advantage that he should know the truth himself and that others should not know it, it may often happen that speculators have a strong interest in circulating false reports as to an anticipated shortage, say, in the cotton crop. But the general question of speculative markets we will reserve for treatment in connection with the stock market, to which we may now proceed.

The market in stocks and shares, as well as giving occasion for all we need say on the subject of purely speculative or gambling markets, furnishes excellent examples of many of the points we have already touched on. Only a very broad and general treatment will be attempted here. In practice there are innumerable complications and refinements, the consideration of which would only be confusing. We will begin with the issue of loans. If a Government attempts to raise a loan at 6 or 4 or $2\frac{1}{2}$ per cent it makes a definite promise to pay so much a year. It calls this promise £100 at 6 per cent, or whatever it may be. What it really is, is a promise to pay £6 per annum with the option (under whatever conditions may be named) of cancelling this promise by the payment of £100. This promise, with this condition, it offers for sale at a certain price, £99 or £86 or whatever it may be, which is its estimate of what will be the marginal value of its promises (when issued to the extent contemplated) to pay such and such an annual sum. If its anticipations are correct, or are an underestimate, the loan will be successfully negotiated. If it has overestimated the marginal significance of its promise the loan will fail.

The stock market. New issues.

But some of those who purchase the Government's promises will do so merely as tradesmen buy goods for stock, in order to sell them again at a profit. This they do on a speculative estimate of the place which the promises will ultimately take on the collective scale of the public. Their calculations may be correct; or it may be that they have formed an underestimate and that they, or those to whom they first sold, make handsome profits before the stock settles down into the hands of those who themselves really want to draw their £6 or £2 : 10s. a year in return for their money. Or, on the other hand, it may happen that the speculative buyers overestimate the interest of the public, and although the loan is " negotiated " successfully, yet when the original purchasers for stock attempt to place their shares among the public they find that they can only do so at a lower figure than they had anticipated, perhaps at an absolute loss.

An interesting case of this occurred a few years ago. In April 1902, towards the end of the Boer War, the British Government desired to negotiate a loan of £32,000,000. They offered a nominal £100 at 2½ per cent (that is to say, a claim for £2 : 10s. per annum) at £93 : 10s., and whereas they asked for £32,000,000 only, no less than £350,000,000 was "subscribed" for; that is to say, persons representing an aggregate demand for a nominal £350,000,000 declared that they were desirous of purchasing for £93 : 10s. a claim for £2 : 10s. per annum. This would seem at first sight to mean that, whereas the Government believed that an issue of three hundred and twenty thousand fresh promises would bring the marginal significance of a Government promise to pay £2 : 10s. a year down to £93 : 10s., the buyers, who either wished to hold the promises or expected to be able to sell them at a profit, estimated that it would require three million five hundred thousand such promises to bring the marginal value down to that figure. But this is not really the case; for many of those who applied for a certain number of shares did not either expect or wish to get them all. They believed indeed that the whole three hundred and twenty thousand promises, and more, could ultimately be placed out at something above £93 : 10s., so that they could get a reasonable profit on any that were assigned to them, and they believed that if every individual purchaser applied for as many as he wished to hold or expected to be able to sell at a profit more than the whole issue would be applied for. In that case, obviously some would get less than they asked for. So the best chance for a man to get as many as he wanted was to apply for more. It is true that every one would not be able to get all he wanted in any case, for there would not be enough to supply them, but the man who made a modest claim for the amount he wanted might get a fraction of it only, whereas if he applied for two or three or ten or twenty times as much as he wanted he might come nearer his true mark; and if he turned out to be amongst the boldest and shrewdest he might get just what he wanted. But this is risky. It all depends on what other people ask for. A man might find that he had overshot the mark, and having asked for twenty times as much as he wanted might actually get twice as much. It is the consideration of this risk that limits his application. Thus three million five hundred thousand was not a genuine record of how many promises the buyers, speculative and other, collectively desired to hold, or expected to be able to sell at a profit over £93 : 10s., but was the complex resultant of each man's estimate of what he himself could profitably hold or deal in, and what he expected other men would ask for, beyond what they could profitably hold or sell. Leaving this aside, we return to the fact that the speculative buyers thought that the whole stock could be placed well above £93 : 10s. On the day of issue the market value of the stock was £93 : 15s.

Soon afterwards the war came to an end, and the natural expectation was that the holders would be in a still better position than before; for the Government was now sure not to borrow any more money, that is to say, not to put any more Consols on the market, and seeing that an additional supply lowers the marginal value of any stock, this averted a danger. But to every one's surprise Consols fell, and ultimately, on December 9 of the same year, they reached their lowest point of £92 : 2 : 6. This shewed that the purchasers had overestimated the marginal significance of the stock to persons who actually desired to buy a right to £2 : 10s. a year on Government security. The Government, however, had negotiated their loan on their own terms, and it was the speculators (not necessarily the original speculators, some or all of whom would have got rid of their Consols before this time) who bore the loss.

It must be carefully observed that when Consols rise or fall there is never at any time the slightest doubt as to the exact promise that is being purchased or the certainty that it will be kept. The revenue a holder derives from his stock in Consols is in no way affected by a change in their price, and when the "credit" of the Government is said to be better or worse than it was this does not mean that there is the slightest estimated risk of its failing punctually to fulfil its promises. It merely means that the marginal significance attached by the public to the certainty of receiving from the Government £2 : 10s. per annum has risen or fallen.

If it is a question not of negotiating a loan but of floating a Company the process might take many forms. It might be in part similar to the one we have just examined. The Company, on the credit of its rights or property, might issue " debentures," or definite promises to pay so much a year in return for such a sum of money paid down. As the public will always prefer Government security to any other, the Company in that case would have to promise a higher rate of interest than that offered by the Government in order to induce people to invest in it. That is to say, it would not be able to sell its promises to pay £1 a year for so much as the Government can. But in principle it would be selling the same thing, namely, a claim to an annual (or half-yearly or quarterly) revenue. It might also issue "preference shares" in the form of promises to pay the holders sums dependent, up to a certain point, upon the degree of success which the Company realises. That is to say, the Company might undertake, after paying the sums due on the debentures and making proper allowance for a reserve fund, for replacement of stock and so forth, to devote any surplus to the payment of dividends to the holders of preference stock up to, say, $4\frac{1}{2}$ or 5 per cent. Then there would be "ordinary shares." The holders of these might be entitled to nothing at all unless there was a further surplus after the holders of the preference stock had received their full percentage, but might then be entitled to the whole of that surplus, however great, without sharing it with the holders of debentures or preference stock.

In such a case the holders of debentures know exactly what they are invited to buy: it is so many pounds and shillings a year; and it is as safe as the credit of the Company can make it. The holders of preference shares do not know so well what they are buying; for the Company may remain solvent, but may not be able to pay the full percentage up to which these preference shareholders have the first claim. They know that they will not get more than a certain revenue, but they cannot be quite sure that they will get as much. And, again, the holders of ordinary stock know still less what they are buying; for the Company, while remaining solvent, may pay them no dividends at all; but, on the other hand, if it turns out to be successful, there is no limit placed on the dividends they may receive.

R

All these different stocks may therefore be offered to the public, and, as in the case of the loan, they may be applied for, partly by people who want to hold them, and partly by people who think they can sell them at a profit. The different stocks—debenture, preference, and ordinary—may, on the day of issue, all stand at different prices in the market; but there are regulations against allowing Companies to issue their stock at a discount. That is to say, a Company that says its capital is £100,000 must actually have received at least that sum, minus such charges as may be legitimately put down to expenses of issue, and are set forth as such in their published statements; whereas a Government or a Municipality may call its obligation to pay £3 : 10s. or £6 a year £100, and may sell it at £99 or £93, or what it can get.

When once the stock is issued, however, though it goes on being called £100, it is really a claim for a certain fixed sum per annum, or for a fixed fractional share in a sum of undetermined amount dependent upon the success of the concern and the judgment of the directors; and it will sell in the market for what it is worth.

Turning now from new issues to dealings in existing stock, we ask, "When equilibrium is once established, why is it ever disturbed?" New issues are analogous to annual crops. A large amount of the commodity comes into existence at a certain point or points of the commercial organism, and must be distributed thence over the whole. But when a stock has been thus distributed, and is in a state of equilibrium in the hands of those on whose relative scales it stands highest, so that no one who does not possess it values it, relatively to other things in the circle of exchange, as highly as any one who has it; why is there still a market in it?

Why and how stock changes hands.

The amount of the stock is by hypothesis fixed for the time being. At this moment, in the spring of 1909, British Consols, for instance, amount to £577,342,017, the 5 per cent Preference Stock of the Great Western Railway to £11,925,808, and Fiji Debentures to £70,900. These amounts will satisfy the demands of holders down to a certain point, and if that point of equilibrium were once reached, and if conditions of exchange supervened, it could only be because the relative position of the stock at the margin on some of the scales (whether of holders or non-holders) had changed. But this may happen for many reasons. The credit of the Government or the prospects of the concern may have changed, and the change may be differently estimated by different persons, thus producing a disturbance of equilibrium. Or the position and circumstances of the holders themselves may change. "There is a time to buy and a time to sell," says the Preacher. The man who is making a handsome income, and who wishes presently to retire from business (or fears that business may "retire from him"), wishes to save. The man who has been saving in his early married life with a view to heavy expenditure on the education or establishment of his children wishes to spend his savings. And men are continuously passing from one of these states to the other. Or men die, and their investments are not in the most convenient form for carrying out the provisions of their wills, or their heirs have their own view as to the significance of various stocks. Or for a thousand other reasons, good, bad, or indifferent, but all of them connected with actual circumstances, wants, and estimates, the stock shifts its place on the scales of certain individuals. Its marginal significance rises on some scales and falls on others, or rises or falls unequally on different scales. And so it will come about that though the great majority of the stocks are still in the hands of persons who value them at the margin as highly as any one else does, so that on the great majority of scales they are still in equilibrium, there will nevertheless be a few shares which are marginally lower on the scale of their possessors than they are on the scale of certain others, who either possess none or who possess some, but are ready to purchase more. If this is so, the conditions for exchange exist; and since it is difficult for the persons concerned to find each other out individually, there is room for the services of agents and dealers, who will buy from those who are prepared to sell (either with a reserve price or unconditionally), and sell to those who are prepared to buy at suitable prices. Any one, therefore, who has reason to believe or to know that there are or may be persons on whose scales the marginal significance of any of his stock is higher or lower, as the case may be, than it is on his own, may instruct a broker to sell or buy for him either unconditionally or at any moment at which he can get such and such terms. And the broker, at a moment determined by the nature of his order, goes to a jobber whose business it is to deal in such stocks. He does not tell the jobber whether he is instructed to buy or to sell, but simply tells him *how much* stock he wishes to deal in, and asks him to "make a price" for (technically "in") that quantity. Suppose the price the jobber makes is $98\frac{3}{8} - \frac{5}{8}$. That means that he offers either to sell the specified amount of stock at £98 : 12 : 6, or to buy it at £98 : 7 : 6 per nominal £100, and undertakes to produce the money or the stock on the settling day, which (in London and in the general market) occurs twice in the month. If the price made by the jobber complies with the terms of the broker's instructions, and the latter does not think he is likely to get better terms elsewhere, the bargain is struck, and the broker sells or buys for his client at the jobber's price, and charges a commission.

It is clear, therefore, that the ultimate buyer and seller will not meet unless the difference in the marginal position of the stock on their scales is pronounced enough to leave a surplus of advantage on each side after payment of a double commission to the broker and the subtraction of the difference between the buying and selling price of the jobber; for what the seller receives is short of what the purchaser pays by these sums. Thus there will presumably be disturbance of equilibrium, that the market does not rectify, of every degree within these limits, but the market will not allow the disturbance to transgress these limits.

Now the jobber, being a dealer, buys only in order to sell, and in making a price he may be regarded ideally as estimating that the price at which he buys (technically known as the "selling price," because it is the price at which the public can sell) will induce as many sales on the part of the public as the price at which he sells (technically "the buying price") will induce purchases. That is to say, he estimates that there are as many shares in the hands of holders, on whose scale they are below his buying price minus the broker's commission, as will suffice to bring the marginal value of this stock on the scales of all other persons down to his selling price plus the broker's commission.

But this estimate, just because it is an estimate, is to

some degree speculative and liable to error; and the jobber may find that in order to sell what he has bought, or in order to put himself into the position of being able to deliver the stock he has sold, he may have to lower his selling or raise his buying price, and thus the prices may change because the jobbers have miscalculated the dispositions of the public. And, again, the dispositions of the public may actually change between the day on which a bargain is made and the settling day; either because something has really happened to affect the credit or prospects of certain Companies, or because new possibilities of investment have been opened, or because there is a growing feeling of confidence and enterprise abroad, or because some general shock, or disaster, or rumour has affected the public resources or the public nerves, or for any other reason. And, therefore, it may happen that before the settling day comes, persons who have bought stock at a certain price may find that they could sell it again at a profit even after paying another commission. And it may be that the causes which have produced this change of price do not affect them, so that, while preferring to hold the stock at the price they gave for it, they prefer selling it at the price it now commands. Naturally, a man who prefers £4 : 10s. a year to £100 may prefer £101 to £4 : 10s. a year. So a man who had bought at £100 (including all commissions) with the full intention of holding, and drawing his dividends, might be glad to resell before the time for settling came, at a net price of £101. In that case his broker would debit him with the price of the stock when he bought it, and credit him with the price when he sold it, charge his commission, and then pay over the balance; and there would never be any "settlement" in the shape of transfer of stock and payment of money at all. Into the machinery by which such "clearances" of mutually cancelling transactions are conducted we need not enter.[1]

But this change in the market price of stock, which is a modifying influence affecting a genuine buyer's or seller's estimate of the most eligible alternative, may be considered in itself, and may become the subject of a purely speculative transaction. That is to say, a man may buy stock not because he wants to hold it and draw *Speculation in stocks.*

[1] Cf. Book II. Chap. VII.

the dividends, but because he expects it to rise, and means to sell it again before the settling day, when he would have to pay for it; and in like manner a man may sell stock not because he wants the money instead of the dividends, but because he expects the price to go down, and means to buy the stock back before the settling day, when he would be required to deliver it. And in such cases, manifestly, the buyer need not possess the ready money, and the seller need not own the stock. They will only have to receive or pay on the settling day the difference between the prices at which they have bought and sold, minus or plus the two commissions. And this transaction, if deliberately engaged in, is of the nature of a speculation or bet on the rise or fall of the stock. An immense majority of the commissions given to brokers are thus " cleared " before the settling day, and are presumably of a consciously speculative character. It is to be noted that neither brokers nor jobbers, as such, are speculators in the proper sense. The broker works for a commission, and the jobber, though obliged to form speculative estimates, relies for his profits upon the difference between his buying and selling prices, and would make his profit if there were not any change in the level of prices; whereas persons who buy to sell, or sell to buy in, are actuated solely by anticipations of a rise or fall sufficient to cover the commissions and leave a margin of profit. As a class they must lose, for what the gainers gain is not all that the losers lose, but that sum with the commissions subtracted. When we hear that a private individual is ruined because he has " made unfortunate speculations on the Stock Exchange," it is probable that it is the extent and not the nature of his transactions that has ruined him. It is the commission that has broken him. His luck has not been prevailingly bad or good, but he has tried his luck so often, always paying for the privilege, that he has nothing left with which to try it again.

It is not necessary for our present purpose to enter any further upon the machinery or the proceedings of the Stock Exchange; but a very few words may be useful. If a transaction has not been cancelled by a transaction in the opposite sense before the settling day, it must then be settled. But on " contango " day, which is the day but one before " settling day," persons who are under contract to pay money, or to deliver stock which they do not possess, will have to make arrangements for the settlement, and this they may do either by borrowing money or borrowing stock to meet their obligations, thus settling their account with the Stock Exchange, but remaining liable to persons outside the market; or by making arrangements to "carry over" their obligations to the next settling day, which is equivalent to borrowing within the market itself. Borrowing stock (a comparatively rare operation in most markets) consists in receiving stock, depositing money in security for the return not of the identical certificates, but of others of the same stock, and undertaking meanwhile to secure the lender in all the pecuniary privileges that would have accrued to him had the stock remained in his name. Into the technicalities of "carrying over" we need not enter. Nor need we discuss the purchase and sale of "options," which is merely another form of betting on the rise or fall of stocks.

The reader will perceive that the element of speculation enters by imperceptible degrees into such transactions in wheat or cotton "futures," or in stocks, as we have been examining. At the one end are the genuine buyers and sellers, whose requirements are different, so that the article dealt in signifies at the margin more to the one than to the other; at the other end are the pure speculators, who have no notion of either buying or selling, but bet on the points at which those who do buy and sell will find their equilibrium from day to day. And between these are the dealers who are forced to form estimates, and to that extent to speculate, and the buyers and sellers, who are keenly alive to the changes of the market, and who are influenced more or less, but not wholly, by their anticipations of its movements. But so long as there is any real market at all, that is to say, so long as there is any commodity or privilege which is actually being bought and sold, the quantity of that commodity that exists, and the communal scale of preferences, determine its marginal significance, and therefore its price, at any moment. Speculative purchasers and holders count just as much as others do if they actually purchase and hold, but, as their ultimate purpose is to sell, they are speculating on the prices at which they will be able to unload. That is to say, they speculate on the conditions of the market as they withdraw from it; and these conditions depend of course, ultimately, on the values attached to the stock by the genuine purchasers who mean to hold. The speculators who do not buy at all, but merely bet, can only affect the market in an indirect and transitory manner.

The great law of the market, then, holds its way, in the main, subject only to secondary disturbances from the fringe of speculative and gambling transactions that twines around it. But when the speculation consists in the establishment of a " corner " or monopoly [1] it may produce a disastrous disorganisation, and the gambling is always ruinous collectively to those who engage in it and profitable only to the agents.

We have now completed our analysis of various types of the open and competitive market; and we shall have no difficulty in understanding other forms of sale in which some of the conditions we have assumed are modified. It will be remembered that the function of a market is to bring into communication with each other persons on whose scales one or more commodities occupy different relative places; and henceforth we shall speak of a market wherever there is any institution, machinery, or system of connections that performs this function. The wider the area of communication and the more intimate its nature, the more nearly do we approach the ideal market. But however contracted the area and however imperfect the communication, the essential characteristic of a market is manifested *pro tanto*, if there is any contact or communication at all. Thus, in an oriental bazaar where the principle of fixity of retail price does not exist even nominally, the seller declines the function of putting present and absent potential purchasers into open relation with each other. He tries to isolate each customer, and should he succeed, it is more than likely that if half a dozen of his customers met, after transacting business with him, they would find that they were very far from having brought their several scales into equilibrium with each other, and they might probably be able to transact business with each other on terms of mutual satisfaction. In such a

Other forms of sale. The oriental bazaar.

[1] See pages 256 *sqq.*

case the bazaar can hardly be said to establish a market price in any sense, except so far as it affords a field of observation for any one who has time and skill to profit by it. All we can say is that in each bargain the seller's bottom price is still determined (for the moment) by his speculations as to what he could get from other customers or (ultimately) by what the article would be worth to himself, whereas the purchaser's top price is determined (ultimately) by the place the article occupies on his own scale or (for the moment) by what he believes he could induce some other dealer to part with it for. And the question of what other customers will pay depends on their scales and the question of what other dealers will take depends upon their estimates of the amount of the commodity on sale and their surmises as to the scales of possible purchasers. Thus even here the same facts ultimately govern the situation, but the sellers make no pretence of helping to reveal them to the buyers.

At the opposite extreme to this individual bargaining on each transaction is the fixed price of commodities and services which is said to be determined in Indian villages by rigid tradition. Here the economic pressures fail to break the resistance offered by a mental conception of the fitness of things; but they are effective within the limits so prescribed. A man will not buy unless the article or service is worth the price to him; and he will hardly continue to make the article, or render the service, if any preferable alternative is open to him. I have known a Scandinavian peasant decline an order for a baling-spoon because it was not worth his while to make it at the traditional price, and he would not charge, or even consent to receive, anything above it. There was no other artist that could supply his place in the neighbourhood, so that he could have raised his price with perfect security. But even if the force of tradition had not only prevented him from raising his price, but had also compelled him to accept the order, he would still have had the resource of executing the order at his leisure and meanwhile turning to more eligible alternative applications of his time. *Traditional prices.*

In the case of the retail sellers in any city or district, there is a loosely organised market of the same type as that in the country market-place, but it may be more difficult for the individual purchaser to know the different prices of goods in all the different shops than to compare the prices in the different stalls; and as distances are greater one shop may perhaps safely charge the customers in its neighbourhood a rather higher price than they would have to pay half a mile or a mile farther from their home, even if they are aware of the difference. Here it will be a question of each individual customer estimating the marginal significance of the penny spent or saved, and the sacrifice involved in travelling the extra distance. Again, a very high percentage of the marketers in a country town are more or less expert purchasers, and can judge accurately of the quality of the goods and grade them with some fineness, whereas a large percentage of the customers at the shop will have to take the shopman's word, in many cases, for the superiority of a more highly priced article. Hence there is a general feeling that the shopman is bound faithfully to communicate his special information both as to current prices and as to the true quality of the goods to the customer. It is understood that a small fee to him as an expert adviser is included in the price he charges, and if he does not honestly render the corresponding service some resentment is justified. All these considerations constitute special features and limitations of this market, but they leave the essential principles unaffected.

<small>Retail trade.</small>

Retail prices, however, sometimes offer a stubborn resistance to economic pressures even in a highly organised industrial community. The retail price of some articles seems to acquire a traditional fixity of an almost constitutional nature. When, a generation ago, a celebrated firm of London hat-makers raised the price of their silk hats, people were so much startled and shocked that they began to wonder whether they would be charged 1s. 1d. at the turnstile of the Royal Academy. In the retail market all kinds of frictions and conventions obstruct the action of changed economic conditions. The effect of these changes has to force its way through narrower channels in the case of retail than in the case of wholesale prices. Hence wholesale markets are notoriously more sensitive than retail. No doubt this is partly because many retail prices can only be modified

<small>Resistance of retail prices to change.</small>

by relatively large units. Fluctuations of even a farthing on a half-quartern loaf constitute a considerable percentage on the price, and this is the smallest variation that can express itself in the retail trade; whereas much smaller proportional differences may express themselves in the wheat and flour markets. But this does not explain everything. Sometimes there is a combination amongst the retailers to keep up the price, and limit the sale. An importer of bananas found that he could not sell his imports in Liverpool because the retailers would not lower the selling price, and the customers would not buy the increased supply at the current prices. He was obliged to import six London costermongers to hawk the bananas at the cheap rate in order to break down the combination. Sometimes on the contrary there is a custom that prevents prices being raised. The supply of milk in the country is often uncertain, but if the farmer cannot meet all the requirements of his customers he does not raise the price, as he often could do, and so cut off the demands lowest on the relative scales. He tells each customer how much "he can let him have" that day, and charges the usual price. It is difficult to give any reason for this except that it is the custom. In London, too, the retail price of milk is constant, but a milk famine caused by a heavy fall of snow will break through the tradition, and famine prices will be charged. But it is interesting to note that in such a crisis the milkman may probably assume, within limits, an uncommercial attitude, and may ask some of his customers to go short of a little of the supply they would have taken even at the famine price so as to enable him to allow more to a neighbouring house where there is a baby. In this case the price is not strictly competitive. It may be noticed, further, that retail prices often retain an obstinate connection with the units of small change. It has often been observed that minor expenses are lighter in a country in which the unit is the franc than those in which it is the florin. And sometimes the effect of a system of coinage long abolished may still be traced in the scale of retail prices. But we need not enter into further details. It is enough to have pointed out how the law of the market manifests itself in retail trade, and how many varied forces combine with it, react upon it, and impede it.

Sale by auction furnishes an example of another type of market. Here, as in the oriental bazaar, the seller declines to name the price, and tries to get the maximum amount for each separate lot. His public, however, is restricted, and as each lot is put up and disposed of in its announced order he cannot hold back his goods on an estimate of the wants of possible purchasers not present at the moment but likely to appear before the market closes; whereas the purchasers may regulate their bids by their knowledge of possibilities of purchase elsewhere open. Where there are a number of lots of approximately the same character and value, offered in succession, the purchasers undertake the speculative estimate of each other's scales of preference, and a man who would give £10 for any one of eight lots sooner than go without, may decline to bid more than £5 for the first because he thinks that when the seven relatively highest demands have been satisfied, no unsatisfied demand will be left that stands above £5 on any one's scale. He may be disappointed. Others may be playing the same game, and when the last lot is put up, a rival who would have let him have the first lot at £5 : 5s. may run him up to his £10 limit for the last, or may take it from him at £10 : 5s.

The notorious uncertainty of the results of a *bona fide* sale by auction, if the purchasers are not experts, illustrates the important part that accidental circumstances may play in an imperfect market, the operations of which are contracted to a few minutes. And the failure of such a market to secure a final equilibrium is illustrated by the frequency with which bargains are made and re-sales effected on the ground, before the company disperses. But the fundamentally determining conditions are just the same as in the ordinary market. The quantity of the commodity on the spot, or elsewhere conveniently accessible, and the relative scales of the persons present, as affected by their own wants or their estimates of the wants of others with whom they can subsequently deal, are the underlying facts which determine the prices.

It is hardly necessary to follow this line of inquiry any further. Sales by Dutch auction, and clearance sales in shops, for instance, will readily yield to the same analysis.

The sellers of a commodity often succeed in establishing

two or more markets and keeping them separate. That is to say, they manage to deal with several groups of purchasers who are not aware of each other's doings, and who therefore never come to constitute a single market. Their object is to extract a higher price from those more willing or more able to pay, and at the same time to draw in the poorer purchasers by offering them lower terms. It is currently and credibly stated that the same milkman in London will supply the same quality of milk at different prices in different streets. A lady who happens, through any circumstances, to be living in a house which suggests a larger income than her dress or general style does, may easily find that as long as she takes her purchases away from certain shops without leaving her address she gets things at what she regards as reasonable prices, but if she yields to the urgent request of the shopman to be allowed to send the goods home, as soon as her address is known the prices are raised against her. The shopmen in some fashionable streets are said to have different morning and afternoon prices, and cases are reported of wealthy ladies, of an economic turn, who have sent humbler friends or dependants in the morning to ascertain and note the price of a number of articles, and have themselves come in their carriages in the afternoon to make their selection, and have insisted on paying no more than the price mentioned to the pedestrian witness of the morning (whom they have brought with them), as against the very different prices cited to them in the afternoon.

Deliberate separation of markets in the same commodity.

In this and similar cases, where a differentiation is successfully carried out, the purchases of those to whom the higher tariff is charged are no doubt less in extent than they would otherwise have been; and the tradesman must either be willing to do a smaller amount of business at a larger profit, or must find a market for his surplus goods at a still lower figure than that at which he might have sold them to his better-class customers. To have made all into a single market, however, would have involved a lowering of prices over the whole area of his transactions; and the still greater lowering of the price of a portion of them which is now necessary may be more than compensated for by the maintenance of a high level over the

The theory of "reduced terms" and of "dumping."

rest of his dealings. Nor does it follow that such a tradesman is making exorbitant profits. It is conceivable that he could not carry on trade successfully by any other process; for it may be that his general expenses are such that if he had but one price, whether high or low, he would be unable to conduct business remuneratively; if high, because he would not have a sufficient volume of custom, if low, because it would not be sufficiently profitable. But if, having secured his expensive site and all other needful apparatus, he can secure high prices for a considerable portion of his wares, and without any considerable addition to his initial and general expenditure can increase his volume of trade by adding a low price section, then this latter addition may just enable him to carry on his business; for it may afford him some advance on the out-of-pocket expenses on the particular stock, though not on a high enough scale, were it uniform, to meet his whole expenses and yield him a suitable income.

A particularly clear and familiar case that illustrates this process is that of a private school in which pupils are freely received on reduced terms. Where the school is so well established that the Principal could, if he chose, always keep it full at the nominal terms, or would only run a comparatively small risk of having vacancies, then of course to take a pupil at reduced terms is to make a genuine commercial sacrifice; and unless it is made for the sake of securing a valuable connection, or some other similar purpose, it will be an act of benevolence towards the persons who are allowed to pay the lower terms. The Principal in that case is actuated by other than economic considerations in the transaction. But it may well be that the prospect of filling the house with pupils at the nominal terms is remote, or at best uncertain; and seeing that all such expenses as rent, salaries, and so forth, must be incurred whether the house is full or, say, only two-thirds full, it will be better to have boys who pay anything more than their keep than to have absolute vacancies. The expenses, it is true, could not be met or the establishment run on these terms if they were general. But there are always a certain number of full-paying pupils, and there are occasional runs of good fortune during which the house is full or nearly full of such. And pupils at reduced terms break the severity of the loss when vacancies are not filled by pupils on full terms. But occasionally mistakes will be made. A boy will be taken on reduced terms, and it will be found that he actually excludes a full-paying pupil who subsequently applies, though it was not anticipated that he would do so. Under these circumstances it will be to the master's credit if the poor but favoured boy is treated with the full measure of cordiality which might naturally have fallen to him under other circumstances. Or again it may happen that a boy who is eligible on account of his connection, or of abilities which seem likely to do credit to the school, or who for any other reason excites the genuine interest, goodwill, or compassion of the Principal, cannot afford full terms, and is refused owing to the expected arrival of a paying pupil who does not actually arrive. In such a case the Principal may be left lamenting (according to the circumstances, or more probably according to his mental habit), either that his prudence was at fault, or that his benevolence suffered a temporary eclipse at an unfortunate moment.

This example of a private school further illustrates the difficulty of carrying out the system of two scales of charges; for since it is well known that pupils are pretty freely taken at reduced terms, there is always a large class of parents who come to regard the terms mentioned in the prospectus as a mere basis for negotiations; and the Principal will often find it difficult to extract his full terms from clients who, though wealthy, have a keen eye for the "most favoured nation" clause in any treaty to which they are parties. Perhaps the only case in which a differentiation of charges is widely accepted with open eyes by all concerned is that of medical attendance. The differentiation is said to be elaborately systematised by the medical faculty, and probably their clients are very imperfectly acquainted with its details, but, broadly speaking, they are aware that they pay more or less according to their means, and perhaps comparatively few of them would complain, however well they knew the difference in the charges made to their poorer neighbours and to themselves. Even here, however, it is probable that doctors, and still more dentists, could make interesting revelations of attempts on the part of clients to beat down their charges on a variety of pleas ultimately based on the knowledge that they are charging less to others who are poorer.

Before turning to another special type of market it will be instructive to note that in all these cases of high-price and low-price markets, kept apart from each other, the purchasers in the low-price market have an advantage. It is (naturally) those who are charged high who complain. The others have part of the price paid for them. They are served on terms which could not be permanently offered to them unless others were paying higher. But when the transaction is looked at not from the purchaser's point of view, but from that of a would-be seller who, owing to any circumstance, is excluded from the high-price market, it is resented as a wrong and an injury and is described as "dumping."

Let us now go on to examine the monopolist's market. In the open competitive market the sellers pursue their several interests independently of each other, and the buyers are in such communication with each other that each knows what bargains the others are making. We have just been examining cases in which the communication between the buyers is imperfect, or in which tariff or other barriers prevent them from acting on the information it gives them. Let us now examine the effect of monopoly or combination amongst the sellers. Starting from the principle that, given the state of the scales of preference of the community, the price is determined by the amount of the commodity in the market, we see at once that if any one could control the amount of the commodity he would be able (within certain limits) to determine the price. Or if all the dealers in the market agreed on a certain price, the amount which the customers would take would determine itself automatically. So if any one controls the total supply, instead of attempting to strike the equilibrating price for the whole stock he may fix on some higher price, and sell as much of the stock as he can at that price. Perhaps he thinks he could sell two-thirds of his stock at a price twice as high as that at which he could sell the whole. If so, by destroying or withholding from sale one-third of the stock he could realise four-thirds of the sum for which the

Monopolist markets.

whole stock would sell. We have seen why this cannot be done in an open competitive market. Each seller is afraid that the unsold third may include his stock, in other words that it may be he who withdraws his stock from sale and his rival that secures the higher price. But if there is a monopoly, or, which amounts to the same thing, a combination amongst the sellers, then the monopolist or syndicate have the option between fixing the price and letting the quantity sold fix itself, or fixing the quantity that they will sell and letting the price fix itself. In the one case they form a speculative estimate of the amount that will sell at the price, and in the other of the price at which the amount they put on the market will sell. The theory of the monopolist market rests, of course, on the same broad principles as those on which the theory of the competitive market is based. The price is determined by the relative scales of the consumers (or their speculative representatives), and the quantity of the commodity that enters the market. But the seller (or syndicate of sellers) is not confined to ascertaining the equilibrating price. He can himself modify it by determining the amount of the commodity offered for sale, or can directly determine it and thereby modify the total amount of sales. But whichever he fixes the other will fix itself. He cannot fix both the quantity he will sell and the price at which he will sell it. Thus the specific difference between a monopolist and an open market is that in the open market the sellers, as such, are simply more or less imperfect mirrors of the minds of the buyers, and know that the point on the collective scale down to which the wants of the buyers will be satisfied is fixed beyond their control by the quantity of the commodity available, whereas in the monopolist market the sellers not only attempt to ascertain the wants of the purchasers but also determine to what point it will serve their own purposes to satisfy them; and it will be observed that at any given moment the open competitive market so far conforms to the monopolist type that the sellers speculatively fix a price and thereby determine the rate at which the commodity shall flow into the hands of the consumers. Only their tentative estimates are based on

s

the supposition that the whole available amount of the commodity will be disposed of during the period over which the market extends; and there is no necessity that any such underlying supposition should determine the prices fixed by the monopolist or the syndicate. The special problems connected with monopolist or syndicate markets have been forced into prominence by the course which industry has recently taken, and they merit a much more elaborate discussion than can be given to them in this treatise; but the main characteristics of monopoly have perhaps been sufficiently indicated for general theoretical purposes.

Hitherto (apart from the stock-market) we have taken our examples chiefly from the class of concrete wares which we usually think of as produced pretty nearly in the form in which they are consumed; and moreover most of them have been things which are ultimately applied either to one object only or to various closely related objects. Potatoes, it is true, must be boiled, or otherwise transformed by fire, before they are consumed; and only a few of the damsons will be eaten in the state in which they are brought to the market; but both potatoes and damsons in whatever forms, and in whatever combinations they are finally consumed, are for the most part still recognisable. That is to say, it needs no effort of imagination to feel the identity of what we eat with the tuber or fruit as it was sold in the market. Whereas, though we all of us know that some of our chairs, tables, and bedsteads are made of wood, that boats are built of it, that broom handles, spade and rake shafts, rafters, doors, window-frames, props to hold up the roofs in coal-mines, and sleepers to underlie railway lines, are all made of it, yet we are not usually strictly conscious of the tree in all these articles; and it takes a craftsman like King Alfred or a poet like Walt Whitman to reverse the process and see all these things in the trees themselves. A tree, then, can be transformed and disguised, and applied to an enormous number of varied purposes. When it is sawn into planks, seasoned, and recognised as "wood," some of the alternative uses of the tree have been irrevocably renounced, but an

Markets in raw materials.

immense number of varied applications are still possible. If a commodity exists in a form, such as timber, which awaits a number of skilled and varied transformations before it assumes the shapes in which it will directly minister to human wants, does that introduce any essential modification into the machinery of the market? Or is it all just the same as if it were, like a potato or a plum, in a form in which it only awaits domestic operations before it is consumed? In technical language: Is the market in raw materials governed by the same psychological laws, and does it work by the same machinery as those that dominate the market in completely manufactured articles or in products ready for the consumer?

Broadly speaking, the answer to these questions has been given in advance. We have seen that the various applications of milk, for instance, economically administered, must all be in marginal equilibrium with each other, and that they all constitute claims on the general stock. And if we pass from the individual to the collective scale, we see that though one purchaser has both a cat and a baby to provide for, and another has a baby but no cat, and a third a cat but no baby, the cats and babies alike will be normally supplied to a point at which their marginal wants, as estimated by their several providers and expressed in their equivalents in gold, occupy identical places on the several relative scales. The variety of application then makes no difference to the law of the market. And neither does the necessity for further operations before consumption. The damsons which are to be eaten raw, those which are to be baked in a pie, and those which are to be made into jam, must all be brought into equilibrium of marginal significance in a perfectly administered household; and, in a perfectly organised market, they will all fall into equilibrium of price, though one person buys for one purpose, another for another, and yet another for three or four at once. What matters to the formation of the market price is where the thing stands on the individual scale, not why it stands there. And if wood of a given quality takes a certain place on a certain man's scale, it does not matter whether it is because he wants to play with it in his amateur workshop, or to make book-shelves for himself with it, or to build a summer-house, or to make tables and chairs and washstands with it not for himself but for others. It is enough that he wants it so much as to give it such and such a place on his scale. And those who stand at or near the goal of use and those who stand more or less remote from it, but in a direct line to it, enter into competition with each other on the same terms. Unless some special convenience or immunity is offered, the plum-seller does not ask whether the purchaser wants plums for private use, or for the supply of a great jam factory; and in the same way a timber-seller deals with any one who will give him a convenient order whether a long or short series of transformations awaits the material after it leaves his hands, and whether it will be exchanged many or few times or not at all before it reaches the actual user. All the different applications that can be made of wood constitute demands. It occupies a certain place on the scale of this man in virtue of its possible application to this purpose, and of that man in virtue of its possible application to that, and on a third man's in virtue of many possible applications, held in marginal balance with each other; and whether they wish to apply it to these varied purposes on their own account, or on account of another man with whom they have made a bargain, or on a speculative estimate of the wants of others with whom they intend to deal, all their demands will enter into competition with each other, and will find their equilibrium at the point at which their marginal valuations coincide.

If a craftsman wants timber in order to make washstands and tables for sale, then it has a derivative value to him, because the things made out of it will have a direct value to others, so that the ascertained or estimated place of washstands and tables on other people's scales, gives timber a certain place on his, and so helps to constitute the demand for wood, and to determine its place on the collective scale; and naturally the ascertained or estimated place of ploughs, waggons, book-shelves, props, platforms, roof-trees, and a thousand other things, has precisely the same action, all of them giving to wood a derivative value dependent on the immediate value of the things that can be made out of it. And all the derivative values, balanced against each other, determine the place that wood, of a given quality, itself occupies upon the collective scale.

We can now answer a question which must often have risen in the reader's mind. We have spoken hitherto of the amounts of any commodity which exist, at any moment, in the possession or under the control of the persons who constitute a market, as though they were fixed; and so, of course, for the moment, they are. *The supply of one market a demand upon another.* But what has determined these quantities, and to what extent can they be modified? The damson crop is affected by the number of trees, and by the season. When once matured it cannot be increased by anything I can do to-day or to-morrow; and even when the trees were planted, none could tell the exact amount of fruit that they would bear in any given year. In like manner when I sow wheat or oats, I can have no assurance of the exact amount of the return that I shall get. But we are well accustomed to this speculative and uncertain element in all problems of administration; and seeing that I may be able to apply the same land to growing cereals and other crops in rotation, or to pasture, or to fruit-growing, or to market-gardening, I may increase the output of any one of the products, or groups of products, at the expense of the others, on an estimate of the marginal significance that the average yield, year by year, is likely to have. The determination of the supply of damsons or wheat, therefore, is arrived at by considering alternative applications of land, just as the supply of tables and washstands is determined by a consideration of the various applications of wood. And as the immediate desire for these articles of furniture constitutes a derivative desire for wood, and puts in a claim on the market in wood, so the immediate desire for wheat and damsons constitutes a derivative desire for the possession or control of land, and puts in a claim on the market in land of exactly the same essential nature as the claims on any other market.

The supply of one market then, so far as it is capable of regulation by the action of man, constitutes a demand upon some other market. As we go higher and higher upstream towards the ultimate sources from which all human wants are satisfied, and examine them in less and less differentiated forms, we shall find that the market in them embraces, and directly or indirectly balances, an ever-wider range of the tastes and desires of the community. But the law of the market never changes. The price is always determined by estimates of the quantity of the commodity available and estimates of the relative scales of the community. Nothing can affect the market price of anything which does not affect one of these factors.

We can see now very clearly how marketing and the law of the market connect themselves with domestic administra-

<small>Domestic and commercial reserves and stores.</small> tion. The consumption of such goods as we have generally taken for our examples, damsons, potatoes, wheat, and so forth, is continuous. The housewife buys her damsons for the year in one or two lots, but she makes the greater part of them into jam, and they are consumed throughout the whole course of the year. She keeps proper control of the key of the store-room, and only issues jam to meet a certain urgency of requirement. She may, therefore, be regarded as speculatively holding back the greater part of her store in anticipation of needs that will arise in future. She endeavours in her mind to estimate the whole series of demands which will be made throughout the year, and to reach an equilibrating standard of urgency up to which any demand must rise in order to justify the issuing of a pot of jam to meet it. If at first she is too easy, she finds her store running out too fast, and as it were " raises the price." If at first she was too strict she finds that the rate of consumption is unnecessarily slow and she lowers the standard of urgency. All this may be seen in miniature even in the helping of a single pudding. A certain lady of narrow means, when she gave her children a jam-roll, used to begin helping the elder children liberally; after a time she would see that it would not go round on that scale, would draw up and economise in the middle, and then, finding she had made enough economies, would relax again for the younger children. (*N.B.*—The observation was made and the record preserved by one of the children that came towards the middle.) The principles, therefore, on which the housewife

holds back or issues her stores, and those on which the merchant or dealer reserves or sells his wares, are identical in so far as they both aim at equilibration of marginal values, only the housewife is estimating the ultimate vital and social importance of increments on individual scales with which she is conversant, and the merchant, as such, is only considering places on the collective scale, the equivalence of which to each other is purely objective.

The actual distribution of any harvest over the time which it has to cover may be shared in any proportions by the consumer and the dealer. Plums, as we have seen, may well be bought for the whole year at once by the consumer; but this is not likely to be the case with wheat. The ultimate consumer as a rule takes his wheat in the form of bread, and never stores more than the supply for a few hours, or at most days. Some few people still bake at home; and there is also a demand for flour for other cooking purposes, so that a small part of the wheat for the year will be stored by housekeepers for some weeks or months in advance, in the shape of flour. But the greater part will remain in the hands of the miller and the dealer, so that the work of distributing it over the claims of the year, which in the case of jam is (at least in old-fashioned houses) still a branch of domestic administration, is in the case of wheat a branch of commerce.

A different type again may be found in the case of new potatoes. Here there is never any accumulated stock that needs to be distributed either commercially or domestically over a long period. The potatoes mature day by day; and week by week, perhaps, they are brought into the market and sold without any speculative or vicarious reserve price that looks beyond the close of the day. The continuous flow of actual consumption is maintained by the purchases made at these weekly markets. So that here the relation between the ultimate scales of preference and the stream of supply is very direct and continuous, and there would seem to be little room for speculative estimate of future wants, whether domestic or commercial. With winter or store potatoes the case is different.

An equally close analogy and the same fundamental difference may be traced between domestic and commercial administration when we consider the mistakes and miscalculations that may occur in them. If the housewife assigns her store of damsons unwisely, and makes jam of what would have been better eaten as fruit, or if she buys a disproportionate amount of the fruit altogether, there is so much waste. And in exactly the same way if a man has made wood into washing-stands which would have met wants standing higher on the collective scale if it had been made into tables, he will try to avoid a repetition of the mistake, but he cannot undo it. To him, as a business man, there has been so much waste. The wood has actually been applied at less business advantage than might have been. A stock of washstands when made can no more be transformed into the tables that might have been made instead, than the milk that was bought this morning can be transformed at four o'clock this afternoon into the tea-cakes or muffins that might have been bought with the same money, or than the milk that has been sipped by the cat can on reconsideration be put into the tea. And just as, since closed alternatives are no longer open, the milk may be consumed at a relative significance too low to have justified its purchase, had the state of things been accurately anticipated, or may have been given to the cat at a lower significance than would have justified the application had we known how much we should want it at afternoon tea, so the washstands may have to be sold at a lower price than would have induced us to make them, had we realised that the tables we might have made instead would be more valuable; or the timber may have been bought under the impression that both tables and chairs would satisfy wants standing higher on the collective scale than is found to be the fact. And just as the total order for milk may have been in excess or defect, so that even if internal equilibrium is preserved, the milk is all consumed at a higher or lower marginal significance than good husbandry would justify, so the whole stock of timber from the business point of view may turn out to supply wants at the margin that would have made it good business to buy more, or bad business to buy as much, had their exact place on the collective scale been truly anticipated.

Effect of errors in domestic and commercial distribution of resources.

So the law of the market holds for any commodity whether it is near or far from the condition in which it will be finally applied to the satisfaction of human desires. Only, when it is still relatively far therefrom, that is to say in a relatively undifferentiated state, in which numerous alternatives are still possible, a wider circle of claims will have to be balanced against each other and brought, by estimate and experiment, into relation with each other, than when it is in its later stages of differentiated elaboration.

Hence there may often, for a time, be a difference in the terms on which it is possible to buy a thing that is in stock and the terms on which it is possible to get it to order. A manufacturer may have made largely to stock, thinking that the time would come when he might sell on terms which would justify him in having done so. But this is a matter of speculation, and if within months or years, as the case may be, the place of this article on the collective scale does not rise to the anticipated height, he may at last be glad to sell it for what he can get, because he has no alternative and can transform it into nothing else more valuable. But he would never have made this thing to order at the price at which he has now to sell it; for before he made it he had many alternatives. He might have made other things, which he now knows would have been a more eligible employment of his resources, or he might have made nothing at all, thereby saving expenditure on raw material, and perhaps, if he reduced his establishment, on wages. So it may happen that if you ask A to make the article to order, he will only consent to do so at a higher price than that which B will be willing to take for what he has in stock.

CHAPTER VII

MARKETS (*Continued*). INTEREST. TOOLS. LAND

SUMMARY.—*The market in advances follows the law of other markets. One man could administer his resources for a given period more economically if he could quicken their flow for the first part of the period at the expense of slackening it in the last; and the case is reversed to another. Or both may be in the same case, but to one the advantage of anticipation may be relatively greater than to the other. Between these two the conditions of exchange exist; and if, when equilibrium is reached, there is a premium on anticipation, that constitutes one source of the phenomenon of interest. Current savings of perishable things may be paid by one man to another who is accumulating wealth in more permanent forms, that may afterwards be paid back in compensation. Hence each individual may transform perishable present into more permanent future possessions, or permanent present into more perishable future possessions; or may transmute more into less perishable commodities, or vice versa. Effort may also be diverted from the immediate production of desired things into the production of tools, or the acquiring of skill that, when obtained, will make effort more fertile; and out of that increased fertility a premium may be paid to one who advances tools or apparatus. Land may be regarded as yielding either a revenue of commodities or a revenue of directly enjoyable services, and in either case it may be regarded as partly given by nature and partly manufactured. A man may desire to hire it (i.e. to have it without buying it) for the same reasons for which he may desire to hire a house or a tool, viz. either in order to distribute his resources more to his advantage or in order to increase them. Both these advantages of anticipation obey the general law of declining significance as the margin advances; and they both, together with the mere prodigal's desire to anticipate future resources, constitute a claim on the total resources at present available, and find their place of equilibrium amongst other claims. The resultant premium on advances constitutes interest. Some cannot help saving; but it is not always wise to save for a distant future. Saving beyond a certain point is never wise. The existence of interest as a normal phenomenon reacts upon the distribution of personal resources, and also has its analogues in things not in the circle of exchange. The rate at which a society accumulates exchangeable things depends upon its wealth, upon the distribution of its wealth, upon the providence of its members, and upon the wisdom and honesty of those that direct its industries. Hire and rent contain elements in common with interest, and hire deals with a problem of fractional purchase analogous to that with which insurance is concerned.*

There still remains for examination a special class of transactions which, although they come under the general law of the market, have been found so perplexing, and have given rise to so many strange speculations, that I have reserved them for special treatment.

The phenomenon of interest has engaged the attention of theologians and moralists, as well as economists. Calvin has the reputation of being the first great theologian who frankly defended the receipt of interest. Possibly (but not probably) Ruskin will be recorded as the last great moralist and social reformer who ever succeeded in catching the ear of a wide public for a denunciation of it. But be that as it may, in spite of all that has been written on the subject, the true nature of interest, its relation to other economic phenomena, and the play of forces of which it is the manifestation, still seem to be very imperfectly understood, and some attempt must now be made to elucidate them.

<small>Interest.</small>

We have already seen that a man's expenditure must be

distributed between what may be called short-service and long-service commodities; that is to say, between commodities which are used up and perish and have to be renewed, and commodities that last for longer or shorter periods in continuous or intermittent use. It follows that the man who is to provide himself with a suit of clothes that will last him six or twelve months must, at the beginning of the period, be in possession of his whole provision for six months' wear; whereas at the beginning of the same six months he only needs to be in possession of bread that will last him a few hours, and will find it inconvenient to have provision for more than a few days. We see from this that if a man should start with little or nothing in hand—that is to say, with no provision of anything he requires that will last him more than a few hours—and during the next six months expects to come into command of a certain defined amount of things in the circle of exchange, it would not be a matter of indifference to him whether this command came in an even stream, day by day, or week by week, or in a stream of changing volume, broad at first, and narrower afterwards. It may be a matter of vital importance to him to bring the rate at which his command of commodities accrues into some kind of correspondence with the irregular way in which the necessity for providing for his wants asserts itself. If instead of £1 a week for twenty-six weeks a man could receive, say, £5:1:3 for the first week, and 16s. 9d. each of the other twenty-five weeks, he would only receive £26 altogether during the twenty-six weeks, but he would be far better off, for he could provide himself with a due proportion of long-service commodities, and yet keep his expenditure on short-service commodities even throughout the period. It follows, therefore, that he will be willing (if that is the only alternative) to accept something less than £26 distributed over the time in a way that will suit him, instead of £26 distributed evenly over the whole six months.

And if we take a longer period, and include articles of greater permanence than clothes, such as furniture, standard books, or even houses, the same principle applies still more obviously. These things must exist in the mass before they

Short-service and long-service commodities. Irregularity with which demands on resources occur.

can be used continuously or in fragments. And unless a man has something in hand—that is to say, unless he has saved something, or has come into possession of what others have saved or otherwise command—he will be very willing, if he can, to make some kind of bargain in virtue of which he can get possession of things at the start, and pay for them gradually as he uses them and as his resources continuously accrue. That is, given the prices of the several commodities, he will be willing to contract the whole range of his options if thereby he can get leave to anticipate the exercise of some of them. His future command of commodities will then suffer a double contraction, partly due to the anticipation he has been allowed to make, and partly owing to the price he has paid for this privilege.

But the opposite case is equally conceivable. We have taken the case of a man whose command of resources is expected to flow in at the rate of £1 a week, so that in twenty years he will have had roughly £1040. But suppose a man has not any prospect of earning, or otherwise receiving, any continuous command of things in the circle of exchange for the next ten or fifteen years, but has present command of £1000. If he were required there and then to exercise his privilege and call out of the circle of exchange the actual things that he will require for the next ten years, what would he do? He would ask, say, for a house, for furniture, for books, for clothes, and so forth. But moth and rust corrupt. He will require larger premises than he would have needed had he been able to get these things as he wanted them; and a constant deflection of energies from other channels will be needed to keep them from deteriorating. When it comes to providing many years' stock of food, the man will be at a terrible additional disadvantage, for he will be confined to kinds of food that will keep indefinitely; and finally, it will be absolutely impossible for him to lay in a stock of direct "services"—that is to say, of the output of human effort to meet the recurrent requirements of his life.

Thus the man who is to receive his resources in a regular stream may find it difficult to provide himself with certain things, and impossible to provide himself with others, which his total resources could easily command if he could distribute them in time according to his taste, taking more now and less afterwards. And the man who should be required to exercise at once the whole power of calling things out of the circle of exchange which will accrue to him during a series of years, would be severely restricted as to some things and would have to go altogether without others which his resources would command if he were able to distribute over future years some of the options which he is required to exercise at once. The same difficulties would arise if he were expecting to receive a given income for a certain period, after which it was to decline or cease. He could not during one term of years gradually store all the things that he would need during a subsequent term. We shall soon arrive at a clearer conception of the process by which saving and accumulation are actually conducted, and shall understand why, as a matter of fact, no man is ever called upon thus to store up in times of prosperity the actual concrete things that he will want in future years. But the point that I am emphasising at the moment is that if he were called upon to do this he would be placed at a terrible disadvantage.

Advantage of anticipating or postponing expenditure.

We see, then, that two men situated as we have supposed would both of them wish to redistribute their resources in time, but would wish to do so in contrary senses. The one would prefer present to future command of a part of the wealth that is to accrue to him in a given period, and the other would prefer future to present exercise of a portion of the options which have already accrued to him. Now since each of these men has relatively too much of that of which the other has relatively too little, it is manifest that the conditions for a profitable exchange are present. The man who has present command of things in the circle of exchange, and would willingly forgo a part of it for the sake of future command, meets the one who anticipates a stream of future command and would gladly contract it if he might exercise a certain measure of present command as a compensation. Each of them therefore can give what he values less, and receive what he values more. And the preferences of each alike are subject to the law of declining marginal significance. For it is obvious that as each of the two men is better supplied with that of which he is in relative lack and worse supplied with that in which he relatively abounds, there is a gradual approach to equilibrium.

We have supposed that to one of the exchanging parties an extra £1 down would actually have more value than an extra £1 distributed over a stretch of the future, and that to the other an extra £1 distributed over the same period would actually have more value than £1 down; but exchange might take place even though both preferred £1 down to £1 distributed evenly over a given period of the future, if the preference were greater in one case than in the other, and if the man whose preference was the lower possessed £1. For in this case the advantage of present over future command would stand relatively higher on one man's scale than on the other's, and it would be possible to fix on a premium so high that the one man would accept it and yet so low that the other would pay it. This is exactly what lies at the basis of the ordinary law of the market. In order for an exchange to take place some commodity must stand relatively higher with respect to another commodity on one man's scale than it does on another's, though it may be valued by both; and the man on whose scale it stands relatively lower must possess a supply of it. In the case in hand the things exchanged and to which the parties attach different relative values are a defined command of things in the circle of exchange now, and the same command in the future; or, to put it in another way, the thing offered for sale is the privilege (valued by both men, but not equally) of anticipating future resources.

The uneven incidence.

The extreme suppositions with which we began this investigation may now be modified. We need not necessarily assume that there are some who have little or nothing in hand but have prospects of incomings in the future, and others that have no prospects of incomings in the future (or after a certain period of the future) but have something in hand. All we need suppose is that there are certain persons whose wealth in hand and wealth in prospect are so proportioned as to give the present a higher relative place on their scales of preference than it occupies on that of certain other persons.

Here, as in any other market, the individual scales might

be combined into a communal scale. The possessors of accumulations in relative excess would cede present command of things in the circle of exchange to those who anticipated a relative excess in the continuous stream of their future command of them. On the scales of these latter such future command would stand relatively low, until they had ceded so much of it that equilibrium was reached. If, when the equilibrium point was reached, there was a premium on present command of accumulated wealth, what would this mean? It would mean that those persons who had surrendered a portion of their present wealth, but had also retained a portion, valued the present more than the future, at the existing margins, in a ratio at (or just above) that represented by the premium. They would be in the position of the stall-keeper who has a reserve price and refuses to sell any more of her wares at the current market price. In many cases the exact parallel would be that of a stall-keeper who at first has wares in such abundance that they are a discommodity to her (that is to say, in such abundance that she would, if necessary, be at pains to get rid of some of them), but at the same time desires to have some, though not so much as she has. She would pay the market price for some, if she had not got any; and having a stock, she will retain some of it, and refuse to sell it at the market price. But she gets the same price for that which, if necessary, she would have paid some one to take away, and for that which she is only just willing to part with at the price, that price being fixed by the equilibrium valuation on the communal scale. So, too, in the market we have now imagined. It is but natural that amongst those who offer present command in exchange for future command of commodities there should be some who, to begin with, have so large a relative excess of the power of present command that they would, if necessary, pay any one who would enable them to defer exercising it till some future date; and who at the same time so highly value some of this command, that if a certain part of their stock has already been transmuted they would decline to transmute more except on increasingly exacting terms. How much of it they will actually transmute depends on the market price they can realise. When one

The market in "anticipations" of wealth.

man transmutes present command of wealth-in-volume to future command of wealth-in-stream, his correspondent effects the reverse transmutation; and therefore the price he pays, which will be the market price of the commodity, is the equilibrating value, on the collective scale, of leave to transmute a stream of wealth that is about to accrue into a volume of wealth that has accrued. This price the seller receives for those portions of his own counter transmutation which he would have paid for being allowed to make, no less than for those portions of it which the premium he receives is only just enough to induce him to make; just as the stall-keeper receives the market price for that portion of her wares which she would, if necessary, have paid some one to remove from the market-place for her, no less than for that portion which she would have taken back home for her own use had the price realisable been a halfpenny a pound less than it actually was.

And, in like manner, just as the consumer of tea or of any other commodity pays the same price for the increments which satisfy his keenest wants and those which satisfy a want only just keen enough to make the price worth paying, so the man who buys the privilege of transmuting the stream of wealth that will accrue to him in future into a present volume of wealth gets those portions of this privilege which are necessary to make any kind of civilised life possible to him, and those which merely provide him with some relatively slight convenience, at the same price. And that price corresponds to the significance of the least valued exercises of the privilege.

It will be well to note at once (inasmuch as no one can actually give to-day a command of commodities which will not accrue till to-morrow) that what is actually received in return for the exercise of present command can only be a promise; and as the value of the promise (that is to say, the assurance that it will be fulfilled) may vary indefinitely, the question of the price at which the exchange between present and future command of wealth is effected may be indefinitely complicated by questions of insurance or covering of risk; but we have seen that, if we were altogether to eliminate this element of uncertainty, the mere fact that some persons can make credible promises to give future command of wealth, and other persons have actual command of wealth at the moment,

T

is enough to constitute a market. And under given conditions as to the quantity of wealth accumulated and the relative wants of members of the community as to short-time and long-time expenditure, it might happen that a man, by handing over to another his immediate power of calling £100 worth of goods out of the circle of exchange, might receive the right to call for £2 worth of goods every week throughout the course of a year. In that case, at the end he would have called altogether for £104 worth of commodities and services; and the extra £4 would be the price or premium he had received for enabling his correspondent to exchange a stream of wealth about to accrue into a volume of wealth that had accrued.

Now suppose that this man saves the £100 and only spends the £4. He may then be in a position to repeat the transaction and spend another £4 in the course of the next year, and still have his £100; and so on for an indefinite series of years. Moreover, the period of one week is clearly arbitrary. The arrangement might be that the instalments should be paid once a fortnight, once a month, or once a quarter. The person who receives the £100 worth of goods may not be sure exactly when he may find it most convenient to pay his instalments. He may expect to earn larger sums one week than another, and he may find it difficult to pay £2 every week, though he might be sure of being able to pay £26 in the thirteen weeks of the quarter, one week taken with another. He might even wish to be allowed the whole year over which to collect, according to his own circumstances or discretion, the total sum due. Or he might pay small sums quarterly, amounting to the premium and the lump sum at the end of the year. All such variations in the bargain would be matters of convenience and arrangement, and the terms for each might vary. But the general rule is obvious. By hypothesis the present possession of £1 stands marginally higher on the collective scale than the promise of £1 to be paid by instalments in the future; and it follows that a promise to pay a sum by instalments, over a given period, stands marginally higher than a promise to pay the same sum in a lump at the *end* of the period. But each instalment as it is received will, by hypothesis, be worth more than if the payment of it were to

[margin note: One source of the phenomenon of interest.]

be spread over all that remains of the period. In the limit, therefore, instalments over any period, however short, will be worth more than the whole sum paid in a lump at the end of that period. The man who defers his instalments, and concentrates them at certain points, will therefore have to pay a further premium for being allowed to do so. Thus we could imagine that the man who could get £100 in return for a promise to pay £2 a week for a year (£104 in all, £4 premium and £100 returned) might find that if he wished to pay his premium quarterly, and to return the lump sum at the end of the year, he would be required to pay 30s. a quarter premium instead of £1, or £6 in the course of the year, and £100 at the end of it. The lender, on his side, might spend his 30s. a quarter premium as he received it, and when he got his £100 at the end of the year might repeat the arrangement. In that case he will no sooner receive his £100 back than he will exchange it for a promise of £106, to be paid in instalments of 30s. a quarter and £100 at the end of the year. Then why not accept this promise at once instead of the £100 ? Why insist on first having the £100 and then exchanging it for the promise instead of accepting the promise at once ? If this arrangement is made it may go on indefinitely. The one man may always be liable at the end of every year for £100 to the other man, and may always offer him 30s. a quarter for accepting a promise to pay in a year instead of payment now. Or the terms might be such that the whole transaction may be closed at the end of any quarter if the borrower likes to pay up the whole sum of £101 : 10s., or if the lender chooses to require it.

Such a transaction as we have described, therefore, may be regarded in two lights, either as a hire or as a purchase. If I lend you £100 at 6 per cent, the interest to be paid quarterly, we may either consider that you are paying me 30s. a quarter for the control of £100 worth of goods as long as you retain it (in a word, that you are hiring £100 worth of goods from me), or we may say that at the beginning of the quarter you buy £100 worth of present goods by the promise to pay £101 : 10s. worth of goods three months hence, and that when the promise becomes due you pay the £1 : 10s., and substitute for the payment of the other £100 the promise to pay £101 : 10s. three months hence again; that is to say, the process of borrowing £100 at 6 per cent, the interest to be paid quarterly, may be looked upon either in the light of hiring the command of commodities, or in the light of purchasing present commodities in terms of a promise of future commodities. Some writers have laid stress on the theoretical superiority of one or the other of these views, but on this matter we need not trouble ourselves. There may be special transactions which are more conveniently regarded in the one light than in the other; but, broadly speaking, borrowing at interest may be equally well thought of as a species of generalised hire, or as a constantly renewed exchange of present wealth for promises of future wealth. The essential point is that we should recognise the identity of the underlying principle in either case, and should understand that what is hired or bought is the anticipation of resources which the hirer or purchaser himself does not yet command.

We can now perfectly understand that any one who wishes to receive present command of resources in any form, in return for promises to pay a lump sum in the future, on going into the open market and trusting to economic forces to supply his wants, will find that he has to pay a premium in one form or another. He will have to promise more wealth in the future than he receives in the present; and this will be the case whatever the terms of the bargain may be, whether the borrower promises to pay back by instalments, or in a lump sum at the time the lender chooses or at the time he chooses himself.

There are persons, then, who actually control present wealth and desire to increase their control of future wealth, and there are persons who expect to control wealth in the future and desire to increase their control of wealth in the present; and these two sets of people will exchange, on terms, until all their relative estimates of present and future wealth coincide. At that point there will be subjective or vital equilibrium between the marginal value of the unit command of things in the circle of exchange to-day, and the unit command of them at any given period in the future, on each individual's scale; and there will be objective equilibrium between these units on the communal scale. The market in which men buy and sell power to anticipate the command of things in the circle of exchange appears to conform exactly to other markets.

But we have much more to do before we have completed our examination of this market. To begin with, we must give a wider extension to the branch of the subject which we have already examined. We have spoken of wealth in hand as a stock already existing. "Advances" must obviously be made out of this existing store. Accumulations and how they are made available. But we must now consider how a stock can be accumulated. Mere hoarding of precious metals and the like obviously constitutes but a very small part of the process of accumulation. Any one who puts work continuously into the construction of an implement, a house, a suit of clothes, or, briefly, any long-service commodity, is accumulating, though perhaps not for himself. He may be paid, or bought out, day by day or week by week, by short-service commodities, and in that case it is the person who pays him that is accumulating; but in any case the accumulation is going on. But besides long-service commodities that last over a long period, there are slowly maturing commodities that must be secured by efforts spread over long periods. A man may tickle trout and receive an immediate return for his efforts; but he will have to work during many months of the year to secure a crop at harvest-time. We may rightly regard the corn he harvests at last as a short- rather than a long-service commodity, but it can only be secured by a process that is equivalent to accumulation, whether we call it so or not. Commodities of many kinds, then, may be secured by the accumulation of efforts and resources, and some of them, when obtained, may be susceptible of use over a longer period than others. Our attention was first called to the subject of accumulation by the consideration of long- and short-service commodities, but we now see that the process of accumulation is as necessary to secure slowly maturing as it is to secure long-service commodities, and in our further examination of methods of accumulation we must bear this in mind.

In the process of accumulating, as elsewhere, the machinery of exchange and the principle of division of labour come into play. If I accumulate for ten years in order to have a house,

I probably neither build it myself by efforts spread over the ten years, as I can spare them from other purposes, nor pay another man for so building it. What happens is in principle something like this:—By such agencies as Savings Banks and the like a number of persons club together, generally unconsciously, so that the tiniest streams and dribbles of savings (that is to say, refrainings from drawing things out of the circle of exchange) are gathered together, and are continuously embodied in long-service commodities, some of them being houses. Thus, when I have been saving a few months, and have diverted from current use say a twentieth part of the resources necessary for the construction of a house, I have unconsciously combined with nineteen others to furnish housebuilders with things they want, and from which we have abstained; and they in return have constructed for us, not for themselves, a house which represents our joint accumulations. Now we have seen that under existing conditions we may expect to find a man who wants a house but has not saved up for it; and he will be willing to pay something for the privilege of anticipating the resources which he expects will accrue to him in the future. That is to say, while retaining our collective right to appropriate to ourselves the house which represents our accumulations, we may expect to receive periodical payments for allowing some one else to use it instead. I shall have my share of these payments, and, if I like, I may add it to my accumulations. If we are all doing the same we shall have our next house ready in something less than six months, and shall then be in receipt of another series of premiums, and so on, until in a period considerably shorter than ten years I shall find that my continued savings at the original rate, with the addition of my share of the premiums which we have received, will amount to the price of a house. Or put it in this way:—Week by week I may abstain from short-service commodities and cede them to others as payment for embodying their efforts in long-service or slowly maturing commodities. The abstinence is mine, not theirs. They have been enjoying immediate returns to their efforts, but I, through them, have been accumulating; and at any moment, by advancing my accumulations, I can, in virtue of the premium on anticipation which the market offers, secure the promise of a larger sum than I have saved, in a series of subsequent payments.

No attempt has been made in this example to represent the immense complexity and variety of the actual relations involved. It is merely intended as a concrete illustration of the way in which a man is able continuously to contribute towards the construction of long-service or slowly maturing commodities until such time as his command has risen to the point at which he can exercise it by summoning from the circle of exchange the commodity for which he has been saving up; and it shews that whoever does this may, so long as the market offers a premium on anticipation, expect to draw out more than the sum of his puttings-in.

Now suppose that a man expects to come into possession of a house, or other long-service or slowly maturing commodity of given value, at a certain time, and that he desires, instead of possessing it when the time comes, to command a series of short-service commodities during the intervening years. He might, even without the machinery of a bank and the combinations it makes possible, find another man who wished to save up for a house, and he might receive from him the command of short-service commodities for a series of years, and then surrender to him the long-service commodity at the end. And in this case (always under the same supposition as to the state of the market) he would draw out a smaller total sum by instalments during this series of years than the house would have realised had he not trenched upon its worth in advance. The other man is saving up and he is spending. The "advances," in this case, are made to, not by, the man who will ultimately cede the slowly maturing, long-service, or large-unit commodity; and it is he who will have to pay the premium. But that is because he does not yet possess this commodity that embodies accumulations. He only expects it. If it already exists, then the man who has present possession of it can command a premium for advancing it.

We can now give a certain extension to our conception of the market between wealth in the present and wealth in the future; for we have seen that exchange may be effected not only between a large sum in the present and a series of small sums in the future, or a single present sum and a single future sum, but also between a series of small payments over a period of time and a lump sum to be received at the end of it, or a series of small sums in the proximate future for another series of small sums in the remoter future. And if in any one of these transactions there is a premium in the market on the present, or the proximate future, as against the relatively remote future, there will be a like premium in all of them. And in this market, as in others, the man who carries either saving or anticipation to the point that brings its marginal significance to him personally into correspondence with the market price, gets what is worth as much as he gives for it at the margin, and more than he gives for it at all points short of the margin. That is to say, a man who postpones his expenditure may be supposed in many cases to receive a far greater return for his initial savings than would have been enough to induce him to make them. It is only at the margin that what he gives and what he gets will balance. And so also with the man who anticipates expenditure.

Hitherto we have dealt with cases in which the total resources which a man commands over a given period are supposed to be constant, and we have shewn that they will have a different vital significance to him according to the way in which their flow in upon him during that period is regulated. To one man they would naturally accrue evenly throughout the period, and if he can secure a broader flow at first by accepting a narrower flow subsequently he will be the gainer. To another man they will naturally accrue at the beginning of the period, and if he can narrow the flow at first and thereby secure a broader flow afterwards he will be the gainer. Or both will be the gainers, but one more than the other, by broadening the initial and narrowing the subsequent flow. But in every case we have supposed that the total of each man's resources for the whole period covered has a defined volume, and the only question is what distribution and regulation of their flow will maximise their vital significance to him. We have seen that this problem will solve itself on the general principles of the market, and that under existing conditions there is a premium on present as against future wealth.

Therefore any one who has saved or has otherwise secured accumulations or possessions is in a position to exchange them for a sum total of future possession or enjoyment larger than themselves—not, indeed, because he has accumulated a present command of resources, but because he possesses it. Here, as elsewhere, he may accumulate painfully, because accumulations will command a premium; but they will command a premium not because they were accumulated (painfully or otherwise), but because they are there.

But now we must turn to another "market" (in the larger sense of the term), in which a man can exchange resources in the proximate for resources in the remoter future, and in which nature and art offer him a direct premium for doing so. This "market" is independent of any difference of need between different members of a society, and was as open to Robinson Crusoe on his island as it is to us in England.

Nature and art—that is to say, the whole complex of conditions that has risen out of the reactions between man and the forces of nature, throughout the ages—offer perpetually open opportunities of applying accumulated resources in such a way as actually and objectively to *create* revenue. *Industrial sources of interest.* In the cases hitherto examined we have supposed that future revenue will accrue to me, whereas you have command of present accumulations. You transfer to me some of your accumulations, and I shall transfer to you still more of my future revenue when it comes, so that you get a larger and I a lesser share of the total wealth, but that total itself is not changed by our transaction. Your share is increased, and mine, though decreased, is more conveniently distributed over time. The material total is unchanged, but its psychological significance is heightened. In the cases which we are now to examine, on the other hand, my application of the accumulations you put at my disposal will create revenue, so that the "more" which you obtain will not mean a "less" remaining to me; for it will have actually come into existence in virtue of our transaction, and there will be a "more" for me too. This is (or ought to be) the ordinary case of commercial interest. We shall approach the consideration of it most easily by examining the significance of tools.

Beyond gathering mushrooms, nuts, wild strawberries, birds' eggs, shell-fish, and the like, it is difficult to see what a man can do to supply his wants without tools. Even the botanist who boasts that he can fare sumptuously where another man would starve will probably need some kind of tools to extract his succulent roots from the soil. Those tools may be extremely simple. He may find a stone, or break off a twig, that will enable him to grub them out; but even that is increasing his ultimate efficiency by diverting his immediate efforts from the direct accomplishment of his purposes to securing the means for effecting them more adequately. When the savage shapes one flint with another, constructs his bow, twists grasses (or his mother-in-law's hair) into a bow-string, and fixes a flint head upon his shaft, and, still more, when he constructs a canoe for fishing, he is, in a very notable degree, accumulating resources and diverting his energies from the direct pursuit of his purposes. The gardener would be helpless without his spade, and would be at a cruel disadvantage without his wheel-barrow. The possession of a few nets makes a vast difference in the proportion between the amount of fruit which the birds get and the amount which he gets himself; and the pitchfork, the syringe, and many other articles which come under the general denomination of tools and apparatus have various degrees of efficiency in making the same labour, bestowed on the same land, yield a larger revenue of desired results. Walls and glass yield a yet further increase. And none of these things can be secured save by diverting human energy from its direct purposes, and accumulating it in such a form as to make it yield a revenue in the increased efficiency of the effort which it supports. The huge factories, the railway cuttings and embankments, the machinery, locomotive and stationary, by which the great industries of an advanced industrial community are supported, all of them represent accumulations, in return for the judicious application of which nature and the complex of industrial relations between man and man offer a revenue in the increased efficiency of human effort and resources.

Here, then, we may note an extension in our conception of the meaning of the processes of saving. We have already considered saving as a diverting of effort from the increase of short-service commodities to the increase of long-service commodities—say, from catching more fish to building houses; and further, as the diverting of effort from directions in which it meets quick returns to the production of slowly maturing commodities—say, from gathering wild fruit to sowing and tending corn; and now we may think of it further as the deflection of effort from the direct to the indirect acquisition of desired things—from "tickling" more fish to building boats and making fishing-nets; from weaving cloth to making looms; from printing more books to founding type and constructing engines; from digging over the garden once more to making nets; from carrying consumable things from place to place, to making railway cuttings, embankments, etc. Or, to repeat it once again, saving seems to consist in (1) increasing our stock of relatively permanent or slowly maturing commodities by the application of resources and efforts which might have been applied to the increase of our stock of relatively perishable or quickly maturing ones, and (2) deflecting energies and resources to relatively indirect means of securing our ends (by embodying them in tools and apparatus) from relatively direct means of securing them (by employing the tools and apparatus we already have).

<small>Re-examination of the nature and process of saving or accumulating.</small>

We will now take up this latter aspect of saving. It does not necessarily involve exchange, for the man who is cultivating his own land for his own use might make his own nets, for example; and in that case the saving would be effected by the same man; whose future efforts become more productive in consequence of it. Yet it may, and certainly often will, happen that one man is in a relatively favourable position for saving, and another in a relatively favourable position for fertilising the result of saving. Thus it may involve relatively smaller distress on my part than it would do on yours to deflect a certain sum from my current expenditure from the direct supply of my wants to the construction of tools; and you, on the contrary, may be able so to apply these tools as to make them increase the efficiency of your efforts more than any use to which I could have applied them would have increased mine. In that case it may well happen that the increased yield so secured, while it would less than compensate you for the relatively severe process of saving, will more than compensate me for the relatively light one. If, then, I transfer the tools in which my saving is embodied to you, and you assign to me anything less than the whole increase of revenue which results to you, I may be satisfied, and you may have a clear gain.

And here, too, the law of diminishing marginal significance very obviously comes into operation. To begin with the simpler case of the tools handled by a craftsman. I have known a carpenter of exceptional skill and resourcefulness do a wonderful day's work of a miscellaneous description with no tools but a flat-tailed hammer and an old broken chisel. The difference between his efficiency with these implements and with none at all was certainly far greater than the whole extra difference which the command of his complete basket of tools would have made; for no number of men, absolutely without tools, could have done his day's work at all, whereas a full supply of tools would probably not have enabled him to increase the yield of the same time and the same effort by more than from ten to twenty per cent. The tasks in which he was engaged on that particular day were no doubt of a comparatively simple nature, and if he had been engaged in building a cart his hammer and chisel would have been cruelly inadequate. But he could shape the wheel-hub perfectly with an axe, and a very small equipment of tools would have enabled him to do all his ordinary tasks as carpenter and wheelwright with fair expedition and efficiency. More elaborate tools, had he cared to command them, would have had a rapidly declining significance. They would have made his labour more fertile, but not at anything like the same rate as the initial supplies of the most useful tools. The principle hardly needs to be elaborated, for it will not be disputed. Successive increments of tools and appliances, after a certain point, while they still increase the efficiency and economy of efforts and resources, will do so at a decreasing rate.

The case is exactly the same with the manufacturer. A man may see his way to making £10,000, spent in improved machinery and appliances, yield him £1000 in the increased efficiency of his staff and materials. Perhaps by spending yet another £10,000 he could still further increase their efficiency, but possibly the further addition would amount not to £1000 but only to £500 a year. So if he went into the open market to raise the money, and found that under all the conditions of the case he would have to pay 6 per cent premium or interest, he would think it worth while to raise the first £10,000 and not the second. The declining significance, however, would be gradual, and he would not be confined to increments of £10,000. The first portions of the second £10,000 might have the power of increasing the output at less than the rate of 10 but more than the rate of 6 per cent, and therefore some portion of the further sum would be borrowed. In short, whatever the rate of interest at which the manufacturer can command an advance (that is to say, the immediate use of concentrated or accumulated resources), a balance must be struck between the industrial efficiency of increased apparatus and the price that has to be paid for it in the market. The point will come at which the man would lay down a certain machine, if interest were only 5 per cent, because he expects it to fertilise the concern to the amount of 5 per cent on the money expended, with a sufficient margin to cover risks, replacement, etc.; but if interest is 6 per cent he will not lay the machine down.

Here, then, is a vast army of fresh claimants on existing accumulations. They too will have to submit to the law of the market and will be able to secure its benefits. They will all compete, not only with each other, but with the other claimants; and the wants of all will be satisfied down to the same point of relative significance. *Competitors for the stock of accumulations.* That is to say, if I want to pay for my house-room as I use it (instead of paying for a whole house before I begin to use it), because that way of fitting my burden to my shoulders suits me best, and if you want an engine before you have saved up for it, because the possession of it will itself put you in possession of a larger revenue, we shall bid against each other in the market, and the man who has something in hand will not ask either of us *why* we want to anticipate the resources he has accumulated, but will only ask *how much* we desire it, or rather how much we are in a position to pay him for gratifying our desires; and whichever of us offers most efficiently to further his purpose will find him most willing to further ours; provided only that either or both of us offer him better terms than he can make for himself by direct applications of his accumulations to his own concerns.

Lastly, we will introduce, if only for form's sake, our friend the "prodigal," to whom a few words are frequently devoted in books of Political Economy. He is a person who thinks, possibly not altogether without reason, that he is capable of enjoying £100 now more than he will be capable of enjoying £200, or, for the matter of that, £2000, at some remote period when he is likely to come into possession of it. He may think so, partly because he will then have larger annual resources and can therefore cut back from an objectively more advanced margin, and partly because he thinks he is himself capable of higher enjoyment now than he will be then, so that even if his revenues were evenly distributed throughout his life he would get a larger subjective value out of them by spending freely in his youth and economising in his age. Or he may not even have so good a reason as the worst of these for valuing future command of resources relatively low. He may be simply careless as to the future. But in any case his estimate of the present in terms of the future is presumably subject to the law of declining marginal significance. As his future resources dwindle, and the prospect of retrenchment or want comes nearer, he will probably cease to pawn the future still further in obedience to every whim, and will only do so to escape serious difficulties or secure objects of keen desire. If not, then the time will soon come when his promises of future payment are no longer current, and then he falls out of the market and we "see him no more." Meanwhile, as long as he draws the line anywhere, and has anything still in hand for the future, he too competes with the rest and has his claims satisfied down to the same relative point, for he is in the same market.

The prodigal as a competitor in the market.

We have now examined a variety of cases in which a man may be willing to promise a premium in future wealth for the possession of present wealth; and two points have come out very clearly. Firstly: Whatever a man's reason for this wish may be, he comes into competition with all other men who, for the same or any other reason, are willing to make similar promises; that is to say, he comes into competition with all those upon whose relative scales a unit of future wealth (which they can convince people they command) stands lower than a unit of present wealth, irrespective of the reason why it so stands. It does not matter what a man wants wood for so long as he wants it, but it does matter how much he wants it relatively to other things in the circle of exchange. In like manner it does not matter whether a man wishes to anticipate wealth because it will enable him to administer the resources on which he can already count more advantageously by suitably distributing them in time, or whether he wishes to increase the total of his resources, by equipping himself with a better supply of tools or cultivating his own faculties, or what other reason he has for his wish. What does matter is the magnitude of the premium he is prepared to offer. Secondly: The premium he will actually have to pay for the whole advance that he receives is not determined by the premium he would have been willing to pay for some of it sooner than go without, but by the equilibrating value of present as measured in future wealth, which is the resultant of the collective forces that play upon the market. This resultant proclaims the position of a unit-at-any-given-time-in-the-future, relatively to that of a unit-at-the-present-time, on the communal scale. It is open to any one to bring the significance of the marginal units on his own scale into harmony with this resultant. In a state of equilibrium every individual has done so; and where there is not equilibrium every individual has something (in his own estimate) to gain by approaching it. This is but the common law of the market. We have therefore succeeded in bringing the phenomena of interest under our general law.

Let us now consider the case of a man who desires to store his own energies in such a way that at a certain point of time in the future he will command in the market an accumulated volume of resources (instead of commanding a stream of resources during the whole period) in return for this continuous output of his energies. Suppose him to be provided with the proper supports, the following alternatives, amongst others, are open

Alternative ways of storing effort.

to him; and whichever of them he adopts he will expect the whole volume of resources he ultimately commands to be greater than the sum of those that would have come to him in a regular stream had he drawn upon them currently. He may cultivate and sow land, the crop of which will not be ready for marketing for some months and will require continuous expenditure until that time comes, but will then be capable of ministering to the immediate satisfaction of people's wants and will perish at once in satisfying them; or he may devote himself to the construction of some long-service article, such as a house, which will likewise be capable of directly satisfying human wants but will only gradually be consumed over a long period of years in satisfying them; or he may devote his resources to constructing machinery, which will not immediately satisfy any human want but will fertilise human effort and make it more productive than it would otherwise be. The body of persons who select amongst these alternatives will turn their efforts along the different channels in such proportions that the product of the same amount of resources in the present and in the proximate future, however directed, will have the same marginal significance at that point in the future at which they will all ripen. The conception of such a marginal balance offers no difficulty. We have seen that as a fact there is, in the general market, a premium on anticipated as against deferred satisfactions, and it follows that if a certain quantity of wheat is to balance in the market a certain house, since the total services rendered by the house will extend over a longer period than those rendered by the wheat, the total of those services must be higher, in order that it should weigh equally in the market, that is to say, command the same price. Again, if an engine can so fertilise a man's efforts and other resources that the same output with the aid of the engine will, in a given number of years during which the engine lives, produce a given surplus yield of resources, the total of that surplus must be larger than the satisfaction that the wheat can render, in order to balance it, or command the same price, in the market. For it will have to be gathered over a longer period.

So if I judiciously direct my resources to any purpose which involves waiting for the result, I shall be able to get a larger return than if I direct them so as to secure an immediate or proximate result. And if that result when it comes will be realisable only over an extended period of time, it must offer a larger total of advantage than if it is realisable at once, for otherwise it will not fetch the same price and I shall be a loser by choosing it. If the premium on the present is low a small excess will justify me. If it is high only a great one.

In reckoning the services that a house will render, year by year, we have to bear in mind that in order to avail ourselves of them without waste we shall have constantly to make expenditure upon it, and that probably or possibly it may gradually become unsuited to our requirements. And the same is true of an engine, the possibility of its being superseded in structure before it is mechanically worn out being a very important consideration. In the case both of the engine and of the house, therefore, we may set against the gross revenue of satisfaction in the one case, or of extra fertility of effort in the other, a fund for repairing and a fund for redeeming or replacing, and if we do this adequately we may regard the house or machine as immortal; and if a surplus revenue of enjoyment or efficiency remains we may regard that stream of future satisfactions, to be weighed against the present satisfactions of the corn, as flowing for an indefinite period, and therefore as having an indefinite total volume. But we shall presently see [1] that such indefinitely large volumes, accruing over an indefinitely long stretch of time and flowing at a definite rate, are always estimated at a definite sum. And as between the estimated stream of satisfactions which the house will yield (when such deductions as the purchaser thinks fit to make for redemption, etc., have been measured off) and the estimated stream of increased efficiency which the machine will give him or his successors, there is no theoretical difficulty whatever in striking a balance.

But the tool commands a price, not because it represents accumulations (that is, diversion in the past of resources and efforts from ministering directly to current wants), but because it has value in the present and future as a source of efficiency. No matter how

<small>Land as a tool.</small>

[1] Pages 298 *sq.*

much has been sacrificed in the past to secure it, it will only sell for what it is worth. And if it happens to be worth a great deal it will command its price quite independently of its history. If a tool fell down from heaven or sprang out of the bowels of the earth, and society granted any man a legal right to destroy it, to use it, or to allow or prevent its use by others, according to his discretion, he could sell it for a price determined by the sum of extra resources which the command of it would confer upon any one who should put it to its use. All forces of nature, in so far as they are available in insufficient quantities, seem to come under the conditions now contemplated. And so far as "land" is taken to mean mere space on the earth's surface it must be regarded in the same light. What we mean by "land" in ordinary life, however, is very largely a product in which effort has been stored just as much as in a plough; and from the point of view of commerce or industry there seems to be no difference between them. Both are matter that has been given us by nature so manipulated and modified as to make it indirectly serviceable to our needs. Fences, gates, roads, processes of reclaiming, permanent manures, and what not, all of them embody stored effort, and they all have as their substrate something that was never saved or accumulated, unless it were by nature. And whenever this original something, of the quality or in the places in which it is desired, exists in less than the desired quantity, subtractions from it would cripple, and additions to it would expand, the efficacy of human efforts. "Land," then, whether regarded as purely a gift of nature or partly as a manufactured article, has its marginal value, exactly as the tool has. It may be hired for its marginal annual yield or may be bought for the estimated significance of the indefinite succession of these annual yields, just as an engine or a house may be; and it will be balanced on the same principles against wheat or anything else that can directly minister to human satisfactions.

It should be noted, too, that land itself may yield a direct revenue of enjoyment when used as a garden, park, or hunting-ground, and that the desire for this direct revenue of pleasure will enter the market for land, and compete there with the desire for its services as a tool, or increaser of the industrial efficiency of effort.

At any given moment in the life of an industrial society a certain portion of its resources is already in a form in which it cannot administer directly to any human need. Such are tools or machinery, whether for carpentry, for agriculture, for spinning and weaving, or for whatever other purpose. *Supply in the market in "advances."* Another portion consists of articles ready for direct use, such as food for short service, or houses for long service. All these are composed of substances and occupy space which were originally the gift of nature; and any article may be at any stage of elaboration towards the form in which it will render its direct or indirect services, and in any stage of transit towards the place in which it will render them. At the present moment, too, there are wants to be supplied, impulses that demand expression, and energies that are capable of directing and modifying the forces and substances of nature. These wants, impulses, and energies will rise and flow in continuous streams during the future also, and the direction our efforts take in the present and proximate future will affect the balance between our wants, our impulses, our capacities, and our resources in the remoter future also. The remoter future, then, has at any moment some sure provision appropriated to it in the ripening crops and commodities, the machines, the indestructible or not immediately exhaustible forces and gifts of nature, and the prospective flow of energies; and the present and proximate future have assigned to them exclusively all rapidly perishable commodities from the rocket that has just been fired, to fresh fish and fresh butter, and on by insensible steps to stores that will keep for a year without serious deterioration, and so forth. But, except where we are dealing with things that have passed out of our control, though we are still enjoying them (of which the rocket that has already been lighted, and the febrifuge that has already been mixed, are types), we are not compelled to use at once the things we can so use. However short the period during which fresh fish will deserve the name, the nearer and the remoter future are competitors, within that period, for it. And just as the future competes for things capable of immediate consumption, so the nearer future competes with the remoter future for things capable of use over a long period, and designed for such use, but capable also of being used up quickly. A house may be used up in a few years, or nursed for a century; a farm may be run down in a year or two, or may be maintained or improved; a machine may be racketed to pieces to save a day's stoppage for repairs; and the perpetually renascent energies and opportunities that are comparatively uncommitted may be turned in any proportions we choose towards provision for the nearer or the further future; and at every stage of elaboration and transport some alternatives may remain open, though many are closed; and from that point onward the original intention may be modified in the interests of a nearer or a remoter future.

Thus there is always an enormous area over which the present and the future (or, more correctly, the nearer and the remoter future, at whatever point you choose to divide them) are in competition with each other, and there is always a premium to be paid for command in the present and the nearer future, as against the remoter.

We have seen that the "demand" for advances is just like any other demand, that it follows the law of diminishing marginal significance, and that the reason why advances are demanded does not affect the market price of them. It depends upon the position they take on the collective scale and the available supply of them. We know also that the supply of one market is always a demand upon another, and that in that larger market a wider range of demands is brought into balance. Now, we see that the market on which the supply of "advances" is a demand is the whole range of the realised utilities, or desired things, that are in the circle of exchange, so far as they are capable of being used at once, and that in that market all present and future satisfactions compete with each other, the resultant being a premium to be received on relinquishing the present.

Advances are made by the men who, for whatever reason, prefer a future (with the market premium) to be secured on some one else's credit, both to the immediate satisfaction of present desires and to the utilising of their resources in securing their own future at their own risk and by their own exertions. Advances are received by those who are willing and able, for whatever reason, to secure to their correspondents payment in the future of the market premium on present as against future resources. In both cases this preference, or willingness, will depend on anticipations of the future and on the provisions already made for the present and future respectively. And every man can so distribute his resources between present and future as to bring their marginal significance to himself into coincidence with the market price as registered in the premium.

And this brings us back to the administration of individual resources, from which we started. We now understand the exact nature and meaning of saving; and we understand that, as one man can make chairs for another, and get something from him that he wants more than anything he could have made for himself, so one man may save for another (that is, make something for him in advance) and get from him in the future something that he wants more than anything he could have made for himself in advance. This fact enters into the very penetralia of our ordinary affairs, and intimately affects the distribution of all our resources. If a man were confined to saving for himself; that is to say, if he could only embody his present resources in the things that he could himself make use of hereafter, he would be utterly unable to make provision for his future. For we have seen [1] that many of the things he will want this day ten years cannot possibly be kept so long if they exist already. Nor would he be able to embody indefinitely large resources in articles of lasting significance to himself, or in tools and appliances that would economise or fertilise his labour. No man, therefore, can adequately provide for his own future by the direct product of his own saving, nor can he indefinitely apply present resources to any kind of provision for his future. And, on the other hand, if no man could enjoy, or utilise, any accumulations, except in the shape of such specific articles as he himself had made or stored out of current revenue, or such as had been provided for him by persons obeying other than economic forces, the vast majority of us would never be able to begin living a civilised life at all. It is the exception for a man to possess a house, or to have "where to lay his head," on the strength of his own accumula-

Saving and providence.

[1] Page 269.

tions, or of possession that has come to him by gift. Most men, therefore, are dependent for civilised life upon the accumulations of others, and upon the market in which they can be commanded in exchange for currently accruing resources.

To sum up, no one can make or save for himself all the things he will want in the future, and few can live in the present without command of some forms of concentrated or accumulated wealth that they have neither made nor saved, neither concentrated nor accumulated, in advance. Therefore, A may want in the remote future something which he has not got, which he cannot make and which in any case would not keep, but for which he is very willing to spare or to make some equivalent-in-value in the present or the proximate future. He cannot himself transmute the one into the other; so what he does is to look for B, who can make (or put him in touch with C who can make) the thing he expects to want by the time when he expects to want it; and who will do so in consideration of receiving now or in the proximate future some of those equivalent-in-value things which A possesses or can make in the proximate future. Such a B he will always be able to find on certain terms. Thus any individual, however large his resources, can always find means of embodying them in tools and apparatus for the use of others; and under existing conditions he can always get a premium for doing so. And, on the other hand, any one who can give security (that is, any one who can make people believe that he can and will keep his promise to give them command of future wealth) may secure the tools and apparatus that he needs without saving up to secure them; or if he likes he may get them first and save up for them afterwards, instead of saving up first and getting them afterwards. But under existing conditions he will have to pay a premium for being enabled to do so.

When it is wise to save and when not. A millionaire is not only able to save but unable not to save, because he cannot spend all his accumulations at once, and he is always able to transmute present into future command of wealth. And under existing conditions persons who desire to anticipate wealth compete with each other in the premiums they offer him for doing that which he cannot help doing; so that he not only keeps but increases his wealth. A very rich man, then, cannot help saving; and a poor man cannot save enough to provide himself with a civilised shelter. These have no choice; but it may be wise and good husbandry for one man to save, though he is not compelled to do so; and foolish and wasteful for another to save, although he could do so if he liked. The last of this series of assertions is perhaps the only one that would be even thoughtlessly challenged; and it is therefore the only one that we need especially elaborate. And even this should hardly be necessary, for the proposition is directly deducible from our fundamental principle that marginal significance declines as supplies increase. The difference between 15s. and 20s. a week is psychologically greater than the difference between 20s. and 25s. It follows, then, that unless there are special conditions to make it so, it would not be worth a man's while to live on 15s. a week instead of £1 a week for twenty years, in order that he might have 25s. a week instead of £1 for twenty other years. Let us take an extreme case and suppose that a family with £1 a week were to live on 7s. 1d. a week, all told, for three years, saving 12s. 11d., in order that at the end of this time they might buy a cottage for £100, instead of renting it, at say 3s. a week, all their lives. Now of that 3s. a week we may say that 5d. represents the maintenance of the cottage, which they would have had to see to if it had been their own. If they buy the cottage, then, they are thenceforth 2s. 7d. a week better off, for the rest of their lives, than they would have been had they not saved; and in a little under fifteen years they will, objectively, have recovered the whole sum of advantages which they sacrificed during the three years of saving. The extra 2s. 7d. a week, which they will enjoy as long as they live, after that will be, objectively, pure gain. But psychologically? We know that 12s. 11d. off £1 is psychologically more than five times as significant as 2s. 7d. off £1. The privation of the three years, therefore, will be less than compensated by the advantages of the fifteen years, even if there is no loss of positive income from permanently lowered vitality. If we extend the period of saving, so as to bring it within the range of easier possibilities, the principle still holds. The terms on which a house can be rented may of course be so hard as to turn the balance the other way at any given point. But it is clear that to a poor man an evenly distributed income of smaller amount may be of more value than an unevenly distributed income of larger amount. It might, no doubt, be very wise for a young man to live hard as a bachelor for a few years and then start life as a married man with a house of his own; for a man may control not only the distribution of his resources but the incidence of the claims and liabilities upon them, and this is an enormously important branch of administration; but the mere fact that only a small percentage of prudent men own their houses is sufficient *prima facie* evidence that it may be better husbandry to hire than to buy, that is to say, better to borrow than to save.

Even to a rich man, saving may be bad economy; or if it is good economy it may be better to borrow first and save afterwards, than to save first and not borrow at all. Suppose a man to be in the enjoyment of an income of £700 a year. He believes that by putting an extra £10,000 into his business he could make it yield £1000 a year more, and he could raise the money at 6 per cent. This would leave him a balance of £400, raising his income to £1100. If he is willing to live on a comparatively small income for twenty years in order to enjoy a revenue of £1700 after that, he can do it either by borrowing the £10,000 and saving £500 a year out of his income of £1100, or by not borrowing at all and saving £500 a year out of his present income of £700. Obviously the first course is the more rational. But there is an element of risk and anxiety in it that must be duly estimated. The principle remains unchanged if we reckon for the gradual rise of income, in the first case by the gradual paying off of the sum borrowed, and in the second by the gradual investment of the savings.

Thus for poor and rich alike the wisdom of any particular act of saving may depend upon the magnitude of the accumulation contemplated in proportion to the total estimated resources of a lifetime. We have seen that it may be impossible or ruinous to save up for a house, if there is the alternative of renting. But even where there is no such tempting alternative saving may be ruinously expensive. For example, a very poor man cannot make adequate provision against old age, or even long sickness, except by encountering the certainty of present misery as great as that from the risk of which in the future he seeks relief. Hence it is contended that old-age pensions are more likely to stimulate than to check providence. In many cases it seems highly probable that this will be so; for there are many men who could not make full provision for old age without reducing themselves to premature penury, but who can hope, without placing an intolerable burden on their years of vigour, to improve the conditions under which an old age, secure in any case from extreme privation, may be passed. To save enough to secure the probability of 1s. a week after seventy would be almost futile, for 1s. a week would not be likely to keep a man out of the workhouse; but it might be worth much thought and self-denial to secure the difference between the bare independence of 5s. and the comparative affluence of 6s. a week. The first few shillings-per-week in old age may have a rising, not a falling significance, and securing a sixth shilling per week may in many cases be worth a greater effort and sacrifice than securing a first.

This, however, is a digression. Our immediate point is that if a very poor man were called upon to make complete provision for his old age or leave it unprovided for, it might be wise to take the latter course; whereas if he were a little richer he would be able to secure himself against extreme penury in old age without squeezing the life out of his youth. Thus it would seem that there is a point at which poverty makes it not only hard but unwise to save for distant objects; though it is always wise to save out one week's or month's expenditure to meet heavy and seldom recurrent expenses. For the extremely poor it would not be wise to save even against death by starvation; for a man can but die once, and it is not wise to deepen misery and eliminate from it any gleam of relief and enjoyment in order to protract it. Nor is it wise to provide for old age, unless there is fair prospect of making old age tolerable without making youth and maturity intolerable. As we have seen, it is only a minority of even well-to-do people that consider it wise to save up for the purchase of a house. And however rich a man may be it is obvious that there is always a natural limit to the wisdom of saving.

Indeed to the rich man the problem often is how he can avoid saving too much. The exigencies of his business may drain him of his income. It is always demanding to be extended, till he no longer controls it, but it controls him. It has become a kind of Frankenstein's monster that dominates his life. It must grow or die. And he cannot let it die, partly because he is dependent upon it, and partly because it has become a kind of entity to him, and, independently of all the things in the circle of exchange that it represents to him, has acquired a kind of independent claim upon his affection and his imagination, and is bound up with all manner of personal relations and obligations. So he curtails the indulgence of his tastes in every direction in order to provide for its extension, and is living in relative poverty in order that he may die relatively rich. Regarded simply as provision for the future, his saving is foolish, wasteful, nay, positively aimless; and if he is wise he will seek the means of escaping from it, though it may need years of scheming to do so. For the wealthiest, then, as well as for the poorest, there is a point at which saving becomes folly.

The fact that saving may produce revenue for an indefinite period does not really affect the matter; though a sophist might urge that, however little a man thinks of the future, an infinite series of future gains must outweigh any finite sacrifice. The answer is that even if a man's thoughts extend beyond his own life, and beyond those of his children and grandchildren, yet all human things are subject to uncertainty, and it is impossible so to forecast or control a very remote future as to secure that our purposes shall be even approximately realised in it; so that even if we could be sure that a definite saving would produce an unending revenue (that is a series of sums of money accruing "for ever"), yet the whole sum of the series, as valued in the mind of any given man, would only carry a definite and limited weight of significance and would be comparable to some definite sum of purposes, to be realised within periods which the imagination can grasp and the judgment handle with a certain degree of precision. There may be persons to whom the conception of establishing or controlling something that is to last as long as the planet is inhabited may have a certain value, but it will be a defined value. And even the diseased estimates of the miser will not escape the general law; for if his passion for saving suffers no sensible abatement as his wealth increases, yet the rate at which he saves will determine the degree of his present privation and abstinence, and the point will come at which sooner than make that privation and abstinence still more severe he will abstain from the minute additions to his savings which such a proceeding would secure. The principle of price as a determining condition of exchange asserts itself inexorably. If it did not the miser would—not as we sometimes say he does, "practically," in the course of years—but actually, in the course of days, die from starvation and exposure.

In fine, every man who is not living absolutely from hand to mouth will make some attempt so to distribute his resources over time as to apply them where they will give the best psychic return. Even if he is so constituted that he values the future more than the present, still, as long as he attaches any value to the present at all, there will come a point at which the receding margin of present satisfaction balances the advancing margin of contemplated satisfaction in the future. The balance between the present and future will be determined partly by a man's comparative poverty or wealth, partly by his individual disposition and circumstances, partly by the premium on savings which the markets to which he has access offer him; but that balance will always be struck somewhere, and it will be struck on precisely the same principles that determine us in striking the balance between potatoes and carrots, between dress and charity, between abundance of possessions and leisure in which to enjoy them, or between any of the other alternatives which are open to us whether they are or are not concerned with things that enter the circle of exchange.

Let us now return to the individual administration of resources, and let us consider how all that we have now learned bears upon it. We may suppose that a man who has arrived at a settled administration of his annual resources receives a legacy of £100. He may invest it, and if he does so he will have to consider what risks he will take. He may be content with a trifle over $2\frac{1}{2}$ per cent, or he may consider that the extra risk in an investment which will give him a higher return is worth incurring at the price. Suppose he considers 4 per cent a suitable interest. He will then expect (subject always to the risk he has deliberately taken) to have an extra £4 a year as long as he lives, and to leave his heirs the option between enjoying this £4 a year as long as they live, or exercising any of the other alternatives that are now open to himself. What are they? He may draw out £100 at once. He may make arrangements by which he will receive £4 : 10s. a year for forty years (£180 in all, the extra £80 being his premium on waiting). Or he may take £7 a year for twenty years (£140 in all, receiving the lower premium of £40 for the shorter period of waiting). Or he may choose £12 a year for ten years (£120 in all). If he has reason to think that the marginal significance of £1 to him during the next ten years will be considerably higher than during the ten or thirty years that will follow, he may be wise to adopt this last arrangement. Or if he makes a permanent investment and receives £4 a year he may spend it on insuring himself against fire, or he may save it up now in order to spend it later on, together with the premium he will then have received on it. Or, on the other hand, he may spend the whole £100 upon fireworks, thinking that the pleasure of making one grand display in the course of his life, and being able to look back upon it as long as he lives, will weigh against all the sum of advantages which he is forgoing. Or he may spend it on a holiday, either because he hopes it will renew his vigour and make him efficient industrially, or because he thinks it will be a keen delight at the time and will bring him a perpetual revenue in the pleasures of memory hereafter, or that these two considerations between them will equal in value anything that he could get for his £4 a year for life, together with the thought of the capital sum being passed on to his heirs. Or he may devote the sum to study or education, whether his own or his children's, and whether technical (in order to make himself more efficacious in creating commodities, or rendering services, which pass into the circle of exchange) or liberal (rendering him more capable of receiving and giving satisfactions that do not enter into it), or sharing

Reaction of the phenomenon of interest on the personal administration of resources.

the characteristics of both. Or he may effect some improvement in his house, or he may buy a picture, expecting to derive from the one or the other a revenue of enjoyment. Or he may combine any number of these things. He may spend 10s. on fireworks to celebrate the happy event. He may relieve a feeling of discomfort in his mind by spending £2 on a wedding present, when he had meant only to spend 10s., but was not feeling happy about it. He may spend £10 on furniture, £10 on the singing lessons he has been promising his daughter " as soon as he can afford it." He may devote £20 to a much-needed holiday, and after a few other " extravagances" he may lay by £50 "for a rainy day"; and out of the £2 a year that he receives on it meanwhile he may take out a modest policy in a fire insurance office, and may still enjoy the feeling that he can indulge himself in a little more tobacco, or a few more tram rides, than he has hitherto allowed himself. Some such distribution amongst a variety of applications would indeed be theoretically normal; for a number of margins would have to be advanced *pari passu* if there was already equilibrium in the man's expenditure and if that equilibrium were to be preserved. Very often, however, there would be no real attempt to distribute the sum in accordance with rational principles. Many people have a preconceived idea of what is proper to do under such circumstances. We have already noticed the force of tradition, and in such cases as this tradition often takes the form of some maxim or "general principle" which supersedes thought. The thought it supersedes in any special case would perhaps have been foolish or impulsive, and the collective experience embodied in the saw may be superior to it. But since the general principle takes no account of the special circumstances (on which after all everything really depends), it is also possible that thought would have been a better guide than tradition. Even such wholesome maxims as " Never trench upon your capital," or " Some saving should be made out of the narrowest income," though they have doubtless saved many people from folly, have also had their victims, and even their martyrs.

One or two further examples of the bearing of the rate of interest upon the administration of our resources and our selection between alternatives may be added, not because they introduce any new principle, but by way of exercises. Taking interest at 4 per cent, a man who is building a house and considering some improvement which will cost £100, and will effect economies in service or will render repairs less necessary, should ask whether it will save £4 a year. If so, it is just worth spending £100 upon it. If interest had been 2 per cent, it would have been worth while making not only this, but further and less important labour-saving improvements. Or it may be that the proposed improvements will add to the pleasure, but not reduce the expense, of living in the house, and the question then is, will it yield a revenue of satisfaction year by year equal to that which £4 (or £2) spent on horse and carriage hire, or on books, or on hospitalities, or in any other way, could yield? Thus, the lower interest is the better shall I be inclined to build. The substantial quality of the houses in many Dutch cities is attributed to the fact that at the close of the eighteenth century interest, on good security, was as low as 2 per cent.

So, too, the man who refuses an offer of £2000 for an old family portrait by a great master, practically pays, say, £80 a year for the privilege of keeping it on his walls. Does it secure him a revenue of enjoyment equal to anything he could get for that annual sum? Perhaps he has never asked himself the question, and hardly realises that the economy or extravagance of keeping it depends on the rate of interest. In like manner a man may buy a house for £1000, and then, by a few judicious purchases of adjacent sites, and a few suitable clearances, altogether at the expense of £200 or £300, may double its value. But he does not always realise that he has now practically doubled the rent. He might now let or sell his house, and have twice as much to spend on other alternatives as he could have had before. Therefore he sacrifices twice the value in other things for his house that he did before; and he has, without reflection, determined to apply the whole of the proceeds of his successful strokes of business to one item in his own expenditure. Neither of these men realises exactly what he is doing, nor do we, as a rule, admire the man who obviously does realise such things. But why? Only because we suspect that it is a sordid habit of mind that has made him realise them. The man who does not value personal relations and associations, and who is in the habit of looking at all his possessions apart from their atmosphere of association, their individuality—one might almost say their personality—who regards them merely as "things" that can be exchanged for other "things," is probably a sordid person. He is thinking more of the value that things have for others than of the value that they have for himself, and it is only in comparatively gross forms that he is susceptible to the flavours of life. His consciousness that it costs him £80 a year to keep a picture on his walls, or £50 a year to be able to sit in his garden and enjoy a pleasant prospect on Sunday afternoons, appears to indicate that he is in the habit of considering these things under their most material and detached aspect, as separable possessions, rather than as ministrant to inalienable experiences. The habit of perpetually dwelling on the exchange value of things suggests an undue preoccupation with means and appliances and an undervaluing of ends and experiences, an overvaluing of things that are and an undervaluing of things that are not in the circle of exchange. But it need not be so. A man accustomed to generalised thought on such matters would necessarily realise the facts that have just been mentioned, and on due occasion would act upon them; but he would also realise the value of the finer experiences that these things can provoke in him but in no other, and will understand that it may be very wise to keep a thing, if its roots have struck down into his life and its memories and associations have made an atmosphere around it, on terms on which it would be very foolish to acquire it as a naked material object or opportunity, on the mere chance of its clothing itself with "living garments" at some time or other.

Thus the balancing of present against future and of long-period against short-period satisfactions, and the saving up and investing of revenue in the hope of securing increased revenue hereafter, are not processes confined to what enters into the circle of exchange. The man who curtails his indulgences and his holidays in order to accumulate capital in his business that will yield him a revenue of things in the circle *Analogues to interest in things that do not enter into the circle of exchange.*

of exchange, and the man who turns aside from literary and artistic pursuits that he enjoys to severe and exhausting mental effort in order to acquire the elements of a new language or a new science, not because he enjoys the process but because he expects a revenue of enjoyment and power from its results in the future, are both of them measuring short-service against long-service expenditure, and are reckoning on a premium for choosing the latter; and both must be in command of certain resources in order to make such expenditure wise. But in the latter case there is no public market, and there is no objective measure of results. I cannot say that just as £100 will secure me £12 a year for ten years, or as a saving of £10 a year will secure me a lump sum of £118 ten years hence, so such and such a capitalising of mental effort will yield me such and such a series of mental experiences of defined magnitude; but nevertheless I must form, however unconsciously, some rough estimate of the value of the sacrifices and of the results. And though there may be no market in which I can barter these results against the commodities and services in the circle of exchange, I must always be adjusting their relations to them in my own life as best I may, and the two sets of considerations perpetually and inextricably work into each other. In determining my business or profession, and at every turning point of my life, I may consider the congenial or uncongenial character of the occupation itself, or of the course of action I am contemplating, its moral implications, its social connections, its personal relations, what it will allow for leisure and relaxation, and very likely its opportunities for influencing the lives of others in directions that I desire. And all these things will take their places in my mind and will weigh for something, but not for everything, as against the excess or defect of income that I should expect to accrue from this course or that.

Again, we have already seen that purposes concerned with things that are not in the circle of exchange cannot be accomplished except with the support of things that are. If I am a student who can earn more money by one kind of work, and a larger measure of enjoyment or imagined usefulness by another, the books that I need for the pursuit of the latter study are in the circle of exchange. How much energy am I to divert from the present pursuit of it with the resources I have, in order to increase my resources for pursuing it in the future? It is in the strictest sense a problem of saving in order to acquire and invest capital that shall henceforth yield me a revenue. I trench upon the enjoyment and usefulness of the present in order to gain a more than compensating enlargement of enjoyment and usefulness in the future, and the things I sacrifice and the things I seek are alike personal and spiritual, and cannot enter into the circle of exchange; yet the transmutation of the present sacrifice into the larger future command of them can only be effected by the instrumentality of things that do enter into that circle. Once again, therefore, we see that the underlying laws which regulate the market have an application beyond the range of business. The fundamental laws of economic science, in fact, are the laws of life, and our economic life not only derives its meaning from things that lie outside its own domain, but also submits to and illustrates laws which cannot be rightly formulated with exclusive reference to its phenomena.

Returning now to the narrower economic field, we may add to what has already been said a few words as to the forces which tend to dissipate accumulations when made or to retard their formation. We have already referred incidentally to the prodigal. His disposition to underestimate the significance of the future is plainly hostile to saving, and it is a disposition which a very large proportion of mankind share with him. We read of tribes of savages who so little realise the future that, however frequent their experience of want may be, they cannot be induced to lay in any kind of stores. When food is accessible they will literally eat as much as they can hold. They do not consider it a more desirable alternative to have a good meal every day for a week than absolutely to gorge themselves one day and have nothing at all for the rest of the week. A Neapolitan rubbing his shoulders against a street corner, when offered a lira for carrying a portmanteau, answered, "Ho già mangiato"—"I have had my dinner." The fact that he would want a dinner to-morrow was not effectively present to his mind. He did not realise that although he had no present wants the satisfaction of

Providence and its effect on accumulation.

x

which would compensate him for the proposed effort, he would have such wants to-morrow, and might not be able to satisfy them on such easy terms as those on which he could provide against them to-day. Still less can the mind at a low stage of reflectiveness realise the value of a revenue. A savage tribe might be capable of storing food and yet be incapable of maintaining a herd of cattle. They might be able to realise that famine a month hence was worth averting by some exertion or some degree of restraint exercised to-day, and yet they might not be able to grasp the subtler idea that by abstaining from eating up a herd of cattle that they had captured they might obtain a permanent revenue of milk and calves. The same Australian black-fellow who took great pains and made great efforts to make a bottle of milk last a kitten, that he had in charge, over a journey of a hundred miles, pronounced the white man in general "big fellow fool" because he did not kill his herd of cattle and have a feast with his friends.

All tools and apparatus of every kind, and all breeding stocks of plants and animals, owe their existence to the realisation of the fact that the same output of energy will produce a higher return the more adequately it is supported by suitable instruments and possessions—that is to say, to a vivid realisation of the future. It is clear, then, that the more provident a community is (that is to say, the higher the general level of realisation of future wants), the more favourable will the conditions be for accumulation.

But we have also seen that even if the poor man is as prudent as the rich man he will probably save a smaller part of his income; therefore both the total wealth of the community and the way in which it is distributed will affect the rate of accumulation. Much that is true, but much also that is false, has been written on the subject of the improvidence of the working classes. That improvidence is unquestionable and is often disastrous. But we should bear two points in mind. (1) For the extremely poor it is no paradox to say that providence is improvident. (2) The fairly well-to-do workman is far more provident and has far more accumulations than is commonly realised. I am thinking not only of the sums in the savings bank and of the property of the cooperative societies, the sick clubs, and so forth, but also of the weekly subscription paid by so many artisans to their trade societies for trade and political purposes. The power of the trade unions in controlling the industry and shaping the legislature of the present day is due entirely to the providence of the working classes, whether or not that power is providently exercised. It represents a sustained self-denial and an effective realisation of a remote and problematic future. The full significance of this is seldom realised. It may or may not be wise. It is certainly a striking manifestation of providence. While these pages are passing through the press we are waiting for the highest court of appeal to determine whether this form of providence, as now exercised, is legal or illegal; and the discussions that have taken place as to the issues dependent on the decision shew that some who deplore the improvidence of the working classes fear their providence still more. It is, at any rate, formidable enough to be regarded as a danger by those who fear the influence of organised labour in politics, and as one of the best promises of our times by those who welcome it. And indeed, apart from these far-reaching aspects of the question, many of those who know the working classes best are much readier to recommend them to spend more wisely than to urge them to spend less and to save more. But this is a digression. Our main inquiry is not into the actual level of prudence in any class of the community, but into the effect of its rise or fall upon accumulations and the rate of interest; and the general proposition is safe that the providence or improvidence of the members of a community is, together with the amount and the distribution of its resources, a determining cause of the rate of its accumulations. As these conditions become more favourable, a lower premium will induce accumulations, and accordingly accumulations will grow and will reach a lower marginal significance. Other things being equal, then, the rate of interest will fall as the community increases in wealth and in the intelligence and self-command needed for a vivid and effective realisation of future wants and enjoyments.

Having considered the conditions that determine the formation of accumulations, let us glance at some of the forces that dissipate them. If the poor man is improvident and forms no accumulations, at any rate he has no opportunity of dissipating them. His improvidence can at most only retard their formation. But the rich man who is improvident dissipates accumulations. If his wealth is to accrue to him in the future he enters the market and demands present wealth, promising future wealth instead of it; and since his offer or promise appeals to the economic forces just as powerfully as the offer of another man who will preserve and fructify any accumulations of which he gets control, the prodigal curtails the supply of the industrial and impoverishes the community by determining the flow of its resources into barren channels. But the prodigal is very far from being alone in this. Everything in the future is uncertain, and the man who lays down apparatus, or who sinks a shaft, in the anticipation of future wealth, may be disappointed by the event. So far from securing him a premium, the future may fail to give him back his principal. In this case there has been waste and misdirection. The length to which this waste and misdirection go will depend on the sagacity and honesty of the directors of commercial enterprises, and the nature of these enterprises themselves. The risk is there and must be taken; but if the risks are taken wisely as well as boldly, there is, properly speaking, no waste, for the failures are incidental to the successes, and the more cautious conduct which took fewer risks would secure lower average or aggregate results. The risk, being part of the price, must not be reckoned as waste. But we have constantly to remind ourselves that the very service which a successful business renders may itself be destructive. It is on his power of giving men what they desire that a man's success depends; and what they desire may be ruinous to the accumulations of themselves and of the community, though incidentally profitable to the man who supplies it. Moreover, a man may get what he wants from others, not by rendering them anything which they regard as a service even in the blindest and narrowest way, but by ignorantly or fraudulently persuading them that he is doing so. Prodigious sums of money are perpetually being diverted to enterprises which will swallow them up and never render them back, and which no one who knows anything about them seriously expects to make

Dissipation and waste of accumulations.

an adequate return. Those who know about them persuade those who do not to think that they will give a return, and in one form or another get a commission from them for their "services" in inducing them to misdirect and destroy their resources under the impression that they are increasing them.

Thus the rate at which a community accumulates its resources, or, in other words, the comparative breadth of the stream which is turned to long-service expenditure and to indirectly productive effort, will depend partly on the nature of the tastes, desires, and impulses of the community, partly on the amplitude of its resources, partly on their distribution, partly on the vividness with which the wants and pleasures of the future are realised, and partly on the sound judgment and integrity of all its members, more especially of those who are most active in directing its industrial affairs. *[margin: Causes that determine the rate of accumulation in a community.]*

As the premium on the present as against the future falls, it is clear that the annual net revenue in increased fertility which a tool must render in order to justify the expenditure upon it of resources which would have produced a given volume of corn will become smaller and smaller. For as £1 one, two, or twenty years hence comes to be estimated more and more nearly as equal in significance to £1 to-day, it is obvious that the revenue accruing from a tool will reach farther and farther out into the future before its attenuated and continuously attenuating significance ceases to influence our estimate; and thus it will have a longer period over which to run in order to make up the given volume of significance with which we·compare it. There is no theoretical limit above zero to this decline of interest.

Under like conditions the value of anything that cannot be accumulated or increased (if in the last analysis any such thing is found to exist), say, space on the surface of the earth, would acquire indefinite value, for it would have a marginal significance in fertilising labour of indefinite volume, and the fact of that volume's only accruing over a period extending through an indefinitely protracted future would not, under the conditions we are supposing, reduce it to a definite estimate. The extreme remoteness from practical conditions of these suppositions will be obvious to the reader, and will probably be sufficient reason in his eyes for not entering on the speculations that have sometimes been indulged in of the possibility of negative interest—that is to say, of a condition of industrial life in which there should be a premium on the future, and in which men should think it worth their while to devote present effort to the securing of future wealth, although if devoted to present satisfaction it would positively produce a larger volume, and should actually find it necessary at the existing margins to do this if they wished to "save" any more. While declining, however, to enter upon these purely academic discussions, it is well to observe that with increasing intelligence, integrity, and providence we have no means of fixing on any definite limit above zero to the fall of interest. Zero may conceivably be the limit, *i.e.* the point that will never be reached, but may be approached as nearly as we please, but certainly it will not be any point below zero. The question is often discussed whether the fall of interest will reduce the volume of accumulations. Normally the fall of interest must rise from increased accumulations; and accumulations increase because people are willing to make them on the terms they can command. Those terms become less and less favourable, and doubtless this will prevent some people from saving, or prevent them saving as much and as eagerly as they would have done had the terms remained more favourable. But the decline in the premium is itself due to the very fact that a smaller reward is enough not only to maintain but to increase the volume of accumulation, and therefore to ask whether the check which that decline puts upon accumulation will diminish its volume is to ask whether the drag you put upon a carriage as it goes down hill will make it back up the hill again.

I will conclude this chapter by trying to determine the meaning of the words "hire," "rent," and "interest," as generally used. This will involve some useful analysis which may help to give consistency and firmness to our conceptions; and incidentally it will lead us to a brief consideration of the principle of insurance, which has not found a place elsewhere in our investigations.

Hire, rent, and interest.

We have already spoken of the difficulties which the existence of large units introduces into the individual's budget. Much of the present chapter has borne upon some aspects of this problem, but there are others on which it has not touched. We saw that a large unit may threaten to disturb the administration of a small income by demanding concentrated expenditure before due preparation can have been made for it; and also that even if the payment for the large unit could be extended over its whole term of service, it might still happen that since two-thirds, or one-half, or one-tenth of the service is worth more than two-thirds, or one-half, or one-tenth of the whole, many persons who cannot afford the whole of a thing, and who therefore go without it, could and would, if they had the option, afford to get one-tenth of it at one-tenth of a price the whole of which they decline to pay for the whole of it. When a man keeps a stock of any articles, horses and cabs, bicycles, pianos, or anything else, for hire, he lets people actually buy them in fractions. And for the business to be sound it is necessary that each purchaser of a fragment should pay for the fragment he actually uses (which includes maintenance in the case of animals), should pay a premium to the jobber on his accumulations as high as he (the jobber) could get from any one else by placing them at his disposal, should pay him an insurance against the risk of there being interspaces during which no one applies for the commodities (which meanwhile deteriorate or run to waste, and demand maintenance, so that a certain fraction of them perishes without being sold), and lastly should remunerate him for the services he renders in conducting all the necessary business on a scale sufficiently high to induce him to pursue this trade instead of applying his energies to something else. We usually speak of "hiring" concrete things that can be moved, and which we undertake to return identically; and all the elements now enumerated normally enter into the payments made for them. The desire to have them on hire will only be gratified down to the point at which it is (objectively) high enough to make an effective bid in all the markets of capital, energy, enterprise, and so on, which we have indicated.

The man who lets houses may also be regarded as selling in fractions. For though the tenant uses (or at any rate buys the right to use) the house continuously, yet he may retain it for a few years only, and in that case he only buys a fraction of it altogether. Here there is the same liability as before to interspaces between lettings—that is to say, fractional periods during which the house must be looked after and kept in repair and when no one is paying for it. Thus the same elements may be distinguished in the rent of a house as in the hire of a cab. In addition to any remuneration the landlord may be able to command for his own attention to the premises, there is the charge for maintenance, which may be regarded as paying for the fraction of the house actually used up, the insurance against no-rent periods, and the revenue which the market offers to any man who has made accumulations and who places them at the service of those who have not. There seems to be no difference in theory, then, between rent and hire, except that the tenant of a house frequently undertakes the maintenance of it himself—that is to say, he actually replaces (or partially replaces) that part of the house that he has used up; whereas the man who hires a horse and cab does not. Similar arrangements are often made in letting and renting land. The distinction between hiring and renting, then, appears to be mainly one of usage. We generally speak of "rent" in the case of things that cannot be moved (houses and lands), but which have to be handed back to their owners identically.

Very closely connected with this fractional consumption of large units is the whole range of provision for uncertain future events which are best met by insurance. It is obviously bad economy to provide for an uncertainty as though it were a certainty. Any one's house may be burnt down, but nobody knows either when or whether his own house will be. It is impossible to make instant provision for it, and if each of a thousand men made express and adequate provision for the event, and it only came to one of them, each of the others would have distributed his resources on the assumption that at such and such a time he would require to make a great outlay, which assumption would have turned out to be false. Here a difficulty analogous to that of the large unit presents itself in a complex and aggravated form. The demand for a heavy expenditure may come before provision can possibly be made for it, or it may not come at all. It may be impossible to provide against the event; and if provision can be and is made, it will most likely not be

Insurance.

wanted. And yet if the man whose chance of needing the provision any one year is one in a thousand could contribute a thousandth part of the provision and then be safe, it might be very wise for him to do so. The system of insurance enables him to do this. He may tell off the fraction which corresponds to his computed risk, and no more, and may then be safe. A thousand men have each paid for a fraction of an ideal house, which they may be regarded as holding in common, with the agreement that actual possession shall be given to the one amongst them whose present house is burnt down. The premium paid by each of them to a certain insurance company may be analysed on the principles that we have already illustrated. Each policy-holder must pay a fraction of the sum he will possibly receive corresponding to his chance of receiving it, so that all the policy-holders together pay for all they get. They must also pay a premium on the accumulations or capital with which the company starts; and they must pay a further sum out of which the staff is remunerated. The privilege they enjoy of being allowed to secure themselves by paying for their risk and no more must be worth these two premiums. The same analysis applies to insurance against sickness or accident; and part of it applies to provision for old age.

What is called "life insurance" stands on a somewhat different footing. In many, perhaps in most, cases it is at first what might more rightly be called an "insurance against some of the consequences of early death." A man earning a certain income cannot at once make adequate provision for his family against the improbable event of his dying within a few years; but he can make a fraction of adequate provision against it corresponding to the fractional chance of its being needed. This he does by insurance. If, as may well be the case, the risks against which it was originally intended to provide have after the lapse of years been safely passed, the payment of the premiums changes into a method by which a man can save up for his heirs on better terms than would be possible by other investments, though the urgency of saving for them at all is no longer there. Further analysis has no special bearing on the matter now in hand.

"Interest" is usually spoken of when the borrower does

not receive and return things that he wishes to use and enjoy, but nominally money and actually the command of such items as he chooses to draw from the circle of exchange to a specified value in gold. In this case the borrower has to see to it that he either maintains throughout, or is able to restore at the close, the full value that he has received; and therefore he makes no payment for maintenance. The whole payment in this case is the premium on the accumulation that has been made for him. It is usual, however, to include in "interest" the payment that is made in compensation for the risk incurred in accepting a promise which it may not be in the power of the party making it to keep.

<small>Interest.</small>

It will be seen that the distinction between rent and interest has little theoretical value. If a man takes a house on a repairing lease he pays "rent" for it; but if he borrows money, buys the house, keeps it in repair, and pays the man who lent him the money, he pays "interest," not "rent." Into "hire," "rent," and "interest" alike, the premium on enjoying accumulations without having accumulated enters as a factor, and except in cases where risk is negligible this premium never constitutes the whole payment.

CHAPTER VIII

MARKETS (*Continued*). EARNINGS

SUMMARY.—*The market of services or efforts follows the general law of the market. The flow of services of every kind determines the point down to which the desire for them is satisfied, higher or lower on the collective scale according as the stream is narrower or broader. The market in human effort is characterised by the fact that effort cannot be stored (except in a secondary sense and to a limited degree) unless embodied in some material thing, animate or inanimate; and therefore it runs to waste if not used as the capacity for it rises. Further, in many cases it is impossible for the holders to maintain an effective reserve price. And again it is impossible to detach it (unless embodied) from its source. Under these restrictions the law of the market dominates the exchange of human efforts with each other and with commodities. But the markets are often imperfect. The supply of each separate market of human effort constitutes a demand on the general market, and whereas its flow into the several markets is to a large extent dominated by economic forces, the original supply or production of human raw material is to be regarded almost entirely as incidental to expenditure of resources and expression of impulses, and scarcely at all as produced in response to a demand. Economic forces tend to secure to every one in the market as much as his effort is worth to any one else at the margin. It does not follow either that he has no claims beyond this, or that his marginal worth might not be increased; but seeing that the better society is supplied with the thing he makes the lower will be its place on the collective scale, it follows that each group of workers has an interest in society being rich in all things else but poor in what it itself supplies. Hence the lump-of-labour economics and much misdirected sympathy with anti-social action. A full recognition of the hardships involved in the uneven advance and the fluctuations of industry is a necessary condition of successfully combating anti-social ways of attempting to remove them.*

We have now dealt with markets of commodities under various aspects, and have seen how the same underlying principle may be traced through the whole range. No economic consideration ever urges a man to give more for any commodity than it is marginally worth to him, and every economic consideration urges him to give as much, rather than go without it. In so far as there is free communication and independence of action, economic considerations will tend to produce a uniform market price for any commodity at any given time, which price will coincide with the marginal place of the commodity on the collective scale. We have further seen that every commodity has its own market, and that, wherever the nature of a commodity allows of its being stored, or secured, for a lengthened period in advance, a class of considerations will affect its place on the scales of the consumers (and therefore on those of speculative holders) which could not affect rapidly perishable articles. And this last consideration has led us on from the consideration of speculative "holding" to an examination of the whole system of hiring, loaning, and "advancing," whether of specific articles or of general command of things in the circle of exchange. And further, we have seen how we may treat the supply of any market as itself constituting a demand upon some other market, until we ascend at last to the least differentiated material sources of our wealth.

<small>Recapitulation.</small>

We must now expressly note that not only commodities but services are in the circle of exchange. This fact has entered implicitly into all our investigations into the market of commodities. The supply of tables and bookshelves is a demand not only on the market of timber, but also on the market of services, for the skill and

<small>Services are in the circle of exchange.</small>

effort of the carpenter is as essential as the supply of wood to the production of these commodities; and to the consideration of the markets of human effort, or service, we will now turn.

It is obvious, to begin with, that we have been justified in assuming throughout our investigations that services as well as commodities do actually enter into the circle of exchange. A man may be paid for speaking, writing, singing, performing antics for others to look at, conducting ceremonies or rites which are believed favourably to affect our relations with the spiritual world, or delivering exhortations which will be conducive to our inward harmony. All these services, then, are in the circle of exchange. Moreover material commodities have received the form or have been brought into the place in which they can satisfy human wants by the exercise of human energies. Many writers have pointed out that man's share in all the processes of manufacture and agriculture, in all "making" or "producing" of material things, consists merely in changing the places of things. The direct activity of man appears indeed to be confined to this; but sometimes his object in placing things together is to initiate transformations effected by nature, upon which he has to wait. He has placed the seed in prepared ground and must await the transformations in the laboratory of nature, by which the constituents of the soil and atmosphere are transformed into things he wants to eat, or which he will manipulate by manufacture into the things he needs. In such cases the action of man is disguised and falls into the background. It hardly leaves a visible trace on the resulting possession, and we think most of the action of nature. In other cases, as in the whole class of manufacturing operations, man is anxious that things should not be transformed by nature after he has placed them, but should retain as long as possible the form and relations which his direct action has given them; and in these cases the record of human effort is stamped in clearer and more permanent form upon the thing itself. Or again, the visible movement may be that of his own organs only, as is the case with speech, causing vibrations on the atmosphere which raise valued sensations, conceptions, or states of mind. In such cases the traceable physical record of man's activity is in the highest degree transient. Or a man may move the fiddle-bow over the strings, in which case the physically traceable effect is equally transient, though produced with the aid of an external instrument that remains. Or he may move his brushes to his paints and his paints to his canvas, in which case the physical modifications produced have a high degree of permanence, but the mechanical energy expended sinks into insignificance in comparison with the rarer qualities that direct it. These examples will suffice to illustrate the indefinite varieties and combinations that may be traced in the qualities of mind, of muscle, of ear, and of eye, that direct and render effective any output of human energy; and the like varieties in the effects involved, whether as to the permanence of the modifications in visible physical structures that directly follow, and in the relations of these direct results to the natural processes initiated by them. But there is apparently no kind of effort, or output of energy, that can enter directly or indirectly into the circle of exchange which does not involve some degree of intelligent thought and some degree of physical movement, and which does not produce some more or less permanent modification in material things. In the case of the singer or musician, it is impossible to preserve the modified material, viz. vibrations in the air (except indeed as far as the invention of the phonograph may be held to qualify this statement), so that if I wish to enjoy the results of the musician's output of energy I must command his services directly; and if when he sings or plays there is no one there at the moment to hear him, then all enjoyment except his own is lost. Whereas if a carpenter has made a table, the results of his effort are more permanently embodied, and even if no one has any use for these embodied results to-day, some one may have use for them to-morrow, or this day twelve months.

The fundamental conditions for the exchange of services for services, or of services for commodities, obviously exist.

<small>Services exchange for services and for commodies.</small> The wants that services can supply have their places on the individual and on the collective scales, in and out amongst those which commodities can supply. Moreover the persons in a position to render services can often produce something with them that takes a higher relative place on the collective scale than

anything that they could produce for themselves occupies on their own. Again, the power to please me with a song has a primary value; whereas the value of skill to draw fish out of the ocean is derived from the value of the fish when safely landed; that is to say, the one skill can be directly, the other only indirectly, applied to the satisfaction of human desires or tastes, but in either case we find that services, like commodities, have their declining marginal value. Whether, for instance, I prefer so much food to so much music depends on the breadth of the stream of the supply of each which I already enjoy. And the manufacturer who has a large supply of material and plenty of orders on his books, may be willing to pay higher for appropriate services and lower for more material than he would be if he had "hands" enough to work through his orders as rapidly as he received them, but was short of raw material.

The conditions for the formation of markets in human effort, therefore, are present; and just as every commodity has its own market and its own market price, so we may expect every kind of human effort to form its own market, in which earnings will appear as market prices. Human effort that derives its significance from more or less permanent modifications of material things, becomes merged, as soon as exerted, in commodities, and its concrete and material result is dealt with in the market of commodities, so that when we speak of the market of services we must be understood to have primarily in view transactions in which a price is paid to a man in consideration of his putting forth some effort, not in consideration of the result. This includes such speculative transactions as undertaking to pay a doctor for his advice and attendance, not for any actual change in the habit of my bodily functions or tissues which he may produce; paying a lawyer for undertaking to conduct my case, not for conducting it successfully; giving a commission to a painter to arrange certain materials in such a way as to produce the counterfeit presentment of such and such a face, not for the actual material arrangement; or a promise to pay a gardener or a carpenter who undertakes to put forth effort to effect certain physical transfers, juxtapositions, unions, and severances.

Markets in human effort.

Here, as elsewhere, it is practically impossible to draw an exact line, and unprofitable to attempt to do so. Time wages, for example, are technically payment for services; but if the work is easily tested the employer knows exactly what he is paying for, and since his bargain is renewed day by day or week by week, it would be mere pedantry to insist that he is paying speculatively for the output of energy, and not for its ascertained result, embodied in commodities. Human energy, then, may minister directly to human desires or needs, or it may effect relatively permanent modifications in material things; and in the latter case a bargain may be struck either for its output or for the transfer of the thing in which it has been embodied. In this last case we cease to bargain for services and bargain for commodities. Thus the general conception of services and the payment for them, as distinct from commodities, is clear enough, but the two may easily pass into each other. We shall generally speak of "earnings" in connection with the output of human effort, as we speak of "prices" in connection with the transfer of commodities, but it may be well to point out that the term "earnings" does not exactly cover the conception of "payment for services" as we have now conceived it; for if a man puts his effort into a material thing and sells the commodity, we speak of him as "earning" the price he receives just as much as if he bargains for the output of the effort itself. The term "wages," on the other hand, while subject, though in a lesser degree, to the same ambiguity, is much too narrow in its scope for our purpose, since it does not include payments made to the artist or to the professional man.

The popular instinct of language, then, has not recognised a distinct category of speculative payment for services as distinguished from payment for their embodied results, and has provided us with no convenient word for it, but it is important that we should give some special attention to it. Since the power of rendering services flows to waste as fast as it accrues unless it is directly applied, or embodied in material commodities, it follows that the market in services has its nearest analogues in markets of the most swiftly and irrevocably perishable commodities. But any commodity, to be marketed at all,

Their characteristics.

must have a certain degree of permanence, whereas the power to make effective effort perishes as it rises; and if the power generated as the moments pass is not exerted as the moments pass, it cannot be held in store and utilised at a later moment. We must therefore conceive of the supply of available human effort of any kind as perpetually flowing to waste if not utilised the moment it rises. On the other hand, the supply of many commodities is replenished intermittently, perhaps as the seasons of the year come round, perhaps as chance determines the discovery of ores or deposits; whereas the power to put forth human effort is (with the qualifications presently dwelt on) continuously renascent. Now we saw, in considering personal expenditure, that stocks must be reduced to terms of "rate of supply" in order to be accurately treated, because wants, to which they have to be related, are either continuous or recurrent. The supply we are now considering presents itself at once in the form of a stream, and we can have no difficulty in perceiving that in an open and competitive market the theoretical price of services, like that of commodities, will be determined by the breadth of this stream of supply (that is to say, the rate at which the services become available), and the composition of the collective scale of preferences. But in this case the rate of supply can only be adjusted to irregularities of demand within very narrow limits. It cannot be stored, and so, if there is anything intermittent or irregular in the occurrence of the wants which a particular service would satisfy, it will be impossible to accommodate the stream of supply to the stream of demand; for the stream cannot be narrowed down to a trickle for a time, and then swelled to a broad volume by pouring in the accumulations from the reservoir. Commercially, no doubt, a contractor may broaden or narrow the stream he controls by taking on or dismissing men, but it is not this stream of which we are speaking. We are speaking of the stream of continuously renascent power of work, and in the case of a man who has not been employed that power has run to waste. The contractor might talk of drawing upon the reserve of unemployed labourers, but the power of work which has not been used up to this moment is not in a reservoir. It has perished.

Y

It is true that this statement is subject to certain qualifications. No man is capable of continuous effort for a lengthened period; and during times of sleep or rest he may be said to be accumulating power, to be discharged in the times of waking energy. And this fact, which is obvious in its application to the alternations of the twenty-four hours, is also true, in a lesser degree, of longer periods. A man may prepare himself by a holiday for putting out a larger amount of a special kind of effort during a given period than he would otherwise have been able to generate in the time. He may even keep up a strain through a series of years on the strength of energy which he has stored up during some previous period. And yet again, a period of training or technical study is a storing of energy to be realised at a later period. But when all these qualifications have been considered, the perishability upon which we have insisted remains the marked characteristic of the exertion of human power, as distinct from the transference of commodities. Relatively speaking, the one is a stream which perpetually flows past us irrevocably; the other is a store which remains with us for a longer or a shorter period, to be used up at our convenience.

In close connection with this continuous perishability of human powers as they rise is their inseparability from their source. Milk can be transported to London while the cow that gave it remains in Berkshire, but the power of work of a man (or of a horse for that matter) cannot be separated from the being that puts it forth. Hence human power cannot be massed locally, except to a limited degree. The amount of any kind of effort available at any moment in a given community cannot, as a rule, be brought under survey at a special place, as the week's supply of plums or potatoes available for the district may. It must be ascertained through more or less indirect methods.

The characteristic of perishability further prevents the possibility of speculatively holding back effort in order to apply it at some more favourable moment in the future. In so far as a man can apply his own efforts to his own purposes, he has a reserve price in bargaining with others; for unless they will do better for him in return for his effort than he can do with it for himself, he has no economic reason for dealing with them. If he has both a stock of wood and the skill of a craftsman, he may choose between selling his wood and making a bargain with some one else for the application of his skill, or applying his skill to his own material, and putting the resultant articles into the market. *Reserve prices.* Or more generally, whatever opportunities, possessions, and faculties any one commands, he may choose between all the possible distributions of his own faculties amongst his own opportunities (whether for the direct serving of his own purposes or the satisfying of those of others), and the linking of his faculties to the opportunities commanded by others, and the opportunities he commands to the faculties possessed by others. As long as these varied courses remain open to him, the advantages of one determine a reserve price below which he will not consent to devote his resources to the other. But if his own faculties and opportunities can make no fertile combinations, then they are thrown into the market with no reserve price, and will sell for what they are worth at the margin to others. The man, for example, who has a small piece of land, the tools for cultivating it, and enough in hand to buy seeds and await the maturing of crops for his own consumption, has a reserve price for the exercise of his skill. If it is of no use to any one else it is of some use to himself, and he need not sell it except for something more than it is worth to himself. Again, the man who has the faculties and the materials necessary for producing things which he could not directly live upon himself (the case, perhaps, of our man who has a stock of wood and craftsman's skill as well), will also have a reserve price for the application of his services to the materials supplied by others, though it is based not on his ability directly to supply his own wants, but on his ability to enter another market than that of mere services. The case would be the same with the cultivator of the plot of land if he were producing choice fruit for the market instead of wheat and potatoes for his own use. But in all cases alike we shall find that in an open competitive market the price of services, like the price of commodities, will be determined by the rate at which the supply becomes available and the collective scale of preferences.

Naturally every different kind of energy has its own

market, but a man of varied faculty need not sell effort of one kind at any price lower than that commanded by effort of another kind which he is capable of making; nor need he turn the same effort into one channel on lower terms than it would command if directed down another. His energy is in the condition of undifferentiated material, and just as the same wood can be made indifferently into washstands or tables, so the same skill can be applied indifferently to effecting either transformation. Untrained faculty may be regarded as analogous to raw material at a still earlier and less differentiated stage, since it can be trained into any one of many different faculties, and there will always be a tendency to turn it into the direction in which it is anticipated that it will minister to the wants highest on the collective scale.

There is another aspect of this question that must be considered. If the effort in question is irksome the man will, so far, have a reserve price. He will not put forth the painful effort except for an adequate return; and what return he will consider as adequate will depend upon the extent to which he is already provided with the things he desires. The only reserve price to the man who is totally without resources is the price that will enable him to keep alive with just enough vitality to enable him to do the work. He might not refuse to accept even less, but he would not be able to offer his wares continuously unless he received so much. The ampler his provision the less pain will he be willing to encounter to increase it by any given unit, and the higher will be the reserve price he puts upon his efforts. Now we have seen that division of labour has brought about a state of things in which hardly any man can apply his own powers to the direct satisfaction of his own most immediate and importunate wants, and it follows that any man who has no independent provision, but relies upon his own efforts, must throw a great part of them upon the market without any reserve price. Moment by moment his power is generated and perishes. If he can make no direct use of it for himself he must dispose of it at its present marginal value to others. He cannot hold it back till a more urgent demand arises.

What he can do, however, and very frequently does, is to let some of his powers run to waste, as far as immediate and direct results go, in order that he may transport himself to another place in which the powers that accrue to him in a future period may be exercised to more advantage; or, in order that he may bring some kind of pressure to bear on his correspondent (as in strikes), to improve the terms of bargains for the future. This last point leads us to another characteristic of the market in efforts which complicates and qualifies all those we have already noted. It rises from the circumstance that human effort is constantly and directly under the control of the human will. So, of course, are damsons and potatoes, for all bargaining and exchange is an exercise of human option; but the damsons and potatoes have, at any rate, no will of their own, and the man who has once got possession of them, though he may be much troubled by proceedings on their part (such as sagging or sprouting—proceedings which he is sometimes tempted to regard as arbitrary), at any rate has not to reckon with any theory on their part as to market prices and its corresponding reactions upon their behaviour. These general characteristics of the market in human effort constitute a sufficiently formidable and intricate subject for economic speculation. But we must return to the fundamental fact that all dealings in human effort are subject to the primary forces which dominate markets in commodities. Every man will secure what he desires on any terms which give it him for less than he thinks it is worth to him, and will refuse to give more for it than he thinks it is worth to him. And its worth is affected by the breadth of his supply of it.

We may now glance at a few illustrations of the way in which the general characteristics of the market in human effort manifest themselves, and the attempts that are made to deal with them and to remove some of their inconveniences. Let us begin with a single individual. He may be a singer, a lecturer, a physician, a university coach, or a novelist. He *The law of the market as illustrated in markets of effort.* may, or may not, be bound or hampered by traditional customs which prevent his conforming to the economic conditions of his case. For instance, custom may dictate that he shall not charge less than a certain fee, and this fee may prevent his getting work which he would be willing to take and able to secure at a lower fee; and some portion of his time may flow off unused in consequence. Or custom may prohibit his raising his fee above a certain point; and he may consequently work harder and earn less than he could do if he were able to limit the number of his clients by raising his fee. In these cases his market is partly dominated by other than economic forces, that is to say, by other considerations than the place on the collective scale occupied by the want to which he can minister, and the place occupied on his own scale by things in the circle of exchange. If, on the other hand, his market is dominated by purely economic forces, what are the elements which compose it? What corresponds to the " amount of commodity in the market "? Obviously the daily renascent flow of possible exertion on his part. To some extent the thing he supplies can be supplied by others also; to some extent it is peculiar to himself. Just so any commodity in the market supplies wants for which partial but not complete substitutes may be found in other commodities. The analogue of the amount of the commodity is the daily accruing capacity to put forth the effort in question. And the place which it occupies on the collective scale is determined by the corresponding stream of wants that it can supply. This stream, as we have seen, may be very irregular. The season, or the term, or the session may bring an access of requirements which periodically raise the place of this particular want on the collective scale. Individual wants or accidental estimates of the significance of the special services in question on the part of conspicuous persons may suddenly raise the demand, or a brilliant achievement of any kind on the part of the man himself may have a like effect, of a more or less transient nature. Now, to the limited extent to which the man can store his energy, that is to say, recoup himself by previous or subsequent relaxation for an extra strain during a certain period, he can adapt himself to these irregularities as they rise. But this possibility is closely limited. It may deal with the ripples, but it cannot deal with the ground swell of change. Many an intellectual and artistic workman has died in poverty who could have made ample provision for his whole life during the few years when he was the vogue, had it been possible for him to concentrate the working hours of his life into that short period, reserving only his leisure hours for the long period of the world's indifference.

Apart from these fluctuations, the individual workman, regarding the thing that he can do as the special commodity that he brings to market, would, if untrammelled by tradition, proceed economically on such lines as the following :—He would be, to a certain limited extent, a monopolist ; and if he found that he could command as much work as he chose to take on certain terms, he might consider either of two problems. In the first place, he may consider how much work he will take on those terms. And here the principle of the reserve price comes into play. He will not sell at a given price any effort which he could more fruitfully devote to the direct securing of the things he would otherwise have to draw out of the circle of exchange ; and even if he can secure none of these things on advantageous terms by the direct exercise of his capacity, yet he may be able to enjoy it for its own sake when he exerts it in directions that have no economic significance ; and it is manifest that at a certain point effort will become so painful that it will not be worth while to encounter it for the sake of further command of things in the circle of exchange.[1] To put it broadly, both the need of rest and aversion to irksome effort, and all that free command of powers and resources, and application of them to the securing of things that do not enter into the circle of exchange, which we embrace in the term "leisure," will put a reserve price on his wares. He will say, for example, "At 7s. 6d. an hour, or at 300 guineas an operation, I will only undertake so much and no more for the public." But, in the second place, he may raise his terms and say to himself, "I consider it worth the risk to take silk, or to raise my fees. That will limit my ministrations to a range of wants higher on the communal scale. It will subject me to the risk of encountering periods during which the stream of demand, at this high level, is narrower than the stream of the supply of energies which I should be willing to devote to its satisfaction. And I may find time upon my hands, not because of my own mental reserve price in time, but because my announced reserve price in money determines

---

[1] Cf. Book II. pages 522 *sqq.*

a margin nearer the origin than I had contemplated." Custom, convenience, the difficulty of rapidly forming lines of communication, and the fear of future complications will prevent him in such periods from putting a larger amount of his energy upon the market, and taking the lower price that it will fetch.

Another difficulty in markets of effort may rise from the uncertainty that often exists as to what the service bargained for will really effect. Markets of effort are often highly speculative. It may be easy enough to estimate the quality of bricklaying or type-setting, for instance, and when one man employs another he may, in many cases, be able to define with some closeness the character of the services he stipulates for, and to ascertain what quantity and quality has been actually rendered. But if the service required is the exercise of a general vigilance over the conduct of a business, avoiding waste, keeping the persons employed in good temper and harmony, watching over scientific and industrial developments which make economies possible, gaining access to fresh customers, regulating mechanical details, and so forth, it may be very difficult to know beforehand exactly what a man will be capable of doing in all these particulars, or to make sure afterwards exactly what he has done. And therefore a man with a very high degree of capacity for business management may have the utmost difficulty in commanding the ideal market value for his services, that is to say, in getting remuneration corresponding to the marginal significance of the services he can render to a great business firm; for he may have no means of convincing any one that he possesses these faculties, and even if he is exercising them on behalf of a single firm, and their value is fully understood there, other firms may not be in a position exactly to estimate the services he would be able to render them. Again, if he can find no opportunity of setting up on his own account, he may have no personal reserve price; and consequently he may be compelled to accept remuneration which he knows, and which those who pay it know, to be far below the marginal significance of his services on the collective scale. This is because there is no effectively organised market for such services, so that the people concerned do not know of the

<small>Imperfection of markets in some kinds of faculty.</small>

existence of his faculty. The same is perhaps still truer in the case of authors. The taste of the public is exceedingly difficult to gauge, and the history of literature is full of instances in which the men whose profession it is to know what books will sell and what books will not, have been very far out in their reckoning. An author may long be unable to convince any publisher of the high place on the collective scale which his services would occupy if his faculty had a chance of making itself known. Reverse instances are perhaps more frequent, though they are less often heard of. Both business managers and authors often have the money value of their services over-estimated, and receive remuneration more than corresponding to the marginal significance in the market of their output of energy. We see, then, that some markets of human energy are capable of more systematic and precise organisation than others, but the underlying principle of markets in human effort and markets in commodities is precisely identical.

We have dealt hitherto with cases of effort in which the specific quality of each individual's faculty is of importance. If we now turn to cases in which the same service can be rendered almost indifferently by a great number of individuals we shall find the same general principles at work. In an area over which general communications spread, any man who estimates the output of a particular kind of effort as having a higher marginal value to him than is represented by its present earnings from some one else, will have an economic interest in diverting it to his own purposes by offering a higher remuneration. And as this service flows to him and its marginal significance decreases to him, it will rise to the man whom it is leaving and whose supply is contracting. This will bring about equilibrium; and the point at which the equilibrium is reached will vary with the supply of the special kind of power in question, and the ultimate reserve price of those who possess it, and the rise and fall on the communal scale of the wants to which it ministers. This last item may be a very unstable one. For instance, there are fluctuations from week to week, from day to day, and even from hour to hour, in the urgency of the

More perfect markets in other kinds of faculty. But even in them prices do not closely follow fluctuations in marginal significance,

want which the skill of the agricultural labourer can supply. If the fluctuations of the natural market were closely followed, the wage of the agricultural labourer would be in a constant state of flux. But even apart from custom and tradition the inherent difficulties of ascertaining the true conditions of the market at any moment, and the manifest waste and inconvenience of constant attempts to do so, would in any case lead to certain "poolings," that is to say, contracts spreading over a certain period, during which, presumably, the labourer's marginal effort for the day will sometimes be more than worth his wage and sometimes less. But when the wage has thus been fixed by a general calculation and by custom, there will be an expanding and contracting fringe of casual labour. At the moments when the permanent staff are really earning more than they are receiving, the farmer will be anxious to have more labour on the same terms, and, if he can, he will secure it, until his increased command of the commodity lowers its marginal significance to the level of the fixed price. And at periods when they are earning less than they are receiving, he may be particularly inclined to find fault with their work, and let them know that he could do very well without them. And the reverse attitude of mind will more or less pronouncedly characterise the men at the respective seasons.

When harvest comes, the fluctuation is too pronounced to be met in this way. It is universally recognised, in one shape or another, that wages must be higher at harvest-time than at other seasons. This is but natural.

<small>except when pronounced.</small>

For a considerable period the marginal significance of agricultural labour is markedly higher than it is during the rest of the year, so much so as to make it worth while to divert to harvest work the energies of many who have usually some more eligible alternative. Such a marked change in the conditions of the natural market must find its expression. The convenience of fixity and uniformity of wage is not strong enough to suppress it. But in different seasons, in different weeks of the same season, on different days, even at different times on the same day, there may be pronounced fluctuations in the marginal significance of agricultural labour. A highly instructive method of recognising this still survives in many parts of Wales, and perhaps elsewhere. It is the institution known as "cross-wages." In the market-place of a town, early in the morning, the labourers who are in no regular employ gather, and the farmers who want extra work gather also; and there, in consideration of the weather, the state of the crops, the amount of labour available and so forth, the bargain is made for the day. On one day the wage may be fixed at twice or thrice as much as on another day of the same week. The terms so arranged are the cross-wages for the district, and they often regulate the wages paid by farmers, and to labourers, who have not been at the cross, and have had no direct share in fixing the cross-wages. As the conditions will be roughly the same over the whole district, the farmers and labourers may agree beforehand to accept the cross-wages during a certain period without knowing what they will be, being satisfied that they will roughly represent the market value for each day; but of course it must necessarily be the case that if, on a certain day, the farmer had known exactly what the cross-wages he has promised to give would be, he would have taken on an extra man whose services he had declined, or would have declined an extra man whose services he had accepted. And, on the other hand, the man who turned from his own little plot and worked for a neighbouring farmer, on the surmise that cross-wages for that day would be 6s., may wish that he had stayed at home when he finds that they are only 5s. or 4s. 6d. Within the week the cross-wages may have been as low as 3s., but in such a case neither labourer nor farmer, who has the same means of judging of the general situation as those who fix the cross-wages, would have expected them to be as high as 6s., or would have made his bargain on such a supposition.

We shall touch in another part of this work upon other methods which are taken to adapt the actual to the natural market, or, on the other hand, to avert the inconveniences of its fluctuations, or to resist, by voluntary combination, the pressure of its laws.[1] But we have already said enough for general illustration of these points, and have seen how the underlying considerations that affect the terms on which effort

[1] Book III. pages 637 *sq.*, 693 *sqq.*

is remunerated are identical with those that determine the price of commodities.

We will pass on to some considerations as to the supply of effort. In the market of commodities we saw that the supply of one market constitutes a demand upon another. Is there anything analogous to this in the market in efforts? Wherever there are many directions in which the same man can turn his energies and capacities, the different applications in question compete in the market for his energy. His power is the analogue of the timber, which may be made either into tables or into washstands, but which when made into one cannot be transformed into the other. A man may be put on one job when it would have been better husbandry to put him on another; but when he has put forth his effort, it is the result that survives, for what it is worth, and not the effort. We have already seen that urgency of agricultural operations may draw a man from other employments at harvest time. This may be seen everywhere, but in a primitive community it is very conspicuous; for not only the carpenter and the shoemaker, but the schoolmaster and the catechist will devote himself to harvest work during the season. Yet there is a limit to the possibility of these changes of function, and a highly specialised skill cannot be acquired in a day or a week. Some simple forms of harvest work might, indeed, at a pinch, be undertaken by workers in the building trades, unless custom or prejudice forbade; but the building trades could hardly be recruited to any considerable extent from the ranks of the agricultural labourers, and a bricklayer could probably neither thatch nor plough. In artistic and intellectual work the versatility of a Michael Angelo or a Leonardo is rare. This want of fluidity of human capacity confines most men to a very limited market. Prejudices and mistaken customs tend to intensify rather than to mitigate the difficulty, and the solution of the grave economic problem which we shall encounter at the close of this chapter is rendered more difficult thereby; but it must always remain true that, in an age of specialising and of division of labour, manual and intellectual, development of any particular capacity constitutes a demand upon the general

The supply of faculty in the several markets.

store of undifferentiated human power that is perpetually poured into the world in the form of fresh human lives, and limits the amount available in other directions.

The various specialisings of capacity which are perpetually being accomplished are acts of administration of the collective resources of human capacity. What are the forces that control this administration? Obviously there is at present no comprehensive and deliberate scheme in accordance with which it takes place. Individual or domestic resources in the shape of personal energy and capacity are directed with more or less intelligence to the individual or domestic purposes, and their administration constitutes a branch of individual or domestic "economy"; but "political" in the sense of communal resources, in the shape of personal energy and capacity, are, in the main, not collectively directed to any communal purpose at all. Such communal ideals as exist must, for the most part, depend upon the play of individual interests and aspirations for their realisation. It is clear, no doubt, that the position on the relative scale of any desire for service on the part of any member of a community will exercise an influence upon the training and specialising of the faculties of other members of it; for any man who is administering his own energies will consider how he can turn them to the direct accomplishment of his purposes, and how far he can make them more efficacious for those purposes by the indirect means of applying them to the procuring of what others want and will pay for. The prospect of economic advantage, then, will determine a drift towards the supply of the want that stands higher, rather than of that which stands lower on the collective scale. But we have constantly to remind ourselves that this tendency can by no means be equated, off-hand, with a spontaneous movement in the direction of the general good. Even on an individual scale a want stands relatively high not because it ministers to relative worthiness but because it ministers to relative urgency; and we can place no antecedent limit on the urgency of the demands which vice or vanity may prompt. But the place which a want takes on the collective scale does not even coincide with its urgency in any vital sense whatever; for a feeble desire on the part of a man in command of superfluities may rank above the deepest craving of the man who is near the point of total destitution. Only if we acquiesce entirely in the law "to him that hath shall be given," and only if we are further content to accept each man's purposes as worthy to be accomplished in proportion to his eagerness to accomplish them, can we hold optimistic views of the social significance of this spontaneous tendency.

Even if we take it for what it is worth only, this apparently social tendency of individual choice is subject to noteworthy limitations. Perhaps the majority of men and women have had little to say as to the special training of their capacities until it has been to a great extent irrevocably determined. The parents or others who decided for them may have considered their own economic advantage more than that of the immature lives they were directing. It is only on the supposition that they fully identify themselves with the tastes and interests of their children that we can suppose the economic forces to tell in their full strength in determining the flow of undifferentiated human talent in the direction which would best minister to the want highest on the collective scale. Under existing circumstances, a want may remain high on that scale, because most of those who can now direct their own course have already had their training specialised in other directions, and have irrevocably lost the opportunity of acquiring the highest degree of requisite skill, whereas those whose development is directed by the will of parents and guardians may only in a few cases be put within reach of a training of which it is they that will reap the advantages, while others have borne the sacrifices involved. In cases of an expensive special training these sacrifices would not only be greater than many parents are willing to make, but would be greater than most parents can make, for they would presuppose resources positively in excess of the total that they can command. Thus, those occupations which require an elaborate and expensive preparation will, so long as present conditions remain, always be recruited from a small section of society; and the talent which exists in the great mass of the people will be either undetected or left untrained.

It is impossible to guess how much of such unrecognised

Could the flow of faculty into the different markets be made to equalise marginal rewards in them?

or untrained talent for highly remunerated services exists. Some incipient attempts are already being made in connection with our system of national education for its detection and utilising, and there is no limit to the range which social speculation may allow itself in this direction. It is possible to conceive an educational system, which should be not a burlesque of the technical education of a professional man, but an instrument for the detection and development of every conceivable kind of human capacity, a great sorting machine for adjusting opportunities to capacities throughout the whole population. The result of such a system, if in any degree successful, would naturally be to determine a flow from the less pleasant and less highly remunerated occupations to the pleasanter and more highly remunerated ones, with the result of lowering the marginal significance, and therefore the remuneration, of each individual in the latter, and raising it in the former. There seems no reason in the abstract why the result should not approach the utopian ideal of a higher payment for the more monotonous services rendered to society by the manual worker, than for the more varied and pleasant ones rendered by the exercise of the artistic and intellectual powers. It is sometimes spoken of as scandalous that a butler should receive higher remuneration than a clergyman. Documents in Siena shew that there was no great difference between the daily payment made to Duccio when he was painting his great picture of the Virgin, and the fee paid to an executioner for his services in burning the alchemist Capocchio to death. Suppose there were a very large number of persons whose talents and opportunities enabled them to choose between the careers of a butler and a clergyman, or an executioner and an artist, an equality of wage in either case would indicate that the two careers were regarded by a large number of qualified persons as equally eligible in themselves. If the wages of the executioner were higher than those of the competent artist, it would shew that, on its own merits, the career of the artist was preferred by all those exercising it who were competent to take the other, so that the extra command of things in the circle of exchange attached to the latter did not sufficiently attract any one of them to induce him to embrace it. One does not see exactly why this state of things, if it ever came about, should be regarded as scandalous.

Between careers which are actually open to the same class of candidates, both as to means and as to talent, it may be presumed that such a law as we have indicated actually determines salaries. If a career in the army or the Church, for example, is embraced by men to whom the industrial or the professional world is open, with a prospect of higher remuneration, it must be because non-economic considerations tell in favour of it. How far there is a sufficiency of undeveloped talent to bring about any great and startling change in the relative remuneration secured in the several occupations of life, can at present be a matter of speculation only. But in so far as the numbers entering a profession are limited, not by preferences for other occupations or lack of opportunity for preparing for this, but by lack of the special talent it requires, the remuneration it commands will remain above the level which its eligibility would otherwise determine.

Behind all these questions of the distribution of undifferentiated human capacity amongst various occupations, lies the question of the supply of this undifferentiated human capacity itself; in other words, the population question. The supply of raw human material is determined largely, some have thought almost entirely, by non-economic considerations. Children are largely or exclusively brought into existence incidentally to the realisation of the purposes or the expression of the impulses of their parents, irrespective of their economic significance to themselves or to others. It is only under very exceptional circumstances that we can suppose free-born children to be bred with a view to the market, that is to say, produced in order that economic advantages may accrue to their producers. Forecasts as to the state of the markets into which children might be expected ultimately to enter no doubt exercise an influence on the marriage and birth rates in some strata of a community; but broadly speaking, the production of undifferentiated human capacity must be regarded as a branch of direct expenditure, regulated in its relation to other expenditures by prudence or recklessness, by abundance or paucity of total resources, by custom and tradition, by

The total supply of human material not produced in response to an economic demand.

impulse ranging over the whole scale of the material and spiritual nature, by conviction, by deliberate resolve and calculation, in a word, by all the considerations that determine our general administration of resources; but it must in the main be regarded as "consumption" technically, not as production, that is to say, as a way in which people choose or allow themselves to expend their resources, not as something they undertake for the direct convenience of others in order to secure things they themselves desire in return. The whole question of the ultimate supply of human effort, therefore, carries us far beyond the limits of economic inquiry, though not beyond the range of those general laws that regulate the administration of resources in general, for these are no other than the laws of the psychology of choice. Given the supply of human material at any moment the economic law of the market, so far as the special circumstances allow the facts on which that law works to be ascertained, dominates the remuneration of every class of effort, and creates drifts, now towards this, and now towards that special training or special application of effort; and we may feel complete security in considering the remuneration of human effort as simply a form of "price," approximating to a market price in proportion as the conditions of a market are realised.

. The reader may have noticed that in all this discussion I have avoided the term "labour market," and have preferred to speak of remuneration, or earnings, rather than wages. The reason is sufficiently obvious. It is true that writers on Political Economy often shew a tendency to stretch the term "wages" till it covers all remuneration for the output of human energy; but since the word will always carry certain limiting associations with it there is a manifest danger in wrenching its technical employment too far apart from current usage. Such specious attempts at simplification always avenge themselves. If we call all earnings wages we might, for instance, come to the conclusion that certain measures, movements, or institutions, would tend to "raise wages" at the expense of the revenue secured by the holding of property (whether in the form of accumulations or of command of the natural sources of wealth), and we might

Examination of the terms "labour market" and "labour movement" and their associations and implications.

expect such a result to be welcomed by the "wage-earning" classes and their sympathisers; but there might be nothing in the argument to determine whether the "wages" that would rise were likely to be the wages of mechanics or the wages of lawyers, doctors, stockbrokers, or managers and directors of industrial enterprises. Similar reflections apply to the use of the term "labour market" to include the wider "market in human effort." The conclusions that we have hitherto reached are quite general. They are simply these :—(1) that remuneration for human effort, so far as it is determined by economic forces, follows the law of the market, just as the price of commodities does; and therefore it is a matter of no theoretic importance to establish and observe a precise line of demarcation between them; (2) that as there is a different market for every commodity so there is a different market for every kind of human effort; (3) that as the economic forces tend to secure a price for every commodity corresponding to its marginal worth, so they tend to secure to every kind of human effort a remuneration corresponding to its marginal worth to any member of the community; and (4) that continuity of supply and extreme perishability characterise the market in human effort.

All this applies to what is commonly understood by "labour" as to all other direct output of human energy, but it applies to it in no exclusive way. Great social importance and interest, nevertheless, attach to any considerations that directly affect the labour market, even if they do not affect it alone; and we will pause for a moment to examine the feelings and sentiments that rouse this interest. The associations that the words "labour," the "labour market," and the "labour movement" wake are, in some respects, curiously illusory. For, in the first place, they at once suggest industry as against some kind of parasitical idleness, whereas, as we have seen, many highly paid persons whose claims are looked upon jealously enough by "labour" are undoubtedly industrious, and draw their remuneration solely in consideration of the exercise of their talents. And, in the next place, "labour" suggests the solid basis on which life is reared, and the power that carries on the serious work of sustaining the world from day to day; and doubtless "labour" is all this; but it is likewise the power on which all the luxuries and frivolities, all the material elegancies and all the artistic and literary enjoyments of life rest; for the type-setter, the oil and colour hand, the cabinet-maker, the gin-distiller, the silk-weaver, and the cigar-roller, are as much in the labour market as the agriculturist, the carpenter, or the builder; and "labour" decorates the palace just as truly as it builds the cottage. If, when confusions and false associations are cleared away, the "labour movement" commands reasoned and enlightened sympathy it must be because it is taken to represent an attempt to modify the distribution of wealth in the interests of the less-favoured and less-privileged members of society, as against the favoured and privileged.

We have now gained a very precise idea of the economic position of every worker, whether he belongs to the privileged or the unprivileged classes. However high his remuneration is, it cannot be fixed by the economic forces any higher than the estimated worth of his services at the margin; and, however low it may be, it cannot be held down by those economic forces any lower than that marginal worth. Hence, if we say that any kind of service is over- or under- *Economic forces tend to secure to every worker as much as he is worth at the margin to others.* paid in the open market, we must be speaking in accordance with some ideal conception; for instance, the idea of what is due to a man, as such, rather than what he commands in virtue of the significance to others of what he can do. If we say that men and women working at a starvation wage are getting "all they are worth," it sounds harsh and inhuman and wakes an instant resentment. But that is because "worth" is a word of many applications, and carries with it many associations besides those of the market. We speak, for example, of the "infinite worth of a human soul," and we sometimes say in contempt that such and such a man, or his fate, "is not worth a thought." Whereas if we say that the economic forces tend to fix every man's remuneration at the precise level of his marginal worth, we do not mean by "worth" any inherent qualities of the man himself, whether technical or broadly human; and still less do we mean the claim he has to the sympathetic care of his prosperous fellow-beings. The question is—What is the man's output of energy economically worth at the margin? And that means —What is it worth while for some one else to give him, in return for his efforts, as an indirect means of furthering his own purposes? Ultimately we may have to evolve some special word, free from misleading associations, to express this idea concisely and clearly; but meanwhile we must do the best we can with our existing vocabulary. When we say that a man's potatoes are "worth 2d. a pound," we mean exactly that they are "worth to some one else, at the margin, the sacrifice of all the alternatives represented by 2d." When we speak of what a man's efforts are "worth" in the market, we use the word in the same sense.

In considering industrial questions it is of extreme importance that we should grasp the fact that if any person, or class of persons, is habitually "underpaid," that is to say, habitually get less for what they do than it is worth to some one else at the margin, this must be due not to the economic forces but to some obstacle that stands in their way. It may no doubt be due to the working of economic forces that a man is worth as little as he is. For instance, he may have been underfed, and put early to exhausting and unskilled work by his parents, under pressure of want or greed; and so he may have feeble powers and poor training. And the economic conditions of a given society may be such as tend to produce these results. But the economic forces can not cause a man, such as he is, to receive a lower remuneration than represents the worth to others of his work; for the economic forces are always urging those others to purchase anything that they can get for less than it is worth to them, so that if there are any persons to whom the work of an individual (or a class of individuals) would be worth more than he is now receiving for it, the economic forces urge them to offer higher terms and so secure his services. In speaking of "underpayment," therefore, we must be careful to distinguish between payment which is less than the payee is economically worth, to remedy which underpayment we may rely on the support of the economic forces; and payment which, though all that the payee is economically worth, is not as much as he "deserves," because it is not his fault that he is worth so little; or is not as much as he "needs," or not as much as he "ought to have," because he can not live a decent life on it. For "underpayment" in this latter sense it is not fair to throw the blame on the employer; and any general movement that aims at improving the condition of the "underpaid" in this sense must aim either at giving them more than they earn, *i.e.* more than their work is worth, or at making their work worth more.

There is nothing outrageous in the demand that the unfortunate, the feeble, and the economically unsuccessful generally, should receive more than any efforts they can put forth are worth. Children, old people, the sick, and the deficient must receive such excess or die; and the present trend of feeling is in the direction of attempting, by old age pensions and a more humane poor law, for instance, to mitigate the terrors of failure in the industrial struggle; whereas the principle of a graduated income tax, so far as it applies to earnings, recognises the obligation of success to bear an increased proportion of public burdens. *Ought any one to have more than he is economically worth at the margin?* But there is far more than this. We have seen that a man's economic position depends not only on his powers but on his possessions. Those possessions may embody the fresh output of current effort, or they may be accumulations, or they may consist in the control, secured by law, of the prime sources of all material wealth. The differentiation between the taxation of earned and unearned income reminds us that there is a vast revenue that some one is receiving though no one is earning it. Thus it is clear that if no one receives less than his current effort is worth, many receive a great deal more. There seems, then, to be nothing intrinsically monstrous in the idea of looking into this matter. If there are sources from which, apparently, any one or every one might receive more than he earns, or is worth to others, no proposal need be condemned simply because it contemplates certain classes receiving more than their output of effort is worth, as certain other classes obviously do at present. Proposals for land nationalisation, or for the collective control of the instruments of production, are dictated by the belief that we are in possession of a common patrimony which is not being administered in the common interest. But we should distinguish very clearly in our own minds between saying that a person is "underpaid for his work," and saying that he has a claim to something more than "mere payment for his work at its worth."

There is nothing mysterious in this excess of revenue over aggregate earnings. We shall perhaps see deeper into the matter later on in this work, but an illustration may serve meantime to remove any cloudiness that may have risen in the reader's mind. Suppose two men discovered a mineral spring or inherited the possession of a factory. They might find that each of them, working it alone, could make £1000 a year out of it, and that if they both worked they could make £1500 a year. If they are both working, then, the withdrawal of either of them would reduce the total earnings by £500 a year. £1000, then, represents the sum of the worth to the concern of the efforts of the two men (taken severally) when backed by the joint control of the accumulated apparatus of the factory, or the natural resources of the spring. But their total revenue is £1500, which is £500 in excess of the sum of what each of them is worth to the other. If the spring or factory were in possession of a third party who did not work at all, and if the two workers did not combine, the owner might pay each what he was worth at the margin (£500) and would have a balance of £500 which he received but which no one had "earned." Can the earners, or any groups of them, by combining, get control of this unearned revenue, or any of it, in addition to the earnings which they are marginally worth to its possessors?[1]

Relation of earned to unearned revenues. But we must not fail to observe that if the natural opportunities or accumulated instruments produce nothing without work, neither can work produce anything without them; and if work has a marginal value to the possessor of tools and opportunities, so likewise have tools and opportunities a marginal value to the worker. Add or withdraw a little work and you

---

[1] It should be noted that the supposition we have made does not necessarily imply that the material product of the two men is less than double that of one alone. One man might be able to bottle ten gallons of mineral water per hour and the two together thirty, but the marginal value of the water when issued at the rate of thirty gallons an hour might be only half what it would be if issued at the rate of ten, and thirty halves are fifteen; so that while the issue was trebled by the combination of the two men, the earnings might only be increased by one half. Compare further Book II. Chap. V. pages 546 *sqq.*

increase or diminish the output of commodities; but make a small addition to or subtraction from the apparatus commanded by the worker, and you likewise increase or diminish the output. Therefore the accumulations we speak of as capital, by making work more fertile, make the worker worth more, and it is only in virtue of that fact that their owners can enforce their claim to a share in the product. And since, like the worker himself, the owner of apparatus can only exchange or let it out at its marginal significance, it follows that the worker, like the purchaser of any continuous commodity, receives a benefit from it in excess of what he pays for it. This will become clearer in the next chapter, but we can already see that whereas the worker may very well desire and attempt to get apparatus and access to natural sources of wealth on better terms than he now enjoys, he is on a wrong tack if he thinks that he is not already getting them on advantageous terms. He is not paying more for them than, or even as much as, they are worth to him, and he would be worse, not better off without them. He benefits by accumulations, though he may reasonably desire to benefit more than he does by them; and since we have seen that accumulation becomes automatic under some conditions, and can only be accomplished by severe self-control under others, it is clear that in any scheme for diverting the share in the product that now flows to accumulations, due precaution must be taken not to check the process of accumulation itself. The problem may turn out to be a very difficult and delicate one.[1]

Again, if in the open market a man is not likely to receive in return for his effort more than it is worth to some one else at the margin, we must reflect that where there is any kind of patronage, or any system of fixed salaries for elective posts, it is extremely possible that a man may be receiving in payment for his work more than it is worth to any one. And if, as in all public and official posts, those who determine how much a man is to be paid are not those who ultimately pay him, we escape, to an undefined extent, the controlling action of the economic forces. If I am to decide how much

Payments for services in excess of their marginal worth.

[1] Cf. pages 309 *sq.*, 660 *sqq.*

a man is worth to me for my purposes, and am then to pay him, I have a more direct interest in determining his worth than if I am to decide how much he is worth to some one else, and how much he is therefore to receive from him. Theoretically as long as there are any open markets no man need accept less than he is worth in them; but under any system of patronage or election he may easily receive more.

No doubt, then, there is a large number of persons who are receiving from various public bodies, under the name of salary, more than their efforts are worth. Proposals for a minimum wage, coupled with provision for state employment, whenever that wage cannot be earned in the open market, would constitute a method of securing more than they are worth, to a large number of other persons; and though we have just shewn that there is no abstract reason why every worker should not receive more than he is worth (and every non-worker something), it is obvious that the grounds on which his claim to it is admitted and regulated demand very severe examination, and that it involves a confusion of ideas to say that he has a right to a minimum "wage" from the state (when the market will not secure it to him) not as a citizen or as a man, but as a worker.[1]

We have now glanced at some aspects of the problem how to secure to the less-favoured members of society more than the economic worth of their efforts. It is not an inherently chimerical attempt, but it is by no means simple of execution, nor free from dangers. It remains to consider projects for making these same unprivileged individuals worth more than they are. Here we might expect to find ourselves upon firmer ground. If it is a fact that the most miserable earners of starvation wages are getting all their work is worth, the lamentable fact of the existence of a vast population worth so very little must, when once recognised, force us to face the question how we can make them worth more. The indignation that their miserable condition excites will become more enlightened when we understand that we are not to look out for and

The two main ways of making people worth more at the margin. Changing the people and changing their place.

---

[1] See further Book III. pages 693 *sqq.*

denounce some wicked person who is paying them shamefully low wages, but are to understand that as far as the vigilance of commercial instincts and motives can secure any end, we may assume that they are already getting as much as their work is worth, and that our problem is partly perhaps to see that they get (not from their employers and customers but from communal funds) something more than they are worth, but very certainly to see whether they cannot be made worth more.

But there are two main ways of making people worth more. One is breeding, rearing, training, and educating them from the beginning, so that they shall possess the vigour, the habits, and the particular skill which are likely to make them worth most. All this might involve national education—moral, intellectual, and technical—in the most extended sense of the term. And, as we have already seen, that would probably mean some approximation to an equalising of the worth, and therefore the earnings, of the rank and file of the workers in occupations that at present receive widely different remuneration.

The other is to shift them to places and conditions in which they will be worth more than where they are. If you gave some of the workers in an "underpaid" industry the opportunity to migrate into one better paid, you would have put them where they were worth more; and further, since the margin would recede in the industry they had left, you would also raise the marginal significance and therefore the pay of their late companions. *The bacillus of the disease of civilisation.* But you would also lower the marginal significance of a worker in the ranks which they had joined; and this observation brings us to the very root of the troubles with which industrial society is afflicted, and may almost be regarded (in the fashionable language of the day) as enabling us to identify the bacillus of the disease of civilisation. Objectively (and we can have no other test) society is enriched by the change. The comparatively low worth of the work dropped, is replaced by the comparatively high worth of the work taken up. The total revenue of the community, then, is raised. And, moreover, the persons in the most deplorable condition have been relieved; and therefore whoever has suffered the redistribution of wealth has been socially justifiable. But the persons whose marginal significance has been reduced will not see the thing in this light.

We have already glanced at some of the more obvious evils attendant on that great principle of division of labour, on which all material and much intellectual progress seems to depend.[1] But in connection with the market of human efforts, we encounter this prime agent in civilisation and progress once again, and detect its most intimate workings on the fabric of society. The principle of the division of labour differentiates the position, the functions, the opportunities and the capacities of men in such a way that each one is dependent for the supply of all his wants on the co-operation of countless individuals scattered all over the world. Even the wage-earner who lives a relatively simple life, commands a number and variety of services which fascinate and baffle the imagination. In the picturesque language of Henry George, "the miner who, two thousand feet underground in the heart of the Comstock, is digging out silver ore, is, in effect, by virtue of a thousand exchanges, harvesting crops in valleys five thousand feet nearer the earth's centre; chasing the whale through Arctic icefields; plucking tobacco leaves in Virginia; picking coffee berries in Honduras; cutting sugar-cane on the Hawaiian Islands; gathering cotton in Georgia or weaving it in Manchester or Lowell; making quaint wooden toys for his children in the Hartz Mountains; or plucking amid the green and gold of Los Angeles orchards the oranges which, when his shift is relieved, he will take home to his sick wife." But together with this increased command of multifarious resources comes a cutting off of the individual from any direct means of supplying himself with even the simplest things he requires. The miner in the Black Country, or the artisan in the heart of London, can command the varied conveniences and comforts of civilisation just enumerated. But cut him out of economic relations, set him by his own effort, applied to the materials and opportunities to which he has direct and unchallenged access, to make his own direct bargain with nature, and he will not even be able to secure the conditions of life com-

The dependence of the individual on society,

[1] Pages 186 sqq.

manded by the most sordid state of savagery. He has, therefore, no reserve price. He can live only as a portion of a vast organism, and if his organic relations with the whole are seriously disturbed he cannot live at all. The cell that is part of my frame, or the white corpuscle that lives an apparently independent life as a constituent organism in my blood, cannot start the life of an amœba on its own account. It must live as part of a higher organism or die. Now the economic pull that I have upon society (to wit, the other cells or corpuscles of the body politic) consists in my power to do or give something that they want. That is to say, the existence of still unsatisfied wants of others to which I can minister supplies the only economic means by which I can insist on any of my own wants whatever being attended to. If others were completely satisfied as to the thing I can supply, I should either die, or live upon what others did for me on their own impulse; for I should be their pensioner, not their valued fellow-worker.

The idea that all the wants of a society should be completely satisfied is chimerical enough; but we have object lessons every day which make it only too easily and therefore and vividly realisable that the specific want in on some want others to which my faculty or opportunity can of society being im- minister may be so far satisfied, relatively to other perfectly satis- wants, that I can obtain little or nothing in return fied. for satisfying it still further. Were it not so, being "out of work" would be a meaningless phrase. It is not enough that I can give men something they need. I am "out of work" unless I can give them something of which they desire more than they will have if I do not help to keep up their supply. The thing most urgently necessary for sustaining life even for a few minutes is air to breathe; but if all I could offer, in exchange for the things I want, were a supply of atmospheric air at the surface of the earth, I should either starve to death or depend upon other than economic forces for my continued existence; because there is as much air at the surface of the earth as any one wants. If indeed I can bring a continuous stream of fresh air through the galleries of a coal-mine, or into a diving-bell, I am supplying air in places to which no natural process brings it in quantities sufficient to satisfy all requirements, and for doing this I may get a return. If any man could invent a simple process by which a stream of fresh air could be secured in such confined and restricted places as lecture-rooms, concert halls, theatres, and places of public meeting, he would be in a position to perform a valuable service for a number of his fellow-citizens. But when and where every one has enough, the economic forces will urge no one to give anything in return for more.

On the other hand, if we can stretch our imaginations to the conception of a syndicate gaining effective legal control of the whole volume of atmospheric air, and having power to regulate its flow and distribution over the face of the earth at their will, so that every one became dependent for vital breath upon the terms which they could make with the air syndicate, economic forces would urge the air-lords to arrest the supply of air at a point which would give it such a relative position on the collective scale as would secure the highest monopoly value for the whole supply issued. The rest of the inhabitants of the world would then have to devote a large portion of their energies, not to furthering their own and each other's general purposes in life, but to furthering the purposes, whatever they might be, of the great syndicate of air-lords. Prominent amongst those purposes might very well be the addition of an effective control of water and land to their control of the air. But let that pass. Should anything occur to make air free once again, there would be an immense gain of material well-being to the world at large, but it would be accompanied by the destruction of the economic position of the air-lords, and they would regard it as a crushing disaster. Their strength, and the abundance of the supply of all producible things which they command, would depend upon the existence of a vast and imperative want on the part of other men, for a thing which they alone could supply. Let that want be supplied without their control and the increased wealth of the world at large would fatally undermine their economic position.

This extreme and fantastic illustration does but emphasise to the imagination what is the actual condition of things everywhere. Should any circumstances lead to the complete satisfaction of any human want, this general benefit would be accompanied by the undermining of the economic position, or means of "earning a livelihood," of some body of persons; for a body of persons surely exists somewhere trained and specialised to meet that want, capable of earning a living by satisfying it, and dependent for that living on the fact of its not being completely satisfied. Inventions and discoveries of every kind are perpetually and continuously placing civilised humanity in more and more effective control of the natural forces and materials; that is to say, they are putting mankind collectively in a position to meet their material wants on easier terms and in fuller measure. But these advances take place irregularly along the line, and when any one want is satisfied in advance of the others, a disturbance takes place in the industrial position of those who live by supplying it. The general gain is their loss, and the more irrevocably specialised their faculties and opportunities are, the more heavily will the blow fall upon them. *Irregular advances and shifting stresses constantly disturb equilibrium and depress the economic condition of individuals or classes.*

And not only are the means of satisfying wants constantly changing by invention and discovery, but wants themselves as constantly shift. At one time vast countries are to be opened up by railway systems, and navvies and makers of steel rails can supply a want felt with a high relative keenness. At another time, a great country like the German Empire determines to adopt the gold in place of the silver standard for her currency, and the marginal significance of gold is shifted and raised on the collective scale of the nations by this new demand upon it. At another time there is a great war, and those whose faculty and opportunity enable them to make cordite and munitions of war, or to use them in the destruction of life and property, can supply a keenly felt and imperfectly gratified set of desires. This relative elevation of some desires involves a relative depression of others; and when the stress falls elsewhere the now elevated desires will in their turn become relatively depressed. And in any of these cases when the place on the collective scale of the thing I can do falls, the significance of my services and the abundance of the supplies they will secure me fall with it.

Hitherto our attention has been chiefly directed to the

forces which perpetually tend, though it may be slowly and through obscure and intricate channels, to the establishment of equilibrium, and to the even distribution over the period of consumption of the uneven output of the forces of nature; but now we have encountered internal and often incalculable sources of disturbance, and we see that every such disturbance means more or less acute and widespread distress, arising from the fact that the wants which it is some one's business to supply, and in return for which he gets all that he has, become disproportionately well supplied in comparison to other things. General abundance means his particular want.

If all the strains and stresses remained constant, and if discoveries affected the supply of all human wants and desires evenly, or if changes were so slow that specialising of faculties and applications of energy could adapt themselves continuously to them, then the increasing control of the powers of nature and the more ample return to human effort would give us an ever-increasing command of the things which (wisely or foolishly) we desire; the means of satisfaction, good or bad, would steadily increase, and no distress would be incidentally involved anywhere. The irregular and incalculable element in nature would be all that we should have to reckon with. But, as it is, irregularity is both initiated and accentuated by the other causes we have just referred to. Let us consider it once again. If apples are abundant and the stock of store potatoes is normal, the want for apples will be satisfied down to a lower place on the collective scale than usual, and the price of apples reckoned in potatoes will fall. The potato-grower and every one else will get more apples for the things they give and will be so much the richer; but the apple-growers will get less of other things for each pound of apples, and if the fall in value more than compensates the increase in amount, they will be poorer than they would have been, and that just because the crop is so good. But if the harvest of potatoes has also been exceptional, the public will have both their want for potatoes and their want for apples more abundantly satisfied than usual, and the price of apples in potatoes may remain the same. Both potato-growers and apple-growers may be poorer, but each can take the low price of the other's product as a partial set-off against the low price of his own; whereas the rest of the public benefits by the low prices of both alike and has no loss to set against the gain. Thus every one benefits by a good crop in the things he does not grow, but may very well be injured by a good crop of what he does grow, and if his individual crop was for any reason only an average one, then his loss would be certain.

In general, if the want that I satisfy becomes less acute at the margin, because it is more abundantly supplied, and at the same time all other wants are more abundantly supplied in a suitable ratio also, then although the thing that I can do is less urgently needed, yet the things I want in return are less urgently needed also, and society may give me as much of these less-valued things for the same amount of my less-valued services as they gave me of the things that they valued more, for the services that they valued more also. The real trouble is not that my product is too abundant, but that other things are not abundant enough, and the remedy is to make them abundant too. That would give us all a larger volume of satisfaction. But if the thing that I supply becomes *relatively* more abundant, and ministers to a relatively less urgent need, my command of what I want declines just because your command of what I give increases. Hence the paradoxical situation that the advance in well-being which we all desire and are all pursuing becomes an object of dread to each one of us in that particular department in which it is his business to promote it. That is to say, because it is my social function to supply the world as well as I can with a certain thing, therefore I dread the world's being so well supplied with it that I shall be able to get little or nothing for supplying more.

It is impossible to exaggerate the importance of this consideration, or the penetrating and intimate nature of its bearing on every aspect of the social question. The extinction of any desire on the part of mankind, however vicious and destructive, the abolition of any established practice, however vile, will throw a certain number of men "out of work"; that is to say, will render the exercise of the faculty upon which they depend for the supply of all their wants economically impotent. And, in like manner, the more abundant supply of any desired thing, however wholesome the need which it meets, and however great the gain to the well-being of society in general which it secures, may plunge some members of the social organism into penury. If all the world is well supplied with tin, it may make life easier and pleasanter to millions, but it saps the industrial position of the Cornish miner. If all the world turned sober, it would indefinitely increase its well-being, but countless publicans, brewers, distillers, and hop and vine growers would be thrown out of employment. If universal peace were secured, and armaments were reduced to the vanishing point, there would be many an Othello to mourn that his occupation was gone. If a really successful unpuncturable tyre were put on the market, there would be a great increase in collective happiness, clerical and other appointments would be kept with notably increased regularity, profanity, at least in cultivated society, would tend to be more closely restricted to its natural preserves on the golf-links, but there would be a procession of unemployed assistants of bicycle repairers, and the production of "outfits" would be a "ruined industry." If the sanitary habits of the public suddenly improved, there would be a slump in the business of the undertaker, and if no one committed murder, the hangman would be out of a job.

Thus every man who lives by supplying any want, dreads anything which tends either to dry up that want or to supply it more easily and abundantly. It is to his interest that scarcity should reign in the very thing which it is his function to make abundant, and that abundance should reign everywhere else. If the world is starved of the thing he can give, and abounds in the things he desires, then by doing little he can effect much. Now, this position of being able to make our efforts more largely efficient in accomplishing our purposes is what we all aim at. And each of us can attain it just in proportion as the world comes to be starved of the thing he can give it. This disaster to the world, then, is our treasure trove. The whole situation was admirably summed up, from one point of view, by the orator who cried, in all sincerity, "What the British workman wants is *more work*—and less of it." By "more work" he meant a greater and more urgent need of what the British workman can give

The paradox that my full success in my social function would mean my economic ruin.

relatively to what he wants, *i.e.* scarcity of the thing it is his social function to supply, and abundance of the thing it is his individual (not necessarily selfish) desire to command. And by "less of it" he meant that under such conditions he would be able to get a higher price for his work, and therefore could secure a competence at a smaller cost in effort. At the end of his day's work he would be both richer and less weary. The desire for relative scarcity in his own skill, or his own commodity, is, therefore, only too natural and intelligible in any man. It is the desire for the conditions that will secure to him what every one desires. Only these conditions must, by their nature, tend to exclude others from the privileges they secure to him.

Thus every man whose desires are uncontrolled by social considerations will welcome any disaster that raises the relative significance of the thing he has or can do. Where there is an open competitive market, this desire for scarcity may remain a pious (or impious) wish, to which those who entertain it can give little or no effect. It is said that early in the last century the favourite toast at farmers' ordinaries was, "Here's to a wet harvest and a bloody war"; the idea being, of course, that a war would prevent the importation of foreign wheat, and that a bad harvest would raise the price of English wheat more than in proportion to the fall in quantity. There could be no more terrible example of the principle I am trying to illustrate. It shews that the horrors of war and the horrors of famine may be welcomed, whether in sheer callous selfishness or in mere thoughtlessness, by any class to whom they would bring material advantage. It shews how men may grudge any benefit to the world, however great, if it deleteriously affects their own economic position in any degree, however small. But at the same time each farmer individually would try to make his own harvest as ample as possible, and so his own interest would make him act socially, though he prayed unsocially.

But when we pass from the individualism of the open competitive market to the deliberate and concerted action of organised trades, or legislative assemblies, or to the general atmosphere of social ideals and aspirations by which they are supported or prompted, we see at once how fatally perverse this whole way of looking at things must be. The gospel of scarcity cannot be "glad tidings of great joy" to the community at large, however gladly the people may hear it when whispered in the ear of each class in succession as a private promise made to it alone. And yet the average intelligence finds it so much easier to consider any question in fragments than as a whole, that this strange and paradoxical gospel of wealth (to me) by starvation (of you) may be openly preached, and will be openly applauded, by an assemblage, to each member of which 1 per cent of it means life and 99 per cent of it death. Each sees its concentrated truth, if applied only to scarcity in that by the supplying of which he lives, and overlooks its diffused falsity if applied all round.

Anti-social attempts to avert it. The "lump-of-labour" theory.

Hence the "lump-of-labour" way of looking at things that so largely pervades working-class economic theories. "What the British workman wants is more work"; that is to say, "I desire that men should be, and should be kept, in relatively keen want of what I and my companions can give them. If any one else supplies them, he is a traitor or a sneak. He has stolen or filched away what is mine. He has taken 'my work,' *i.e.* he has made that abundant which I have an interest in keeping scarce." If anything happens that makes the want less keen, or easier to meet, it is a disaster.

This point of view, though I have said that it pervades working-class economics, is not confined to them. It is said that when the Tariff Reform agitation began, commercial travellers as a class were in favour of it, but that presently they were converted because they thought that it would destroy their own industry. That is to say, they were converted from their faith in Tariff Reform, not because they believed the assertions of its opponents that it would cause political corruption, that it was an attempt "to make every one rich by making everything dear," that it was a whispered promise in every man's ear to mulct every one else for his benefit, and that it would ruin the foreign trade of the country, but because they believed the assertions of its advocates that it would put a check on the waste of socially unprofitable and devastating competition and rivalry.

The open and unscrupulous selfishness of any threatened "interest" is formidable enough, and its concentrated energy may give it vast social and political power. But it is with something more subtle and pervasive that we are now dealing. The "lump-of-labour" theory and its analogues guide the action and tinge the aspirations of countless disinterested workers, who veritably believe that it points the way to social salvation. And a mere demonstration of the blindness and mutual destructiveness of their methods will not suffice to convert them, if it be accompanied by no manifest zeal for their ends and sympathy with their feelings. "On ne détruit que ce qu'on remplace." We have seen that diffused progress is almost normally accompanied by local depression, and often by local wreckage; and it is right and natural that this local wreckage should catch the eye and excite the sympathy. For, in point of fact, the gain, under such circumstances, must be ampler in volume than the loss in order to make it socially equivalent to it. When a diffused benefit is accompanied by a concentrated loss, the benefit extends the satisfaction of a great number of people, at a declining significance, to a slightly lower margin, but it cuts back deep, at a rising significance, into the supplies of the few whom the concentrated suffering strikes. A loss of 5s. a week to a hundred families, to whom it meant a reduction of 25 per cent in their resources, would be a loss of just 500s. and no more, but it would not be compensated by the gain of 1s. a week to 500 families, to whom it meant an increase of 5 per cent in their resources, though that also would be a gain of just 500s. A loss of 25 per cent is more than five times as significant as a gain of 5 per cent. So if any industry is threatened by a new discovery or invention by which the world will be enriched and a particular class of persons impoverished, not only do the persons whose industrial position is attacked dread it, and desire to disarm and thwart the step of industrial progress that brings it about, but they also find that they have the keen sympathy of the spectator, who is more struck by the concentrated loss, though he does not share it, than by the diffused gain in which he shares.

<small>Misplaced sympathy cannot be met by apathy.</small>

And this confirms the attitude of mind which looks at

every question from the point of view of the person interested in the restriction rather than of the persons interested in the enlargement of the supply of all things that "soothe and heal and bless." I have heard cheap reprints of the classics furiously denounced as "unfair" to living authors, who cannot expect people to pay them a living wage if they can get such noble literature for a few pence a volume. A man who should translate a great classic for nothing in order that it might be issued in a cheap form would not be praised as a benefactor of his country, but denounced as a traitor to his class. A girl of independent means who should teach her nieces, or nurse her mother without pay, would be "taking the bread out of the mouth" of some one less fortunate than herself. It is all a part of the lump-of-labour theory, and it is all in a confused and bewildered way benevolent and generous. It seeks salvation through the gospel of maintaining scarcity. The mischief is that this gospel is always privately true and always publicly false. And to press its public falsity will always be regarded as hard-hearted, until the private truth to which it points is tenderly considered. However much the general resources of the community increase, and however large any man's share in that increase may be, it must always remain true that he personally would have been better off yet if, while all other wants were better supplied, the special want to which he ministers had remained as keen and unsatisfied as ever. That is to say, it is inherently impossible that general command of things in the circle of exchange should be increased by any action, invention, or discovery which does not leave some one worse off than he would have been had all else gone on the same, but had this particular action, invention, or discovery been cancelled. Hence the "lump-of-labour" theory, and the "taking-bread-out-of-his-mouth" reproach, taken as general principles, would absolutely paralyse all material and much intellectual, artistic, and spiritual progress; and there is a woeful waste of social enthusiasm where disinterested efforts and aspirations are directed into the channels these theories and sympathies have dug. Social enthusiasm seeks to resist and control all selfish and oppressive action, but in order that it may succeed it is of supreme importance that it should be enlightened as well as earnest. When we understand more exactly what we have to do, and the unescapable conditions under which we have to do it, we may hope to co-ordinate the truly progressive powers better. Mere demonstrations of the confused and suicidal nature of the " lump-of-labour " and " taking-bread-out-of-his-mouth " theories, however, will not avail. When we understand that local distress is incidental to general progress, we shall not indeed try to stay general progress in order to escape the local distress, but we shall try to mitigate the local distress by diverting to its relief some portion of the general access of wealth to which it is incidental. To mitigate the penalties of failure, without weakening the incitements to success, and to effect an insurance against the disasters incident to advance, without weakening the forces of advance themselves, is the problem which civilisation has not yet solved. No wonder, for it is only just beginning to understand what that problem is, and to recognise the " deeply inherent limits " within which it must be solved.

CHAPTER IX

DISTRIBUTION. COST OF PRODUCTION

SUMMARY.——*The problem of distribution is analogous to the problem of personal expenditure of resources, inasmuch as it involves the balancing and mutual substitution at the margin of factors in the production of a desired result which cannot be substituted for each other at the origin. The same material product may result from different combinations of productive agents, such as tools, land, output of muscular or intellectual effort, and so forth ; and since a marginal subtraction of one may be compensated by a due marginal addition of another, they can all be reduced to a common measure, expressed in terms of each other, and therefore summed up in terms of a common unit. The product divided by that sum yields the unit share in the distributed product. The last problem we shall discuss is that of the relation of cost of production to exchange value. What a thing has cost cannot determine its value, but what a thing will cost may determine whether or not it will be made. If it has cost more to make than it is worth at the margin, it will not be made again in such large quantities, and if it is worth more at the margin than it has cost to make, it will be made in larger quantities. Thus there is a constant tendency to equality between price and cost of production, but not because the latter determines the former. But the cost of production sometimes exerts a sentimental reaction on the conduct of the producer which is an effective though not an economic force ; and low prices may sometimes produce a genuine effect in lowering the cost of production by stimulating invention and economy, since a man will fight harder to escape ruin than to increase his fortune.*

CH. IX DISTRIBUTION. COST OF PRODUCTION

We have now gathered all the material for the last branch of our inquiry, for we have solved by implication two of the problems which have given rise to the stubbornest debates amongst economists; the problems, namely, of "distribution," and of the relation of "cost of production" to exchange value.

What is understood by "distribution" as a branch of Political Economy is the study of the principles on which the product of any complicated industrial process is distributed amongst those who have in any way contributed towards securing it. Manufactured articles are sold, and in a going concern the price must pay for the rent of the premises on which the process was conducted, for the remuneration of all the persons who have contributed by mental or physical effort to the result achieved, for the cost of the materials out of which the article has been manufactured, for the wear and tear of the tools and apparatus that have aided in their transformation, for commodities, such as coal and oil, that have been consumed in the process, for the premium on any waiting for results that has been necessary, directly or indirectly, to reach any stage or accomplish any part of the process, and so forth. What determines the share of the proceeds that each of these agents or factors will receive when the finished article is sold? Our first answer must be that the question never actually arises in anything like this form; for the firm, that is to say, the responsible person or persons who receive the price of the manufactured article, will already have made bargains of one kind or another with many or with all of those concerned in its production. They will already have paid the greater part of the wages and salaries of the human agents. They will have bought the machinery and raw material. They will hold the premises, perhaps, at a yearly rent. Moreover, they will very probably be working, not wholly on their own accumulations, but in part on those of other people, which they will have secured by offering in the future a certain premium for present use. In other words, they have already bought in the market (on speculation) things, services, and privileges, which are factors in production, and they now put the product in its turn upon the market. But what determined the price they were willing to pay for

The problem of distribution.

all these things? Obviously the effect they expected them to have in giving value to the product; just as the price which the housewife is willing to give for her stores is ruled by the significance she expects them to have in ministering to the wants of her household. Only in the case of the manufacturer, who buys things that enter into the circle of exchange, and then combines them into something which he returns into the circle of exchange, it is easy to apply an objective test to the accuracy of his estimates, whereas in the case of the housewife, who draws things out of the circle of exchange, but does not return the product into it, there is no such easy and objective way of determining whether or not she has given for any group of commodities more than they were worth. In both cases alike, however, it is obvious that there may be any degree of success or failure.

We will pursue the analogy further, and place it on a broader basis. Everything that I want, and can get out of the circle of exchange, has its market price; that is to say, there are terms on which it is obtainable as an alternative for other things that I may desire. Given my resources, the question I have to decide is how much I am to spend on each commodity in order to bring all their marginal significances into balance with their respective prices. Now, though we cannot think of a supply of water and a supply of literature, taken as wholes, as alternatives, yet at their margins they may perfectly well be so. The water company may make an extra charge for a garden hose, and I may consider whether I will command that extra supply of water and pay the extra rate, or go without it and spend the money on 1s. or 1s. 6d. classics. Thus, the supplies of all the articles that I buy in relatively large quantities and in relatively small units are clearly and directly alternatives at their margins. That is to say, each of them ministers to a sense of heightened vitality and enjoyment of life, or relief of pain, or assuagement of anxiety, or sense of power, or other ultimately desired experience, or gives vent to impulses and allows a passage to some drift in my nature that demands to have its way, or in one way or another can be placed on the balances in my mind, so that I can say "so much of this is worth so much of that, but no more."

Analogies between domestic or personal and industrial administration of resources.

They all have a common measure, then, in the strength with which they all appeal with defined and comparable weights to my general sense of vital significances or values. The administration of my pecuniary resources, then, is a buying of things and services, which in their totality are not, but at their margins are, capable of taking each other's places. Successful administration of resources is buying them in such quantities that the marginal significance of each shall be equivalent to that amount of any other which could be obtained as an alternative.

And just so a firm of manufacturers (or the "entrepreneur" or "undertaker" who deals on their behalf with all the persons and for all the things necessary for the enterprise) will require certain things that cannot be substituted for each other in their totality. The firm must command a place where the industry may be conducted, some output of human energy, physical and intellectual, material on which to work, tools and apparatus with which to work it, and subsidiary substances, such as coal, gas, or water, which will be consumed or transformed in the process. *Balance of marginal efficiency and market price of factors of production, and substitution of factors for each other at the margin.* Now probably no one of these things can be entirely dispensed with or its place taken by any one of the others. And within the limit of any one such group there will be several classes of requisites that can hardly be substituted for each other. Intelligence cannot entirely take the place of physical strength, nor one kind of trained skill for another. Nor can a building be a substitute for machinery, or machinery for a building, or one kind of machinery or one kind of tool for another. And yet, within limits, the most apparently unlike of these factors of production can be substituted for each other at the margins, and so brought to a common measure of marginal serviceableness-in-production. Thus, though no amount of intelligence or industry can make bricks without straw, yet intelligence may economise straw, and one man with more intelligence and less straw may produce as good bricks as another with more straw and less intelligence. There is a limit to this. To withdraw straw beyond a certain point would be to render it impossible for a given degree of intelligence to produce a satisfactory brick, so if that limit is passed we have come to a point at which a less intelligent man with a better supply of straw might produce a better article. In general terms, therefore, intelligence, care, and fidelity can be substituted at the margin for raw material; and raw material can be substituted at the margin for intelligence, care, and conscientiousness. A little more of one may be an exact compensation for a little less of the other; in the sense that the result will be the same whichever alternative is taken. But as the margins change, as, for instance, the intelligence of the man is increased and the raw material diminished, the marginal significance of the increasing factor falls and that of the diminishing factor rises, so that it would take more of the former to compensate in the result for a given sacrifice of the latter. The terms on which any two factors may be accepted as equivalent to each other change as their margins advance or recede. Whatever their price in the market, the individual undertaker will advance his margin of one at the expense of the other till their significance to him coincides with their prices.

The undertaker, then, will provide himself with all the factors of production in proportions determined by the state of the market and their marginal effectiveness in this industry. It may well be that, though additional intelligence would save him something in waste, that same intelligence would have higher relative significance in some other application. In that case some one else will outbid him for it, for he will not spend any more on intelligence, to save material, than the worth of the material which it will save; and if it will, at the margin, render more valuable services to somebody else, the market price of it will rise above his figure. We are exceedingly familiar with this in practice. People often complain of the carelessness of those they employ, when they are quite aware that they could get a higher class of men by paying a higher wage. But they are also aware that it would not be worth their while to do so. A sense of bitterness in such cases may be natural enough, for we do not see why any one should be careless; but a general grievance against the level of character and intelligence in any rank or class of humanity, however easy to understand, in no way affects the matter we are considering. There is a market for intelligence, and even for character. It may be very deplorable that the market is not better supplied, but well or ill supplied it obeys, as a market, the market laws; and every manufacturer has to balance character against other things that he can get in the market and has to bring their marginal significance into coincidence with the terms on which the market offers them to him as alternatives. The fact that it is not always easy to know whether you have really got what you have paid for in this particular market does not affect the theory. There is always a speculative element in all purchases. In sum, then, just as we saw that in private expenditure fresh eggs and the pleasures of friendship may come to be balanced at their margins,—so much of the one being just equivalent to so much of the other,—so we now see that material things and mental and moral qualities may, at their margins, have exact quantitative relations as productive agents, so much of the one being worth so much, but not more, of the other.

Again, the unintelligent or unconscientious exercise of physical power not only wastes the material on which it works, and the tools it works with, but wastes itself also. The same physical power obviously produces widely different results according to the greater or less intelligence by which it is directed. Some intelligence is required for the efficient performance of even the simplest task, and a very high degree of trained skill will be required for others. In some cases, and to some extent, the physical energies of one man may be directed by the intelligence of another. In other cases, and always to some extent, the directing intelligence must be the man's own. Here again, though neither intelligence and muscular strength, nor my own intelligence and the intelligence of some one else who directs me, can be substituted for each other in totality, yet each can be substituted for the other at the margin. "I can get any kind of work out of any kind of man" is obviously a vaunt that cannot be made good; but one manager can get better work from the same man than another can, or as good work from a worse man; so that managing ability may, at the margin, be a substitute for skill and intelligence in the hands, and *vice versa*. And the question of the proper adjustments may be of great importance.

We have now theoretically reduced intelligence, moral

character, physical power, directing skill, and material objects to a common measure by which they can be quantitatively compared and equated with each other at the margins. And every undertaker is constantly engaged in making practical calculations of this nature, when he considers whether he will dismiss a man for want of smartness or keep him because of his trustworthy character, or whether an extra hundred pounds spent in lighting a store-loft will save enough time in looking out patterns to justify the expenditure, or whether an extra hand will save in waste more than he costs in wages, or whether such and such a draughtsman or manager is worth his pay. In every case his test is to consider which course of action will yield the highest value in the final product.

In agriculture it has long been recognised that though land, labour, instruments, and so forth, are all necessary to produce a crop, and no one of these can be substituted for any of the others in its totality, yet they can be substituted for each other at their margins. It will be possible to produce the same crop off the same piece of land, with slightly inferior implements or less effective manuring, if the requisite amount of extra labour is judiciously applied, or with less labour if better appliances are provided. Or the same crop may be produced on a smaller area of land, by the employment of more labour upon it; or the same amount of labour may produce a better result on a larger than on a smaller piece of ground.[1]

Nor is it in agriculture alone that labour and skill can be marginally substituted for land, and *vice versa*. Any London tradesman or manufacturer may meet, in an acute form, the problem of balancing the marginal significance of increased area against that of increased height in his premises. Shall he build a relatively low structure on a relatively wide area or a relatively high structure on a relatively narrow area? Each will give him, say, the same cubical capacity, but the tall building will cost more to erect and will involve more labour and expense when erected. A given increment of land will enable him to dispense with a given amount of labour both in constructing and in working his premises. More land and less labour, or less land and more labour,

[1] Cf. Book II. pages 551 *sqq.*

therefore, may produce the same result, and the balance will be struck according to the condition of the markets. Will the extra amount I must pay for the land be covered by the saving on wages?

We need not work out any more details. It is already obvious that the main groups of factors of production, and within each main group every distinguishable sub-variety of effort, tools, skill, material, and so forth, may find a substitute, at the margin, in some other. All must be balanced against each other at their margins, and the market price of each factor will determine to what point it will be well for any individual to supply himself with that factor in preference to relying on some other as a substitute.

It will be well at this point to note how very unsatisfactory, from the theoretic point of view, is the popular division or classification of the factors of production as land, labour, and capital. The distinction between land and capital is obviously arbitrary. What we mean by land in practical life is something which admittedly consists very largely of the accumulated result of human effort, and accordingly it is usually regarded in books of Political Economy as capital, the term land being reserved for the "original and inalienable" properties of the soil. And these it has been found practically impossible to define or separate. Just where we have an area of the earth's surface which, physically speaking, owes little or none of its value to anything that has been done to it or on it,—for instance a bare site in the centre of a great city,—we find that its value depends more than ever upon capital, that is to say, upon the results of accumulated effort. Only it is the capital that has been expended not upon the site itself but upon the surrounding areas. Land, therefore, even as economically defined, cannot be considered in isolation from capital. And since, as we have seen, the principle on which things balance each other in the market is independent of whether they have been accumulated or not,[1] the distinction between land and capital, which it seems difficult or impossible to draw, would be theoretically worthless if drawn.

Objections to the popular classification of the factors of production as land, labour, and capital.

[1] See pages 289, 290.

Moreover, the conception of capital as a third factor, distinct from land and labour, is in flagrant and irreconcilable contradiction with the usages of language. In estimating the capital of a company, for example, we include its land, at a proper valuation. Under an industrial system of slavery we should also include its live stock of men as well as of animals; and in countries such as our own we should include not only money that is to be spent on labour devoted to the production of tools or apparatus, such as the sinking of a shaft in mining operations, but the wages to be paid to men engaged in preparing the product for the market before that product is ripe for marketing. So that alike in slave and free countries the capital of a concern includes land, tools, raw material, products in every stage up to the finished goods waiting to be marketed, and command of the efforts of the workers, whether or not secured by legal possession of their persons. It is impossible that any precision of conception or any clearness of speculation should be based on a classification and terminology so outrageously at war with the usage of language.

Moreover, even if we were able satisfactorily to define three or more distinct and exhaustive groups of the factors of production, we should get no greater advantage from it than we should if we were able scientifically and exhaustively to classify the different branches of personal expenditure, as material, intellectual, and artistic for example. The attempt would fail in itself, but even if it succeeded it would throw no light on the laws of the market, for all our different satisfactions balance on the strength of that vital significance wherein they have a common measure, and can be substituted for each other at the margins, not in virtue of the generically different services which they render us at the origins. As a matter of fact there seems to be no possible scientific division of the factors of industry into great groups, and still less any possibility of an exhaustive enumeration of them. A firm, for example, may devote its resources in any proportion that seems fit to the laying down of plant in order to produce things, to advertisement to inform people that the things are produced or to persuade them that they are good, or to the enforcing of practices or traditions which they believe will in the course of long years gain them a desired reputation for straight dealing and intelligence, which will fertilise or economise advertisement, and secure confidence which will itself be a revenue. A good name, then, or almost any kind of notoriety, may be a factor of production in the commercial sense just as much as tools, site, raw material, strength, intelligence, or conscientiousness. In proceeding, therefore, to a closer examination of the laws of distribution and the function of the undertaker we shall entirely ignore all attempts to enumerate and classify the factors of production. We know already that the same principle determines the claims of them all so that the division, could we accomplish it, would have no theoretic importance.

What, then, is the problem of the undertaker? By hypothesis he is dealing with limited resources, and in applying these resources he must draw commodities, services, and privileges out of the circle of exchange, and so combine and direct them as to produce a result, that can itself be returned into the circle of exchange with a value higher than that of the factors or ingredients that were drawn out. *The problem of the undertaker.* He desires to maximise this result, just as the housewife or any other administrator desires to maximise the result of her expenditure. And as the housewife's attention is fixed upon marginal considerations, while she takes the initial increments for granted,[1] so the undertaker takes for granted the early increments, near the origin, of all the factors of production, land, labour, tools, and so forth; for some supply of all of them is necessary for any production at all; but at the margins, where each performs a service no longer distinctive and irreplaceable, but capable of being rendered equally well by some substitute, he carefully balances them, and the smallest change in their market prices may induce him to substitute a little of one for a little of another. Here, therefore, a common measure can be found; and just as the price the housewife is willing to pay for any article of consumption is determined, not by the fact that some of it is very important, perhaps essential to life, but by the relative importance of a little more or a little less of it,

[1] Cf. page 46.

as against a little more or a little less of something else, so here the prices that the undertaker will pay for the different factors are determined not by the peculiar service that each renders near the origin, but by the extent to which the units of each can respectively perform at the margin the common service they can all render alike. In a former example we determined the equivalence of so much bread to so much water not by considering the nature of the specific functions of bread and of water in supporting the human frame, but by comparing them on the common ground of their satisfying a human craving.[1] On this ground the value of each can be expressed in terms of the value of the other. It is not because they are unlike, but because they are like, that they come into comparison with each other. So if land and labour are to be compared and equated, and are to settle their respective claims on the common product, it must be because they are reduced to a common measure so that the significance of each can be expressed in terms of the significance of the other. And this must be accomplished by finding the aspect under which their significance is identical, not that in which it is specific to each. Lastly, here as in all markets, what each man is *willing* to pay for a thing is determined by its relative place on his own scale, what he actually *has* to pay (or go without it) by its relative place on the scales of others. There is equilibrium when these places coincide.

Reduction of factors of production to a common measure. Their summation and the distribution of the product. It is obvious that if we dispense with the undertaker altogether and think of different groups of persons, controlling different agents or factors of production, as freely combining and bargaining with each other, exactly the same principles will hold. We may suppose that some possess land, some tools or buildings, some material, some manual skill, some knowledge of the markets on which the product must be placed; and that all are willing to wait for their share till the product is made or sold, and so to take their share in the speculative risk of the undertaking. Some may contribute several factors, but all wait and all speculate. This supposition is necessary for

[1] Pages 71 *sqq.*

our hypothesis, for if any one demands instant payment the value of his contribution is discounted and bought on speculation by the rest, and they are collectively taking the place of the undertaker with respect to him. Where there is no undertaker the co-operators must themselves determine how they are to share the proceeds, and it is at the margins, where the things that they respectively control can be substituted for each other, that they must find their common measure and come to terms. A marginal addition or subtraction of any one of the factors, the others remaining constant, may be expected to have such and such an effect on the product, and it is thus, and thus only, that they can make comparisons. The withdrawal of the whole supply of labour or the whole supply of land would annihilate the industry. The withdrawal of any one class of tools, or any one kind of intelligence or experience, would severely cripple it; but the withdrawal of a defined small amount of one factor, at the margin, would produce a definite result. How much of any other factor must be withdrawn to produce the same result? When we have answered that question we have determined the relative marginal efficiency of a unit of each of the two factors, and have arrived at the principle on which they must share in the proceeds; for we can now express the contributions made to the result by all the different factors in one and the same unit, and if we divide the proceeds by the sum of these units we shall determine the share to be claimed on account of each.

Now if any number of groups (whether spontaneously organised or brought together by an undertaker) are in a state of equilibrium with regard to each other, the relative marginal significances of all the factors will be identical in all of them. If not, then say that in one group the addition or withdrawal of a unit of land would affect the result twice as much as the addition or withdrawal of a given measure of some other factor, say of labour or of apparatus or intelligence, whereas in another group that same unit of land would produce an effect only equal to that of this given quantity of the other factor. Clearly a regrouping would be advantageous on both sides. The second group should cede a certain amount of land to the first, and the first should cede some of the other

2 B

factor to the second. Each would be able to offer advantageous terms of exchange to the other, till equilibrium was reached. In the two groups the units of the two factors would then occupy the same relative positions. Thus the proportions in which the various factors that combine in any one group are to share in the product is determined by their relative significance at the margins in increasing or diminishing it. And the same proportions will tend, in the open market, to establish themselves in different independent groups. This will be the case whether the two groups are engaged in the same industry or in different industries that make use of certain common factors of production.

And again, if the total to be shared is proportionately larger in one industry than in another, though the factors employed in them are essentially the same, then clearly the group that reaps the lowest remuneration will divert the whole or a part of its energies to the more remunerative industry, thereby raising the marginal significance of the deserted and lowering that of the invaded industry, by respectively contracting and expanding the stream of their products put upon the market. Or if the different factors in any one group can severally distribute themselves among other groups, or form fresh combinations where their proportional claim in the product, determined by their relative marginal efficiency, represents a larger sum than they are now entitled to, the group will break up, and its constituents will distribute themselves amongst other groups, till equilibrium is reached. This gives us a complete theoretical solution of the problem of distribution with the undertaker eliminated.

Returning to the more familiar case of the undertaker, and stretching the term to include all the functions of promoter, director, and manager, we find him making bargains with those who control the several factors of production. Some of them will receive fixed payments or promises, and will have no further claims on the concern. On this method he may secure raw material, labour, machinery, and land, and may pay some part of the necessary premium on waiting (debentures). Others will take or share the risk, and will give their co-operation on an expectation as to the result, their respective claims on which are suitably

Marginal worth of the undertaker's faculty.

defined. These others may be a distinct and separate class of persons with possessions for the direct enjoyment of which they are willing to wait (shareholders). Or the undertaker may himself take some, or all, of this risk, for he may be his own capitalist. Or he may be employed, at a fixed salary, by those who take the risk. In any case, on his own account, or on the account of his employers, he will make whatever initial bargains have to be made; and will then direct and combine the several factors, and determine their respective amounts. These functions may be separated or subdivided. A syndicate may be formed in the first instance to raise the capital, that is to say, to make speculative bargains with possessors who will wait, and then all other bargaining and directing may be handed over to a manager. Or the original syndicate may retain some control of the business, that is to say, may themselves exercise a part of the functions of the manager. But, in any case, whatever resources the undertaker commands, he must so balance their application that the marginal significance of a pound is identical whether expended in wages, rent, interest, or however else. He will, therefore, fix the proportions in which the different factors are to be combined on the principles we have already examined. He will have to make definite payments or promises in some cases, and he will raise more or less elastic expectations in others; and in every case he will have to pay, or to promise, or cause to be expected, as much as the open market offers, in order to command the factors of production he requires. To succeed, then, he must be able so to arrange the proportions of his factors, and so to combine them, as to make them all worth as much at the margin in his own concern as other people expect them to be in theirs. For he will have to give as much as other people offer for them, and he will get as much as they turn out to be worth to him. If he succeeds, the product will recoup him for all his payments, will enable him to meet all his promises, and adequately satisfy all the expectations he has raised, and will leave a balance which he considers a satisfactory remuneration for the exercise of his own sagacity; that is to say, not less than he supposes he could have obtained by some other application of it. This is on the supposition that he has no fixed salary, but has made his own bargains with all the others concerned and is the residuary claimant. If he has a salary that will be included amongst the payments and the syndicate, or whoever takes the ultimate risk, must include that salary amongst their speculative payments or promises.

If the result transcends or falls short of this mark, it may be due to the undertaker's skill or want of skill, or it may be due to the conditions of the trade. In the former case the marginal significance of the undertaker's services has been under- or over-estimated by himself or by his employers; and the price of these services will tend to rise or fall as the case may be; for the undertaker too is a factor of production, and his remuneration, whether it consists in a definite payment or in an expectation, was determined on an estimate of the marginal significance of his services. He too has his market, though the special conditions may make it a very imperfect one.

If the result is due to the general conditions of the trade, the undertaker's anticipations are falsified, but it becomes clear that no other undertaker will be able to do what he has failed to do; so that the blame attaching to him will be that of having made the promises and payments in question, not of having failed to justify them. An adjustment will now take place between the collapsing or languishing industries which either cannot keep the promises or cannot fulfil the expectations they have raised, and the flourishing industries which can keep their promises and can fulfil the expectations they raise. And so the contracting and broadening streams of supply will restore equality of result. But in no case will the amount of the payments and promises that have been made, and the expectations that have been raised, determine the value of the product in the circle of exchange. In all cases it is the anticipated value of the product to be secured that determines the estimated marginal values on which payments, premiums, promises, and expectations were based. These estimated relative marginal significances of the properly grouped and distributed factors determine the proportions of their respective claims for remuneration, and the sum of the unit claims, expressed in the common measure, when divided into the total anticipated value of the product, determines the actual rate at which the concern believed it could afford to remunerate them. To have acted on that belief does not secure a result in accordance with it. If the result falsifies it, the belief will be corrected. But action—in this case costs incurred, promises made, and expectations raised—will always be determined by anticipated results, and will never itself determine what the actual results are. And thus we are insensibly brought to the consideration of our second problem, that of the relation of cost of production to value in exchange.[1]

To solve this problem also, we have only to array the facts already examined, and to draw the principles which we have been illustrating throughout the course of our investigations into explicit reference to the matter now in hand. At the risk of perhaps wearisome repetition, I will therefore throw this last section partly into the form of an epitome of the whole argument. *Cost of production and exchange value. Recapitulation.* The guiding principle of all administration, as we have often seen, is so to select between open alternatives as to direct our resources towards the fulfilment of that purpose which, given the terms on which it is open to us, takes the highest place on our scale of preferences. And seeing that the securing of that alternative perpetually lowers its marginal significance, and the neglect of other alternatives raises theirs, we shall always be able to bring our marginal increments of satisfaction into balance with the respective terms on which they are open to us. The purposes that the same resources will fulfil will then stand at the same height on our scales; and so long as we can keep them there, there will be equilibrium and a maximising of desired results. But if we have made an error of judgment, and have made a choice which we cannot now reverse, which puts us in possession of that which turns out to be of less value to us than something else we might have had in its place, the error so far as it goes is irreparable. We

---

[1] In 1894 I published (London, Macmillan and Co.) a short mathematical treatise entitled *An Essay on the Co-ordination of the Laws of Distribution.* In paragraph 6 I made a premature attempt to solve the general problem of distribution, which was at once pronounced by Professor Flux to be worthy of attention, rather on account of its presentation of the problem than on account of the solution offered; and Professors Edgeworth and Pareto subsequently shewed that the solution itself was erroneous. This paragraph of the *Essay*, therefore, must be regarded as formally withdrawn, and the solution now offered in the text must take its place.

may, indeed, learn by experience. To-morrow, or months or years hence, the choice may present itself again, and we may then correct for the future the mistake of judgment which has already produced its full effect upon the past. And within that area of our lives which is irrevocably affected by the waste involved in our misdirection of efforts and resources, better and worse alternatives still remain, though the best of all has been shut out. A contracted range of alternatives may still be open to us, and we must still make the best of them by trying to bring them into equilibrium at the margins, so as to involve no further waste. To revert to our old illustration, even if she has taken in too much or too little milk, the housewife has a wide range of applications open to her. By carelessness in selecting between them, she may add many more mistakes and much more waste to what has already been perpetrated, and by care she may make the very best of the contracted opportunities which her initial mistake has still left her.

Now this principle of administration of resources is applicable as much to our getting as to our spending. Our getting, indeed, is very largely of the nature of spending. It is the spending of time, of energy, of thought, of resources of every kind. And even where it does not naturally come under the conception of spending, or administering resources, it comes under the wider conception of choosing between alternatives, which, as we have seen, follows the same law. If I encounter irksomeness, weariness, or positive pain, it may perhaps be straining language to call this an expenditure or administration of vital resources or powers of endurance, but in any case I am choosing between alternatives, on the principle of a balance of marginal significances. Practically speaking, then, the problem of getting is either identical with the problem of spending to the greatest advantage or strictly analogous to it. If I am devoting my efforts to the direct accomplishment of the things I desire, I shall be guided in my distribution of them by the several marginal significances to me of the experiences they will beget when turned down this channel or that. But if I am pursuing my purposes indirectly, doing things in which my interest is not direct,

Flow of resources under the economic stresses.

because that is the most effective way of securing what I want, then I shall be guided not by the place which the results of the various services I can render occupy on my own scale of preferences, but by that which they occupy on the collective scale, as indicated by the money price which they will command. If I am in control of a stock of timber (however I come to be so) which I desire to transmute into the maximum of literature or art or missionary activity, or political propaganda, or knowledge of mathematics, or silk and satin garments, or anything else that cannot be made of wood, I shall sell it at the highest price I can get; that is to say, I shall direct it to the supply of that want which, by the price offered for its satisfaction, proclaims itself to be objectively highest on the collective scale. In other words I shall go to market with my timber, and by the process of always selling to the best customer I can find, I shall be continuously producing or maintaining an equality between all customers, from which there will only be slight departures. The moment one customer becomes better than another, he will command supplies until the marginal value of the article has no higher place on his relative scale than on that of his neighbour. The market will perpetually tend to an equilibrium of prices. In the same way if I have any services to render, I shall render them in such a way as to maintain an equilibrium between all the different purposes which they can further, as expressed in their places on the communal scale.

If I am thinking of my son's future life, I make a forecast of what I suppose will be, some years hence, the relative place on the collective scale of such services as can be rendered by an electrical engineer, a mechanical engineer, a mining engineer, a barrister, a doctor, and so forth. I try to estimate the likelihood of his achieving eminence or respectability in any of these occupations. I think, if I am wise, of his tastes as well as his talents, and consider which line of activity would be most desirable as an occupation apart from the command it would give him over the services and commodities of others. And I consider the resources I should have to devote to preparing him for each one of these careers and the alternative applications of them which I might make in furtherance of any of my purposes in life other than his establishment. Now all of these considerations will weigh with me, and amongst them my forecast as to the strength of his future economic position, that is to say, the place on the collective scale occupied by the services he will be able to render in one or the other of these professions. Not, as we have seen, that individual tastes and other considerations will go for nothing, but that they will not go for everything, even where they are pronounced; and there will be many cases in which they are not pronounced. Thus, there are persons whose selection of their own career, or of that of others whom they partly or completely control, will be influenced by the anticipated place which these or those services will take on the collective scale. And there will be a tendency to bring them into equilibrium.[1]

<small>Tentative direction of flow of faculties and resources. Misdirection tends to correct, not to justify itself.</small>

Thus, if in the general estimate, or the estimate of a sufficiently large number of persons to whom the alternative is open, the positions of a mining, a mechanical, and an electrical engineer are in themselves equally desirable, and if the expense of the education in each case is approximately the same, and if the progress of science has opened immense possibilities to electrical engineers, so that at present their services are marginally more effective, and therefore stand higher on the collective scale, than those of mechanical or mining engineers, then those who anticipate that this state of things will last for some time, will have a reason for training themselves or their sons to electrical rather than mechanical or mining engineering. Those who have already qualified as mechanical engineers may think that they have made a mistake. They have acquired one skill instead of another, which other they might have attained at the same effort and sacrifice, and would have found more valuable. But this does not in any way affect the market price of their services. It is affected solely by the number of persons in the market possessing this particular skill, and the place of the wants it ministers to on the collective scale. Slowly, however, this state of things will correct itself. As those to

[1] Cf. pages 203 *sqq.*

whom the two careers are in themselves indifferent are drafted into the electrical branch, the stream of supply of electrical engineers is constantly broadening and that of mechanical engineers narrowing until the balance is effected. Now it is likely enough that the general estimate may have exaggerated the extent of the initial departure from equilibrium, or underestimated the rapidity with which equilibrium will be restored. Just at the moment when I become convinced that there is a better career for electrical than for mechanical engineers, a vast number of other *patresfamilias* may have been visited by the same inspiration, and a considerable though smaller number were visited by it several years earlier. As my son enters upon his long and laborious training, other people's sons are issuing from theirs, in a broader stream than before; and the stream perpetually broadens till, when my son comes out of his training, it is of very different dimensions from what I anticipated. So that by this time the position of the mechanical engineer may even be better than that of his brother the electrician. Here, again, I have made a mistake, and as far as it goes it is irreparable. The fact that, if my sagacity had been greater, my son might have been performing the service of a mechanical engineer does not make his worth as an electrical engineer any higher. The value of his services is dominated by the law of the market. But though my mistake has been made, and its consequences must be accepted, I and others need not make it again. We shall not put the sons that are now entering upon their training into the same profession. Thus the result, though it does not influence the past, influences the future. The stream of supply will be checked, and a tendency in the counter direction will set in.

Now, the whole work of the world is done, and all the wants of the world are supplied, by the direction of human faculties to the accomplishment of human purposes. And every step in personal training or in manipulating the materials of the planet modifies human power or the materials on which it works in some specific direction, and therefore constitutes a specialising of resources and a relinquishing of one set of alternatives by the embracing of another. Nor has the alternative that has been relinquished any influence on the value or significance of the alternative that has been embraced; for I can no longer equilibrate the two against each other. But if the specialising has not been carried to the last point, if alternative applications are still open, then the anticipated significance of each of them tells upon my mind and influences my action as I equilibrate one against another. I shall not devote my powers or my possessions to the realisation of any purpose as long as they will serve another that seems to me preferable. So the resources, personal and material, of all men are perpetually being directed towards certain goals, alternatives are being perpetually accepted to the exclusion of other alternatives that are rejected, and each such selection narrows the possibilities still open, and at last closes them altogether, the ultimate result having been realised. At every step the alternatives relinquished may cause regret, but at no step do they affect the value of the alternatives realised. So far, then, as my selection between alternatives is dictated not by the value to me of the things that they directly secure, but by the command of generalised services and resources in the circle of exchange which they will indirectly give me, that is to say, so far as I am influenced by economic considerations, my determination is guided at every stage by anticipations of the place which services and things take, or will take, on the collective scale; and my success is measured not by the significance of the alternatives I have relinquished, but by the significance of the alternative I have embraced.

If a number of men have already made chairs the price they realise will not be affected by the knowledge that if they had made tables they would have been in a better position; but their conduct in future will be affected by that knowledge. They will redistribute the undifferentiated resources, which are still capable of being turned to the production of either tables or chairs indifferently; they will broaden the stream of supply of tables, and contract that of chairs, until the falling price of tables and the rising price of chairs bring the prices into conformity with the output of energy and resources respectively required to produce them. Just in the same way the housewife who finds that she has been buying vegetables and fruit in such quantities that, when they are consumed, a halfpennyworth of vegetables meets a less urgent want than a halfpennyworth of fruit, will henceforward contract the purchase of vegetables and increase that of fruit, till the rising significance of vegetables and the declining significance of fruit bring them into balance with the prices. Both alike, craftsman and housewife, have made a mistake in accepting a less eligible alternative than was open. The mistake of neither is itself removed by after-recognition. But both may learn wisdom; and when the alternatives are again open may choose the more eligible one.

But if a man, in full conviction that he could most profitably devote his resources to the production of chairs, had laid down special machinery which was only capable of producing chairs, the production of tables with it would not be an open alternative, and he would consider not whether it would be better to make it produce tables than chairs, but whether, having made a mistake by laying down that class of machinery, it is better for him to scrap it or to go on producing chairs. The question depends for its answer on the range of alternatives still open to him. His machinery will enable him to make chairs, but will not enable him to do anything else. So far there is no alternative. But his stock of wood, if he has any, may be employed in making chairs or tables or in many other ways; and his own thought and effort may likewise be turned into many channels, though he cannot go back to the time when he learned his trade and choose to have learned some other instead. His money may be turned to buying anything that is in the circle of exchange. It need not be spent on wood or wages for the kind of skill that deals with wood, if he can find anything that serves his turn better. Thus he has a certain acquired skill, a certain kind of stock, and a certain general command of commodities and services. Can he without the help of his machinery so combine these as to produce something that stands higher on the collective scale than the chairs which he could produce by applying the same resources to making chairs with the help of his machinery? If not, he will go on producing chairs however bitterly he may regret not having adopted a better alternative when it was open to him.

Closed and open opportunities and alternatives.

Cost of production, then, in the sense of the historical and irrevocable fact that resources have been devoted to this or that special purpose, has no influence on the value of the thing produced, and therefore does not affect its price. Cost of production, in the sense of alternatives still open which must now be relinquished in order to produce this specific article, influences the craftsman in determining whether he will produce it or not. Thus, the price of the chairs when produced will be determined by their marginal place on the collective scale; but the maker's anticipation of what that place will be, compared with the place of anything else which it is still open to him to make instead of the chairs, will decide whether he will make them or not. These two propositions need no qualification, but the significance of the phrase, " anything else which it is still open to him to make instead of the chairs," is subject to continuous change and narrowing as the process of specialising proceeds and the concrete result is approached. Money and untrained talent may be turned into any channel, but every decision as to the channel into which to turn them shuts out certain possibilities and limits the range of the things that it is still " open to the man to make instead of chairs," until the chairs at last are actually made, and it is no longer possible to him to make anything else at all instead of them. At every stage the cost incurred in making a thing is the relinquished possibility of making other things, and its extent or amount is determined by the value, or marginal significance on the collective scale, which those other things would have had. So the " cost of production " of any one thing is only another name for the marginal significance of certain other things, which have been forgone for its sake. The marginal significance of things that can no longer be produced instead of it has no effect on its present price; the marginal significance of things that can still be produced instead of it will determine the lower limit of the price at which it will be made to order, and the extent to which manufacturers will continue to make it at all.

These reflections will explain the great ambiguity of the term " cost price." Even members of the same trade, meeting for conference on their common affairs, and speaking with perfect freedom and sincerity, will use the word in different senses. One will declare that he is "making no profits at all," but is "selling at a loss," and another will say that "things are bad enough with him, but not quite so bad as that," when they both mean to indicate exactly the same state of affairs. Men will declare in good faith that they are "selling below cost price," and yet will never think of suspending operations. Or again, we may hear that a business goes into liquidation although it is really "perfectly sound in itself," and we may see that it actually does go on without apparent disturbance. All these phenomena are easily explained. The one man says that he is "selling below cost price" because he takes as his measure of "cost" the estimated value of the things he might have produced when all his original opportunities were still open. Allowing a reasonable percentage on the money that he might have put into another business, though he did not, and a reasonable remuneration for the talents which he might have directed into other channels, though he did not, and adding to this his out-of-pocket expenses for wages, raw material, and so forth, that he need not have incurred, though he did, he finds that altogether they amount to more than the price which he can realise for the articles he has put upon the market; so that he gets less for the thing than it has cost him to make it. But the other man uses the phrase "cost price" in the sense of the sacrifice not of alternatives that once were, but of alternatives that still are open to him. He contemplates only the possibilities of turning his resources, as he now has them, to some other purpose, and he finds that there is nothing else he can now produce or do which would yield a more satisfactory result than what he is actually doing. He is indeed disappointed and dissatisfied at the range of alternatives still open to him, but, since his business still offers him the best of the yet remaining alternatives, now that it is once established, the marginal significance of what he relinquishes to keep it going is lower than that of what he gets by it; and his product, therefore, realises more than its actual "cost of production" as measured in the open alternatives that he relinquishes for it. He would be worse off if he declined orders and closed his works.

Ambiguity of the term "cost price."

In the case of a firm that is "over capitalised" the state

of things is this. Expectations were entertained and promises made on the supposition that certain results would be realised. They have not been realised, and to keep all the promises that have been made would be impossible, unless the persons who keep them are able and willing to pay more than they receive. If they do this, after a time they probably will be unable to pay at all. But if the persons to whom the promises were made can be induced, or forced, to face the facts in time, and to consent to take a share in the loss caused by the misdirection of resources, or bate something of the excessive hopes which the original misrepresentations or mistaken estimates caused, the continuance of the business may be a better alternative for all concerned than any other that is now open. If the fulfilment of all the promises is acknowledged as part of the "cost price," it is above the value of the product. If the alternatives that are open now, or even those that were in real truth open at the beginning, are taken as the "cost price," it is below that of the product.

We can now see how "cost of production," which is simply and solely "the marginal significance of something else," directly affects the quantity of anything produced, and thereby indirectly affects its price, so that there is a constant tendency for prices to conform to cost of production; that is to say, for the price of the thing I make and the price of the thing I might have made instead of it to coincide; for, obviously, I shall always embrace that one of the alternatives still open that offers the best result, and I shall thus increase the supply and lower the marginal significance of the best, and reduce the supply and raise the marginal significance of the others, till they balance. And if I have cut myself off from better alternatives than are now open to me by specialising my resources in a particular machine, it is true that I cannot immediately recover from the false step, but if I am a large manufacturer, and my machines are perpetually being replaced, I shall be able rapidly to recover from small errors of judgment. As my machinery for making chairs wears out, instead of completely replacing it, I may increase my stock of the machinery for making tables. As long as I have the machinery I shall be ready to make chairs

The cost of production of one thing is the marginal value of another thing.

for anything above the out-of-pocket expenses, but as I should not have made the machinery had I foreseen the state of things, so I shall not replace it now that I see it.

Resources flow down from their undifferentiated condition through a series of differentiations to the ultimate realisation of concrete purposes, and when I am about to lay down a new machine, I am considering alternatives higher up the stream than any that were open to me when I was considering how to use the machine I had already made. I may direct them now to a point which was inaccessible to me then. And exactly the same reasoning applies to the acquiring and training of special skill; that is to say, to the turning of human energy and faculty into channels from which it cannot be recalled, or can only be recalled partially and with loss. The misdirection of energy which makes me regret that I devoted myself to the study of Greek and took my University diploma in Arts, instead of in Brewing, is irreparable so far as I am concerned; but others may take warning by my fate, and may give the more remunerative direction to their energies when still *in statu nascendi*, and thus the abundance of the better remunerated skill and the paucity of the other may bring their rewards more nearly into balance, and if equilibrium were actually reached there would be no professors of Greek in the world who wished that they had turned their talents into more remunerative if less pleasant channels.

The flow of resources.

Thus from first to last, so far as economic forces direct the application of energies and resources, they will aim at the highest place on the collective scale accessible to them. The results of alternative applications of the same resources will be brought rapidly into equilibrium if they remain open almost up to the end, slowly, and through many reactions, if the resources which bear upon them respectively were differentiated with reference to them at a point high up the stream. But a principle is always at work, corresponding to that of the mechanical "governors" of an engine. It should hardly be necessary to explain what these "governors" are. They are the twin balls that even the most casual observer must have noticed spinning round an upright rod. When the engine is going at a high speed the

The analogy of mechanical "governors."

balls fly out, and in so doing raise a throttle that shuts off steam and so reduces the speed of the engine. The slower movement of the engine communicates itself to the rotation of the "governors," and as they drop inwards they open the valve and let out more steam. Thus when they are duly regulated, the very fact of the engine working at a higher than the desired speed sets forces at work that reduce the speed, and the very fact of its working at a lower than the desired speed sets forces at work that raise it. Thus every departure from the normal speed constantly tends to correct itself. In like manner, the mere fact of any one price being lower than any other which the same application of energies and resources might have secured, will tend, at a point low down or high up on the stream, as the case may be, to divert the flow and effect a redistribution. The fact of low prices will tend to check off the supply that makes them low, and of higher prices to broaden the stream, the narrowness of which it is that makes them high. But at any given moment the economic forces will never in themselves have any direct tendency to make a man refuse the best price he can get because he would not have made the article unless he had expected a better price, or to accept a lower price than he can command because that lower price would have been a sufficient inducement to him to make the article even if he had anticipated nothing better. In no case will considerations of past sacrifices bring any economic force to bear which will prevent a man from embracing the best alternative still open to him, or that will induce him to accept anything short of the best.

There is probably no difference of opinion amongst serious thinkers as to the facts I have been insisting upon, and indeed they are so obvious that it is impossible for any one who begins to think at all to fail to recognise them when they are clearly put before him. But the words "value," "price," "cost price," and "cost of production" are so ambiguous and are used in so many senses that a statement which is perfectly true in the sense in which it is made may be wholly or partially false in the sense in which it is understood. And these ambiguities react upon our thought and cause confusion. Nay, it is perfectly possible for one and the same man to make a statement to himself in one sense, and the next moment to understand and act upon it in another sense—and that sense one in which he would never have made it in the first instance. The history of Political Economy abounds in instances of the careful definition of such words as "land" and "capital," the construction of elaborate arguments based on the defined meanings of the words, and the insensible transference of the conclusions to what are ordinarily and currently understood by the terms; this last step being sometimes taken by the original framers of the definitions and arguments, and sometimes by their disciples. This danger is acute in the matter we are now considering, and it will therefore be well to take detailed and even minute precautions.

By the true exchange value of a commodity at any moment I mean simply the place, relative to other things in the circle of exchange, which its marginal unit would take on the collective scale if it were so distributed as to secure present equilibrium. And this true exchange value determines what I have called the equilibrating, or sometimes the "ideal" price at the moment. By cost of production, or cost price, when the phrase is used without qualification, I mean the estimated value, measured in gold, of all the alternatives that have been sacrificed in order to place a unit of the commodity in question upon the market. And in this sense it is clear that cost of production can have no influence upon exchange value, and therefore none upon the "ideal" or equilibrating price. But we have seen that the ultimate facts which determine this exchange value can never be completely known. Ideal exchange value depends upon the composition of the collective scale and the amount of the commodity, and in most cases neither of these can be the subject of complete knowledge, but only of more or less intelligent conjecture. Hence the dealers or possessors name a price based upon their estimates of the ultimate facts as they are or will be. And human estimates may be influenced by irrelevant considerations. We have seen [1] that in private life we are often unwilling to recognise the folly of our expenditure, and try to make out that we value a thing which is really no better than rubbish to us

Sentimental influence of "cost of production" on commercial actions.

[1] See page 118.

2 c

because we paid a high price for it. There is a natural unwillingness in the human mind to face unpleasant facts, and having committed an error of judgment we often shrink from recognising the fact, even though we thereby aggravate its results. In the same way, a commercial man who has made an error of judgment and has produced things which he cannot sell at cost price (that is to say, which he cannot sell at a price which would have justified him in producing them, at the moment when he determined to do so) will be unwilling to recognise his error, and will make a struggle to secure a price high enough to justify his action. Thus he may hold back from selling a thing at less than cost price, even when he has no sufficient prospect of getting a better price by waiting. That is to say, a price is offered him which is really as good as he is likely to get, and which nothing justifies him in refusing. Had it covered the cost price he would have accepted it without demur, but a certain shrinking from facing the facts induces him to hold on. If such motives really influence a man he is not obeying an economic force, but is making a sacrifice of things in the circle of exchange in order to gratify his desire to postpone as long as possible the recognition of his own error of judgment; for his hesitation to sell at a given price is either justified by the chance of his getting a better price by waiting and bargaining, in which case the economic forces would urge him to do so whether the price be above or below cost price, or else there is no such justification, and in that case by refusing to sell at what he can now get he is subjecting himself to the expenses of storage, as well as the continuous output of energy, and the vexatious wear, of striving unsuccessfully to mend a bad bargain, for all which there is no economic justification.

In such a case the man who fixes his price with reference to the cost of production is either allowing an irrelevant consideration to affect his judgment or else is deliberately taking a commercial risk to gratify a personal feeling. And it may be noticed that such personal feelings seldom influence men's conduct in businesses in which mistaken estimates as to the value of the thing to be produced are of normal or frequent occurrence. In such a business a man will not hesitate to sell at what he can get, or if he should judge that this may have a deleterious influence on other branches of his business he will actually destroy the stock which it was a commercial error to have created. If a publisher, for instance, has brought out a work wholly or chiefly at his own risk he may find that there is no chance of its selling at cost price or anything like it; and then (after a suitable interval, determined amongst other things by a consideration of indirect effects upon the minds of purchasers of other books in the future) he may sell his stock as a "remainder" for what it will fetch, or, if he thinks it will be better in the long-run to do so, he may destroy the stock. But in any case he is entirely uninfluenced in his present conduct by considerations of what his costs have been in the past. He thinks only of what he can best do with his stock in the present and future.

Even in a necessarily speculative business, however, it is easy to conceive cases in which the judgment may be warped by the personal feelings engaged. It is notorious, for example, that persons who habitually deal in stocks will sometimes hold on to stock contrary to their better judgment. They "backed their judgment" some time ago when they bought for a rise, and though they would now never think of touching the stock if the whole transaction could be reopened, they will not sell, because to do so would be the formal admission to themselves that they had made a mistake in buying; though had they bought at such a price that they could now sell at a profit, they would be eager to do so. But this clearly is not business; and the man who is least subject to such impulses will be, so far, the best business man. Temper is expensive. And again, if it is not business to refuse the best price you can get because it is not good enough to cover cost price, neither is it business to accept something less than the best price that can be obtained, simply because this something-less-than-the-best already more than covers the cost of production, and is so far good. The best, though bad, is better than the second best; and the second best, though good, is worse than the best.

Nevertheless, an important relation exists between price and cost of production which is frequently illustrated in the history of industry, and of which our theory gives a perfectly satisfactory account. It is true that, if the cost of production of any article exceeds its value in exchange, the cost cannot raise the value to its own level; but by a curious reaction, the exchange value often lowers the cost of production. The idea that the business man is actuated by a uniform desire to make money, never sated and never varying, is, as we have seen,[1] in flat contradiction with human nature. No man will fight as hard for an extra £1 if he possesses £1,000,000 as he will if he wants to keep himself and his family supplied with food. He may conceivably fight as hard for "money," but if so it must be more money that calls forth the same effort. A man, then, will fight to avoid ruin harder and in closer detail than he will fight to make a large fortune larger. As long as he is fairly prosperous, he may be content to let things go on as they are, and to put forth no very great efforts in order to make himself a little more prosperous yet. But if his wares permanently command less than cost price in the market, ruin stares him in the face, and the whole resilience and energy of his nature will come into action in order to avert it. He will look into every detail, he will take nothing for granted, he will search for improved methods and improved machinery. He is driven back upon his base line, and must make his last and most desperate stand. History presents noteworthy examples of industries thus threatened, so husbanding their resources and so stimulating inventiveness and energy, that cost of production has been reduced and a new era of prosperity initiated; for many a man "looking for silver has found gold," and in searching for small economies has hit on great ones. And then, again, since selling below cost price, except incidentally, means failure, and normally selling above cost price means success, it is natural that the level of cost price should make a powerful appeal to the imagination, and should even affect the judgment when it is not economically relevant; so that a man may largely take cost price as marking the level of solvency and be content when he is above it without seeking to secure any further gain. Moreover, a trustworthy and independent judgment is one of the very things of which a man may

Real reaction of low market prices in reducing cost of production.

[1] Pages 83, 84, 197.

know that he has an inadequate supply, and which he may rightly desire to economise; and there may be some branches of trade in which he finds it an economy of thought and trouble to take the price that he has given for an article as the basis of the price that he will ask for it. Thus there are some second-hand booksellers who habitually sell the same book at different prices, and will even have two copies of the same book, in equally good condition, marked at different prices, in their shop-windows at the same time. Such dealers will of course be careful never to give a price for a book unless they think they will be able to sell it at a profit; but apparently it saves them trouble to have a mechanical system by which they fix their selling prices. Possibly they think that the occasional appearance of exceptionally cheap books may stimulate their trade. If so it is a naïve and half-unconscious form of "salting," which preserves the dealer's dignity, for it obviates the necessity of his recognising exactly what he is doing, and at the same time it avoids the shock that it would give his feelings to sell one copy at a lower price than that at which he bought it in the hope of making some one buy another copy at more. But it is obvious that the effect is the same as if he habitually fixed his price at the highest point which he thought he could realise, and now and again deliberately sold a book for less than it was worth in order to give his shop a reputation for "bargains." From the business point of view it is an anomaly to have the same article in your shop avowedly at two prices.

But these phenomena are far from constituting the main source of confusion as to the connection between the cost of production and exchange value. In all the examples we have hitherto discussed, "cost of production," or "cost price," has been used in the sense of the expenses already incurred; and the price we have discussed has been the price of something already possessed or already in existence. But whenever in serious discussions cost of production is said to exercise any direct control on price, the cost of production intended is cost that has not yet been incurred, and the price meant is not the price at which an existing commodity is offered, but the price at which a promise is made to produce

Distinction between past cost of production incurred and future cost of production estimated.

it. Now in this sense of course it is perfectly true that price, or rather the lower limit of price, is strictly determined by cost of production. That is to say, no man will, in the way of business, promise to procure or produce a commodity at a certain price when he deliberately believes that it will cost him more. But there are a hundred different ways of estimating this cost. When a man sits down to calculate the cost of production of an article, he may only consider the out-of-pocket expenses which he would incur in executing that particular order; or he may make an allowance for a suitable proportion of the whole expense of keeping the concern going; or to these he may add a suitable charge for interest on the capital originally invested; and he may or may not add something to represent his own remuneration. And on whatever basis he makes his estimate he may then make any addition which he thinks the state of the market will bear; or if he has made his estimate on any basis except that of the actual out-of-pocket expenses which the execution of the individual order will involve, he may be obliged to deduct something from the estimated cost price because the state of the market requires it. And he may be willing to do so sooner than lose the order, for perhaps it is only so far as these out-of-pocket expenses for the specific order are concerned that any alternatives are still open.

Thus the calculation of the cost of production, in any sense except this narrowest one, will be no more than an attempt to reach a basis which may offer some guide and support to the judgment. A man may know fairly well, from the general conditions of his business, how it is doing on the whole. That is to say, he may know roughly what relation the best values that he can now produce bear to the alternatives successively relinquished when he specialised free resources in more or less permanent forms of building or machinery, got together his staff and made engagements with them, and generally organised his business; and on making a detailed estimate of the proportions of these relinquished opportunities that should be debited to the production of any particular article, he forms a conception of the fraction of the total output which it represents; and this gives him a basis for considering its relations to the other things which he might produce instead of it. If the trade is in a normal condition he knows that the proceeds of this particular industry are neither so great as to induce a rush into it, nor so small as to scare people from it. That is to say, he knows that the value of the product and the cost of production about balance, so that his rivals will not allow him to get much more, nor will the state of the market compel him to accept much less, than the full cost of production. But if the business is especially prosperous or depressed, his calculation of the full cost of production will merely give him an idea of the proportion that the execution of this particular order will bear to his general output, and he will raise his tender far above or sink it far below the full cost price according to the state of the market.

To sum up, then :—In no case can the cost of production have any direct influence upon the price of a commodity, if the commodity has been produced and the cost has been incurred; but in every case in which the cost of production has not yet been incurred, the manufacturer makes an estimate of the alternatives still open to him before determining whether, and in what quantities, the commodity shall be produced; and the stream of supply thus determined on fixes the marginal value and the price. The only sense, then, in which cost of production can affect the value of one thing is the sense in which it is itself the value of another thing. Thus what has been variously termed utility, ophelemity, or desiredness, is the sole and ultimate determinant of all exchange values. *The only sense in which cost of production can affect the value of one thing is that in which it is itself the value of another.*

We have now reached our goal. We have traced the identity of the great laws of the psychology of choice through all our commercial and private life, have shown that the principles on which we choose between further indulgence of our literary tastes and further support of social movements in which we are interested are the same as those on which we choose between the different wares in the market, that our resources are administered on the same principles whether directly or indirectly applied to our purposes, that our conduct in the presence of market rates itself explains how those rates are *Recapitulation.*

constituted, and that every man's desire to fulfil his own purposes will ceaselessly urge him to search out the means of fulfilling those of others.

What, then, is our picture of the movement of the industrial and commercial world, as we have now studied and analysed it? At every point we see both human faculty and the materials which nature supplies, in various stages of specialisation and combination, controlled by forces which are ever thrusting us to feel forward towards that further specialisation which, of all the wants that can be reached, will touch the one that stands objectively highest on the collective scale. As the stream sweeps down and approaches the region that seems thirstiest, news of success or failure in really finding it is signalled back to some point higher up on the stream where the channels part. The water that has once passed such a point cannot return to it, but in one channel its swift flow shews that it has found the thirsty spot, and in another it lags and lingers and shews that it has found the ground saturated: and so the sluices of the one channel may be lifted and those of the other dropped, and the flow of the ever-running waters regulated. Thus at each point the water that flows this way or that, though never itself to return, tells us how best to direct the future stream. And at each dividing point, or (to vary the metaphor) at each ganglion in the industrial organism, the flow of vital energy is directed forward along this passage or that, and news of the total they will carry is shot back to some higher ganglion that in its turn will co-ordinate a wider and yet wider system of centres.

At the one extreme we have the actual services and commodities which directly minister to human desires or modify human impulses, bewildering in their diversity yet all comparable, and all capable at their margins of being substituted one for the other as ministers to the fulfilment of human claims. In one sense the goal is million-fold, in another sense it is one. And at the other extreme we have the ultimate forces and materials of nature, and the eternal stream of nascent humanity with its limited, but as yet undifferentiated, capacities. Human society at any moment finds itself the heir of all the then existing specialisings and combinations of these primitive resources. Nature herself has specialised her own constituent elements in the primeval forests, in the coal-beds, and in all the living things she has produced, and man has modified or undone her specialisings or made new combinations of her material, sometimes in age-old workings, the prehistoric draining of a morass, or shaping of a mountain side, or the building of a Roman road. And every individual, since man was, has specialised his own faculties, sometimes in transient ways that directly affect only himself and those around him, sometimes in discoveries that widely affect for good or for ill the powers, the opportunities and the desires of men— whether it be the discovery of fire, of distilled or fermented drinks, of letters, of poisoned arrows, of music, of gunpowder, of telegraphy (that is said to transmit two gambling messages for every one upon any other matter), of the rack or of chloroform. And at every stage of the world's history living humanity, entering upon her heritage, directs her means towards the accomplishment of her ends, pushing out her tentacles, feeling forward and signalling backward; every step being in a sense irrevocable, but none irreparable.

At the goal, where the wants and desires of men are actually satisfied, and where the different commodities and services are directly comparable at their margins, as ministrants to human wants, we come upon the ultimate seat and source of value. "Everywhere hath she sway, there is her Imperial throne." It is there that the direction of human effort is put to the economic test, and thence that the signals are flashed back all along the line, stimulating and checking the distribution of resources at every point of division. No raw material, no machine, no specialised talent, no natural or artificial combination of things, has any value except the derived value which it draws from its anticipated contribution to some ultimate service that shall be placed on the scale, tried, compared and appraised, before this imperial throne of Human Demand.

But society, though we may speak of it collectively, is made up of individuals, and these individuals organise themselves to some extent deliberately with a view to collective ends, to a much greater extent spontaneously with a view to their several particular ends. As the result of the whole outcome of history up to any moment, we find each man in enjoyment of certain faculties, in possession and control of certain things, inspired—by instincts, impulses, unreflecting habits, and deliberate choice—with certain purposes, some of which he can accomplish by the direct application of his own powers and resources, but for the accomplishment of the vast majority of which he is dependent on the co-operation of other men. This co-operation of other men in many cases he can only secure by co-operating in his turn towards the accomplishment of their desires, and it is the part of his life which is determined by this necessity that we speak of as economic. The ultimate cost at which the drift of his total effort reaches the objects of his desires consists in any degree of positive pain or distress that may be involved in the efforts made. His ultimate alternative often lies between securing something he desires and encountering painful or irksome experience, and avoiding the latter but foregoing the former. But when the pain has been faced, or when there is no question of pain at all but only of a choice between desired things, then we may say that the cost of the fulfilment of any specific purpose is the relinquishing of the alternative purposes which could have been accomplished on the same terms instead of it. Those outputs of energy therefore, which a man had rather not make than make, are his ultimate cost of production; and he will strive with what roughness or delicacy of adjustment the circumstances allow to effect a marginal balance between the pain of his efforts and the desiredness of what they secure.[1] And in administering and expending his efforts he will pursue his purposes directly or indirectly according as the one or the other method is the more effective, and so he will secure a marginal equilibrium of results between the economic and non-economic applications of his energies. The same principle dominates these two regions of application of resources internally. Everywhere he brings the marginal significance of the things he gets into equilibrium with the terms on which he can get them. The flow of energies and resources towards the direct accomplishment

[1] Cf. Book II. pages 416 *sqq.*

of his desires will seek the points of highest subjective significance on his own scale. The flow of his energies and resources towards the indirect accomplishment of his desires will seek the points objectively highest on the scales of others. Thus with perpetual liability to error, which experience is continuously checking and correcting, the whole resources of society, so far as they obey economic forces, tend to flow towards the accomplishment of each man's purposes just in proportion to his individual command of personal energies and things desired by others, for in that proportion can his demands be met without falling objectively below the point on the collective scale at which they will cease to be regarded.

Inventions and discoveries of every kind steadily tend to place mankind in fuller control of the powers of nature, and to give them larger means of accomplishing their desires. But this enlarged power has no direct or inevitable tendency to make those desires wise or worthy, or to correct the inequalities that have historically emerged between the powers possessed by different men to direct the resources of others towards the accomplishment of their own desires. The network of interchanges created and sustained by the economic forces is, morally, socially, and aesthetically, absolutely indifferent. It serves to enable every man to pursue his purposes, such as they are, beyond the range of the direct applicability of his own faculties and resources to them. It enables the saint who has the will but not the power to do some great deed to enlist the co-operation of the sinner who has the power but not the will to do it. But in order to make the sinner help him to the accomplishment of his purposes he has been obliged himself to help the sinner to the accomplishment of his. It is an arrangement by which each will further the other's purpose, irrespectively of what he thinks of it, in order to further his own. And the man who is in the best position to get anything he wants is the man who already has most of everything else; for he it is who can best, and at least sacrifice, help others to what they want. And so, under the all-covering cloak of money payments for services and commodities, and sales of instruments and supports of life for money payments, all purposes and impulses, of love and of lust, of narrow greed and of broad beneficence, of enlightened and productive insight, of blind, tangled, and self-confuting gropings, all destructive and reckless passions, all wasteful and desolating vices, all noble ambitions, all vulgar or refined enjoyments, all fruitful enterprises, and all foolish or wicked schemes of industrial waste, enter the open market and draw to themselves the efforts and services of men in proportion not to their worthiness or fruitfulness, but to the means they command of furthering the purposes of others; for they secure the co-operation of all sorts and conditions of men, not in the measure in which such men sympathise with them, but in the measure in which by serving them they will forward their own purposes. Neither the urgency of his want nor the nobility of his purpose determines the extent to which a man may rely on economic forces to help him. Cobbett's halfpenny can influence the flow of productive resources no more than the halfpenny of a millionaire. The shopman will further each alike to the extent of one red herring in return for his coin. Nay, if an agent of the white slave traffic and an emissary of a rescue society apply for tickets to travel by the same train they will be impartially furthered in their respective purposes on the same terms, and if both are faint for want of food the restorateur at the station will for the same consideration impartially " restore " them both, and enable them to carry on their several purposes refreshed and invigorated. And yet more, indirectly each of them may be said to be helping the other to perform the journey, and the light-hearted tourist is helping them both, for all alike help to create the public demand in anticipation of which the railway was built, and in response to which it is run.

The purposes of men are often not only diverse, but mutually destructive, and this both on the large and on the small scale. The wars by which one set of men devote their energies and resources to extinguishing the energies and resources of another set of men, and the perpetual diversion, in times of peace, of national energies and resources towards the preparation for such acts of destruction, are the types of a yet more intimate and incessant conflict by which men devote their energies not towards increasing the collective resources, but towards competing with each other for the command of them. When we add the perpetual errors of judgment which lead men to turn their resources into relatively futile channels because they know no better, and the further industrial wreckage which is perpetually and deliberately planned by those who shew false lights in hope to pick up some fragments of the wreck upon the shore, the imagination begins to form some conception of the moral and social chaos which may lie concealed beneath the apparent cosmos of that economic system, which outwardly displays the fascinating picture of a huge federation, as wide as the world, organised automatically upon a scheme which perpetually determines the flow of all resources, personal and material, to the point of the social organism where "the demand for them is most urgent and their significance highest."

We know that through the blind interplay of all these forces the collective means of forwarding human purposes steadily advance, and this shews that in point of fact the destructive and wasteful tendencies less than balance the constructive and conservative ones; and so far as we may believe that the progress of ages has brought, if not an increased yet at least a more widespread refinement of manners, so far as we can look forward hopefully to the gradual elimination of the most wasteful forms of savagery, so far as we have reason to think that in spite of all fluctuations and reactions a slow growth of the sense of responsibility and a slow purification of collective aims are going forward, we may perhaps draw encouragement even from the darker side of our general reflections. For so long as it was believed that the economic forces, if left to themselves, would create out of a chaos of individual impulses a cosmos of social order, and would result in the best of all possible worlds, there seemed to be nothing left but to harden our hearts in the presence of the major evils of social life. They seemed to be necessary and there was an end of it. If this is and must be the best of all possible worlds we need not hope to mend it. But now that we know better, and perceive that the economic forces never have been, never can be, and never should be, left to themselves, and are seeking deliberately to subdue individual action into harmony with collective purposes, the more clearly we can detect the evils which accompany the strength of spontaneous organisation, the more effectively we may hope to check them. A profounder insight into the nature of the economic forces and their action may enable us to control and enlighten them. But this was not possible either to the optimism of a blind idolatry or the pessimism of a despairing acquiescence. If laws and institutions are not omnipotent neither are they wholly impotent. The play of individual desires produces many results that outrage the general conscience, and, as we can control the lightning so soon as we understand it, we may hope, as we come better to understand the economic forces, indefinitely to increase our control of them, till we can make the ever-present vigilance of the individual's desire to accomplish his own purposes subject to the control of public aims, and so harness individualism to the car of collectivism, avail ourselves of its prodigious economies and yet say to it, when it would rage destructively, "hitherto shalt thou go and no further."

The purpose of the investigations we have now completed has been to make some contribution towards that understanding upon which all fruitful action must be based.

BOOK II

EXCURSIVE AND CRITICAL

Cum rerum natura nusquam magis quam in minimis tota sit.
                                             PLINY THE ELDER.

Nowhere is the nature of things more intimately revealed than in the calculus of infinitesimals.

CHAPTER I

MARGINS AND THEIR DIAGRAMMATIC REPRESENTATION

SUMMARY.—*This chapter is devoted to a fuller examination of the principle of declining marginal significances. It is always the provocatives, opportunities, or supports of desired experiences or vents of impulse, and never those experiences themselves, that this law illustrates; but within that area it seems to be universal. It may appear, at first sight, that the claims of duty, of faith, or of humanity are not (or at least should not be) subject to any declining urgency as they are more fully met; and also that some satisfactions are habitually indulged in down to the point of satiety, whereas, according to our theory, the last and least significant increments of the things that minister to them should be less valued than increments of other things that would minister to still unsatisfied wants. But a careful examination will shew that these objections either rest on some misapprehension or are due to the fact that, under any given set of conditions, there is always a "minimum sensibile" below which conscious estimates cannot be carried. Another set of difficulties arises from a confusion between the positive and negative sign of increments of satisfaction and a positive or negative state of satisfaction. The attempt to dispel this confusion, in connection with the diagrammatic method, leads us to an examination of the reactions of various kinds of indulgence upon the organism itself and its future capacities for enjoyment. This again leads to the discovery of interesting relations between a hedonistic calculus and current moral judgments. Our method, however, does not imply a hedonistic theory of conduct. The chapter closes with some notes on the dangers and limitations of the diagrammatic method it has introduced.*

The whole structure raised in the First Book of this treatise rests upon the principle of declining marginal signifi-

<small>The law of declining marginal significance.</small> cance as supplies increase; and though we have established and illustrated it with sufficient firmness and accuracy for the immediate purposes of that Book, yet a number of problems to which no precise answers have been given may well present themselves to the reflective reader; and the extreme importance of the principle itself makes it desirable that it should be investigated and tested, not only in its immediate applications to economic problems, but in its fuller scope. Any misgiving as to its general validity might throw a taint of suspicion on its special applications. Moreover, we shall find that the closer investigation upon which we are now to enter will throw much light upon the connection between the narrower problems of Economics and the broader problems of Sociology; or perhaps we might say, between commercial Economics and the true Political Economy, in the sense of the economy of the *polis*, or regulation of the resources of the community.

Let us begin by noting that in speaking of declining significance we are never dealing with the ultimately desired

<small>Distinction between experiences and the things that generate them.</small> experiences themselves, but always with something that we value as likely to produce such experiences. Thus, we spoke of concerts which a man wishes to attend because he thinks he will derive enjoyment from them; and we saw that, other things being equal, he would value a fifth concert per week less than a fourth. We did not say that a fifth "unit of enjoyment of music" would be less valuable to him than a fourth, for our only conception of a unit of enjoyment must be a quantity of enjoyment which equals some standard amount; so that each unit, being equal to the standard, would be equal to every other unit, and to say that the fifth unit was of less value than the fourth would be to say that two amounts were equal to the same but not equal to each other. Indeed it would obviously be nonsense to say that equally desired experiences have a declining sig-

nificance, for if their significance declines they are not equally desired. In the same way, if we declare that opportunities of study have a declining value to a man, we may mean that if he has twelve hours a day clear for study he will attach less value to a thirteenth hour than he would to a fifth hour if he had only four; but we can hardly mean that successive acquisitions of a unit of information have a declining value, for we can hardly define a unit of information; and we cannot mean that successive increments of the pleasure or advantage he derives from the results of his study have declining value, for our only conception of equal increments of satisfaction must be increments that have the same value. And so throughout. So we are never speaking, in this connection, of units of experience, which (if we can form any conception of them at all) must be regarded as equal, but of units objectively measurable, roughly or accurately—whether by time, space, weight, number, or otherwise,—which are valued for the sake of the states of consciousness they are expected to produce or the vent they afford to impulses.

What we assert, then, is that after a certain point successive increments of external stimulants, or opportunities, produce successively declining increments of the desired internal experiences. And this principle applies not only to things provocative of delight to the senses, but to means of artistic and literary enjoyment, and even to opportunities for securing the satisfactions, or obeying the impulses, of friendship or affection. But it is sometimes asked, "Is not the case different when questions of duty are concerned? Does not duty always remain paramount, however much of your powers and resources you have already devoted to its demands? And are not the claims of compassion always superior to those of selfishness, however much you may have indulged the former and starved the latter? Is it possible for a well-regulated mind to bring about a marginal coincidence of value between the means of satisfying desires which are on essentially different ethical levels? Can such qualitative distinctions be reduced to questions of quantity?" That they are so reduced, it will be admitted, is a fact (whether lamentable or not), and in dealing with ordinary humanity we might be safe enough in assuming that such a reduction would take place; but when we find that the martyr who has borne the rack is ready to be burnt to death sooner than depart a hair's breadth from the formula of his confession, we seem to have reached a region to which this law of diminishing significance does not apply. However much the martyr has given to his faith and however little he has kept for his comfort, it would appear that the escape from no quantity of physical anguish, however great, will weigh against any concession in the matter of faith, however small.

Such questions may seem to take us very far from our proper subject, and so indeed they do, and it is for this reason that they have been excluded from consideration at an earlier period. But I have maintained from first to last that the laws of Economics are the laws of life, and consequently if a law declares itself to be paramount on the economic field, it proclaims itself by implication as a general law of life and conduct. It may therefore be legitimately challenged on any field, and if it cannot hold its own everywhere it must at least lie under suspicion in its economic applications. In any case, a closer inspection of our general principle, in other applications, is almost certain to throw light upon the special applications in which we are most interested. To begin with, then, it is not only consistent with our theory of "prices," but is actually involved in it, that to any man, at any given time, there *may* be some alternative so horrible that sooner than accept it he would endure all the physical and mental torment that can possibly be inflicted on him. This does not necessarily mean that he does not feel the torture, though even that might be the case, but it means that the whole sum of torture which he is capable of enduring before his frame cracks will not be enough to overcome his shrinking from the only alternative open. Something must give way first, and if his resolve, or his aversion, is stronger than his physical vitality, the tissues of his frame will be disintegrated or his vital functions unhinged before his choice is reversed.

History shews that these conditions have from time to time arisen; and we contemplate with awe the heroes who have supplied the demonstration. We probably think that few people could rise to this pitch of heroism in any cause;

Are the claims of duty and of faith exempt from the law?

but, on the other hand, it is no more than we have a right to expect of every normal human being, living a normal life, that there should be certain things which he would not do for any amount of money, however large; perhaps because he regards the actions as detestable or dishonourable, perhaps only because he regards them as intensely disagreeable. This only means that to him the total difference between the command of things in the circle of exchange that he already enjoys, and an indefinite or unlimited command of them, does not weigh as heavy in his mind as the dishonour or the discomfort of the specific thing that he is required to do. It does not mean that his objection is "infinite." It merely means that it is larger than his estimate of all the satisfaction that he could derive from unlimited command of articles in the circle of exchange, and this is a strictly, perhaps narrowly, limited quantity.

These considerations, it is true, do not completely satisfy us; for they would seem to imply that although the offer of money may not be enough to make an honourable man do a dishonourable action, yet if he is in want of money at all the offer must tend in the direction of making him do it, so that raising the bribe would strengthen the temptation. If it is true, as we have said, that every force tells for all that it is worth whatever other forces are already on the field, would it not follow that if a man is in want of money the offer of money must tell for what it is worth, whatever other motives actuate him? And if so, must he not be nearer to doing the dishonourable action (though he does not do it) than he would have been had the bribe not been offered to him? And if the bribe is raised (so long as he would still value the increased sum), must not the tendency to make him do the dishonourable thing become more marked? Or in the case of the martyr, if he shrinks from pain at all, must not the infliction of greater and greater degrees of pain tend to make him renounce his faith, though the inducement is not high enough actually to bring about the renunciation? It is true that there is nothing in these conclusions that greatly shocks our general experience or observation. We hear men say, "I confess I was almost tempted by the prospect, for a moment," or "It required all my resolution to hold out, I can assure you," when they are speaking of actions the commission of which would have filled them afterwards with shame and self-contempt. But nevertheless we can by no means admit that every man can be at any rate tempted, though not seduced, by a bribe, or shaken, though not broken, in his resolution by torture. We are certain that this is not even approximately true as to the bribe, and we cannot believe that it is completely and universally true as to torture.

On this we may note, in the first place, that the very offer of the bribe or application of the torture may wake resisting forces which were dormant before.[1] I might be considering whether or not an action was really dishonourable before the bribe was offered, and as soon as a bribe is proposed I may have a conclusive reason for associating it with dishonour. Or again, if a man offers me half a crown for doing or saying something I may be contemptuously amused, but if he offers me £1000 I may be deeply insulted. For I might take the first proposal as a naïve attempt to overcome my inertia, but the second as revealing a serious intention of finding out the price at which I would sell my honour. Thus the increased inducement might itself touch the spring of increased resistance. If the briber can contrive to associate his material offer not with dishonour but with some appearance of honour, and can make his insult take the semblance of a tribute of respect, it will perhaps be found that £1000 does indeed weigh more than 2s. 6d. in the scale. But even here a finer perception might detect the finer insult, and might resent it the more deeply for its deliberate subtlety.

But there is something deeper even than this, and its examination will lead us back to our economic and commercial investigations. Just as it is very easy to suppose *The minimum sensibile.* that a man could tell the difference between a half-pound and a quarter-pound weight by trying them in his hand, but very difficult to suppose that he could tell the difference between 14 stone and 14 stone plus a quarter of a pound by lifting them in a basket, so it is very easy to imagine a man's refusing to give 1s. for a thing that he would be glad to have for 6d., but very difficult to imagine him willing to give £1000 for some object but refusing to

[1] Compare the qualifications to the Principle of Superposition on page 204.

give £1000 : 0 : 6 for it. That is to say, 6d. is appreciable when the whole matter at issue is only 1s., but inappreciable when the matter at issue is £1000. It is a case of proportion. When the stake is of any given magnitude there is a certain *minimum sensibile* or minutest quantity that can be felt or appreciated in connection with it; and this *minimum sensibile* will vary with the magnitude of the thing at issue. The same principle applies in the moral world. When my feelings are deeply moved and I am vividly realising any one of the main issues of life, things to which I should give careful attention on other occasions do not affect me in the least. The mind does not readily adapt itself at one and the same time to the higher and the lower end of the scale. When it is experiencing great things it is not sensitive to small ones. When some grave disturbance of equilibrium has occurred or is threatened, or some vast issue is at stake, small things are not felt. Only if the great things were secure and had not recently been disturbed would the small things be able to assert themselves as significant. If I hear of the sudden and unexpected death of a dear relative and immediately begin to speculate about his will, why am I ashamed of myself? Because I had imagined that my affection for him was so great that immediately on the news of his death the significance of a few hundred or thousand pounds would have sunk below the *minimum sensibile*. And when I find that it is not so, I perceive that I have given myself credit for a higher appreciation of the things that are not in the circle of exchange, relatively to those that are, than I really possess. It is a startled sense of my own sordidness that brings my shame. It is not that I believe I ought not to care whether I have or have not the sum of money, but that I should have supposed that at that moment there would have been no room in my mind for such a thought, any more than for the fit of my trousers, or any other subject of consideration in itself perfectly proper but not sufficiently important to claim a share of my attention at the moment. I might experience the same kind of shock if, in catching up a child wounded by a passing dog-cart or motor-car, I found myself annoyed because my cuffs were stained or my clothes damaged by his blood. And the proof that this correctly represents the psychology of the case is that if the question of the legacy or of the stained cuff merely presented itself to me externally but failed to touch the springs of interest or emotion, if it were a mere shadowy presence with no weight or "tactile value," I should note it as something strange, but should not feel it as anything shameful. The same analysis applies to occasions on which some great happiness comes to a friend accompanied by a slight incidental inconvenience or disappointment to oneself. The examination of such cases reveals the possibility of any given consideration sinking beneath the *minimum sensibile*, but it also reveals the fact that in an enormous number of such instances the feeling or the motive that we neglect without one moment's hesitation is nevertheless actually felt. It is negligible, but if we look for it, it is there. It does weigh something, but it does not for a moment threaten to turn the scale.

Returning now to the martyr or the "incorruptible," we see that it is perfectly possible for the extremest pressure that can be brought to bear upon either to be quite negligible, so that it would no more be recognised as a reason (even an inadequate one) for doing the abominable thing than fear of staining my cuffs would be recognised as a reason against helping a wounded child. And it may be that it is not only negligible and practically unrecognised, but absolutely imperceptible even when we look for it. There is ample room for these facts within the limits of our theory.

Another point suggests itself for consideration in connection with moral questions. There is much confusion and ambiguity in our use of the word "duty." I may say that no personal or private considerations however urgent ought to affect the performance of my duty, even in the minutest point; but I shall not allow that I ought to leave a burglar despatching his business in my house rather than be a minute late at the office. "Of course not," it will be said, "because it is your obvious duty to protect your family, to say nothing of your property." Apparently, then, it is my "duty" to attend to whatever I conscientiously consider the most important matter at stake; and to say that nothing should interfere

<small>Ambiguity of the word "duty."</small>

with duty simply means that I ought to do the thing, whatever it is, which a high-minded man would regard as most important. Certain family claims which are not "duty" in a general way become so when they reach a certain point of urgency; and when satisfied down to a certain point they will again cease to be duty. In this sense "duty" is not a label which is attached to certain classes of action and not to others, giving precedence to the smallest volume of that to which it is attached over the largest volume of everything else. It is a name we give to the resultant course of action when every consideration has been given its due weight and no more, and nothing that is irrelevant has been allowed to weigh at all. And we shall generally find, on analysing any dilemma, that the dictum "Duty before all things" is only maintained by giving the name of "duty" to whatever, under the circumstances, properly comes first; and that our determination on this point is influenced both by the terms on which the alternatives are offered to us and by the extent to which we have already paid tribute to the one or the other claim. The label can only be attached after the conclusion is reached, and cannot indicate any short cut by which to reach it. If I insist on allowing no weight to any consideratious that cannot be labelled "duty" in advance, I shall generally find that I must include in my "duties" not only my duty to my family and to my friends, but also that trump-card of the casuist, my "duty to myself." And I shall find myself speaking of a "conflict of duties," thereby implying that duty itself is a quantitative conception. It is of course true that if we are to allow no more than its due weight to a certain consideration we shall often allow it no weight at all, because it is irrelevant. If I am asked, for instance, to arrange a number of candidates in order of merit, I shall probably regard it as absolutely irrelevant to the matter in hand that a widowed mother is dependent on the success of one candidate, while another is a man of property himself and has no one dependent upon him, or that I am attached to one and am repelled by the moral character of another, or that I believe that success will react prejudicially on the character of one and favourably on that of another. And if I take this view, then undoubtedly it is my duty not to give any weight to considerations that ought not to weigh, and it may or may not require some heroism on my part to act up to my convictions; that is to say, the temptation may tempt or it may not, as in the cases already noted. Or I may find that the real temptation is to incline to the verdict counter to my wishes, in order that I may escape the reproach of having been influenced by them. We may note that it is usual to protect examiners, as far as possible, from all knowledge of facts that are to be regarded as irrelevant; and this shews that the difficulty of ignoring them, if known, is generally recognised.

On the other hand, if I am making an appointment I may think that some or all of these considerations are relevant, and in that case it may be my duty carefully to appraise them all and weigh them against each other. When we have admitted that considerations of extreme strength in their personal appeal may be wholly irrelevant, and ought not to be realised as motives at all, even if they are felt, we shall have done full justice to the absolute conception of duty; but it is interesting to note how very many cases there are in which we are inclined at first to regard a consideration as irrelevant in principle, but find on close examination that a mere quantitative change in the things considered, if sufficiently pronounced, appears to us to raise the irrelevant into relevancy. In any case, our theory only asserts that when a consideration that "ought" not to weigh at all does as a matter of fact weigh—that is to say, is felt as a temptation—it may be felt more or less according to the magnitude and urgency of the issues at stake.

It is highly instructive to turn from the objection to the doctrine of declining significance which we have just examined to another which is quite as frequently urged. It is said that the whole theory of distributing our resources so as to gratify our wants *pari passu* and keep the marginal wants balanced, is false to fact and experience. The truth is, it is said, that there are certain things that we "must have," and we get "as much as we want" of them before we begin to consider less urgent requirements at all. For instance, we all eat as much as we want several times a day,

<small>Do we secure "as much as we want" of one thing before we secure any of another?</small>

and do not stop short of satisfaction because our desire for literature or travel is unsatisfied. Now to begin with, this is obviously an argument of the well-to-do. It is flagrantly untrue of the very poor that they get as much food as they want before they begin to trouble about keeping up their supply of clothes.[1] We have already spoken of the thousands of young people, well above the line of actual want, who in managing their own slender resources consciously and constantly bring their meal to a conclusion at a penn'orth or two penn'orth short of satisfaction in order to advance some other margin. In its crude form the whole contention that we are examining is palpably false. Where do we or can we find in civilized society the man who gets as much food as he wants "before" he gets any clothes or any shelter? All that can be seriously maintained is that if a man's resources are sufficient to provide him with a certain amount of the things he needs most urgently, including food, he will soon come to points in every other branch of his expenditure at which he will be content to rest until he has completely satisfied his desire for food as far as mere quantity, apart from quality, goes.

In the contention so formulated there is a great deal of truth, but it need not disturb our confidence in our general theory. Any one who has tried saving pence out of his meals by restricting them in quantity, not quality, will know that the significance of these pence rises very rapidly as they are successively withdrawn. A halfpenny-worth of bread (two thick slices of a half-quarter loaf) may carry a man from a sharp sense of hunger to a sense of satiety. To save 3d. a week on bread might involve a very considerable volume of unpleasant experiences, and therefore, unless the 3d. would minister (as in Cobbett's case) to very keenly felt wants in other directions, it would be bad husbandry to save it. "Yes," it may be said, "but by your theory to save $1\frac{1}{2}$d. a week would involve less than half the sacrifice of saving 3d. a week, and its expenditure on something else would secure more than half the gratification of three pennyworth; and since by hypothesis the expenditure on bread is taken down to a point at which it ceases to have any significance at all, there must be some small quantity [2]

---

[1] Pages 34 sq. [2] Cf. pages 66 sqq.

of the resources expended upon it that could be profitably turned elsewhere." This is theoretically true as far as it goes; but theory also tells us that this adjustment would be an exceedingly delicate matter, and that it might demand an amount of attention and exercise of will that could be more profitably employed somewhere else where it would have a higher marginal significance.[1]

We have now examined two attempts to invalidate the general principle on which, as I have maintained, we administer our resources. It has been contended both that the sense of duty *ought to be* completely satisfied down to the last and minutest demand, and that the appetite for food *actually is* so satisfied, before anything else is attended to at all. The collocation of these two contentions is amusing; and before we leave them we may note that the sense of duty and the desire for food may become direct rivals. In that case I may perhaps cheerfully go without a meal at the call of "duty"; but presently I shall find that it has become my imperative "duty" to suspend the direct performance of my "duty" for a short time in order that I may eat something to enable me to perform my "duty" more strenuously (or to perform it at all) afterwards; and the graduated formulæ of "it is an imperative duty," "I almost think it is a duty," "I really think that without any dereliction of duty I may allow myself," etc., ease the (in this case) *difficilis descensus* from the pretentious heights of absolutism to the *avernus* (shall we call it?) of practical relativity.

Another and closely related aspect of the question of declining significances is suggested by charitable appeals. For instance, there is a famine in India, and I subscribe a guinea. That would appear at first sight to mean that I consider the want of food in India more urgent than any other wants of my own or any one else's to which the guinea would have ministered. But if so, why not give a second guinea? Has the want in India been sensibly reduced by my subscription? In bulk, yes. But in intensity? Even if I could suppose that my guinea had met the most urgent case, would there be any perceptible

The relief of suffering.

---

[1] For a worked-out example see my *Alphabet of Economic Science* (London, 1888), pages 128 *sqq.*

decline of urgency in the next case waiting to be met? It is exactly the question of the increments of tea over again. We saw that there was no perceptible decrease in the significance of tea as we passed from one quarter-ounce to the next at the margin of 4 lbs., though there was a perceptible satisfaction in the consumption of either.[1] So I must suppose that a perceptible relief of suffering has been effected by my guinea, but I can hardly believe that a second guinea would relieve suffering perceptibly less intense than that relieved by the first. The marginal significance of a guinea, then, in relieving distress in India, appears to remain the same. Why do I not pay a second guinea and a third, and so on? The answer is twofold. In the first place, in the majority of cases it is not really the famine in India but my own conscience that I am appeasing, and my own conscience becomes perceptibly less clamorous after the first guinea has been paid. It may still grumble, and dispute the ground with other applications, but it may no longer dispute it successfully. My conscience may be right or wrong in insisting that I should take a share in the burden, and in being appeased when I tell it I have done so; but that is not the question. The point is that the demand I am meeting is, as a matter of fact, perceptibly reduced by what I have done to meet it. It is otherwise, however, if I really am directly appraising the urgency of the want that my guinea relieves when given to the famine fund, and the wants it can supply in other applications. In this case it is true that the want in India does not perceptibly decline as I give guinea after guinea, but it is also true that the wants that I neglect in order to meet it perceptibly rise as guinea after guinea is subtracted from the supply of them, until at last they rise to the level at which they balance my sense of the urgency of the need in India. This point may not be reached till I have reduced myself and all those dependent upon me to the level of misery of those that I am relieving; and some moralists are courageous enough to hold this up as an ideal. Our theory of marginal significance is elastic enough to adapt itself to their creed; for all that we assert is that, whatever the grounds on which we form estimates of the

[1] Page 54.

relative significance of rival applications of resources, we can so administer these resources as to bring their marginal significance in each application to equality. The urgency of the Indian claim is no doubt gradually declining if the administration of the fund is even approximately sound; but within the limits of the influence of my fortune it does not decline perceptibly. The balance is therefore found when all other expenditures are curtailed to the point at which their rising marginal significance equals that of the Indian claim.

Curious light is thrown on this class of problems by the added joy and relief which is not unfrequently felt by the recipient of a present that comes with the condition that it is to be spent on a holiday or on some personal indulgence. Presumably the recipient, if free, would have spent the sum as he wished. Why is he pleased at being forbidden to do what he would have wished? Because it is the sense of his duty to do the thing, not his sense of the importance of the thing's being done, that would have successfully contested the first place; and his "sense of duty" is entirely extinguished by the prohibition. The demand that would have had to be appeased before the other could be indulged is withdrawn from the lists, and the indulgence can be secured without a drop of gall. A goad has been blunted, and the hedonistic gain is obvious. In cases where this analysis would be untrue and where the wish to do something else with the money is really inspired by the eagerness of direct sympathy, the restriction would be actually felt, and perhaps resented, as a reduction in the value of the gift. Perhaps by the painful associations it waked it would altogether annul it or leave a balance to the bad.

Examination of an apparent paradox.

We have now concluded our examination of the class of objections to the law of diminishing psychic returns which is based on the absolutism of ethical or social conceptions; but in the course of these investigations we have been incidentally led to contrast a demand or craving that has to be appeased with an enjoyment that may be secured. This opens in its entirety the important subject of positive and negative satisfactions, their relations to each other, and the proper notation to be employed in their calculus; and to this subject we must now turn.

Positive and negative increments and states.

If we regard pain as negative pleasure, and discomfort as negative satisfaction, then a supply of anything that gradually relieves me from acute suffering leaves me in a state of (decreasing) negative satisfaction throughout the process. But the reduction in the volume of this negative satisfaction, which is taking place all the time, is a movement in the positive, not the negative sense. It is an addition, not a subtraction, of desired effects; for it is a subtraction of undesired experiences. The acquisition, therefore, is a positive quantity, and must be noted by a plus, not a minus sign. Here we may introduce the familiar notation of curves. On Fig. 1 we measure the supply of any commodity per unit of time along the line OX, or the axis of X; and on OY, or the axis of Y, we measure rates of satisfaction. Thus the curve

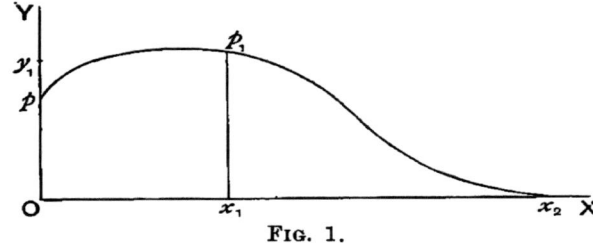

Fig. 1.

pp_1x_2 would represent that the initial increment of the commodity per unit of time satisfies some kind of desire at the rate of Op per unit of commodity; that by the time the supply is increased to Ox_1 the rate at which it is satisfying desire has risen to x_1p_1 or Oy_1, and that when the supply reaches Ox_2 per unit of time, the desire is completely satisfied. The quantities measured along OX, which are called abscissas, indicate the breadth of the supply per unit of time, or the breadth of the stream of supply. Quantities measured along OY, which are called ordinates, indicate the marginal values investigated on pages 47-71 of Book I.,[1] and areas such as Opp_1x_1 sums of satisfaction per unit of time, secured by the consumption per unit of time of the quantity of the commodity indicated by the corresponding abscissa. Generally speaking, such an area must (as we have here supposed) itself be taken as representing a rate of total enjoyment per unit of time, rather than a

[1] For the full justification of this statement, see below, pages 440 sqq., especially pages 446 sqq.

sum of total enjoyment;[1] but sometimes it will be convenient to take the whole figure as representing not a rate of consumption, but a single act. And in such cases we shall take x_1p_1 as representing the marginal value, and the area Opp_1x_1 as representing the "value in use" or total significance of the definite quantity Ox_1. For instance, the figure might roughly represent the experiences of a single meal, during which for a time "the appetite comes as we eat" and we are conscious of increasing enjoyment, whereas after that point our hunger is gradually appeased to the point of satiety.

Now this diagrammatic method is useful as an instrument of research, as a means of demonstration and exposition, and, most of all, as a vivid and comprehensive form of statement. But it is very dangerous, and if not used with due caution and precision it may lead to grave confusion and may encourage loose and irresponsible thought. In the next chapter, accordingly, we shall examine the construction of one particular curve in great detail; and whenever we make use of curves we must try to bear in mind the necessity of giving an exact account of what they mean, so that the results obtained may not be in any way equivocal. The necessity for caution in this matter is illustrated on the very threshold, for (apart from the difficulty of determining how we are to measure a unit of satisfaction[2]) we have to note at once that this first curve which we have introduced is ambiguous in relation to the very matter we are now discussing, viz., the relation between assuaging a craving and securing a positive enjoyment, or, more generally, between removing negative and securing positive objects of desire. We have seen that the removal of a pain must have the positive sign, and it must therefore be represented by a positive area, so that if we begin in pain and the supply of a commodity gradually removes that pain, the result must be represented as positive—comparable with, and to be weighed against, a gain of positive satisfaction. Our figure, therefore, will not tell us whether we begin in a state of positive satisfaction, a state of indifference, or a state of negative satisfaction, or pain. It will only tell us that if we command the quantity of the commodity represented by Ox_2 our state will be the *better*,

---

[1] Cf. page 101.   [2] See Chap. II. of this book, and cf. Chap. III.

by the whole area Opp_1x_2, than it would have been had we had no supply at all. If we only command Ox_1 our state will be the better by the area Opp_1x_1. The area $x_1p_1x_2$ will then represent either an unassuaged pain or an unrealised pleasure, but in either case the area Opp_1x_1 must have the positive sign. It is a gain, not a loss. The existence of the possibilities represented by the figure may in itself constitute a misfortune or a privilege; but granted their existence, the command of Ox_1 of the commodity, whether it means plus a pleasure or minus a pain, is a gain (in the estimation of the subject), and must be regarded as positive.

If we draw Fig. 2, it will represent the effects of the supply of a commodity which ceases to act in a positive

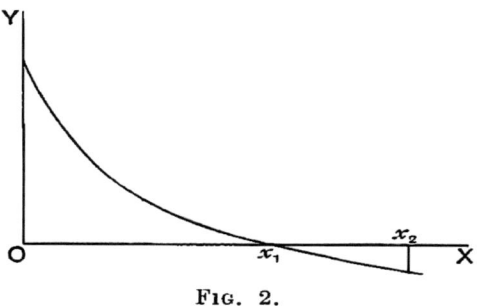

Fig. 2.

sense when it exceeds Ox_1 in quantity. Thus at a given temperature the consumption of fuel might begin by being extremely acceptable, and when it had reached the rate of Ox_1 per hour it might cease to be acceptable at all, and might, if raised still higher, become positively undesirable, or negatively desirable. Now one man may be so constituted that whereas he does not feel any positive distress by sitting without a fire, he may be conscious of a distinct pleasure if a fire is lighted; and another may be consciously miserable without a fire, and as the warmth increases may be conscious only of more or less adequate relief from discomfort till the quantity Ox_1 is exceeded, after which another kind of discomfort ensues from excessive heat. Yet another may at first be conscious of relief from suffering; then, before the quantity Ox_1 is reached, may feel that all his discomfort is gone and a positive enjoyment of the cosy warmth has succeeded to it; until, as the quantity Ox_1 is exceeded, he feels that although the room is still positively pleasant it would be pleasanter yet if the fire were kept a little lower. To all these men alike the supply of the commodity up to the quantity Ox_1 will produce a result that should have a positive sign and should be represented by a positive area, though to one it is minus pain, to another plus pleasure, and to the third at first minus pain and then plus pleasure; and to all of them the further increments represented by the line x_1x_2 produce a result that should carry the negative sign and should be represented by a negative area, though to one it is plus pain and to another minus pleasure. All of them are in a state more to be desired as the supply grows from zero to

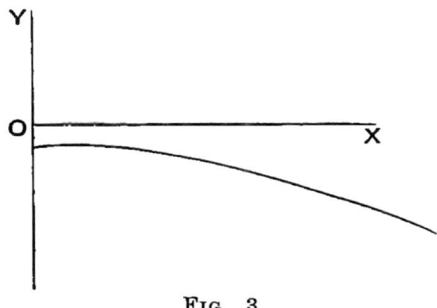

FIG. 3.

Ox_1, and in a state less to be desired as it grows from Ox_1 to Ox_2.

It follows from this example that an area below the axis of X, which represents negative satisfaction, may mean a subtraction from pleasure that leaves a positive balance, just as well as an addition of pain. Fig. 3 would represent a supply, or an experience, that, whether it detracts from the happiness of a happy state or makes a neutral one positively painful, or a painful one more painful yet, in any case produces a negative result, of increasing intensity per unit, as one increment follows another. If we are speaking in terms of positive satisfaction we shall still say that these increments have a declining (positive) significance, though if we were speaking in terms of negative satisfaction, or pain, we should say that they had a rising (negative) significance. Thus the fact that things which cause discomfort normally act with increasing intensity as unit is added to unit does not affect the generality of our proposition that additional increments, after a certain point, produce decreasing (positive) results.

It sometimes happens that a positive quantity (in the technical and ambiguous sense in which it includes the subtraction off a negative quantity) is only to be had in association with a negative quantity. In that case probably the positive ordinates of the first will decline, and the negative ordinates of the second will increase, the movement in both cases being technically in the sense of positive decline. Thus a man who has bitten his tongue or has bitten a piece half out of his cheek may be in need of food, and yet eating may cause him acute annoyance. As his hunger or sense of faintness

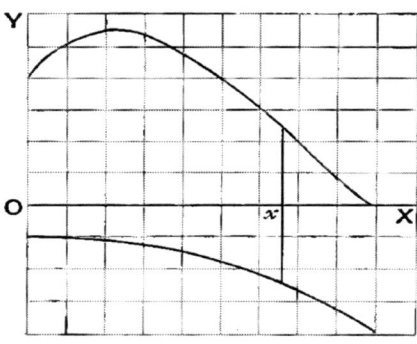

Fig. 4.

gradually yields, and his demand for food becomes less urgent, the increasing painfulness of the terms upon which alone he can assuage the declining urgency of his want will soon balance it, and his meal will come to what would else have been a premature conclusion. This might be represented either analytically by Fig. 4, or synthetically by Fig. 5. Both figures alike represent the fact that up to Ox an advance from the origin is accompanied by a balance of advantage, and that after that point the reverse is the case. And both figures agree in the magnitude of the advantage or disadvantage in either case.

Where there is no indication to the contrary a curve must be taken to indicate not a history but an anticipation, and an anticipation that has discounted (not necessarily for what they are worth) all conflicting elements, risks, and reactions as far as they come within the ken of the person who makes the estimate. It will be a synthetic and resultant estimate of the balance of advantage to be anticipated from the acquisition of each successive unit of the commodity, of the type of Fig. 5.

We have noted that positive and negative quantities may be balanced against each other, and also that mathematically positive and negative quantities may both alike be ambiguous psychologically; for just as a subtraction from pain and an addition to pleasure are alike positive, so a subtraction from pleasure and an addition to pain are alike negative. Thus Fig. 2 (page 417), where the increments of the same commodity

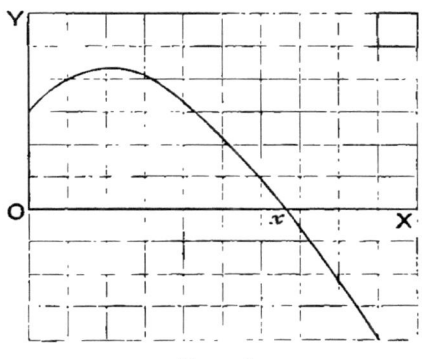

Fig. 5.

at first have a positive and then a negative effect, is explicit as to the positive or negative sense of the process in question, and as to declining (positive) significance of all increments after a certain point; but it is equivocal as to the positive or negative state of the person affected. He might be either in a state of suffering or a state of enjoyment throughout the process, or he might pass from suffering to enjoyment at any point on the line Ox_1, or from enjoyment to suffering at any point on the line x_1x_2; but in any case he has either more enjoyment or less suffering as he passes from O to x_1, and either less enjoyment or more suffering as he passes from x_1 onward.

Now, although the relief from a pain and the securing of a pleasure, or the deduction from a pleasure and the addition of a pain, have respectively the same signs, and may be taken as equivalents, yet they are in themselves very different things. Given my constitution and circumstances, a certain relief from pain must be regarded as equivalent to a certain positive pleasure, a certain deduction of pleasure to a certain access of pain; and certain pleasures and pains taken together, or certain relinquishments of pleasure and escapes from pain taken together, must be regarded as balancing or neutralising each other; but it makes all the difference in life whether my constitution and circumstances are such that my energies have to be given chiefly to escaping or minimising undesired things or are mostly free for securing or developing desired ones, and whether I can often or only seldom get a pleasure without a concomitant pain or escape a pain without a concomitant loss of pleasure. And it is just here that our immediate choices react upon our future possibilities. Difference between relieving pain and securing pleasure.

This subject of the reaction of our enjoyments, privations, and endurances upon our future capacities for enjoyment has already been touched upon in Book I.,[1] but the investigation we have just completed will now enable us to enter upon it more fully. We have to make constant adjustments between the immediate gratification of desires and the building up of capacities. A great part of wise conduct obviously consists in forgoing a present gratification, or incurring present pain, or making irksome effort, in order to acquire a capacity for future enjoyment, or power ultimately to secure or promote desired ends. Wise administration of vital resources must therefore take constant note of this reaction of the present upon the future.

Every wise man must desire to build up for himself such habits of mind and body from within, as well as to surround himself with such outward circumstances, as will make life as little as possible an escape from wretchedness and as much as possible an experience of well-being and an achievement of desired ends. We must therefore cultivate the power to endure such undesired experiences as are inevitable, and to forgo such desired experiences as are unattainable, with the minimum of suffering, and to derive the maximum of satisfaction from the realisation of things desired. An

[1] See page 85.

example may make this clear. Two men are on a tour together in a beautiful and sparsely inhabited country. They find themselves out of their reckoning, and when dinner-time comes they are far from any opportunities of dinner. The spirits of one of the companions begin to sink, his temper becomes unstable, he cannot enjoy the scenery through which he is passing, the exhilaration of mountain air or of the battle with the waves is a thing he knows not, the suggestion to turn aside and spend half an hour in ascending a rock or exploring a cave is fiercely resented, and, in fact, the man's whole moral, æsthetical, and physical being is swept up into one hideous craving for food. At last the friends (if they still deserve the name) reach hospitable quarters. Their hostess wishes to do justice to her reputation and keeps them waiting for an hour in order to set a noble repast before them. But when it comes it is too late. The poor wretch can now eat nothing, and goes sick and miserable to bed. His companion (so far as his sympathetic heart allowed) has meanwhile been drawing in delight at every pore, keenly enjoying the tussle with the waves or the stride across the heather, with an eye that (like Wordsworth's) finds no hairbreadth of earth, sea, or sky from which it does not gather delight, ready at any moment to turn aside and delay the end of the journey in order to increase the enjoyment of its progress, conscious indeed of keen hunger, but conscious of it rather as a prospect of future pleasure than as a present experience of pain; and when at last he finds himself opposite his victuals, a harmony is established between the organism and the environment which almost rises to the dignity of a spiritual experience. The less fortunate of these travellers derives the maximum of suffering and the minimum of enjoyment, the other the minimum of suffering and the maximum of enjoyment, from the necessity of taking food. The one is the victim of a craving; the other has a capacity for enjoyment. To the one it is agony to be thwarted, and only a negative satisfaction to be humoured; to the other privation is no pain, but a supply "adds sunshine to daylight."

The wise or happily constituted man has a mind so regulated that many of his desires only become rampant as the prospect of satisfaction approaches. Till then they are dormant potentialities of enjoyment. Thus the man who on coming in sight of a public-house declared that he " had a thirst on him for which he would not take £5 " was perhaps to be congratulated if he had been thoroughly happy before he saw it; but if he had been miserable himself and a cause of misery to his companions for the last hour or two because there was *not* a public-house in sight, he was an unenviable person as well as an undesirable companion.

What, in the instances we have given, may be regarded at any rate primarily as a difference of physical constitution has all manner of analogies in acquired habits of mind and body; and every wise man would desire for himself and others such habits and impulses as would conform to the happier type. Now, though all means or opportunities of gratification seem to have this in common, that the immediate effect of successive increments is (after a certain point) of declining positive value, yet different kinds of gratification differ enormously in their after-effects upon the organism itself. Is our present enjoyment building up an increased capacity for future enjoyment? Is it leaving us permanently unmodified, so that after a time we shall return to exactly the same state in which we were before? Is it undermining our power of future enjoyment, so that after every act of indulgence we return not to the same, but to a lower power of enjoyment than we had before? Or is it substituting a craving for a capacity for enjoyment?

_{Building up capacities for satisfaction, or desired habits and impulses.}

The characteristic of ruinous enjoyment is that it not only tends to satisfy us at the time (as do all enjoyments), but that it also tends to undermine our capacity for future enjoyment. The most pronounced forms of ruinous enjoyment are probably those which are popularly regarded as vicious, such as intemperance. The characteristic of a vice, from a hedonistic point of view, is that it tends to replace a capacity for enjoyment by a craving. Intoxication may be extremely delightful, but the more habitually a man drinks, the less pleasure it gives him to be drunk and the more pain it gives him to be sober. He begins, perhaps, by hitting on a means of heightening enjoyment; but he ends by being

_{Ruinous satisfactions and vice.}

in a state of chronic misery, from which he gains occasional respite in an intoxication which no longer gives him any positive pleasure. His whole conscious being has been swallowed up in the vortex of one frightful and incessant craving. This is a typical case of ruinous enjoyment. I am not here concerned with any attempt to analyse the ultimate grounds of the reprobation implied in the terms " vicious " and " vice," but it is interesting to note that the popular moral judgment stands in intelligible relation with the results of a hedonistic calculus. And note that our diagrammatic method gives us no notice of this change from a source of pleasure to a craving. Diagrammatically the appeasing of a craving is indistinguishable from the securing of a satisfaction; and if the acquired craving is more imperious than the natural desire for pleasure originally was, we should have to represent the change by an increased height of the curve indistinguishable from the representation of an increased capacity for enjoyment.

But there are many enjoyments which, so far from producing a vicious craving, rather tend to beget a sense of satiety, or even disgust, unless kept within very moderate limits. The danger here is not of converting a possible source of enjoyment into a craving, but simply of deadening by indulgence the susceptibilities from which the enjoyment springs. For example, most people enjoy a little salmon occasionally, and are inclined to regard it as something of a treat; but it is pretty generally known that, if used as a staple food, salmon very soon loses its charm. The provision long customary in the indentures of apprentices, that they must not be required to eat salmon more than so many times a week, is the historical record of this fact. Salmon therefore could not well take the place of the Englishman's traditional rasher of bacon as the breakfast dish for all the year round. It seems to be a fairly general experience (though of course by no means universal) that you may eat fried bacon for breakfast whenever you are inclined to do so, and may continue to be so inclined day after day and year after year; whereas if you were to eat salmon whenever you were inclined to do so, you would very soon cease to be inclined to eat it at all. The appetite for bacon, then, when extinguished for the moment, rapidly recovers its pristine

Wasteful satisfactions and luxury.

vigour; whereas the appetite for salmon, unless it is allowed a long period of recovery, becomes permanently lowered or deadened. If a man, though eating salmon as often as he feels inclined, does not eat as much at a time as he is inclined to do, the effect may be deferred. But even so, salmon will soon cease to be much of a treat.

Again, a man is not likely to eat oatmeal porridge for the pleasure of the palate when the appetite (as an index of an organic demand of the system) is assuaged; whereas the skilled cook, "by successive intensifications of his diabolical art," may tempt a man from excess to excess by appeals to his palate, even when his appetite has long been sated. Now

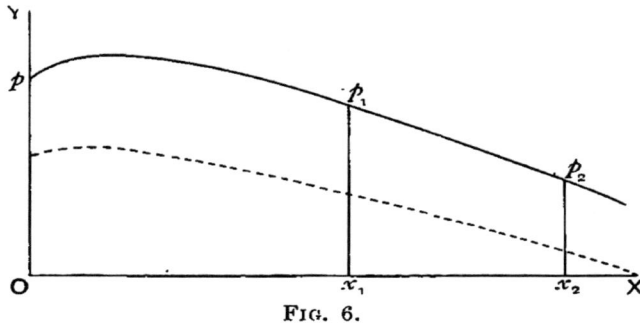

FIG. 6.

healthy and vigorous persons who are accustomed to simple and frugal ways are perhaps conscious, or subconscious, on most days that they would enjoy a rather more elaborate diet than they are accustomed to. But every one who has had experience of the two ways of living will tell us that those who live with severe simplicity get more enjoyment out of their meals than those who have an elaborate dinner every day. It is very easy to see why. The man who tries to extract the maximum of sensuous satisfaction out of every meal is securing trifling increments of satisfaction at the margin to-day, and is thereby deadening his capacity for enjoying the more significant increments nearer the origin [1] to-morrow. He is not indeed substituting a craving for a source of satisfaction, but he is lowering his possibilities of satisfaction. Thus, if a man has a moderate supply of any such luxuries as we have been discussing, his enjoyment may be represented by Fig. 6.

[1] "Origin" is the technical term for the point marked O in all our figures.

He stops at x_1, and there are still unexhausted possibilities of enjoyment. But if he habitually goes on to x_2, though at first he secures the additional area of enjoyment $x_1 p_1 p_2 x_2$, yet he gradually lowers the significance of the initial increments, and ultimately only enjoys the smaller area bounded by the dotted line above Ox_2 instead of the larger area $Opp_1 x_1$. Again, the man who eats or drinks as soon as he is inclined to do so, often falls into the habit of eating and drinking as soon as he is able to do so; and, as he never recovers a state of healthy hunger, he too always remains at the low level of enjoyment.

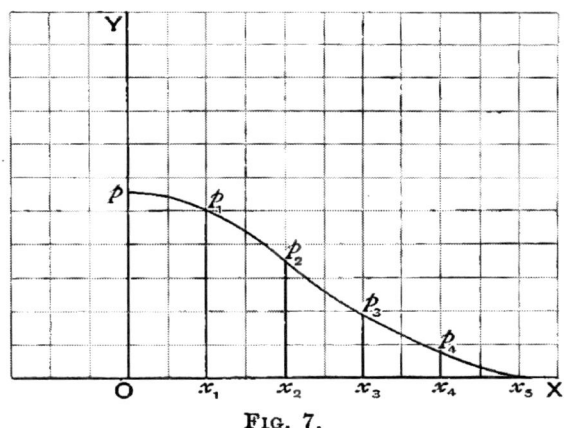

Fig. 7.

Let us take another illustration. Some moderate smokers will declare that a pipe two or three times a day gives them great satisfaction, but that they do not miss it, in the sense of feeling any positive discomfort, if for any reason they are deprived of it. For the time being a single pipe completely exhausts the possibility of enjoyment, so that they would find no pleasure in further smoking. Let Fig. 7 represent the total pleasure, declining from the initial point of intensity to the point of complete satisfaction.

It is obvious that after a pipe has extinguished the present possibility of further enjoyment a certain time must elapse before it is recovered; and it will not be recovered suddenly. Let us suppose that after an hour the area of possible enjoyment $x_4 p_4 x_5$ has been recovered; that is to say, the man is in the condition in which he was when he had smoked four-

CH. I MARGINS AND THEIR DIAGRAMMATIC REPRESENTATION 427

fifths of his pipe. He may now enjoy a cigarette that contains one-fifth of a pipeful of tobacco as much as he enjoyed the *last fifth* of his pipe; and if he repeats this every hour he enjoys five times the area $x_4 p_4 x_5$ in the course of five hours. Whereas if he had not smoked for five hours he would then be just where he was before he smoked his last pipe and could enjoy the whole area Opx_5 again.

We have seen that our diagrams do not distinguish between the assuaging of a craving and the conferring of a positive satisfaction, and that in many cases the earlier incre- ments of a commodity may perform the first function, and the later increments the second; and, moreover, that the two may overlap. In the case of smoking it is possible, though not usual, for a man who enjoys it to be able to abstain completely from it without positive suffering. In the case of food or drink this is impossible. Thus, if a man had a suitable allowance of food and drink, he might divide it up into a number of rapidly succeeding nibbles and sips (like cigarettes), or he might take larger portions at longer intervals. It would seem that in such cases the man who does not allow his organism time to recover its full sensitiveness to pleasure before he endeavours to extract renewed enjoyment out of it, and the man who pushes abstinence to the point of positive pain and craving before he assuages it, supposing them both to eat the same amount, would be alike wasteful in their administration. The man who lets his organism recover its power of yielding enjoyment without inflicting positive suffering on it (or, if the two states overlap, goes back to the point at which the pain incurred and the pleasure secured just balance) is administering his resources to the best advantage. *[margin: Self-indulgence and asceticism.]*

Note here again the extreme care that must be taken in the use of diagrams. If our curve in Fig. 7 represented the value of successive increments of any commodity per month (as in the case of tea in Book I. Chap. II.), or per year, or per day, it would take no note of the different effects of the same rate of supply differently distributed within the period in question, which is the problem we have now been discussing. Some system as to this internal distribution is tacitly assumed (as it was in our former tea problem) as constant during the whole inquiry, or as modified according to some consistent system as the supply contracts or expands. This is as it should be, for whatever particular condition we are examining and are supposing to be subject to variations, it must always be assumed that the other conditions are constant.

To return to our main inquiry. We have seen that certain kinds of enjoyment, and certain habits of consumption, while apparently innocent in themselves, are eminently wasteful from the hedonistic point of view, either because they more or less permanently deaden the keener powers of enjoyment, or because they never give those powers the opportunity of recovering themselves. And yet deliberately to stop eating salmon when you would like more, in order that you may be able to get more pleasure out of a help of salmon this day week, is a piece of self-conscious sybaritism from which the healthy mind revolts. Even the man who will not eat when he is hungry and has suitable food before him, for fear of "spoiling his appetite" for a more sumptuous repast which he expects in a couple of hours, fails to excite our admiration. We seem then to be in the presence of a kind of waste against which it is impossible to provide without unworthy attention to appetites that are only wholesome so long as they are unreflective. And so indeed we are. But our analysis has resulted in a triumphant vindication of certain instincts which we may henceforth trust more completely, and which, if we follow them, will effect the desired saving and give zest and vigour to life, without any habitual self-consciousness. Luxurious living has always lain under suspicion as hostile to a vigorous life, as something which, if not absolutely culpable, deserves a certain disapproval, and moreover as self-defeating even on its own chosen ground of physical enjoyment. Self-indulgent habits which, on the face of it, only seem to open up innocent sources of enjoyment are nevertheless regarded with a certain contemptuous impatience by healthy and vigorous minds. The man accused of self-indulgence retorts on his critic with a charge of asceticism; and his mentor, while repudiating the charge, often finds it difficult to defend by logic the position to which he is guided by an obscure instinct. But that obscure instinct, we now see, is perfectly sound, and it warns us against forms of enjoyment which, if not viciously ruinous, are yet wasteful.

We seem now to have got at something like the philosophy of it. The self-indulgent person is perpetually nibbling and never giving himself the chance of a hearty meal. The ascetic is always cutting back to the point at which the potentiality of a satisfaction passes into the realisation of a pain. And both alike debilitate their frames, and unduly concentrate their minds upon material sources of satisfaction. For, be it observed, persons who have practised genuine asceticism (as distinct from persons who by nature or training have become indifferent to what most men enjoy) will generally tell you that they were never so greedy in their lives as when they fasted severely; and perhaps that they have never quite recovered from the effect of the practice. A sufficient effort of will, or a strong enough preoccupation, may extinguish or indefinitely suspend a craving, but to maintain a want at the stage of craving, without extinguishing it, is to fix the mind upon it. Hence many curious parallels in the moral effects of luxurious and ascetic living; and hence the justification of the instinct for a robust and simple life that shuns both.

We can now fully understand the recognised failure of all elaborate attempts to make life enjoyable by luxuries. A rich man trying really to enjoy himself in the midst of his wealth often suggests a man attempting to bathe in his Sunday clothes. He cannot feel the sweep of wind and water over his limbs. Hence the genuine but futile wail of persons surrounded by luxury, hence their craving for the "simple life," and their restless longing to break away from their surroundings and to put themselves into circumstances where money positively will not command any but the simplest supports of life. Only so can they get into contact with the initial satisfactions which are reserved for those whose nerves have not been deadened and blunted by being called upon to respond to fresh supplies before they have recovered from the last, or to seize a little more excitement at the margin to the detriment of their tone at the origin. There can be little doubt that those who constantly go without things, not

Hedonistic value of a simple life.

because they do not want them, but because they cannot get them, and who have an unfailingly abundant supply of nothing but a few simple things, selected by experience for their staying qualities, get more physical enjoyment out of life, and a larger amount of physical delight out of their contact with things, than all the devices of luxury can secure. And, very happily, this mode of ordering life, with all its invaluable reactions, may be maintained, when once deliberately embraced, not by thinking but by not thinking about it. The man who cares most for other things will act with the greatest wisdom in these matters; and he will instinctively form habits, or, if you like, contract prejudices, which without self-consciousness will secure the best fruits of reflection.

This question of self-consciousness enters closely into another problem, which has to be faced in all housekeeping above the lines of poverty and below the lines of luxury. We have seen that "second helps are never so good as first," and it would seem to follow that there is a *prima facie* gain (under the reserves indicated on pages 82 *sq.*) in having no second help to-day, but another first help to-morrow or this day week. That is to say, if green peas or new potatoes (in themselves, let us take it, of the "staying," not the "cloying" order of commodity) are a treat which cannot be indulged freely, it would seem to be better to have a little often than a great deal seldom. And many housewives follow this line. But it is by no means above challenge. Children who are habitually stopped at the first help when they keenly desire more will almost certainly become greedy, if the reason given for stopping is that they may have the rest to-morrow; whereas if they had sometimes had as much as they wanted, and none at other times, they might have remained healthily animal. And so we are back again at the point which we encountered early in our inquiries.[1] We may pay too heavily for securing the best possible administration of certain defined resources in their application to their immediate purposes. On the whole, may we not say that the popular instinct regards as the most desirable life one which is simple to the verge of severity,

The perfect Epicurean.

---

[1] See pages 21, 82, etc.

but which allows a certain amount of variety, and prefers long or even complete and permanent abstinence to stinted and watched indulgence? Bread and water, Epicurus declared, were good enough for him; but for all that he would like a bit of cheese, so that he could have a blow out when the fancy took him. We may be sure that when he did have cheese he liked to have plenty. I once heard of a servant girl who every year bought and cooked for her single self a peck of green peas. She said she liked to "have her fill o' peas" once a year, and when that was accomplished she was in a state of equilibrium for the rest of the season. She was a true Epicurean.

As far as material indulgences are concerned, then, the instincts of popular moral judgment condemn the most ruinous forms of enjoyment as vicious, regard less ruinous but still wasteful forms as undesirable, if not exactly culpable, and look askance at too scrupulous attempts to economise and maximise enjoyment, as savouring of self-conscious materialism and wanting in directness and robustness. The man who so orders his life that, with small or great variety, he periodically pursues his enjoyments down the slope of diminishing returns to a point determined by his general resources and the claims upon them, but never dulls his capacity for periodical renewal of them, escapes the censure of the most rigid moralist. He is "living the simple life."

But there is another kind of satisfaction, the indulgence of which positively increases the capacity for future enjoyment. The man who enjoys himself in such ways as neither to reverse nor to destroy nor merely to maintain, but to increase his hedonistic capacity, gets a curious kind of credit for his conduct. Intellectual, literary, and artistic enjoyments (to those who really enjoy them) belong to this class. Most of them demand at some period or other a certain more or less painful effort and discipline.

Capacities for enjoyment which indulgence develops.
Painful training of capacities.
"Superior" tastes.

Probably no one can get the highest and most sustained form of enjoyment out of literature without a considerable amount of drudgery of one kind or another; and the same is true of art, and at least equally so of science. Even exercises or studies which are in the main enjoyable must often be pursued all down the scale of diminishing returns of satisfaction until they cease to give any pleasure at all and become in various degrees painful, if we are really to make anything of our studies. Some wise man (is it Ruskin?) has said that if we wish to do our best we must never work against the grain, but if we wish to do better than our best we must often go on when the work is irksome. We shall spoil it, but next time we shall do better than our former best.

Now this kind of gratification, sometimes merely pursued past the point of enjoyment, sometimes associated with painful training or irksome preparation, but always tending to create an increasing fund of possibilities of enjoyment, is regarded by the popular instinct as " superior." We speak of people who cultivate such sources of satisfaction as having " superior tastes." The slight half-veiled contempt for the " superior " person that we can often trace is apparently due, partly to a doubt whether he really does enjoy his superior pursuits, and partly to a suspicion that he may be starved into them by the lack of a wholesome and vigorous appetite for the robuster enjoyments of his neighbours. Lady Jane Grey appeared to prefer reading Plato to hunting and hawking; but did she really prefer it, or did she only wish to prefer it, or wish to be thought (by herself and others) to prefer it? And if she did prefer it, was it because she got more out of Plato or because she got less out of hunting and hawking than the others did? Was it the presence of a faculty they had not, or the absence of a faculty they had, that made her choice differ from theirs? Our respect for "superior" tastes when they are genuine is shewn by our extreme desire that the " working-man " should contract them, by our distress if more fiction than history and science is taken out of our public libraries, and our willingness to bear a part of the expenses of lectures on " superior " subjects—for others to attend.

Roughly speaking, these more fruitful enjoyments seem as a rule to be less exclusively and often less directly connected with the senses than the neutral or ruinous enjoyments are. It is true that the eye and ear are directly concerned in the enjoyment of music or of art, but the element of intellectual analysis and judgment, and, far more, the element of imaginative and emotional association, play a preponderating part in them. In the enjoyment of literature or of scientific investigation the place of the senses is still more subordinate. Now it is generally regarded as an axiom that mental and spiritual enjoyment is of a higher order than the enjoyment of the senses, and it is interesting alike for those who are, and for those who are not, prepared to receive such a judgment as axiomatic, to note that at any rate it finds itself, like the other moral judgments we have examined, in easily traceable relations with the hedonistic calculus.

But the coincidence is not quite complete. For capacities that can be developed and rendered fruitful, perhaps at the expense of initial pain, sometimes yield material, not spiritual or intellectual satisfactions. They are then on a level with "superior" satisfactions hedonistically. But the moral judgment declines to consider them "superior." The process of learning to smoke wakes no moral enthusiasm even if it results in a power of enjoyment free from any vicious or wasteful craving. Having the ears pierced for earrings, in the old days, was only regarded as really praiseworthy by those who thought it a woman's first "duty" to make herself attractive. No one gets moral credit for what has been called "the long and painful apprenticeship to the art of liking olives." We have got some light, I trust, in this chapter on the relations of instinctive moral judgments and the results yielded by a hedonistic calculus; but it is far from my own belief that the one can be completely resolved into the other. This last set of instances may serve as a warning against any such belief. *The relation between popular moral judgments and the result of a hedonistic calculus.*

The tendency, not fully accounted for by hedonistic considerations, to attach a note of intrinsic inferiority to pleasures of the sense is curiously illustrated by the case of connoisseurship in wines. If an interest in wines and a delicate judgment of them is combined with strict moderation it presents many of the qualities of an artistic enjoyment; and the old-fashioned elaborate conversation about wine presented a curious analogy to the discussion of the merits, say, of pictures. Yet to have given such close and earnest attention to things of sense suggested a more or less material view of life. Hence a somewhat confused feeling. Connoisseurship in wines seemed

2 F

in itself to belong to a "superior" order of enjoyments, but by its associations and suggestions, to an "inferior" order; and accordingly it often provoked in the mind of the impartial outsider curiously mingled and conflicting feelings, now bordering on contempt, and now rising to something very like respect or even envy.

It will hardly have escaped the reader's notice that our examination of the reactions of different enjoyments upon the organism, and especially the section on the wastefulness of enjoyments of the intrinsically cloying order, or enjoyments carried to the cloying point, has been a running commentary on the dangers of civilisation and of increased command of material comforts. If wisdom does not grow with power, our latter state, even from the material point of view, may well be worse than our former, as material wealth increases; and the action of the economic forces, unguided and unchecked, naturally favours the growth not only of a class of ministers to vice, but of a class of persons who live by enabling people to get another drop out of the squeezed orange of to-day's capacity for enjoyment, reckless of its reactions upon to-morrow. And further, it will be seen that the "simple life" comes, if at all, rather incidentally as a natural result of caring for worthy things than as an object self-consciously aimed at for its own sake. The remarks on pages 186-189 may be re-read in the light thrown on them by this chapter.

The hedonistic value of civilisation.

Nothing that has been said in this chapter must be taken as committing the author to a hedonistic theory of ethics. Suppose a man deliberately desires to cultivate impulses, and to train himself to a sense of values which he does not expect to give him the maximum of personal happiness. Suppose there are things that he really does care for more than his own happiness, or impersonal objects that he wishes he did care for, and hopes he one day will care for, more than for his personal enjoyments. Such a man would endure suffering, sacrifice pleasure, and fight against many of his impulses, in order to secure a permanent set or habit of will and a firmly established scale of values which could only be justified by reference to some social or religious test. These purposes would have secured his loyalty,

Hedonism not involved in our general principles.

CH. I MARGINS AND THEIR DIAGRAMMATIC REPRESENTATION 435

but not on the ground that they promised to secure his happiness. But the formation of such habits and the cultivation of such affections would, in this case, be the man's active desire, for whatever reason; and he would sacrifice the gratification of other desires in pursuing it. His self-discipline and his renunciations would be, from our point of view, of the same order as those of the man who undergoes irksome discipline for the sake of acquiring a hedonistically valuable taste, though he would not be moved by hedonistic considerations. It is not my purpose, however, to discuss ethical theories, but merely to shew that the general principles on which our investigations are based, while throwing light on the hedonistic calculus, do not presuppose a hedonistic theory, but are equally applicable to any other.

I will conclude this chapter with a few additional notes on the nature and limitations of the diagrammatic representations we have used. They may be best regarded as attaching themselves to the examination of roused and dormant desires on pages 422, 423. A large number of personal curves probably rise for some time before the ordinates reach their maximum and begin to decline. The matter is a little difficult to decide, for it is not easy to keep it clear from the considerations, entered upon above, of changes in the ethos of the individual during any considerable period. But it may well be that the same man with the same tastes and capacities would be willing to pay a larger sum for, say, a second chance in the month of hearing good music than he would for the first, possibly more for a third chance than for a second (and then less for a fourth and fifth, and so on), not because his musical taste is improved, but because his musical appetite is roused. In any case, when a dormant capacity or desire is roused, or a mild one stimulated, an abrupt or early cessation of the means of satisfying it may leave us in a balked or aching state, which constitutes a pain in excess of the original sense of want or privation (hunger, or what not) which is as yet imperfectly relieved. It is possible that, starting with any given condition, and regarding relief from discomfort and positive pleasure alike as positive, the sudden arresting of satisfaction might leave a legacy of actual pain which would not be represented on our

Limitations of the diagrammatic method.

diagram; because the supply of the commodity has a positive value as long as it lasts, and would continue to have a positive value if it proceeded. Fig. 8 might give some kind of representation of such a case. It might mean that the man started from a state of indifference, but pursued some occupation or enjoyment with growing keenness, and derived a pure access of satisfaction as the appetite was at once roused and gratified. Up to the amount Ox_1 he has secured the area of satisfaction Op_1x_1, and there remains an unexhausted possibility of satisfaction represented by the area $x_1p_1x_2$. But if the supply is now broken off, the unsatisfied desire continues and the satisfaction ceases. The result is a pain represented by the negative area

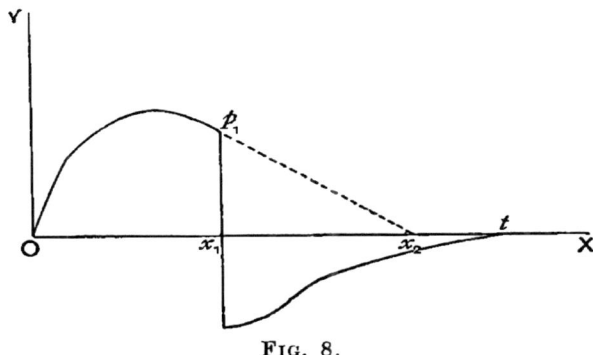

Fig. 8.

below x_1t. It is only after a lapse of time represented by x_1t that the pain wears itself out and the man returns to his initial state, having experienced both a positive and a negative satisfaction, the latter of which might in some cases be the greater. In such cases we say we had rather have had none of a thing at all than the tantalising amount we secured, even though we thoroughly enjoyed that little while it lasted. Fig. 8, however, is a monstrosity; for progress along the axis of X means increments of commodity up to x_1, and for the positive area above, up to x_2; whereas for the negative area it means the passage of time from x_1 to t. It is really two figures, and the units of area alone are common to the two.[1]

Returning to the phenomenon itself, we note that it may occur in every case of gratification arrested short of complete satisfaction. As a rule we may suppose that the lower the

[1] Cf. page 441, and the whole of Chap. II.

point to which we have reduced the ordinate the smaller will be this offset of dissatisfaction. And in a well-filled life it will often be absolutely eliminated; for although the lowest increment of satisfaction has not been squeezed out of some indulgence, and a theoretical sense of want might supervene if the next occupation or experience of the man were inherently neutral, yet if there is some other pleasant or desired occupation to which to turn, the anticipation of it substitutes eagerness for something else in the place of a languid desire to continue the present experience on the declining slope. Perhaps the best theoretical defence of smoking that has yet been discovered by the numerous and able advocates engaged in the cause is the assertion that it prevents listless and self-indulgent persons from over-eating, because when the keen demands of appetite have been satisfied but there is still enough left to dally with, the seductive prospect of a smoke turns the mind into another direction and offers a greater satisfaction from the arrest of the process of eating than can be gained from its continuance.

It is a fact pointed out and abundantly illustrated by the psychologists, that the very same present sensations may be pleasant or painful, according to the anticipations of the immediate future with which they are associated. The hunger that is a conscious pain, if the prospect of a meal is at all remote, may be a source of keen pleasure to the man who actually has his victuals before him, even before he has eaten the first mouthful. And in the same way the man who is accustomed to associate self-control with vigour, enjoyment of life, sense of command, and self-respect, may derive positive and immediate satisfaction from the absence, at the end of every meal, of that "sense of repletion" which in itself, according to Alexander Bain, is "massive and serene."

The conclusion of the whole matter, so far as our diagrams are concerned, is that it is generally an abuse of the diagrammatic method to attempt to make a curve represent, with any closeness, an isolated and concrete experience. A curve must represent the *estimate formed by the consumer* of the value to him of the successive increments of the commodity, and that estimate will be formed in view of all the immediate effects and remoter reactions and implications which he is capable of appreciating. All these considerations therefore will tell on the height of the ordinates, which must be regarded as registering the resultant estimate. The anticipations on which they rest will perhaps never be perfectly justified; but as anticipations they have already made all the necessary discounts, and they need no kind of supplementing or correction. Declining ordinates mean that the consumer, taking at his own valuation all the considerations that can influence him, desires successive increments of the commodity with declining eagerness; and his estimates are based upon anticipations which are constantly being checked and modified by experience.

CHAPTER II

ON THE DIAGRAMMATIC METHOD OF REPRESENTING AREAS OF SATISFACTION AND MARGINAL SIGNIFICANCES [1]

SUMMARY.—*The method of representing economic phenomena by curves demands closer examination than we have yet given it, and turns out on inspection to present many problems both of interpretation and construction. The measurements on the axis of* Y *indicate limiting rates of marginal significance, and, while expressed in an objective rate-unit, they must ultimately rest on estimates based on psychic experience. Hence difficulties arise as to the relation between objective and psychic units, the possibility of keeping that relation stable, the meaning we are to attach to accuracy of estimate and the conditions which limit that accuracy. If we express the data of Book I. Chapter II. as to the significance of tea in the form of a tea curve we are led to examine* (a) *the implications of the special formula to which our data conformed, and* (b) *the possibility of any simple mathematical formula approximately representing the facts. An attempt accurately to interpret the curve further leads us to distinguish between a curve of total satisfaction and marginal significance on the one hand, and a curve of price-and-quantity-purchased on the other hand. We find that these curves can, at best, only coincide approximately, and that an individual curve purporting to represent both series of phenomena can theoretically only be a " temperamental " compromise.*

In the preceding chapter I have represented satisfactions

[1] Chapters II. and III., though important from the theoretical point of view, are of an abstract and somewhat academic character, and some readers may prefer to go on at once to Chapter IV.

by areas bounded by curves, though with the express reservation that this procedure raised questions and required explanations upon which it was not convenient to enter at the time. We will now proceed to a more careful examination of this method. We shall frequently employ it hereafter.

The representation of a given satisfaction by an area of any kind, whether rectilinear or curvilinear, involves by implication the conception of a unit to which different satisfactions can be reduced, and in which they can be expressed for diagrammatic comparison with each other. And though this idea is far from familiar and presents great difficulties when first expressly suggested to the mind, we have nevertheless seen that it is directly implied in all our practical dealings and deliberations; and it underlies all the investigations upon which we have hitherto been engaged. For to say that two things are of equal value to us, and that another thing is just as valuable to us as both of them put together, is to say that the latter is worth twice as much to us as either one of the former, or that we anticipate a satisfaction twice as great from the one as from either of the others. If we say that a thing is just worth a penny, we are thereby equating the satisfaction we expect it to yield with all the other satisfactions which we believe a penny would secure at the margins of other branches of expenditure, and if we went on to say that something else was worth exactly three shillings and not a penny more, we should be saying that we expect it to yield as large a satisfaction as any thirty-six things we could get for a penny each, or a satisfaction thirty-six times as large as that which any one thing just worth a penny is expected to yield. Now it is quite true that such estimates are often vague, and almost casual, and that they are subject to every kind of fluctuation and inconsistency; but every deliberate act of choice, or of administration of resources, is an attempt to make them more precise and consistent; and even an impulsive choice is a declaration that at any rate one thing is more valued by us than another, and this involves an act of quantitative comparison. Such as they are, these choices, impulsive or deliberate, are verdicts as to comparative volumes of satisfaction, considered

Implications of diagrammatic curves. Unit of satisfaction.

as magnitudes, and they often express themselves in units of pence and shillings.

Now all commodities, services, or opportunities that enter into the circle of exchange are ultimately estimated not as physical or objectively measurable magnitudes, but as sources of anticipated satisfaction; and we frequently estimate things that are not in the circle of exchange in terms of things that are, and constantly choose between things that are and things that are not in this circle, weighing them against each other. Thus it is clear that for each one of us, at any given moment, the ordinary conduct of life unmistakably implies and involves the conception of satisfactions as magnitudes, and therefore as expressible ideally in units, which may be represented diagrammatically by unit lines, or areas, or otherwise, as suits our convenience. And just as, in measuring and comparing lengths with a view to determining their relative magnitudes, it does not matter whether our unit is an inch, a metre, or a mile (the difference being only in the numerical expression of the results obtained, not in the results themselves), so it is of no consequence whether we take our unit of satisfaction as that represented by 1d. or that represented by £1. But in comparing different satisfactions, expressed as areas, we must always remember that to be comparable as magnitudes the satisfactions must be estimated by the same person. With these reservations we may now proceed to the diagrammatic representation of the estimates dealt with in the second chapter of Book I. and generally to the interpretation of curves of total and marginal satisfaction.

We may take (arbitrarily) a small square on the ruled paper of Fig. 9 to represent one-quarter of the satisfaction anticipated from the expenditure of a farthing. Then four squares will represent the satisfaction corresponding to a farthing, sixteen squares that corresponding to a penny, and $12 \times 16 = 192$ that corresponding to a shilling. Any rectangular or curvilinear area, irrespective of its shape, if equal to 192 small squares would then represent this shilling volume of satisfaction. It might, for instance, be a rectangle with a base of 1 and an altitude of 192, or one with a base of 16 and an altitude of 12.

Taking a side of a small square as our linear unit, let us

442   THE COMMON SENSE OF POLITICAL ECONOMY   BK. II

now agree that the unit length (not area) measured along any base line shall represent a periodic (monthly or as otherwise defined) supply of one ounce of tea, and a base of 16 such units a supply of one pound. We can now represent diagrammatically any of the data as to tea which we assumed in Book I. Chapter II. For instance, the fourth pound was expected to yield a satisfaction equal to the significance of 8s. in any other application. This would be represented by an area of 8×192; and as we have agreed that a basis of 16 shall represent a pound, a rectangle of base 16 and altitude 8×12 ($=96$) will be the proper representation of the satisfaction anticipated from the consumption of the fourth pound per month (Fig. 9 (*a*)). But of this fourth pound we saw that the first half was estimated at 4s. $5\frac{1}{4}$d. and the second at 3s. $6\frac{3}{4}$d. These values would be represented respectively by rectangular areas containing 852 and 684 small squares, and since the basis of each would, by our convention, be 8 (corresponding to $\frac{1}{2}$ lb.), their altitudes would be respectively $106\frac{1}{2}$ and $85\frac{1}{2}$ (Fig. 9 (*b*)). We can now interpret units of altitude. They will not signify positive quantities, as the units of the base do, but penny rates of satisfaction per pound of the commodity, or halfpenny rates of satisfaction per half-pound, and so forth.

Now, taking *ad* in Fig. 9 (*b*) at an altitude of 96 as in Fig. 9 (*a*), it is obvious that the rectangle *ab*, which is added to the original rectangle at the left, is equal to *cd* subtracted from it at the right, since the total area of the two differentiated rectangles is to be exactly equal to that of the integral rectangle that represents the satisfaction yielded by the whole pound; and we may suppose that this differentiation between half-pounds, quarter-pounds (or any other fractions, for it is not necessary to proceed by bisection of a pound rather than trisection, for instance), may be carried as far as we choose. The area of any succession of differentiated rectangles will always remain equal to that of the integral areas that present them collectively as a single magnitude. In Fig. 10 let us carry out this process to different degrees of advancement for the different pounds; and let us draw a curve such that in the case of the small and the large rectangles alike it always adds on an area to the left equal

Interpretation of abscissas and ordinates.

THE DIAGRAMMATIC METHOD   443

to that which it cuts off to the right, so that for any base the area bounded above by the curve shall be exactly equal to the rectangle standing on the same base. Such a curve may be regarded as integrating any number of contiguous rectangles which we choose to take in succession. That is to

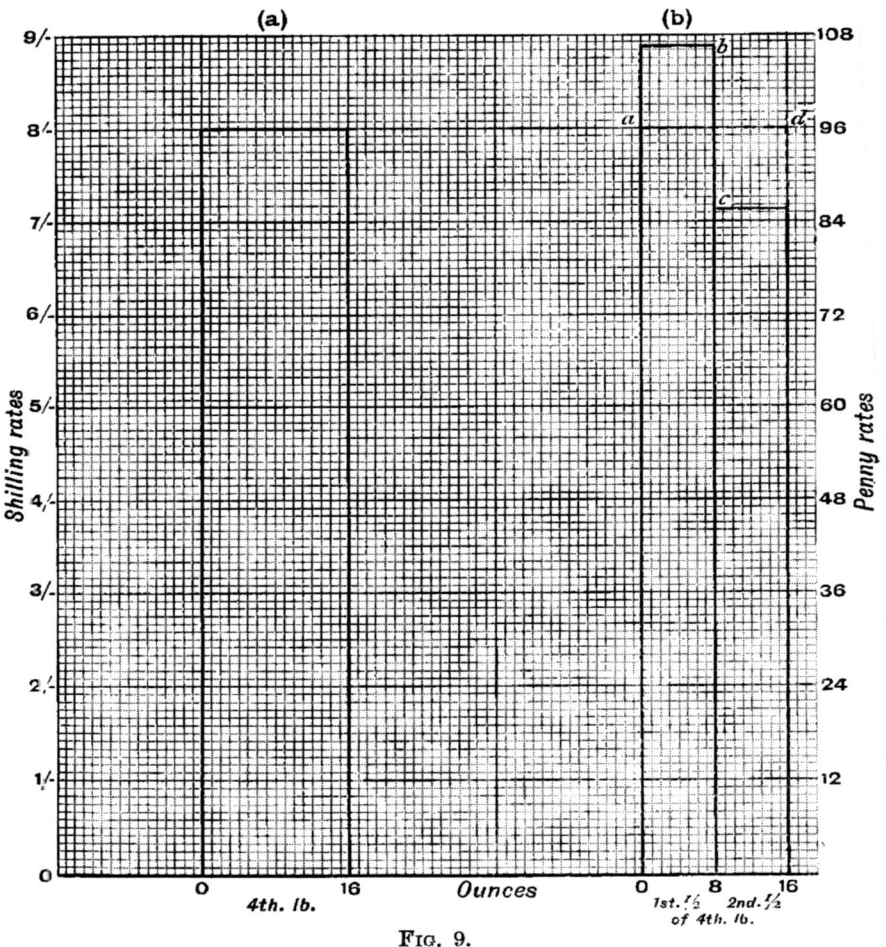

Fig. 9.

say, the area intercepted by the curve above any line measured along OX will be exactly identical with the area contained in the whole series of rectangles standing upon the same base.

This is a curve of total satisfaction, and its meaning is now obvious. We have seen that ideally, and in the limit, the significance of any commodity is a magnitude continuously

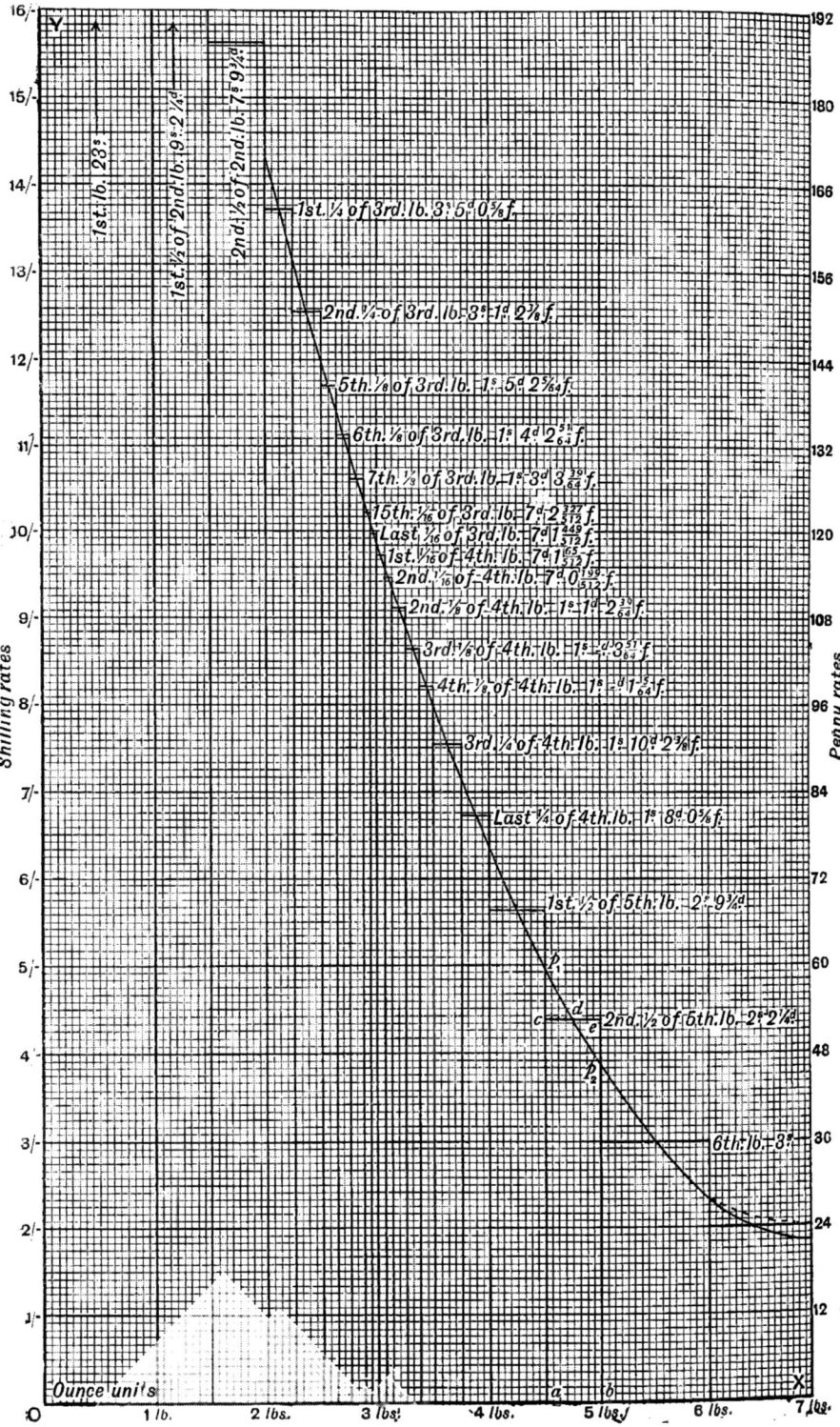

Fig. 10.

changing as we recede from the origin, so that, however small the increment we are considering, the change cannot be regarded as suspended during the progress of its consumption. The whole process, then, ideally considered, is properly represented not by a series of steps or discrete areas, however small, but by a curve-bounded space. Such a curve, could we obtain it, would give us at a single view the whole infinity of facts to be registered. If we take any portion of the weekly, monthly, or other periodic supply of a given commodity (whatever our conventional units may be), e.g. the third unit, or the quarter of a unit between $7\frac{1}{3}$ and $7\frac{7}{12}$, or generally the portion represented by the line ab on the axis of X (Fig. 11), then the curve is constructed so as to bound an area, ap_1p_2b, exactly representing the satisfaction anticipated from the consumption of the portion of the commodity represented by ab. And note that whereas in Book I. Chapter II. we directly assumed data as to pounds and binal fractions of pounds only, a curve assumes that we have all conceivable data, and can begin and end anywhere we like.

This continuity and entire accuracy of data is, of course, purely ideal. We may conceive approximations to it, but to imagine that any one could distinguish between the rate at which tea was ministering to his satisfaction at the beginning and at the close of his consumption, say, of the 7·9432th pound, and could express this difference in fractions of a shilling-per-pound rate, is an absurdity. Indeed the reader who has some tincture of mathematical culture will perceive that even an underlying assumption of commensurability between the satisfactions accruing from successive conventional units of the commodity and those represented by the conventional units of the currency is inconsistent with ideal accuracy. These reflections reveal at once the great convenience and the ingrained artificiality of the method of representing economic quantities by curves. The very nature of a curve is incompatible with the nature of the phenomena we are investigating; but it is of high value as an ideal simplification, and as a means of mentally arresting phenomena, which in their actual existence are unmanageably complex and fluctuating. If we professed in our diagrams to present possible or actual facts, we should have to undertake the hopeless task of determining in each case what degree of accuracy might reasonably be assumed; whereas by frankly presenting the unattainable limit in every case we declare at once the ideal nature of our hypothesis and of our representation of it.

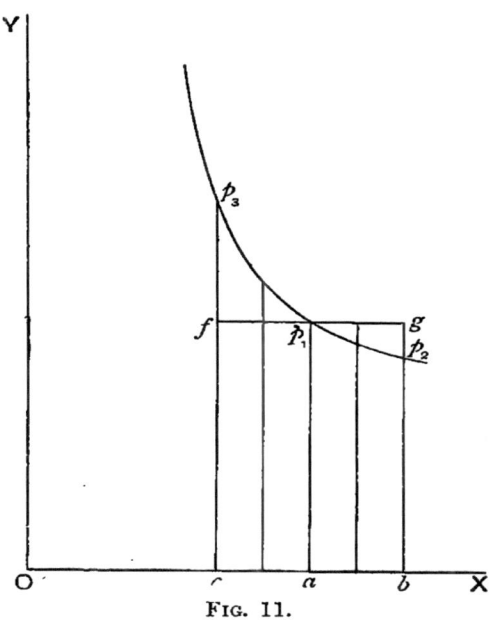

Fig. 11.

This being understood, the reader will have no difficulty (if he turns back to our investigations as to "limiting rates" on pages 60 sqq.) in recognising the height ap_1 of the curve above any point a as the graphic representation of the limiting rate of significance (in whatever unit measured) of increments or decrements of the commodity taken from the point a. For on considering the errors ($p_3 f p_1$ and $p_1 g p_2$ respectively) that would be involved in treating the areas above ab and ac as equal to each other and to the rectangle on base ab (or ac) and with altitude ap_1, we shall find that they become smaller not only absolutely but proportionally to the areas themselves as we make the increments ab and ac smaller; and this without limit. For if we halve the lengths ab and ac and erect perpendiculars on them and then compare the rectangles on these bases, and with altitude ap_1, with the areas above the bases bounded by the curve, we shall see that

Ordinates represent limiting rates of marginal significance.

the error involved in treating them as equal is in each case less than half of the corresponding error for the wider basis. The proportion of error, therefore, decreases, without limit, as smaller bases are taken. Thus the height ap_1 represents a rate of satisfaction per unit to which no increment or decrement taken from the point a ever conforms, as a whole, but which always lies between the rates proper to any given increment and to the corresponding equal decrement, and to which those rates approximate without limit as they decrease in magnitude. The units on OY, therefore, measure limiting rates of the significance of units of the commodity (per unit of time) as the increments are taken smaller. Or, in abbreviated terminology, the ordinates represent the marginal significance of the commodity for any given supply. So, too, in Fig. 10 the areas p_1cd and p_2ed respectively will be not only smaller, but smaller in proportion to the rectangles da and db as c or e approaches d.

We have now a provisional conception of what a curve of marginal significance would mean if we had it, and we may go on to the examination of the bearing upon the determination of the form of such a curve of any data we may suppose ourselves actually to command. Let us rule our paper, as in Fig. 10, so as to mark rectangles of base 16 and altitude 12. Returning to our example of tea, we may retain the significance of all our units, and for convenience may register successive pounds (each pound being 16 ounce-units) of supply along OX, and successive shilling-per-pound rates of significance (each being 12 times a penny-per-pound rate) along OY. Each large rectangle, containing 192 small squares, will indicate, as before, the area of satisfaction represented by a shilling.

Construction of a curve of total satisfaction.

It is obvious, to begin with, that any datum we may be able to obtain will give us some information as to the course of the curve. If we know, for instance, that the fourth pound of tea yields an area of satisfaction valued at 8s., we shall know that the curve must be such that the area ap_1p_2b equals the area ac, and the area p_1df equals the area fcp_2. (We shall express compliance with this condition by saying that the curve "satisfies the datum" of the area ac.) But there is an infinite number of curves that would fulfil this condition.

Some of them might bisect dc, and others might cut it at points indefinitely near to d or c, and they might intersect the verticals from a and b at any variety of points. But if we have the additional data that the first half of the fourth

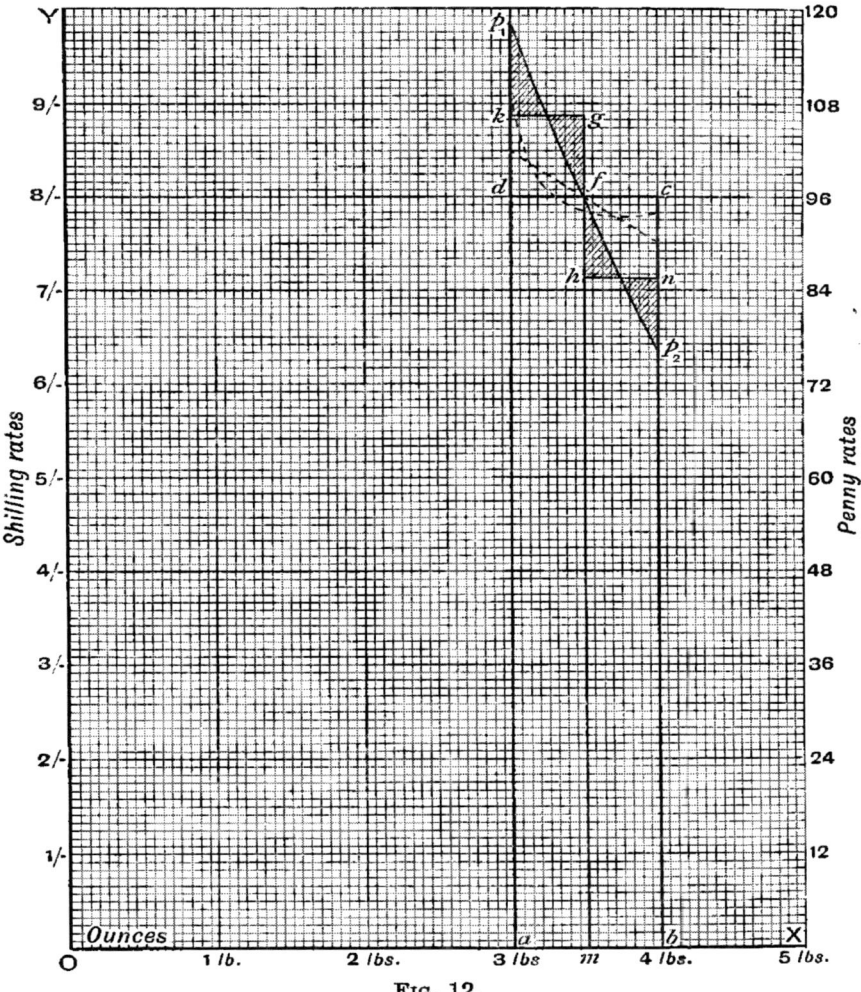

Fig. 12.

pound corresponds to the area ag, and the second to the area bh, many of these possibilities will be excluded, for the area which the curve adds to ag must equal the area it cuts off from it; and the same must hold for bh. The course of the curve, therefore, will be more closely determined by the two rectangles *ag* and *bh* than by the one rectangle *ac*, which is equal to their sum. In our original hypothesis we supposed the estimates of successive pounds of tea to reveal an easily detected law which enabled us at once to calculate any smaller areas we liked to choose. This formula would absolutely determine the form of the curve, and tracing it would only be a matter of calculation. But if we assume no such property, and imagine each datum to stand alone and not to involve any derivative data (assuming only the general property of continuous decline, after a certain point, which we may take as fixed by the nature of our inquiry), then it is clear that the minuter the increments for which we can obtain estimates, the more closely can we determine the course of the curve. For instance, we have set out on Fig. 10 (page 444) a series of data as to pounds, half-pounds, etc., and we see that, *so far as they shew* (that is to say, apart from our knowledge that our formula would enable us to split up the larger rectangles as finely as we choose), there would be room to suppose that the curve undulated with considerable violence over the portion corresponding to the increment from 4 lbs. to 7 lbs., but that our data enable us to assert a more regular course for the portion corresponding to the increment from 2 lbs. 12 oz. to 3 lbs. 4 oz. Seeing then that if we have given any two contiguous rectangles of satisfaction, *akgm* and *mhnb*, the curve must always pass between the points *g* and *h*, it follows that if we could determine the areas corresponding to indefinitely small increments we could determine the position of the curve at any part of its course within indefinitely narrow limits; for just as we determine a point absolutely if we can determine any position we choose of points, that approach each other without limit, between which it lies,[1] so we can determine a curve absolutely if we can determine, as closely as we like, two mutually approximating points between which the value of *y*, corresponding to any given value of *x*, lies.

But here it will be well, for our security, to establish the fact that whereas (as we have just seen) a curve may satisfy the datum of a certain area, but may fail to satisfy the data of two smaller areas into which it can be broken up, it is

[1] See page 60.

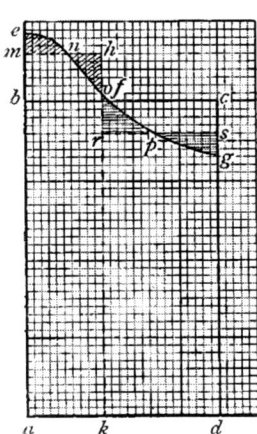
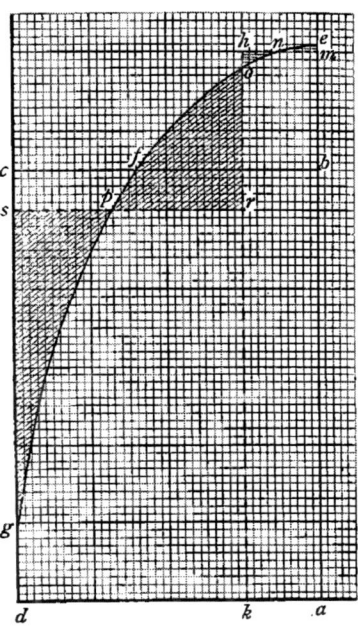
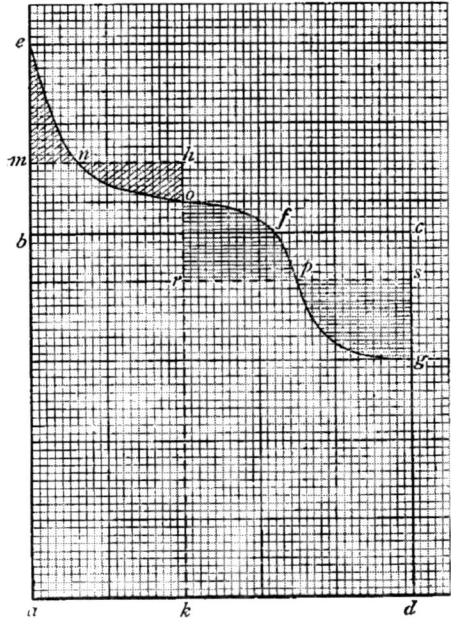

Fig. 13.

not possible for it to satisfy the data of two adjacent areas, severally, without also satisfying the data of the total area which is their sum. The general proof of this proposition, to which we will now proceed, applies to all the different forms of curve shewn in Fig. 13.

We start with the two rectangles ah and ks and construct a curve, $enofpg$, such that it adds and subtracts equally from each of the two rectangles. The equal areas we mark by oblique or horizontal lines respectively. There are, of course, an indefinite number of such curves; but if we construct an integrating rectangle, ac, by drawing a line, bc, that makes the rectangles bh and rc equal, the area which the curve $enofpg$ cuts off from the rectangle ac will be equal to that which it adds to it—that is to say, the area ebf will equal the area gcf. Since we have $emn = nho$ we may substitute the latter for the former, and we shall have $ebf = bmhof$. Again, since we have $bh = rc$, we can obtain by substitution $bmhof = scfor$. And since we have $rop = psg$, we can again obtain by substitution $scfor = gcf$. Therefore we shall have $ebf = gcf$. Q.E.D.[1]

Thus, if we have any series of rectangles arranged as in Fig. 10, on bases measured continuously along OX, a curve which adds to and cuts off equally from any contiguous pair of these rectangles, severally, will have the same property with respect to the integrating rectangle that is equal to their sum. The rectangle so obtained may then be substituted for the two rectangles of which it is the sum, and we may again integrate it with another rectangle, still relying on the same result, so that the curve will always add and subtract equally from the area of the integrating rectangle that sums any number of contiguous areas with the data of which the curve complies severally.

It is evident, therefore, that since we can always rely on the curve's retaining its fundamental property when we add together the data on which we build it, but never when we subdivide them, the accuracy with which we can determine it will depend on the accuracy and the fineness of the data on which we can construct it.

[1] This analytical proof is, strictly speaking, unnecessary; for since we have $ah = aeok$ and $ks = kogd$, we have also $aegd = ah + ks = ac$; and this involves the equality of bef and fge. But the proof by substitutions may probably be found the more enlightening.

To what degree of approximation, then, can we hope actually to determine such a curve? Or, rather (since the question so put hardly admits of a definite answer), what are the principles which will determine the degree of approximation to an ideal curve that may be realised in any particular case? In the first place, let us consider the question of accuracy. In the case of the tea curve, for instance, we have to ask what will determine or influence the limits within which we can reasonably suppose our housekeeper's estimates to be exact. But on the very threshold of this inquiry we are met by a grave difficulty. What do we mean by accuracy of estimate? If we are speaking of the estimate a man forms of the length of a stick, for example, or the height of a top-hat, we are speaking of something which can be tested by actual measurement. Thus if we say that a man can be trusted to judge a yard to within a quarter of an inch, we mean that if he declares such and such a thing to be exactly a yard long, or undertakes to measure with his eye a yard length from any given point, we shall find on testing it by standard measure that what he pronounces to be a yard will not be less than $35\frac{3}{4}$ inches, nor more than $36\frac{1}{4}$ inches. But what could we mean by saying, for instance, that you could rely on a housekeeper's estimates of the significance to her of such and such an amount of tea, under such and such circumstances, to a farthing? She is making an estimate, and if that *is* her estimate, what is the meaning of calling it accurate or inaccurate? Even if you try to bring it to the test of experience, and ask her afterwards whether her estimate is justified by the result, she can only tell you that it has or has not procured a satisfaction equal to what she now supposes she could have got by the sum she mentioned, if she had applied it otherwise; and this is itself an estimate. Though her estimates, therefore, are based on experience, and are checked and modified by it, yet no objective standard of experience can be kept for reference, or can be applied objectively as a check, like the standard yard.

Apparently, therefore, what we should mean, in the first instance, by saying that a housewife's estimates, under certain conditions, will be reliable to a farthing, would be something like this:—If we are dealing with estimates, as such (and not

Conditions that determine degrees of precision in determining such curves.

with the experiences which might or might not correspond to them if the experiment were made), we shall find that they may be made in various ways. We might ask a housekeeper to say how much another half-pound of tea would be worth to her if she already had $2\frac{1}{2}$ pounds, and then some time afterwards, when she had not that question and answer in her mind, we might ask her what half-a-pound would be worth if she had 3 pounds. Then again we might divide the amount into other fractions of a pound, thirds or fifths, and begin at some other base than $2\frac{1}{2}$ pounds, but include the former area in our new inquiries. And finally, we might ask how much a whole pound would be worth if she already had $2\frac{1}{2}$ pounds. Now if she answered all these questions independently, giving every answer on the strength of a direct estimate, without mental reference to previous answers, and if the answers when compared never revealed inconsistencies of more than a farthing in the pound, and if similar tests produced similar results wherever applied, we could say with confidence that her estimates were not mere guesses or random selections of prices or quantities on which her mind was accustomed to rest, but were direct and genuine quantitative estimates, accurate as estimates, and therefore consistent, to within a farthing a pound. Another test would be to present the same question at different times in such different lights or connections as to suggest different answers, and see whether such suggestions or associations influenced the answer.

This must be the primary meaning of accuracy and reliability of estimates as such. But behind this we may think of the correctness of the estimates as attempts to realise hypothetical experiences. We may have a clear and consistent idea of the value we should attach to such and such a supply of a commodity if we already commanded just so much of it and no more, and it may be impossible to shake that estimate by the most skilful cross-examination; but yet if the experience comes we may find that we had formed a very erroneous conception of it, and our estimates may be very different now from what they were when the experience was only hypothetical. Thus remoteness of the supposed case from experience may either affect the precision of our estimate as such, or it may make our estimate

Meaning of accuracy in estimates.

now (whether precise or vague) unreliable as a forecast of what our estimate would really be under other circumstances. These two things must always be distinguished in our minds, though it may not always be necessary to insist on the distinction in any particular context.

But yet again. It is impossible to banish the idea that as well as more or less imperfect estimates there are certain definite and ultimate facts to be estimated, and that faults or errors of estimate do not affect these ultimate facts. How can we get at precise conceptions in this matter? Clearly we are still dealing with subjective experiences and not with external magnitudes. But just as we know that many impressions are received by the eye but not consciously registered by the mind, so there may be many sensations and experiences that actually go to making us happy or strong or the reverse, but of which we are not conscious as causes, or which are in themselves so slight that we have not learned to pay attention to them. An ideally perfect estimate would identify every cause and register every effect, and would actually assign to all experiences the values they *would* have for us if we distinctly realised them. We can reach no conception more nearly approaching objectivity than this.

Returning now to our actual estimates as such, we may go on to examine some of the influences which make a greater or lesser degree of accuracy, in the sense of precision and consistency, possible in any given case. But it will be well at this point to develop a distinction that has already been made, though not emphasised.[1] Accuracy is not the only valuable quality in our data, for we have seen that the curve which satisfies the minuter will always satisfy the broader data, and the minuter data determine the curve more closely than the broader. Minuter data of a certain relative inaccuracy might therefore determine the course of the curve more closely than the broader data of relatively greater accuracy. In Fig. 10, for example, we might suppose that the area of satisfaction corresponding to the sixth pound was given with great accuracy, but if we had no minuter data the curve might, for anything we should know, undulate in an indefinite number of ways, within wide

Margin: Conditions that affect precision and minuteness of estimates.

[1] At the bottom of page 451.

limits, over that portion of its course. We should have one accurate datum, but the course of the curve would be indeterminate; whereas we might suppose a considerably higher degree of proportional inaccuracy in our data at and about the end of the third pound, and yet be more certain that we had determined the course of the curve about that point within narrow limits. The relatively inaccurate data, because narrower, would exclude many possibilities which a more accurate datum, if broader, might admit. And, as we shall see, it may very well happen that the broader data are, as a matter of fact, proportionally more accurate than the narrower. In such a case the narrower data may be of service to us in determining the general course of the curve within the limits of the broader data, but owing to their relative inaccuracy in detail their summation might give results incompatible with the broader data, and in such cases we should be guided by them only in such a general way as is consistent with compliance with the less determinate but at the same time more accurate conditions implied in the broader data.

With this proviso we will proceed with our examination of the conditions favourable to precision and consistency of estimate. Some general remarks on precision in estimating objectively measurable magnitudes may precede our examination of the more evasive estimate of satisfactions as magnitudes.

We must not blink the difficulty and complication of this problem, or the fact that any general principles we can lay down will be subject to every kind of disturbance from the personal idiosyncrasies or the special experiences of the individual who makes the estimates. It will, however, be admitted that in estimating quantities of any kind, a given individual will have a range, or theoretically a point, of maximum accuracy. Take an observer whose experience, professional or other, gives him no particular guidance in the matter, and present him successively with two pieces of wire, one an inch and the other an inch and a half long; then, successively, with diagrams shewing spaces of $\frac{1}{32}$ in. and $\frac{3}{64}$ in. respectively, intercepted between fine lines. Then take him to a place from which he has a variety of views, and under conditions identical as to distance, angle of observation, and so forth, ask him to notice the distance between the trunk of a tree and a boulder (known by you to be 1000 yards), and subsequently the distance between the edge of a tarn and the edge of a snow patch (which is 1500 yards). In each case ask him what proportion the first length in each pair bears to the second. You will probably expect a more accurate proportional estimate in the case of the inch and the inch and a half than in either of the other cases. Perhaps there will be some other length which he will be able to estimate more accurately still, but there will be some point, between the thirty-second of an inch and 1000 yards, in the neighbourhood of which his estimate will reach the maximum of accuracy. And as he recedes from this in either direction his estimate will become less reliable. It does not follow, however, in individual cases, that this departure from accuracy will be regular and continuous. There may be certain definite magnitudes which, for one reason or another, the individual has been accustomed to measure with unusual accuracy, and these may be irregularly distributed. Thus, if we take a carpenter who is also a professional cricketer, and who, when a boy, sometimes ran along a mile of road keeping pace with a stage-coach, and if we submit to him pairs of lengths which are really the same fractions of each other in every case, and not very remote from equality (say that one is nine-tenths of the other), probably if their mean is a foot he will estimate them with greater proportional accuracy than if their mean is 9 yards. But again he will measure them with greater accuracy if their mean is the 22 yards of a cricket pitch than if their mean is 9 yards; with less accuracy if their mean is 1000 yards than if their mean is 22 yards; but with greater accuracy again if their mean is a mile than if their mean is 1000 yards. Thus, the general principle that there is a certain magnitude in the neighbourhood of which estimates reach a maximum of accuracy from which they depart in either direction, may be qualified by any vivid experience or frequent practice which may have cultivated particularly accurate observations of certain lengths. And whatever the points of maximum accuracy may be the man will attempt to reduce his problems, when possible, to terms of the lengths he can best judge. Thus if a length is unmanageable he will try to divide it into halves, thirds, or quarters, or to multiply it by two or one and a half, and see whether these fractions give him lengths that he can judge immediately with some confidence and from which he can then calculate the others. The boy who, when asked how he would estimate the distance of the sun from the earth, answered, "Guess a quarter and multiply by four," had a confused sense of a sound method in his mind, though he was not fortunate in his application of it.

Now in the case of our tea curve all these complications are present, and certain others as well. The ultimate quantities to be estimated and compared, here as elsewhere in the administration of resources, are not tea-leaves and pence, but quantities of satisfaction; and yet the housewife is never accustomed to think of these as quantities at all. *Relation of psychic quantities to units of the currency.* She thinks in pounds and ounces of tea, and in shillings and pence of money, but the half-unconscious and wholly unanalysed processes which emerge into conscious deliberations under these denominations of ounces and pence really concern lots of satisfaction. Hence a divergence between the points on which her deliberations crystallise themselves in her own consciousness and those on which they actually depend.

It is not difficult to see why this is so. In order to estimate tea with reference to other commodities we must express its value in terms of money, as the common measure between all the commodities in question; and we shall estimate it in the quantities in which we are accustomed to buy it. But our direct experience of its value is based on much smaller units, for while we pay for tea by the pound we consume it by the cupful. If a man drinks two cups of tea of a certain average strength every day for breakfast, his estimate of the value of a pound of tea must be arrived at by considering it as supplying, say, sixty-four breakfasts, and the marginal value of a quarter-pound by considering the significance of substituting a cup and a half for two cups at these sixty-four breakfasts. The enjoyment of tea at one breakfast is the quantity of satisfaction he really estimates, but in order to bring it into correspondence with his problems of expenditure he must reduce it to the terms in which he actually deals in it. If we express our estimate of one sixty-fourth of a pound of tea in terms of money we fall into manifest absurdity. For money is an instrument of practical exchange, and since we cannot give effect to these minute estimates of a fraction of a farthing in any actual transaction, this method of expression loses all its value. Hence the sense of intolerable unreality in our previous working out of the tea problem (pages 44-63). As we narrowed the areas of our estimates and so brought ourselves nearer to the actual basis of realisable experience we continued to express those estimates under a denomination that was becoming more and more hopelessly inappropriate and unconvincing.

Thus the point at which we deliberate as to alternative expenditures of money is likely to be remote from that at which our experience gives us the most direct and vivid sense of the immediate value of a commodity. In a word, to compare one *expenditure* with another we have to recede indefinitely from the points at which we can best compare one *experience* with another. Commodities are not practically exchanged with each other, or obtainable as alternatives, in the quantities in which the experiences they provoke are most directly comparable with each other. And as we are more accustomed to deliberate consciously as to expenditure than as to satisfaction (though our whole expenditure is ultimately regulated with a view to satisfaction), a difficulty inevitably arises. The careful administrator does occasionally revert consciously to the primary and ultimate basis. She may from time to time calculate, for instance, how many rice puddings can be made out of a pound of rice, or how many breakfasts a pound of tea will provide, in order to establish a kind of bridge along which she may pass either way from the quantities in which she buys commodities to the quantities in which she experiences their services. She sometimes travels from her expenditure per pound or per annum to her satisfaction per quarter-ounce or per diem, in order to base herself upon experience, and she sometimes calculates how much a saving too minute to be estimated in coin of the realm day by day would amount to in a month or a year, in order that she may bring one set of experiences into terms under which it may be compared with another and alternative set.

As we are now to deal with the ultimate limits of accuracy in the construction of a curve, it is obvious that we are concerned not directly with shillings and pence per pound, but with the estimates of satisfactions per cup, and so forth, as quantities. Obviously it is with these that the housewife must ultimately wrestle. For instance, if an economy is to be effected she may have tea at fewer meals, never supplying it at certain times of day unless it is expressly asked for, or in the last resort saying that it cannot be had; or instead of this she may make it weaker, or she may practically limit the amount of the infusion at each meal while not limiting the amount of hot water that passes through the pot, or she may look for a cheaper tea, or (*horresco referens*) one that will not be so popular in her household. She may or may not be subject to such more or less unsympathetic pressure from her family as is implied in some of the foregoing suppositions, but in any case she is dealing with certain alternatives, and in considering them she is estimating and comparing volumes or areas of satisfaction, and it is a reference to these that underlies her estimates in money of the marginal value of an ounce of tea, and determines at what point of pressure she will buy more or less of any given quality at any given price.

Ultimate psychic basis of estimates.

It is therefore here that we must apply the principle of the magnitude that is estimated with greatest proportional accuracy; for there may be some one or more of the satisfactions she habitually considers which, as magnitudes, are realised with especial distinctness and vividness, and to which others are consciously or unconsciously referred as to a kind of standard. Suppose, for example, there is one member of the household whose wants, for any reason, good or bad, the housekeeper considers it specially important to satisfy, and whom she occasionally disappoints, as to quality or quantity, in the matter of tea. The significance of this occasional contretemps may well constitute the actual unit of greatest proportional accuracy of estimate, and it may be by unconscious reference to it that the housewife can determine most accurately the relative values of all the alternative refusals, indulgences, evasions, devices, and pecuniary expenditures, with which she is concerned in the matter. Here, as in the case of the carpenter, there may be other points impressed by other experiences that give an exceptional degree of firmness to estimates of certain other quantities; but, neglecting this consideration, we may follow up the special clue we have grasped.

Note that our housekeeper will probably never deliberately incur or inflict the specific privation we are considering, merely in order to economise the tea needed to avert it. It will occur through some inadvertency or miscalculation, and it will be the delay, or trouble, or want of courtesy to a guest, or incidental (as distinct from primary) waste, that would be involved in correcting the error that will determine her to accept the result. But when the housekeeper is asked to make a number of hypothetical estimates as to what successive increments of the supply would be worth to her, and comes to think of a contraction of supply great enough to make this specific privation normal and permanent instead of occasional and accidental, she finds she has a very clear conception of that particular " lot " of satisfaction, that she has been accustomed to translate it into a great variety of equivalents, and that she has from time to time defined it pretty closely as worth just so much of certain other things, but not even a little more. She can now translate it, by a deliberate calculation, into so much tea per month, and can estimate it with some precision at its money value. This may form a kind of standard unit of reference, and may be the magnitude she is capable of estimating with the highest degree of proportional accuracy and precision. The area thus determined will be that of the elements out of which our curve can be constructed with greatest accuracy. For in considering the value of other increments nearer to the margin or further from it, our housewife (we are supposing) will find it easiest to make accurate estimates of areas of satisfaction of this particular magnitude; and she will find, of course, that if she has to think of herself as compelled by the further contractions of her supply to cut deeper back into the satisfactions of her household than she has ever actually done, she will realise that a smaller amount of tea, at the higher significance so reached, would yield the standard unit of satisfaction, and that in like manner at a more advanced point it would require a correspondingly larger amount to secure it. Geometrically the standard area will stand on a narrower basis as we approach the origin, and on a broader one as we recede from it.

Thus, subject to all the qualifications hinted at or developed, we may suppose that the ultimate elements out of which data for the curve would be obtained with the greatest proportional accuracy would consist in estimated satisfactions of a magnitude about equivalent to that of the satisfaction relinquished on the occasions of disappointment that have impressed themselves most vividly on the housewife's mind. *Elements from which the curve is constructed.* They would be represented on our diagram (when reduced to the terms of a month's supply, and expressed in shilling and penny rates per pound) by a series of rectangles of uniform area standing on progressively larger bases as we recede from the origin.

Now seeing that every day the housekeeper deals with the whole supply for the day, and has the opportunity of experiencing or observing the actual service rendered by every increment from the initial to the final one, we might be tempted to think that she could base her whole conjectural construction of the curve from the origin to the margin upon direct experience. *Range of experience.* But this is not so. We have seen that recurrently satisfied wants never take us back to the real initial significance of the things that satisfy them.[1] If our supplies were very much contracted (even apart from any reaction upon the organism that might ultimately take place) we should gain experience of significances that had evaded us before; for the want which to-day's first increment supplies is a different want according to the point up to which our want was satisfied yesterday. And as soon as we begin to contract or increase our supply at all this process sets in, though its effect at first may be hardly perceptible, and it may only become pronounced as we recede considerably from our present margin. Thus an additional element of uncertainty enters into all estimates far behind or far in advance of the present margin, and our ideal equal areas will become correspondingly more speculative. This speculative element may reveal itself consciously in a refusal to make equally precise estimates, or unconsciously in an inability to make equally consistent ones, as we recede from the actual

[1] Cf. page 426.

margin. Past experiences, vividly remembered, may establish at irregular intervals other bases of comparatively direct and immediate estimates; or critical points may so appeal to the imagination as to give a firm but illusory precision to speculative estimates; or some changed unit of maximum accuracy may assert itself in certain regions of the curve; and throughout we must distinguish between precision and consistency in the sense explained above, and approximation to the estimates which would be formed under the pressure of immediate experience should it ever be realised.

When formed, our curve, such as it is, will be an estimate, or a register, more or less reliable, both of the total significance to be derived from the consumption of any given quantity of the commodity, and of its marginal significance at any point.[1]

Before leaving this branch of the subject we may note that if we asked for estimates of the significance of a series of objectively equal increments of the commodity we should have a series of rectangles, not of equal area but on equal bases, from which to construct our curve; and we may ask what conditions would influence the delicacy and accuracy of our estimates of the difference of area between them. Two considerations are relevant here. In the first place, the same magnitude is less easily perceived and estimated as part of a larger than as part of a smaller whole. The difference of an inch is more conspicuous in the length of two men's noses than in their heights. Small differences will therefore be less delicately noted when the areas are large than when they are small, and therefore a given difference between two contiguous rectangles might escape detection near the origin but might be distinctly felt farther from it. But in the second place, our whole investigation has shewn us that the significance of successive increments of the commodity changes more rapidly in some regions than in others. Between two successive rectangles on equal bases, therefore, we shall sometimes have greater differences and sometimes have keener powers of observation. The first condition is indicated by a rapidly falling curve, and the second by a higher positive altitude of the curve. In our example of the tea, and in Fig. 14, *a*, these two conditions tend to counteract each other; for as the

[1] But see below, pages 467 *sqq.*

differences themselves decrease, our power of perceiving them increases. But in Fig. 14, *b*, they reinforce each other. As the differences themselves become greater our power of observing them also becomes more acute.

Enough has now been said to shew in the first place how extremely precarious any actual evaluation of a curve of total significance of any commodity must necessarily be, but also, in the second place, that this value, which it is so difficult to estimate, is actually a definite and a highly significant quantity.

The area bounded by the curve represents what the older economists called the " value in use " of the commodity, that

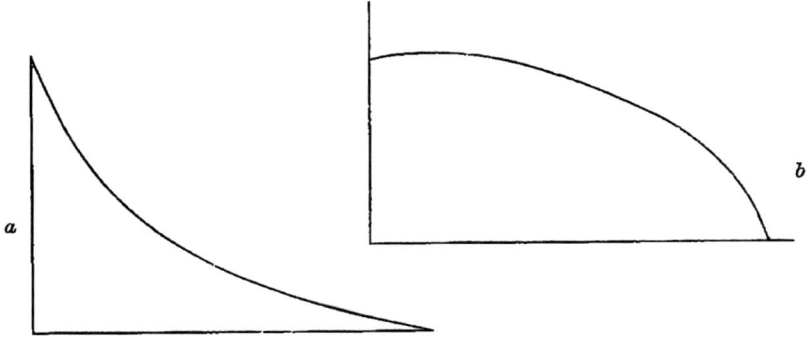

Fig. 14.

is to say, the total satisfaction or advantage derived from its enjoyment; and the height of the curve above any point on the abscissa represents its marginal significance, which, in the case of exchangeable things, will always tend to be brought into coincidence with its " value in exchange." And note that if our expenditure is wise a decline in marginal significance due to an increased supply will always coincide with an increased volume of satisfaction. A reduction in the " exchange value " of any commodity, taken in itself, should always result in its increased " value in use " to us.[1]

We have now sufficiently examined the general meaning of a curve of total significance or satisfaction, and we have seen the very precarious nature of the data upon which any attempt actually to evaluate the total significance of a

[1] Cf. pages 45-47.

commodity must depend. But we have still to take note of certain points, a neglect of which might lead to erroneous or inaccurate thought.

It will be understood that a curve proves nothing whatever as to the facts from which we start. It is merely an idealised picture of facts and their implications. It may therefore enable us to understand the full meaning of any set of supposed facts, but it cannot establish them. At most it can only shew us the relations in which certain facts, if they exist, stand to each other. But by doing this it may bring out implications involved in our data that we had not fully realised, and this may throw back light on the validity of the data themselves. For instance, a glance at the tea curve at once suggests that it will not decline any further after the point to which we have carried it; and as there is no reason why the law of declining significance should become invalid after seven pounds, we begin to suspect our data of being in some way self-contradictory or impossible. And this is really the case. We supposed our original data as to the values of successive pounds of tea to conform to a perfectly rigid and easily discernible algebraical law. But this is strictly impossible. In the first place, it is impossible that the estimates should be mathematically accurate at all. That is to say, it is impossible that an infinitesimal change in the quantity of the commodity could be actually and directly appreciated, and its significance registered in terms of money. But if we are dealing only with approximations it may possibly happen that the more or less loose estimates given may conform loosely to some simple algebraic formula. Since, however, an immense number of heterogeneous factors would enter into the composition of every region of the curve, some of them changing as it proceeds, we may be very sure that no simple algebraical formula would be able to represent them all even approximately, though it might approximately fit a certain portion of the curve. So if we had assumed this precise algebraical law as determining the whole curve, we should have assumed in the first place an impossible precision, and in the second place a highly improbable (and, as it turns out, impossible) simplicity and regularity. As a matter of fact it will be found that our original data themselves assumed

Form of the supposed tea curve.

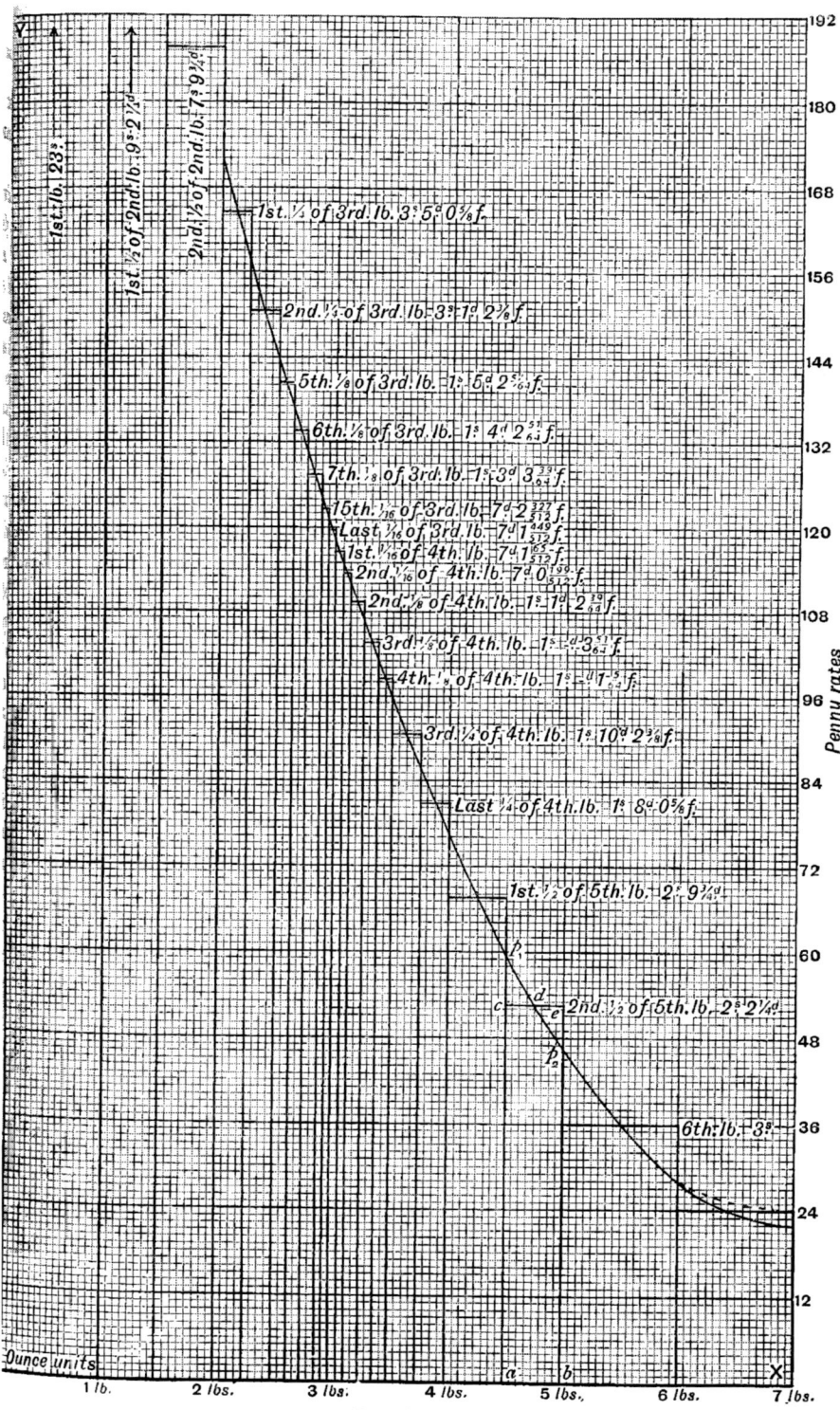

Fig. 10.

that after the sixth pound the law of the curve would change; for the series 23s., 17s., 12s., 8s., 5s., 3s. would give as its next term 2s., and we have constructed the curve on this estimate. But this contradicts our original data, for we started with the supposition that at 2s. a pound the purchaser would take 7 lbs.; and the figure makes it very clear that if the whole seventh pound is only worth 2s., then the first half-pound is worth more than a shilling, and the second half-pound worth less. The second half-pound therefore would not, on this supposition, be bought at all. Our curve would give about 6·42 lbs. as the ideal point at which the purchase would stop. So if we are to suppose that 7 lbs. would be bought at 2s. we must suppose the character of the curve to change after 6 lbs. It might take some such course as that indicated by the dotted line.

In very many cases a curve that approximated to a similar formula during a part of its course might reasonably be expected to change its character as it approached the origin; for we have seen that at first a commodity may have increasing significance, and may only enter upon the period of declining significance "after a certain point."[1] In the case of tea, however, there is nothing palpably absurd in supposing our curve to follow approximately the formula we have assumed, at any rate up to a very close proximity to the origin. It is easy to imagine that as tea (or coffee) became dearer and dearer a careful housekeeper, whose family still retained a taste that they were less and less able to indulge, might limit the purchases more and more till at last it was only on occasions of special festivity that the precious infusion was consumed. When the price of £1 : 6 : 4d. a pound was reached, a quarter of a pound, or two ounces, might be bought for Christmas Day, and none at all at any other time. This consumption (four or two ounces a year) would be at the rate of one-third or one-sixth of an ounce per month, and would be represented on our figure by a point only one-third or one-sixth of the side of a small square from the origin. And if we had lowered the whole curve by, say, two of the large units on Y so that it intercepted the axis of X at a little under 6 lbs. 7 oz., the whole series of marginal values from the initial

[1] Cf. page 435.

CH. II   THE DIAGRAMMATIC METHOD   467

increment to the one that completed the full satisfaction of the desire might, without palpable absurdity, have been supposed to be represented by this particular curve. As it is, it is clear that our original data involve the supposition that the law indicated by the successive steps in declining value from 1 lb. to 2 lbs., etc., up to 6 lbs., would not continue to hold for the decline from 6 lbs. to 7 lbs.

Even if we do not assume an algebraical formula for a curve, we can seldom use this diagrammatic method without expressing more and expressing it more precisely than we desire, and this constitutes a grave disadvantage in the use of curves for popular demonstrations. If, for example, we say that successive increments of a commodity will decline in significance after a certain point the statement remains general. But if we illustrate it by a curve, the "point after which" will be determined and the rate of decline at every point will be determined, and a general conception of the modes of variation will be suggested. And so the incautious student may be misled by the characteristics of the individual curve selected, and may fail to distinguish between them and those characteristics really involved in the data. The utmost caution is needed to prevent a curve from surreptitiously insinuating into our minds suppositions which are not included or involved in our data, but which we nevertheless receive into our conclusions. Nor is it beginners only that have fallen into this trap.[1] But this by the way.

We might now suppose that in such a diagram as Fig. 15, if properly constructed, we should have an ideal presentation of the amount of the commodity Ox that would be purchased by a certain individual at any given market price Oy; of the total satisfaction Oy_0px that its consumption would afford; of the volume of other satisfactions Op sacrificed in the total sum paid for it; and of the surplus of satisfaction yy_0p which is secured over and above what is sacrificed. If this were so, then this last-named area would represent the advantage which the consumer derived from the existence of this particular market, and the volume of

Interpretation of a curve of total satisfaction. Instability of the psychic meaning of the unit of currency.

[1] Cf. pages 552 and 568 *sqq.*

satisfaction of which he would be deprived if it closed or became inaccessible to him, all other things remaining equal.

These conclusions, however, are still subject to sundry modifications and qualifications which we must now examine.

In constructing our curve, we have used denominations of shillings and pence simply as measures of certain definite satisfactions, and we have tried to shew how, ideally, the area of total satisfaction corresponding to any given supply Ox of the commodity could be actually evaluated in these denominations. But on closer inspection we become aware of a disturbing instability and ambiguity in our unit when regarded as a psychological magnitude. We have often noted that 1s. has a different psychological significance to two

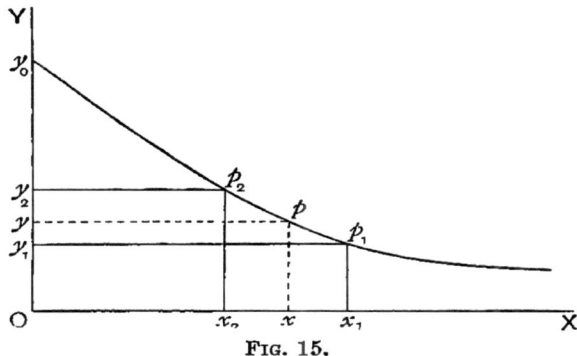

Fig. 15.

different men, and also to the same man if his income rises or falls. Theoretically, then, the marginal significance of a shilling will be affected by the sum the man has already paid to secure a certain satisfaction. We supposed, in our example of the tea, that the housekeeper gave us the outside value of the first pound of tea to her, and then *supposing herself to have paid that sum for it* went on to give us the outside value of a second pound, and so forth. If our Fig. 15 has been constructed on this system, then $x_1 p_1$ will represent the marginal value of a commodity to a man, on the supposition that he has actually paid the money represented by the area $Oy_0 p_1 x_1$ for the quantity Ox_1. But will Ox_1 represent the amount he would actually buy if the market price were Oy_1? Not unless the sum of money represented by the whole area $Oy_0 p_1 x_1$ is so insignificant a part of the man's total expenditure that it makes no perceptible difference to the marginal significance of a penny whether the area $Oy_0p_1x_1$ or only the area Op_1 has been spent upon tea. If this is not so, then the fact that he can actually get Ox_1 for the expenditure of Op_1 will leave him better off than on our first supposition by the area $y_1y_0p_1$; and this being an appreciable sum it will enable him to get a little more of everything or anything (including the commodity under direct consideration) than he would have been able to do had he spent $y_1y_0p_1$ (as well as Op_1) on the supply Ox_1. A little more than Ox_1 may therefore be purchased. And again, since all the man's wants will be satisfied down to a lower point of urgency, the significance of what a penny will buy at this advanced margin is lowered. Thus the psychological significance of our unit will be smaller if the whole supply is purchased at the lower price than if the full sum represented by the mixtilinear area had been given for it. As we imagine Ox to advance or recede, the changing values of the total or the rectangular areas will react upon the psychological significance of the unit, and the difference between them will prevent the abscissa from accurately representing the amount that would be consumed at the price represented by the ordinate.

This is not a mere fanciful speculation. If a careful housekeeper were giving any such estimates as we have supposed, when she came to think of herself as paying 50s. or 60s. a month for tea instead of something like 14s., she might be perfectly conscious of the constraint she would feel in all branches of her household expenditure, and might realise that she was estimating the increments of tea in a unit of higher significance than that by which her actual expenditure is regulated.

The curve as constructed, therefore, does not represent the relation of price to quantity purchased with any theoretical accuracy at all, and it represents the psychological value of the satisfaction secured in a fluctuating unit.

We will begin with the latter difficulty. How can we maintain the stability of our psychological unit throughout a series of estimates? What we really want is to fix in our own minds or the mind of our informant the actual psychological magnitude represented by the objective unit at the margin of our current expenditure; and then to estimate *in that unit* the significance of small increments of the commodity at various margins. We should then have, for any given quantity consumed, what we set out to obtain, viz. an evaluation in a stable unit of the total estimated satisfaction enjoyed, as distinct from the sum paid. These estimates, however, are such as we could only imagine experts trained in a psychological laboratory attempting to make. The naïve, however careful and acute, answers we could expect from practical administrators would never be based on so subtle a conception as that of the psychological unit. We should have to assist our informant by putting our questions in some such form as this: "If when you had bought your tea for the month and paid for it at market prices, you lost half, three-quarters, nine-tenths, or all of your stock, what in each case would you pay for a first small increment, sooner than go without it?" The smallness of the increment estimated would reduce to a vanishing point the reaction of the sum to be paid upon the psychologic value of the money unit, and the fact that in every case the full amount that is actually paid for the commodity, and no more, is already written off, would keep that psychological value uniform. The ingenious reader may still think of disturbing influences, the shock of the loss, the changed significance of other enjoyments caused by the reduction in the supply of tea and so forth; and he may imagine any system of discounts that pleases him. It is clear that in any case absolute fixity of the psychological unit is only an ideal conception, and that actual estimates in money will never be more than approximately consistent in their psychological significance. The essential point is that the total psychic value of the satisfaction derived from the consumption of a given amount of a commodity is a finite quantity, capable of ideal evaluation in a fixed unit, and that over a vast field of our current expenditure it exceeds, in our own estimate, the value of the alternatives we relinquish for it.[1] This total area of satisfaction may, in theory, be represented accurately by a figure which sets forth the marginal significance of every successive increment of the commodity; but if we have taken as our psychic unit the satisfaction which the money unit

[1] But compare the following chapter.

commands at the actual margin of our expenditure under existing conditions, then any hypothesis which sensibly changes those conditions (as by increasing or diminishing the amount actually spent on our commodity) will change the significance of the unit; and therefore, if we measure penny or shilling rates on the axis of Y, it follows that the same figure cannot represent, with theoretical accuracy, the meaning of a number of different hypotheses, regarded as co-existing. Given any price and the actual administration of resources that corresponds to it, we can ideally construct a curve of total satisfaction, the unit of which corresponds to the marginal satisfaction now secured by a penny or a shilling; but if the price changes we cannot preserve the same figure and get an accurate result by simply changing the point on OX at which we erect a perpendicular to cut the curve; for under the changed conditions the satisfaction secured by a penny or a shilling will have changed.

I have been careful to speak of the Figure as giving, ideally, a representation of the total satisfaction derived from the consumption of Ox, in the mixtilinear area above it. I have not said that the surplus of satisfaction over payment would be accurately represented by the area yy_0p. For this again would only be an approximation. In evaluating the price actually paid at Op cur Figure implies that if the market for the commodity in question were closed, or if the commodity ceased to exist, the purchaser, while losing the total area above Ox, would gain the released area of the rectangle Op. This means that the whole of the money now spent on this commodity could be expended on other commodities at a marginal significance represented by xp or Oy. But theoretically this is not true, for if the supplies of other commodities were increased, it would of course be at a declining significance, and consequently, when the whole sum Op had been distributed amongst them, their marginal values would have declined to some extent, however small, from the height xp. Some portion of them, therefore, would have less value than if their marginal significance had remained at xp; and in the sum they will not equal Op. And here again, as we recede from the actual point of departure towards the origin, there will be another source of

Interpretation of the rectangle of payment.

disturbance in the psychic significance of the money unit, independent of the advancing margin, viz. the change in the whole significance of remaining sources of satisfaction as the one to which the Figure refers dries up. Here again, therefore, all attempts to guard against and discount sources of disturbance in the psychic value of our objective unit must be at once subtle and clumsy. The only ideal method is to conceive of a mind trained to hold a psychic magnitude firmly and apply it consistently as a unit. That magnitude would be the satisfaction represented by the money unit under existing conditions, but it would be applied to hypothetically changed conditions directly, and not through the convenient but treacherous intervention of a money unit which might be perpetually changing its significance.

If we traced our original curve with a stable psychic unit, based on the satisfaction secured by a penny or a shilling at present margins, and if we then allowed for the decreasing values of other commodities as the margins advanced, represented by a decline in the height of the ordinates as we pass from xp to Oy, we should have a consistent representation of total satisfaction, and of surplus of satisfaction over the sacrifice represented by the price, corresponding to the actual state of things. It would shew how much satisfaction I get and how much I pay for it, measured in a stable unit. But it would not give us accurate information as to any other than the actual state of things.

If, on the other hand, we were to ask, not "how much would you give for an ounce of tea under such and such circumstances?" but "how much tea would you buy if it were such and such a price?" we should get a curve with just the opposite characteristics.

Curves of price-and-quantity-purchased.

It would give us information about a number of different hypothetical conditions, but its different parts would have no consistent significance. Thus, by asking "how high would the price of tea have to rise before you would stop buying it altogether?" we might find a point on the axis of Y, and then, by asking how much would be bought at the several prices descending from that to zero, we might obtain points on a curve which would accurately represent the relation between price and quantity purchased for every hypothesis at once. But on each hypothesis the psychological significance of the unit would be different, and as it would always make a (theoretical) difference whether the whole sum represented by the mixtilinear area above any abscissa, or only that represented by the rectangle, were paid, the area would never represent accurately either the total sum that the consumer would pay for the amount Ox, or its psychological evaluation in any fixed unit.

A curve, therefore, which professes to give, for every price, (1) the quantity that would be purchased at that price, (2) either the pecuniary or the psychic evaluation of the total satisfaction it would yield, can only be a compromise, for it endeavours to comply with two incompatible sets of conditions. Its construction would illustrate the principle of "temperament" by which a note on the piano which is neither D sharp nor E flat, but a compromise between them, is made to do duty for both alike. This is only possible if the interval between them is small. In our case the errors involved in confounding the two curves become negligible in proportion as the total expenditure on the commodity in question is a negligible part of the man's whole income.

Temperament.

The psychological curve always remains the ultimate and basal fact, and though we can never rely on its precise evaluations it is essential that we should form a precise conception of its nature and should realise that it has a definite value. The price-and-quantity-purchased curve is the most accessible and is the one with which we shall usually work; but unless the contrary is expressly stated we shall assume that our curves have a "temperament" which allows us to read them either way.[1]

[1] Cf. Appendix to Chapters II. and III. pages 490-492.

CHAPTER III

ON THE NATURE OF CURVES OF TOTAL SATISFACTION

SUMMARY.—*Curves of total satisfaction are purely abstract; that is to say, they represent the subjective value attached by a consumer to each increment of the commodity, or the amount he would purchase at any given price, apart from any consideration of the causes that might be supposed in actual experience to limit his supply or raise the price of the commodity, and apart from all reactions upon the price of other commodities. They are also isolated; that is to say, we cannot conceive of a system of such curves being so constructed as to be valid simultaneously. Nor can we sum their areas, taken successively, without omitting some values and counting others more than once. Nor can we read on them the effect of a rise or fall in the consumer's income. Nevertheless their general form has a high theoretical significance. Communal curves of price-and-quantity-saleable cannot be interpreted psychically, though they rest on a psychic basis. A system of such curves cannot possess simultaneous validity.*

<small>Ideal and isolated character of personal curves.</small> The refinements dwelt upon in the preceding chapter are usually ignored. A curve of price-and-quantity-that-would-be-purchased is supposed to be constructed by a direct process of estimates; and its area is taken to represent the total satisfaction accruing from the consumption of any given amount of the commodity, while the rectangle of price-multiplied-by-quantity is taken to represent the value of the sacrificed alternatives, the surplus satisfaction being secured without corresponding sacrifice or payment. But, independently of the difficulties thus ignored,

the legitimacy of the whole conception has been seriously challenged. Probably this is due to the fact that a personal curve of total utility, though its formation is in itself entirely legitimate, is nevertheless of such an ideal and isolated character, that it cannot be regarded as co-existing with other curves of the like nature, for the same individual, nor can it, and its analogues for other individuals, be made, as they stand, the basis for the calculation, by summation, of a communal curve of the one commodity. And therefore when we try to bring a curve of this nature into relation with any practically realisable hypothesis as to the conditions of markets, it assumes an elusory and evasive character which has tempted the bewildered and impatient student to fling it aside as a mere illusion. All this must now be explained.

We shall best avoid the confusions in which the controversy has often been entangled, and shall at the same time best vindicate the fundamental value and significance of the method itself, by examining more closely the meaning of the condition that "other things must remain unchanged" while we are obtaining our successive data as to how much of the commodity the consumer would purchase at such and such prices. To begin with, amongst the other conditions that are to remain unchanged, we must include the power of purchasing substitutes at the prices now current. For example, when our housekeeper is considering how much tea she would buy if it were 6s. a pound, she will probably think of herself as increasing her purchases of coffee or cocoa as she contracts her purchases of tea; and she will suppose that she will still be able to buy coffee and cocoa at the present prices. Now this shews us at once the isolated nature of our hypothetical tea curve. For suppose we had constructed a coffee curve, as well as a tea curve, on the same principles. We should then find that the conditions we supposed to be stable when we were drawing up our tea curve included the possibility of getting more coffee at the present price; and, in like manner, the conditions we supposed to be stable when we were drawing up our coffee curve will have included the possibility of buying tea, as required, at the present market price. Thus, as soon as we suppose the price of tea to rise, we are violating

Meaning of the condition "other things remaining the same." Substitutes.

one of the conditions on which the validity of our coffee curve depends; and, in like manner, if we supposed the price of coffee to change, we should thereby be violating one of the conditions on which the validity of our tea curve depends; for it is sufficiently obvious that the amount of coffee which a housekeeper would buy at any given price might be affected by a change in the price of tea; and *vice versa*. It seems impossible, then, even ideally to draw up a system of curves which shall be valid simultaneously; for any curve purports to represent a number of simultaneous possibilities, indicating what quantities would be purchased at any given price; but a change in the price of any one of the commodities will, or may, affect the quantity of other commodities that would be taken at *any* given price. That is to say, if we change our supposition as to the price of any one commodity, that very supposition will change the form of the curves of other commodities, throughout their course. This perhaps needs some further elaboration and explanation.

Let us start on the assumption that the consumer's income is as a matter of fact distributed in a certain way. He buys Oa of commodity A at the price aa, Ob of commodity B at the price $b\beta$, Oc of commodity C at the price $c\gamma$, etc. We construct the curves severally as in Fig. 16, on the principles already illustrated, in every case starting from the same initial hypothesis. Each commodity is measured on the axis of X in its own conventional unit, but the unit on the axis of Y is uniform. We can now suppose *any one* of the curves (say the curve of B) to set forth (as a first approximation, subject to the secondary inaccuracies and inconsistencies dwelt on in the last chapter) the marginal significance of B at any point of supply, the quantity that would be purchased at any given price, and the surplus of satisfaction over enjoyment attendant on the consumption of any quantity, provided always that A, C, etc., can be obtained in any quantities desired at the prices aa, $c\gamma$, etc. But the moment we suppose the price of B to rise and the consumption to contract we may find the consumer taking more of A or C as a substitute, and in that case Oa would no longer represent the amount of A that would be consumed at the price of aa. Nor would the curve as it stands

Reaction of changed supply of one commodity on the form of the curves of other commodities.

CURVES OF TOTAL SATISFACTION

(unless by accident) represent the relation between price and quantity at any other point either. The curves of A and C therefore may change their form for every value of $b\beta$ and are drawn up on the supposition that it is constant, whereas the curve of B is drawn up expressly to illustrate the significance

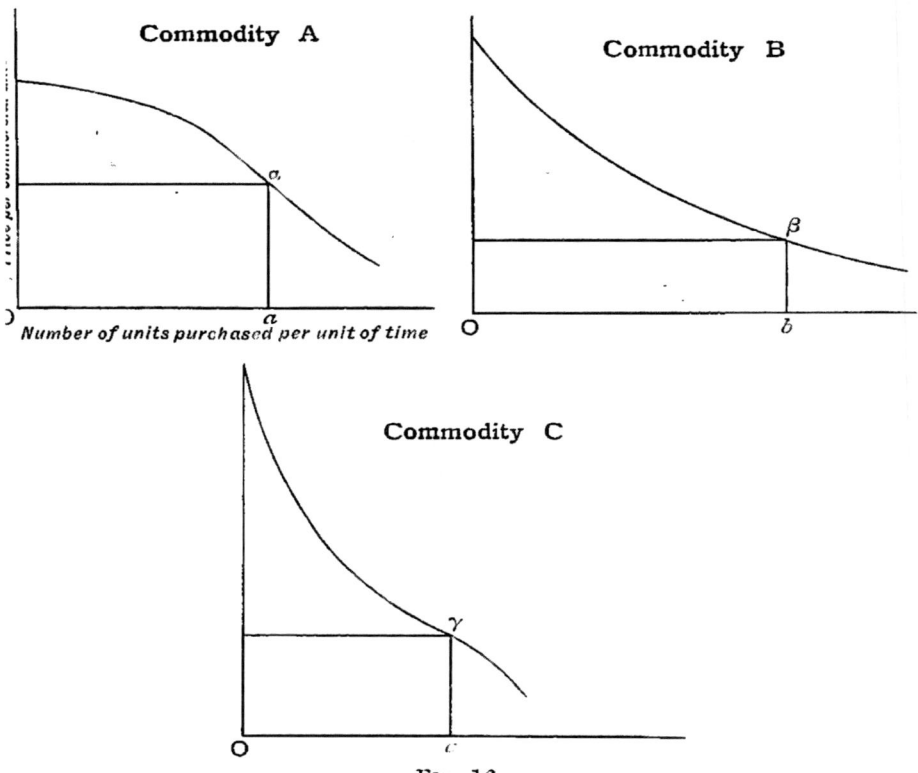

Fig. 16.

of changes in that value, regarded as causes or effects of a change in the magnitude of Ob.

In constructing the curve of B we must be supposed to register the value of $b\beta$ for any value of Ob, or *vice versa*, as the resultants of all the complex readjustments of expenditure caused by a change of supply, or a change of price, in B, the prices of A, C, etc., remaining constant. And if we start in every case from the actual prices $a\alpha$, $b\beta$, $c\gamma$, etc., we may thus trace the curves of A, B, C, etc., severally and independently, and *any one* of them will then be valid as long as all the others are cancelled and the original data (*aa*, etc.) treated as constant; but no two of them will represent a system of relations between changing quantities and marginal values which holds contemporaneously for both of them.

We have now sufficiently developed the fact that we can only regard such a curve as we have been discussing as valid in isolation. But it will be instructive to consider a little further the nature of the reaction of a change in the price of one commodity upon the demand for another. A glance at any of the figures will shew that a rise in the price of a commodity (A), while it will always cause a contraction of the quantity purchased, will sometimes increase and sometimes diminish the amount of money spent on it. And in either case it may cause an increased expenditure on the readiest substitute (B). Thus a rise in the price of A, whether causing an increased expenditure on A or not, may easily cause an increased expenditure on A and B between them. This may extend to other commodities also; but since the man's total resources are not increased by the rise in the price of A, economies must be effected somewhere. Thus a rise in the price of A may cause an increased consumption of B but a diminished consumption of C.

In some cases this result might be the direct, not the indirect, effect of the rise in the price of A; for there are commodities which are complementary to each other as well as commodities which are substitutes. Thus a man may have a taste for *café au lait* but not for *café noir*, so that if the price of coffee rose it might check his purchases of milk. If the total expenditure on the two commodities were reduced, then some other expenditure would be increased.

<small>Complementary commodities.</small>

Thus every modification in the price of any one commodity reacts on the demand curves, or curves of total estimated value, of some other, ideally of all other, commodities, services, and opportunities. A system of such curves purporting to represent the whole range of any man's scale of preferences would be mutually destructive, for each one only represents the possibilities of a sliding scale of purchases and prices on the supposition that there is no movement in any of the others. Any one curve represents a track, movement along which incidentally modifies some one or more of the other tracks, and which is itself modified by a movement along any one of them. This is the meaning of the principle so constantly insisted on by Pareto, that the marginal significance of any commodity is a function not only of the quantity we possess of that particular commodity but also of the quantity we possess (including zero as a quantity) of other, ideally of all other, commodities. The quantities of all desired things, services, and opportunities which we command, and the marginal significances we attach to them, are therefore a system of magnitudes which mutually determine each other within the limits imposed by our total command of resources.

Well, then, taking these curves as indicating, severally, the consumer's own estimate of the addition to his total satisfaction which the existence of each market confers upon him, his resources and alternative opportunities being what they are, can we say that as the market in A does under existing circumstances yield the net additional satisfaction corresponding to the mixtilinear area shewn by the curve of A, and the market in B the corresponding area shewn by the curve of B, the two areas added together will indicate the total additional satisfaction yielded by the two markets?

Manifestly not. Let A and B be tea and coffee. Now there are (or may be) services that can be rendered either by tea or coffee indifferently. If the rise in the price of tea, while making the consumer buy less tea, makes him buy more coffee, this is manifestly the case. The curve of A, therefore, shews the value not of the whole service which is actually rendered by the tea the man consumes, but that part of the services only which could not be rendered by coffee. And in like manner the curve of B represents that part of the services rendered by coffee which could not be rendered by tea. Thus, if we first take the advantage we derive from the tea market on the supposition that the coffee market is open as an alternative, and then the advantage we derive from the coffee market on the supposition that the tea market is open as an alternative, and then add the two together, we shall have arrived at something very different from the total advantage which the two markets together confer upon us; for

Impossibility of summing areas of surplus satisfaction.

that range of wants which can be indifferently satisfied by tea or by coffee will have evaded our estimate altogether. When we estimate tea it escapes and is transferred to coffee, and when we estimate coffee it escapes and is transferred to tea.

If we suppose the effect of the closing of the markets to be cumulative, then if we take tea first this common service will escape to coffee, changing the form of its curve and increasing the mixtilinear area for any given abscissa. If we then close the coffee market too, the value of the common service will be apprehended and registered under the head of coffee; whereas if we had taken coffee first it would have been the tea curve that would have been modified, and the common service would have been evaluated there; but in neither case would the sum of the areas shown by the original curves, drawn out severally on the basis of existing alternatives, give us any evaluation of the service that can be rendered indifferently by either of the commodities.

And again, the service which can be rendered by tea or coffee indifferently, but not by anything else, does not exhaust the whole service that they do now severally render. If when the tea and coffee markets are closed the cocoa market remains open, the alternatives still available may enable a considerable portion of the services now rendered by tea and coffee still to be performed. Perhaps, indeed, an important part of the services which they render is discharged by the hot water and not by the infusions or solutions it contains. So that we shall not capture the whole of the significance of the service actually rendered by tea till we have closed all access to hot water— nor then either, for the most important of all its services could be rendered by cold water.

But when commodities are complementary to each other, the several curves, instead of not counting certain values at all, will count them twice (or many times) over. To enjoy tea we require fuel and a kettle, and we value a teapot and cup, and the value we attach to tea depends upon our command of these things. Or there might be a man who found cream with his tea essential to high enjoyment. If such a man declared that he would go up to £1 for two ounces of tea sooner than give up his Christmas Day treat, the estimate might be made on the supposition that he could command an adequate supply of cream for a few pence. If he were asked about cream he might say that he would give £1 for a small jugful once a year sooner than give up his Christmas celebration, but that would be on the supposition that the tea would cost him a few pence. If we added the two estimates together we should have counted nearly all the enjoyment of tea-with-cream twice.

These sources of confusion have, as a matter of fact, puzzled many a student of marginal and total significance, and obscured many an exposition of them. For example, we are told that a man gets a loaf of bread for a few pence, for which he would give his whole fortune sooner than go without it. Nay, by a still deeper confusion we are told that the value of an initial supply of bread is "infinite." And it has been suggested that a wheat curve should stand at an infinite height at the origin—that is to say, should be what mathematicians call asymptotal to the axis of Y. This at once prompts the question, "How about water?" Should the curve of water be asymptotal to the axis of Y too? If it were so, we should have an extreme case of repeated counting of the same value; for a man dying of thirst would certainly not attach an "infinite" value to a crumb of bread. He would not give a drop of water for it. But of course the truth is that price cannot be "infinite." If a millionaire paid his whole fortune for the smallest crumb of bread he could see, the price would be high but not "infinite." Moreover, even if we substitute more accurate language for talk about "infinities," and say that if a man had plenty of water he would give all the rest of his possessions for a certain supply of bread, or if he had plenty of bread he would give them all for a certain supply of water, it remains true that if he is without either bread or water he can but offer all the fortune he has for both, and we cannot take the two previous suppositions as applicable concurrently.

Current confusions of thought on the subject.

Nor must we raise the initial value of bread by crediting it with relieving us from all the agony we should endure if we had water but nothing to eat, and credit water with relieving us from all the agony we should endure if we had bread to eat but nothing to drink, and then put down the

2 I

sum to their joint credit; for to be without both food and drink would not involve suffering equal to this sum.

The outcome of all this inquiry is a more enlightened perception that the importance to us of increased supplies of any one commodity depends not only on the degree to which we are supplied with that commodity, but also on the degree to which we are supplied with all other alternative or complementary commodities. And since our general state of vitality and sensitiveness may be regarded as complementary to every desired experience, we may venture on the generalisation that theoretically the marginal significance of any commodity depends primarily on our supply of that commodity, secondarily on our supply of the most obvious substitutes and complements, and remotely on our supply of all things, whether in the circle of exchange or not, which in any way affect our vitality.

Hitherto we have been trying to evaluate the loss of desired experiences which the closing of a market would involve to a given individual, on the supposition that he could still obtain the same total amounts of all other commodities that he would be able now to obtain, should he choose (from change of taste or convictions or for any other reason) entirely to give up purchasing the commodity in question. We may express this by saying that his total resources or income are to remain the same, but that this particular market is to be closed to him. We are neglecting the lowered marginal significance of other commodities which would follow his increased purchases.[1] Now let us suppose the reverse case, that while his income remains the same some new possibility is opened to him : bicycles or motor-cars are invented, or new fruits are imported, or opportunities of study or of hearing good music or of travel are organised, and he finds that by contracting his expenditure on other articles to the total amount of Ox (Fig. 17), and expending the sum thus saved on the freshly opened alternative represented on the figure, by the sacrifice of an area equivalent to yx he will gain the total area contained between the axes, the line xp, and the curve. This newly opened opportunity then will present

Loss and gain as markets are closed or opened.

[1] See page 477.

him with a total advantage of the mixtilinear area above yp for the expenditure of the same income. Whether this will be for his ultimate good or not is of course quite another question. We have seen ample reasons for declining to assume anything of the kind.[1] But at any rate he has now got something for which he would have been willing to sacrifice the whole mixtilinear area, and has only surrendered the area yx for it. Measured by his own immediate desires, then, there is the gain indicated.

But now let us suppose that a man's income increases

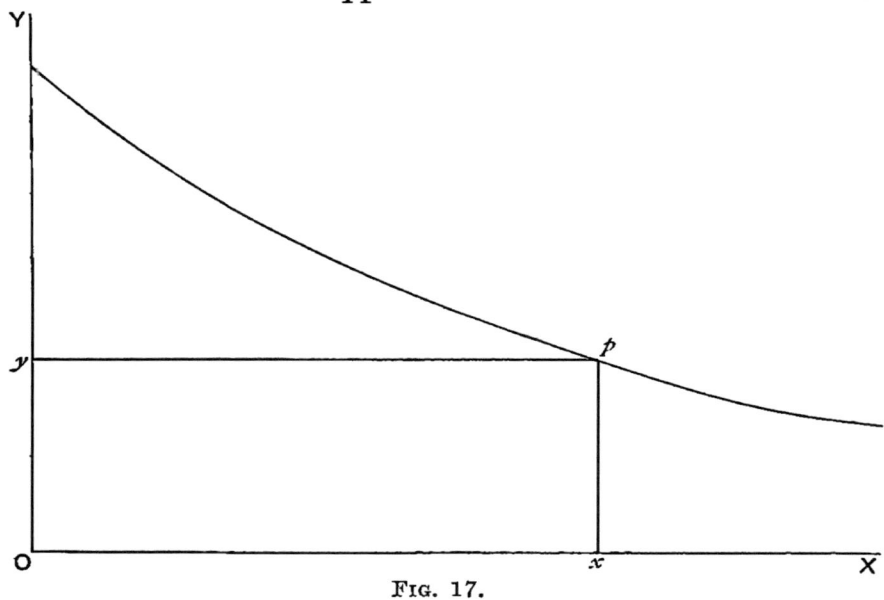

Fig. 17.

or diminishes. This will obviously affect the whole system of his scales of preference. Possibly "pop and cockles" may completely fall out of his list of purchases, and "champagne and oysters" may appear on it; but in an ordinary case (especially where the change is not so great as to declass the man), while some modes of expenditure will probably be dropped and some almost certainly introduced, a large number will be extended. He will perhaps increase the scale of his hospitalities, will pay more for houseroom, and so forth. That is to say, on a great

Effect of rise or fall of income.

[1] See pages 15 *sqq.* and 423 *sqq.*

number of individual commodities the amount of his purchases will increase, but he will pay for land, railway tickets, concerts, and provisions at the same rate as before, and, as before, will gratify his tastes to the point at which the *relative* marginal significance of the things he buys is the same to him as it is to his competitors in the market. But the price of things, though the same, will not represent the same sacrifice, for he is better supplied with all the things in the circle of exchange that the price represents. But as for those things that do not enter into the circle of exchange—irksome effort, for example, or the sacrifice of personal tastes or the thwarting of personal affection—he would not now incur the same sacrifice in these things to avoid a slight decrement or to secure a slight increment of any of the things in the circle of exchange that he would have done when his smaller income gave each of these latter a higher psychic significance to him at the margin.

For instance, if one of his children shews signs of ill-health, and by the expenditure of £100 a year he can place him under more favourable conditions, he may not hesitate to sacrifice the alternatives of things in the circle of exchange at the margins of his other expenditures which will be necessary; whereas when his income was narrower he could not have faced the acuter hardships and sacrifices which would have been involved in drawing back these margins. Thus his marginal estimates of the significance of things on which he still expends his money, relatively to other things in the circle of exchange, are the same as they were; but relatively to things not in the circle of exchange they have taken a lower place. Whatever his income he will always bring his expenditure into equilibrium with the market prices; that is to say, the marginal units of the things he buys will always occupy at the margin the same fixed place on the objective scale of things in the circle of exchange, but on the subjective scale they have advanced to a point of lower significance.

It would be useless to attempt to indicate this change diagrammatically, for, as we have seen, every curve is changed by a change in the supplies of other commodities as well as that to which it specially refers. If we were, therefore, to draw up a man's curve of a certain commodity on the supposition that he was poor, and then again on the supposition that he was rich, the only fixed point on which we could rely would be that if he continued to consume the commodity at all, he would consume it down to the same point of objective value as before, but that the objective unit would have a lower psychic significance. Whether he would consume more or less of the commodity, whether his surplus satisfaction would, measured in coin, be greater or smaller, and if greater in coin whether it would be greater psychologically or not, and what its proportional significance to his whole satisfaction would be, we should have no means of determining. The two curves, therefore, would have no significant relation to each other. All we can say is that if the man's expenditure is wise, he enjoys a larger total area of satisfaction as the marginal satisfaction which a shilling will command diminishes; but that it really is so would be a rash assumption.

There is still another source of confusion. We have been attempting to evaluate the surplus satisfaction, over and above the sacrifice involved in the payment, which a consumer actually derives, under existing circumstances, from his normal consumption of a given commodity, and to evaluate it in terms of the actual significance of pounds, shillings, and pence under the actual conditions of his resources and expenditure. *Possible confusions from inconsistent hypotheses as to causes of contracted supply.* Our questions as to what he would give for such and such an increment at such and such a margin, or how much he would buy altogether at such and such a price, have merely been a device for discovering the actual value in use that things have for him; and he will not give us the answers we require unless he treats the hypothesis of an increased price as purely ideal and applying to himself alone. For as soon as he begins to think of any actual circumstances under which the price would rise, it will involve the supposition that causes are at work which affect not only him, but others also. And if he imagines that the supply of tea, for instance, is contracted, and that is why he has to pay a higher price for it, he may assume that other people are in the same position as himself; and if that is so, then obviously the general demand for substitutes such as coffee and cocoa will rise, and the prices will rise correspondingly, and the condition "other things remaining the same" will be violated, for he will not be able to purchase the substitutes at the prices for which he can now obtain them. If he is a commercial man he may instinctively take this into account, and give us estimates of what he would do under given conditions, modified by an instinctive sense of what others would be doing under pressure of the causes which had brought these circumstances about. And even the non-commercial student, as he imagines himself retreating towards the origin in his consumption of some particular commodity, often frames half unconsciously some hypothesis to account for the fact, which reacts upon his suppositions as to the supply of other commodities.

Thus when we imagine a curve that rises rapidly as we recede from the actual rate of supply towards the origin we may very generally detect ourselves arbitrarily and tacitly assuming both a gradual (or sudden) exclusion of all natural substitutes and a continued command not only of the strictly complementary commodities but of all the other things necessary to continued life and sensitiveness. That is to say, we begin by considering how much we give for a loaf of bread, all our other supplies and open alternatives being what they are, and consider what inconvenience we should actually suffer if we happened to be "short of bread" one day; but when our imagination travels back towards the origin we not only cut down our supply of bread, but silently cut ourselves off from increased supplies of potatoes, etc., until at last we find ourselves in a besieged city—but always with a good supply of water. And during this process the significance of money has itself indefinitely changed. Money, as we have seen, represents open alternatives. And in a besieged city a shilling represents less and less of the common objects of desire. Many things it cannot get at all. Of many other things it can get very little. The only things of which it may possibly be able to get more than before are such as have little relevancy to our distressed condition and narrowed opportunities—jewels and works of art, for instance. So the value of the unit in which we estimate our rising want as we approach the origin is itself declining, owing to the changed conditions that affect the whole society in which we live.

Thus an attempt to trace an individual curve back towards the origin is legitimate, and its results are interesting, suggestive, and enlightening, in proportion as the condition "other things remaining the same" is observed. But as in the case of any great and essential article or group of articles of consumption we can scarcely imagine the origin to be approached owing to an actual rise in the price while other things remain equal, such curves must depend for their construction on imaginative estimates of the value we ourselves should under present conditions attach to small increments of the commodity at given margins; not on attempts to reconstruct conditions that might really raise the market price to a high figure.

It may well be asked whether a method that needs so much guarding and explaining is worth adopting at all. The answer is that the principle of declining marginal significances is absolutely fundamental. The doctrine of surplus value in the thing bought over and above the value of the price paid, is an inevitable deduction from it. The awakened mind must, and as a matter of fact does, speculate upon it. It underlay the old distinction between value in use and value in exchange. It underlies modern discussions of the significance of a more even distribution of wealth. It is intimately connected with the relation of Economics to life. A want of a clear understanding of it brings perpetual confusion into our speculations and entangles the student in perplexities and contradictions. And it is therefore of the very first importance that we should try to find out exactly what it is and how far it takes us. *[margin: Essential significance and value of curves of total satisfaction.]*

Moreover, though we cannot assume a system of curves of total significance to co-exist and to retain its general validity while modifications take place in one or more of the supplies, yet we may assume that, in spite of all the modifications which are perpetually taking place, all the curves of commodities, some supply of which is still enjoyed, continue to be such that in the neighbourhood of the actual supply an advance would mean an increased, and a retreat a diminished, marginal significance. That is to say, at and about the point of the actual supply, the curve, however fluid we may consider its form, will always preserve the property of declining as we recede from the origin.

What we have regarded as a source of disturbance and confusion in our attempts to construct individual psychic curves would become an essential element for consideration in the construction of a curve representing the collective or communal scale spoken of in Book I. (pages 142 *sqq.*). That scale, as we saw, is purely objective, and is not susceptible of any consistent psychic interpretation, though it ultimately rests on psychic phenomena. If we take any given commodity, and ask not how much any individual would take of it at a given price, other things being equal, but how much the community would take, other things being equal, the term "other things being equal" has essentially changed its significance. When dealing with the individual, "other things being equal" would mean that all the substitutes were to be had at their present prices. When we are dealing with the community we cannot mean any such thing. For obviously if the price of any one commodity were seriously changed, the consumption of substitutes or complementary commodities would also be changed, and if this were done on the large scale it must alter their prices also. By "other things remaining equal" then, we must now mean "no changes taking place in the conditions on which other commodities may be obtained, except such as are directly involved in the reactions of the supposed change of price in the commodity under direct consideration." Those changes themselves must necessarily be considered, and the estimates as to how much the public will take of any given commodity at such and such prices must be based on the consideration of the actual effect which the price would have on the general expenditure of the public, at the prices which that general expenditure would determine, if no independent causes changed the supply of other commodities. Dealers might be able to form a fairly accurate estimate of the course the curve would take in the near neighbourhood of actual experience, but might have no means of forming a close estimate at points near the origin, for example, or near the point of intersection with the abscissa.[1]

Communal curves of price-and-quantity-purchased.

In such a communal curve of a single commodity, the mixtilinear area above the rectangle of price paid would have

[1] Cf. further pages 521 *sq.*

no consistent psychic significance. It would be made up of satisfactions corresponding alike to the halfpence of Cobbett and those of the millionaire. The figure would merely represent the objective fact that persons could be found who, under existing circumstances, would pay for so much of the commodity at the rates represented by the successive ordinates; and, therefore, the area in question would represent satisfactions for each of which some one would pay the money unit sooner than go without it, but they would have no psychic parity or equality at all. They are not susceptible of psychic interpretation,

If we compare a communal curve with an individual one, the former certainly appears to have a firmer and more defined significance, for it represents the tangible fact that so much of the commodity would be bought at such a price. But it will be noted that this objective fact is merely the resultant of the play of innumerable psychic forces which take causal precedence of it. It is a perfect illustration of the Aristotelian distinction between that which is first relatively to the observer, and that which is first in the order of nature. The observer of the market who has little concern with psychology finds the phenomena of the market directly accessible; and, if he works back towards the psychic phenomena at all, he does so from the basis of the objective facts. But the apparent firmness of these objective facts really rests on what has perhaps appeared to us the quagmire of the psychic data which are first in the causal order of nature. though they rest on a psychic basis.

Finally, we have to note that with the collective, as with the individual curves, it is impossible to construct a system the members of which shall be simultaneously valid; for any change in the selection between the alternative points presented by the form of any one curve reacts upon the forms of all the others. If we start with the existing state of things, we might trace a curve for any one commodity, shewing the prices which would result from a reduction of the supply by one-tenth, two-tenths, etc., on the supposition that the supply of all other commodities remained what it is; and then, returning to the supposition of a normal supply of the first commodity, we Like individual curves they mutually cancel each other.

might trace a curve with respect to a second, and so forth. But the members of the system thus created would each start from the basis of the present state of things and on the supposition that no change took place in the supply of any commodity but the one under direct treatment. The conditions, therefore, on which they are constructed would mutually cancel each other, and only one could be regarded as valid at a time.

APPENDIX TO CHAPTERS II. AND III.

We have generally assumed that the same curve may represent, with a sufficient approximation to accuracy, both the total excess of satisfaction over payment for a given amount purchased, and also the system of relations between prices and the quantities that would be purchased. But this assumption will not always be justified.

If a man's income rises or falls, he does not increase or diminish his expenditure upon every article of consumption.[1] The consumption of bread *per capita* is likely to be larger, not only relatively but absolutely, in a poor man's household than in a rich one's. Thus a marked diminution in a man's effective income may actually increase his purchases of bread. Now if such a practical diminution is caused by a rise in the prices of articles other than bread, there is nothing surprising in an increased consumption of bread resulting from it. But it may be that it is a rise in the price of bread itself which contracts the man's general resources, and we may then have an apparently anomalous result, for in that case a rise in the price of bread may make him buy more of it; and within certain limits he may therefore take more bread when the price is higher than when it is lower.

This, however, does not affect the principle of declining marginal significance. It still remains true that if the man were deprived of half his stock of bread he would suffer more than twice as much as if he only forfeited a quarter of it.

[1] Cf. page 483.

APPENDIX TO CHAPTERS II. AND III.

On the principles finally formulated on page 461, we may construct the curve of marginal significances, shewing the surplus of satisfaction over payment for any given quantity purchased at a given price. But this curve, so far from representing with approximate accuracy the curve of price-and-quantity-purchased, will be of a wholly different character from it. The latter curve will, at this point, be sloping upwards as we recede from the origin. Within certain limits the higher the price the more the quantity purchased; but this will not be because the price is higher, but because the man is poorer. This example is an emphatic warning that no curves which depend for their validity upon the condition "other things remaining equal" can be fruitfully applied to any hypothesis that covers more than a small fraction of the whole area of a man's vital experiences.

Before leaving this illustration we may note that if the rise in the price of bread is caused by a defective harvest, then, the total amount of wheat being reduced, and the consumption of a certain class of the community being increased, it is obvious that there must be a diminution of consumption in other classes of the community sufficient to cover both the deficiency in the crop and the extra consumption; and that means that the poor would outbid the rich for bread to a certain point, as they already completely outbid them for tripe.

If it is true that for a large proportion of the community the curve of price-and-quantity-consumed really has this rising slope in the neighbourhood of the actual supply, it seems possible that the poor may be forced deeper into this disastrous necessity of outbidding the rich as an incidental consequence of "corners" in the wheat-market manœuvred for financial purposes.

There is another case in which portions of a curve of marginal significance will entirely fail to coincide with the curve of price-and-quantity-purchased. We have seen that some curves of marginal significance rise in the region near the origin. Fig. 18 represents such a case. For any price, Oy, the figure suggests that there are two possibilities of purchase, Ox_1 and Ox_2. But a moment's reflection will shew that the earlier portion of the curve cannot be interpreted in this way. To buy Ox_1 would be to sacrifice yx_1 and only to gain Ozp_1x_1. The curve, therefore, only begins to be a curve

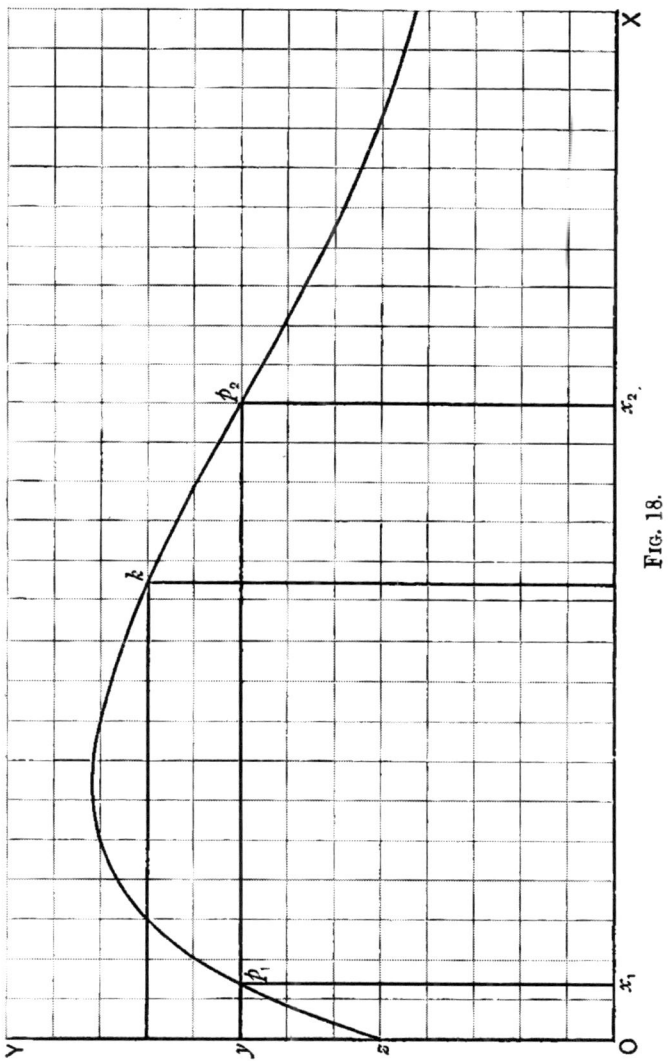

Fig. 18.

of price-and-quantity-purchased after the point k, at which the total area of the price would equal the total significance of the commodity.

CHAPTER IV

BUYER AND SELLER. DEMAND AND SUPPLY

SUMMARY.—*This chapter deals with the application of the diagrammatic method of curves to the phenomena of the market. Individual curves of price-and-quantity-taken, if properly constructed for the purpose, can be added into a communal curve, on which the price corresponding to any given supply can be read. A disguised method of reaching the same result by means of intersecting curves is frequently employed, but though legitimate in itself it is misleading when used, as it generally is, in conjunction with a distinction between buyers and sellers, which is irrelevant to the issue. The same principle that determines the flow of any given commodity to the various consumers also determines the flow of the factors of production to the different industries. Capacity for productive effort is distributed between economic and non-economic employments, or is reserved and not put forth at all, on the general principles of the distribution of resources or choice between alternatives.*

We have seen that the curves of the total significance of different commodities to the same individual cannot be added together, though a joint curve of two or more commodities can be constructed independently. When we pass to the consideration of the summation of curves of different individuals referring to the same commodity, we see at once that so far as we interpret them psychologically there can be no sense in speaking of addition at all, for there is no common psychological unit. But so far as we interpret them as curves of quantity-taken-at-the-price, there seems no reason why they should not be added. If we know the quantity that each individual would take at a given price, we know the quantity that they would take amongst them, and if we know the total supply of the article, we can find the price by determining to what point of relative marginal significance that supply will satisfy all the individuals concurrently.

But here a difficulty presents itself. If the price rises because the supply is reduced, the amount that A will take at this higher price is affected by the terms on which he can get all the available substitutes; but if B is having his stock reduced at the same time as A he will probably run to the same substitutes, and since this will raise their market value A will find that the conditions under which he made his estimates have been violated. We asked him how much he would take at such a price, "all other things remaining equal," and we constructed his curve from his replies; but now we find that (in the normal case) as the price rises all other things do not remain equal, for the price of substitutes rises also; and the modifications which this will introduce into A's estimate of the relative significance (expressed in the objective unit) of the commodity at any given margin cannot be determined simply by analysing his present sense of values, for the terms on which the alternatives will be offered to him will be changed to an extent which he cannot determine and which does not depend on his own estimates of different satisfactions.

Addition of individual curves of quantity-and-price.

It is the dealer's business to forecast the effect which a change in the supply will produce upon the price of the commodity when all these reactions have had their full effect, but he will not individualise the different demands. He will estimate the nature of the sum of all the individual curves, but he will think of it (or at any rate estimate it) as a single thing, not as arrived at by the addition of a number of individual demands. Thus, neither the mind of the dealer nor the minds of the individual consumers contain material out of which we could construct a number of personal curves of price-and-quantity-consumed, which could be added together into a total curve. The dealer's mind contains the material for the (speculative) construction of such a total curve, but not for the construction of the elements out of which it is composed; and the minds of the individual consumers contain the material out of which the first approximation to the individual curves might be made, but not the material for estimating the modifications which will be produced in those individual curves by the reaction of the changing prices of substitutes, which the dealer estimates in the mass.[1]

Nevertheless, it remains true that these effects, which are only estimated by the dealer in the mass, are actually composed of the sum of the effects on individual demands, and we may therefore conceive ideally of a series of individual curves of price-and-quantity-demanded, in which these reactions have been discounted, and which can therefore be added together.

They will represent for each individual the prices which he would give for each successive increment sooner than go without it, under the modified possibilities as to substitutes which would accompany the contracted supply which caused the rise in price; and the sum of them will constitute a collective scale shewing at what price any given quantity of the commodity could be sold, or what quantity could be sold at any given price, all other supplies remaining constant, though the demand upon those other supplies varies.

In Fig. 19 let (a), (b), (c), etc., represent the curves of one commodity for the individuals A, B, C, etc. On the axis of X the commodity itself is measured in its proper conventional unit, and on the axis of Y the corresponding price or marginal significance is marked. Now take (d) equal to the sum of (a), (b), and (c) read laterally. That is to say, for any ordinate of determined length Oy the abscissa on (d) is to equal the sum of the abscissas on (a), (b), and (c).

Supposing A, B, and C to represent all the potential consumers of the commodity, this would mean that (d) represents its collective or communal scale of significance. If we have the three curves and know the total amount of the commodity at command, we can construct the collective curve (d), measure off the total supply on its abscissa, as Ox, and find the corresponding ordinate Oy. This will be the point

[1] Cf. pages 485 sq.

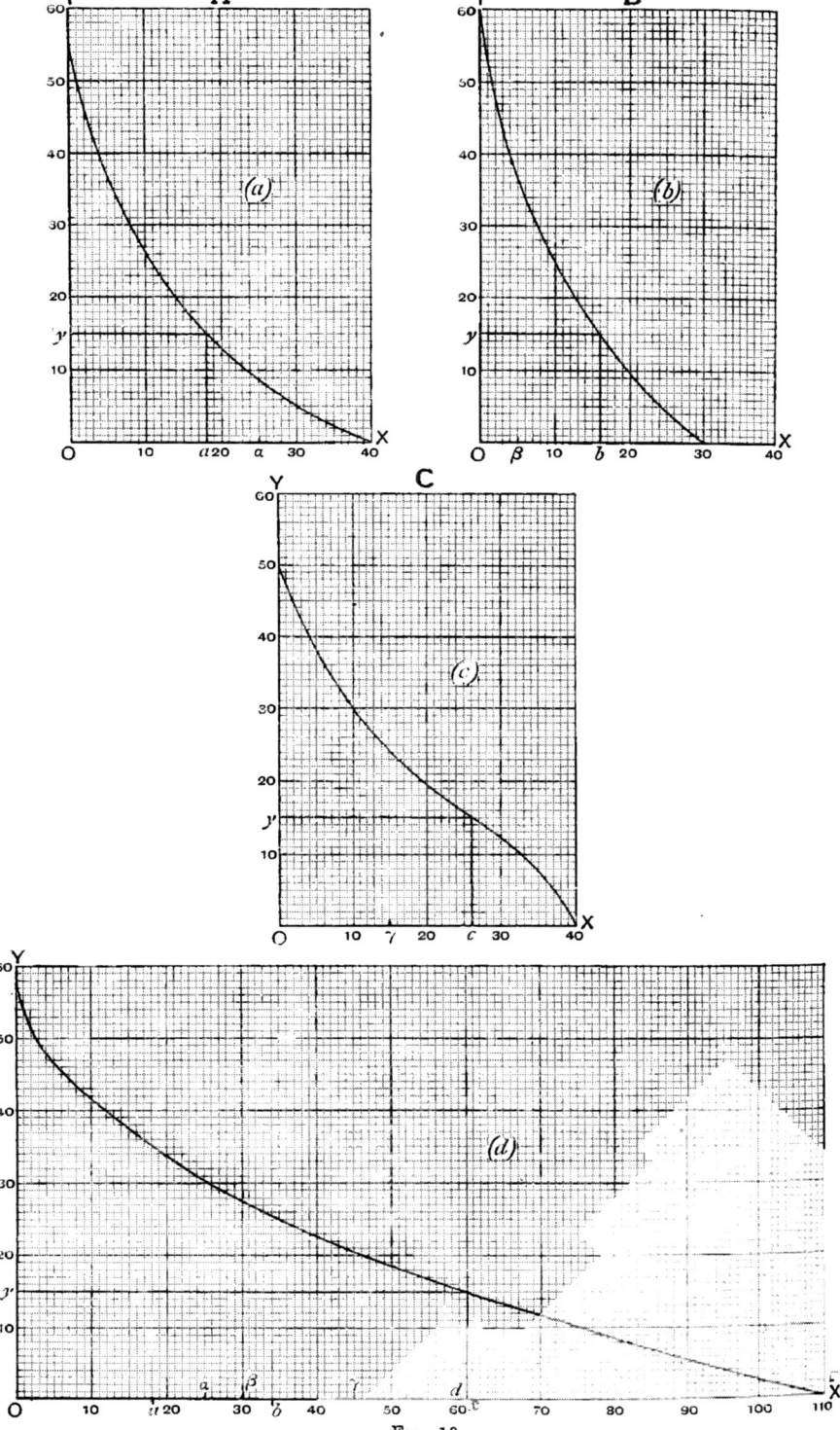

Fig. 19.

CH. IV   BUYER AND SELLER.   DEMAND AND SUPPLY   497

of relative significance down to which all the claimants will be satisfied; and we can measure off the several abscissas on (a), (b), and (c) that it will determine. They will shew the amounts of the commodity that A, B, and C will respectively take out of the market. The communal curve will be represented by (d), on which equal areas, though they represent satisfactions that correspond to the same objective unit, have not the same psychological significance.

This addition of curves is given primarily as a graphic device for finding that point on the ordinates of the curves which will make the corresponding abscissas amount, in their sum, to the total supply. This distribution is actually determined by the play of the demands represented by the several curves. If the supply were distributed in any other way, there would be no equilibrium, and the conditions of further exchange would exist. But we have seen that the collective curve directly represents the facts of the market in the form in which the sellers actually endeavour to estimate them. They have more knowledge by experience of the collective scale than they have of the individual scales, and each purchaser may find a price ruling in the market which has been arrived at by a direct attempt on the part of the sellers to construct a portion of this collective scale, without reference to the elements out of which it is composed; and the purchaser will then regulate his purchases in accordance with this price. Thus the graphic process of determining the price by finding the ordinate on the collective scale that corresponds to the total supply, and then determining the share that falls to each individual by ascertaining the abscissas that correspond to the ordinates on the individual curves, closely corresponds to the facts of the market.[1]

We may now, therefore, pursue our investigations into the constitution of the market by aid of this system of diagrams. Our figures, so far, have given no indication of the amounts of the commodity (if any) which the individuals concerned possessed before the market opened. And we shall find that no suppositions we can make as to this will affect the result so long as the curves and the total quantity of the supply are supposed to remain the same. If neither A,

[1] Cf. pages 218 *sqq.*

B, nor C possesses any of the commodity when he comes into the market, and the whole of the supply Ox (d) is brought in by sellers who have no reserve price, A will be the purchaser of Oa, B of Ob, etc. If each of the individuals A, B, etc., already possessed the exact amount that we have arrived at as his ultimate portion, no business would be done at all, and the "price" would be virtual, not actual. But now let us suppose A, B, etc., to possess respectively the amounts Oa, $O\beta$, $O\gamma$, (Oa, $a\beta$, $\beta\gamma$, on (d)). And let us further suppose that an amount γd, bringing the total to Od (which we will call Ox), is thrown upon the market without reserve. The total Ox remaining unchanged, and the curves remaining the same, the final distribution will also be the same, but A will have sold aa, B will have bought βb, C will have bought γc, and the sellers who are not potential buyers on any terms will have sold γd.

Thus the initial distribution of the stock affects the amount of business done and the movements that bring about equilibrium; but it does not affect the price or the ultimate distribution, which depend solely on the total amount of stock and the curves of the individuals. If we know what the stock is we know where the ideal equilibrium will be, and if we also know how the stock is distributed we know the extent of the disturbance of equilibrium from which we start; but this latter piece of information does not affect the point of equilibrium itself.

The facts of the market, however, are very generally presented in a disguised form, determined by considerations *Intersection* irrelevant to the result, and fostering what I take *of curves a* to be a mistaken conception of the whole matter. *disguised form of* If we had a number of curves to deal with, we *addition.* might suppose them to be divided (on any or no principle) into two groups, and then reduced by addition to two collective curves. We should then be able to escape the cumbrous process of addition as far as these two curves were concerned, and arrive at the resultant price by the graphically simpler method of intersection. In this case too, of course, it would be necessary to know the total amount of the commodity in the market, and unnecessary to know its initial distribution. Thus in Fig. 20 let us add together in (d) all

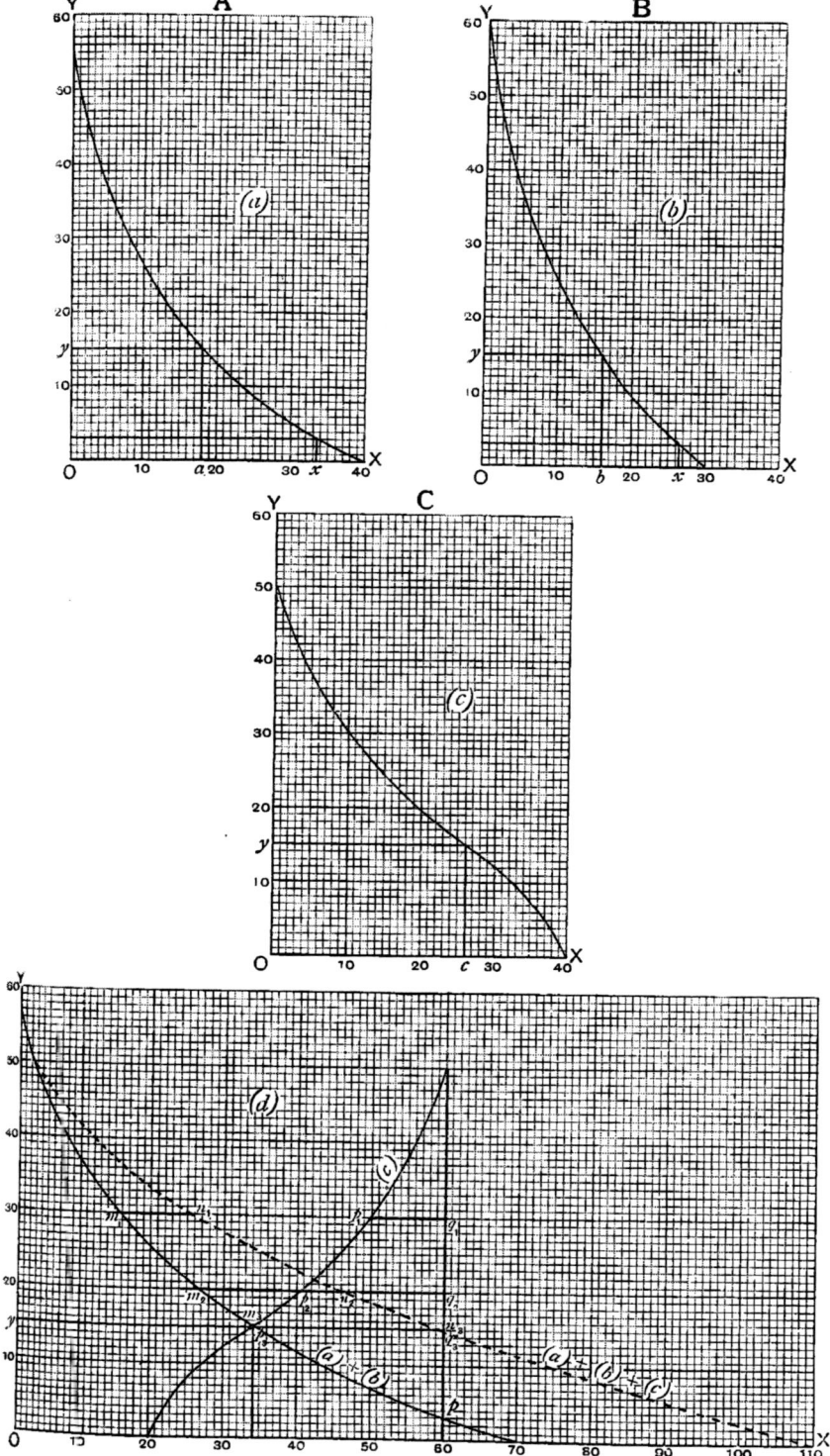

Fig. 20.

the constituent curves except (c), and instead of adding (c) as before, let us measure Ox (the total amount of the stock) along the axis of X, and taking the point x as the origin of the curve (c) let us reverse that curve. The point of intersection will have the same ordinate which we obtained by addition in Fig. 19. This is easily seen from a study of the dotted line, which is constructed, as before, by adding all the curves together. Thus every mn will equal the corresponding pq. In the figure, $p_3 q_3$ and $m_3 n_3$ coincide. Therefore (Ox being the whole amount of the commodity, and the dotted line being the collective curve) xn_3 is the price that was determined by our former method (Fig. 19). And it coincides with the height of the point of intersection of the sum of $(a) + (b)$ with the reversed (c). Every point on every curve has been taken into equal account in obtaining this result; and it does not matter which curve or curves have been reversed. It is the height of each point that affects the result, not the question whether it has been registered and combined with the others in a curve rising towards the left or one rising towards the right.

What we have now got is an ordinate such that the portions of all the curves which are above it have abscissas that collectively make up the length Ox, representing the total amount of the commodity.

But this method of intersection can only be applied once. It cannot be applied cumulatively, for it confuses the record while registering the result. Thus if we add (a) and (b), and suppose the stock still to be the same, we arrive at xp as the price which would rule between A and B if C were not in the market; and having C's curve we can then arrive at the modification in the price effected by C's entrance into the market either by the method of addition or that of intersection. But suppose we had originally treated (a) and (b) by the method of intersection. We should have arrived at the same result as far as they are concerned (Fig. 21), but we should not now be able to combine it with the data of (c). Thus it will be seen that the method of addition is the only fundamental one. Intersection is a disguised form of addition, and this very disguise obliterates the record. We shall see the importance of this more clearly as we proceed.

CH. IV   BUYER AND SELLER.   DEMAND AND SUPPLY   501

The methods of addition and intersection may both be applied in cases where our data are less complete than we have hitherto supposed; for the process of addition may be regarded as beginning at any point of the collective curve which we like to select. Thus, if we knew, for instance, not how much of the commodity A, B, C, etc., possess collectively, but how much more (or less) than would satisfy them down to the urgency represented, say, by 20, and if we knew the course of the curves in the neighbourhood of the 20 point in each case, we

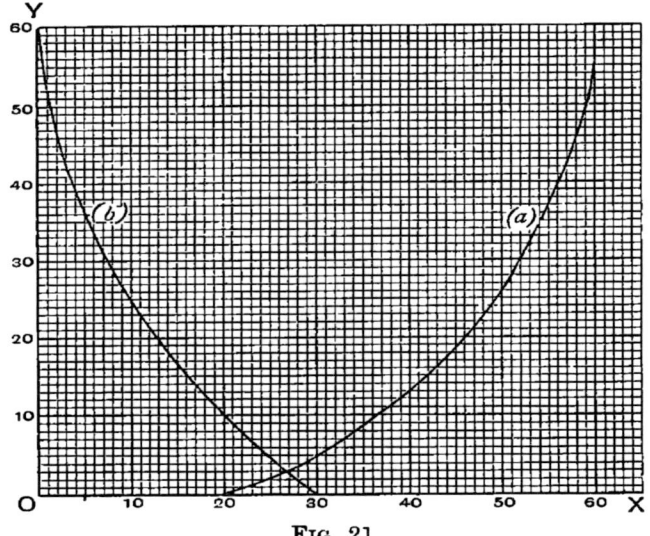

FIG. 21.

should have all the material necessary for determining the equilibrating price that would satisfy all the consumers, and the ultimate distribution of the aforesaid excess amongst them; but we should not know how distant that point might be from the origin either of the collective or of the individual curves.

We shall enter upon the detailed examination of a case of this kind presently, and it will be seen that it is a perfectly natural one. Our present business is to illustrate it diagrammatically. We are not supposed to have complete knowledge of the curves. We do not know where they start or how they arrive (Fig. 22) at the points in (*a*), (*b*), and (*c*), which

Addition and intersection of uncompleted curves.

bring A, B, and C respectively to the margins at which the commodity has a value of 20 for them; nor do we know the total amount of the commodity; but we know how much of it is left when the 20 points in (*a*), (*b*), (*c*) have been reached, and we know the course of the curves for some space about these points. Assuming data consistent with those of Figs. 19, etc., let us say that the supply is 14 in excess of that required to bring all the margins to 20. We simply have to add the curves as before, beginning at this point, and we shall

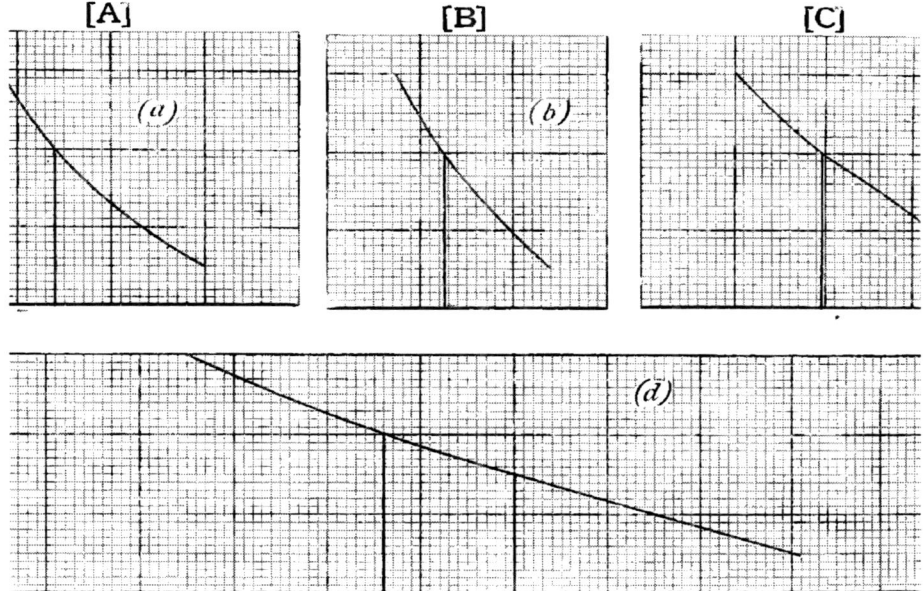

FIG. 22.

obtain a portion of the identical curve (*d*) which we had in Figs. 19 and 20, only we shall not know how far off the origin is. We measure off the length 14 from this point, and obtain, as before, 15 as the price. If we preferred the method of intersection we could first add (*a*) and (*b*), and then reverse (*c*), making the space between the highest point of (*a*) + (*b*) and the highest point of (*c*) equal to 14; so that wherever the curves intersect we shall have the collective abscissas of all the curves taken together, above the height of the point of intersection, subtending abscissas to the amount of the stock (Fig. 23).

It would be a great mistake to suppose that in such a case the portions of the curve and the stock about which we have no information are without influence upon the result. It is because the total amount of stock is what it is and because the curves are what they are that the whole amount of the stock, minus fourteen, is capable of satisfying all the demands down to the ordinate 20. There might, of course, be other combinations of data which would yield the same result, but that would be a coincidence. At any rate the result from which we start is determined by definite data, and our final result is as much determined by those data, of which we only possess the registered results, as by those which are represented by the fragments of the curves and the surplus of the supply which are given us in detail. What

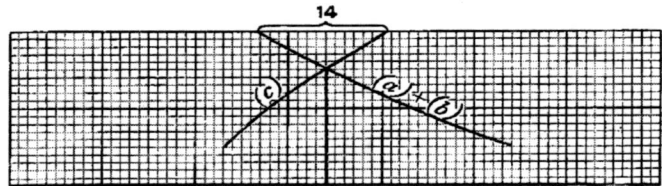

Fig. 23.

ultimately determines the price, then, is the whole amount of the commodity and the character of the individual curves.

We may suppose our information to be given in yet another form. Suppose a whole body of curves (no longer the same body we have represented in Figs. 19, etc.) has been reduced to two (Fig. 24), and we have one of these collective curves given us from the origin onwards (a). Concerning the other we are told that the total amount of stock (unspecified), if distributed exclusively amongst the consumers represented by this second curve, would satisfy them to the point with the ordinate 4. The course of this curve upward from the point in question towards the origin is given us for a certain distance (b), but we do not know how far off the origin is. We measure 4 on the ordinate of (c) at the origin, and then reverse (b). The point of intersection will give us the price 17. But this again is only a disguised addition of the partial character that we have just

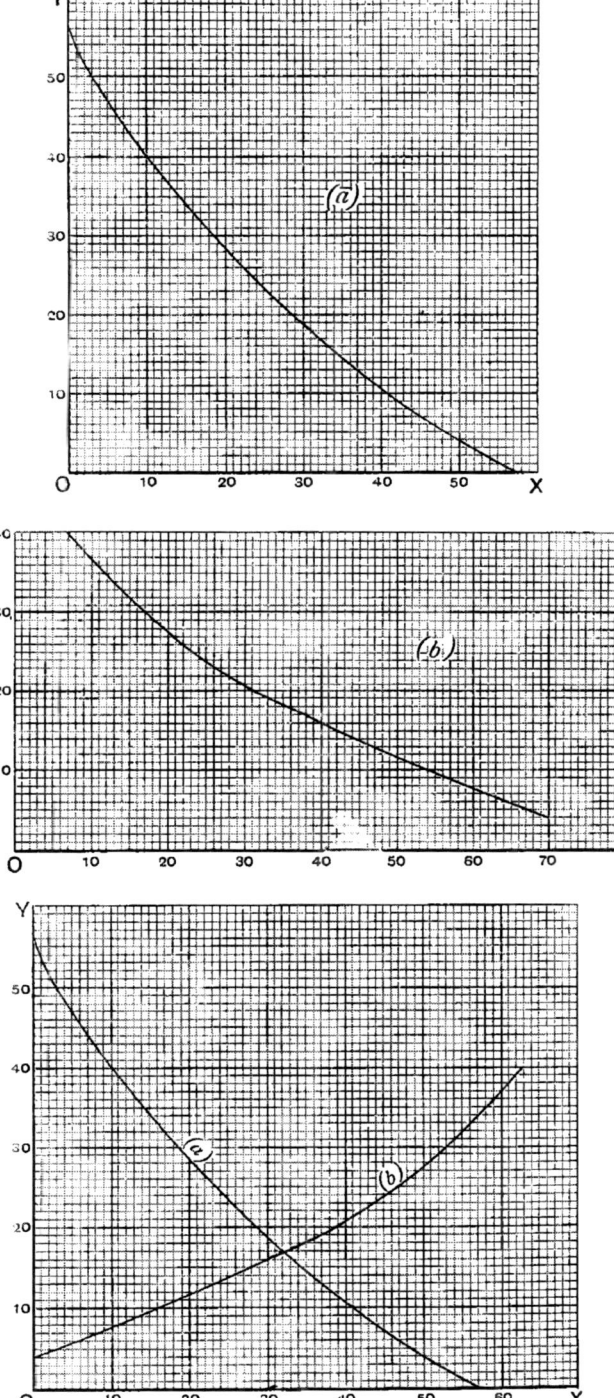

Fig. 24.

examined. We do not know what the quantity of the commodity is, but we know how much it is in excess of any ordinate on curve (b) which we choose to select, within the limits of our information. Thus we know that it is 63 in excess of the amount required to bring the ordinate of (b) to 40, 39 in excess of that required to bring it to 20, and so forth. The reversed curve (b), therefore, will secure that every point is at such a distance from the origin, or highest point of curve (a), as to comply with the conditions specified in connection with Fig. 23; and the data of the latter figure can be reduced to the form presented in the other with perfect

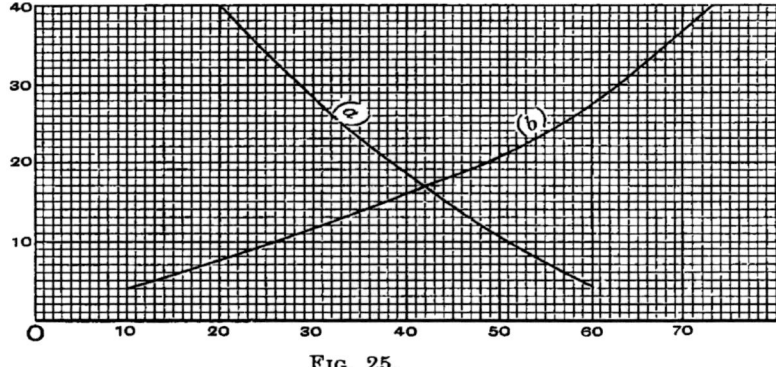

Fig. 25.

ease. The total amount of the commodity required to bring the ordinate of group (b) from 40 to 4 is 63. We know from curve (a) that 10 would be required to bring group (a) to the same point. Starting then at the points of the two curves with ordinate 40 we have $63 - 10$ ($=53$) as the surplus of the supply; and we can present the two curves from the points of ordinate 40 onwards, with a space of 53 between these two points, and obtain (Fig. 25) the price by intersection precisely as in Fig. 23. But here, as before, the real process is one of addition. We could of course have started at any other point of (b) lower than 40, and the corresponding point of (a), with the same result. In fact our Fig. 25 includes all such alternatives in itself.

We can now understand the exact meaning of the confirmed habit of presenting the phenomena of the market under the form of a curve of "supply" and a curve of "demand."

the intersection of which determines the price. It is based in the first place on a division (irrelevant as we have seen) between those persons in the market who have, and those who have not, a certain stock of the commodity in question. The curve of the latter is given in its completeness, or, at any rate, the origin is marked and the portion of the curve which is sketched is made to begin at a defined distance from the origin. This is called the curve of demand. The other curve in then inserted as a reversed curve, and a definite ordinate is assumed either for the point at the origin or for a point at a defined distance from the origin; and this is called the supply curve. Now this curve is a curve of reserve prices, which, as we have seen,[1] is merely another name for the demand curve of those who possess a stock of the commodity; and its reversal is merely a quick way of arriving at the results of addition. But in connection with it information is tacitly given us as to the surplus of the total stock over the amount required in order to gratify the whole market down to some given ordinate. The connection between these two pieces of information is arbitrary; for the vital information as to excess of supply over that required to bring the ordinates to a certain point, might just as well have been given us in connection with the other (so-called "demand") curve, or partly in connection with one and partly in connection with the other, or without any specified connection with either of them. Thus, if we had not had the two curves given us at all, but only the whole collective curve, without distinction between possessor and non-possessor, and had also been told that the stock was enough to satisfy all claims down to the ordinate of 40 with a surplus of 53, we should have obtained exactly the same result. And if we suppose curve (a) and curve (b) alike to be miscellaneous groups, both of them made up of some persons who possess and some who do not possess supplies of the commodity, we shall still have precisely the same results.

Marginal notes: Intersecting curves of supply and demand, and their illusory character.

But the distinctions which are irrelevant to the determination of the market price and of the quantities ultimately possessed by the individuals constituting the market do affect,

[1] Pages 229 *sqq.*

as we have seen,[1] the specific steps by which the price is discovered and the equilibrium reached. It is in the failure to distinguish between the methods by which that price is *discovered*, and the ultimate facts by which it is *determined*, that the current analysis of the market appears to me to fail. Though the division between buyers and sellers is not absolute (for we have seen[2] that a man may be a buyer or a seller according to circumstances in the same market, and that the buyer may be a possessor of stock also), yet it is undoubtedly the "higgling" of buyer and seller that discovers the actual price. Hence the seductive character of the current representation, and the insidious character of its concealment of the ultimate nature of the market and market prices.

We will now proceed to the examination in detail of examples of the way in which relevant and irrelevant facts are usually confounded in the analysis of markets and market prices.

In his book on *The Economics of Distribution*[3] (pages 11 *sqq*.) Mr. Hobson supposes that in a horse-market there are eight "sellers" (of horses of uniform quality) who have reserve prices running from £10 to £26, and ten "buyers" willing to give prices running from £15 to £30. The details may be thrown into the form of Fig. 26. The figure is necessarily defective, for if H will sell at £26 and P will buy at £26, this involves a difference in the place of a horse upon the scales of preference of H and P, but Mr. Hobson does not tell us how great the difference is. It may be less than a farthing; that is to say, it may be that H would not sell at a farthing less than £26, and P would not buy at a farthing more. But that H would sell at £26 shews that he prefers £26 to the horse, though by never so little; and that P would buy at £26 shews that he prefers the horse to £26. A horse, then, stands on H's scale at a little below £26, and on P's at a little above. This is not shewn on our figure; but neither is it necessary for the purposes of our investigation.

Mr. Hobson's horse fair.

Mr. Hobson proceeds to argue that if a price of anything above £21 : 10s. were set there would be more sellers than

[1] Page 498.
[2] Pages 233 *sqq*.
[3] Macmillan, 1900.

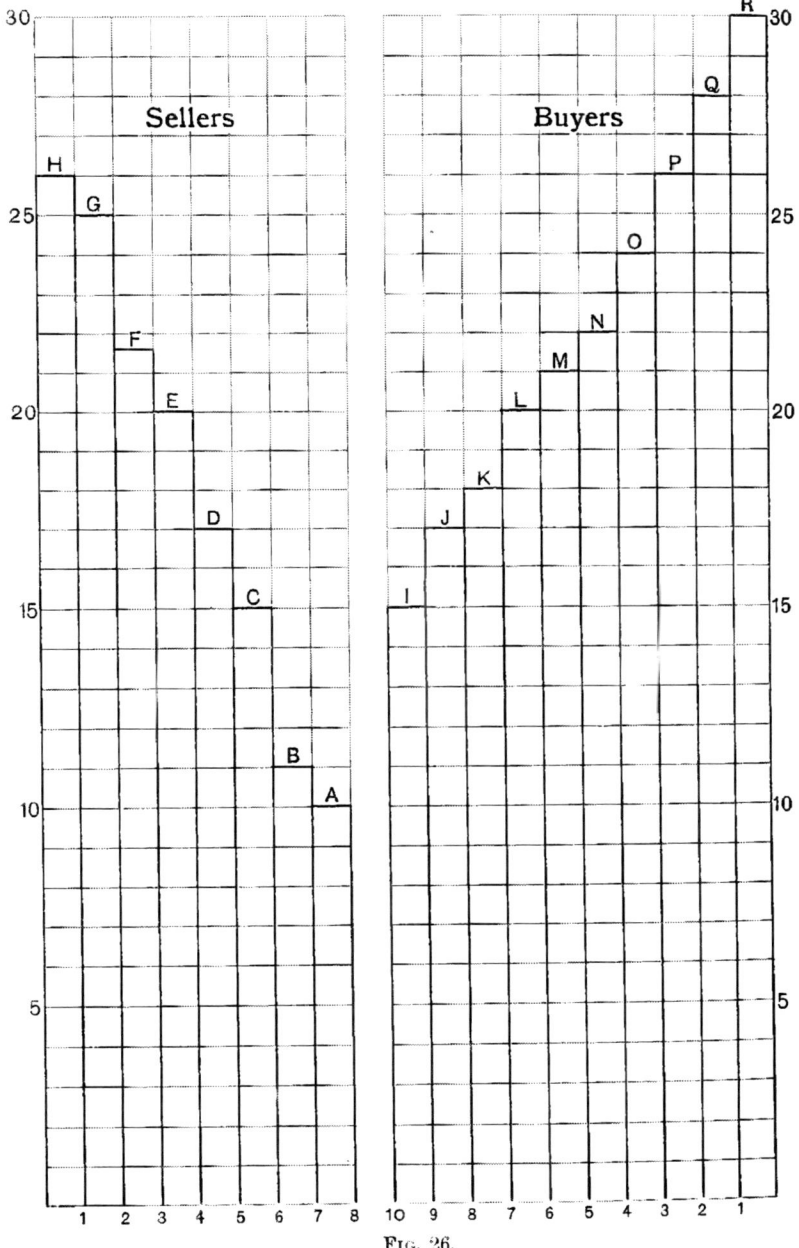

Fig. 26.

buyers, and if anything under £21 were set there would be more buyers than sellers, so that the price would settle somewhere between £21 and £21 : 10s. Anywhere within this range there would be an equal number of buyers and sellers.

This is all perfectly true, and it corresponds to our elaborate exposition of the market as a machinery for discovering the ideal equilibrating price.[1] But if it is given as a statement of the data which determine that price it is quite needlessly complicated and gives us a number of irrelevant facts. If we know nothing at all as to who possess the horses but know the position a horse occupies on the relative scale of each of the persons concerned, we shall have, on Figure 27, a statement of what prices would rule for any supply of horses from one to eighteen, and shall see that for eight horses it might be anything from £21 to £21 : 10s.

The relevant facts for determining the price, in the case supposed by Mr. Hobson, are found to be that there are eight horses altogether, and that the places that a horse occupies on the scales alike of A–H and I–R are as stated, and as represented in the diagram. The irrelevant facts are that the eight horses are at present in the possession of A–H, and that I–R are all without horses. When I say that the possession or non-possession of a horse is irrelevant, I mean that it is irrelevant if we know the position of a horse on the scale of preferences of each of the persons concerned. The possession or non-possession of a horse may no doubt affect that position, but so may the man's health, or the health of his wife, or his age, or the fact that his wife has recently read Mrs. Hayes's *Horsewoman*, or that his daughter has read Xenophon *On Horsemanship*, or a thousand other things. There may, in short, be an indefinite number of reasons why the horse occupies just this position on his relative scale, but as long as we know the fact we are indifferent to the causes. Given, then, the relevant facts, you may distribute the items between the groups just as you like. You may arrive at your conclusion by the method of addition or the method of intersection. You may deprive the whole alphabet from A to R of horses altogether, and throw eight horses from some other source upon the market, without reserve

[1] Pages 219 *sqq.*

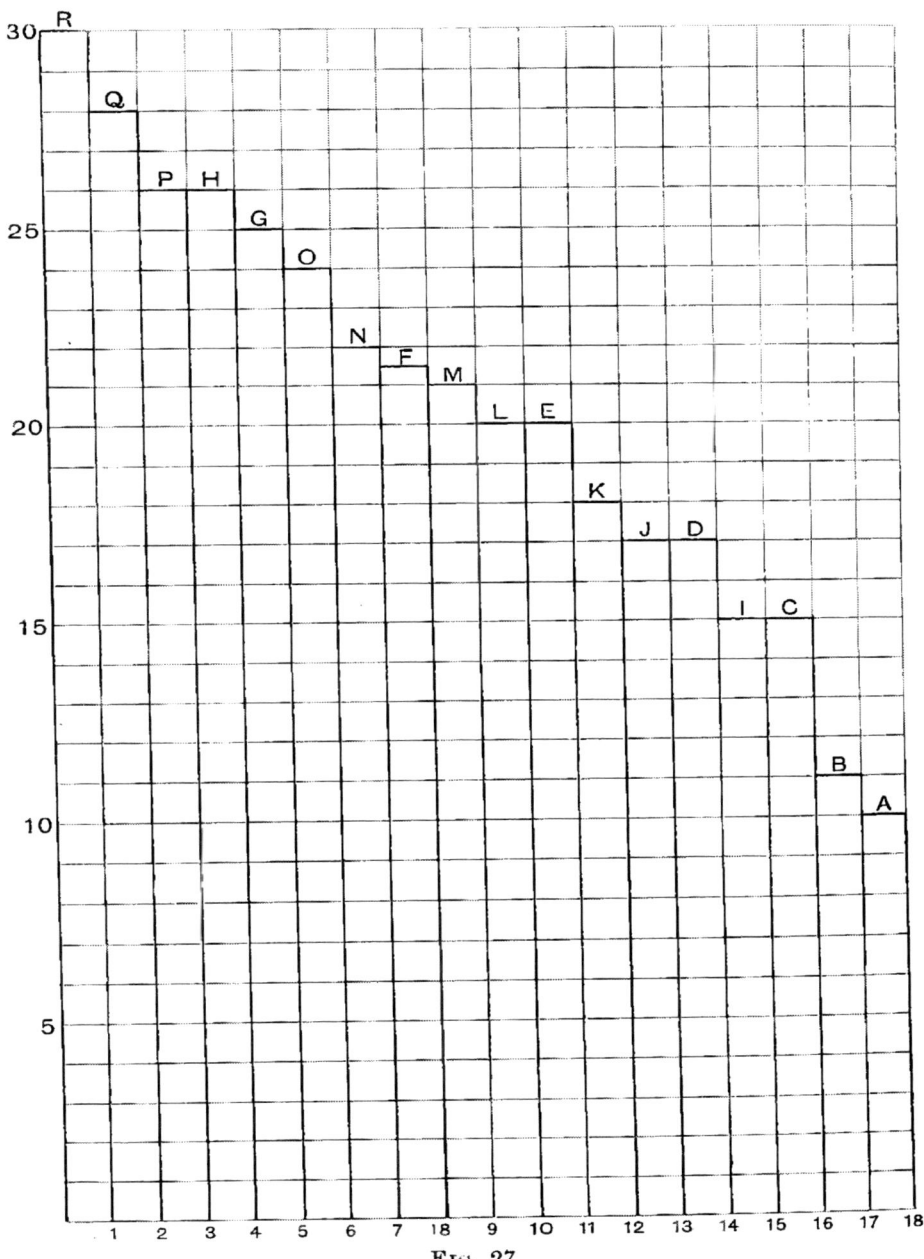

Fig. 27

price; you may suppose that some in group A–H possess horses and others do not; but you will always bring out the identical result that the market price, virtual or actual, will be somewhere between £21 and £21 : 10s., and that the ultimate possessors of the horses will be H, G, F, R, Q, P, O, N. Naturally. They are the eight persons on whose scales of preference a horse (whether they have him to begin with or not) stands highest, and there are only eight horses altogether.

If the fundamental method of addition is adopted, it is obvious at once that no hypothesis as to which of the persons brings the horses into the market will in any way affect the result, and, on examination, the same will be found true if we adopt the method of intersection. On Mr. Hobson's supposition, group I–R possess no horses, and group A–H possess eight. We know, then, that as there are eight horses altogether, we must so arrange the curves that between the highest of one group, R, and the highest of the other group, H (both included), there shall be eight units, so that whatever the point of intersection may be there shall be eight and only eight letters above it. This will give us Fig. 28,[1] which will bring out the same ultimate possessors of horses and the same prices as we had in Fig. 27. But if we suppose that the eight horses were originally possessed by A, C, F, H, K, L, M, O, and that B, D, E, G, I, J, N, P, Q, R were without them, and proceed by intersection to determine the price and the ultimate possessors, we must again see to it that between R and H (both included) there are eight units, and again we shall obtain identical results (Fig. 29). But this rearrangement of the individuals is really superfluous. We may suppose the down and up sloping series in Fig. 28 each to include possessors and non-possessors, according to the data of Fig. 27. This will in no way affect the result; nor is it necessary to have any information on the subject in order to split up the data of Fig. 27 in any way we like and place the two groups cross-wise, with the interval between their highest members determined by the datum as to the total number of horses.

[1] I have preserved the convention by which the "demand" curve is made to run down and the "supply" curve to run up, from left to right. Of course it has no significance and might just as well be neglected or reversed.

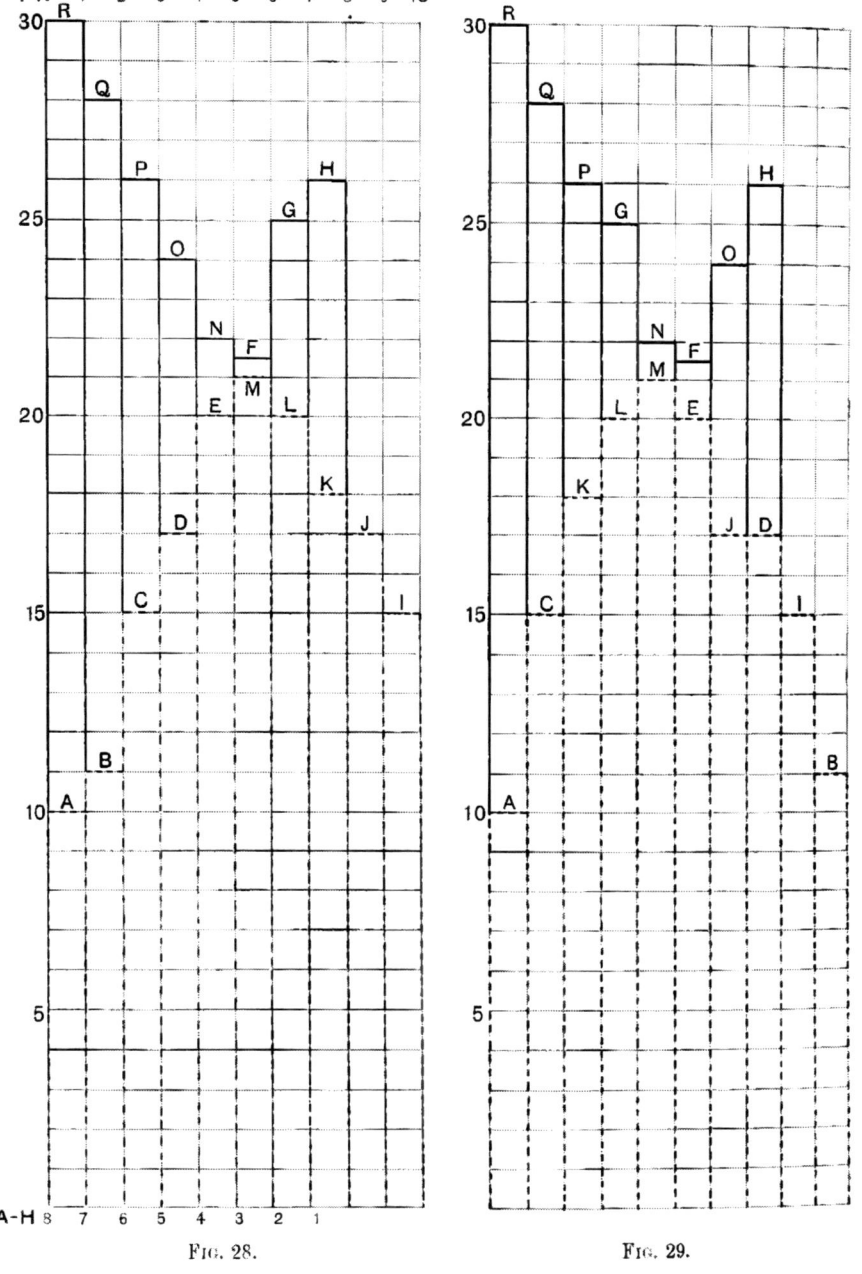

FIG. 28. FIG. 29.

It will be noted that Mr. Hobson gives us the whole of the facts. Mr. Marshall (*Principles. of Economics*, ed. 3, page 410) has a parallel example in which he only gives some of them. He supposes, in a corn-market, that at 37s. a quarter there will be "sellers" of 1000 quarters of wheat and "buyers" of 600; at 36s. "sellers" of 700 and "buyers" of 700; at 35s. "sellers" of 500 and "buyers" of 900.

Mr. Marshall's corn-market.

The facts given us may be tabulated thus:—

A	B
Sellers will sell—	Buyers will buy—
1000 . . . at 37s.	600 . . . at 37s.
700 (keeping 300) at 36s.	700 . . . at 36s.
500 (keeping 500) at 35s.	900 . . . at 35s.

Therefore (subtracting from the B figures the 600 required to bring the B's to the 37s. point) we find that when all are satisfied down to the point of 37s., it will take—

A	B
300 more to satisfy the A's to the point of 36s.	100 more to satisfy the B's to 36s.
500 more to satisfy the A's to the point of 35s.	300 more to satisfy the B's to 35s.

It appears, then, that in the market altogether there are 1000 quarters more than would satisfy the group A, called "sellers," down to 37s. (for they have 1000 quarters that they value at less than 37s., or they would not sell them at that price). It would take 300 of these to satisfy them down to the point of 36s. (for we are told that at 36s. they would hold back 300), and 200 more to satisfy them down to 35s. What we know of the curve of the group called "sellers" is therefore represented on Fig. 30 (*a*). As to the group B, called "buyers," we do not know to what point they are already satisfied, *i.e.* we do not know at what price they would begin to buy, but we know that 600 quarters (or 600 more than they already have) would bring them to the point 37s., and then another 100 would bring them to 36s., and another 200 yet to 35s. What we know of their curve, then, from the 37s. point onwards is represented on Fig. 30 (*b*). In neither case do we know how far from the origins the curves start.

2 L

Let us add the two curves, starting at the points with the ordinate 37s. Fig. 30 (c) gives us the result. Now we know that after all parties are satisfied to the point of 37s. there are 400 quarters left; and these will satisfy all parties to the point of 36s. Or we might adopt the method of intersection, placing 400 quarters between the 37s. points of the two curves. The result, of course, will be the same (d). Both (c) and (d) can be constructed and read without reference to the initial distribution of the corn. If all the corn had originally been in the possession of the group A, or if half of it had been in A's possession and half in B's, or whatever the proportion had been, so long as the curves of significance remained the same, and the excess over the amount required to bring them all to the point 37s. remained 400, we should always have the same result. The course of the curves, then, and the amount of the excess, constitute our relevant information — relevant, that is, to the determination of the market price and the ultimate distribution of the excess. The irrelevant information is that the corn is now in the possession of group A.

A psychological objection may here be raised. It may be said that it is impossible that the curve of preference should be conceived irrespective of the possession or non-possession of the commodity. In the case of the horse-market it may be admitted that every man has a more or less determined relative estimate of the significance of a horse, and that we need not inquire how he came to form it. But in the case of the wheat we are asked to suppose that each man has a scale on which successive quarters of wheat are continuously registered with continuously declining significance. Now it may very well be that the man who comes into the market with the intention and hope of selling may buy when he becomes better informed of the facts, or *vice versa*, yet some mental friction would have to be overcome, so that the curve would not decline regularly, but would break at certain points determined by the amount of corn the man possessed. The answer is that this may be, though it need not be, the case; but that in a large market such individual considerations will counteract each other, and the whole body of persons conducting the business will present a sensibly continuous curve.

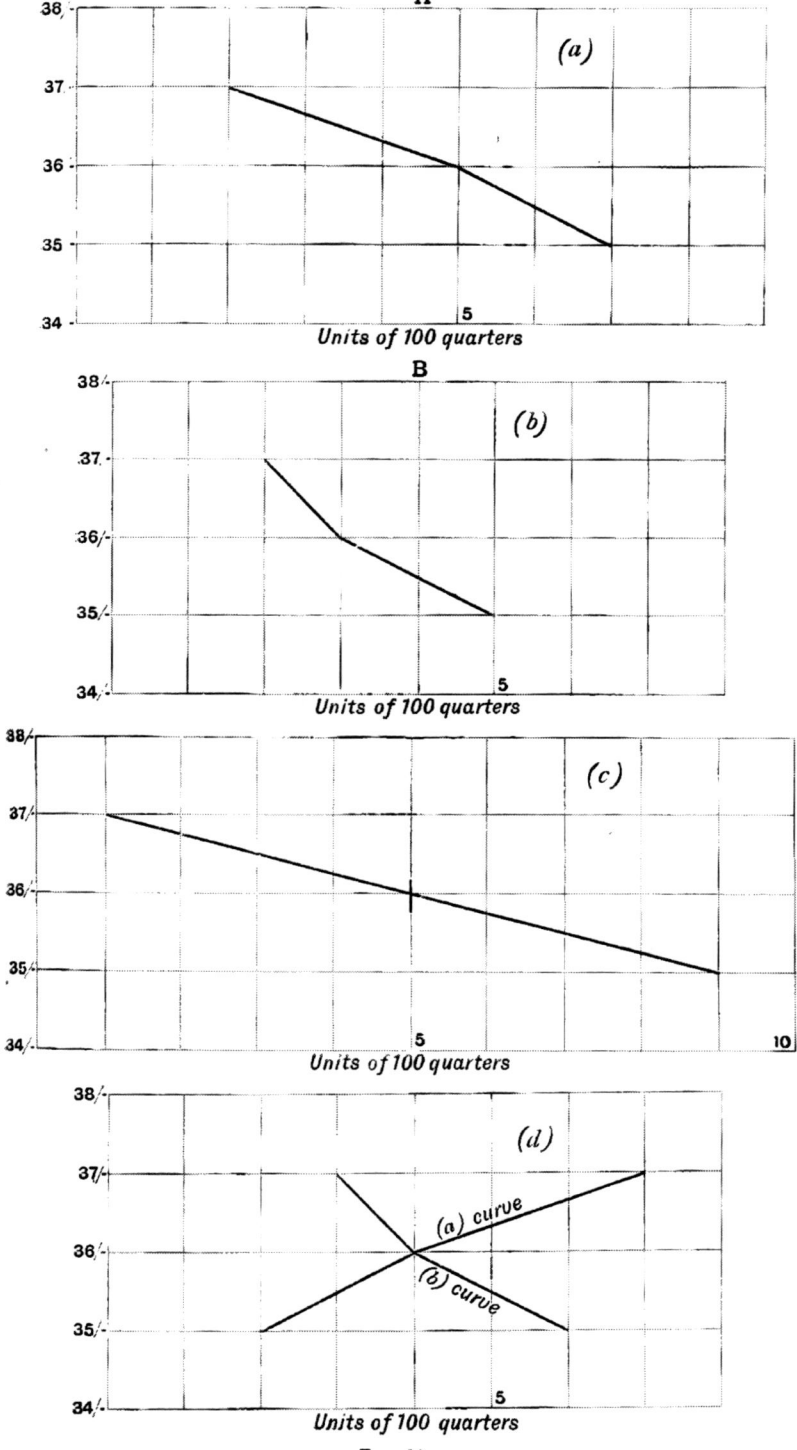

Fig. 30.

The final outcome of these investigations is that the diagrammatic method of taking a buyers' curve and a sellers' curve and shewing by their intersection what the market price will be is perfectly legitimate if properly understood, but that if it is supposed to represent the ultimate facts which determine the price, it embodies and emphasises irrelevant matter. If it is supposed that the two curves are different in kind and represent two principles, that they could not equally well be represented as a single curve, or that the transference of any constituent elements from one to the other would affect the result, or that either curve might not contain the register of both buyers' and sellers' preferences, then the method is misleading and mischievous. In the higgling of the market the price *emerges* as the result of the play of a conflict between buyers and sellers as such, which is not relevant to the ultimate facts and forces which *constitute* that price. The method of intersection is, in fact, a mere disguise of the method of addition, and it might ignore the distinction between buyer and seller without affecting the result, as far as price and ultimate distribution are concerned. If adopted to shew the amount of business done under given conditions, the distinction between buyers and sellers and the intersection of their curves is a legitimate method; if adopted to shew the ultimate considerations that determine the market price, it is, to say the least of it, seriously misleading.

Our main conclusions are nothing new. They merely restate the results of the analysis of markets entered upon in Book I. Chapter VI. Given the total supply of the commodity, the market price that any single customer finds established is determined in the main by the demands of all the other purchasers, but in some degree by his own. If his demand is, in bulk, a very small portion of the whole, then its effect on the price will be correspondingly small, that is to say, the total curve will decline so slowly that the addition or withdrawal of an amount of the commodity sufficient to carry this one purchaser from his initial to his final increments will not perceptibly raise its ordinate. And therefore in dealing with any one individual separately we may assume the market price as already fixed by all the other individuals, and may then simply measure it

Restatement of the Law of the Market.

off on the axis of Y of the particular curve we are examining, and may draw a parallel to the axis of X through that point. The abscissa of the point at which this parallel cuts the curve will measure the amount that this particular purchaser will take. We may put it in this way: the amount of any commodity which will flow, in obedience to the economic forces, to the satisfaction of any one consumer's wants will be determined by his curve of preferences, by the similar curves of all the other claimants, and by the total amount of the commodity. This is the general law of distribution.

If we go on to ask what determines the quantity of the commodity, we find ourselves dealing once more with the identical problem that we have just solved. The flow of the productive forces into this or that industry is determined on exactly the same principles as the flow of the stock of any single commodity to the different consumers. *The "supply" of one market itself a "demand" upon other markets.* To breed horses you need land, buildings, corn, apparatus of many kinds, and trained human faculty. In supplying horses, therefore, you demand all these things. To raise corn you need land, buildings, ploughs, waggons, gates, ships, machinery, and human faculty. In supplying corn, therefore, you demand these things. And so with all other commodities. Thus the supply of any commodity is itself a demand upon other commodities and services, and if we separate out the demand, say, for woodwork implied in the supply of each of the commodities into which it enters, we shall be doing just the same thing that we did when we separated out the demand for potatoes from all the individual budgets of the persons that composed the market. Here, as there, the share that each one gets is determined by the curve representing the urgency of the want it satisfies, by the similar curves of the other industries, and by the total available resources of the community. Thus the supply of any commodity is regulated by the combination of productive factors needed for its production and the rival claims of other commodities for the factors of this combination. Ultimately, then, we have at one end the undifferentiated and unmanipulated forces and materials of nature, the faculties (trained and untrained) of man, and the various modifications of the former by the latter, which exist at the moment. This constitutes the total available stock. And at the other end are the tastes and resources of each individual. The amount of the supply, at any moment, of this or that commodity (in its final and united form, or in any of its intermediate states or constituent elements) is determined by the attempts of the commercial community to gauge and anticipate individual wants and to regulate the flow and the combinations of the ultimate sources of supply in accordance with them.

We have seen that all the different items of the ultimate sources of supply, and all the existing products, can, at any given moment, be expressed in a common unit. Therefore, in considering any single industry, we have first to determine what unit we will take to measure amounts of the productive agents. We might take, for instance, the amount that would exchange for an ounce of gold, or a ton of pig-iron, or a quarter of wheat of given quality, or any combination of these or other articles we choose to select. This will be our arbitrary unit-of-products-and-factors-of-production, and as we are now applying it exclusively as a measure of factors of production we will call it the unit-factor of production. The unit of the special product we will take as that amount of it which the unit-factor of production can produce. What will the unit on the axis of Y be? It will represent the general command of articles in the circle of exchange which corresponds to the ounce of gold, ton of pig-iron, or what not, that we have taken to measure our unit-factor of production. We may think of it in terms of money. It may be a pound's worth or a shilling's worth of anything that is in the circle of exchange, including the factors of production themselves. The curve, then, will indicate the place on the communal scale of preferences of each successive unit of the commodity; and the flow of productive forces into that industry will be regulated exactly as the flow of fish or carrots to this or that purchaser's larder is regulated. It will bring it down to the (objective) level determined by its marginal significance elsewhere. If the total amount of the resources of society which will in any case be deflected to this particular industry is an infinitesimal portion of the whole, we may take this margin as independently fixed.

The curve (Fig. 31) gives us the rate at which the unit-factor of production will satisfy human wants (measured objectively) in this industry at any margin. At what rate (measured by the same standard) will it satisfy human wants

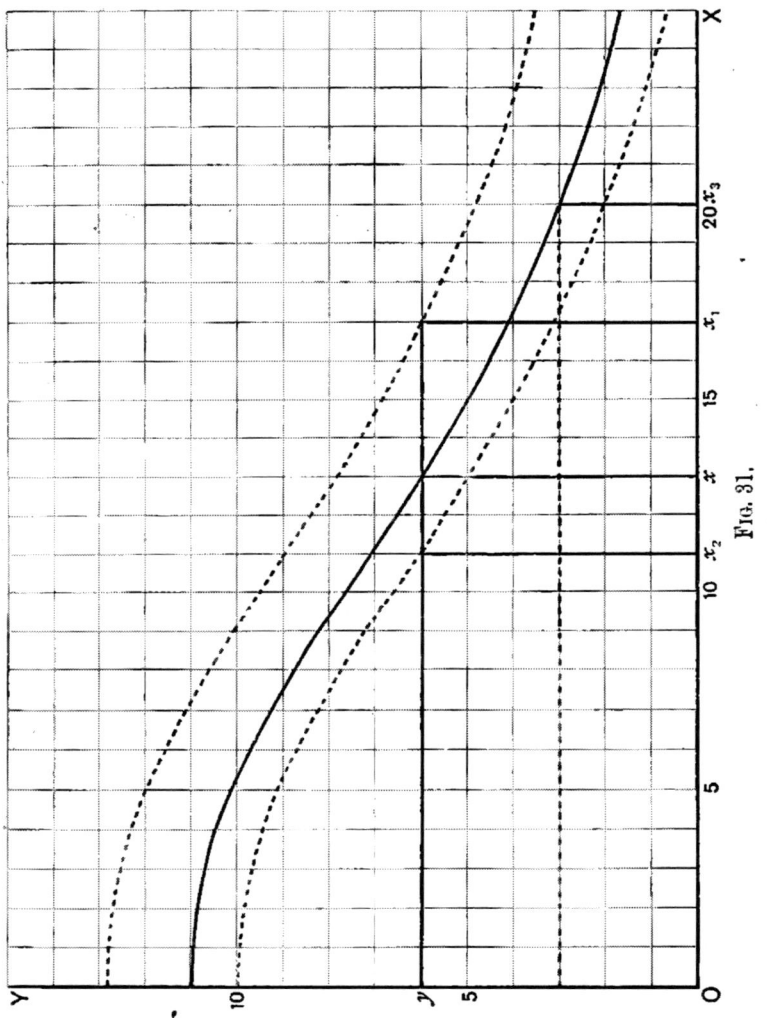

Fig. 31.

in other marginal applications? Whatever that rate may be it can be represented by a line. Measure off that line on the axis of Y, draw through the point thus determined a parallel to the axis of X, and the abscissa of its point of intersection with the curve will determine the flow of the productive resources to this industry, and the corresponding amount of the product. The curvilinear space above this line will represent (objectively) the satisfaction which the creation or destruction of this particular industry would add or subtract from the community. Its revenues of enjoyment (or at least of anticipated or estimated satisfaction) will be increased to that extent by the existence of this industry. It follows, of course, that whereas the communal curves of demand for, say, a certain kind of timber in the furnishing, the building, the shipping trades, and so forth, can be added, under the conditions laid down on pages 494 *sq.*, the communal curves for different commodities (houses, ships, race-horses, diamonds, books, fruit, music, etc.) cannot be added, since each such curve assumes that all other conditions remain the same, and to travel along any one of them constitutes a change of the conditions for some or all of the others.

If the demand (estimated significance) for a commodity increases, as represented by the upper dotted line in Fig. 31, the product will be increased from Ox to Ox_1. If it declines, as in the lower dotted line, the industry will shrink to Ox_2. If, while the demand remains the same, some invention is made which doubles the quantity of the commodity which could be produced by the unit-factor of production, or, which is the same thing, halves the amount of the productive forces required to produce the units we have hitherto registered along Ox, the dotted line parallel to the axis of X will indicate the quantity which will be produced. We might equally well represent this latter change by retaining the length Oy unchanged and doubling the height of the ordinate at every point, because the factors that would give the value Oy in other industries will now be producing the units of our product, and therefore the anticipated satisfactions they yield, at double the previous rate. The unit of Ox, therefore, will represent twice as much of the commodity, measured in its own proper unit, as before (Fig. 32).

Representation of the effects of a change in demand or in the conditions of production.

We have now to note that any very extensive departure from the existing state of things might affect the whole constitution of the unit on which we are working, for it might disturb the marginal relations between different kinds of human effort and different products or gifts of nature. And, as the value of anything can only be expressed objectively in terms of something else, changes or discoveries that affect

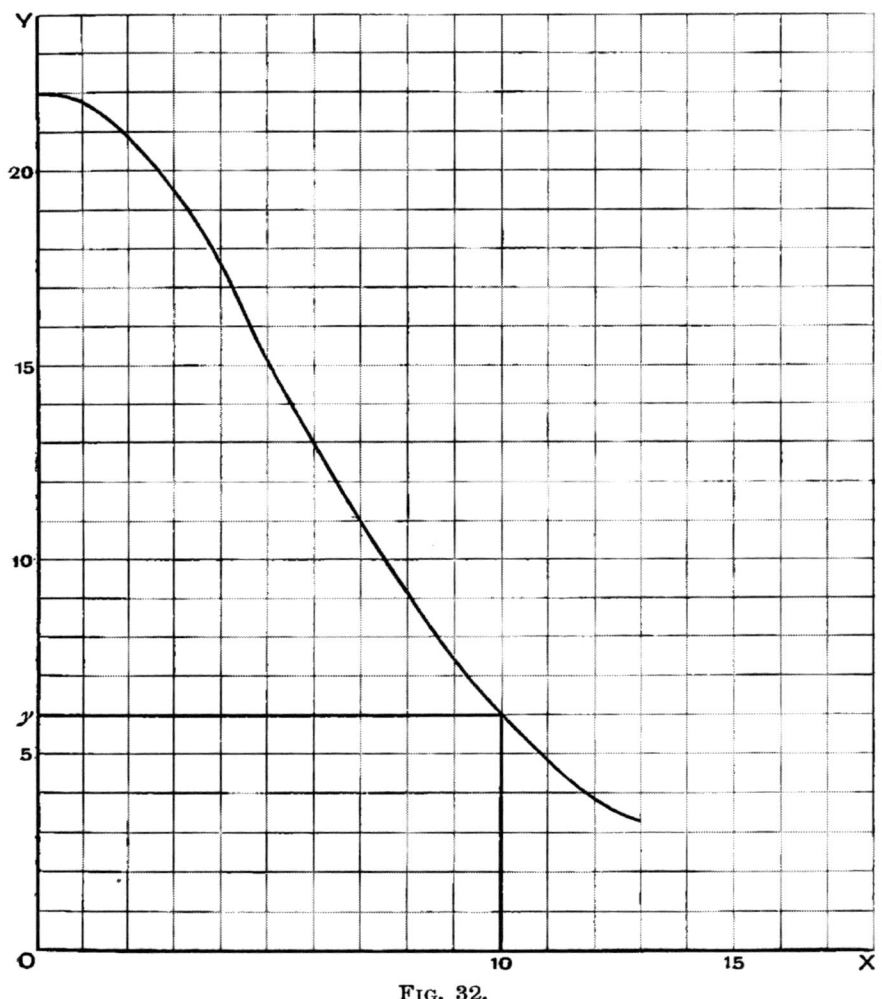

Fig. 32.

the general fertility of human effort, and the significance of natural products and agents, cannot be recorded by any consistent objective method. Further, the diagrammatic illustrations which we have been using can only be regarded as applicable to cases in which we are examining a very small part of the whole field, so that we may consider the general conditions as stable. An attempt to draw up the whole scale of significance of any one of the main factors of production, carried back to the origin, would of course be quite futile. It would be impossible to imagine the origin at all nearly approached without such a disturbance in other conditions as would deprive our units of all continuous significance.

One other point of theoretical interest remains for investigation here. We have seen [1] that the creation of the supply of undifferentiated human capacity is to be regarded in the main as itself constituting a branch of expenditure or "consumption." It is determined, at any moment, by the scale of relative significance of this particular form of expenditure, "consumption," or expression of impulse, which has ruled in the past. But the total capacity-for-effort that exists is not employed "economically." What determines the amount that is devoted to the production of things that enter, or might enter, into the circle of exchange? Here, as in previous instances, we must begin with individual curves. Writers who have paid attention to the subject have usually regarded the output of human effort (spoken of under the rather dangerous abbreviation of "labour") as limited by its irksomeness, and have represented its significance (at least after a certain point) as a negative quantity.

The supply of labour. Irksomeness as a negative and leisure as a positive magnitude.

We will begin with Robinson Crusoe. Along the axis of X (Fig. 33) we measure units of effort. The proper basis for such a unit would be foot-pounds if we were considering mere muscular effort, but it will be convenient to take an hour's work as our unit, including all physical and mental effort, and ignoring the fact that during different portions of the day, and so forth, the actual output of effort made per hour, measured by any objective standard, will vary. The p curve will now represent the marginal significance to Crusoe of the result of successive unit-outputs of effort, and the l curve will represent the marginal irksomeness of the output of effort itself. The unit on the axis of Y is essentially psychic, and we may for the present read the figure as

[1] Pages 336 *sq.*

CH. IV   BUYER AND SELLER.   DEMAND AND SUPPLY   523

meaning simply that at the margin of six hours' work per day the value of the product compensates threefold the irksomeness of the effort; that is to say, Crusoe would make the effort even if its results accrued at only a trifle above one-third the rate at which they actually accrue. Thus the balance is

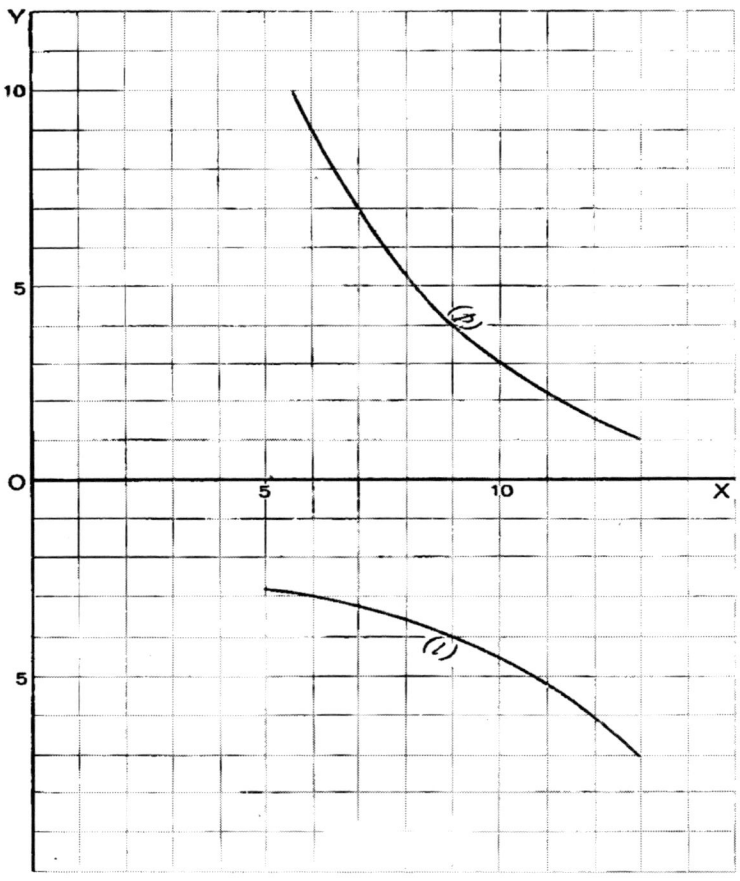

FIG. 33.

favourable up to 9 on the axis of X; after that it would be unfavourable, and therefore the output of effort is carried to that point and no further.

Leaving the island and returning to civilisation, we take the remuneration of each man's effort per hour as a datum fixed by the general laws of the market, and, still reading the curve psychologically, we find that at the margin of six hours a day the individual whose curve we are examining estimates the advantage of the increased supplies of all commodities and services in the circle of exchange as threefold compensation for the irksomeness of the work that secures them. And the advantage is on the side of doing more work for wages up to nine hours a day, but no further. This, then, is the amount of labour he chooses to supply on the terms which it will command in the market. Well, then, he sells his time with a system of reserved prices, which constitutes his own demand for it; just as the stall-keeper sells her plums.[1] Each individual can get for his work economically as much as his doing it is worth to others, and he will require for it as much as his not doing it is worth to himself. The total supply of any kind of effort is the whole capacity of the persons capable of making it, and this supply is distributed between economic and other applications in accordance with the general laws we have studied so fully.

This way of putting it at once suggests that the man who sells his labour is selling something for which he himself has a demand of some kind, and that this demand should be represented as a positive, not a negative quantity. Reflection fully justifies this suggestion. The irksomeness of the labour by which we earn money is not really the only thing that we have to set against the advantages the money secures. It is only a negative expression of one element in the desirability of rest or leisure. This latter is a positive conception, and it includes all output of effort upon the direct securing of things not in the circle of exchange, as well as rest. Our previous studies[2] of the relations of positive and negative satisfactions and their diagrammatic representation will remove all difficulties from our path in this matter. We may treat " desirability of leisure " as positive, and may represent the l curve with positive ordinates, as in Fig. 34. We shall then get the same point as before, viz. 9, by intersection, and shall see that the whole diagram is no more than another disguise of the process of addition of curves.

We may read the l curve, whether in Fig. 33 or in Fig. 34, thus:—We have no information as to the total of

---

[1] Pages 229 *sqq.*   [2] Pages 414 *sqq.*

BUYER AND SELLER. DEMAND AND SUPPLY 525

exchangeable commodities which the man could conceivably secure to himself by his extreme output of effort, reducing his leisure to the minimum requirements of rest and nutrition which would enable him to continue at the same level. But we know that if he had already reserved as much leisure as would reduce its marginal significance to 7, he would still have thirteen hours a day, to distribute between the further gratification of his desire for more leisure and the total gratification of his desire for things in the circle of exchange. The p curve shews us that it will take seven of those thirteen

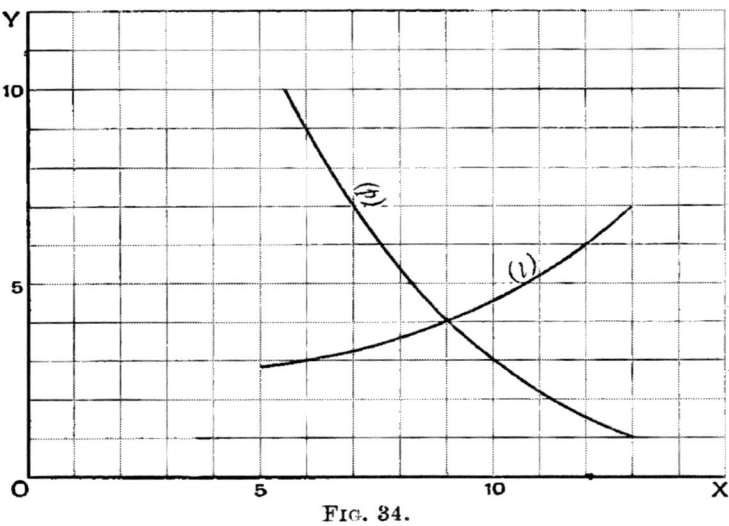

FIG. 34.

hours to bring his desire for things in the circle of exchange down to the point of 7. That is to say, the marginal value of leisure, when eleven hours have been reserved for it, and of the reward of labour, when seven hours have been devoted to it, stand alike at 7. There are six hours more to be distributed between them. Add the curves together from this point, reversing l (Fig. 35), and we shall obtain our former result as to the point to which both sets of desires will be gratified. Two more hours will be devoted to work, making nine hours altogether, and four more to leisure, making fifteen hours altogether.[1]

[1] It is necessary, however, to note that in thus reversing our original l curve we have assumed a stability in our psychic unit on the axis of Y that was not

For obvious reasons we have not carried our curves back to the origin. The assumption that "other things are equal" would be patently absurd at any great distance

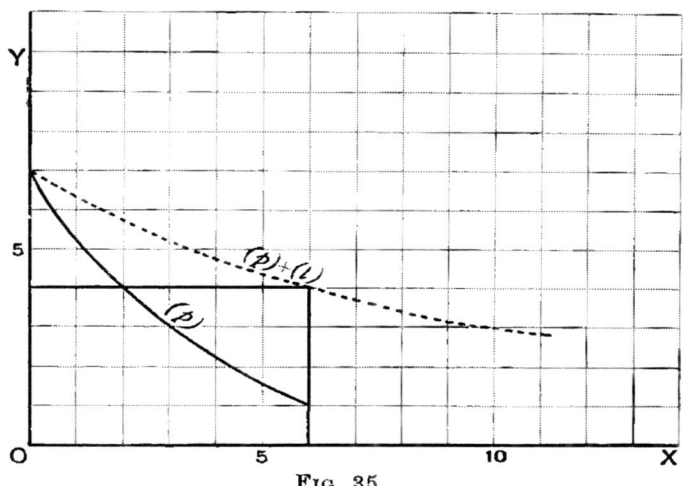

Fig. 35.

from the actual point of equilibrium. Even the range that we have actually allowed our curves to cover can only be justified by considerations of facility of demonstration.

granted in our first construction of the figure. The ordinates of the p and l curves for any abscissa were determined with reference to each other, at that point, and consequently our ordinate of 7 for the l curve, when the abscissa is 13, means that irksomeness of effort (or desire for its cessation) at that point is seven times as great as the advantage accruing from labour at that point. It does not follow that it is just equal to the advantage accruing at the abscissa 7, unless we can be sure that the psychic value of the unit remains stable for p throughout its course; and we have seen (pages 469 *sqq.*) the extreme difficulty of securing even a fair approximation to such stability in far simpler cases than this. If we retain the form of the p curve, and reversing the l curve relate each ordinate to the now corresponding ordinate of p, we may get a different form of the curve, representing the same relations and the same psychic values. But the point at which the two ordinates are equal to each other must obviously be the same.

CHAPTER V

THE THEORY OF "INCREASING AND DIMINISHING RETURNS"

SUMMARY.—*The laws of "increasing and diminishing returns," as currently stated, are in no sense co-ordinate, and do not form an antithesis. The use of the terms in economic argument seldom coincides with the definitions given to them. As applied to "cost of production" the conception of diminishing returns is often misleading and confused; and a fatal graphic resemblance between two intersecting curves of demand on the one hand, and a curve of demand intersected by a curve of "cost of production" on the other, has (together with other misleading influences) produced a habit, in graphic demonstrations, of treating increasing cost of production, as the amount produced increases, as the normal case. Other and less academic influences are at work to foster an irrational dread of "decreasing returns" to labour in the near future.*

Diagrams of intersecting curves have been used with many different meanings, and a failure to distinguish precisely between them has given rise to much confusion. Our path to the further investigation of this subject lies through a consideration of what are known as the laws of "increasing" and "diminishing" returns.

In books on Political Economy our attention is called to the following facts. If successive doses or increments of labour (or labour and capital) are applied to a piece of land, we find that, at any rate after a certain point, doubling the amount of labour does not double the product. As we increase the amount of labour, therefore, each successive increment secures a smaller "Diminishing and increasing returns."

return in the shape of product. This is called the "law of diminishing returns," and is said to apply generally to agricultural and extractive industries. On the other hand, if an industry such as that of the cotton or iron trade so increases that, say, twice as much labour (or labour and capital) is employed in it as before, it will generally be found that the result is a more than doubled output. This is said to illustrate the "law of increasing returns," and to apply generally to manufactures.

When the statements are made thus baldly the reader can hardly fail to see that the two "laws" are in no sense co-ordinate, and cannot be regarded as standing side by side and proclaiming " divisum habemus imperium." The cases are not parallel. In stating the law of diminishing returns, it is assumed that the factor of land is constant, and if, when a number of factors co-operate to produce a result, you double some of them without doubling others, of course you cannot expect to double the result. If you double the pastry without doubling the apples, you do not double the pie. If you double the diners without doubling the dinner, or double the dinner without doubling the diners, you do not double the dining experience. In like manner if you double the land without doubling the operations on it, or double the operations without doubling the land, you cannot expect to double the crop. This principle would apply to manufactures just as much as to agriculture. If, for example, you had doubled the number of hands, retaining the same machinery and buildings, or if you had doubled the raw material without doubling the labour bestowed upon elaborating it, or if you had doubled the labour bestowed on the same raw material, you could in no case expect the exact doubling (or other proportionate increase) of the product. Or if a tradesman doubles his accommodation without doubling his stock and staff, or doubles his stock without doubling his accommodation and his staff, he will not double the effectiveness of his whole establishment. There are circumstances under which any of these operations might more than double the total result. If a business were desperately under-staffed or under-stocked, for instance, doubling the defective factor might more than double the

A false antithesis.

effect of the whole; but if doubling any one of these factors without doubling the others exactly doubled the efficiency of the concern, it could only be a coincidence; and "after a certain point" it would certainly less than double it. The "law of diminishing returns," then, is really no more than an axiomatic statement of a universal principle that applies equally to all forms of industry, and to a great range of non-industrial experiences and phenomena as well.

The law of increasing returns, on the other hand, includes all those cases in which economies may be effected in one or more of the factors by increasing the scale of production. There is no kind of parallel or contrast between the two principles. If you double *some* of the factors and not the others you will not exactly double the product (except by a coincidence). If you increase *all* the factors in a suitable proportion you will in many cases be able to secure double the product without more than doubling any of the factors and without as much as doubling some of them.

The law of increasing returns, then, is an intelligible formulating of a very interesting and important phenomenon. Production on a large scale makes certain economies possible. A man who is cultivating 50 acres of land may require a waggon, but if he were cultivating 200 acres he might only require two, not four. And if, instead of supposing one man to increase his holding, we imagine four holders of 50 acres each to be working in co-operation, we may still suppose the same economy to be effected. Or, without any "co-operation" in the technical sense, a man may own a steam thrashing-machine, and may do the thrashing for all the farmers and holders in the neighbourhood more economically than they could do it for themselves; but it is only if there is a great deal of wheat grown in the district that this can be done. No limit seems yet to have been reached to the possibility of economising in one direction or another as the bulk of any industry increases. It seems always possible, at every stage, to introduce some new process of specialising or division of labour, and so to effect some new economy for which the industry was not ripe until it had reached its present dimensions. And note that the phenomenon we are now examining is independent of the question how far the business of a single concern, or under a single management, may be carried advantageously. The economies which a large volume of production, as such, renders possible are in principle independent of the question whether the industry is in few or many hands.

The principle of increasing returns, therefore, is intelligible and important; and it directs our attention to a significant point in the analysis of the processes of production. The "law of decreasing returns," on the other hand, as ordinarily stated, is, as we have seen, the mere enunciation, with special reference to land, of an axiomatic and sterile proposition. Of course you cannot indefinitely increase a product in proportion to the increase of certain selected factors of production if you do not increase the other factors.

This utter disparity of the two "laws" is sometimes veiled by stating the case merely in terms of "labour," or, it may be, of "labour and capital." Thus it is said that in agricultural and extractive industries the increase in the output will not be proportional to the increase in labour and capital, whereas in manufactures it will be more than proportionate. But manifestly this is only a partial statement. There is a suppressed assumption that you do not (or a suppressed postulate that you cannot) contemporaneously increase the other factors in the one case, and that you do (or can) increase them in the other. The enunciation of the "law" of diminishing returns, then, reduces itself to a veiled statement, or hypothesis, as to facts. Sometimes writers perceive this, and base their argument on explicit statements as to the actual limitation of the supply of land on the surface of the earth, or place their whole investigation on the footing of a hypothetical isolation, say, of England in time of war. On the relevancy or legitimacy of these statements or hypotheses we may have something to say presently,[1] but meanwhile it is abundantly evident that there is no possibility, along any of these lines, of formulating two co-ordinate "laws," in the proper sense, parallel one to the other. The only "law" is that (within limits that do not appear as yet to have been ascertained or realised) successive economies in the administra-

Attempts to veil the disparity between the two "laws."

[1] Pages 533 sq., 539 sq.

tion of the factors of production may be introduced as the volume of production increases. But of course that does not mean that these economies are always such as to secure an increase in the product more than proportionate to the increase of *some* of the factors, if the other factors are not increased at all. The two " laws " therefore hold united, not divided, sway over industry.

But the semblance of a parallel in the statement of the genuine law of increasing returns on the one hand, and of the axiom and the disguised assumption (or hypothesis) which jostle each other under the cloke of a " law of diminishing returns " on the other, has led to a frequent treatment of the two as parallel, and this has reacted upon the conception of the " law of diminishing returns " itself. This " law " accordingly has made a series of masked movements by which it has in some degree approximated itself to a parallelism with the other. Modifications in the conception of the " law of diminishing returns."

If we were to construct an interpretation of the phrase *law of diminishing returns* in strict analogy to the rational use of *law of increasing returns,* we should formulate it thus :—" There are some industries of such a nature or in such a stage of development that you could double the output without more than doubling any of the factors of production, and by less than doubling some of them ; but there are other industries of such a nature, or in such a stage of development, that you cannot double the output except by as much as doubling all the factors of production and more than doubling some of them." This would be an enunciation of two parallel principles which really might divide the realm of industry between them. It would remain to be shewn what industries, if any, came under the latter law. But this completely consistent use of the terms has never, so far as I am aware, entered either consciously or unconsciously into books of Political Economy ; and that for a very sufficient reason. The terms in which we have attempted to give precision to the law of increasing returns are not the terms in which we habitually think. " No more than doubling any of the factors of production, and less than doubling some of them," is not a working formula. We might more than double some, but the economies effected by the reduction of others might more than compensate this increase; and, moreover, the question is complicated by substitutions, by the introduction of totally fresh factors, by the partial or complete elimination of existing factors, and so forth. And in order to make comparisons we need a common denominator to which all these entering and vanishing, waxing and waning factors can be reduced. This common denominator, as we have already seen,[1] we have; and its index is the value in exchange of the several factors, that is to say, their marginal efficiency in other industries; and this we measure in terms of gold. What we practically mean, then, by the law of increasing returns is that in certain industries (or conditions of an industry) an increased output means a cheaper production, as measured in gold values; and, by analogy, we should interpret the law of decreasing returns to mean that in certain other industries (or conditions of an industry) an increased output would mean an increased cost of production.

Here, then, we have an intelligible use of the two terms in a parallel and consistent sense; and in most generalisations and inferences concerning "industries which obey the law of increasing returns" and "industries which obey the law of diminishing returns" this seems to be what is in the mind of the writers. But the reader will see that by a process of attraction the meaning of the "law of diminishing returns" has been drawn completely away from its original basis. Both laws have effected a masked movement from terms of specific factors of production, measured in their proper units, to terms of generalised productive resources measured in the unit of gold. And the law of diminishing returns has effected a further, and if possible more important movement, from the statement that *if* you do not adequately increase some important factor you must not expect an increase in the product proportional to the increase in the other factors, to the statement that in certain industries it will not be normally possible largely to increase certain important factors or to find adequate substitutes for them, except on terms so unfavourable, pecuniarily, that the net result will be an increase in the cost of production as the volume of the output increases.

Increasing and diminishing cost of production as the scale of production increases.

[1] Pages 361 *sqq.*

These ambiguities would hardly have maintained their place in the textbooks had they not been supported by the assumption that in the case of agriculture there really is a normal difficulty or impossibility in obtaining at will an increased command of land, whereas in the case of manufactures there is no such normal and permanent limitation to the increase of any factor. Thus, the axiomatic statement that if you do not increase the land you will not increase the product in proportion to the increase of the other factors, coupled with the postulate that you cannot increase the land, yields the result that you cannot increase agricultural products except at an increase in the cost of production; and this result (flagrantly as it contradicts the facts in many instances) is accepted as representative of an important though undefined class of industries, the characteristics of which are often developed without further challenge, and without examination as to the extent to which such industries, or such conditions, actually exist. The generalisation, which still seems to pass loosely current, that the law of "increasing returns" applies to manufactures and the law of "decreasing returns" to extractive and agricultural industries, when translated into terms of cost of production, seems to derive little or no support from history, nor is it easy to apply it to the analysis of the actual phenomena of industry. It is true, of course, that land is ultimately limited in quantity, but at present there is plenty of land to be had for any specific use, either by withdrawing it from other uses,[1] or by taking in fresh land not at present used for anything. And, on the other hand, if any specific manufacturing industry calls for an increase of labour, that labour can only be had by being withdrawn or withheld from other occupations, or taken up from labour-power that is not at present being used at all. As a matter of fact, no practical difficulty has been found in increasing to any required extent the area of the earth's surface applied to the production of wheat. And seeing that the men who, in an English manufacturing centre, construct thrashing-machines or other agricultural implements for use in Russia, are just as truly and certainly taking their part in the agricultural industries of Russia as the peasants who are on the spot,

[1] Cf. below, page 540.

we cannot even say that the land of the great wheat-growing countries of the old and new worlds is out of the reach of the inhabitants of English cities; for they are actually harvesting the crops. In truth, the great industry of wheat-growing might be taken as affording a typical example of the economies of large scale production, and the abundance and cheapness of wheat in the world market indicates the fact. And, on the other hand, it is monstrous to assume it as self-evident that all the factors of production in a manufacturing industry can be increased at will. The raw material of many of them, as of the cotton industry, is itself an agricultural product, and none of them can at short notice indefinitely increase the factor of adequately skilled labour.

<small>Contrast between the immediate and the ultimate effect of increased output on cost of production.</small>

The most general case alike in manufactures and in extractive industries appears to be that a large and sudden increase of output must be made at an industrial disadvantage, because the supply of one or more important factors cannot be largely increased at a moment's notice. The increase, therefore, must be made at more than proportional sacrifice, since the proportions of the factors will necessarily be disturbed; and unless a sufficiently higher price is offered an increased product will not be forthcoming at all. On the other hand, if an increased demand continues for a long period, an increased flow of all the requisite factors will set in, and ultimately the advantages and economies of large production, with the factors of production duly balanced against each other, will be realised. Hence, whether in agriculture or manufactures, it seems to be a fairly general rule that when an increased demand causes an increased production that presses against the existing limits, at first cost of production will rise, but ultimately it will fall. There may, of course, be numerous and important exceptions; for there may be real and permanent difficulty in increasing the supply of certain materials; but the cereals, and generally the great vegetable staples, are a singularly unfortunate example to allege. Here at any rate there is no theoretical difficulty, and has been no practical difficulty, in increasing all the factors of production *ad libitum*.

We are now in a position to examine various diagrammatic

CH. V   "INCREASING AND DIMINISHING RETURNS"   535

methods which have been employed to exhibit the relation between value in exchange and cost of production, determining the normal price of an article by the method of in- Intersecting curves of "demand" and "cost of production."
tersection. It is usual to speak in this connection, as in that of the market,[1] of a demand curve and a supply curve, but to distinguish between the cases that illustrate diminishing and those that illustrate increasing returns. Thus, we might take Fig. 36 to illustrate the case of an industry following the law of increasing returns. This would mean that if the quantity Ox of the commodity

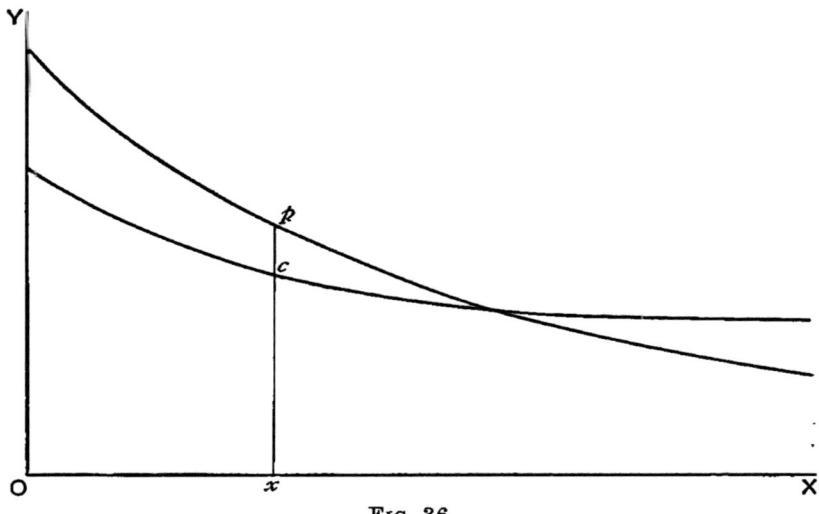

FIG. 36.

were produced its market value would be xp per unit, and the cost of production of a unit would be xc. Under these conditions there would obviously be an inducement to extend the industry. As Ox increased xp would, of course, fall. But so, by the action of the law of increasing returns, would xc; for as the output increased, economies could be introduced which would bring down the cost of production. There is a limit, however, to the decline of xc, whereas there is no limit to that of xp, and therefore a point of intersection must ultimately be reached. If the production were carried beyond this point, the cost of production would be greater than the price; that is to say, the effect of applying the necessary combination of

[1] Page 504.

factors of production at the margin of this industry would be the sacrifice of (objectively) higher values at the margin of other industries; and there would consequently be a tendency for these factors to flow from this industry to others, and so to contract the supply.

We may note, once for all, that what appears to be in the mind of writers who use this diagram is prevailingly cost of production as measured in the standard unit (gold). But as the distinction between this measurement and the measurement of the factors of production themselves, in their proper units, has seldom been kept steadily in view, there has naturally been some ambiguity in this matter.

Apart from this, we must carefully note that the two curves cannot be interpreted in the same manner. The demand curve represents a group of facts or possibilities which all of them exist contemporaneously. It is a synopsis. The high values near the origin represent possibilities as to market price, should an isolated change take place in the supply of this particular commodity, and they represent actualities in the shape of the (objective) value of certain units of the commodity to the persons who actually consume them; whereas the supply curve does not represent a series of co-existing facts. It is not true that some units are produced at the high cost represented by the points of the curve near the origin. The economies resultant on the larger output affect the conditions of production generally, and if the amount produced is Ox, the cost xc (except for temporary and individual reasons) will apply to one unit as much as to another. Scrupulous writers are also careful to note that the curve is often used with a historical significance, and in that case the high values near the origin no longer represent even potentialities in case of a reduced supply, for many of the economies which have been effected are permanent and might be applied even to a smaller supply. The supply curve, in such a case, represents a historic development on which the industry has travelled forward, but on which it could not travel backward without modification. This being so, it would be an altogether grotesque supposition that during the whole of this historical process the demand curve had remained constant. Thus the two curves could hardly be regarded as co-existing on the same plane, and no satisfactory interpretation can be given to their intersection.

It is undoubtedly true, however, that in some cases economies can at once be effected, if the scale of production is increased, without awaiting the elaboration of new methods. In such cases all the possibilities represented by the declining cost of production curve may be conceived as actually co-existing, *qua* possibilities, though not as actualities. In the same way an amount-of-the-supply and market-price curve represents a series of prices that co-exist as *possibilities* but not as actualities; whereas a curve of marginal significances represents, if properly constructed, a group of co-existing *actualities*. With these limitations a curve (as in Fig. 36) may be accepted as theoretically giving a closer approximation to the truth than the straight line of Fig. 31, in cases where the whole curve of demand is given from the origin onwards, or in which a large part of the whole curve is under consideration. Within the limits of actual oscillation, while "other things remain the same," a straight line will often best represent the facts. {Legitimate use of intersecting curves to illustrate "increasing returns."}

The case is far worse for the application of the method of intersection of supply and demand curves, as in Fig. 37, to instances that are supposed to illustrate the "law of diminishing returns," and this unfortunately has been its favourite application. We have seen that it is normal for a sudden increase in the demand which provokes a sudden increase in the supply to meet with the check caused by the difficulty of suddenly increasing certain of the factors of production, whether land, or skilled labour, or elaborate machinery, or premises. Hence an up-sloping curve will represent the immediate effect on cost of production of an expansion of the supply. We have seen, however, that these effects are transitory. It is only a question of time; for if time be given, all the factors of production will probably be made to flow into this particular industry in proportions corresponding to, if not identical with, those that prevailed before; and the increased scale of production will give scope to all the usual economies. Broadly speaking, then, the up-sloping curve of {Confusions and errors in their use to illustrate cases of diminishing returns.}

supply, as contrasted with the down-sloping one, represents not a class of industries, but the condition that the increased demand is recent and has been sudden. There is not only a difference but a contrast between the immediate and the ultimate effect of an increased demand accompanied by an increased supply. The obvious application, however, of the up-sloping curve of supply to the *immediate* effects of an increased demand has, I think, misled students into the assumption, never sufficiently examined, that there is a large and normal class of industries to which this form of curve *permanently* applies.

The remark which has been made with reference to Fig. 36 is also applicable here. The lower curve represents a succession of facts and is not a synopsis of co-existing ones. Lower ordinates of the supply curve nearer the origin do not represent any actual facts which exist contemporaneously with those represented by the ordinate of the point which the production has actually reached; whereas the higher (objective) significance of the units nearer the origin, as represented by the demand curve, does represent facts that co-exist with the lower objective significance of the marginal units.

But the same form of curve has often been used for quite a different purpose to which this last objection does not apply, but which is open to other objections still more grave. If we select some factor, such as land, to exclude from consideration, and then draw a curve on which we arrange the individual units of the product in order of the proportion in which they depend on this factor and not on the others, we shall again obtain a curve of the form presented in Fig. 37. Thus, if land were the factor excluded from representation in our supply curve, we should register at the origin that individual unit, say of wheat, which had been produced by the smallest output of labour and capital because it was raised on the most fertile land; that is to say, the land employed in its production, having the highest marginal efficiency, would have been combined with the smallest amount of the other factors.

In every industry the different units will be produced under very different conditions, and when they are brought to market the ratio in which wages, rent, transport, expenses

CH. V   " INCREASING AND DIMINISHING RETURNS "   539

of management, and so forth, enter into their costs of production will be different in each case, whether we measure some or all of these agents in their proper units, or measure all of them in the general standard (gold). And we may of course arrange them if we like in the order dictated by the proportion in which any one selected factor or factors (or all the factors except one or more selected ones) have entered into the process of their production. We should then have a curve of the form represented in Fig. 37. Here the ordinate of a certain unit would not be xc because the

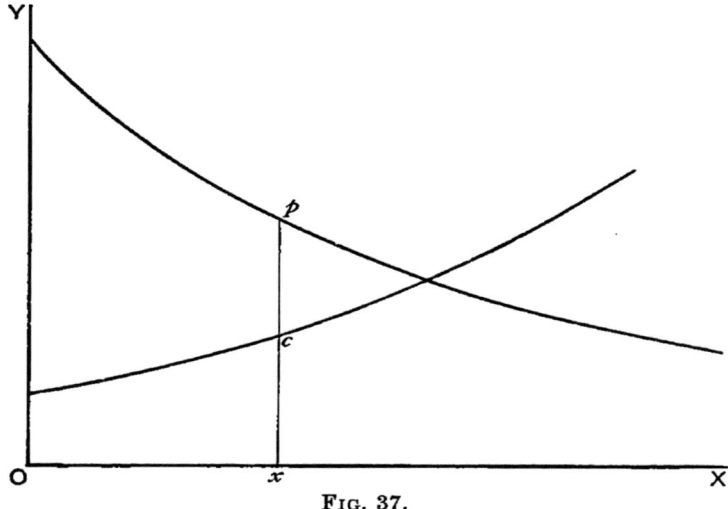

FIG. 37.

total number of units produced is Ox, but that particular unit would be registered in that place because its ordinate is xc. It is as if you were to collect a number of men and arrange them in order of their heights. A certain man would not be, say, 5 ft. 11 in. because he was the twentieth man originally brought in, but would be put into the twentieth place because he was 5 ft. 11 in.

The habit of treating land as something wholly exceptional that does not enter into production on the same footing as other factors has led to a frequent use of this form of diagram as though it represented cost of production. It will be worth while to dwell on this point for a moment. It is usual to speak of wheat which has been grown on specially fertile ground as having been raised "under favourable conditions." This is quite natural and intelligible in itself, but if we translate it into a statement that the cost of production of this wheat has been less than that of other wheat grown on less fertile ground, we at once land ourselves in a tangle of confusion. There is no presumption that the cost has been less to the man who raised it, for he has had to pay higher rent for the more fertile land. Nor is there any reason to suppose, from the communal point of view, that a smaller sacrifice of open alternatives has been made for this unit of wheat than for any other. Just as in a broad generalisation we assume that labour might be withdrawn from the margin of any one industry and applied at the margin of other industries, not indeed without loss, but without great and conspicuous loss if the transfer were only small, and with a loss that diminishes without limit as we suppose the transfer to be smaller, so we must also assume that if land were withdrawn in small quantities from any given use, agricultural or other, it could be applied to some other use where it would be only a little less valued. The cost of production of any commodity, as we have seen, is determined by the significance of the alternatives sacrificed in its production, and there seems to be no kind of justification for excluding land, and the other purposes that it might have served, from the cost of production either of wheat or of anything else. If we ask the origin of so strange a practice as that of excluding land (which, moreover, we cannot separate from capital) from consideration when estimating the cost of production, the answer seems to be as follows: It was taken as an axiom that cost of production determined the value of the product. It was then seen that wheat raised upon land for which a high rent had been paid sold for no more than wheat of the same quality that had been raised on inferior land. Hence the syllogism: "Cost of production determines exchange value; rent does not affect the exchange value of wheat; therefore rent is not part of its cost of production." The major premise was false and the conclusion absurd, but so firmly was the premise established as an axiom that even

The use of an up-sloping curve to indicate increasingly "unfavourable conditions."

Aftermath of the "cost of production" fallacy.

a *reductio ad absurdum* did not lead to its revision. The argument, such as it is, would of course apply just as much to labour, raw material, or capital, as to land. For some wheat less has been paid in wages than for other wheat of the same quality; it would follow that if cost of production determines exchange value, wages are not part of the cost of production. The general truth is, as we have seen, that the value of the factors of production is derivative from the value of the product. The price or hire of some land is higher than that of other land because its products or services are more valued, but the same is true of all raw material and of all kinds and grades of skill. Their value is derivative from the value of the commodity, or ultimately the experience, they produce. This derivative nature of the value of factors of production was perceived in the case of land earlier than in other cases; and thinkers who were still under the impression that in general the product derived its value from the value of the factors of production, and who perceived that this was not true in the case of land, at once set land on a footing of its own, with the resultant confusions which we have been examining.

A certain semblance of rationality has been given to this arrangement of the units of wheat in the order of the decreasing ratio in which the cost of land stands to the cost of the other factors in their production, by dwelling on the idea that the most fertile land is likely to be occupied first, so that every extension of agricultural industry will be from more to less suitable land; and then the reaction of the considerations already dwelt on[1] in relation to the immediate effect of a rise or fall of demand has enabled writers to pass from this specific conception of progressive recourse to inferior land in wheat-growing to the general conception of the necessity of progressive recourse to less and less favourable conditions as any industry expands; and so again a rising curve has been taken, without adequate examination, as representative of a large and normal class of industries. But this whole conception is illusory. The conditions that are favourable or otherwise to any particular industry are constantly changing, and an increasing scale of production is itself a factor in the change.

[1] Page 538.

A man may be at a positive disadvantage because he set up his machinery yesterday as against the man who is to set it up to-day. Manitoba may offer more favourable conditions for growing wheat for the London market than Essex does. It is quite as likely that the established man has to work at a disadvantage because he is committed to less favourable conditions than are now open, as it is that the man who is entering upon the industry is at a disadvantage because he finds all the most favourable sites and conditions preoccupied.

But probably the most deeply seated of all the predisposing causes which keep the up-sloping curve of cost of production in favour is one that has no connection whatever with the theory of decreasing returns. Neither of the intersecting curves of Fig. 20, on page 499, has any connection with production, or cost of production, at all. Yet one of them slopes up as the other slopes down. If we place all the holders on the up-sloping curve, so that all the "supply" is in the hands of the persons whose desires it represents, it is easy to fall into the habit of calling it the "supply" curve. We have seen that it is no such thing. It is the demand curve of a certain number of the persons in the market arbitrarily grouped together. The supply is not represented by a curve at all, but by a length on the abscissa. But once use crossing curves to illustrate the determination of the market price, and call the up-sloping one the "supply" curve, and you have at once a figure that you can transfer bodily, and without knowing that you are doing it, to the illustration of the regulation of "supply" as determined by cost of production. Thus crossing curves may come to be used indifferently to represent "demand and supply" or "demand and cost of production," the term "curve of supply" may be used indifferently in either case, the up-sloping curve of the one (which is merely a down-sloping curve of exactly the same nature as the other, reversed for convenience, and having no constitutional connection with "supply" whatever) may be transferred to the other; it may then be read as a curve of diminishing returns and increasing cost of production, and may create a habit of mind to which cases of "increasing return" present themselves as graphically inconvenient phenomena which must be recognised from time

A false analogy imported from intersecting demand curves of "buyers" and "sellers."

to time but can generally be comfortably neglected. A more disreputable origin for a respected figure in the economic world it would be difficult to conceive!

It remains true, however, that there may be industries in which an increased volume of production must normally imply increased cost, and under the limitations insisted on in the parallel case of decreasing cost of production [1] such industries might legitimately be illustrated by a diagram such as that of Fig. 37. But when this very ambiguous diagram is employed without examination to represent unspecified industries that obey the "law of decreasing returns"; when that law, as originally defined, has been the mere statement of a truism that applies to all industries; when the unwarrantable exclusion of rent from a place amongst the costs of production, and unwarranted assumptions and delusive analogies as to increasingly unfavourable conditions and as to the nature of supposed "supply" curves, have presided over the construction and the interpretation of the curve and strengthened its hold on the imagination, and when purely geometrical deductions from it have then been applied to important practical matters, it is surely time to submit all the emergent theories to a thorough revision, based on a severely precise definition of the meaning to be assigned to the curve, and a demonstration that it actually represents an important body of industrial fact.

Legitimate use of intersecting curves to illustrate "decreasing returns."

We may now summarise our results. A curve representing the conditions of increasing or diminishing returns, if properly constructed, would be an attempt to register a continuous series of changes of the nature of that represented by the transition in Fig. 31, page 519, from the unbroken to the dotted lines parallel to the axis of X. It might be in the same sense (increasing returns) or in the opposite sense (diminishing returns) to what is there represented. It would have no connection or relation whatever to the up-sloping curve on Figs. 20, etc.

A final word as to the processes illustrated in Figs. 19, etc., may be introduced. We must distinguish between the process by which the ordinate Oy was obtained, and the merely graphic presentation of the quantities which each

[1] Page 537.

of the consumers, A, B, C, etc., will take out of the market. The height Oy was only obtained by a process which involved the securing by A of the precise amount Oa, and by B of the precise amount Ob. These amounts were determined by the form of the curves (a), (b), etc., and the device of adding them together indicates that a claim is met or is not met, without reference to whose claim it is, according as its position is high or low on the relative scale. The shares which A, B, etc., have respectively taken in determining the final result are registered on the curves (a), (b), etc.; but though the results may be registered separately, the process could only be conducted in combination. We start with the marginal significance of the commodity to A at about $8\frac{1}{2}$, to B at $36\frac{1}{2}$, etc., and we learn from combining all the curves that if the total quantity of the commodity is Ox (d), the market will tend to bring the marginal significance to all the consumers to the magnitude Oy, and in proportion as its action is frictionless and effective will actually do so.

Return to the general law of the market.

In the same way if we take any individual industry, the price is determined by the collective curve of demand and the quantity possessed. This corresponds to the ordinates of the points a, β, γ in the curves of Fig. 19. It may be, like the ordinate of β, above, or like the ordinate of a, below the ideal equilibrating ordinate, but the curve itself enters, together with other curves, into the determination of that ideal ordinate; and the amount produced, that is to say, the amount of the productive resources which flows into this particular industry, tends to coincide with the abscissa corresponding to that ordinate.

If the amount of the product can be increased or diminished by the inflow or outflow of the productive resources of the community in relatively fluid forms, the approach to the equilibrating ordinate will be rapid. If the forms in which the factors of production can be added or withdrawn are such as require a long period of time to mature or to wear out (deep shafts, for instance, or extensive premises and elaborate machinery), the movement will be slow; but in any case the price will only be changed by a change in the amount produced. Except as it affects that, the ideal equilibrating ordinate can have no influence on the price. Thus, if we know the course of the curve in the neighbourhood of the actual point reached by the supply, and know what the supply is, we know the price. If we wish further to know whether the tendency will be in the direction of expanding or contracting the supply we must know what the cost of production in the existing state of the industry actually is. This cost of production is represented by the ideal equilibrating ordinate and is no other than the marginal value of other commodities, measured for convenience in the standard (gold); just as the equilibrating point to which A's desire for plums can be satisfied is determined by the place of plums on the relative scales of B, C, etc. If by any combination of factors (and there will probably be a number of different combinations realisable under different conditions, and equivalent to each other as measured by the standard) a unit of the commodity can be produced at a cost less than its present price in the market, the tendency will be for the supply to increase. If no such combinations will produce it except at a cost which exceeds its present price, the tendency will be for the supply to contract.

But as we advance from individual curves to the collective curves of great industries it comes out more and more clearly that all the elements of a commercial civilisation mutually determine each other; that any marked change in the conditions disturbs the whole structure, composition, and significance of our units; and that the diagrammatic method can only be regarded as precise, even ideally, when it refers to an industry or a portion of an industry that is too insignificant a fraction of the whole to cause serious disturbance in general relations. In other words, it is only in the neighbourhood of present margins that our standard units can be regarded as stable. In an individual curve we may fruitfully imagine ourselves, if due caution is exercised, as travelling far; but only on the supposition that the general margins are maintained. In great collective curves we must never think of ourselves as commanding, even conjecturally, more than a minute portion of the tracing, in the neighbourhood of the actual point of realisation.

We have been engaged throughout almost the whole of this chapter in the discussion of theories about increasing and diminishing returns, and our conclusions have been almost entirely negative. One important point, however, remains, as to which we may hope for more positive results. The habit of isolating "labour," and tacitly assuming sometimes that it is, and sometimes that it is not, proportionately backed by other factors, has caused us a great deal of trouble, but it is not difficult to explain. It is the reward of labour, in the general sense of output of human effort, about which we are ultimately concerned, and all the questions about increasing and diminishing returns derive their interest from attempts to estimate or to forecast the conditions under which humanity conducts or will conduct its attempt to secure the satisfaction of its desires from the resources and opportunities of nature. If the law of diminishing returns *to labour* is, or will ever become, dominant, these conditions will become less favourable, and the thought of this possibility has sometimes been a nightmare to the speculative thinker. I am not about to enter upon any investigation of the terrors that haunt many minds as to the ultimate limitation of the resources of the planet. Though it be true at the present moment that the whole of the inhabitants of the globe could stand shoulder to shoulder on the surface of the Isle of Wight, it is of course easy to shew that if the increase of the population proceeded uniformly at a moderate rate, a state of things would come about within a calculable and imaginatively not a very remote period at which there would be no room for them to stand shoulder to shoulder on the face of the dry land and on the floor of the ocean. For the matter of that, it would be equally easy to shew that within a calculable period the atmospheric envelope of the planet would not contain sufficient nitrogen to renew the tissues of the population, if all other obstacles to their increase were removed; and possibly the one speculation may be found as suitable food for melancholy as the other to one whose temperament promotes "going far to seek disquietude."

But apart from these speculations which are too remote to cause any rational anxiety if they stood alone, there is a reason why a perpetual suggestion of the possibility of decreasing returns to labour, as an instant possibility, should force itself upon our minds irrespective of any foundation that

"INCREASING AND DIMINISHING RETURNS" 547

t may or may not have in reality; and if we can rob this
ismal suggestion of the unfair advantage it derives from a
wholly irrelevant group of phenomena we may perhaps have
ontributed in some modest degree to the gaiety of nations.

Let us then suppose that some individual industry
llustrates the law of increasing returns in the sense *This terror is*
hat if an increasing volume of human effort were *fostered by*
levoted to it, land, capital, and so forth, could be *phenomena that in*
btained on such terms that the marginal effective- *no way*
less of labour, measured by product in bulk, would *justify it.*
ncrease. Now, taking Fig. 38 in which as usual we measure

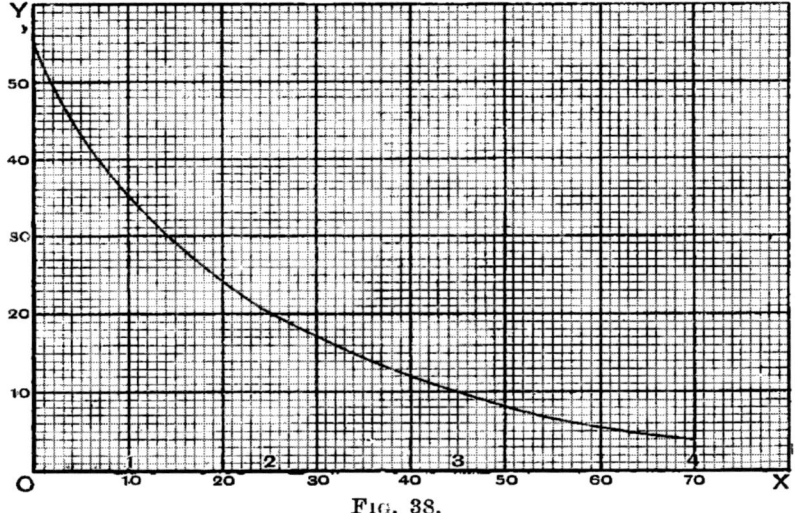

FIG. 38.

on the axis of X units of the product, and on the axis of Y
heir marginal exchange value, we are to suppose that if we
louble, treble, or quadruple the amount of labour devoted to
his industry we shall in each case more than proportionately
ncrease the material output. The divisions of the paper then
epresent the selected unit of the commodity, and the numerals,
., 2, 3, 4, placed at increasing intervals, represent the succes-
ive additions to the product caused by the doubling, trebling,
r quadrupling of the output of effort. The figure would then
nean that whereas a given number of men, which we take as
our unit, properly backed by capital and so forth, would pro-
luce an amount of the commodity represented by 10, double

that number of men would produce not 20 but 25, three times the number not 30 but 45, and four times the number not 40 but 70. But we are dealing with the material product in bulk, not with its value, and as the amount of the product increases, its marginal significance per unit will decline. If the curve takes such a form as that indicated in the figure, we see that doubling the number of men will give a more than proportional increase not only to the amount of the output, but also to its value, for the declining height of the ordinates is more than compensated by the increased length of the basis from 1 to 2. But when we pass from doubling to trebling, and from trebling to quadrupling, the original number of men, the still increasing proportional bulk of the output is now more than compensated by its decreasing value. Thus, although the industry obeys the law of increasing returns as interpreted in the return to labour of the material product, the law of diminishing returns is illustrated in the return to labour as measured in command of other commodities. For the units on the axis of Y which represent the value of the product must be interpreted in terms of other commodities. Men will give less of them in return for a unit of the commodity under investigation, because they are now better supplied with it.

But suppose they were better supplied with other things also. Suppose that the gradual increase of the population, accompanied by a suitable increase of capital and applications of fresh land or fresh and improved applications of land, enabled all the other industries to increase in volume also; and suppose that all likewise obeyed the law of increasing returns of material product to labour. Every one, then, having not only more of the particular commodity we first took into consideration, but having in suitable proportion more of all other commodities as well, will give as much of these other commodities for a unit of the first as they did before, and every one, therefore, will have more of everything, including opportunities of leisure and every form of self-expression. This would be the ideal condition of a progressive community, in which every generation, partly because of progress in the arts, but partly also from the mere increase of population and the resultant economies in every industry, would find itself wealthier than the last, and able to secure the co-operation and alliance of nature on ever pleasanter and easier terms. But it would still remain true that in each individual industry the position of its members would be strengthened if the other industries absorbed a relatively larger amount of the new energies and resources, and weakened if it absorbed a relatively larger amount itself. Every one would be aware that however much the ordinates of his industry were being raised by general processes that made all other commodities more abundant, and therefore to be had on easier terms, they would be falling in virtue of his own advance along his own line.

Thus generalising from his own industry every one will argue that the law of decreasing returns is already in full swing, that the more persons there are engaged in producing things, and the more abundantly they produce them, the poorer every one will be.

Thus we have arrived at a more exact analysis of the phenomenon which we have already described as the microbe of the disease of civilisation,[1] the fact, namely, that every man is convinced (except in exceptional periods) that his own industry or profession is overstocked. However true it may be that an increase in the numbers engaged in every industry, accompanied by a suitable increase in tools and appliances, would secure a larger general command of resources, it remains true that in any industry, taken in isolation, the reverse must seem to be (and in a sense must really be) the truth. Hence it is to the interest of the existing members of every industry, taken severally, that every other industry should recruit its staff and increase its output, while they themselves retain the exclusive right of ministering to the increased demand for their own product thus created. They will then reap the full benefit of the raising of their own curve which the advance of other industries down their declining slopes secures, and will themselves escape the obligation of raising the curves of others by advancing on the down-slope of theirs. But it is obvious that if the advance were even in all industries the remuneration of each factor of productivity, measured in the sum of things in the circle of exchange of which it represented the command, would increase.

[1] Pages 345 *sqq.*

CHAPTER VI

THE DIAGRAMMATIC EXPOSITION OF THE LAW OF RENT AND ITS IMPLICATIONS

SUMMARY.—*The current exposition of the law of rent, based on a diagram of "decreasing returns" to labour, for a constant of land, mistakes the characteristics of the constant for those of land. Hence many errors in nomenclature and in thought have arisen. It is equally easy and equally legitimate to represent the same facts in the form of a diagram with labour for the constant and land for the variable. This will shew that both rent and wages are shares in the product determined by marginal efficiency; and that when all the factors have received their share in this marginal distribution there is no surplus or residuum at all.*

The roots of the error concerning the exceptional treatment of land, which we examined in the last chapter, go down far deeper than the point to which we have as yet traced them, and the process of extirpation cannot be completed without an elaborate examination of the current exposition of the theory of rent. We will therefore go on to the examination of the ordinary diagram given to illustrate both the supposed "law of decreasing returns" and the "law of rent" derived from it. In Fig. 39 increments of "labour" applied to a constant of land are reckoned along the axis of X, and rates of increment to the crop per unit increment of labour along the axis of Y. The total yield for Ox_1 "labour" is Orw_1x_1, and labour being rewarded at the rate of x_1w_1 per unit receives the area Ow_1

The diagram of rent. Its form, its interpretation, and its implications.

altogether, the balance $y_1 r w_1$ being rent. If Ox_2 only had been applied to the same amount of land the total yield would have been the smaller area of $Orw_2 x_2$, but the reward of "labour" *per unit* would have been higher, namely, $x_2 w_2$. Rent would only be $y_2 r w_2$, a smaller proportion of a smaller total. Thus decreasing returns to land per unit and increasing returns to "labour" per unit are read as we recede from the margin, and decreasing returns to "labour" per unit and increasing returns to land per unit as we advance from the origin. More labour bestowed on

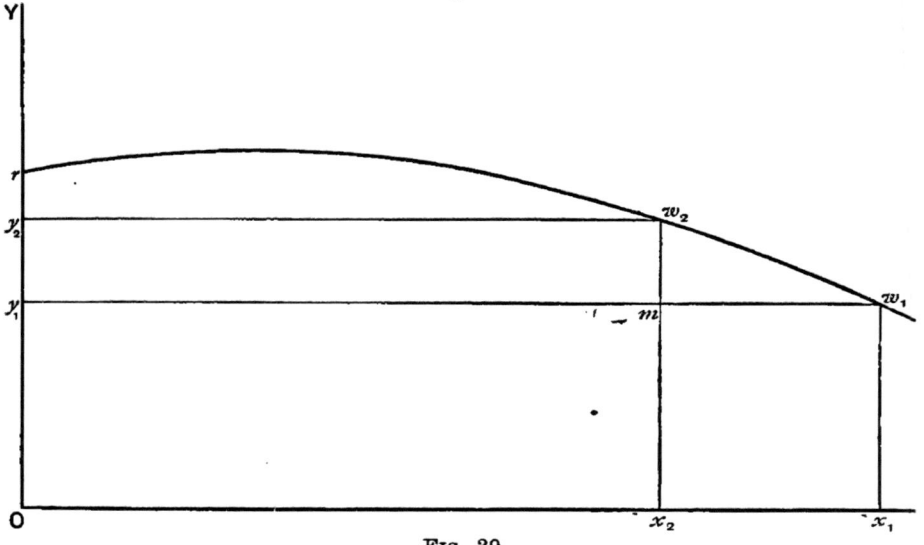

Fig. 39.

the same land means less land under the same labour. So we have these results: More labour on the same land or *less land under the same labour* means a larger rent per unit of land and a less "wage" per unit of "labour"; whereas less labour on the same land or *more land under the same labour* means a lower rent per unit of land and a higher "wage" per unit of "labour." Those of the results just formulated which are directly illustrated in the figure are very familiar to all students of Political Economy, and familiarity has made them appear axiomatically true. But those of them which are just as explicitly contained in the data, but are only indirectly illustrated by the figure, and which have been italicised in the statement just made, are unfamiliar to most students of Political Economy, and may appear startling and perplexing, though they are absolutely identical with those expressed in the more familiar form and at once accepted as axiomatic.

Thus every one sees that if (after a certain point) more labour is applied to the same land the return to the land will be higher. But every one does not see that this is exactly the same as saying that after that point if more land is brought under the same "labour" the return to labour will be higher.

In our figure rent appears as a mixtilinear area and "wages" as a rectilinear one; and this has usually been assumed to be due to some special characteristic of land, but if we work out our data under the other form of statement we shall find that these graphic forms are simply due to the fact that land was taken as the constant. Had we thought in terms of less or more land under the same cultivation instead of more or less cultivation bestowed upon the same land, we should have found "wages" represented by a mixtilinear area and rent by a rectilinear one. This I shall go on to shew in detail. But before proceeding to the demonstration it will be well to note certain special points.

I have explained why certain phrases have been italicised above. I must now explain why I have put "wages" and "labour" between inverted commas. It is because labour is taken to include capital. In short, "labour" means all the factors of production except land. And "wages" means the remuneration of all these factors. To measure them all in one unit implies that they have all been reduced to a common denominator, and this must have been done on some such principle as that expounded in Book I. Chapter IX. It would be useless to attempt to express such a unit accurately every time we have occasion to speak of it. Even to call it a "unit of labour-and-capital-reduced-to-a-common-denominator" would be too cumbrous. To call it a unit of labour is in the highest degree dangerous; but the danger is reduced, though not altogether avoided, by systematically writing "labour" for this complex of factors,

CH. VI RENT

and "wages" for its remuneration. We must add that the distinction between "labour" in this sense and "land" is artificial and arbitrary; for all the land we ever deal with embodies capital, and so does "labour" as now defined.

We have next to note that the figure, and the argument that usually accompanies it, do not really give us any theory of rent at all. They assume our own law of remuneration in proportion to efficiency for all the other factors (tacitly reduced to a common denomination), and then simply tell us that whatever is not anything else is rent.

Further, we must note with extreme care that the number of units of "labour," Ox_1 or Ox_2, applied to the constant of land, will be fixed by the alternatives open to land and "labour" respectively. "Labour" is devoted to, say, wheat-growing till the marginal return is only x_1w_1, because it cannot find any more eligible alternative, and it is not devoted to it beyond that point, at a lower marginal significance, because it can find alternatives as eligible. And in like manner so much land and no more offers itself at a declining marginal significance to a given amount of wheat-growing "labour," because it cannot find anything else better, but can find other things as good, to do with itself. So land will not come to a man unless he offers it as good terms as it can get anyway else, and men will not come to land unless it offers them as good terms as they can get anyway else. The quantities Ox_1, x_1w_1, y_1rw_1, are determined by the general conditions of industry and the markets; and if under conditions which would justify these proportions an individual should choose to take land and work on it at the rate represented by Ox_2, instead of earning Ow_2 and paying y_2rw_2 in rent, he would find that out of his total crop of Ow_2 he would have to pay a rent of y_1rw_1, and would only have Om minus the mixtilinear triangle w_2mw_1 for himself. If rent were at the rate of y_2rw_2, and "wages" at x_2w_2, it would be because more eligible alternatives had been opened to "labour," or a more abundant supply of land had become available to it as against the conditions that determined y_1rw_1 and Ow_1. It should be noted incidentally that any such change would be sure to affect the internal constitution of the complex unit of what we have called "labour"; it would not act upon interest on capital and wages for every different grade and character of work, for instance, in exactly the same proportion.

Lastly, we may note that the figure deals with yield per unit of land of a given quality, as it is plied with more and more "labour." It takes no account of different grades of land, each of which would present a curve of different form. Neither does the figure take account of the different conditions that might prevail on larger and smaller holdings.

With reservations, the nature of which will presently appear, as to the general form of the curve, we may now proceed to the detailed demonstration promised on page 552. It will be well to begin from the beginning and build up our curves step by step.

Suppose a man holds 50 acres of land and bestows 3000 hours' personal work upon it in the course of the year, *Construction* backed by tools and apparatus of every kind, stock, *of curves of* seed, manure and so forth, and also hired labour. *the marginal* An hour's labour will in this case be a mere *significance of labour to* symbol of an aggregate of factors of production, of *a constant of* defined magnitude, expressed under a common *land, and of the marginal* denominator, and will mean "the totality of the *significance of land to a* applications and combinations which may be *constant of* supposed to accompany, or to be included in, *labour.* the expenditure of an hour's work on the land by the tenant." Let us suppose that the crop is about equivalent to 5 quarters (or 1280 quarts) of wheat per acre. For convenience of subsequent operations we will take it at 1260 quarts, and this would be 630 quarts per half-acre. Thirty "hours" a year will be devoted to each half-acre. So the crop will be at the rate of 21 quarts per "hour" expended. We will take this as our starting-point. But it will be convenient to take a smaller unit of land than the acre or half-acre. Let it be the twentieth of a rood (which would be two poles), or the fortieth of a half-acre. The selection of the unit is determined merely with a view to diagrammatic convenience. Then our supposition will be: Land cultivated to the point of 60 "hours" to the acre yields the equivalent of 1260 quarts of wheat per acre, which is at the rate of 21 quarts per hour, or 15·75 per (two-pole) unit of land.

The scale of
1260 quarts per 80 land-units under 60 hours' cultivation
is the scale of
630 quarts per 40 land units under 30 hours' cultivation,
and the yield is at the rate of
630 ÷ 30 = 21 quarts per hour, or
630 ÷ 40 = 15·75 quarts per land-unit.

Here the reader must note carefully that these rates per unit of land and labour are not shares which fall to each of the factors, nor estimates of the value of their respective contributions. They simply indicate the ratio of the gross crop to the land or to the labour, taken severally. Yield per unit of land is a familiar conception. Yield per unit of labour is equally important for our present investigation, and the reader must try to make himself equally familiar with it.

Let us now suppose that if the man only cultivated at the ratio of 25 "hours" per half-acre his crop would be at the rate of 531·40 instead of 630.[1] Here note that we are imagining our cultivation to be less intensive than on the first supposition; that is to say, the cultivation or "labour" is spread thinner on the land. This we may think of in terms either of the unit of land having less labour spread on it, or of the unit of labour being spread over more land. Thus, if we pass from 30 "hours" on 40 land-units to 25 "hours" on 40 land-units, we get the same ratio (5 to 8) which we should have got had we passed from 30 on 40 to 30 on 48 (5 to 8 again); but of course the total crop on 48 land-units under 30 "hours'" cultivation will be greater by a fifth than that on 40 land-units under 25 hours' cultivation.

Thus if, as we have (arbitrarily) supposed, the crop on 40 land under 25 labour is 531·40 quarts, it follows that the crop on 48 land under 30 labour will be 637·68 quarts (six-fifths of the other); and whichever way we measure it we shall have a yield of 13·285 quarts per unit of land and of 21·256 quarts per unit of labour.

[1] It is of course admitted and understood that such minuteness of estimate takes us absolutely away from all contact with practical business or practical possibilities. It is adopted merely for graphic purposes and to illustrate the principles involved in the current expositions.

We may tabulate these results :—

	Quarts per "hour."	Quarts per land-unit.
30 to 40 gives a yield of	21	15·75
25 to 40 or 30 to 48 ,, ,,	21·256	13·285

Thus as we pass from 25 to 30 units of cultivation on 40 units of land we have decreasing returns to labour, but increasing returns to land. To say that we have a decreasing or increasing "total yield" would have no sense unless we had established some common denominator (pecuniary or other) under which we could express land or labour indifferently, or both collectively. This lies outside our present inquiry; and we see that "increasing" and "decreasing" returns, from our present point of view, are merely relative terms and may be applied to the same phenomenon simultaneously according to whether we are speaking of land or of "labour." To this important conception we will presently return, but meanwhile we are to follow our investigations along another track.

Our hypothesis is that at 30 "labour" to 40 land we have a crop of 630; so that we may call this the return either to 30 "labour" or to 40 land, on the supposition of the ratio of 3 to 4. When we alter the ratio to 5 to 8, we may keep either 40 land (with 25 "labour" spread on it), or keep the 30 "labour" and spread it over 48 land. In the one case we shall have a crop of 531·40 instead of 630, and in the other a crop of 637·68 instead of 630; that is to say, if we spread so much less labour on the same land we shall decrease the yield *to the land* by 98·60 quarts, and if we bring so much extra land under the same "labour" we shall increase the yield *to the "labour"* by 7·68 quarts.

We may now begin to plot out our results on Fig. 40. In (*a*) we may assume that the half-acre (40 of our land-units) is constant. We mark along the axis of X the number of "hours" per half-acre put in annually, and on the axis of Y rates of yield measured in quarts, so that the crop per half-acre, for any ratio between land and labour, will be represented by areas in which every small square is

CH. VI RENT 557

a quart. In (*b*) we will take 30 " hours " of cultivation per annum as our constant, and will measure along the axis of *X* the units of land (twentieths of a rood) over which it is spread. The meaning of the units on the axis of *Y* will still be rates of yield measured in quarts, and areas will represent the crop per 30 " hours' " cultivation, for any ratio between land and " labour." In (*a*) as we advance from 25 " hours " to 30 we secure by hypothesis an addition of 98·60 quarts per half-acre, or if we move in the opposite direction, from 30 to 25, a diminution of that amount. This may be plotted on (*a*) by erecting a rectangle of an altitude 19·72 on the base line between 25 and 30. This means that, land remaining constant, the addition or withdrawal of these 5 hours per half-acre will make the difference we have assumed in the crop. But, as we have seen, to pass from 30 to 25 on (*a*) is equivalent to passing from 40 to 48 on (*b*), since each of them means changing the ratio of 3 : 4 into that of 5 : 8 ; and the effect of this change is to increase the yield to 30 " hours " of labour by 7·68. In (*b*), on the base line between 40 and 48, we must therefore erect a rectangle of area 7·68 or altitude 0·96, which means that, " labour " remaining constant, the addition or subtraction of these eight land-units will make a difference of 7·68 quarts in the crop.

Note that movement towards the origin in (*a*) corresponds to movement away from it in (*b*). We may either start with the ratio 3 : 4 and move to the left in (*a*) and to the right in (*b*), or we may start with the ratio 5 : 8 and move to the left in (*b*) and to the right in (*a*). That is to say, our data imply that if we increase the number of " hours " spread over the same land we shall increase the yield per unit of land and decrease the yield per unit of " labour," whereas if we bring more land under the same output of cultivating labour we shall increase the yield per unit of " labour " and decrease the yield per unit of land.

Let us now change the ratio of 3 : 4 in the contrary sense. Let us suppose (as an arbitrary datum) that a ratio of 7 : 8, that is to say, of 35 " labour " to 40 land, or 30 " labour " to 34·286 land, would yield a crop of 705·98 per half-acre, or six-sevenths of this, viz. 605·13 per 30 "hours." This would mean that the difference made to the

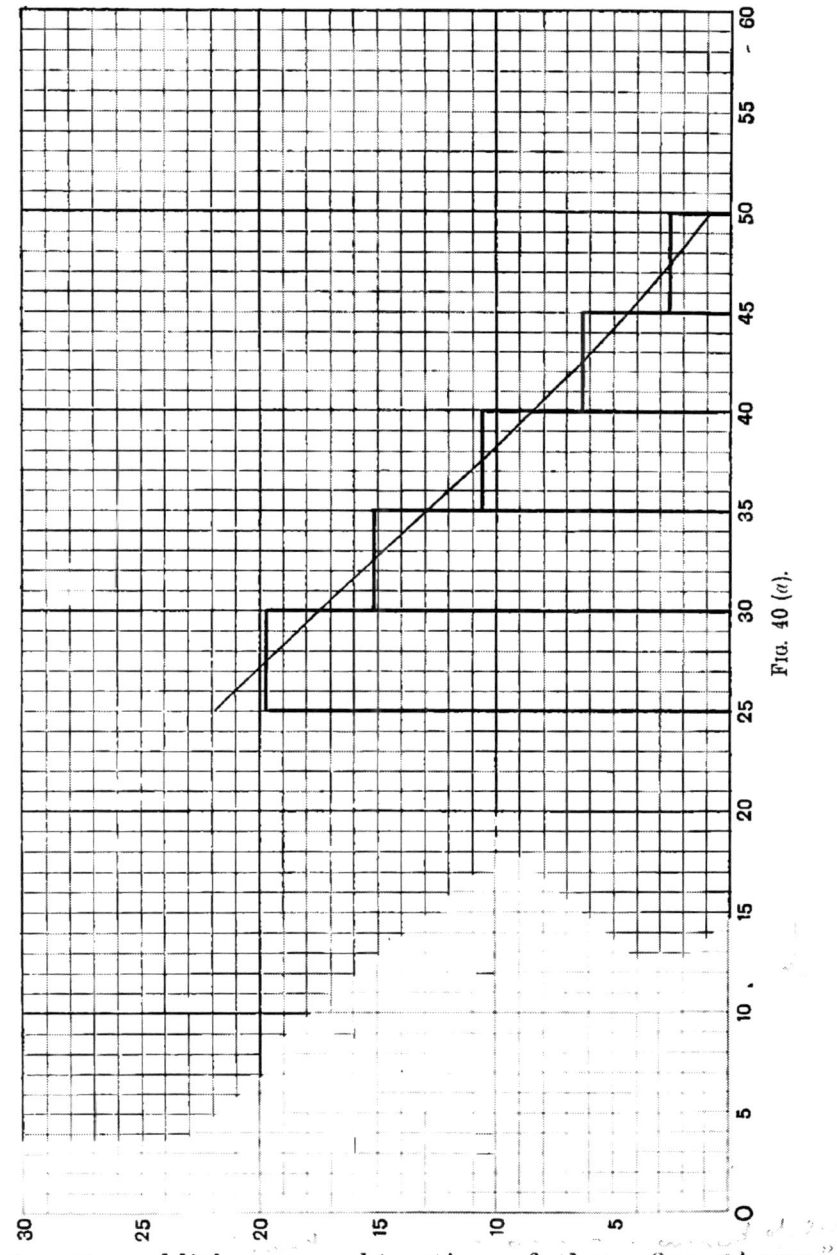

Fig. 40 (a).

crop by the addition or subtraction of these five "hours" on 40 land-units is 75·98, and may be represented on (a) by a rectangle on the base line between 30 and 35 with an

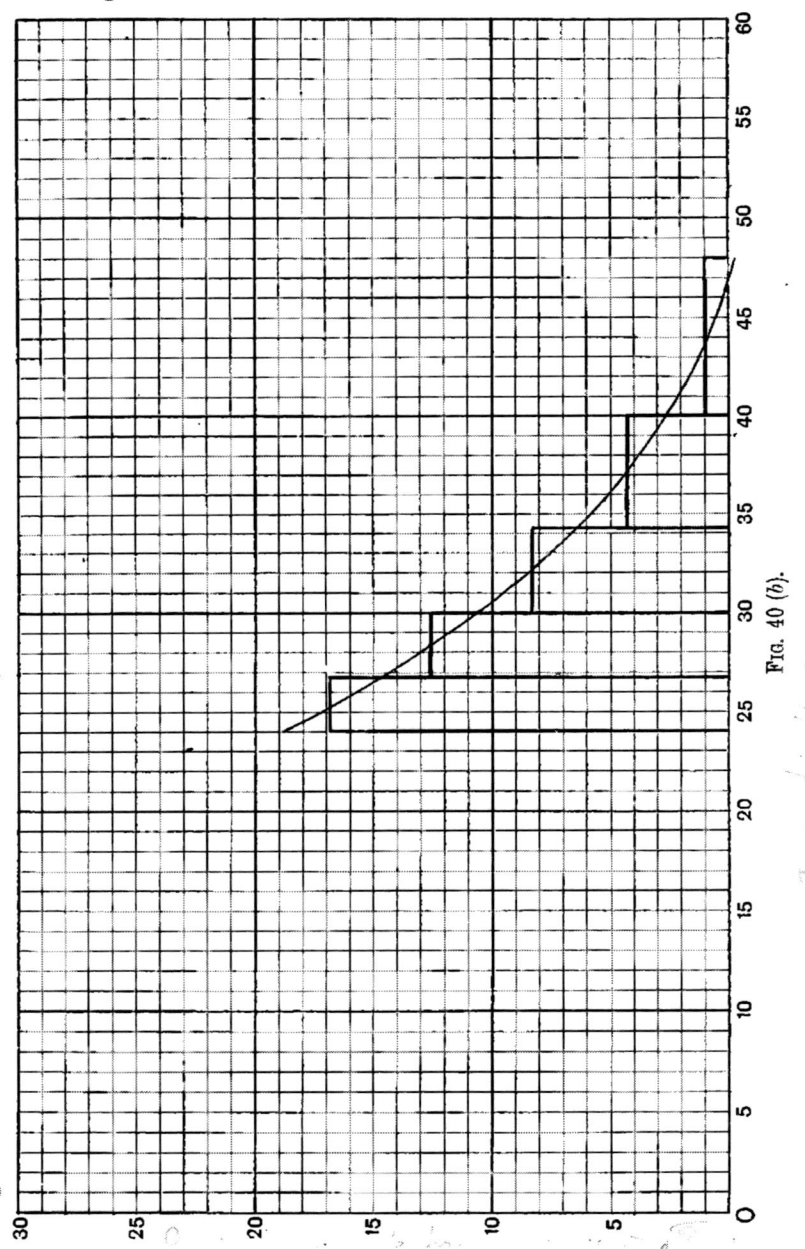

Fig. 40 (h).

altitude of 15·20; whereas the difference made by the addition or subtraction of these 5·714 land-units under 30

560   THE COMMON SENSE OF POLITICAL ECONOMY   BK. II

"hours" of cultivation is 24·87, and will be represented on (b) by a rectangle whose base is the line between 34·286 and 40 on the abscissa, and its altitude 4·35.

We can now tabulate and extend our results. If we start with the rectangle on the left in (a) and move to the right, and with the corresponding rectangle on the right in (b) and move to the left, we shall have a series of increments to record on (a), and of decrements to record on (b). But the figures may be read either way, and if we read (b) towards the right and (a) towards the left we should have increments to record on (b) and decrements on (a). We shall therefore not mark positive or negative signs on our table; for if we read it down the differences in column 6 will be positive and those in column 7 negative, and if we read it up it will be the other way, and either reading is equally legitimate.

Ratio of "Hours" to Land-units.	"Hours" to Constant of 40 Land-units.	Land-units to Constant of 30 "Hours."	Crop to Constant of Land (on Arbitrary Hypothesis).	Crop to Constant of "Labour" (on same Hypothesis).	Difference in Yield to Constant of Land.	Difference in Yield to Constant of "Labour."	Height of Rectangle on (a).	Height of Rectangle on (b).
5 : 8	25	48	531·40	637·68				
					98·60	7·68	19·72	0·96
3 : 4	30	40	630	630				
					75·98	24·87	15·20	4·35
7 : 8	35	34·286	705·98	605·13				
					53·18	35·76	10·64	8·34
1 : 1	40	30	759·16	569·37				
					31·85	42·03	6·37	12·61
9 : 8	45	26·667	791·01	527·34				
					12·99	44·94	2·60	16·85
5 : 4	50	24	804	482·40				

Now, as the effect of increasing the labour bestowed upon the same land in the one case, or increasing the land brought under the same expenditure of cultivation in the other, will obviously be continuous, we may trace curves on the principle fully explained on page 447, which in the case of (a) will correspond to the ordinary curve given to illustrate rent in the books, and in the case of (b) will be the complementary curve in which labour is supposed to be constant.

Thus, for any abscissa on (a) the corresponding ordinate will mark the marginal efficiency of labour per hour, at that point, in increasing the yield to a constant of half an acre of land (40 land-units); and for any abscissa on (b) the ordinate will represent the marginal efficiency of land per unit, at that point, in increasing the yield to 30 "hours" of labour.

What we have got in (a), therefore, is a portion of the familiar rent curve. It shows us the "decreasing returns" to "labour" as successive increments or doses are applied to the same piece of land; and since "labour" is remunerated at the rate of its marginal efficiency, the rectangle of the ordinate multiplied by the abscissa, that is to say, the rectangle contained by the curve, is the total amount that would be paid in "wages." There remains the rest of the crop for rent; and if the curve were completed, that would be represented by the mixtilinear area above the rectangle.

This last point may easily be established. The land would produce no crop at all unless some labour were expended on it. Thus, if we start with the crop for x "hours" per land-constant, and successively account for, and register as an area, the part of the crop dependent on the difference between x and $(x-1)$ "hours," the part dependent on the difference between $(x-1)$ and $(x-2)$, and so on, up to the part dependent on the difference between 1 and 0, we shall have accounted for the whole crop. Now our curve is constructed precisely on these principles. Over each successive base it bounds an area which represents, by construction, the part of the crop for which the corresponding portion of the abscissa is responsible. Thus, if we had completed it, it would account for the whole crop. For example, at the ratio of 3 "labour" to 4 land, or 30 "labour" to 40 land, we take the abscissa 30 on (a) and read $17·50$ as the marginal significance of "labour" per hour. If this represented a state of equilibrium, $17·50 \times 30 = 525$ would be the amount of the crop that would fall to "labour," and the rest would measure the rent of half an acre.

In (b) we should have a portion of a precisely analogous curve shewing the "decreasing returns" to land as successive increments are brought under the same amount of "labour"; and since land will also be remunerated at the rate of its marginal efficiency the rectangle contained by the curve is the total paid for rent. The rest of the crop will remain for "wages." The point 40 on the abscissa of (b) corresponds to the point 30 in (a). Reading the ordinate for the abscissa we find it to be $2 \cdot 625$. The rent then will be $40 \times 2 \cdot 625 = 105$, and the rest of the crop will be the "wages" of thirty "hours" of labour.

If our curves have been accurately drawn and correctly read these results must coincide. And so they do. For returning to page 554, where the total crop for 30 "hours" bestowed on 40 land-units is taken at 630 quarts, we find from (a) that wages will be at $30 \times 17 \cdot 5 = 525$, and from (b) that rent will be at $40 \times 2 \cdot 625 = 105$. And $525 + 105 = 630$.

Let it be clearly understood that all we have proved is that the same data may be diagrammatically expressed in two different ways; and that these two representations, if correctly made, will be consistent. That our sum comes out right proves nothing; and if it came out wrong it would disprove nothing. The curves are to be drawn in accordance with the calculations, and they can be calculated more accurately than they can be read. They illustrate the calculations; but they do not prove them to be correct. The calculations, as legitimate inferences from the data, must stand or fall on their own merits. The curves simply illustrate the relation in which the different inferences stand both to each other and to current (or recently current) economic teaching.

The essential and all-important point of the demonstration, up to this point, is that in the ordinary diagrams rent is set forth as a mixtilinear and "wages" as a rectangular area, not because there is any inherent appropriateness in these geometrical forms as representatives severally of the respective industrial factors, but simply because return to the constant, whatever it happens to be, will always come out as a mixtilinear area, and that to the variable as a rectangular one. And whether a distributive share is represented as a mixtilinear or a rectangular area, it is the same quantity and it is marginally determined.

This will become still clearer if we plot the total crop (for each ratio of land and "labour") to 40 land-units and to 30 "hours" respectively, in conjunction with the marginal returns to "labour" and to "land." I must refer my readers to the short mathematical treatise already mentioned [1] for the detailed justification of the general form of the curves which our data imply; but it is sufficiently obvious that the form of figure usually given (as in Fig. 39) is an exceedingly crude representation of the facts. The more careful writers always state that the law of diminishing returns will only come in "after a certain point," and assume that when we are near the origin increments of labour will produce more than a proportionate increase in the product. Further, it is clear that if I were to distribute a few hours' labour over many acres of land (really distributing it over the whole, not selecting a portion of it), I should produce no appreciable effect at all. The difference between giving so much labour and no labour would not be perceptible. If, on the other hand, I were already giving 300 days' work to a holding of 40 acres, every extra hour of work would produce an appreciable result. Thus I have attempted, in the work referred to, to shew that our curves will pass through the origin, will rise for a time, and then decline. Our data have hitherto been assumed in accordance with this theory, and we may now extend them so as to carry our data for (a) back to the origin in one direction, and some way farther to the right than it has yet reached in the other.

Construction of the rectangles of the gross crop to constant land and variable labour, and *vice versa*; and distribution of the whole product in accordance with marginal significances.

We will assume, then, the following data, some of which have been already tabulated, the rest being now introduced for the first time:— [2]

[1] *Co-ordination of the Laws of Distribution*, London, 1894.
[2] As a matter of fact the assumed data throughout conform to the formula, crop $= 2\cdot 248 x^2 e^{-\frac{x}{150}}$, in which x stands for the number of "hours" put in per annum per 40 land-units. The corresponding formulæ for the pair of curves on Fig. 41 (a), page 566, will naturally be $2\cdot 248 x e^{-\frac{x}{150}}$ for the curve containing the rectangle, and $2\cdot 248(2 - \frac{7}{150}x)xe^{-\frac{x}{150}}$ for the curve the integral of which equals the rectangle.

[TABLE

TABLE I.—Land-Constant at ½ Acre (40 Units).

Ratio of Labour to Land.	"Hours" of Cultivation per Constant of Land.	Crop per Constant of Land (Assumed).	Total Crop per Unit of Land (Derived).	Total Crop per Unit of "Labour" (Derived).
1 : 8	5	46·26	1·16	9·25
1 : 4	10	152·36	3·81	15·24
3 : 8	15	282·24	7·06	18·82
1 : 2	20	413·08	10·33	20·65
5 : 8	25	531·40	13·28	21·26
3 : 4	30	630·00	15·75	21·00
7 : 8	35	705·98	17·65	20·17
1 : 1	40	759·16	18·98	18·98
9 : 8	45	791·01	19·78	17·58
5 : 4	50	804·00	20·10	16·08
11 : 8	55	800·91	20·02	14·56
3 : 2	60	784·74	19·62	13·08
13 : 8	65	758·22	18·96	11·66
7 : 4	70	724·01	18·10	10·34

If we take the figures in the second column as a series of abscissas and those in the last column as the corresponding ordinates, we shall have a series of points in a curve the rectangle contained in which gives the total crop per half-acre (40 units) at any ratio of land to labour. And if we add the curve of marginal significance of "labour" applied to a constant of 40 units of land, we shall have on our Fig. 41 (*a*) one curve *c* (which stands for "crop") containing the rectangle of the total crop per 40 units of land, and another curve *w* (which stands for "wages") containing the rectangle of the share of labour in that total. The first of these rectangles minus the second will obviously represent the share of land, also as a rectangle. And this last rectangle will be equal to the total area of curve *w* minus the rectangle it contains. If we divide it by 40 we shall have the figure in the last column but one of our table.

But the assumed data of Table I. can be presented in Table II. for a constant of 30 "hours" and a variable of land-units. We have taken our points on the abscissa of (*a*) at uniform intervals of 5 units and assumed data to match them. The corresponding intervals on (*b*), being reciprocals, will not be uniform. It would, of course, have been equally easy to have gone the other way about, so the regularity in one case and the irregularity in the other has no theoretical importance. We will tabulate for 30 "hours'" constant the data corresponding to the abscissas from 60 to 15 in Table I.

TABLE II.—For 30 "Hours'" Constant.

Ratio of Labour to Land.	Land.	Crop per Constant of "Labour" (Derived).	Crop per Unit of "Labour" (Derived).	Crop per Unit of Land (Derived).
3 : 2	20	392·37	13·08	19·62
11 : 8	21·818	436·86	14·56	20·02
5 : 4	24	482·40	16·08	20·10
9 : 8	26·667	527·34	17·58	19·78
1 : 1	30	569·37	18·98	18·98
7 : 8	34·286	605·13	20·17	17·65
3 : 4	40	630·00	21·00	15·75
5 : 8	48	637·68	21·26	13·28
1 : 2	60	619·62	20·96	10·33
3 : 8	80	564·48	18·82	7·06

Here again, by taking the figures in the second row as abscissas and those in the last row as the corresponding ordinates, we shall obtain a series of points on a curve c, Fig. 41 (b), the rectangle in which gives the total return to 30 "hours'" cultivation applied to the amount of land marked by the abscissa; and if we add the curve of marginal significance of land, we shall have in (b) a curve c (crop) containing the rectangle of the total crop to 30 "hours," and a curve r ("rent") containing the rectangle of the share of land in that total. The first of these rectangles minus the second will represent the share of "labour," also as a rectangle. And this last rectangle will be equal to the total area of curve r minus the rectangle it contains. If we divide it by 30 we shall have the figure in the last column but one of Table II.

Thus the readings of (a) and (b), either in Fig. 40 or Fig. 41, will give absolutely identical results, if the figures are correctly and consistently drawn. The reader will be able to check this roughly by reading the curves for any two

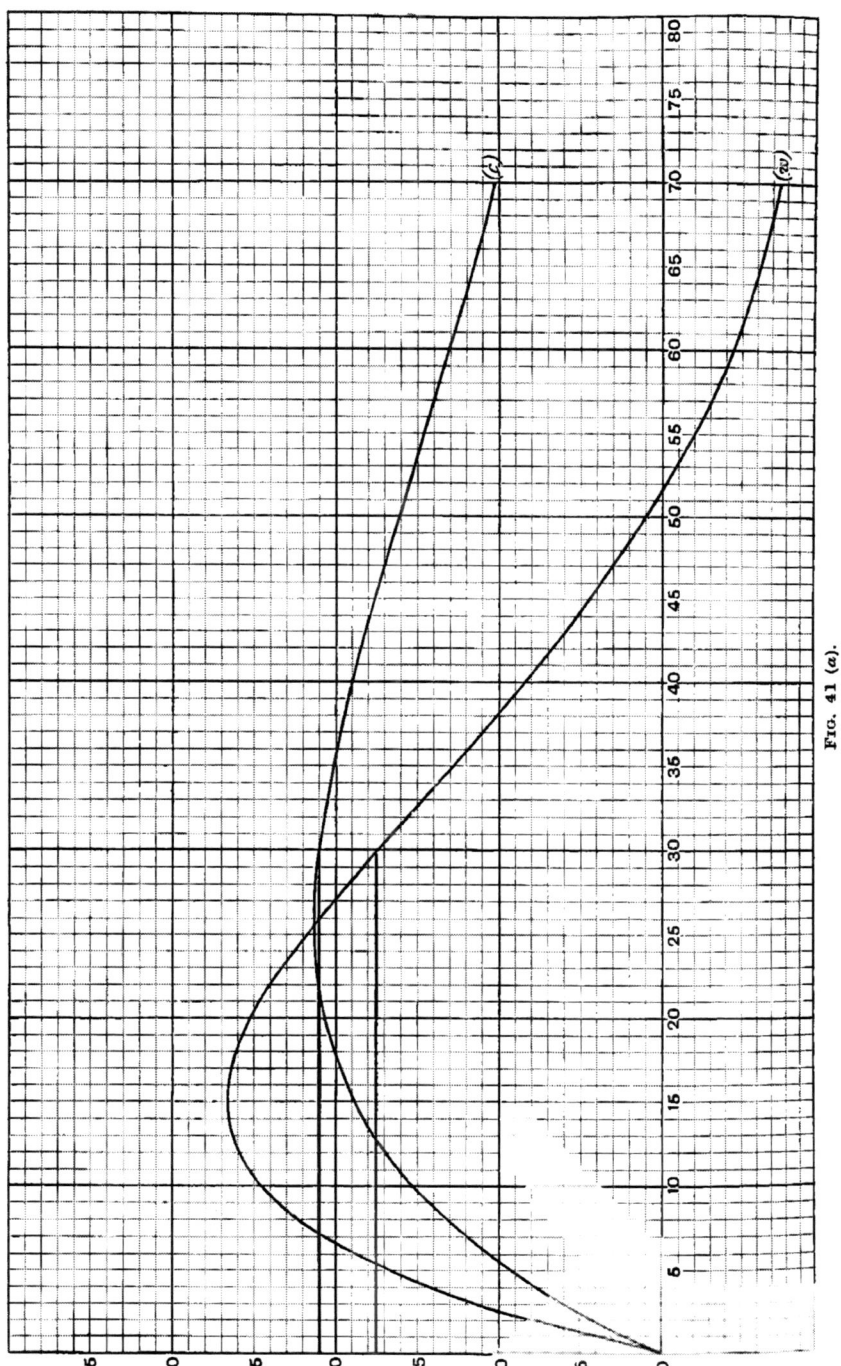

Fig. 41 (a).

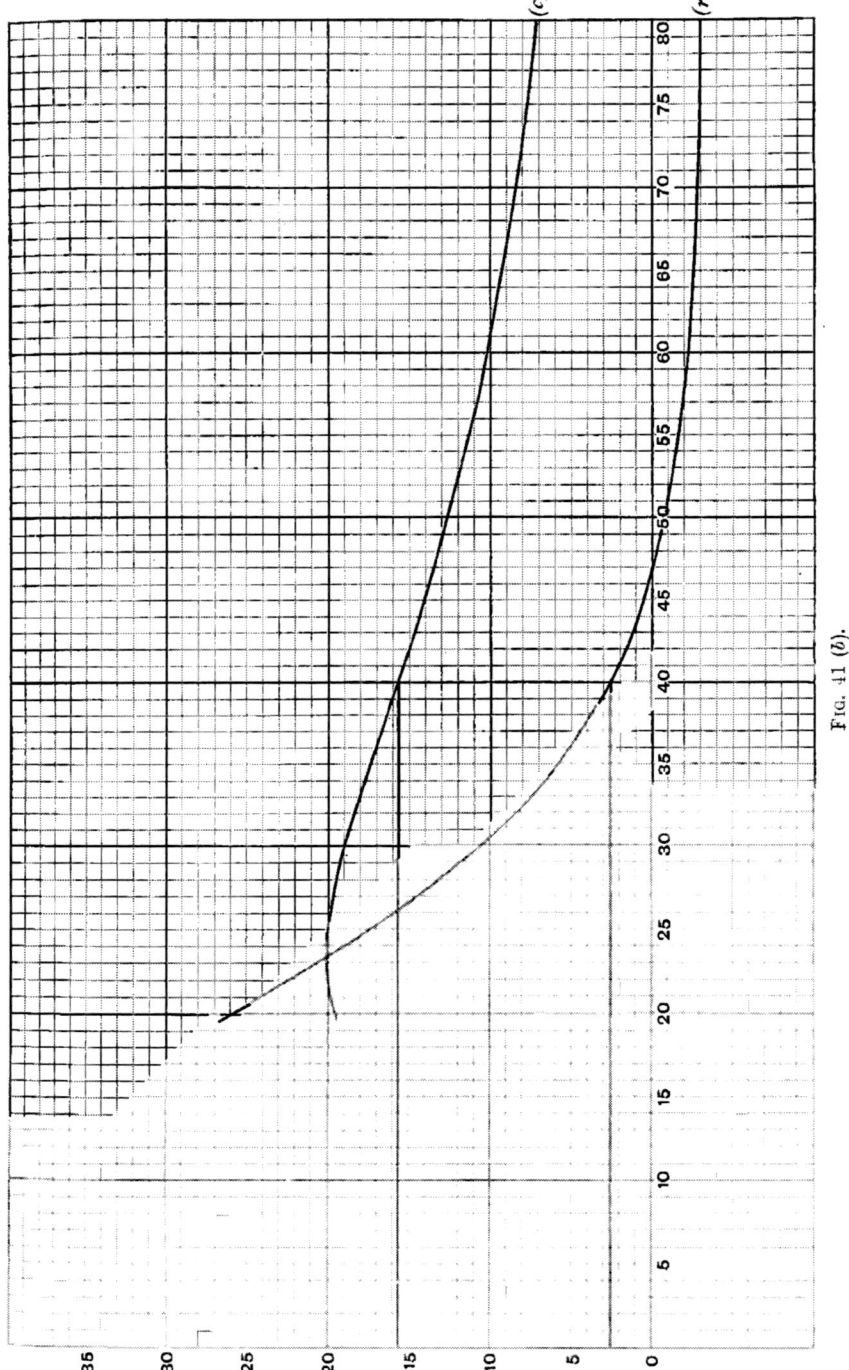

Fig. 41 (*b*).

corresponding points that lie between the tabulated points. For example, on (*a*) take the rate of 35 "labour" to 40 land. This gives us 12·9 for wages per hour; and 7·3 × 35 for the rent of 40 units of land, or about 6·4 per unit. Now 35 to 40 is 30 to 34·3. Therefore the corresponding point on (*b*) will have the abscissa 34·3. If we read the ordinates we find that rent is about 6·4 and the wages 11·3 × 34·3 for 30 hours, or 12·9 per hour.

We have now thoroughly established the important conclusion that there is no special propriety in regarding rent as a residual share in the product, nor is there any special or necessary appropriateness in representing rent diagrammatically as a mixtilinear area, in contrast to the representation of wages, for example, as a rectilinear area. But the mistaken conceptions now dissipated have led to what I cannot but regard as disastrous confusions both in thought and nomenclature which may long impede the progress of Economics. It has been assumed, in the first place, that every economic quantity that presents itself graphically, under any treatment, in the form of a mixtilinear area has some specific analogy to rent. And here we may note that what is known as the "Ricardian" law of rent may be presented in this same form. Thus a diagram of the form in Fig. 39 (page 551) might be regarded not as shewing the relation between marginal-return-per-unit-of-labour-and-capital and ratio-of-labour-and-capital-to-land, but as an arrangement of the several units of labour and capital employed in the wheat industry, referred to the varying fertility of the land to which they are applied. We should then have the mixtilinear area representing the excess of the yield of the more fertile over the yield of the least fertile land under cultivation. The Ricardian theory of rent usually (though quite unnecessarily) assumes that the least fertile land will bear no rent at all, and in that case the mixtilinear area would represent the whole rent; otherwise it would represent the excess of rent over a minimum. Now, if you take a number of persons who possess different talents and arrange them in the order of the marginal value to the community of the exercise of their talents, you will have

Examination of errors resulting from a misconception of the rent curve.

near the origin an individual the product of whose efforts per annum is relatively high, and as you go forward you will come to individuals the exercise of whose talents produces a smaller and smaller pecuniary return. If we draw a line on the level of the return to the efforts of the least efficient of the men in question, the area above it will represent the excess over that minimum return that accrues to the more able individuals; and simply because this is a curvilinear figure the revenue it represents has actually been called "rent of ability."

It is clear that at this rate any excess in the value of one article above another that is nominally the same would be entitled to the name of "rent." Thus, if a pound of one kind of manure produces the same result as two pounds of another, and so forth, you might register pounds of the different manures, in order of their efficiency, along the axis of X, and treat the excess of efficiency of a pound of the one over a pound of the other as "rent of superior efficiency." Indeed, if any two things could perform the same function, but one of them could perform more of it than the other, you might regard the excess of the price of one over the price of the other as a case of "rent." And in very truth that is all that the Ricardian law of rent amounts to. If two pieces of land can each of them yield wheat to labour and capital, but one yields more wheat than the other, the value of that land will be proportionately higher, just as the value of an apple-tree that bore an average of two hundred apples of given quality per annum would be higher than that of one that only bore an average of one hundred and fifty of the same quality. In fact the Ricardian law of rent is nothing whatever but a statement that the better article commands an advanced price in proportion to its betterness. The introduction of the hypothesis that the lowest quality of the article is to be had for nothing would make the whole price of the better article due to its "betterness." If there is no such gratuitous supply, then only the excess of the price of the more expensive article in the market would be due to its "betterness," and the rest to its "goodness" up to the point of lowest goodness in the market.

Again, reverting to our former interpretation of the

figure (waiving all scruples as to the course of the curve in the neighbourhood of the origin), and bearing in mind that the form of the mixtilinear area is determined simply by the fact that land is constant, we shall see that by representing any other factor as constant we shall obtain a representation of it as a mixtilinear area. Thus, in all the individual and communal curves which represent the declining marginal significance of successive supplies of any commodity, we may regard the *psyche* or sensitive organism as the constant, and the areas as psychic. If the sensitive organism, or body of sensitive organisms, remains constant, successive increments of the provocative or stimulus will, after a certain point, produce decreasing revenues or volumes of the experience in question, and we shall therefore have the mixtilinear area representing an excess in the experience provoked by the earlier over those provoked by the marginal increments. When students perceived this they promptly dubbed that excess " consumer's rent."

But misleading as these uses of " rent " appear to me to be, they constitute but a small part of the evil that we have to deal with.

We have seen that the figure constructed on the hypothesis of land being constant, and labour and capital variable, may equally well be regarded as an illustration of the Ricardian theory of rent when associated, as it usually is, with the hypothesis of " no-rent " land being under cultivation. The general attitude of mind with regard to rent that results from all this may be thus described:—Rent is a residuum which is determined by the subtraction of the shares of the other factors of production, and what those shares are is determined by the remuneration they can secure on " no-rent " land—that is to say at the margin of cultivation.

<small>Rent not a residuum.</small>

We may notice in passing that this treatment of rent as a residuum incidentally stultifies the claim of the current economic science to have established a " law of rent " at all. For if rent is simply what is left when the other factors have been satisfied, we have not established a law of rent, but have assumed that we know how to determine the shares of everything except land, and then simply stated that what is not anything else is rent. If we start from $x = a+b+c+$ etc., we cannot determine a simply by the equation $a = x-b-c-$ etc., unless we have independently determined the values of b, c, etc. Thus, what is usually given as a derivation of the law of rent from the law of decreasing efficiency of successive doses of labour and capital on the same land is really an assumption that every other factor of production obeys the law of marginal efficiency which we have taken as our guide to the whole theory of distribution. Instead of elaborating a theory of rent the current exposition tacitly assumes a (correct) theory with reference to everything except land, and then claims that no theory at all is necessary for land. But our elaborate examination has shewn that the diagrammatic exposition strictly involves the conclusion that that same law really applies to land just as much as to the other factors. In truth, then, the mixtilinear area represents rent, not because it is all that is left when the other claimants have been satisfied, but because it represents the marginal efficiency of land, and would be represented by an ordinate if we had taken labour as the constant, just as labour is represented by an ordinate when we take land as the constant.

But we are concerned at present not with the inconsistencies already involved in regarding rent as a residuum, but with the further conclusions that have flowed from it. If rent, it is argued, is a surplus or residuum which can be arrived at by deducting the remuneration of the other agents, as measured by the return to them on marginal or "no-rent" land, why should not profits be regarded as the residuum or surplus to be arrived at by deducting the remuneration of other agents, as measured by their returns in a marginal or "no-profit" business? And when, by these or similar processes, we have arrived at satisfactory "laws" which determine rent, profits, and so forth, surely we can determine wages (as General Walker did) by making them, too, a residuum when the other factors have been paid off. It is clear that all such attempts are based on the system of equations $a = x-b-c-$ etc., $b = x-a-c-$ etc., $c = x-a-b-$ etc., and so on, none of which adds anything to the original datum

Consequences of the conception of rent as a residuum.

$x = a + b + c +$ etc., but each of which assumes that data have been independently obtained, with respect to all agents except that one to which it specially refers.

Nor is this the last or the worst of it. The reader will have noticed that the use of "margin" or "marginal" which we are now examining is quite different from that in which we have defined it on page 40 *sq.* and used it throughout this work. "Marginal land," for instance, or "marginal ability," in this connection, is not land or ability considered with reference to the volume of the supply, at the margin of which it is added or subtracted, but land or ability of the lowest intrinsic quality which is devoted to the industry in question. And the marginal conditions are not the conditions determined throughout the industry by the "margin" in our sense, that is to say, by the marginal significance of adding or subtracting a small increment, but are certain specified conditions applying to the production of specified units of the product. On this conception of margins many writers have conceived of one distributive category after another as consisting of an actually existing "surplus," mounting backwards towards the origin from the "margin," and constituting a great reservoir untapped by marginal distribution; and bewildered and bewildering attempts have been made to get at the marginal (least efficient) man working with the marginal (least efficient or least abundant) capital on the marginal (least efficient) land, and to calculate everything backwards from this point. But it must now be clear to the reader that all such attempts are based either on the mere arrangement of units on the abscissa in the order of their efficiency, which neither illustrates nor proves anything except that the better article commands the better price, or else are based on a misunderstanding of the geometrical form necessarily assumed by the area that represents the constant, whatever it may happen to be, in a diagram constructed on the principles of Fig. 39 (page 551). The ambiguous use of the term "margin" has obviously added to the confusion. We now see once for all that the marginal distribution in our sense (that is to say, the distribution of the product amongst the claimants in proportion to the

Errors arising from the ambiguous use of the terms "margin" and "marginal."

significance of the addition or withdrawal of a small increment, at the margin determined by the present supply), exhausts the whole product. The curvilinear area represents a margin just as much as the linear ordinate does, and may just as well be represented in the same geometrical form.

In our phraseology a unit "at the margin of x" is not contrasted with the other units in the group, which are in some way superior to it. All the units in the group are at the margin. The distinction is not between the x units of the group severally, but between the significance of each of a number of qualitatively indistinguishable units when forming one of a group of x and when forming one of a group of $x + 1$. The one use of the term implies qualitative differences, the other presupposes qualitative identity, within the group. In our sense of the term, therefore, all the units of every group are always marginal units, whatever the margin may be; and therefore, naturally, the marginal distribution accounts for the whole product.

It is open to any one to examine or to dispute the ethical or social claim of any factor of production to a share, in accordance with its marginal significance, or to argue that there is no industrial necessity to allow such a claim; but it is not open to any one who understands the facts to argue that when, by a marginal distribution, every factor, reduced to the common term (on the principles of equivalence of marginal significance expounded in Book I. pages 368 $sq.$), has been satisfied, there remains any residuum or surplus whatever to be divided or appropriated. The vague and fervid visions of this unappropriated reserve, ruling upward as we recede from the marginal distribution, must be banished for ever to the limbo of ghostly fancies.

Before we bid farewell to the current or recently current expositions of the law of rent, we have still to notice one curious and instructive point. There is no connection whatever between the definition of rent given by the economists and the demonstrations by which they seek to determine its amount; for the economists first carefully define land as the primitive and inalienable properties of the soil, and explain that any ordinary piece of agricultural land is, to an indefinite

The expositions of the law of rent have no connection with the definition of rent.

extent, not land at all, but capital; and then proceed to examine the law of rent (almost invariably drawing their illustrations from agricultural land) on principles that take no account whatever of this distinction; for, as far as concerns the "Ricardian" law, it is clear that if one man commands a rich alluvial soil, and another man commands soil which by drainage, permanent manuring, and other devices, has been made equally desirable, both the one and the other, and both in equal degree, will pay a higher rent than they would pay for unmanipulated moorland which it is just worth while for some one to cultivate. And again (to take the law of rent as expounded in connection with the principle of "decreasing returns"), whether the land which we rent has been made what it is by mixing marl with the original soil, by drainage, or by other deliberate process, or is what it is by virtue of its original properties, or has become valuable because of the opening of a railway line or the building of a number of houses in the neighbourhood, in any case it will be cultivated more or less intensively on exactly the same principles. The law of rent, then, as expounded by the economists, has no connection with land as defined by them, but connects itself readily enough with land in the popular sense, which is an amalgam of economic land and economic capital.

There is nothing surprising in this, for we have seen over and over again that it is impossible to draw the line either between land as a primitive gift of nature and land as embodying capital or the results of human effort, or between a change in the value of a piece of land caused by something that has been done to it and that caused by changes that have taken place elsewhere. And, finally, since we know that land and capital are remunerated on one identical principle, in conformity with their marginal efficiency, we can see that the attempt to distinguish accurately between them is as unnecessary as it is hopeless.

Indeed it may be roughly said that everything that we read in Economic books as to the pure theory of distribution, whether it refers to wages, interest, rent, or profit, is either false when asserted of the category under discussion, or else true of all the others as well.

CHAPTER VII

BANKING. BILLS. CURRENCY

SUMMARY.—*Banking had its origin in the practice of depositing money with goldsmiths for safe custody. It was found that most of the money so deposited was never taken out again, but was transferred from one credit to another. Hence it was found safe to invest the greater part of it in revenue-yielding ways, and only to hold a comparatively small reserve in gold. The miscellaneous forms of property held by the bank represent the sums that their clients hand over to each other by cheques and so help to transact the business of the country, and are in truth media of exchange. The actual transfers of gold necessary to settle balances, after all the obligations in the country have been "cleared" as far as possible, is undertaken by the banks without specific charge. But not so in the case of balances between one country and another.*

International trade is generally carried on under the denomination of gold (or silver), but the Englishman who owes money in France might buy goods in England to the value of his debt, export them to France, sell them there, and ask his correspondent to pay his debt for him. Thus gold transactions within the countries would be substituted for cross gold transactions between them. And if an Englishman owes gold in France he would find an advantage in liquidating his debt in this way, even if he made no independent profit on this subsidiary transaction, so long as he lost less on it than it would cost to transport the gold. This machinery for discharging debts in goods when it is cheaper to do so than to pay for them in gold is simplified and generalised by the use of "bills," and its action is registered by the " rates of exchange" prevailing between different countries.

We measure changes of value in commodities by changes of price, and as all prices are measured in gold and the price of gold therefore cannot vary, it is difficult to realise that gold varies in value just in the same way and on the same principles as other commodities do. The resistance of retail prices, and other relatively fixed scales of payment, to change, prevents the ratio of exchange between gold and certain classes of commodities and services from adapting itself rapidly to changed conditions. But in principle all values are determined by the same considerations of quantity and place on the relative scale. But whereas the use of gold as a standard of value does not affect its place on the relative scale, its use as a medium of exchange does, for it withdraws a portion of it from other uses and so raises its marginal significance. A minted sovereign is a piece of gold certified by the Government as to weight and quality. The certificate may be of value, and persons may be willing to pay for it. Hence a sovereign may be worth a little more than the gold it contains. But its cost of production (i.e. the expense of minting it) cannot maintain its price if for any reason the certificate should fall in value. This only happens rarely, for short periods, and within narrow limits. A paper currency can only be maintained so long as the paper is directly or indirectly convertible into actual commodities or immunities. A Government cannot make it circulate by saying it shall, unless it puts some actual meaning and power into it by effectively relating it to actual values.

We have now closed our critical investigations directly relating to the construction and interpretation of diagrammatic curves and the economic problems they suggest; but a somewhat isolated branch of inquiry, indicated by the title of this chapter, still demands our attention. It is not my purpose to enter in detail upon questions of finance and currency, but the very short examination of the subject with which we contented ourselves in Book I.¹ must be supplemented by notes on a few topics, selected partly for their fundamental nature, partly for their important bearing on current discussions, and partly because, as I believe, false conceptions of a peculiarly insidious kind are current concerning them. Much will be omitted that would have to appear in even an elementary treatment that aimed at completeness within its own limits.

We have already distinguished between two functions of gold. It is a standard of value by which a survey of the terms on which all manner of alternatives are offered can be facilitated, or, in other words, it furnishes the scale on which exchange values are expressed; it is also an actual medium of exchange, inasmuch as it constitutes a universally acceptable commodity, and is thus a convenient means of dividing into two stages the operations by which we transform the things we have into the things we want; for it enables us first to generalise the special forms of wealth or capacity we have, and then specialise this generalised wealth into what we want. It is obvious at once that the former function is of the wider scope, for two persons directly exchanging their wares might do so in terms of gold without using gold as an intermediary. A farmer who has hay which he will have to sell at the market price in order to buy turnips at the market price may find another farmer with turnips to sell who wants hay. In this case there may be no necessity for the material intervention of gold at all, even though it be employed mentally as a means of enabling each of the farmers to realise the other alternatives that are open. Each of them may estimate both the hay and the turnips in gold to help him in determining their relative values. When they have both determined that they can do no better than exchange, the one so much hay for so many turnips, and the other so many turnips for so much hay, they have simply to make the exchange; and if each farmer makes out a bill of the same amount to the other and they then exchange receipts, though in form there will be two distinct transactions in which each farmer assumes that the other will pay him in

(margin: Gold as a standard of value. Cancelling obligations to pay gold.)

¹ Pages 127-141.

gold, as a matter of fact this is a mere customary fiction, and there are not two transactions but one. The turnips and the hay are exchanged for each other, but their values are expressed in terms of gold.

Now it may well be that two men have frequent dealings with each other in which each receives goods from the other, without at the time giving him anything in exchange for them, but promising to pay him gold to the amount required. Here the obligation to pay gold is not a mere fiction. There is no agreement to give anything else and no obligation to enter into further transactions, and the gold promised may ultimately be paid. But if at the end of six months one man finds that forty sovereigns are due from him to his neighbour, and thirty-eight sovereigns due from his neighbour to him, there is obviously no necessity for him to hand over forty sovereigns and to receive thirty-eight; it will be the same if he pays over two and the men exchange receipts. And if some such approximate balancing of claims can be anticipated with confidence there will be no occasion for each of the two to keep by him a stock of sovereigns in order to meet the claims of the other. And of course the mere fact of A owing fifty pounds to B may suggest to A the possibility of hitting upon something that he can sell him. And if (as may probably be the case) it would be inconvenient to him to find the ready money he may try to tempt B by offering him a slightly advantageous bargain. Thus he goes a little out of his way to *create* a counter obligation against which he may cancel his. Thus, one way or another, instead of requiring between them to keep eighty or a hundred sovereigns in order to be able to settle with each other, the two men will find it enough if each of them has five or six sovereigns ready to pay any balance that is likely not to be cancelled when they compare their mutual claims. This is a great advantage, for each wants to put all his available wealth into his land and crops. Here all the accounts are kept in terms of gold, but very little of the business is transacted through gold as a medium. Nevertheless each transaction is in itself a promise on the one side to deliver the goods and on the other side to pay gold. Now this incurring of obligations to pay gold which never have to be fulfilled is a phenomenon of extreme importance in the industrial world, and the machinery by which such obligations are met without the transfer of gold repays careful study.

The simplest case would be such as the one we have already examined, where A has supplied B with commodities or services and has a claim for gold against him, and B in like manner has supplied A with other commodities and has a claim for gold against him.

$$A \rightleftarrows B$$

These two claims for gold, so far as they go, will cancel each other, and only the balance need be paid. Gold as a standard of value and a potential medium of exchange has been associated with the whole transaction; gold as an actual medium of exchange, only with a small part of it. But suppose A is under obligation to pay gold to B, and B is under obligation to pay gold not to him but to C, who in his turn is under obligation to pay gold not to B but to A. Then A is to receive gold from C and pay gold to B, B is to receive from A and pay to C, and C is to receive from B and pay to A—

$$A \to B \to C \to A$$

so that in the end the gold will be exactly where it was at the beginning, if the obligations are equal; and if the various transactions are not of the same value in gold, the final state will only differ from the initial state by the margin beyond the area of coincidence. Here again it is clear that a sum of gold passing from A to B, and from B to C, and from C to A again, is making the same superfluous journeys that it was found easy to avoid in the simpler case when it passed from A to B and then back again from B to A.

Now any one of these three, B for instance, might say to C: " I owe you money, but A owes me money. Instead of paying you I will tell A to pay you, and will accept your assurance that he has discharged my obligation to you in lieu of his payment to me." If C accepts this arrangement, then the form

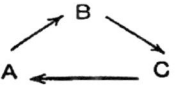

has been reduced to the form

$$A \rightleftarrows C$$

and, as we have seen, these claims cancel each other; so that the whole of the three transactions can be cancelled, so far as the gold is concerned, except for the settlement of the balances. If A, B, and C are in easy connection with each other, it does not matter whether they live in the same house or in the same city or in the same country. They might be one in New York, one in Berlin, and one in London; or they might be next-door neighbours; or they might be (as they often are) members of the same family liquidating their obligations across the table. It is easy to see that the same principle might be successfully applied to any number of persons and to any network of cross obligations and combinations if a system of cancelling could be established that involves less expense and inconvenience than the keeping and transferring of the metal would. Now the actual transfer of gold may be a more serious matter between Glasgow and London than between two streets in Glasgow, and a more serious matter between Glasgow and Berlin than between Glasgow and London. Therefore if two persons, A_1 and A_2, live within easy access of each other and are in habitual communication, and two other persons, B_1 and B_2, are similarly situated with respect to each other, then suppose A_1 is under obligation to pay gold to B_2, and B_1 under a similar obligation to pay gold to A_2, we should have

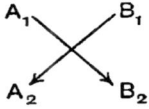

that is to say, A_1 and B_1 are to pay, and A_2 and B_2 are to receive. Then let A_1 pay A_2 on behalf of B_1, and let B_1 pay B_2 on behalf of A_1—

$$A_1 \qquad B_1$$
$$\downarrow \qquad \downarrow$$
$$A_2 \qquad B_2$$

the result being the same, namely, that A_2 and B_2 have received money, and A_1 and B_1 have paid it. Thus, if we regard A_1 and A_2 as a single group, and B_1 and B_2 as another single group, the form

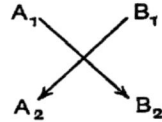

may be regarded as reducing itself to the form

and only the balance between the total obligations of the A's to the B's or the B's to the A's will have to be settled by the transfer of gold. And in the same way the A, B, and C of a former example may be groups of persons living respectively in London, Berlin, and New York.

This is the whole theory and principle of foreign exchanges and international trade, but we must further examine the machinery through which it is applied. Before proceeding with this branch of our inquiry, however, we must consider another closely connected but also contrasted financial scheme.

Let us suppose that a man who has numerous transactions with his neighbours both buys and sells with most of them, though there are some from whom he buys only and others to whom he only sells. This still is, or recently was, very much the case in remote country districts. Such a man may, by the cancelling process already described, conduct a great part of his exchanges under the denomination of gold but without the intervention of gold as an actual medium. But he both receives and pays in gold to some extent, and he must take care to keep by him enough of the gold that he receives to enable him to make his payments. And there are periods during which a considerable amount of coin is simply lying in his cash-box in anticipation of claims that will be made before any more cash has come in. Indeed, to be safe he always aims at having a little more than he is at all likely to want. If he could be sure of its safe custody he would be glad to be rid of the anxiety and risk of keeping this cash himself; and we are told that it was the lodging of sums of money with goldsmiths for safe custody that first gave rise to the system of banking.

The origin and nature of banking.

Let us suppose, then, that a bank is established and that it receives the greater part of the stock of money which the community finds it convenient to have available for paying their balances in gold. The banker credits each of his clients with the amount of his stock. When A has to pay a sum in gold to B, instead of handing over the sovereigns he now gives him an order for those sovereigns upon the banker, and B, if he likes, can go to the bank and get them out. But if he too wants gold chiefly for paying balances, and if he too lodges the greater part of his stock with the banker, it is unlikely that he will draw the sovereigns out at all; he will simply hand over to the bank A's certificate that so many sovereigns are now his, not A's, and the banker will transfer the amount from A's credit to B's.

This system could be carried on either in conjunction with the cancelling process described above, or apart from it; for A and B may either give each other orders on their bankers for the full amounts of their obligations, or may exchange their bills as far as they go, and only settle the balance by an order on the banker for the transfer of credit from one to the other. And where the accounts of a whole community are thus kept by the banker, it is obvious that machinery is at once established by which many cross transactions may be simplified. Thus, in the instance given on page 579, if A has given an order on his banker to B, B may simply transfer the order to C without knowing that C owes money to A. C, in any case, may go to the bank and draw out the money, or he may leave it there to his own credit. Or if B prefers it he can draw a cheque on his bank in C's favour, and at the same time pay in A's order, so that he would at once have the credit transferred to him from A's account out of which he can meet C's claim. The more complicated the transactions are the greater the simplification that can be effected by one central recipient who has the whole field under his survey. The transactions of the community, therefore, when banking is firmly established, will be to a very great extent conducted without any physical transfer of gold at all. But so far we have not seen that the banking system effects any further economy in the amount of gold required to carry on the business of the community.

It is true that the gold need not be shifted. If it lies at the bank and is now B's, whereas it was A's, the shifting is only in the books, not in the cellars, of the bank; but A, B, and C must severally, and therefore collectively, have credit at the bank for the full number of sovereigns that they must otherwise have kept at home. Indeed in some ways the banking system rather tends to limit than to extend the cancelling of obligations, in the strict sense, as between individuals. Every one knows that it often conduces to simplicity and clearness of account-keeping actually to go out of the way to avoid cancelling transactions, and to exchange cheques as well, when exchanging receipts; so that a man may have to keep a larger balance at his banker's than the reserve of sovereigns that would be necessary if he did business with his neighbours by cancelling accounts. Otherwise there would be danger of overdrawing, at any rate for a few days or hours. For if A owes B £40, and B owes A £38, and neither of them has more than three or four sovereigns, they can settle their accounts when they meet; but if they avail themselves of the conveniences of banking, and without waiting till they meet send each other cheques, if one presents his cheque at the bank a few hours before the other there will be no credit to meet it unless balances of £40 or so are kept at the bank. Thus in some cases the conveniences of banking may be an alternative to those of cancelling, and may involve the maintaining of a larger balance of money in hand. But it is also possible that banking may be resorted to in conjunction with a system of private cancelling, and in any case it may obviously facilitate the interchange of obligations by which A can make his credit with B discharge his obligations to C, and so forth. But all the while it would appear as yet that the gold, whether for paying of balances or total amounts, must exist in the hands of the bankers though it is not transferred. The economy is in moving the gold, not (so far as we have yet seen) in the amount of gold that is kept.

But now we must take another step. The banker finds that only a comparatively small part of the gold with which his clients are credited is ever taken out: the greater part of it is left with him *Bankers' investments and reserves.*

and is simply transferred now to one credit and now to another. The consequence is that he does not find it necessary actually to keep all the gold which stands to the credit of his clients. He can transform the greater part of this wealth into revenue-yielding forms, provided he keeps enough cash to meet all claims that he can in reason expect will be made on it. For, as we have seen, if A gets an order for gold from C, whether he wants it immediately to settle B's claims, or wishes to keep it ready for any other and future purposes, he will generally not draw out the actual sovereigns, but will simply leave the credit he has received in the banker's hands, or request him to transfer it to some one else.

But the persons in the neighbourhood of Bank A will not deal exclusively with each other. They will deal to some extent with persons in other parts of the country; so that persons dealing with Bank A may be under obligation to pay sums of money to the clients of Banks B, C, etc., and customers of these banks will be under similar obligations to the clients of the others, including A. All these transactions may also be carried on by means of orders to the bankers to transfer credits, only now the client of Bank A will order his banker to transfer his property not to another of his own clients but to a client of Bank B. Here then is an actual order to transfer gold from his cellar to that of another banker, not from the credit of one of his clients to the credit of another, and it would seem that the gold must be shifted. But there will be a number of such obligations on the part of Bank A to Bank B, and a number of counter obligations on the part of Bank B to Bank A, and now, so far as the transfer of gold is concerned, a genuine cancelling of obligations may take place. Bank A sends a number of orders for gold on Bank B, and Bank B meets a part of these by counter orders for gold on Bank A. Perhaps a balance is still due from Bank B to Bank A in gold, but a balance may be due to Bank B from Bank C, and so forth; and—since all the banks will be connected with each other directly or indirectly, through local branches of the Bank of England, through their agents in London, or otherwise, and since they will all (as we shall see) ultimately have balances at the Bank of England,—partly by a system of cancelling obligations and partly by a system of cheques on the Bank of England, they will probably arrange all their affairs without the material transfer of any coin whatever.

Thus it is only a portion of his property (if he is in trade a small portion) that each individual will wish to command in the form of gold; and of this portion, again, he will only desire to have a fraction, probably a small one, actually in his cash-box in the form of gold; the rest he will hold as a balance at his banker's, which he is entitled to realise in gold at any moment he chooses. Now of these balances the banks will hold the larger portion in the shape of revenue-yielding forms of wealth; and of the portion which they desire to command in the form of gold the branch banks will, again, only keep a fraction in their tills; the rest will be held by the great houses in Birmingham, Liverpool, Manchester, and so forth; and these, again, will hold only a portion of their reserves in gold, and the rest in the form of credit with the Bank of England. The Bank of England in its turn will hold the greater part of the property with which it is entrusted by the other banks, and which they may at any time claim in the form of gold, in the shape of revenue-yielding forms of property, only maintaining such a reserve in actual coin and bullion as it deems sufficient both to meet the claims that will actually be made upon it and to maintain its credit unshaken.

Thus we see that enormous economies in the use of gold as a medium of exchange are effected. The whole metallic reserve held by all the banks constitutes a very small fraction of the collective liability of the banks to pay gold on demand; for note that every depositor in every bank is entitled at any time to draw out the whole of his property in coin of the realm, or in Bank of England notes, which in their turn he may present at the Bank of England, demanding gold in exchange for them. Every one, then, is entitled to draw out the full amount of his balance in gold, and *any one* can actually do this as long

By the banks all kinds of property are converted into media of exchange, though gold remains the only standard of value.

as the machinery is working smoothly; but it would be impossible for *every one* to do it, because the immensely greater part of the property does not exist in the form of sovereigns or gold at all; it consists of all kinds of property and obligations, of a value equivalent, at the marginal terms of exchange, to the total sum which the public has the theoretical right to draw out in gold. It all exists, however. Every man's balance severally, and the whole amount of the deposits in the banks collectively, represent real property, and all this property is in the possession of the banks at every moment, to its full amount. It is the greatest mistake to suppose that the whole body of banking transactions reduces itself to mere entries and transfers in books, and that if the banker had simply squandered the property entrusted to him, everything would go on just the same so long as nobody knew it. For it is just because the property is there, and is most of it yielding revenue, that the banker is able to pay his staff and support his own expenses. The property of the clients, represented by their balances at the bank, is real property and is doing real work; and the revenues that accrue to it in virtue of that work are paying for all the privileges and conveniences that the clients enjoy. If five hundred people draw cheques on the same bank on the same day to the extent of £5000, and only 50 sovereigns, one per cent of the whole, are actually drawn out of the bank, nevertheless, each individual cheque has behind it a basis of actual property to which the drawee has received a valid title. If the bank is solvent, then even if it had to "stop payment," that is to say if it were unable to meet all the simultaneous claims for actual coin made upon it, the holder of credit in it would be the holder of actual property. Thus the man who pays a cheque, hands to his correspondent a document which gives him a substantial claim; and the sum of these substantial claims (unlike the formal right to draw coin) can be met simultaneously; for the holders of the cheques and credits in the bank are entitled, in the last resort, to enter into acknowledged and legal possession of miscellaneous property that is actually bearing revenue and is negotiable, like all other property, in the public markets. So when I receive a cheque in exchange for valuable possessions or services, though I do not thereby enter into possession of the commodities and services that I myself require, yet I do get actual property, not a mere pretence or symbol of property. The actual property I get is valued by some one else, and I can hold it until I find it convenient to exchange it for property that I value myself. Thus by the banking system a vast amount of miscellaneous claims and possessions other than gold are converted into "media of exchange" just as real as gold itself; for they mediate between the things I have and the things I want, and enable me to transform the one into the other without the necessity of a double coincidence between my wants and those of my correspondent. The whole mass of cheques which is exchanged day by day is therefore not an economy of "media of exchange" at large. It is a calling into partnership with gold, as a medium of exchange (but not as a standard of value), of an immense amount of other property. To regard the banking system of England as consisting in a cunning device to make sovereigns that only exist as entries in a book do the work of real sovereigns, is a fundamental misconception.

The great bulk of the business of the country, therefore, is still carried on by the intervention of media of exchange, but only a little of it by the medium of gold; whereas almost the whole of it is carried on under the denomination of gold. Gold, therefore, has a far wider application as a standard of value than as a medium of exchange. But even in this last capacity it is still active. Actual transfers of gold are constantly made from individual to individual, from bank to bank, and from city to city. The obligations of the bankers in Edinburgh and the bankers in Liverpool may not accurately balance each other, and even if the balances are settled by cheques on the Bank of England the receiving banks may find it convenient to demand cash and not a credit from the Bank of England itself. Or at any time and independently of other banks any given bank may desire to draw cash from the London (or other) agent with whom its reserve is deposited. So there will be a pulsation and ebb and flow of gold not only within any given district but from one district to another, and the banks undertake, as part of their business, to convey the actual coin from one part of the country to another, as may be needed.

Thus if I live in Birmingham and owe money to a man in Leeds, I may send him a cheque on a Birmingham banker, and this will save me the expense and risk of actually sending him the gold. It may turn out, as the result of the whole series of transactions between Birmingham and Leeds, that gold actually has to be transferred directly or indirectly from Birmingham to Leeds, or it may turn out the other way. In the first case the fact that I have transferred a portion of my credit in Birmingham to the credit of some one in Leeds will aggravate the situation. In the other case it will relieve it. And this will make a difference to the bankers, but it will make no difference to me. The banker will conduct my business on the same terms whether this particular transaction happens to increase or to diminish his own expenses. It is indeed possible that if I am dealing with a distant part of the kingdom he may charge a special commission on all cheques, but this commission will be uniform and will not depend on whether this particular transaction tends to involve him in the expense of the transfer of gold or tends to relieve him from it. The expenses of the transfer of gold, then, whenever it may be necessary, are a part of the general obligations incurred by the bank to its clients, and no individual dealing with other individuals through a bank in the United Kingdom has to consider whether this particular transaction is likely to involve the expense of a transfer of gold, for if it does he will not have to pay anything extra, and if it saves such a transfer he will derive no benefit from the fact.

In home trade the expense of actual transfer of gold, in settlement of balances, is not made a separate charge by the banks on the persons on whose behalf it is undertaken.

But if a London merchant is under obligation to pay gold to a Paris merchant there is no machinery by which he can once and for all contract himself out of the liabilities or privileges that may be incidental to the money being due in Paris and the gold being in London, when the time of settlement comes. And it is here that the economic difference between home and foreign trade clearly emerges.

In foreign trade the responsibility for the transfer remains with the contracting individual.

There is obviously no reason why the purely economic forces which urge men to further the purposes of others in order that they may thereby further their own, should in any way be limited or qualified by national boundaries. And from the economic point of view it therefore seems impossible to conceive that there should be any essential difference between foreign and domestic trade. Whatever differences there are must apparently be differences of condition or of machinery, not of economic principle or theory. But what are these differentiating considerations? Some of the conditions under which, and obstacles in the face of which, the economic forces act may indeed be determined by a difference of government or language, or both. But it is difficult to assign any general or dominant efficacy to them even when they coincide with the areas of "home" and "foreign" trade. Familiarity and confidence are essential elements for the carrying on of business, and this may, in a vague way, be furthered by a common nationality, language, or government; but it is hard to see why a merchant in Dover should necessarily have more familiarity with or confidence in a merchant in the Hebrides as against a merchant in Calais. English and Americans speak the same language, yet their dealings constitute a branch of foreign trade. Englishmen and Welshmen deal with each other, and their dealings are a branch of domestic trade, even if they habitually speak different languages. English and Irish trade is domestic, and English and French trade foreign quite irrespective of the *cordialité* or otherwise of any *entente* that may exist between the peoples. Colonial trade is usually (and rightly, as we shall see) classed with foreign rather than home trade, though by the sentimental tests it should belong to the latter. Tariff boundaries seem to promise a more important distinction; but the trade between England and Denmark is foreign trade though there are practically no tariff barriers to overcome, and the trade between Florence and the surrounding agricultural districts is domestic although a tariff barrier is drawn round the city. Where, then, are we to look for any essential differences? Is it in the different systems of currency? No; for the standard coins minted by any one of the countries forming the "Latin Union" were made legal tender in the public treasuries of all the others by a treaty of 1866, and were practically received as such in all private transactions. Moreover, even where there is no such legal or conventional equivalence of currencies, transactions are conducted under a common standard. The affairs between Germany and England are conducted in terms of gold, and the sums of gold which people in London and people in Berlin have engaged to pay each other can be cancelled directly or indirectly, as between Liverpool and Glasgow; the balances in either case being ultimately paid in gold which has to be physically transported from the one centre to the other. But, as we have seen, there is a real difference in the machinery by which the cancelling is effected and the form in which the individual trader meets his share in the expense of the necessary transfers; and it is to the examination of this point that we must now return.

Let us revert to the case examined on page 579. We suppose that three persons, A, B, and C, are in such relations with each other that A owes to B, B to C, and C to A. That is, B having supplied things to A, sends him in a bill, C sends in a bill for the like sum to B, and A to C. Let A send in his bill to C and request him not to pay it, but simply to acknowledge that he owes the money and will pay it to any one A may nominate. Let C send back A's bill with this undertaking endorsed on it, and then let A write on it a statement that it is B to whom the money is to be paid, and let him then forward the document with these two endorsements upon it to B. B has now a claim upon C for the money which A owes him, and as C has a claim for the same amount on B, the two claims meet each other and there is no transfer of coin at all. A has settled his account with B by giving him a bill upon C; and this is the type of the instruments by which international obligations are cancelled. We have only to suppose that A lives in London, B in Bombay, and C in Amsterdam to transform this into an actual case of settlement of international accounts by bills.

Importance of "bills" in foreign trade and the nature of the economies they effect.

We may note at this point that theoretically there are three exactly equivalent ways of settling such a group of accounts.

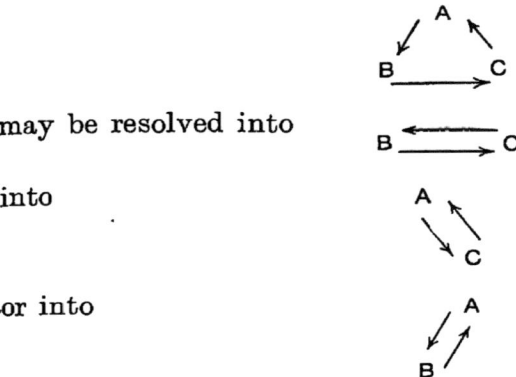

may be resolved into

into

or into

according as A "draws a bill" on C, B draws a bill on A, or C draws a bill on B. All these processes are identical in principle and in effect. Custom determines the prevailing practice in each important case.

But the "double coincidence" implied in this example will be rare. An English merchant may well export woollen goods to New York, a New York merchant wheat to Amsterdam, and a Dutch merchant dairy produce to London; but it is not likely that it will be the same English merchant that sells the woollen goods and buys the dairy produce. And so with the others.

We shall therefore have, in the simpler case of the two countries, dealing with each other both ways,

resolving itself, by the agency of a bill, into

$$A_1 \longrightarrow A_2$$

$$B_2 \longleftarrow B_1$$

That is to say: the Paris merchant B_1 who owes money to the London merchant A_2 will find another Paris merchant B_2 who has a bill against another London merchant A_1; he will pay it and will then send B_2's order on A_1 in payment of his own obligation. B_2 will then have been paid by B_1, and A_2 will draw upon A_1, who will pay him.

In the more complex case we have

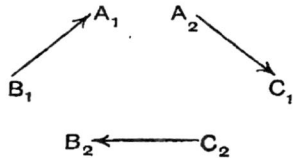

An English merchant A_2 has bought dairy produce from a Dutch merchant C_1. C_1 finds another Dutch merchant who has bought wheat from a New York merchant B_2 and wishes to pay him. C_1 sells his bill on A_2 to C_2, who forwards it in payment to B_2. B_2 finds another New York merchant B_1 who owes money to an English merchant A_1 for woollen goods. He buys the bill on A_2 from B_2, and forwards it in payment to A_1, who presents it to A_2 and receives payment for it. Thus A_2 has paid A_1 instead of C_1; C_1 has been paid by C_2 instead of by A_2; C_2 has paid C_1 instead of paying B_2; B_2 has been paid by B_1 instead of by C_2; B_1 has paid B_2 instead of paying A_1; and A_1 has been paid by A_2 instead of by B_1.

The movement has been

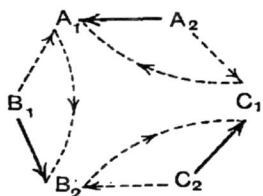

A_2, C_2, and B_1 have paid, and A_1, C_1, and B_2 have received, as was due; but the settlements have all been made without transfer of coin from country to country.

The instrument of liquidation has been a bill on London; but theoretically it might equally well have been A_1's bill on B_1 in New York, or B_2's bill on C_2 in Amsterdam. But it is manifestly unnecessary for more than one bill to circulate.

Thus we see that in international or colonial trade (for we might just as well have had Quebec as New York in our example), through the instrumentality of bills payments within a country may be substituted for payments from one country to another, even when all the transactions are conducted and all the obligations incurred in terms of gold, and even if every one of the creditors requires and receives full payment in gold.

But the most important and complex part of the investigation still remains. How are balances settled? They might be, and sometimes are, settled by the actual transfer of gold, but the expense of transferring gold from Berlin to London, for example, is about $\frac{1}{4}$ per cent. More closely, if a German has to fulfil an obligation to a London merchant for £1000, it would cost him about £1002 : 9s. if he actually sent the gold. Now in any given state of trade there will always be German merchants who would be prepared to export, say, musical instruments or glass to London, if they could get a very little better price than they can actually command. A German merchant who would just not be induced to accept a certain order at £1000 might just be induced to accept it at £1001. If such a man, having an offer of £1000 for certain goods, were to say to the German who owes £1000 in London, "I will discharge your debt for you by sending goods to London which will be accepted as the full value of £1000, if you will give me £1 for doing so," it would pay the German debtor to accept the offer. The German manufacturer would present him with a bill against his correspondent to the full amount of £1000, he would despatch it to London in payment of his obligation, and it would have cost him £1001 only, instead of £1002 : 9s. Thus the exports to England will increase, and the balance "against" Germany (that is to say, the obligations of Germany to England in excess of those of England to Germany) will be reduced. But it may be that in spite of this Germans are still buying more from England than England is buying from Germany, so that the obligations of Germany are still mounting, and German debtors, having exhausted all the possibilities of finding German manufacturers who are within £1 on the £1000 of striking bargains in England and so creating bills on her, will have to offer better terms and make use of those who are, say, only within £1 : 5s. on the £1000. And this process may go on until there is no German manufacturer or

The settlement of balances. Rates of exchange between different countries. Their effect upon trade.

2 Q

exporter who will undertake to deliver any goods in London which will have the market value of £1000 there, unless he receives a premium of £2 : 9s. for doing so. When it comes to this, if there is still a balance to be paid, the German debtor will have nothing to lose by despatching the gold, and he will therefore do so.

If the balance is the other way it will be the English debtor who may have to pay a premium on getting his debt discharged, and the English manufacturer of woollen or leather goods, or hardware, who may be induced to sell his wares in Berlin at a lower price, after allowing for transport, than he would accept in England, because he will receive a premium for discharging a debt in Berlin. In a word, when there is a balance due from London to Berlin, a claim for money in Berlin being worth more to a London merchant than a claim for money in London, the export trade will be stimulated. And when the balance is the other way of course the reversed relation holds.

Sums approximating to £99 : 16s. and £100 : 5s. are known as the *gold points* between London and Berlin. Naturally the gold points between any other two centres are different. They are the points to which the premium must rise either way in order to make the actual export of gold the cheapest way of settling a balance. Within the gold points balances are settled by exporting goods which would not have yielded a profit had exchange been at par.

The gold points.

The gold balance will, normally, be "against" gold-producing countries, where gold is a staple export and obligations are normally discharged in it, for these countries normally export gold and receive other commodities in exchange; whereas in other countries the balance will prevailingly be "favourable," that is to say, they will receive their share in the increasing supply of gold in return for export of other commodities.

On the basis of these actual "bills" a fabric of drafts and instruments of every kind is raised, by which international obligations are liquidated. Thus a cheque on my London banker sent to a friend in Berlin becomes a "bill" on London, that is to say, a claim for so much gold in London; and if such claims are at a premium in Berlin, it will sell for more than the metallic value of the gold it represents. And so, too, with Bank of England notes.[1] The case of actual coin seems anomalous. By hypothesis gold in London is of more value to the Berlin merchant than gold in Berlin. Yet when, for that very reason, bills on London are at a premium, English sovereigns follow the bills and will exchange for more than their metallic weight in German coin. *Qua* gold they are worth less, but *qua* instruments by which obligations can be discharged in London they are worth more, and persons who are intending to go to London and spend money there will pay more for them, just as willingly as for notes. If there were a large number of them, and their export to settle obligations in London became a business, a man who undertook to send them to England for the convenience of others, instead of desiring to take them across for his own convenience, would have to be paid. But as there are not enough to satisfy all the wants of those who desire them, not as gold but as English coin, they remain at par with the notes this purpose of which they serve equally well. The chief centre of the "bill" business in the larger sense is London, and "drafts" on London are drawn by all nations in settlement of their accounts.

Expositions of the theory of foreign exchanges often dwell too much upon the form which the transactions take without connecting it sufficiently closely with the ultimate movements of trade which it represents. We do not find in practice that one man goes to another, as we have supposed, and says, "I will discharge your debt for £1000 in London if you will give me a commission of £1 for doing so." But the man who owes £1000 goes into the market to buy a bill by which he can discharge his debt, and finds he has to pay £1001 for it. This of course simply means that to induce some one to create a bill for £1000 on Berlin, that is to say, to supply goods for which he will receive £1000, he must offer him a premium of £1 for doing so. A man who has a bill must sell it for what it can fetch, but he will not create a bill, by a transaction which taken alone would involve a loss, unless he can sell it at a profit. If there is a profit of £1 to be made on creating a bill for £1000, any one can do it if it is worth

---

[1] Notes that are at a discount, and will not discharge gold debts to their face value, in their own country, will of course be at a discount elsewhere too, independently of the balance of indebtedness.

his while. And as a matter of fact bargains are struck by telegraph all over the world in accordance with the rate of exchange, which varies from day to day; and the amount for which a man can negotiate a bill on such and such a centre is a material consideration in the terms which he can offer his correspondent. All this is perfectly understood, but a delusive simplicity can be given to the exposition by simply treating bills as though they were themselves commodities, and saying that if bills on Berlin are scarce they will rise in value like any other commodity, and if they are abundant will fall, only that they cannot rise or fall beyond the gold points because there would then be cheaper substitutes for them. The superficiality of this treatment need hardly be pointed out. The bill is not a commodity, and we must go behind the phenomena of the bill market to the actual commercial facts which it represents.

Difficulty of tracing the similarity of the effects of an increase or diminution of gold and those of an increase or diminution of other commodities, due to the confusion caused by the reversing of our terminology when we are speaking of the standard commodity.

Our treatment of the principles of banking and of foreign exchange has necessarily been extremely brief and imperfect, and it is not compatible with the scope and aim of this work to go into further detail. There is, however, one branch of the subject which still remains for examination, and it cannot be wholly neglected. It is the question of the principles which regulate the distribution of the precious metals, and specifically gold, between its uses in the arts and in the currency.[1] The difficulties that surround this question do not arise so much from the use of gold as currency as from its use as a standard of value, and with this we will therefore begin. There should be no real difficulty in understanding the fundamental relation between gold and other commodities. But it is extremely difficult not to be confused by the language in which we have to express

[1] As I believe that the line of investigation here pursued is somewhat novel, and as I have no technical knowledge of minting or of the gold market, the whole of this section should be regarded as a tentative suggestion rather than a dogmatic exposition. My reason for giving it at all is that I believe the usual treatment of the subject to be theoretically unsound (cf. pages 610 *sqq.*), and therefore it seemed desirable to attempt a fresh analysis.

the facts. Thus high gold prices mean low price of gold; for the gold prices of other things are the amounts of gold that must be given for them, whereas the price of gold is the amount of other things that must be given for it. Thus, abundant gold means high prices (in gold), and scarce gold means low prices (in gold). Whereas abundant wheat means low prices (of wheat), and scarce wheat means high prices (of wheat). This is perfectly consistent; but since, when we are speaking of gold, "prices" mean the prices *in* the commodity of which we are discoursing, and when we are speaking of other things prices mean the prices *of* the commodities of which we are discoursing, the terms constantly confuse and frequently betray us when we are considering the theory of finance and currency. The most experienced scalers of the Alpine heights of speculation in the currency have constantly to steady their heads in these regions of discourse, and the novice is almost certain to be the victim of aggravated *vertigo*. The facts, however, that lie behind these bewildering phrases are intelligible enough. We will approach them by forgetting gold for a moment and speaking of wheat. If there is a good wheat harvest, a given amount of wheat will exchange for less of any other commodity or service, and any other commodity or service will exchange for more wheat than if the harvest is bad. High wheat prices would correspond to a relative abundance of wheat; that is to say, a value which was expressed as ten pecks of wheat when wheat was relatively scarce might be expressed as eleven pecks when it was relatively abundant. Consequently if a man had a fixed income of so many quarters of wheat, independently of its abundance or scarcity, he would find when wheat was abundant that prices had risen against him, and although his nominal wheat income would be the same, his real income in the general command of commodities and services would have fallen. But if the man's nominal income were increased so as to make his real income the same, he would find that wheat being cheaper than before relatively to other things, that is to say, the sacrifice of other things involved in consuming a peck of wheat being smaller than before, there would be a tendency in his administration (imperceptible if he were rich, very marked if he were poor) to consume more wheat in proportion to other things than he had done previously.

On the other hand, if the crop of wheat relatively to the number and habits of the population remained constant for a long series of years, and the amount of gold increased, people would gradually discover that all articles made of gold became relatively cheaper, whether measured in wheat prices or in the equivalents of other services and commodities; and men who had hesitated to pay the extra price for the use of gold in dentistry, or publishers who had refrained from attractive touches of gold in the make-up of their cheap issues, would find that it was now worth their while to incur the lessened expense. Thus, if a man were considering whether he would order a set of artificial teeth, containing a certain amount of gold in the plate, he would find that whereas the extra cost would formerly have been a quarter of wheat, now that gold is cheaper it will be less by a few pecks. He may think this lower (wheat) price worth giving for the additional advantage, in durability and comfort, of having the gold in his plate, whereas at the former price he would not have ordered it. Gold being cheaper it can be had at less sacrifice of other things.

Now these consequences of an increased crop of wheat or an increased output of gold will remain exactly the same if gold, instead of wheat, is the standard. If gold becomes relatively more abundant, gold prices rise, and the man whose real income remains the same (his nominal income being raised, as in the case of the wheat standard) finds gold articles relatively cheaper because all other things are dearer in gold prices, so that the amount of other things he would be able to get instead of the gold in his plate is now smaller than it was, and the sacrifice of other things now involved in securing the plate being therefore smaller, he may be willing to incur it. If, on the other hand, the relative supply of gold remains constant for a series of years and wheat becomes more plentiful, there will be a tendency to substitute the consumption of wheat for that of certain possible alternatives. Thus the relative value of wheat or of gold in relation to other things, and the extent to which they are used by individual consumers, depend on the

CH. VII   BANKING. BILLS. CURRENCY   599

relative abundance of wheat or of gold, and are entirely independent of the standard in which values are measured, though the position of a man with a fixed income is naturally dependent on the article in which that income is fixed.

If our general thesis is correct that the economic forces tend to secure remuneration to every man and prices to all articles in accord with the marginal significance of the services they render, then there would always be a tendency for nominal wages in wheat to increase if wheat became more abundant and for nominal wages in gold to increase if gold became more abundant; but this tendency may have serious obstructions to overcome. Confining ourselves to the case of the gold standard and the gold prices with which we are familiar, it is obvious that even if a man has not a fixed salary expressed in terms of gold, there may be a traditional price of his services which will offer a certain opposition to change. It would not be easy for a man to change his terms from 7s. 6d. to 7s. 8d. an hour for some kind of instruction, or from 4s. or 10s. a thousand words for translation to the same sum for 1010 words, if the ratio in which gold exchanges for wheat and other commodities had changed. This inertia, or friction, affects all kinds of bargains, the terms of which ought, on the general principles of exchange, to fluctuate not only with the supply of the commodity or capacity concerned and its place on the communal scale, but also with the change in the significance of the unit in which it is expressed; and schemes of a complex standard of value that would automatically preserve the ratio between established prices and their purchasing power have been designed; but they have never come into use; and therefore any man may find himself prejudiced or advantaged by a contract or convention that only yields to the changing facts under severe pressure; and he may therefore be giving either more or less than the value of what he gets, because the terms of his bargain have ceased to correspond with the facts. There is a specially marked tendency to retain certain retail prices at a fixed nominal level, and the fact that this

Friction caused by traditionally or contractually fixed salaries and prices.

can continue—that the price of a hat, for instance, or the admission to an exhibition remaining fixed through great fluctuations in the purchasing power of gold—shews how much friction counts for, and how much the action of the general economic trends is impeded when it has to force itself through the narrower channels of the commercial system.

But when the amplest allowance has been made for all this friction the general proposition remains true that whether wheat or gold were the standard an increased crop of wheat would at once raise wheat prices and encourage the consumption of wheat, whereas an increased supply of gold would raise gold prices and encourage the use of gold. We have, therefore, to keep in mind that, under a gold standard, high prices correspond to cheap gold and low prices to dear gold; and that in principle and in the long-run this difference of expression is the only difference which the selection of gold as the standard of value really makes, *except in so far as the use of gold as a standard of value involves its use as a medium of exchange.* This use as a medium of exchange constitutes an extra use for gold, and consequently raises its value, just as every additional use for any other commodity would, and does. Every individual finds it convenient to hold a portion of his property in the form of gold (or the subsidiary currencies, into the relation of which with gold we need not enter), and therefore a certain amount of gold is withdrawn from other uses, and its marginal significance in these other uses rises. How much does each individual thus set aside? If he is living from week to week or from year to year upon his current earnings, he will practically desire to have the whole of his income immediately available in this form, for he never has enough property for a long enough time to enable him to invest it in revenue-yielding ways. But if he is engaged in any kind of trade or any occupation which involves the acquisition and maintenance of capital, or if he is spending less than his income, or if his earnings are considerable and his expenditure is irregular over long periods, there will be a perpetual question in his mind how much of his property to keep immediately realisable in

Marginal note: The use of gold as a medium of exchange, unlike its use as a standard of value, constitutes an actual demand for it, and therefore raises its marginal significance.

CH. VII BANKING. BILLS. CURRENCY 601

gold and how much to employ remuneratively. He will not, indeed, in any case keep any large stock of actual coin about him, but he will keep a certain amount of his property as a fluctuating balance at his banker's, and all of this is available at any moment in the form of gold. This balance he will not make larger than necessary, for (neglecting the details of the arrangement with his banker) it will be practically "lying idle." The adjustment, then, of the portion of his income which he keeps available in coin to the rest of his income will be determined on exactly the same principles as all other distributions. A very small balance might be inconvenient, a somewhat larger balance less inconvenient, and the marginal inconvenience of this larger balance might not be sufficient to compensate the advantages of investment. When we come to the bankers we are in face of exactly the same problem. They must be prepared to meet all claims for coin. This they will do by keeping actual coin in their tills and by keeping a balance, that is to say, a claim for gold which will ultimately lie for the most part against the Bank of England. They do not wish this balance to be more than enough to keep them safe, for it is from the revenues derived from the rest of the property which they hold in trust that they derive their own incomes. And the same is true of the Bank of England itself.

But we have still not quite come to the question of the currency. We have been speaking chiefly of gold rather than of sovereigns, and the great reserve in the Bank of England is, as a matter of fact, largely in bullion, not in sovereigns. What determines the amount of gold which is actually coined? The answer to this question is at bottom quite simple. The process of converting bullion into sovereigns or sovereigns into bullion is supposed to cost about $1\frac{1}{2}$d. an ounce either way, and if any competent firm were allowed to undertake the minting of sovereigns, and were to do it at that price, it is clear that the value of an ounce of gold in sovereigns could not remain greater or less than that of an ounce of gold in bullion by more than $1\frac{1}{2}$d. an ounce (which is about 0·16 per cent), for the one could be converted into the other at that price. For the purpose of actual currency the gold must

Distinction between a gold reserve and coin.

What determines the amount of coin?

be in the form of sovereigns, for that is the certificate (of the Government in the actual fact, of the issuing firm in the case we are supposing) of the quality and quantity of the gold, and such a certificate would be required by all persons, not experts, as a guarantee that they were really receiving the gold. Now it might be worth any one's while to pay something for this convenience; that is to say, he might be willing to receive a little less gold in a form in which it would be accepted and could be exchanged by any one, rather than a little more in a form in which it could only be accepted by or exchanged with experts. The ordinary man, indeed, desires to have no gold except in this form and incidentally in his bookbinding, jewellery, and so forth. But the goldsmith, the bookbinder, the dentist, and others who put gold into their business in the most literal sense, desire gold both in coin and otherwise, and they will not take a smaller quantity in sovereigns in preference to a larger quantity in bullion unless they derive some corresponding convenience from it. And this they will only find to be the case to a limited extent. Thus, with the goldsmith in particular, the balance which we have seen other men strike between the amount of property which they keep in their business and the amount which they keep at the banker's will resolve itself to a great extent in his case into a distribution between the amount which he keeps in bullion or manufactured articles and the amount he keeps in coin or as a balance with his banker. Now, seeing that it costs the equivalent of $1\frac{1}{2}$d. an ounce to convert bullion into sovereigns, one might naturally expect under the conditions we have supposed that sovereigns would be worth more than bullion at the rate of $1\frac{1}{2}$d. an ounce, for why should any one be at the expense of making them to such an extent as to bring their marginal significance below that point? Whereas until it has reached that point there will be a profit in coining; so it will not rest anywhere above it. But we have seen that there is always a risk of the price of manufactured articles being less than their cost of production, and it is therefore conceivable, in the abstract, that such changes should take place in the demand for sovereigns and the demand for bullion as to reduce the marginal value of sovereigns below the point which alone would have justified their manufacture.

But neither could the departure in this sense be more than $1\frac{1}{2}$d. an ounce, for if bullion rose above that point it would become profitable to melt sovereigns. Now the gold contained in sovereigns is at the rate of an ounce to £3 : 17 : 10$\frac{1}{2}$. It follows, therefore, that the price of gold, if any one were at liberty to mint it, could never, except for a short time and under quite exceptional circumstances, sink below £3 : 17 : 9 an ounce, or rise above £3 : 18s.

Now this state of things, which we should expect if coining were an ordinary industry, corresponds exactly to the actual facts. In explaining this we will confine ourselves to the conditions established by law in England. Every man has a right to take properly assayed and certified gold to the Mint and have it coined into sovereigns gratuitously, at the rate of £3 : 17 : 10$\frac{1}{2}$ the ounce. Any valuable alloy there may be in it belongs to the Mint, but *per contra* the Mint makes no charge for the alloy in the sovereigns. *Limits between which the value of coined and uncoined gold may vary. The Royal Mint and the Bank of England.*

But though the Mint is compelled by law to coin and return the gold handed in to it, yet it is not bound to give it back at once. It is to treat all customers without favour in the order of application; and since there are always orders on hand from the Bank of England that it would take months to execute, any one who should apply to have his gold coined would be likely to have to wait, say, six months for his turn. If you reckon interest at four per cent the delay would be equivalent to a payment at the rate of about 1s. 7d. an ounce for mintage. The consequence is that no one ever does take his gold to the Mint. There is, however, another legal provision by which the Bank of England is bound to buy all the gold that is offered to it at the rate of £3 : 17 : 9 per ounce. This is only 1$\frac{1}{2}$d. on the ounce, or a little above a third of a penny on £1. Any one, therefore, who wishes to have his gold coined can legally command better terms from the Bank of England than he can from the Royal Mint. The Bank of England is not bound to pay in sovereigns; it may pay in its own notes. But the cash department of the Bank of England is compelled to give gold for the notes of the issue department, on demand, and consequently any one who likes may take his gold to the issue department and receive notes for it at the rate of £3 : 17 : 9 per ounce, and may then go round the corner to the other department and receive the gold. If he does this it will not hurt the Bank of England, for the Bank of England does not pay for having its gold minted; nor will it be embarrassed by an excess of gold in its cellars, for the gold will be drawn out in sovereigns as rapidly as it is put into the cellars in bullion, and the Bank may have its gold coined as fast as it pleases by the Mint. The Bank of England, therefore, will be the gainer by $1\frac{1}{2}$d. for every ounce of gold that is thus given it. The country, indeed, will be the loser by the expense of coining, for which it, not the Bank of England, pays. Whether by a coincidence or not, it happens that this $1\frac{1}{2}$d. that the Bank of England may take off the value of the gold in the sovereigns it returns, coincides with the best estimates of the cost of minting, so that while the country loses and the Bank of England gains $1\frac{1}{2}$d. on every ounce of gold that is minted, the net result to the man who sells the gold is exactly the same as if he had paid for the minting. There is, therefore, exactly the same check on reckless turning of gold into sovereigns that there would have been under the conditions we imagined of a country in which any firm might mint gold into coin, the cost of doing so being $1\frac{1}{2}$d. an ounce.

As a rule, however, the persons selling gold to the Bank of England will not at once cash the notes. Bank-notes are legal tender, and it will be convenient to the man who has disposed of a large amount of gold (if he does not wish to open a credit with the Bank of England[1]) to take away the legal tender that he desires in the form of bank-notes rather than in the actual sovereigns. The Bank is compelled to hold actual gold against every one of its notes that is in circulation beyond the eleven millions guaranteed by the nation. Consequently, the Bank will hold the gold that is brought in, against the notes that it issues, and if the country already has as many notes in circulation as suits the convenience of the public a large fresh issue will determine, not immediately but in a short time, the presentation of a corresponding number of notes at the cash department, in which case the effect will be the same as if the sovereigns

---

[1] See below, page 606 *sq*.

had been taken out directly. If the number of notes issued is not such as materially to swell the body of notes in circulation, no perceptible effect will take place, but in any case the Bank cannot be inconvenienced. It gains its $1\frac{1}{2}$d. an ounce and loses nothing.

Our investigations so far would lead us to expect that the market price of gold bullion in the open market would be £3 : 17 : 9, and this may in truth be regarded as the normal state of things, but there are occasions on which the price rises not only to the metallic par of £3 : 17 : $10\frac{1}{2}$, but even to £3 : 18s. We saw but now [1] that such a state of things is not inconceivable, but the examination of the conditions under which it may arise will lead us to the most difficult part of our subject.

We have seen that the Bank of England holds a great part of the gold reserve of the world, and occasions arise on which the bankers of some one or more countries may wish to withdraw a large amount of the gold which stands to their credit. There may be danger that when called upon thus actually to pay an abnormal proportion of the claims for gold which some of its clients are in a position to make, the Bank may feel that the remaining reserve threatens to be reduced to an alarmingly low proportion of the total claim which it is still nominally liable to have to meet. It must, therefore, "protect its reserves," that is to say, prevent their being further depleted. Now what is really wanted is some means of inducing people not to draw gold, but to settle their affairs by transfers of credit; and a very small charge on actually cashing cheques in gold instead of paying them in to the accounts of the drawers, or on withdrawing gold from an account instead of transferring the credit, would suffice to accomplish this. But it is impossible to make such a charge. The value of a cheque or of a bank credit is due to the fact that though you are not likely to cash it you always can. And to place any obstacle in the way of cashing it would amount to a qualified "stoppage of payment," and it is of the essence of the security and credit of the Bank that it should be prepared at any moment and to any extent to meet its nominal obligations

Causes that may raise the price of gold. Protecting reserves.

[1] Page 603.

to pay gold. The difficulty, then, has to be met by circuitous and wasteful processes. In the first place the Bank of England does a great business in discounting bills. We have hitherto [1] spoken of bills as though they were claims for the instant payment of money at such and such a place, and so they may be; but many of them are claims for money, not now, but six months hence; and a merchant who holds such a bill, that is to say, who has supplied goods to a customer, whether at home or abroad, for money that will not be due for three or six months, may want to have the money either in cash or, more probably, in credit with his banker, at once. If the Bank accepts his bill, that is to say, the promise of his correspondent for money three or six months hence, and gives him present cash or credit in exchange for it, it will, of course, make a charge corresponding to the interest on the money which it lends, so that when the bill becomes due it will not only repay the loan but pay interest on it also. This charge is discount. Now the Bank of England cannot prevent its clients who actually have credit from withdrawing as much gold as they choose, but it can discourage the formation of credits by raising the terms on which it discounts bills. It can, therefore, to a great extent regulate the proportion between its reserves and its liabilities by refusing to enter into fresh liabilities and so contracting its business. It thus limits the potential calls for gold, and thereby restricts the actual calls which stand in a definite relation to them. This is a wasteful and indirect process, and it affects the terms on which loans are made all over the country, often to the extreme embarrassment of business; but no more direct or economical device has yet been hit upon.

But the Bank has another means of protecting its reserves, —the very curious one of bidding for gold in the open market and offering more sovereigns for it than would make its own weight if melted. This may seem at first sight a strange way of increasing its reserves, for it is offering more than an ounce of gold in payment for an ounce; but the Bank will pay for the gold either in bank-notes or in acknowledgments, that is to say, in credit, and it calculates that the credit of the importer of gold will not actually be

---

[1] Pages 590 *sqq.*

drawn out in sovereigns to any greater extent than the credit of its other clients will, and, therefore, by buying gold for notes or credit it will increase its reserves in larger proportion than its business. Thus, by buying gold and at the same time raising discount it protects its reserves from depletion, partly by contracting its general business and so reducing the claims on its reserve, and partly by increasing its dealings with a particular set of clients who will actually bring gold into its cellars, to the full amount of their accounts, and will only draw the ordinary proportion of them out again in gold. These are the conditions under which the value of bullion in the market per ounce rises above the value of sovereigns per ounce. But except for a very short time and in very exceptional circumstances this excess cannot exceed $1\frac{1}{2}$d. an ounce, for if the Bank of England bought gold at a higher rate than this its clients would proceed to draw out sovereigns simply for the purpose of melting them down, and bringing them back again to sell at a profit as bullion.

But we have not even yet answered the question what determines the amount of gold that is actually minted into sovereigns. The whole reserve of the Bank of England need not be, and is not, coin; and the means the Bank takes to protect its reserves has no immediate connection with the amount of gold that is minted. What then determines this amount? The answer is simple. The private individual, who deals in gold little and indirectly except as coin, places an amount of his property determined by considerations already explained[1] with his banker. It is registered in terms not of bullion but of sovereigns, and he can draw out absolutely as much of it as he chooses in the form of sovereigns. Provided he has a balance at the banker's, or a claim on any one else's balance, it costs him absolutely nothing to get it in the form of coin. Hence the celebrated declaration of a Member of Parliament: "We all of us have as much money as we want." So the depositors in the banks can, and do, take out as many sovereigns as it suits their convenience to have, and the Bank of England has to see to it that enough sovereigns are minted to meet the demands. The answer to the question, "What

What determines the amount of the gold minted.

[1] Pages 600 *sq.*

determines the number of sovereigns coined?" is therefore, "the estimate formed by the Bank of England of the number of sovereigns that the depositors in the banks collectively want to have." As it costs the Bank of England nothing to have the sovereigns coined, and as it always has plenty of gold, there is no reason why any one should be stinted. The country, therefore, bears the expense of providing all the depositors with as much coin as they call for.

But the importers of gold are in a different position. They cannot generally exchange their gold for sovereigns at weight par. They may have to pay ·16 per cent premium. Thus there is generally a check, not indeed to the minting of gold, but to the flow of gold into the cellars of the Bank of England, where it lies ready to be coined. But the Bank may reduce or remove this check or substitute a stimulus for it within certain limits, whenever it conduces to its credit to do so. On the other hand, there should be a normal check to the flow of gold out of the currency into the form of bullion again, and so to a certain extent there is. If it were not for a certain abuse, to be explained presently, all persons who required gold for their business would have a slight advantage in buying it direct from the importers rather than drawing it out of the currency. For it would seem that if the market price of gold is £3 : 17 : 9 an ounce, a man would be able to get more gold by ·16 per cent in return for his cheque if he paid it to an importer than he would get from his banker by drawing out the sovereigns and melting them. And there would be the additional expense of the melting. If we put that at $1\frac{1}{2}$d. he would lose ·32 per cent by drawing his gold out of the currency instead of out of the market. And if the market price rose for any reason, though this advantage would be diminished, it would still always be on the side of buying gold in the market. It is true that most persons whose business requires them to deal in gold will tell you that they are not conscious of being influenced by this consideration, and that whether they buy gold from a merchant or take it out of the currency is determined by considerations of convenience quite independent of this premium, even supposing that the market price of gold perceptibly affects transactions of the scale on which they conduct them. But in the nature of things this cannot be universally true. A market price is after all a market price, and means that gold or sovereigns are actually at a commercial premium, that is to say, that a preference for one or the other is actually felt by some one, presumably by the large dealers in bullion.

But this difference between the market price of gold and the gold weight of the sovereigns in which that price is paid, is crossed in the case of the working jewellers by a practice which we must now examine. Those A leakage in the currency. of them who deal with branches of the Bank of England are in the habit of requesting their bankers to select the heaviest sovereigns and put them aside to meet the cheques that they draw in their own favour, for purposes of melting.[1] Now the standard weight of a sovereign in England is 123·27447 grains. But a "remedy" is allowed to the mint-master; that is to say, an allowance for the imperfection of workmanship; so that if a sovereign does not weigh more than 123·474 or less than 123·074 it may be issued by the Mint; and it is legal tender, and may be issued by the Bank of England against its own notes and cheques, until it has sunk by abrasion to 122·50047. Between the heaviest and the lightest sovereigns paid out by the Bank of England and its branches there may therefore be a difference of ·97353 grains, which is about ·79 per cent. But presumably the Mint keeps very well within the allowed "remedy," and we may suppose that there are few sovereigns in the currency much above the standard weight, whereas the sovereigns issued against a cheque in the ordinary way would, on an average, be far above the lower limit. We shall therefore perhaps not be far wrong if we say that the average weight of the selected sovereigns exceeds the average weight of the unselected sovereigns by something less than ·387 gr. or ·315 per cent, which would be very close to the full amount of 3d. on the ounce, which marks the maximum theoretical advantage on buying in the market as against melting the currency. The subject is one as to which it would be a matter of some delicacy to make close inquiry, and I do not profess to have

---

[1] The prevalent idea that private melting is illegal is without foundation. It is illegal to deface or intentionally abrade (sweat) sovereigns. Any one may melt them.

any accurate information. The practice, as far as it goes, is obviously an abuse, and together with the fact that the Mint (and therefore indirectly the Bank of England) throws in the excess of the alloy in the sovereigns which it issues above that in the gold it receives, it establishes a permanent leakage in the currency for which there is no theoretical necessity, and which constitutes a loss to the nation.[1] The activity of the Mint must be sufficient to keep the public stocked with all the sovereigns it wants in spite of this leakage; and the Bank of England must maintain its reserves against it.

The "quantity law." We have concluded our positive examination of the selected points of financial science; but one theory must still be examined, for it seems to be not only unsound in itself but a fruitful source of confusion throughout the whole range of monetary science.

A treatise on currency frequently expounds what is known as the "quantity law," as regulating the value of the currency. The supposed law may be stated as follows: "The exchange medium of every country (coined gold in the case of England) has to carry on the business of the country, and this business consists in the whole volume of exchanges conducted day by day or year by year. Seeing then that the whole body of the currency, consisting of so many pieces, has to conduct the volume of exchange, each passage of a coin from hand to hand will have to conduct a certain fraction of it, and this fraction will be determined by a division sum; the dividend being the volume of exchanges, and the divisor being the number of coins employed multiplied by the average number of times that each coin changes hands during the period over which

[1] This is only a particular case of the general phenomenon which is defined under "Gresham's law" as the tendency of bad money to drive out good. This is not really a special law affecting the currency. It is merely a special application of the general principle that if S_1 and S_2 are units of two specified commodities (in this case heavy and light sovereigns) which are equally capable of serving the purposes of A (who cannot indeed distinguish between them), whereas S_1 will serve certain purposes of B (who can distinguish between them) better than S_2 will, there will be a tendency, as they pass in exchange, for B to "secrete" the S_1's for his own special purposes and pass on the S_2's to A. Or in more general terms, if S_1 will serve some purposes as well as S_2 and other purposes better, there will be a tendency to assign S_1 to those purposes which it can serve better than S_2 rather than to those it can only serve as well. A light sovereign (within the limits of legal tender weight) will serve the purposes of the ordinary citizen as well as a heavy one, but the latter will serve the technical purposes of the jewellers best.

the volume of business has been taken." Hence the name "quantity" law, from the supposed determination of the value of each unit of the currency in inverse ratio to the quantity of the currency as a whole.

The unsatisfactory character of the statement must be obvious at once, and it is noteworthy that there is (unless it has escaped me) no mention of any such law, nor any implication direct or indirect of its existence, to be found from end to end of the numerous works on currency and finance of the late Professor Jevons. To begin with we may eliminate all mention of the number of coins and the "average" number of times that each changes hands. For this "average" can only be arrived at by adding together the number of times which each coin has circulated and then dividing by the number of coins. When we multiply a (number of coins) by b (number of times each circulates on an average) to obtain c (total number of transactions) we have really already assumed c and obtained b by dividing c by a. We start with c then, and as it is c we want we may dispense with the process of first dividing by b to get a and then multiplying by b again to get back to c.

The simplified statement of the quantity law would then be: "A certain total volume of trade has to be conducted by a given number of changes of a sovereign from hand to hand. Therefore each one of those changes has to conduct a given volume of exchange, arrived at by division. And as it 'has' to do this, it will do it. The amount of work we set it to do determines the amount of work it does. That is to say, the value in exchange of a sovereign is determined by the work it 'has' to do every time it shifts."

Prima facie this is an inversion. How can we make a sovereign do a certain amount of work by telling it it must? The total business that the sovereigns collectively do is the sum of what each of them does whenever it changes hands. The business the sovereigns *do*, one would say, depends on their efficiency severally. How can their efficiency severally depend on the work they *have to* do amongst them? Obviously no one would suggest that the services rendered to the community by a pound of potatoes or a ton of iron could be arrived at by

Prima facie objections to it; and the grounds on which it is defended.

determining in the first place the total services that potatoes or iron *have to* render annually to the community, and then dividing it by the number of pounds or tons in existence ; or determining the amount of earth that a navvy shifts by every swing of his spade by stating how much earth the whole body of navvies *has to* shift, and then reckoning up their number and the average number of spade-swings which each of them performs, and dividing the total work they *have to* do by the figure so obtained. It is obvious, then, that if any such law holds in the case of the currency, it must be owing to some special characteristic which completely differentiates it from every other article. And this is exactly what is asserted by the exponents of the law in question. Their contention is that currency is a purely legal institution. A government, it is supposed, can make anything currency by declaring that it shall constitute the legal discharge of obligations ; and as a proof of this we are referred to the numerous instances in history in which paper currency has been maintained for indefinite periods. In these cases a piece of paper which has an inscription, corresponding to a certain weight of gold, passes as the equivalent of so much gold and is actually received as such an equivalent by persons who deal in gold as a commodity, although it carries no right to demand gold from anybody. A Bank of England note, of course, can be cashed at the Bank of England, that is to say, any one who likes is legally entitled to receive five sovereigns of full weight at the Bank of England in exchange for the note. But in countries where there is no such obligation on the part of any private or public body, nevertheless the dealers in gold are willing to part with it in exchange for paper, and all other persons are willing to receive the paper just as if it were gold. And it is further noted that the value of the notes will not sink below the par of gold unless there has been an over-issue. Thus it seems that the government, by itself giving its servants pieces of paper with the name of an amount of gold upon them, declaring that all its obligations are thus discharged, and that it will regard all other obligations amongst its subjects as discharged in like manner, can actually give a value to the paper that depends on the amount it issues. In other words, by enacting that its paper shall be received in payment of all debts and obligations it can cause all the business transactions of the country to be conducted by its means, and having thus determined the total amount of work that the paper shall do, it can further decree how much paper there shall be to do it; and since the habits of the industrial community determine how much of its business shall be done by the currency, and how much by cheques, paying of balances, and so on, the rate at which the paper will circulate, that is to say, the number of times, on an average, that each piece will change hands in the course, say, of a year regulates itself; and so the amount of the issue will determine the amount of business which each paper unit will conduct each time it changes hands.

These facts being supposed to be established, it would follow that if the business of a country is actually conducted in gold, that is to say, in an article which has an independent industrial value, apart from the enactment which makes it legal tender, this is an unessential incident. Because, as we have seen, all the functions of money can, by hypothesis, be conducted by a unit that has no primary industrial value. If (it is maintained) the currency of any country, England for example, consists of pieces of metal that happen to have a value in the arts and sciences, then there are two independent uses to which a piece of gold can be put, one of them being the natural and direct service which gold, as gold, can render in the arts and sciences; and the other being a fictitious or legally established value, which the legislature has chosen to affix to gold, but might just as well have attached to paper, leather, or anything else, provided it could so stamp its units of currency as to prevent their unauthorised issue by others than itself. Thus, according to this theory, a sovereign as a weight of gold, and a sovereign as a unit of legal tender, are indeed physically identical, but the values that the coin has in its capacity of a legal discharge of debt and in its capacity of a weight of gold have no direct or immediate connection with each other whatever.

But a government which chooses a valuable for its currency saves itself, it is admitted, from the temptation of over-issue; for if it over-issued, then its sovereigns, *qua* currency, would have less value than they would have *qua* gold, and whoever got hold of them would melt them until their contracting number threw more work upon each individual sovereign, and therefore raised its value in the currency; whilst the increased supply in the arts would lower the significance of gold in them. On the other hand, there can be no possibility of the value in the currency being permanently higher than the value in the arts if (as in England) there is a free mint. For any one who has gold can have it coined at will, and therefore if the amount of work thrown on each sovereign were such as to raise its value in the currency above what it bore in the arts, gold would be coined till the increasing number of sovereigns lightened the amount of work that each had to do, that is to say, reduced its value, whereas the deflection of gold from the arts and sciences would raise its value in them, and equilibrium would be restored. Thus, it is maintained, the two capital functions of gold (one primary and specific, the other wholly legal and independent of the natural properties and uses of the substance gold) will keep in balance with each other.

This theory of currency is fascinating by its ingenuity and neatness, and derives enormous practical support from its harmonising with the psychology of the ordinary man, in whose mind there is no practical connection between the value of gold as currency and its value in the arts. No man is conscious of being willing to work or to surrender his goods for a piece of gold, because gold is valuable for dentistry, for gilding picture frames or book leaves, for setting jewellery, or for making plate. His value of it for currency is something which, if he thinks about it at all, he regards as resting on custom or law. This theory then has the enormous polemic advantage of allying itself directly to the ordinary way of thinking, and as it is easy to expound and has a certain elegance, it is equally popular with teachers. But nevertheless the reasoning on which it rests is throughout topsy-turvy. From first to last it goes on the assumption that sovereigns, collectively and individually, will do what they have to do, and that the legislature can determine what that is; and throughout our exposition of the doctrine it has been obvious that we have been compelled to treat the value of a sovereign not as constituted by anything that it can and will do, but by something which in obedience to law it has to do. Now, that the law can enable any assemblage of things to perform a certain service, or conduct certain operations, collectively, simply by saying that it has got to do so, is so startling a proposition as to demand the closest inspection. If we maintained, for instance, that the government could by decree determine that all the agricultural operations of this country should be carried on by persons and with instruments authorised by itself, and if it were assumed that this would not affect the extent or nature of the operations, but that they would all be necessarily conducted by the authorised men and implements, and therefore if there were few men and implements each would do a great deal of work, whereas if the government issued more each individual would do less, but precisely the same amount would be done altogether, we should at once see the impossibility of supposing that the amount done by each unit was determined by dividing the sum of what they all do by the number of units; because as a matter of fact the amount that each of them does is the primary datum, and what they all do together is arrived at by addition or multiplication. If the government had any power of making each individual do more or less it could make a larger or smaller number of them capable of doing a given amount of work, but it cannot decree how much they *shall* do collectively, independently of their numbers, and then determine what each of them does by regulating those numbers.

What, then, are the supposed peculiarities of the work of the currency which have given rise to the belief that these exceptional possibilities exist in this case, though not in others? In the first place, the undoubted fact is pointed out that the amount of transference of goods or services which can be effected under the denomination of a sovereign depends solely upon the value of that sovereign. That is to say, if a quarter of wheat and a ton of hay are each worth the gold in one and a half sovereigns, they can be exchanged under the denomination of one and a half sovereigns. If, on the other hand, they are each worth the gold in a sovereign, they can be exchanged under the

[margin: The difference between the primary and the derived values of all commodities mistaken for a difference between currency and other commodities.*]*

denomination of a sovereign. Thus the same amount of business, namely the exchanging a ton of hay for a quarter of wheat, might be conducted with the intervention of one sovereign, of one and a half sovereigns, or of two sovereigns, equally well. And therefore, if, for any reason, the stock of gold were so reduced that the gold in a sovereign should double its value, then the sovereign would be able to conduct twice as much business as it did before. The services that the currency renders to the community at large, therefore, seem to be independent of the number of sovereigns that are in the currency. And it is undoubtedly true that, within wide limits, the money function could be performed equally well, in any community, by a larger or smaller number of sovereigns. This then, we are told, constitutes a fundamental difference between the money function and the functions of other things, for a large or a small number of potatoes will not equally well perform the nutritive functions of potatoes, nor will a large or small number of men or tools be able to perform the same industrial functions equally well. The derivative nature of the exchange function of gold, therefore, seems to differentiate it from the primary functions of other commodities. But, as we have seen, this derivative value is not peculiar to the currency. To any man who is dealing in anything it is a matter of indifference, within wide limits, whether he receives a large or a small quantity of it for any given consideration, provided the small amount in one case is as valuable as the large amount in the other. If, for instance, a certain class of books is worth 5s. a volume in the second-hand trade, and a bookseller has a considerable trade in them, making on an average 10 per cent per annum on his turnover, and if presently this class of books, through a change in the taste of the public, becomes twice as valuable, and the bookseller with the same general apparatus and machinery, and with the same effort of attention and so forth, deals in half the number of books, his purposes will be just as well served, so long as he makes the same profit on his turnover. For neither his expenses nor his income depend on the value that he attaches to the books for his own use. They depend on the value that some one else attaches to them, so that this derivative function which they perform for him can be performed equally well by a smaller number that are highly valued and by a larger number that are valued low. But to the student purchaser of books it is by no means the same thing whether he has a thousand volumes for which he has given, on an average, 5s. each, or five hundred of the same volumes for which he has given, on an average, 10s. each. The five hundred at 10s. each do not facilitate his studies or serve his other purposes any better than if he had only given 5s. each for them. And he is without half the library he would have had on the other supposition. The distinction, then, that we are at present examining is not one between currency and all other commodities, but between primary and derivative values, between the value attached to an article by the user and the value attached to it by the dealer. And in all cases, whether of primary or derivative value, the total service consists in the sum of the individual services. We can in no case get at the individual services by saying that each individual has got to perform, and therefore will perform, its due fraction of the total, fixed as a total by some external power. Surely we should expect that if the government really has the power of making the currency do certain work, it must be by giving to a definite quantity of gold the power to do a definite piece of work, not by enabling an indefinite sum of gold, whether great or small, to do a definite amount of work by its fiat that it shall do it. If, as we have seen, a little gold can under certain circumstances do as much as a great deal under other circumstances, it must be because under those circumstances each unit of gold is made capable of doing a larger amount of work; not because it is told that there is more work for it to do. This is obvious enough in an ordinary way, and the example of the books will again serve our purpose. If the primary services of the books (to the readers) have mounted on the collective scale then their derivative services (to the dealer) mount too, and each book will convert a larger amount of his energy and thought into a correspondingly larger amount of the things he desires. Just so if the primary services of gold mount, either because of a falling off in the rate of production, or because of increased applications of gold to the satisfaction of tastes and wants, or for any other reason, each unit of gold will be able to conduct a larger amount of business.

These considerations suggest that we should begin our inquiry as to the connection between the amount of gold in the currency and the value of each sovereign at the other end from that by which it is usually approached. Granted that, in a general way, the total amount of work that the currency has to do is fixed by the general business habits of the community (though, as we shall see presently, this is a large assumption), it will follow that if the marginal value of an ounce of gold, in the arts, is high, then a small amount of gold will be enough to conduct that part of each man's transactions for which he employs the currency, and he will become a "dealer in gold" only in small volume. That is to say, the withdrawal of a small volume of gold from its primary applications will suffice to conduct the business of the country because each piece of gold, having a high value, will be able to transact a large amount of business. If, on the other hand, a large output of gold during a series of years, or any cause affecting the use of gold in the arts, should bring down the marginal significance of an ounce of gold in the arts, then each man will find that as a "dealer in gold" he needs a larger volume of gold to do his business for him, and a larger volume will be held out of its primary applications. Thus it is not the amount of gold in the currency that determines how much work each piece shall do, but the amount of work that each piece can do that determines the amount in the currency.

Re-examination of the connection between the amount of gold in the currency and the value of each sovereign.

If we now turn to paper currencies, again, we shall remodel the statement thus: It is not true that a government can confer on pieces of paper, or other intrinsically worthless articles, the collective power of doing the business of the country, but it can within certain limits confer a defined power of doing business on certain pieces of printed paper. For the government, as general guardian of contracts and of property, has the power to enforce or to decline to enforce any contracts, and as guardian of the rights of property it can determine whose property anything shall be. It is possible, then, for a Government at any time to say: "There are in this country a number of persons under legal obligation to pay fixed rents for premises, fixed interest on capital, fixed salaries for services, over such

What makes paper currencies circulate?

periods as their several contracts cover. There are also a number of persons under definite obligations to pay such and such gold, at such and such dates, once for all. Now we, the Government, can, if we like, issue stamped papers bearing various face denominations of one, ten, a hundred, etc., units of gold currency, and we can decree that any one who possesses himself of such papers, to the face value of his debts, and hands them over to his creditor shall be held to have discharged his debt, and we will henceforth defend his property against his late creditor and declare that he has, in the eye of the law, paid the sum of gold which he owed." It is obvious that these pieces of paper will thereby acquire definite values to all persons who are under obligation to discharge debts or to pay salaries or rents or other sums due under contract; for to command one of these pieces of paper will be, for certain of their purposes, exactly equivalent to commanding a sovereign. As these persons constitute a large and easily accessible portion of the community, there will at first be no difficulty whatever in circulating the notes, for those who have no direct use for them themselves will know that there are plenty of people who have, and a certain number of these certificates can, in this way, be floated. Each will be able to transact business to the same extent as a piece of gold of its face value. But as the contracts gradually expire and the debts are gradually discharged, the original force that gave currency to the Government's paper will become exhausted. At first the holder of such a bond will from time to time come across men who will say: "Oh, yes, I was just looking out for paper in order to discharge my debt or pay my rent"; and if there were the smallest tendency to depreciation, competition would instantly rise amongst these persons who would be glad to get, at any reduction whatever, these things which their creditors would be compelled to receive at full value. If people chose to go on making fresh contracts and giving fresh credit, without specifying that the payment should be in gold, and thus went on perpetually bringing themselves under legal obligation to receive paper in full payment, the process might go on for a certain time, by its own impetus, but there would be nothing to compel any one to enter into such a contract; and if at any time, for any reason, there were a slight preference for making contracts in gold, so that there was a dearth of people of whom it could be definitely asserted that for their own immediate purposes, independent of the general understanding, the paper was worth the gold, there would obviously be no firm basis for the structure, and every one would become nervous and would want to make some allowance for the risk of not finding any one who would take the paper at or near the face value.

The Government has, however, a further resource. It has the means of maintaining a perpetual recurrence of persons thus desiring money at its face value, for the Government itself has more or less defined powers of taking the possessions of its subjects for public purposes, that is to say, enforcing them to contribute thereto by paying taxes. Ultimately it requires food, clothing, shelter, and a certain amount of amusement and indulgence for its soldiers and all its officials; and it requires fire-arms, ammunition, and the like. And in proportion to its advance in civilization it may have other and humaner purposes to fulfil. Now, as long as gold has any application in the arts and sciences it exchanges at a certain rate with other commodities, just as oxen exchange at a certain rate against potatoes, pig-iron, or the privilege of listening, in a certain kind of seat, to a prima donna at a concert. The Government, then, levying taxes upon the community, may say: " I shall take from you, in proportion to your resources, as a tribute to public expenses, the value of so much gold. You may pay it to me in actual metallic gold or you may pay it to me in anything which I choose to accept in lieu of the gold. If you do not give it me I shall take it from you, in gold or any other such articles as I can find, and which would serve my purpose, to the value of the gold. But if you can give me a piece of paper, of my own issue, to the face value of the gold that I am entitled to claim of you, I will accept that in payment." Now, as these demands of the Government are recurrent, there will always be a set of persons to whom the Government paper stamped with a unit weight of gold is actually equivalent to that weight of gold itself, because it will secure immunity from requisitions to the exact extent to which the gold would secure it. This gives to the piece of paper an actual power of doing the work that gold to its face value could do, in the way of effecting exchanges; and therefore the Government will find that the persons of whom it has made purchases, or whom it has to pay for their services, will not only be obliged to accept the paper in lieu of payments already due, and which it chooses to say that these papers discharge, but will also be willing to enter into fresh bargains with it, to supply services or to surrender things for the paper, exactly as if it were gold; as long as it is easy to find persons who, being themselves under obligation to the Government, actually find the Government promise to relinquish their claim for gold as valuable as the gold itself. The persons who pay taxes constitute a very large portion of the community and the taxes they have to pay form a very appreciable fraction of their total expenditure, and consequently a very large number of easily accessible persons actually value the paper as much as the gold up to a certain determined point, the point, to wit, of their obligations to the Government. Thus it is that a limited demand for paper, at its face value in gold, constitutes a permanent market, and furnishes a basis on which a certain amount of other transactions will be entered into. The Government, in fact, is in a position very analogous to that of an issuing bank. An issuing bank promises to pay gold to any one who presents its notes, and to a certain extent that promise performs the functions of the gold itself, and a certain volume of notes can be floated as long as the credit of the bank is good. Because bank promises to pay are found to be convenient, as a means of conducting exchanges. After this number has been floated the notes begin to be presented at the bank, and presently it has to redeem its promises as quickly as it issues them. The limit then has been reached and the operation cannot be repeated. After this people will decline to accept the promises of the bank in lieu of the money, or, which is the same thing, they will instantly present the promise and require its fulfilment. The amount of notes in circulation may be maintained, but it cannot be increased. The issuing Government does not, without qualification, say that it will pay gold to any one who presents the note, but, in accepting its own notes instead of gold, it says, in effect, that it will give gold for its own notes to any *of its own debtors*; and as long as there is a sufficient body of these debtors to vivify the circulating fluid the Government can get its promises accepted at par.

Any Government which, even for a short time, insists on paying in paper and receiving in gold, that is to say, any Government that does not honour its own issue when presented by its debtors, will find that its subjects decline to enter into voluntary contracts with it except on the gold basis; and if its paper still retains any value whatever, it will only be because of an expectation of a different state of things hereafter that gives a certain speculative value to the promise. In fact a Government which refuses to take its own money at par has no vivifying sources to rely on except the very disreputable and rapidly exhausted one of proclaiming to debtors, and persons under contract to pay periodic sums, that they need not do so if they hold a certificate of immunity from the Government. Such immunity will be purchased at a price determined, like all other market prices, by the stock available (qualified by the anticipations of the stock likely to be available presently) and the nature of the services it can render. The power, then, of Governments to make their issues do exchange work depends on their power to make a note of a certain face value do a definite amount of exchange work; and this they can effect by giving it a definite primary value to certain persons, and then keeping the issue within the corresponding limits. It does not consist in an anomalous, and, in fact, inconceivable, power of enabling an indefinite issue to perform a definite work, and arriving at the value of each individual unit by a division sum.

Indeed, this division sum is impossible in any case to make; for the proposed divisor is arrived at by multiplying the number of units in the face value of the issue by the rate at which, on an average, they circulate. Now the Government can undoubtedly regulate the amount of the issue, but it cannot regulate the average rate at which the units will circulate. Nor indeed can it rely on the dividend, namely the amount of business which the circulating medium shall perform, remaining constant. For it is a matter of convenience how much of the business of a country shall be carried on by the aid of a circulating medium and how much without it; and as a matter of fact, at periods when there is a dearth of small change in a country a great amount of retail business is conducted on account, and balances are more often settled in kind. Thus business which would ordinarily have been carried on by the circulating medium is carried on without it, because of its rarity. In Italy, for instance, when coppers were rare the exchange value of a copper did not rise because a smaller number had to do a greater amount of work, but each unit did as much business as it could, and the rest of the business was done without them. Again, the history of paper money abounds in instances of sudden changes, within the country itself, in the value of paper money, caused by reports unfavourable to the Government's credit. The value of the currency was lowered in these cases by a doubt as to whether the Government would be permanently stable and would be in a position to honour its drafts, that is to say, whether, this day three months, the persons who have the power to take my goods for public purposes will accept a draft of the present Government in lieu of payment. It is not easy to see how, on the theory of the quantity law, such a report could affect very rapidly the magnitudes on which the value of a note is supposed to depend, viz. the quantity of business to be transacted and the amount of the currency. Nor is it easy to see why we should suppose that the frequency with which the notes pass from hand to hand is independently fixed. On the other hand, the quantity of business done by the notes, as distinct from the quantity of business done altogether, and the rapidity of the circulation of the notes may obviously be affected by sinister rumours. Two of the quantities, then, supposed to determine the value of the unit of circulation are themselves liable to be determined by it.

BOOK III

ANALYTICAL AND PRACTICAL

Verum animo satis haec vestigia parva sagaci
sunt per quae possis cognoscere cetera tute.
Namque canes ut montivagae persaepe ferai
naribus inveniunt intectas fronde quietes,
cum semel institerunt vestigia certa viai,
sic alid ex alio per te tute ipse videre
talibus in rebus poteris caecasque latebras
insinuare omnis et verum protrahere inde.

LUCRETIUS.

But this faint spoor suffices for an alert mind; so that thou thyself may'st come at all the rest. For just as hounds, when once they have found the true track, full often search out with their nostrils the lair of the mountain-roaming quarry, hidden though it be with foliage, even so may'st thou, in such things as these, see for thyself one thing after another, work thyself into the secret lurking-places, and thence drag out the truth.

CHAPTER I

SAMPLES OF ANALYSIS

SUMMARY.—*We may apply the principles we have been studying to the analysis of a miscellaneous set of phenomena in the social and industrial world, both by way of exercise and by way of testing the principles themselves. The subjects chosen in this chapter are gambling, the housing problem, unemployment, depression and crises, the immediate and permanent effects of attempts to relieve distress, or of changes in expenditure, the meaning of the national income and the legitimacy of inferring from it the average command of commodities and services which would accrue to each individual if wealth were more evenly distributed.*

The systematic portion of our task is completed. It remains to illustrate and test the value of the instrument of analysis which is now in our hands by applying it to concrete cases.

We may take our material almost at random. An institution such as Trade Unionism; a programme such as the scheme of "communalising the instruments of production," or the more limited proposals to nationalise or communalise the land, or to feed ill-nourished school children; or matters of discussion such as the housing problem, or the proposals of the "tariff reformers"; or phrases such as the "national income"; or the problems suggested by a concrete action, like that of subscribing to a famine fund, or by practices such as playing cards for money, or betting on the turf, may provide us with subjects for analysis. In the course of our examination of any one of these questions we shall find abundant illustration of that interdependence of economic, social, and moral questions which has been so often insisted upon in the body of this work.

We will begin with the highly complex question of gambling, and we will take it first in the simple and undisguised form which it assumes at the gaming-table. Our treatment must necessarily be brief and inadequate, for it is not within the scope of these concluding chapters, either in this or in any other case, to give more than a bare indication of the way in which our principles may be applied.

<small>Gambling.</small>

From the individual point of view, there can be no doubt that an immense number (I should say an overwhelming majority) of those who gamble intend to win and think that they can do so. In the case of a pure game of chance, such as we are now supposing, a man who thinks that he can win must believe in such things as runs and turns of luck, the occurrence of which may be felt by a natural or acquired sense, or must be the victim of some analogous superstition; or else he must rely on some "system," all which systems reduce themselves either to a belief that in matters of pure chance what has already happened affects the probabilities of future happenings, or to a transformation (by a systematic scheme of successive stakes), of a game in which there are even chances of loss and gain into one in which a gain is made more probable than a loss, but at the expense of the loss being proportionately heavier if it comes. In this latter class of "system" the gambler's attention is absorbed by the increased probability of gain, and he does not realise that the proportional gravity of the loss leaves him in the long-run exactly where he was. So far it is obvious that we are not on economic ground at all. Superstition, and ignorance of the doctrine of chances, can only be eliminated by general intelligence or special study. Meanwhile, we can but stamp as a delusion, and set aside without further examination, the belief that any instinct or system can give a man an advantage in a game of pure chance. The man who thinks he is more likely to mend than to mar his fortunes by gaming is the victim of an illusion, and there is an end of it. But this dogmatic statement cannot now and here be justified.

We now pass to the social aspect of the question. Dropping

for a moment the question of the commission taken in the form of the favourable chances of the table, it is clear that if there is any considerable transference of money from some of the players to others our general principle of declining marginal significance shews us that the gains will, on the average, be of less significance to the winners than the losses to the losers ; so that there will be a net loss in the psychic significance of the collective wealth of the players. The money will have been transferred from the place in which it is more to the place in which it is less significant; for since the relative wealth or poverty of the players has no influence on their gain or loss, we may put it out of consideration, and may treat the gainer and loser as though they were equally wealthy ; and in that case it is obvious that the gain, which advances from the existing margin onwards, will have less significance than the loss, which retreats from the existing margin backwards. We may illustrate this principle by passing for a moment from the gaming-table, and taking the case of a sweepstake on a horse-race. Each player makes a uniform stake, and the names of all the horses that are to run are then written on separate lots, and a sufficient number of blanks is put in to make the number of lots equal to the number of players. Each player then draws a lot, and the holder of the name of the horse that wins sweeps all the stakes. Now it is clear that if there are fifty players, each of them sacrifices his stake at the existing margin, whereas when they accumulate in the hands of the winner they advance, at a constantly declining significance, from the present margin downwards. Each stake, therefore, comes from where it is more and goes to where it is less significant.

Contrast the case of insurance against fire. There is an uncertain loss to be met. The margin of the man upon whom it falls suddenly and notably retreats. He receives sovereigns, each one of which is taken at the existing margin of the other insurers and is applied at his raised, because retreated, margin ; so that the sovereigns come from where they are less and go to where they are more significant. Gambling and insurance, therefore, which have some elements in common, namely the certainty of the stake and the uncertainty of the issue, are, from the social point of view, exactly the opposite of each other. Gambling is a machinery for carrying money from where it is more to where it is less significant, and insurance is a machinery for carrying it from where it is less to where it is more significant.

Insurance companies charge a commission, and, as they render a social service, they are creating a fund (not indeed material, but psychic) in the extra significance which wealth gains by the transference they effect, out of which fund they are paid. And now we will return to the table and reintroduce the element of the "chances of the table," which is the analogue of the commission of the insurance agent. It is not necessary to explain in detail what these "chances of the table" are. It is enough to instance the game of *rouge et noir*, in which the teetotum turns up "zero" on an average once in thirty-seven cases, and what then happens is equivalent to each player forfeiting half his stake. Thus the table has an advantage of one chance in seventy-four over the players. The owner of the table practically draws this commission for facilitating the anti-social work of making wealth less significant, just as the insurance agent draws his commission for his social service of making it more significant. And here we may return for a moment to the individual. He cannot alter the chances of the game, and at the table the chances are not even. It is as if the player paid a small fee for the privilege of staking on an even chance; and as the players collectively would win and lose equally on an equal chance, they collectively lose on a chance which is in favour of the table; so that to the psychic loss which accrues to them collectively from the transference of wealth from one to the other, there must be added the material loss of the subtraction from their collective wealth of the commission of the table. And in the long-run his portion of this loss must come home to every persistent gambler, and must more than swallow up any gains he individually may make; for it is steady and cumulative and bears a proportion to the magnitude of his transactions, whereas his gains are at best casual and have no tendency to repeat themselves. The successful gambler, then, if he persists, will pay all and more than all his gains in return for the privilege of making them, and the unsuccessful gambler in addition to his losses will pay for the privilege of incurring them. These statements, again, can only be substantiated by the doctrine of chances, but they cannot be questioned or shaken.[1]

There remains a theoretical possibility of a man having, say, only one shilling in the world and no prospect of getting another for months or years. It is possible to argue that the best thing he can do with it is to stake it at some game in which the prizes are enormously high and the chance of winning them correspondingly small. Say he has one chance in thirty thousand of gaining £1000. This chance is not actuarially worth 1s. It is only worth 8d. But yet to the man in his present state it may reasonably appear that £1000 would be worth more than 30,000 times as much as a shilling. For whether he goes into the workhouse (or the Thames) to-day or to-morrow may seem to him to make hardly any appreciable difference at all, if he knows that this fate is in any case coming; and so he gets something—a small chance of £1000 —for almost or quite nothing. It is a case of rising margins such as our theory fully recognises.

Doubtless in such cases an element of illusion generally enters, and when the man draws a blank he will probably be conscious of something very like a disappointed expectation; but it is conceivable that the transaction dispassionately considered might really be reasonable. Such a case, however, could only be isolated. For a man to make a practice of thus staking his shillings would imply that he had a flow of shillings to stake; and if the flow and his play continued long enough he would be sure to lose more than he gained. Other cases, in which the unschooled imagination pictures the large gain of one as more than compensating the collective small losses of the many, resolve themselves into various forms of hallucination, and are, above all, inapplicable to habitual or repeated transactions.

We have already seen[2] that the speculating public occupies

---

[1] The only theoretical reservation is that any individual gambler may stop short (if only because he dies) before the run has been long enough to absorb all his gains. But it is a mistake to think that there must come a moment in the career of every gambler at which, if he were wise enough to stop, he would be a winner on his whole transactions. It is probable but not certain that there may be such a moment, or such moments, early in his experience; but the longer he goes on the less likely is it that he can ever stop as a winner on the whole body of his transactions since he began. [2] Page 246.

exactly the same position to the Stock Exchange which the gamblers collectively occupy to the table, and that the ruin of the one, as of the other, is probably due to the commission, not to luck. In horse-racing, the bookmaker, even if perfectly honest, is able to derive a similar commission, from the curious fact that the inner circle of the backers of the horses, whose estimates ultimately determine the "odds," collectively over-estimate the chances. This may be illustrated by an example, much too crude to correspond with actual facts, but manifesting the principle. Suppose there are four horses in a race, and the trainers and owners of each horse, and others who have a special interest in it, estimate its chance of winning at one-third. It follows that their estimate of the collective chances of the horses is $1\frac{1}{3}$,—*i.e.* more chances than there are. It will work out thus: Each owner or backer who thinks that his horse has one chance out of three of winning will regard 2 to 1 against the horse as the proper odds; that is to say, he will promise to pay £1 if he loses on condition that he is to receive £2 if he wins. The first chance being only twice as great, in his opinion, as the second, he regards the odds as fair and the chances even. So a bookmaker betting 2 to 1 against each of the four horses will receive £1 on each of the three that loses and will pay £2 on the one that wins, leaving himself a balance of £1. The bookmaker, then, does not back horses any more than the "bank" makes stakes on the table. They leave that to the public. The difference between staking on the green table and speculating on the Stock Exchange or the turf, is simply that in the two latter cases an element of judgment may enter, though it seldom really does. The judgment of the ordinary speculator or backer of horses being on a level with the "judgment" of the gambler who dots down on his card a certain number of the turns of the teetotum until he considers the proper moment has come for him to back his luck. In so far as judgment really enters into the case of the horse-race, an individual's chance of making money may be better than his chance of losing it, but we must observe that he is only "making" money from the individual point of view. From a social point of view he is merely "taking" it from his less competent correspondent. And on the principle already examined his gain will normally be less significant than his companion's loss. "Judgment" on the Stock Exchange in purely speculative transactions stands on the same footing. But if a property or concern of any kind is speculatively bought with a view to developing and improving it, then nobody need lose and the gains of the speculator may really be "made."

And this will serve to illustrate the transition from the speculation which is of the nature of gambling to the speculation which is not. There can be no doubt that the excitement of taking risks is not only a deeply rooted but a valuable trait in human nature. But the man who devotes his resources to acquiring special skill and training, without knowing whether he will be able to make a living by it, or to prospecting for minerals without knowing whether he will find them in payable quantities, is speculating in a very different sense from that in which the gambler speculates. The former aims at creating wealth, the latter merely at getting wealth that is already created, instead of some one else getting it. Or, to put it in another way, the former class meet uncertainties on their industrial way and deal with them as best they may; the latter go out of the industrial way just to create uncertainties. But it need hardly be pointed out that here as everywhere the line is difficult, or rather impossible, to draw. We know perfectly well that the man who buys for a rise, intending to sell again before settling day,[1] is practically gambling, and that the man who takes shares in a new industrial undertaking, intending to hold them and to draw his dividend, is not gambling. But the point at which fools who came to scoff remain to pray, or saints who came to pray remain to scoff,—that is to say, the point at which the man who bought to sell becomes interested in the concern on its own merits and holds for a dividend, and the point at which the man who bought to hold sells because he thinks the selling price is more than the shares are worth,—can seldom be foreseen or defined. Nor can we tell how the two motives combine even at the beginning. A man may buy partly because he thinks the thing good enough to hold, and partly because he expects a fancy on the part of the public to make it still better to sell. Probably the majority of those who

---

[1] See page 246.

buy stock at all are at least potential speculators in buying and selling.

The gambler's ultimate plea, however, has not yet been examined. Suppose he declares that he knows perfectly well that he loses, that it to say, that he pays for the game, but says that he enjoys the game and is willing to pay for it. This is the account that many people who play cards for money will give of themselves. Some, no doubt, believe in their luck, and unreasonably expect and intend to win. Some believe in their skill and judgment and deliberately intend to profit at the expense of their guests and hosts, or fellow-guests. But the majority, I suppose, will say that their gains or losses are in the long-run trifling, and that, in any case, the game is worth the price. And we may note that as in this case there is no commission, there is no certainty of loss to be taken into consideration. To judge of this plea we must consider the nature of the satisfaction, whether it is of the character of vicious or ruinous indulgence as examined and analysed in a previous chapter;[1] and, finally, we must consider how far it is possible to dissociate it from the incidental cruelties involved in drawing the young, the poor, and the inexperienced into risks in which loss is likely to be crushing and gain corrupting.

We will now turn to another question, without any attempt to establish a link between it and the one we have just examined; for the scheme of this chapter does not imply that any special connection between its successive sections exists.

Many people live under housing conditions which rightly shock every feeling of humanity; and the fact raises a growing sense of social compunction. How it is to be met constitutes the housing problem. But it is clear, on examination and analysis, that it is only in a very limited sense that we can speak specifically of a housing problem at all. In what sense is the question why people live in improper houses, and how we are to stop it, different from the problem why they eat improper and

The housing problem.

---

[1] See pages 423 *sqq.*

insufficient food, or why they are inadequately clothed, or amused? The problem how to house people is obviously only a branch of the problem how to provide for them generally, both in body and mind. Certain persons are ill-provided with everything. In their own eyes they are not ill-provided with houseroom relatively to other things, for if they were they would redistribute their expenditure so as to get more houseroom and less of everything else. But you will answer they cannot afford to give up anything else. Exactly. That is to say, they are as keenly in want of more of everything else as they are of more house accommodation. Their conditions of accommodation possibly strike us as even more terrible than their conditions of feeding and clothing, but they do not strike them so. The housing problem, then, is in the first place the general problem of poverty. In the next place it is the problem of education. We think, perhaps, that people ought to value decent accommodation more highly than they do. And lastly, we think (and here it seems for a moment that we come upon a specific housing problem) that rents ought not to be so high. But why is the house rent of the poor so high? Primarily because they have to live near their work and land is of great value there because it is a highly efficient industrial instrument there. The rich man either does not live where his work lies, or lives there in a good house. If the poor man lives in foul quarters, then, it is either because he is poor or because he does not appreciate the value of better housing conditions as highly as we think he ought to do. Broadly speaking, it would seem that the only ways of dealing with the housing problem are to combat the poverty of the ill-housed, to quicken their sense of the evil of bad housing, to make good houses cheaper, or to give houses to people for less than they are worth. All these plans have been attempted. Miss Octavia Hill and her disciples have done much in educating individual slum-dwellers into desiring better conditions, but the process is too slow and laborious to satisfy the impatience of the demand for improved conditions. Attempts, whether by public authorities or private companies, to build better houses at a cheaper rate, on commercial principles, come under an important class of experiments of which we have already spoken.[1] If, on the other hand, houses are provided by philanthropic companies or individuals, who are content with 3 per cent on their capital (or otherwise on less than commercially remunerative terms), a privileged class of occupants is at once created; and the difficulty may be found insuperable of securing the privilege, even as far as it goes, to the class of persons most in need of it. Possibilities of cheap and easy transport are constantly opening, and perhaps the best hope of depleting our overcrowded centres lies in a development of tram services which would relieve the competition for central business sites. Thus, the housing problem turns out to be a poverty problem, a land problem, an education problem, a problem of locomotion, and a problem of town-planning. Attempts to deal with it merely by saying that bad houses shall be destroyed and none but good ones built in their stead do not in themselves touch the difficulty. They are open to the same danger which we encounter in connection with proposals for a minimum or standard wage.[2] As a minimum wage may mean the multiplication of the unemployed, so minimum requirements of decency and convenience in houses may mean the multiplication of the unhoused; or if the standard only applies to new houses it may mean the crowding into existing tenements of those who cannot afford to come up to the new requirements. At best, if it stood alone, it would mean attempting to force people to pay for what we think they ought to want instead of for what they want themselves. There is no doubt a wide range for insisting on sanitary conditions which do not notably add to the expense of building, but it can hardly be doubted that in some country districts the by-laws enforced by the local authority prevent cottages being built, and therefore aggravate overcrowding.

It should hardly be necessary to add that overcrowding may be brought about by any cause that makes building land difficult to obtain; and if the owners of land object to having cottages on their estates for æsthetic, social, or sporting reasons, the result is just the same as if the competition for the land were purely industrial.

[1] See pages 209 *sq.* [2] See pages 693 *sqq.*, and cf. page 344.

We will now turn to the connected problems of unemployment, depression, and commercial crises, which are admittedly amongst the most baffling on the whole field of applied economic science. I am far, indeed, from claiming that the principles laid down in this work present an obvious and convincing solution of them. But the following points may be considered. Every one knows that persons, not without some dexterity both of mind and hand, may be absolutely unemployable in a given post. Every busy man has had embarrassing offers of "help" from zealous friends who are willing to do anything,—but who can do nothing that does not require more superintendence and correction than the result is worth. In an industrial society of increasing complexity it may reasonably be expected that the conditions which enable the individual to pass from a negative to a positive efficiency will become more and more exacting. An advancing education may be supposed to meet these more exacting conditions, but, so far as it depends on the specialising of capacities, the man who has been made eminently employable in one line of activity may thereby be made all the more unemployable in another. Again, unemployment may be absolute or relative; that is to say, a man may be unable to find any employment at all because he can do nothing that is worth anything to any one else that he can find, or he may be unable to find employment at a living wage or at the wage which he demands. Now the specialising, alike of instruments and of faculties, and the minute division of labour, which are characteristic of the organisation of industry on the great international scale, are accompanied by liability to variations in the stress of demand, and such variations mean accompanying variations in the relative worth, economically considered, of this or that particular skill. Industries in which sliding scales prevail recognise this fact. When, for any reason, the product becomes worth less, there may still be employment for the same number of labourers if they are willing to recognise that their work also is worth less. The sliding scale cannot obviate disputes, for it is based on an evaluation of the significance of labour relatively to the significance of all the other factors of

Unemployment.

production, which can hardly, in the nature of things, be above dispute; but it does at least recognise the fact that with the changing stress of demand the significance of any kind of labour changes also. If this fact could be universally recognised, one cause at least of unemployment would be removed or qualified; for it is obvious that the attempt to maintain a standard wage, or to fix a minimum wage, independently of fluctuations in the market of the product, must, so far as it succeeds, throw men out of work when the demand falls, until the marginal value of the reduced product and the marginal significance of the reduced number of workers bring about equilibrium. The larger product might have been sold at the lower price, and all the workers might have been kept in employment at the lower wage. And the supplies of the rest of the community would have been maintained at a higher level.

There is, however, no limit to the possible fluctuations of demand, and however much the principle of the sliding scale were elaborated and extended, and even if it were applied to all interests, rents, and salaries, fluctuations in demand might reduce all concerned in a given industry to a starvation wage, if not to absolute "unemployment."

Obviously, the only real issue from such a state of things will be found in the draining off of labour from the depressed industry to others. This is a process beset with inherent difficulties in the want of mobility and versatility on the part of the workers,[1] but the difficulties are indefinitely aggravated by the jealousy with which any invasion of other industries (all of which normally regard themselves as overstocked[2]) is sure to be regarded.

Note, further, that every business must be carried on to a great extent on a speculative basis. Promises of all kinds are made[3] in anticipation of the results of an industrial undertaking. Thus, before a great ship is launched or a great building completed, not only an immense number of promises, but an immense number of payments have been made in anticipation of the value that the completed work will have. All kinds of estimates of the marginal

Commercial depression and crises.

[1] It has often been noted that old sailors are scarcely ever out of a job, because of their general resourcefulness and versatility.
[2] See pages 546 *sqq.*   [3] See pages 370 *sq.*

significance of land, tools, technical skill in directing and executing work, and every variety of factor of production, have thus been formed and acted on. These estimates are not necessarily correct. When the whole commercial community is in high spirits and feels successful, vast numbers of overestimates of the worth of things may be indulged in. Payments out of current stock may be made on the assumption that the stock is being more than replaced *pari passu*; and while the country thinks itself growing in wealth, it may in fact be living on its means. At last the time for keeping promises and replacing expenditure comes, and the resources from which this was to be done are found not to exist. In detail this is a chronic phenomenon in all periods, whether of prosperity or of depression. Individual firms are perpetually becoming bankrupt because they find themselves unable to keep their promises; and others who have promised or performed on the strength of these promises are involved in the ruin in their turn. But if business in general is sound, these events do not shake the general confidence, however much they discourage or hamper individuals. If, on the other hand, the general estimate has been at fault and the commercial world collectively, or in a particular country, has consumed more rapidly than it is creating, and has promised what it cannot perform, a general shudder of nervous apprehension will run through it when the discovery is made. People become afraid of promising anything at all, and still more afraid of paying in advance, or of trusting other people's promises, and the whole complex system of mutual supply becomes more or less paralysed. Mechanics and others have been receiving and have consumed more than the equivalent of their marginal significance, and now that this is known they cannot get the same wages any more. Meanwhile, the people who gave them more than they get from them are impoverished or ruined. And not only do many people realise that they have spent more than they had or more than they could afford, and are actually in poverty, but the means of communication and combination by which alone we can prosper have been disorganised and the mutual confidence without which the industrial machine will not work has been shaken. A starves for want of the things that B can make; B starves for want of the things that C can make; and C for want of the things that A can make; because A, B, and C can only be brought into relation with each other by a system of speculative promises which no one dares to make or which no one cares to trust. Now, as soon as a man finds that he cannot sell his goods at the accustomed price, he complains of over-production and says that the markets are glutted. Thus we have the paradoxical situation of general "over-production" and "glutted markets," accompanied by general want. That is to say, apparently, there is so much of everything that no one can get anything. But it is not really the abundance of the things produced, or the abundant power of producing them, that causes the mischief, but the timidity or forlornness of those who weave the vast and intricate maze of promises, through confidence in which alone things can be moved from those who make to those who use them.

For recurrent general depressions the only radical cure seems to be a raising of the intelligence and conscientiousness both of the directors of industry and of the public. It is possible that this may ultimately be furthered by making them state officials, but at present the socialistic Utopias are generally characterised by totally ignoring the necessity of any connection and proportion at all between promises and the means of fulfilling them.[1] It is said, however, that private persons are already beginning to take advantage of slack times for outlay on permanent plant and improvements; and it seems ideally conceivable that the State should pursue a similar course, and should undertake public works, that must be executed some time, in the slack periods when they can be executed at least expense, and will, at the same time, have a tendency to counteract a serious evil.[2]

Note, finally, that it is easy to exaggerate the magnitude of the material difference between prosperous and depressed times. The bulk of the business of the country goes on successfully all the time. It is only over a comparatively narrow margin that inflation and contraction succeed each other.

The question may often have presented itself to reflective minds whether it would be possible, by limiting the area of commercial intercourse, to prevent the inhabitants of a given

[1] Cf. pages 682 *sq*. [2] Cf. page 357.

country from being swept into the storms of the whole industrial world. Just as it is argued that a yeomanry, living largely on the direct products of its own industry, would be less liable to desolating economic disturbances than a manufacturing population, which is helpless to supply its own wants if the world markets cease to demand its product, so it may be argued in the abstract that the fluctuation within a limited area will be less violent and disastrous if it is approximately self-supplying than if a considerable portion of its population are liable to bear the brunt of changes in the currents of the whole commerce of the world. But though the question whether such relative isolation and self-sufficiency are possible, and whether they might be expected to yield a balance of advantage, is perhaps arguable in the abstract, as a matter of fact no scheme of fiscal union is ever based on any such idea of shielding a suitably constituted area from the commercial storms of the world. The fact becomes obvious when we note that actual or proposed areas of fiscal union are always determined by other than commercial or economic considerations. The United States of America are often cited as furnishing a typical case of protection, but we should never lose sight of the fact that there is free trade within the United States themselves, so that it seems safe to assert that there is no other free trade area of so great an extent and embracing so wide a variety of natural and social conditions in the whole world. Moreover, it is generally supposed that the United States would welcome the accession of Canada, and in case of a union would at once throw down the fiscal barriers that now separate the two countries. If this is so, one is led to the conclusion that the tariff is not maintained on economic grounds, and that no economic loss would be anticipated from its removal. In the same way the desire to federate the British Empire fiscally is clearly determined by other considerations than those of an economically convenient and suitable area, containing a due balance of productive resources; and the desire of all advanced industrial communities to find external markets for their "surplus products" shews that they have no idea of cutting themselves off from the great world-streams of commerce and constituting themselves into self-supplying

Tariffs and fluctuations of trade.

2 T

groups of a size and character determined by the prospect of economic stability.[1]

It will be a good exercise to see how far we can trace the meaning of such an act as subscribing a guinea to a famine fund in India. The root fact is that there is a shortage of food, and the inevitable deduction seems to be that man or beast must somewhere go so much short.[2] If the otherwise starving Hindus are fed, they must eat food that some one else would eat if they were left to starve. Now, if I subscribe a guinea, it is exceedingly improbable that I save that guinea out of food. Even if I did we should have to inquire in what way the food that I should have eaten gets, directly or indirectly, to the Hindu; but if I eat just as much as I should have done, the more perplexing question remains: Who abstains from food because I subscribe a guinea? How does my subscribing make him abstain, and how does the food from which he abstains reach India directly or indirectly? Let us consider the special circumstances, which would of course vary if the famine were not in India, but in China or Sicily. To begin with, we may assume that there is no actual lack of food-stuffs in British India as a whole, even in time of the severest famine. Probably there will be plenty of food near the famine-stricken districts, easily accessible. The trouble is not that there is no food, but that the ryot has no money or general command of wealth by which to get it. Nay, it is very possible that the starving ryot has himself managed to grow rice enough for sustenance and next year's seed, but has to sell to enable him to pay taxes.[3] Now a certain not inconsiderable part of the taxation of India is devoted to the payment of pensions and annuities in England. This, then, is the situation. India exports rice in order (amongst other things) to pay pensions in England. Suppose, in the first instance, that English pensioners or annuitants, who would actually have consumed a guinea's worth of Indian rice, determine to subscribe a guinea to the famine fund, and to go short of the food them-

Subscription to a famine fund.

---

[1] For some remarks on unemployment and "tariff reform," see pages 666 *sqq*.
[2] See, however, page 649.
[3] See Vaughan Nash, *The Great Famine*, pages 134 *sqq*., London, 1900.

selves. That is to say, they give up eating the rice and eat nothing else instead. The case would then be perfectly simple. The distressed ryots would either keep their own rice or buy rice from a neighbouring district, and India would export less rice by that amount. Money can in this case be eliminated from the question, and we can regard the English pensioner as simply giving the ryot a bill on himself for the price of the rice which he has never received. The ryot can then either keep his own rice and pay his taxes by his bill on the Englishman, or can buy rice from his neighbour with the bill and pay his taxes out of other resources. It would be exactly the same if you or I abstained from the rice, and subscribed the guinea. In that case the essential facts might be represented thus. I allow India to draw a bill on me for a guinea, and at the same time I abstain from eating rice. India, instead of selling rice to raise a guinea for the pensioner in England, sends him the bill upon me for that amount, and keeps and eats the rice; leaving me to pay the pension. But now, suppose that the subscribers, instead of abstaining from rice, abstain from stalls at the opera, or dishes of early asparagus or strawberries, or that they travel third class instead of first, or go without books they would otherwise have bought, or trench upon their other charities. How does this relieve the famine? The immediate answer is obvious and is the same as before. India has leave to draw a bill upon the subscriber, and, therefore, is not compelled to sell the rice. There is, therefore, so much more rice in India, and so much less in the general market, and it follows that somebody must go short. But the accounts are not "cleared" as they were in the former case, and we must pursue our inquiries further. Two apparently independent centres of disturbance have been established. On the one hand, the rice market in England is to a certain extent depleted. Our previous studies enable us to form a perfectly clear conception of what that would mean if it stood alone. What would have been the marginal demands had the supply been as great as usual would remain unsatisfied. The price of rice would rise, and certain people would either go without rice altogether, or would take less than usual. As we need not suppose that any of the phenomena we are examining affect the incomes of the majority of these abstainers, they would presumably increase their purchases of the most obvious substitutes for rice, let us say sago, tapioca, or Indian corn. And since at present we have seen no reason to suppose that the available supply of these substitutes would be in any way increased, these markets also would feel the reaction, and there would be a tendency to a rise. And so, in widening circles, the effect of a shortage in rice would diffuse itself, and minute abstinences would be the result, until the whole effect of the shortage was exhausted in the diminished satisfactions of a great number of individuals who had unconsciously and unintentionally made minute marginal concessions to fill up the hideous void in India, where for once we watch a margin actually running back, unless arrested, to the origin itself.

So far, then, the effect of my donation to India has been to diffuse the suffering caused by the shortage of the rice crop, and this is entirely satisfactory. But, so far as we have yet gone, though the diffusion is in itself a subject of congratulation, it is a little surprising to discover that the persons amongst whom the actual loss is diffused appear to be entirely involuntary agents in the transaction.

But we have only traced the movement from one of the centres of disturbance. Let us now return to the other. If I economise in my railway travelling or in my payments at the box-office of a theatre, I do not save any expenditure except to myself. The first-class carriage in which I should have travelled is run just the same, and the performance I should have witnessed takes place; but the shareholders of the company or the proprietors of the theatre are a guinea to the bad. So far as I am concerned, the balance-sheet is made up. I have given a guinea to the ryots, and I have gone without a guinea's worth of comfort or enjoyment. But the enjoyment or comfort that I have forfeited is not transferred to some one else. It has perished, or rather it has never come into existence, but has remained a dormant opportunity. I am the loser to the full extent; but nothing whatever has yet been done towards economising rice. And again, though I bear the loss of the pleasure or comfort that has not emerged into actuality, yet the management of the theatre or the shareholders of the company have their resources curtailed by the full extent of the guinea of my subscription, and they must bear the loss too. I, therefore, compel them practically to pay the subscription over again in some shape or another; and they again have the alternative of standing out of some open opportunity already provided for them, or of going without some material transferable thing which is there not potentially but actually. We may carry on this process as far as we like in the imagination, though it is clearly impossible to trace it in the concrete, as the pressures becomes more and more diffused. It is impossible to say how many potential enjoyments, or exchanges of service, are sterilised without in any way affecting the consumption of rice. But, ultimately, the pressure must come home somewhere to persons who economise by going without material things. We need hardly repeat the stock warning that no sharp line can here be drawn. Gathered fruits or cut flowers stand more nearly on the footing of a stall at the opera-house or a journey in a first-class railway carriage than on that of a bag of rice or corn. The opportunity they offer is open, indeed, for a longer time than the opportunity of witnessing the performance or taking the journey, but they are indefinitely more perishable than a bag of grain, and it may well be that if I do not buy them, they cannot be kept and supplied to some one else. In that case the vendors will be the losers, wholly if they cannot sell at all, partly if they are obliged to make a reduction at the close of the market. In the latter case the loss is not complete, but a product which would have satisfied a want higher on the collective scale goes to satisfy one lower on that scale. There is an objective loss, amounting to something short of the whole objective value that would have been realised; but whether there is psychic gain or loss no man can say. In any case nothing has yet been done towards bearing the ultimate privation caused by the shortage of rice except just so far as the enjoyment I have abstained from is directly or indirectly a substitute for the consumption of rice.

But the widening effects of my abstinence are reaching the same diffused markets which the widening effects of the relief of the Hindu's starvation have reached, and they are acting in opposite directions. While the retention of rice in India is raising demands, the enforced abstentions in England are lowering them, and so theoretically we have found the meeting-place, and have seen not only that the relief of the famine in India is directly caused by my abstaining from a certain enjoyment, but also that the effects of these two primary phenomena theoretically meet and counteract each other through a vast network of minute capillary channels. It still remains true, however, that my voluntary subscription causes an undefined series of involuntary contributions on the part of those whom my contracted expenditure affects, and that these are passed on from hand to hand, repeating and multiplying themselves in diffusing circles, and all of them without effect in relieving the markets upon which extra pressure has been put, so long as they affect forms of consumption which are not effective substitutes for the consumption of rice. Further, it remains true that the ultimate abstinences are borne by involuntary, not voluntary, agents, except in so far as the original subscriber actually abstains from such food-stuffs or other commodities as are direct or indirect substitutes for the rice.

Now, note that the unforeseen and sudden nature of the demand is the real cause of the disturbance. If an enlightened administration came to the conclusion that the regular levying of taxes, together with irregular appeals to charity for their practical remission, was a wasteful method; and if the English public were to make up its mind, once for all, to give peace and justice to India on easier terms [1] than are now nominally exacted, and were to regularise and rationalise the methods on which these lower terms were enforced; we might then have a continuous instead of an intermittent abstinence on the part of the British public from certain satisfactions in order to relieve the pressure upon India. The energies which are now devoted to the construction of first-class carriages, the production of operas, and so forth, would be turned into other channels, and might, directly or indirectly, produce food

[1] The salaries of the Indian officials, pensions and all, are surely not higher than the market value of the talent and fidelity which they exercise at their posts. So far as that goes, the justice and peace given her cannot presumably be purchased on any easier terms; but England might give them to India for less than they cost, instead of charging her the full price and then giving her doles when she is ruined.

to make good the diminished tribute in rice from India. And even if no direct provision could in all cases be made, so that an ultimate shortage of food was somewhere felt, at any rate there need be none of that incidental and gratuitous waste that our analysis has traced as due to the intermittent character of the claim upon England's charity and the inability of the machinery of the economic world to adapt itself to it.

Now let us eliminate the fact that the suffering to be relieved is in one country, and the abstinence that relieves it in another. We may suppose that a disaster has occurred in our own country and that subscriptions are made to relieve it. Here the conditions are essentially the same as before. There will be two centres of disturbance, caused respectively by the destruction, say, of crops and herds, due to a flood, and by the contraction of my own expenditure, when I have by my subscription transferred a part of my purchasing power to the sufferers; and unless the things I abstain from are precisely the things which the relieved sufferers consume, my abstinence does not cover their consumption, and the same succession of incidental and, so to speak, gratuitous losses that we have already traced will accompany the process of my compelling some less well-to-do person than myself involuntarily to incur the really effective abstinence that balances my beneficiary's consumption.

Now let us take another step and eliminate the element of suffering or loss altogether, simply supposing that one person in England makes a gift to another. The difference here is that there is no primary loss to be made good. We are not supposing that there is a shortage anywhere. But, if the presentation is not one of a group of actions that has been contemplated and provided for in advance by the enterprise of the industrial world, that is to say, if it constitutes a disturbance in the regular and anticipated course of events, it may be accompanied by all the incidental disturbances that we traced in the other case. If I buy for my friend something different from what I should have bought for myself, or if I make him a present in money and what he buys with it is not the same thing that I abstained from, then two markets are affected. Prices tend to rise in the one and to fall in the other, and there is a suction in the one case and an obstruction in the other, which, if continued, would tend to draw productive resources down one set of channels to the relief of the other.[1] Meanwhile, there is a certain amount of waste of services and of swiftly perishable commodities, and as the relative places on the communal scale of a variety of things are directly and indirectly shifted up or down by the tightening and relaxing demands, certain people are made richer or poorer.

And now, finally, we may eliminate the hypothesis of a gift altogether, and may see exactly how any sudden change of expenditure tends to produce loss and disturbance. The provision already made for the expenditure which ceases will run more or less to waste, and the increased demand on another market will squeeze out certain marginal claimants upon it, driving them to alternative forms of expenditure. But, as the increased expenditure in the favoured market improves the position of those who command its wares, it is probable that some of them may secure, in the falling market, some of the satisfactions from which I have turned aside, and caused others to turn aside, and so far the wastage of accumulated resources and talents which my contracted expenditure has caused will be checked. Some waste, however, there will always be, as well as the disturbance of the raised and lowered values of existing goods. If the new order of things becomes established, the distribution of the factors of production adapts itself to it, and the things more in demand are produced instead of those less in demand, and there is no continuous loss.

The incidental disturbance due to any change, as such, may be ignored when there is a great and obvious purpose to be served, such as in our instance of the relief of famine. Nor need it trouble the most scrupulous conscience when it is of a casual and personal nature, for such irregularities are always taking place, and in the broad cancel each other. But capricious changes in fashion have, doubtless, a depressing effect upon the material and moral condition of the industrial populations they affect; and even where a new invention or reformed administration increases the resources and the well-being of the community, the incidental disturbance may be disastrous in its local effect, and, unless some provision be made to meet it, may be a heavy social offset against the total gain.[2]

In leaving this subject we may note that we have through-

---
[1] See pages 383 *sq*. [2] Cf. pages 352-357.

out been assuming a "rigidity" in the industrial organisation that allows no room for "play." As a matter of fact it would require very extensive movements to complete the circles in the way we have supposed. Any small changes of pressure would probably exhaust themselves long before their effects met and counteracted each other in diffused markets, and at every point spare energies might be released and directed into compensating channels. To take a single instance; a rise in the price of any food might make it just worth while to harvest some small and distant crop in some part of the world that would otherwise not have paid for the picking or saving and transporting.

We are now in a position to enter upon the last inquiry to be undertaken in this chapter, namely, the meaning of estimating the national income at so much, and the value of the speculations as to the average income which it would secure if wealth were more evenly distributed. I may warn the reader in advance that we shall reach no particularly definite or novel results; but the inquiry will itself, I think, constitute a particularly valuable exercise. *Total and average national income.*

What would be meant by saying, for example, that the total income of England is about seventeen hundred million a year, and that this gives an average of £40 a head, or of £200 for a family of five? The total income is arrived at by adding up the estimated incomes of individuals. Both the national and the individual incomes are expressed in terms of gold. But how are these incomes reckoned, and in what do they consist? If a man earns his living by growing vegetables and selling them in the market, he acquires a certain command of commodities and services that other people control and which they consider marginally equivalent—each to each—to the lots of vegetables they receive from him in exchange. The vegetables he produces, therefore, are the communal asset that is represented in his income. They are what he contributes. What he consumes is contributed by others. If he pays rent, then part of this asset of vegetables is represented not in his income, but in that of the landlord. But what if the man earns his living by teaching Greek, or by book-keeping, or by preaching, or by dancing, or by company-promoting? He renders services, in return for which he receives certain things he desires. The communal asset is his services. They are what he contributes. What he enjoys is contributed by others. The communal income, then, though measured by marginal significances in gold, is constituted by the marginal significance of everything made, produced, or done, that enters into the circle of exchange. The revenue of a community for a year is all the desired things, whether material commodities or services, which come into existence that year. Hence, if my income is £500, and out of it I pay a servant the equivalent of £30 in board and lodging and wages, her income will be estimated at £30 and mine at £500. And this will not be counting her £30 twice. I have rendered services that count for £500, and she has rendered services that count for £30, and both are reckoned in the national income, just as much as the wheat grown by the farmer. Many reflections are at once provoked. Naturally, the total income of a nation tells us nothing unless we know how it is distributed. Wealth and starvation side by side may shew as large a total as evenly distributed comfort would. Again, the income of the nation consists only in exchangeable things; but we have seen [1] that the true revenue of satisfaction, enjoyment, or vital realisation and experience (whether of the individual or of the community), though supported by things in the circle of exchange, is neither secured nor measured by them. Probably, if any community realised this, its income would decline and its well-being would increase, for it would create less and enjoy what it created more.

Again, as all wealth is estimated by its marginal significance in gold, it would be possible for an increased supply of any commodity or service, except gold, to appear on the estimate of the national income as a loss. For, if the fall in marginal significance relative to gold should more than compensate the increased supply, the total area of enjoyment would increase while the total exchange value of the commodity declined; and a gain in the means of satisfaction would be registered as a loss of wealth. If gold increased in greater proportion than other things, prices would rise and all supplies would be registered at a higher figure and so the income of the

[1] Pages 152 *sq.*

country would rise all round, whereas only gold would reall[y] be more abundant. In all careful statistics this is allowe[d] for, and an "Index Number" is used which measures value not in gold but in a complex unit that may be supposed t[o] give a much nearer approach to psychic or vital stability.

Innumerable sources of error and illusion, however, remain[.] Since all services and commodities are impartially estimate[d] at their market value, the tools that the burglar buys and use[s] are just as much a part of the year's income as those that th[e] farmer uses. The services of two rival " travellers " who ar[e] endeavouring to capture the same market count as much i[n] the national income as if they had been bringing convenience[s] and utilities within the reach of persons who would otherwis[e] have gone without them. Mutually destructive or inherentl[y] vicious activities and services count for as much as construc[-] tive and wholesome ones. The "services" for which th[e] wages of shame are paid constitute a part of the nationa[l] revenue as much as any other;[1] but if Portia is Brutus' wife and not his harlot her companionship ceases to count i[n] the national revenue. And, moreover, any changes in th[e] tastes, habits, or morals of the community which enabled the[m] to derive increased enjoyment from their own personal activitie[s] or their mutual intercourse would tell for nothing in th[e] estimates of national wealth.

All this, however, and much more of the same sort, i[s] admitted. It must not be lost sight of, but it need hardl[y] be pressed, for it is all generally allowed, and some of it i[s] habitually realised. Any one who says that the nationa[l] income amounts to £40 a head means no more, at most, tha[n] that the resources of the country are such that there [is] enough for every one to have forty pounds-worth, at the rate[s] now current, of the things and services in the circle [of] exchange that, wisely or foolishly, virtuously or viciously, h[e] desires. But it is just this proposition that we must no[w] proceed to examine, for it is by no means obviously true.

If, indeed, we could be sure that, however the wealth of th[e] country were redistributed, the same things would be wante[d] in the same quantities and with the same relative intensitie[s] by the people then in a position to realise their desires as the[y]

[1] Cf. pages 184 *sqq.*

are now by the present commanders of wealth, then, truly, all the activities of the country might go on just the same and the revenue might remain the same, only the things and services now made and rendered would be given to other people. Indeed, less than this would satisfy us, and would justify us in speaking of the "average income" of the country in the usual way. We have learnt to distinguish between the immediate disturbance and the ultimate effect of any change, and the former of these considerations may be ignored. It will be enough for us if the resources now devoted to the production of services and commodities desired by those who are at present in a position to command them, are capable of being so diverted as to produce commodities and services demanded in the new order of things, in such quantity and quality that, estimated at their marginal significance, they would total to the same amount as at present. Have we any right to assume that this will be so? Let us try to see.

The mere fact of a thing being desired by a number of wealthy men gives it a high marginal value objectively. It is possible to conceive, for example, that a man of very great wealth might be willing to offer a larger sum for a great area of land for purposes of sport than a number of poorer men might be willing to give for the same land for purposes of subsistence. Strange and paradoxical as it may seem, the land would in this case occupy a higher place on the scale of preferences of the man to whose pleasures it made a slight addition than on the scales of the men to whom it made the difference between a hard life of unrelieved toil and a fair degree of comfort;[1] because the wealthy man has so great a command of generalised resources and commodities that the whole amount which would make the vital difference between poverty and comfort to a hundred families signifies very little indeed to him, and opens to him no alternative more eligible than that of adding to his game preserves. The price of the land, therefore, is higher because of the existence of a few very rich men than it might be if there were the same general command of resources and services in the community, more evenly distributed. Thus land might stand lower on the communal scale, if wealth were more evenly distributed.

[1] Cf. pages 145 *sqq.*, 189 *sqq.*, etc.

One may see the same fact illustrated in the case of the fees that an eminent surgeon or counsel can command. If there are a number of exceedingly wealthy men in the community, there may be many persons to whom the difference between the services of the acknowledged possessors of the very highest skill in their respective branches, and those whom skilled opinion places just one distinguishable degree below them, might weigh in the scale as heavily as anything else that could be got for, say, £200; and if there were enough of these persons to employ the energies of some two or three surgeons, they might command fees of five hundred guineas; whereas, if there were no very wealthy men, no considerable body of persons would care to spend more than, say, £20, or £10, or 10s., as the case might be, on the mental satisfaction of thinking they had got the services of those whose public reputation was supreme, in preference to the services of others, possibly quite as good, and certainly barely distinguishable from them in excellence. If I suppose that by going to one dentist I can have one per cent greater security against present or future suffering than if I go to another, the extent of my general resources will determine the amount at which I am willing to purchase this extra security. If I am a millionaire and am unfortunate enough to require the amputation of a limb, the difference between three hundred and five hundred guineas sinks, in the presence of such a crisis, below the range of perceptible distinctions. If my whole income is not above a few hundreds, I shall be well content with the services of a man of good local reputation in whose hands I shall feel reasonably safe; and if he will perform the operation for £20 I might not be willing to give £30 (much less £500) for the services of the top man in the profession. Thus the difference between a certain exercise of A's skill and of B's may be valued at £480, or at something under £10, in the estimate of the national income, according to the degree to which the inequalities in the distribution of wealth have been carried.

It is unnecessary to multiply examples. It is sufficiently clear that if the command of the collective resources of the community were more evenly distributed, they would all be there just the same. The surgeon's skill and every other faculty would be there, available for the relief of suffering, and the sustaining and adorning of life, but minute differences would not count for so much, relatively to staple articles, as they do now. Whereas fine distinctions of talent in music-hall " stars " and others, who render services to masses of persons at once, might possibly command greater not less differentiated remuneration. But these latter cases would be exceptional. When we think of the scheme of values in the minds of the rich and poor respectively, we must surely feel that these considerations entirely vitiate the calculations made from the total income of the nation to the ideal " average " which each might enjoy; for if we divide the national income by the population and say that the quotient is £40, what that suggests is that there is now enough to give every one the things that he individually would buy if under present circumstances, and with present prices ruling, he had £40. But this is not so. He would have a share in the national revenue of things and services, the items in which share, taken severally, can each find somebody now who attaches such a value to it that all the values added together make up £40. But to some of them no one not immensely rich could attach the high values they now bear, so that if wealth were evenly distributed they would be there, but would not be valued by any one at such a figure as to make up the average of £40.

This does not mean that there would be a material loss to set against the psychic gain of a more even distribution. It merely means that the averaging of the national income, objectively measured, gives an unreliable estimate of the actual command of the things he desires which his share of that revenue would secure to each individual.

But, it may be urged, although it is obvious that a family with an income of £200 a year would not value jewellery or game preserves, choice bindings or *editions de luxe*, thoroughbred horses or skilled professional services, at the figures they now command, yet this would merely create a disturbance for a time, if the change were sudden; and ultimately the talents and resources that are devoted to the production of these things would flow down other channels and would produce equal values in the things that are now most in demand. But can we really place any reliance upon this? The talents and resources that are now devoted to the breeding of a bull-dog worth £1000 might conceivably, if diverted, produce the year's food, clothes, shelter, amusement, and so forth, which five families of five each would demand, if each family had an income of £200 a year; and our general assumption that all free resources can be turned into various channels at approximately equivalent commercial significances seems to imply something like this; but the assumption is far from safe even as a *prima facie* probability if we are supposing the change in the direction of resources to be not a mere shifting of margins but a substitution in bulk of one set of industries for another. It does indeed seem at least possible that the kind of talent that produces prize bull-dogs might succeed in producing particularly fertile varieties of plants and animals that would be valued under the new conditions. But no one can say how these things would work out in terms of marginal value in gold; or whether, for instance, the general distribution of the population of the earth over her surface could remain substantially the same as it now is if the processes of industry were so completely revolutionised as they would be under the conditions we are supposing.

Forecasts on such subjects must be based on general considerations, and their speculative character should be recognised. An extensive redistribution of wealth would certainly change its psychic significance, but its actual effect cannot be arrived at by any such simple process as doing a division sum. And statements based on such a procedure have a delusive air of solidity and precession against which we should be on our guard. If we are confident that the world, or any particular community, is rich enough to enable every member of it to live in human comfort, our confidence must be based on our general belief in the versatility and resourcefulness of human intelligence, and our anticipation that the reaction of a more even distribution upon the energies, tastes, and morals of the community would be such as to heighten rather than to lower the effectiveness of human effort.

This confidence is not shared by every one, and, therefore, the desire for a more even distribution of wealth, which animates most social reformers, is looked upon with open suspicion or with secret misgiving by many men who would be slow to admit that they were willing to purchase the luxury of the few at the cost of the penury of the many. They believe that all devices for relieving poverty at the expense of wealth will result in impoverishing the rich without enriching the poor in the first instance, and in still further impoverishing the poor ultimately. The only basal answer that can be given to such forecasts is that we must at least try to devise such methods as may make the experiment worth trying; but it is well, meanwhile, that we should try to face the implications of our Utopia itself, suppose we could get to it. And to this we are led by some aspects of the inquiry we have just concluded.

We have asked whether the talents that are now devoted to choice bookbinding, for instance, could under changed conditions produce improvements in the potato crop that would stand on the relative scale of the new community as high as the object of artistic beauty stood on that of the old one. Well, if they could, and if they did, there would doubtless be a psychic gain, but would there not also be a psychic loss? Few of us would dare to say that we prefer a society in which there are both slums and culture to one in which there is no want and no refined artistic taste. But, nevertheless, if the disappearance of poverty meant the disappearance of a wealthy and leisured class, and if the disappearance of such a class meant the disappearance of what we now think of as refined tastes, refined manners, and all the finer artistic enjoyments, we should feel that a heavy price had been paid. A comparison, however, of such social and economic conditions as those of Denmark with those of countries of greater wealth and greater poverty does not support the belief that the higher qualities and finer tones of the intellectual and æsthetic life need fear anything from more even distribution of wealth.

One thing, however, is very clear; namely, that there actually are some satisfactions or indulgences which in the nature of things could not become universal, even if our general command of material resources were indefinitely increased, and which must tend to disappear if wealth is more evenly distributed. And the examination of a case in point may serve to remind us of the necessity of constant vigilance against the tacit assumption that what is possib[le] to any one is possible to every one.

Napoleon may have wished to encourage the belief th[at] every soldier carried in his knapsack a marshal's baton. B[ut] he must have known that, however true it might be that a[ny] soldier might rise to the position of a marshal, that "fool o[f a] word" impossible was the only one to apply to the suppositi[on] that *every* soldier could do so. For the existence of o[ne] marshal implies the existence of a number of soldiers w[ho] are not marshals. In like manner it is possible in a[n] advanced industrial community for any man to becom[e] wealthy; but it is not possible for every man to becom[e] wealthy, with the implications we now attach to the term for, included in our conception of wealth (even in the mode[st] degree to which every middle-class establishment aspires to [a] possession) is the keeping of servants. The personal ide[al] then, at which middle-class people aim, appears to be o[ne] which cannot in its very nature be universally realised; f[or] if we cannot all be marshals, neither can we all belong to t[he] servant-keeping class. This is the most obvious and stubbo[rn] of a great number of facts indicating that most of us wish [to] command the services of others on terms on which we shou[ld] not wish to render them ourselves.

People who for any reason have done all their ow[n] housework know how much of it there is which is n[ot] worth doing for the sake of enjoying the results. Amazi[ng] simplifications of life take place, for good or ill, when t[he] alternative is to work the apparatus of a complicated li[fe] one's self.

Let us suppose that one family enjoys an income of £5[00] a year and another an income of £100. One member of t[he] poorer family goes into service with the richer family a[nd] receives in food, wages, and accommodation, the equivalent [of] £30 a year. The income of the poorer family is now schedul[ed] as £130, and the joint incomes of the two families are £63[0.] Had the girl stopped at home and done the same things f[or] her own family that she does for the other family the joi[nt] incomes would only be £600. *Prima facie* both famili[es] would be the losers, not only nominally but really, for t[he] poorer family prefers £30 a year in other things to t[he]

2 U

services of the girl, and the richer family prefers the services of the girl to £30 worth of other things. But now, suppose that the income of the poorer family rose, from independent causes, to the level of the other. The family, now in command of £500 a year, might not only prefer to keep their daughter at home rather than that she should earn the equivalent of £30 elsewhere, but might further desire to command the services of another girl at £30 a year, and might soon come to consider themselves the victims of extreme social hardship if they could not get her. But "where everybody's somebody, there no one's anybody"; and if the rendering of personal services stands no lower down upon any one's scale of preferences than it is upon yours, you must either (1) render personal services yourself, or (2) get them from other people at terms which you or your compeers would accept, or (3) go without them.

Thus we see that not only an equalised distribution of existing wealth, but changes which should raise the resources of the poorer to a level of those of the richer without any corresponding loss anywhere, would in themselves render the realisation of the usual middle-class ideal impossible.

Such reflections may cause many searchings of heart, and may bring home to us the danger of allowing a not inconsiderable gap to arise, unobserved, between our social sympathies and the goal to which our practical endeavours are directed. On the other hand, it may strengthen our sense of the true nature of independence, and may direct our thoughts to many possibilities of simplification of the apparatus of life by extension of our communal as distinct from our private opportunities, and dissociation of the idea of enjoyment from the idea of exclusive possession and command. The flower-beds in a public park may be enjoyed by hundreds of thousands, and half a dozen gardeners may give as much pleasure as hundreds could have done if each of them had worked at that which only a few could enjoy. In the National Gallery or the Louvre the poorest citizen who has the rudiments of artistic taste and culture may secure opportunities of enjoyment and education which no private collection could secure to even a handful of the community. The extent to which this economy can be carried depends very largely upon the development of two qualities in the general mind : the capacity for dissociating the idea of enjoyment from the idea of possession, and the sense of respect and responsibility in handling or enjoying public property.

CHAPTER II

SOME FURTHER ANALYSES

SUMMARY.—*The subjects dealt with in this chapter are the general nature of taxation, the contention that it may be placed on the foreigner and that properly arranged import duties might relieve unemployment, the meaning of borrowing for unproductive expenditure, schemes for communalising the instruments of production generally or land in particular, and Trade Unionism.*

Taxation is the deflection of the resources of members of the taxed community from purposes which they would have selected for themselves to purposes which are selected for them by the governing power. It is justified only by the belief that the purposes to which these resources are directed are collectively more important than those from which they are deflected. To the question, "What is the test or standard of importance?" the only answer is that the power which imposes the taxes must judge of that as best it can ; and according to the form of government, and the state of public opinion, or of opinion prevalent among the governing classes, this or that material or spiritual consideration will weigh lighter or heavier. It is obvious, then, that importance will be very differently weighed under different political and social conditions, but in any case the individual who differs from the government view as to the relative importance of things has to acquiesce, under penalties, in the judgment from which he dissents.

Taxation.

There is a fairly general consensus that taxation is justified when it secures objects which the great majority of the nation considers extremely important, and which they

believe would not be done at all, or would not be d(
adequately, if they were not done collectively. The mainte
ance of the army and navy, and of the police force, and t
law courts, are usually cited as instances in point. It
generally believed that all these things are necessary to sec
civilized life, and that, if their institution and maintenal
had to depend on voluntary effort and combination, t
certainty as to the action of others would paralyse each ma
efforts, so that nothing effective would be accomplish
These postulates are not granted by every one, and amon
those who grant them acute divisions of opinion may rem;
as to the extent to which provision should be carried,
amount of taxation which it justifies, and the persons fr
whom the taxes should be raised. As to this last poi
again, it seems easy to lay down a general principle, 1
impossible to determine its application except by the ju(
ment of those who apply it. The principle is that t
purposes from which the resources are deflected should be
little significant or important as possible. If any one thir
that the use of great wealth is usually considerate, enlighter
and large-hearted, the use of moderate wealth generally sord
and the use of small wealth vicious, his conception of t
suitable sources of national revenue will be very differe
from that of the man who thinks that the pence of the p(
usually minister to vital needs of extreme urgency, th(
of the middle classes to honourable ambitions and hum
comforts, and those of the wealthy to idle display and dissi]
tion. The man who declines to accept either of these generali:
tions may regard the problem as a highly complex one, and m
not be prepared with any general receipt for the applicati
of the accepted principle. Or he may say that he does r
trouble himself about the value of the satisfactions of tl
class or that; but he sees that some people get a great d(
of what they want, such as it is, and others only a very litt
and he would like to give them more even shares. This
merely the application of the general principle that t
psychic significance of wealth declines as wealth increases.
is not scientifically capable of proof, but it derives stro
support from the common sense.[1]

[1] Pages 148 *sqq.*

But it may, in any case, be safely asserted that to the extent to which democratic sentiment, or an effectively democratic constitution, dominates the action of a community, the more even distribution of wealth will be thought of as a thing to be desired; and there will, therefore, be a tendency to throw taxation upon wealth, qualified by the fear of checking the productive energies of the community; and a tendency to relieve the relatively poor from taxation, checked only by the feeling that all who have a share in controlling the public expenditure should have something directly to lose by its unwise application.

But when questions of taxation and public expenditure are discussed, we often hear it said: "All taxation falls ultimately on the wage-earners, for, if a wealthy man is heavily taxed, he cannot himself spend the portion of his income which is taken by the Government, and since his income is all of it ultimately expended in wages, he will have the less to pay in wages, and will, therefore, dismiss some of his servants and workmen, who will compete with others for employment, and so reduce the average wage." We will not stay to examine the contention that the wealthy man's expenditure, all of it, ultimately goes in wages; and we will admit that, in so far as it constitutes a disturbance of economic relations, the imposition of a fresh tax is liable to produce distress and inconvenience. But, as a general principle, it is just as true, or just as false, of what the Government takes, as it is of what the individual keeps, that it is ultimately expended on wages. If the rich man pays wages to grooms, gardeners, and footmen, the Government pays wages to soldiers, sailors, and schoolmasters; and, barring the strain of change, the question is whether the marginal significance of the work done by the gardeners, grooms, and footmen is higher or lower than that of the work done by the soldiers, sailors, and schoolmasters. This may be a very serious question, but we must not allow it to be complicated by the idea that it has any connection with the problem of unemployment, except in its temporary effects if the change is sudden. And, as far as that goes, a sudden remission of taxation would have just the same effect as a sudden imposition of it. It would throw one set of men out of work and would create a demand for another set.

The introduction of the schoolmaster into the last illust[ra]-tion reminds us that there are many things beside natio[nal] defence (as it is uniformly called among civilians, though if armies and navies exist except for purposes of defence, it [is] difficult to see against whom any one is to be defended), a[nd] the maintenance of internal order and justice, to which t[he] effective will of the community has determined that every m[an] shall contribute, whether he himself thinks it sufficien[tly] important to justify his contribution or not. When compulso[ry] education was introduced into England, it was felt that [the] parent should be allowed to judge for himself whether [he] would or would not devote a certain amount of his resourc[es] to the education of his child. It was felt to be a questi[on] of national importance that the child should be educated, a[nd] therefore, every parent must be compelled to educate [his] children, with such public and private assistance as h[as] already been provided. Presently it was felt that t[he] contribution of the citizen towards the education of t[he] children of the State should be entirely independent of t[he] question whether he was or was not himself a parent and w[as] having his child educated.

On what grounds may we suppose that the individu[al] citizen came to consider the education of every child [his] concern? It may be that he felt he would be relieved fr[om] some personal risk or detriment by the general enforceme[nt] of education. If it were merely argued that a commun[ity] is safer and more comfortable to live in if its children a[re] schooled, the appeal would be to each citizen's personal intere[st]. But, if the argument were that a child who has been schoo[led] is more likely to live a worthy and satisfactory life himse[lf], then the person who decrees taxes for educational purpo[ses] is actuated by a desire for the well-being of the childr[en] and that well-being becomes one of his own direct intere[sts] and purposes. If the argument were that "England" w[ill] be in a better position, commercially, morally, or intellectual[ly] thirty years hence, and if the person who advocates t[he] imposition of the tax is already sixty or seventy years o[ld,] his motive will be of a highly abstract and ideal nature. [He] desires well to a community linked by a certain historic[al,] local, and racial continuity to the one in which he lives (a[nd] perhaps depreciates and denounces) after he is dead, and is willing to forego present satisfactions of a more personal character in order to help towards this desired end. This is rightly praised as patriotism. Or he may etherealise his purposes still further, and may wish well to future " humanity." This may perhaps be considered " emasculated cosmopolitanism "; but if his interest extends to the uncertain boundaries and nationalities of the " Empire " a generation hence, and no further, he may escape that reproach.

These are merely illustrations of the different principles on which different men may estimate the relative importance of purposes and objects, and they will help to explain why a large section of the nation is chronically and normally more or less indignant at the kind of things on which " their money " is being spent. Owing to the tax-gatherer the unwilling and unconvinced leave undone sundry things which they want to do, in order to secure ends which are considered more important by others, but not by themselves.

Before leaving the subject of national taxation, we may examine very briefly two claims that are put forward in favour of taxing foreign imports that compete with home products. It is urged that by such taxation we might either lay the burden of taxation upon the foreigner or relieve unemployment. In so far as we did the one, it will be admitted by the more clear-sighted advocates, we cannot do the other, for, in so far as the foreigner pays the tax he will import his goods, and import them at present prices, and, therefore, the market will be unaffected and the home-producer will neither employ more labour nor reap any other special advantage. But, so far as the one object is not accomplished, it may be urged, the other will be, and both are desirable.

Tariffs and the foreigner.

Both schemes illustrate our general principle that the object of taxation is to direct resources from less to more important purposes. In the abstract the pure-blooded cosmopolitan thinker might boggle at the proposition that the purposes of the foreigner, as such, are less important than our own; but he would have to admit that, as we are at present constituted, they are more important to us; and if he genuinely believed that we are already paying the foreigner's taxes, his last scruple would vanish, and he would earnestly desire to make him pay ours. But can he ? A lengthened discussion would be out of place, but a few general principles may be formulated.

We have seen[1] that although the expenses incurred in producing goods, and in bringing them to the market, do not determine their exchange value when there, yet their exchange value when there does determine how much expense will be deliberately encountered in order to get them there. If the expenses are raised, therefore, goods that would have been produced will be produced no more. If this holds, then, an import tax that did not produce, or was not accompanied by, a rise in prices would tend to close the market against the foreigner who now supplies it. He would not pay the tax, for he would cease to import. If, on the other hand, the price rose by the amount of the tax, he would go on importing, but would recover the tax in the higher price received.

But is it not possible that he has no other market, and that his resources are committed to this particular product ? Certainly he may have no other market that will take the whole of what he sells to us at approximately the same price which we pay for it, and so far we have him at our mercy, much as a sufficiently powerful Trade Union might have in their power the employers whose resources were already committed to one particular trade. But, unless it can be shewn that certain resources in the foreign country are permanently and inherently incapable of producing, except at a considerably lowered efficiency, any other commodity than that for which we permanently constitute the only market, this exaction of the tax from the foreigner cannot be maintained. In any case it would contract, if it did not entirely stop, his importations, and this would tend to raise prices.

If a preferential system is advocated, this may be the deliberate intention. If we wish to get our wheat, for instance, from our own colonists rather than from the United States, Russia, Hungary, or the Plate River, and think this object worth paying for, it seems to be theoretically possible to exclude some of the foreign wheat by an import tax and

[1] Pages 373 *sqq.*

by the consequent rise in prices to encourage not only home, but colonial wheat-growing. If the price were not raised, no result would follow, for our home-farmers and colonists already produce as much wheat as they care to do at present prices. If we contemplate damping the foreign imports and encouraging the home and colonial cultivation through a series of years during which the price of wheat will be artificially maintained at a high enough figure for our purpose, there seems to be no theoretical principle on which we can determine the extent to which the courses of the world's industry might be modified with a corresponding redistribution of its population; but we should have carefully to inquire who pays the cost, what are the risks, what is the significance of the incidental waste of disturbance, and what is the value of the contemplated results. When we duly consider these matters we shall fully understand the phrase in which the late Duke of Devonshire declined to "gamble" in the people's bread.

But by far the most attractive of the pleas urged in favour of such taxation as we are now considering is that it will relieve unemployment. This plea we must examine at some length. The attempt to induce any one, by a system of taxation, to buy at home what he would otherwise buy abroad is palpably an attempt to make him "employ" one set of persons instead of another, to his own economic detriment. But we may urge that such action, though to his own economic detriment, will be to the advantage of those he "employs." And in answer to the objection that it is just as much to the disadvantage of those whom he ceases to employ, we may say that as we are not interested in these last we do not mind that.

Tariffs and unemployment.

Two points must be made clear before we proceed to a further analysis. In the first place, we have seen [1] that there is, properly speaking, no economic theory of foreign trade as distinct from home trade. We may therefore consider putting pressure on an Englishman to deal with an Englishman or a Canadian rather than with a citizen of the United States, or putting pressure on a London publisher to get his printing done in London rather than in Glasgow or Hull, or on a

---

[1] Pages 589 *sq.*

villager to get his table and chairs made by the village carpenter instead of buying them in the neighbouring town, as all raising the same theoretical points for consideration. Thus the matter under investigation is the policy of directing a man's bargaining along lines which he would not choose for himself in order to benefit certain people in whom we are specially interested at the expense of others in whom we are interested less or not at all. The area and the grounds of our interest may be important in many ways, but they do not affect the economic theory. Whether we take the Empire, or the United Kingdom, or the country, or our own district, city, village, estate, or family as the area of intenser interest, the problem is the same. And in the second place, the policy of pushing others, to their economic detriment, into transactions they would not have chosen for themselves, because we desire certain results to accrue, and the desirability of our voluntarily entering upon similar transactions ourselves, at a certain sacrifice, for the sake of those same results, may be discussed together; for their investigation demands the same analysis. In other words, the question of whether it is patriotic to buy at home what it would suit me better to buy abroad, and the question whether it is patriotic to make other people do the same must ultimately depend upon a common principle for their answers.

Let us return for a moment to first principles. The villagers who once did their own spinning and weaving, forging and furniture-making find that they can provide themselves with the products of all these industries more satisfactorily to themselves by not working at them at all, but by sending, say, milk and fruit to the towns, and receiving tools, clothes, and furniture from them. The villagers can get better clothed by keeping cows than by spinning and weaving, and the townsfolk can get better fed by weaving cloth where they are than by going elsewhere and cultivating the soil. The distribution of the population between country and town is determined by the equation of marginal significance between food on the one hand and raiment on the other.

We have insisted[1] that this highly organised industry has very heavy drawbacks, but also that it is an essential

[1] Pages 183 *sqq.*

condition of that materially advancing civilisation which we cannot escape, even if we would. And we have also seen that in spite of the increased general wealth which results from the new order of things, the currents of industry cannot be swiftly changed without loss and possible hardship to individuals. Certain village artisans or tradesmen are hard pressed by the competition of the towns, that is to say, by the existence of persons who, working at an advantage, can do more for the same return than they themselves have been accustomed to do. Theoretically, they should either turn to agriculture where they are, or go where they can work at a better advantage in their present trade ; and whichever course tends to establish the equation of marginal significances is the better one. Anything that obstructs or retards this change is, so far, bad. Anything that softens the hardship of the transition is, so far, good. Sound thought and sound policy must distinguish between these two things with the utmost care ; and the basal fact that now concerns us is that the new equilibrium towards which we are moving is economically more advantageous to all concerned than the old ; and the policy of buying at home, at a disadvantage, instead of abroad tends to retard or to disturb this superior equilibrium. If a patriotic villager determines, at a loss to himself, to patronise the village artisan, he thereby holds him back, or brings him back from whichever of the courses, indicated above, the situation demands ; and at the same time by withdrawing or withholding his custom from the artisan in the neighbouring town, and ceasing to send him food, he drives him to get his food in some other way, which by hypothesis is less advantageous. Thus, at a loss to himself, he has kept one man, for whom he cares, in a position of relative inefficiency, and has forced another man, for whom he does not care, into a position of relative want. There is a collective loss to the two communities jointly and severally. It is sometimes said that the doctrinaire free-trader's golden rule is, " buy in the cheapest and sell in the dearest market, and so fulfil the law of Christ." So far as he neglects, in thought or in policy, the hardships of the transition, and so far as he takes a purely material view of well-being, the taunt is justified. But, nevertheless, it is the most substantial of facts that the constant desire to further our own purposes, whatever they are, of which "buying in the cheapest and selling in the dearest market" is one aspect, is in truth the great underlying force that perpetually draws us into relations of mutual service. Largely understood, "buying in the cheapest and selling in the dearest market" is the best rule that the plain man can find for directing his own energies and those of others along the most efficient lines—efficiency, be it always remembered, being measured by reference to the things, good or bad, that men want done; and each "man" counting for more or less according to the extent of his command of the things in the circle of exchange.

But it may be urged that by neglecting what we have dismissed as "the incidental hardships of the transition," we have really falsified the problem. It is not a question, it may be said, of keeping a man in a relatively inefficient employment or pressing him into a relatively efficient one. It is a question of employment or unemployment for him. Now, so far as this state of things, wherever it really exists, is due to changes and fluctuations of trade, we have recognised it as a problem of urgent importance, but have seen that no tariff proposals touch it.[1] And so far as it is not a question of changes and fluctuations, it can be due to nothing but a relative inefficiency, which we are to regard as permanent. That is to say, one part of the community is asked (or is to be compelled) permanently to abstain from fulfilling certain of its own purposes for the sake of persons who, relatively speaking, are permanently inefficient. This may be, and in some cases obviously is, extremely right and proper, but the admission that a considerable portion of our own able-bodied industrial population comes permanently under this category of the relatively inefficient would be humiliating indeed, and no treatment could be regarded as anything but a palliative unless it aimed at removing, rather than providing for, such inefficiency. This consideration is quite fundamental. The disputants in current "tariff-reform" controversies will generally be found to be working on different underlying suppositions. The free-trader assumes that in considering permanent conditions the man who is employed

---

[1] See pages 640 *sqq.* and cf. pages 356 *sq.* etc.

in one industry must be regarded as withholding himself from another industry. His opponent assumes that the man his schemes are going to employ is now, and but for him will remain, out of employment. But the existence of a body of men permanently out of employment because all who have anything to give find it suits them better to deal with other people means the existence of a permanent body of the relatively inefficient.

But suppose we let this pass and grant that the object is desirable, we have still to ask whether the proposed means would be calculated to attain it. Our examination of this question will lead incidentally to the unmasking of a certain ambiguity in the phrase "inefficiency" so freely used in the argument just closed, and will also open some very wide questions of inter-racial policy.

The terms "finding work" and "giving employment" are unfortunate, for they readily ally themselves with the "lump-of-labour" habit of mind; and, therefore, though we can hardly avoid using them, we must always be on our guard against their misleading suggestions. Let us consider exactly what they mean. The Europeans have "found employment" in abundance for the unhappy natives of Congo-land, but not in the sense that the phrase connotes in Political Economy. Giving employment to a man means enabling him to provide more ample satisfaction for his wants and desires by the indirect means of serving some one else than by the direct means of serving himself. Normally, this is a mutual or two-sided relation. The industrial inhabitants of town and country "employ" each other in this sense, and the whole principle of the division of labour involves the mutual "giving of work." But it is not always easy to keep this in mind as the normal relation; and that for many reasons. In the first place the mutuality is generally indirect. The man to whom I give work is not usually the same as the man who gives me work. In the second place, our habitual use of the terms *employer* and *employed* disguises the fact that the hands really "employ" the manager or the capitalist (in the sense of enabling him to do better for himself by doing well for them) just as much as the manager or capitalist employs them. The term "employment" then conceals rather than reveals the intimate nature of the mutual relations in connection with which it is often used. But, in the third place, mutuality of employment is really subject to certain limitations. We think of the consumer as the employer and the producer as the employed, and although in a general way we know that consumption implies production and production consumption, and that the normal member of an industrial community is both producer and consumer, yet there are many and important cases in which the consumer is not a producer at all; so that we think of him exclusively as employing and not at all as being employed. To such a case we must now turn our attention.

We will go back to our village and will suppose that a wealthy man lives in it whose income is drawn entirely from outside its area, so that for village purposes he is a consumer and employer and nothing else. Now, it is clear that so long as he stays in the village and consumes his wealth there, it must come into the village in some shape or other without anything going out to balance it. Does it make any difference to "employment" in the village in what form this revenue comes in? Clearly it does. The rich man may have many of the things he wants made in London or anywhere else and sent down to him complete; or he may (in the last analysis) have food, beer, clothes, tobacco, and so forth, together with the raw material of the things he wants, sent into the village, and in that case the villagers may eat, wear, drink, smoke, and chew, while they are constructing the article. In the end the patron will get things that he wants, but in one case he will have "employed" outsiders and in the other case villagers. That is to say, villagers in one case and outsiders in the other will have been eating and drinking some of his revenue while making the rest of it available for his purposes. In deciding between the several courses the rich man may be guided by no considerations but those of efficiency. He may simply ask himself what suits him best. But it is also possible that he may employ relatively inefficient workers for the sake of benefiting them rather than "outsiders." If so, he is doing a kindly thing, which, if he has not good judgment, may tend to perpetuate an economically undesirable situation, but which, if he has good judgment, may simply alleviate the hardship of a transition. In any case, he makes a voluntary sacrifice himself and imposes an involuntary sacrifice on the more efficient persons from whom he withdraws or withholds his patronage.

But now, suppose the villagers themselves can determine what the rich man in their midst is to do. Suppose they can keep all others than themselves from entering their area, and can dictate to the consumer that he shall draw his revenue in such forms as to make him dependent upon them for transforming it into the things that will minister to the satisfaction of his desires. They can then make their terms with him as to the share of his revenue which they are to receive in reward for making the rest of it available for his purposes. If they can force him to bring it in in forms, some of which will directly suit their purposes and the rest of which will only indirectly suit his, they can take the part that suits them in return for bringing the part that potentially suits him into the form that will actually suit him. The outsiders would do the same service to the "employer" if he were allowed to employ them, and they would do it on better terms for him; but the villagers may say, "That is your gauge of efficiency, but it is not ours. We ask no more than is right, and we give as much as is due. If other people want to give more and take less we won't have it. We will keep them out and keep you in, and we will have our share of the wealth that comes to our village."

That is a perfectly intelligible position; and it violates no principle of Political Economy. Given the object the means are well suited to its accomplishment, and circumstances are conceivable under which it might be successful. We have had to assume that the villagers can not only regulate imports but can also prevent immigration. Otherwise the patron might be able to import a population which would be, from his point of view, more efficient than the villagers. Thus, if a tariff system could be contrived which would compel all Englishmen who draw income from foreign sources to introduce their revenue in forms, some of which would directly serve the purposes of the working population and the rest of which would only indirectly serve their own, the "amount of work" or "employment" in England might thereby be increased, but since it might be impracticable to prevent the movements of the European populations from one country to another the increase of employment might be rather to England than to Englishmen. England would tend to become a residential country, and persons of all nations who could make themselves useful to the rich residents would come to England, where their patrons might employ them, from other countries in which they might not.

If there is a class of inhabitants who, though not drawing their revenues from outside our selected area, are yet consumers only and not producers (such as landlords or owners of minerals), the situation is to some extent the same, but any " inefficiency " of the workers may in this case react to some extent upon the revenue to be shared. Still a policy might well be advocated either of hampering the "pensioners" in purchasing manufactured goods from outside, or of preventing immigration, or both. The hostility to Chinese labour (apart from any objection to special conditions) that is so marked in our Colonies and elsewhere is due to a feeling that certain classes or individuals are in actual command of the sources of the communal revenue, and that the labour they may consider most "efficient," from their point of view, would cut out the landless White Man from his opportunity. The idea is very probably mistaken. The voluntary presence in a country of an industrious and frugal population, willing to give much in return for little, is probably an economic advantage to all classes of the inhabitants. But the opposite belief is far from unnatural.

Now, let us take stock of our conclusions. It seems to be ideally possible to conceive of a system of tariff regulations which should favour the producer at the expense of the consumer. If immigration can be stopped, the producer who would not have been employed at all without the protection of the tariff may now get a living, and the producer who would have been employed may now be employed on more favourable terms; and all this at the expense of the consumer. If immigration cannot be stopped, there will be a movement of population, especially of the kind that ministers to a wealthy residential community, towards the area on which the "consumer" is allowed to employ people; and this would tend to undermine the privileged position of the producer and to throw the inefficients out of work again. In any case, the consumer who is not a producer might be forced to give "more employment," and that at a higher scale of remuneration, whether to natives or immigrants, within the area which controlled him.

But this whole system aims at benefiting the producer at the expense of the consumer, by prohibiting the import of things directly useful to the consumer and allowing the import of things directly and indirectly useful to the producer; and it is, therefore, entirely inapplicable to an industrial community in so far as the consumer and producer are identical, and in so far as men mutually "employ" each other at home, and also enter into the mutual relation of employer and employed with the foreigner. We may hope that a manufactured article may be excluded in the interests of the producer at the expense of the consumer if the consumer and the producer are two different people and if the consumer's revenues are independent of the terms on which he employs the producer. But if A consumes B's product and B consumes A's, and if each would be hampered in his production by being forced to make worse terms at home instead of better ones abroad, then we can hardly hope to make every one succeed better by allowing him to prevent his neighbour from taking the natural steps to success. The contrast between consumer and producer falls to the ground; for the things that one producer desires to exclude because they are his manufactured article may be those that another desires to import because they are his raw material, or because, as consumer, he wants them for himself and can get them best abroad. Oilcake is the manufactured product of the maker but the raw material of the stock farmer. Tools are the product of one manufacture and the instruments of another; and as long as we talk of "capturing neutral markets," and "finding markets for our surplus products," we cannot contemplate crippling one manufacture to help another. But enough of technicalities.

The central truth is this. If we can separate out persons who are consumers only from consumers who are producers also, we can imagine the interests of the former being neglected without prejudice to the latter. But, if we are considering those who are both producers and consumers, our ultimate consideration must always be for them as consumers. They produce only in order to consume. If you injure them as consumers, you stultify them as producers. Sectionally, you may benefit one man as consumer by giving him an advantage as producer at the expense of others. Collectively, you cannot. And to speak collectively of benefiting the producer at the expense of the consumer would be to speak of strengthening the means by balking the ends. Proposals to tax food, for other than purposes of revenue, are the *reductio ad absurdum* to which this confusion leads. To stay hunger is the first and deepest object of work or production. And if you impede the importation of food because it is an industrial product and should, therefore, be protected, you are "protecting" work against the accomplishment of its primeval and basal purpose.

We will now pass from national to local taxation. There is no distinction in principle between the action of the state and the action of the municipality or other administrative area; and the Poor Law furnishes, as a matter of fact, one of the chief examples of purposes recognised by the community as sufficiently important to justify compulsion in securing co-operation from the unwilling. Drainage, the maintenance of public roads, the establishment or maintenance of public parks and gardens, or of public libraries, offer further illustrations. But the library and the park stand on a different footing from the rest. It is very difficult, even ideally, to conceive of any test by which we could draw up a balance-sheet between the money cost of the army, for example, and the collective estimates of the marginal significance of a company of soldiers, or of a Destroyer, formed by the individuals composing the community. But in the case of the park or the library it is a comparatively easy matter. If a charge were made on entering the park or taking books out of the library, could it be so arranged as to make it cover the public expenditure? If not, then apparently the members of the community taken head by head would have preferred other applications of the communal resources. Each one has estimated the significance to himself of the privilege of taking out books and entering the park, and the sum of them, measured in the objective standard, does

Municipal enterprise and socialism.

not amount to the value of the resources expended upon them. If the community is justified in the expenditure, therefore, it must be because it is convinced that the purposes balked by the levying of the tax, or its diversion to this purpose, though objectively of greater volume than the purposes accomplished by its application, are yet of less vital significance.[1] Such action is, no doubt, ethically and socially justifiable in principle, but its concrete justification can only rest on fallible estimates which cannot be objectively checked. Here, as elsewhere, the rule seems to hold that the higher and more ideal your purpose, the greater your difficulty in gaining any assurance that you have accomplished it. This is probably at the back of people's minds when they say that you must not judge municipal enterprises simply by the commercial test of whether they pay. This is perfectly true; but it is equally obvious that if we come to think that it does not matter whether they pay (or would pay if put to the commercial test) or not, we may open the door to recklessly wasteful and whimsical experiments. That an experiment does not pay is at least *prima facie* evidence that some other application of the resources expended upon it would have stood objectively higher on the collective scale. This may not be enough to condemn it, but it tells against it as far as it goes, and the burden of the proof lies on those who defend the expenditure.

In this connection we may touch on the question of the principle that should regulate the scale of wages, or, generally, of remuneration for services, paid by the government or the community. If it is more than the market rate, the public body is establishing a privileged set of persons; and by "privileged" we need not mean privileged as against the average citizen, but privileged as against other persons with whom they would be on a level but for their having been selected by the public body. The two-fold question will arise: On what principle are they selected? and, At whose expense are they privileged? Neither of these is an easy question to answer, and both are highly important. It may well be, however, that a higher than the current wage will really be economically justified. By paying better the public body may get better men and better work, even if that was

---

[1] Cf. pages 146 *sqq.*, 189 *sqq.*, 215 *sq.*

not the inspiring motive. This would be a case of using the public funds for au experiment of a kind already examined.[1]

We have now opened the way to the consideration of the far-reaching question of the extent to which it is desirable to push the municipal or other communal management of enterprises that stand on a commercial basis. The most natural industries for public bodies to enter upon are those which it is in any case deemed necessary or advisable to make monopolies, whether absolute or qualified. Railroads, tramways, letter-carrying, the liquor trade, gas and water supply, and many others, will occur at once to the mind; and every one of them offers a number of problems and suggests a number of considerations which can be debated from many points of view. The ultimate object may be to restrict trade; it may be to extend and encourage it; it may be simply to effect economies. But in all these cases the services ultimately rendered may be paid for by the individuals who desire them, and the objective test at once exists which we sought in vain in some previous cases, and which we can only apply ideally in others. Here, if the governing body submits to the financial test, it is aiming lower than in some of the previous cases, but it can be more certain that it is accomplishing its humbler aim. Sometimes, as in the case of the liquor traffic, for example, to adopt the financial test would be absolutely to renounce the purpose for which the communal action is taken; but in the case of trams or railways financial success would be a proof that the marginal estimates of the significance of the privilege secured, formed by certain members of the community, raised it to a place on the collective scale that economically justified the expenditure of the resources that had been devoted to it. But, if the money is to be not only spent but raised on economic principles, it must be raised on loan and not by taxation; for only so can we know that all concerned have got what they consider a good bargain. Now, a public body is at a great advantage in raising money on loan, but it is an advantage the basis of which it is instructive to examine. The credit of a municipality, and still more the credit of the nation, is good because no one is afraid of its becoming bankrupt; that is to say, it is not the persons

[1] Pages 209 *sq.*

who lend the money but the persons who do not that will have to bear the loss if the undertaking fails. The risk, far from being eliminated, is in the opinion of some greater (though in the opinion of others it may be less) than that of a well-guaranteed private company. The municipality, however, enters upon the competition with this advantage, an advantage which is denounced as unfair when looked at from one point of view, and should be regarded as gained at the risk of the community when regarded from another. The effective conduct of the business will, doubtless, be placed in the hands of a skilled manager, but the work of the directors and promoters will, to a certain extent, be done by volunteers, who either have a direct interest in the well-being of the community, or value the credit that attaches to public service, or enjoy managing affairs and directing enterprises, especially, perhaps, when detached from the personal risks of private business. Thus, there are sources of economy in the conducting of business by public bodies,—the easy terms on which they can raise capital, and the amount of business talent which they can secure without payment. What does this latter consideration amount to? The question being one of fact must depend for its solution upon experience rather than argument. How far is there really a store of competent business capacity which can be put into harness by motives other than economic? Not only the contractor but the general designer and conceiver of all kinds of work, as well as the mechanic who carries out the physical portion of it, are as a rule supposed to be actuated mainly by the desire to accomplish their own purposes and to put themselves in command of general resources and services to be turned in the direction they desire. How far can you give men a primary interest in the well-being of the community so that they will be willing to exercise vigilance, to give thought, to lay down far-seeing and far-reaching combinations, not in order to put themselves in command of resources to be devoted to other objects, but with the primary object of serving the community? In a word, can a succession of competent men be found to do public work for the sake of the public? And if the idea once becomes well established, will the public spirit that secures the services of such men be subject to a law of acceleration ? Any amount of *a priori* argument may be brought to bear as to the fitness or unfitness of municipalities to undertake this or that class of work, but it can only be decided by experiment how far the persons who are fit for this kind of work can be found willing to do it as a primary object, and whether such machinery can be constructed as will give scope to the continuous and systematic exercise of their ability and goodwill. It is possible, of course, that the work thus got for nothing might be of inferior quality to the work done at high salaries, but the difference might not be worth the salary. In all these matters "collectivism" or what is (perhaps too hastily [1]) called "Municipal Socialism" is not so much an economic theory as a social faith.

People who think that their economic advantage is seriously threatened by the willingness of other persons to do for nothing the work for which they wish to be paid will never be more amiably disposed towards their public-spirited rivals than Shylock was to Antonio, but, apart from trade jealousies, there is abundant room for difference of opinion as to the extent to which it is prudent to push our experiments. Experiments, however, there must be, and they will be the less costly and the more conclusive in proportion as they are watched by honest and competent observers who have no interest but that of the public at heart.

But if ever it is claimed in the name of collectivism or socialism that the *exclusive* ownership of the instruments of production shall pertain to public bodies, we come to questions in the answer to which economic doctrine must hold a much more prominent place. There is nothing at present to prevent the State from acquiring instruments of production to any extent; but a proposal to prohibit private citizens from holding them would seem to rest on a radical misconception of the social function of the instruments of production themselves. If our general analysis of industrial phenomena is correct, then the man who makes a tool has so far benefited the industrial community from the industrial point of view, and he can only get any good out of his tool by making a bargain with his neighbour, to that neighbour's advantage. His

[1] For if the Municipality borrows capital from individual lenders and pays for work and material at market rates, we are far from any accepted definition of socialism.

neighbour, then, is the better for his having constructed the tool. If the public body can increase the advantage, that is to say, if, from public spirit or otherwise, it can offer better terms than private individuals are urged by the economic forces to offer, that is so much to the good ; but to prohibit the private citizen from offering terms which his neighbour will find more eligible than those offered by the State, is to prohibit him from conferring a public benefit. Probably, this would be admitted by most socialists, although many of them appear to be haunted by an idea that capital in private hands is actively oppressive and is necessarily evil, whereas in the hands of a public body it would be helpful and necessarily good. That capital in private hands may be, and often is, used for purposes injurious to some sections of the community is an indubitable fact, but the idea that the capital employed in an industry is an instrument of oppression *to the workers in that industry* appears to be the offspring of mere confusion of thought. The fact of a rich man employing " those who create his wealth " at a starvation wage naturally suggests that it is the existence of the capital that makes them starve, whereas in principle it is the existence of the capital that prevents them from starving. The capital, that is to say the tools and apparatus, is worth more to them than they pay for it, and is so far a benefit to them ; but every humane person will wish that they should get greater benefits at a less cost, and if the State can back them with capital on easier terms, or if any agency can transfer them to other occupations in which their marginal significance will be greater, a real improvement will have been secured. The existence of the capital in private hands does not injure them (unless indeed prolonging their existence is an injury) but it does not benefit them enough to satisfy the demands of humanity. Those socialists who would allow private capital to compete with that of the State apparently admit all this. At any rate, they would concur in the action of those who do.

Returning to the public body, we may ask whether it should borrow capital for its enterprises or should raise it by taxation. Those who regard the receiving of interest as an evil in itself will presumably advocate the former course, but if they exclude the latter they will have to make a material sacrifice, for the satisfaction of their sentimental objection, which it will repay us to examine. Raising capital by taxation means compelling the willing and the unwilling alike to stand out of so much present satisfaction in order to secure a communal revenue in the future. Opinions will differ as to what return is adequate to justify the sacrifice. Suppose it is fixed at 5 per cent, that will mean that the effective majority of the community decides that the communal industries must be fed down to the point at which the marginal yield of capital is 5 per cent, but that less than £5 a year does not justify the enforcing of a saving of £100. Now, some members of the community would prefer to spend the share of their capital that they will be required to surrender and go without their share of the revenue it will produce; and others will think that a lower yield would justify the investment of capital and would like to save more and produce larger revenues. We may, if we like, ignore the unwillingness of the former class, and force them, without compunction, to conform to the communal standard of prudence; but nothing is gained by not allowing the others to be more prudent than the average. Suppose, for instance, that taxation (perhaps withholding dividends, which is simply a special form of taxation) has raised as much as the communal authority cares to exact as capital for the establishment of some new industrial undertaking; and suppose that a marginal significance of 5 per cent determines that amount. There will be members of the community who for one reason or another estimate future revenue relatively to present satisfactions more highly than the enforced standard requires. Suppose another £10,000 would bring the marginal yield of the capital down to $4\frac{1}{4}$ per cent, another £10,000 yet to $3\frac{3}{4}$, and yet another £10,000 to $3\frac{1}{2}$ per cent; and suppose we could raise a loan of £20,000, but no more, if we offered $3\frac{3}{4}$ per cent. We should then know that we could not carry the margin of productivity down lower than $3\frac{3}{4}$ per cent without paying more for our capital than it was yielding at the margin, but that we could carry it down to that point. We may, therefore, borrow £20,000, pay for it at $3\frac{3}{4}$ per cent, and secure to the community the whole curvilinear area which stands above the rectangle of payment, beginning at a height of $1\frac{1}{4}$ above it and gradually declining to it. And this gain, against which there is nothing to set, has been secured by opening an opportunity to the more prudent of our fellow-citizens which they value. If we are amongst those who are personally willing to sink capital in the new industry till it reaches the marginal significance of 5 per cent, our more prudent neighbours have now not only helped us (as they would have done even if we had raised no loan) to drag our unwilling fellow-citizens up to our mark (which we have agreed to regard as an advantage), but have also made us a gratuitous present of further revenue. The sentimental objection against such a proceeding must be strong if it is to overrule its advantages. At any rate it is well to realise what the advantages are.

But the most difficult part of the collectivist problem still remains, and is not always faced. If public bodies were the only employers, on what principle should remuneration of the different agents be fixed? Is it possible to conceive of any machinery by which the marginal significance of each should be determined without anything corresponding to the present system of free experimental combination and transference from group to group, in which each individual is urged by his desire to fulfil his own purposes to seek the place in which his marginal significance to others is highest? It may be possible to give an affirmative answer to this question, but the claims sometimes made in the name of "socialism" seem to indicate that in many quarters it has never been seriously asked. We hear it urged, for instance, that the Government ought to be compelled to "find work" for every one at the standard wage. What is the standard wage? It is something that has been arrived at under the various economic pressures of the present system of industry. And the difference between the standard wage of a bricklayer and a bricklayer's labourer, or between that of a type-setter and a cab-washer, may or may not be due to privilege of birth, position, and opportunity, just as much as the difference between the standard wage of a professional man and that of an agricultural labourer. On principle it would seem as reasonable to demand, without further inquiry, employment at the standard wage for doctors and lawyers who were out of work, as for mechanics and labourers. And what is to secure the State that undertakes such a task from bankruptcy? How is it to know that all the values it secures by its organisation of human effort will cover all those it has promised in remuneration? The receipt given by Bernard Shaw——" to give every man enough to live well on, so as to guarantee the community against the possibility of a case of the malignant disease of poverty, and then (necessarily) to see that he earned it "——is a more rational one, for it would not stereotype the *status quo* of standard wages, and it recognises (parenthetically) that the State must secure assets equal to its liabilities. But if it is a sound receipt it ought to be capable (after the initial outlay of bringing the subject, where necessary, into condition) of reversal, and of being put in this form: " To see that every man earned enough to live well on, and then to let him have it." Let the State try to do this by all means, not recklessly indulging in random experiments and not grudging the expense of promising ones. Let it take care that the expense is laid on the proper shoulders, and finally, while opening all the opportunities that it can, let it close none that are opened by private individuals whether in isolation or in voluntary association.

All this should, of course, be read in the light of facts already laid down,[1] that a large part of the revenue of a community is not earned at all, and that some must, and all may, receive more than they earn.

Expenditure on the part of a public body that brings in revenue in any direct form is spoken of as productive. Expenditure that brings in no direct pecuniary return, such as that on armaments and more particularly expenditure in war, is spoken of as unproductive. When nations are at war they almost invariably meet a part of the expense not out of accumulations in the war-chest, or out of current taxation, but by borrowing. From whom do they borrow? What is the exact process? And who repays? Clearly the resources devoted to manufacturing ammunition, transporting soldiers, and so forth, are not created by the process of borrowing. Resources of every kind that might have been devoted to other things are devoted to the war, and in the process are destroyed or consumed.

Unproductive loans.

[1] See page 341 *sq.*, and compare page 573.

Somebody, then, has actually expended energies and resources. We have seen that expenditure is usually induced by promises. In this case the promise is an allowance of so much a year by the nation for every £100 expended on its behalf. We examined the particular terms of our last great loan on pages 239, 240. When two nations are at war, and one of them raises a loan, the persons who actually find the resources required may belong to the borrowing nation, or to neutral nations, or even to the nation with which the country is at war; but the obligation to pay is taken by the borrowing nation in its collective capacity, and will be handed down to its posterity or successors. It is obvious, then, that if posterity is to be regarded as having any rights whatever, the act of borrowing for unproductive purposes is one of extreme gravity which should only be undertaken under any conditions with compunction and a heavy sense of resultant responsibility. It is one thing to consider that a war is worth waging and paying for currently; it is another thing to determine that a war is worth waging provided that we induce certain people to pay for it on the strength of promises, only a small part of which we can fulfil ourselves, and the rest of which will have to be fulfilled by those who have never been consulted in the matter. Hence, there is some general recognition of responsibility for paying off a war debt within a period which will throw the burden substantially on the generation that made the war. But it is only this unreliable sense of obligation, or the still more spiritualised force of abstract devotion to posterity, that can sustain a determination to reduce the National Debt. If we clear the question from all sense of obligation incurred, and look upon it simply as it concerns ourselves, that is to say as presenting us with alternatives between which we may choose after our own convenience, it would seem that we shall never wish to reduce the National Debt at all, unless for certain secondary considerations which will be developed below.

For without any collective action being taken, it is always open to any one to pay off his share of the National Debt and reap his share of the benefit. Suppose we put an individual's share of the debt at £20 (a little above the average arrived at by dividing the National Debt by the population of the

United Kingdom). All he has to do is to invest £20 in the Funds and leave it there. He will then draw 10s. a year, just the amount, according to hypothesis, that he pays in taxes. If every one had thus bought his share (in some cases, of course, more, and in other cases less than £20, for it depends on what each pays in taxes on this account), the whole could be cancelled without affecting any one's position in any way. It would, in fact, be already virtually extinguished.[1] But why do some people hold more and others less than their share of the National Debt? Some consider £2 : 10s. a year on government security compensates them for saving £100, or is the most desirable way of investing it if they come into possession of it. Others do not. But the Sinking Fund, by which the National Debt is reduced, compels these others, if they are tax-payers, to buy relief from annual payments at the rate of £100 purchase money for £2 : 10s. annual relief, though if left to themselves they do not do it. If a man who does not think permanent investment in the Funds good enough for himself nevertheless advocates the maintenance of the Sinking Fund, it would seem to be because he feels his responsibility to posterity so keenly that he is willing to relieve posterity from an annual charge of £2 : 10s. on terms on which he does not care to relieve himself from it; unless, indeed, he realises that he is a very small tax-payer himself, and that he is compelling others to pay in much larger proportion than himself.

It is, however, true that if we contemplate the odious possibility of making other wars for which we do not pay, the fact of our having retained a Sinking Fund may enable us to raise the loan on easier terms than we could otherwise have done. Indeed, apart from that, it is conceivable that our steady maintenance of a Sinking Fund may, together with other causes, so raise our credit that we may be able to reduce the interest on our National Debt by converting it. This is a process into the details of which it is not my purpose to enter. In principle it amounts to borrowing at a lower interest a sum with which to pay off our present debt, thus substituting for it another of the same amount but contracted on easier terms.

[1] We have neglected the expense of collecting and distributing the revenue and have taken Consols at par, for the sake of simplicity.

How far these considerations actually weigh in the counsels of the nation it would be difficult to say; but I think it is safe to assert that the anxiety of the ordinary citizen to see the National Debt reduced is in fact very largely due to his sense of responsibility to the future; and nothing can conceivably be more wholesome than the sense of our obligation to pay off our debt, for if once we got rid of it, there would be no check on reckless borrowing with the deliberate intention of paying interest only and never redeeming the debt.

The gravity of the act of borrowing for unremunerative or doubtfully remunerative expenditure will be fully realised when we understand that the burden we lay upon posterity thereby is one that must either be borne for ever or paid off, under a sense of public responsibility, by persons who on their own account would rather go on bearing the burden than pay the price of deliverance.

We have seen that a great deal of what is often thought of as municipal socialism works with capital borrowed from individuals. In such cases the municipality applies and manages the capital, but has not full ownership of it. Exactly the opposite condition of things is contemplated by land nationalisers, in the narrower sense, for they advocate the possession of the land by the community, and its application to industrial or other purposes by the rent-paying occupier. Socialists who advocate the complete programme of public possession and administration of all instruments of production are, in a broad and inclusive sense, necessarily land nationalisers, but many land nationalisers declare that they are entirely opposed to socialism. The movement for land nationalisation makes a strong appeal to instinct. It is impossible to think either of a mountain or of the soil of a city as belonging to a private individual without a certain shock. And this instinctive sense of incongruity has undoubtedly been stimulated by the elaborated conception that land, being the free gift of nature, belongs to no one and ought not to be private property, and, further, by the belief that the value of any piece of land is largely determined not by what is done to or on that land itself, but by what is done to or on the land round about it; so that a vacant site in London, which owes nothing to capital directly expended on it, may, nevertheless, be worth £50 a square foot or more. It is easy to riddle with destructive criticism all the arguments for land nationalisation, when they are stated absolutely. Why should the land values of London belong to the nation any more than to the world? If New York and all its inhabitants were destroyed by earthquake, or if Russia were swept bare, it would affect the value of land sites in London just as the destruction of the woollen industry in Yorkshire would. What right has the "nation," then, to land which belongs to humanity? Again, we have seen that it is impossible to draw a line between land and capital. A field is not the gift of nature only. It consists in the gifts of nature modified for human purposes by human toil; and so does a book, a coat, or a picture. This is recognised by land nationalisers to some extent, for they would nationalise only that element in any given piece of land, as we usually understand the term, which is not due to labour bestowed on that piece of land itself. Thus, we should everywhere nationalise the indirect value which the expenditure of capital on one piece of land confers on other pieces of land, but nowhere the direct value which it confers on the land to which it is applied! It is generally recognised, therefore, that some statute of limitations would have to be accepted, and that all values that have become practically indistinguishable from those due to the environment, and to the primitive and inalienable properties of the soil itself, should become part of the national property. The abstract distinction, then, between what nature gave and what man has made cannot be consistently maintained. Again, the value of all our possessions may be affected by the course of social or industrial progress. Changes of taste, or catastrophes, or discoveries, for which we have no responsibility, and for which we can take no credit, may secure unearned increment or inflict unearned decrement on the value either of our talents or of our possessions.

Nevertheless, public opinion seems to be flowing towards the recognition of the desirability in many cases of land being held by public bodies. The very fact of the impossibility of distinguishing between land and capital, and the tendency of all those products of labour which it is difficult to separate or remove from the land—drains, buildings, and so forth—to lapse into the possession of the possessor of the soil, strengthen the feeling that the possessors of the soil collectively hold its inhabitants in the hollow of their hands. The many Allotments and Small Holdings Acts which have been passed testify to the feeling that the powers implied in ownership of the land cannot be safely left to the action of the economic forces with any confidence that they will be used in the best interests of the nation. The scheme of taxing vacant building sites is evidence of the same conviction with reference to non-agricultural uses of land. Public bodies constantly require land and have to buy it, and the questions concerning the value conferred on adjacent sites by capital expended by the public on the public property rise in an acute form. If the whole area were public property, the increased values would automatically fall into that public purse, by expenditure out of which they had accrued. Again, if any industrial opportunity is opened in a particular place, which makes a man's labour worth more within a certain radius of that place than it is elsewhere, the owner of the soil can make him pay more as a condition of allowing him to live there; for the soil on which a man is worth more than on any other soil itself becomes worth more than other soil, and if its quantity is closely limited the marginal increment may be heavy.

These and many other considerations are pushing legislation in the direction both of the taxation and of the communalising of land. Perhaps all social and economic questions are questions of degree, and although we have seen that every kind of property is subject to increments and decrements of value by the action of others than its possessors, yet this is most conspicuously so in the case of land. And its fixity makes it particularly easy to secure its public possession. The instinct, then, that the increase of wealth due to the communal progress should fall under communal control or should be distributed amongst those who have created it, though quite incapable of being logically confined to the land, can, nevertheless, find in the land an eminently suitable subject on which to fasten.

We need not carry our analysis any further. It has

shewn us that many doctrines and many social purposes are blended in the movements which are vaguely thought of as tending to the nationalisation of land. Taxing the unearned increment, when land passes from hand to hand, is an attempt to secure to the nation a portion at least of a value, the creation of which cannot be brought home to any assignable individual or individuals, and may, therefore, be considered as a communal product. Taxing building sites is based on a belief that the economic forces unite individual holders of land in the neighbourhood of cities into tacit combinations, which, while not benefiting them economically as a class, are detrimental to their fellow-citizens. For the theory is that by preventing the natural spread of cities they actually realise the enhanced value of their sites more slowly and in smaller bulk than they would do if they allowed the city to spread. Allotments and Small Holdings Acts, so far as they contemplate the acquisition of land by local authorities, rest to a large extent on the conviction that when cultivation of the land really offers an eligible alternative to the labourer, the small shopkeeper, or the craftsman, there is often a tacit combination to shut him out of it; or, where this is not the case, that he may require some help and encouragement in starting his new career, which it is not to the economic interest of any individual to give him, but which the nation is willing to risk for national purposes. Other points that have been touched upon are sufficiently clear without further comment. And, lastly, the example of great estates managed entirely by agents (or bursars) fosters the idea that land is a convenient form in which public bodies may hold property.

It is to be noted, however, that the nationalisation of land could not, in any direct or immediate form, create wealth. If the nation takes it, it must take it from somebody. No wealth would be immediately or directly destroyed and none would be created; and if any one was at once to be the richer in consequence of land nationalisation, some one else would have to be poorer. In any scheme of land nationalisation, however, a distinction must be drawn between the question from whom the wealth is to be taken and the question in what form it is to be held. Acquiring land does not necessarily mean that the land is to be taken without compensation from the persons who

2 Y

now own it, though it might mean that; but it must mean that the *value* of the land is taken from some one, unless, indeed, it should be borrowed; and in that case the burden of the interest would have to be borne by some one.

It would be out of the question to attempt an exhaustive analysis of the many-sided phenomenon of Trade Unionism.
<small>Trade Unionism.</small> A Trade Union is, amongst other things, an intelligence department, enabling a man to know, better than he could find out for himself, where he is likely to find the marginal significance of his labour highest, and what that significance is likely to be. Further, it may be a benefit club, providing him with sick pay, out-of-work pay, or an old age pension. But its most characteristic functions are connected with the principle of collective bargaining. If a man earning 25s. a week thinks he is worth 28s., and his employer does not agree with him, and each is determined to act on his opinion, the man will leave his employment and will get work elsewhere if he can. The stake with which he has backed his opinion is a high one, for if he is wrong he will suffer heavily before he has found it out. And he may after all be right, in the sense that he really was worth 28s. to his employer, and would be to other employers if he could but get at them, but he may, nevertheless, fail to find any one else who will give him even 25s. On the other hand, the employer backs his opinion by a comparatively light stake, for if he loses the services of a man who would have been worth 28s. to him, and saves the wage he would have paid him, he is only the loser by the undetermined margin of the gain he would have made on employing him, and this will constitute a very small part of his income; whereas the workman risks the whole of his. The workmen, therefore, taken severally, are at a disadvantage in bargaining with the employer. If, however, the whole body, or a considerable number of them, determine to back their opinion, they will bring the stake of the employer individually to something more like equality with the individual stake made by each of them; for though it would make little difference to him to lose the services of one man, it would make a great difference to him to lose the services of many or of all of them. Moreover, by accumulating

a fund they can hope to diminish their risk by gaining a power of resistance which will secure respectful treatment; and by spreading their sacrifices over a long period of preparation and accumulation they may make them at a lower total cost, should the worst come to the worst.

But as far as we have yet gone it would seem that both employer and employed would have an interest in ascertaining how much the man is really worth, and that the competition of the employers will tend to secure him in getting it; for, if the employers are always eager to take a man if he is willing to work for less than he is worth to them, will not every employer prefer making a shilling a week himself to seeing another make 1s. 6d.? And will he not, therefore, bid the man up until he is receiving his full economic wage? It would, therefore, seem that the machinery of Trade Unionism is a rather elaborate provision for the assistance of economic forces which are strong enough to look after themselves. But here an interesting point arises. Suppose two employers of a thousand hands each are paying 25s. a week to each of them, and that each employer knows that every man is really worth 28s. a week to him, *i.e.* if he lost the services of one man, at the margin of a thousand, it would reduce his own incomings by 28s. a week. It follows that it would pay each of them to take on a certain number of extra hands, not only at 25s. but at anything short of 28s. So it is generally argued that each of the employers will compete for the men with the other until the wage is raised to 28s. But this is not really so; for, if an employer took on, say, a hundred more men at 26s. or 27s., he would have to raise the wages of the thousand men he already employs by one or two shillings each. He would, if he raised wages to 26s., get a hundred new men worth 28s. each for 26s. and so make a clear profit of £10 a week, but he would have to pay a thousand extra shillings a week to his present men, and so would lose a clear profit he is now making of £50. If he got the new men at 27s., the gain would be £5 and the loss £100. The employers, of course, perfectly understand this practically, and consequently there is an automatic lock on the competition of the large employers, without the necessity of any formal combination or agreement amongst them. They will decline to bid for a few extra men and a small extra profit which would involve a greatly increased expenditure. Each, then, will contentedly remain at the point at which he stands. Theoretically, it would seem, it is only where there is a fringe of small employers that there is any effective competition amongst those already in the trade. If a small man who is not employing any hands at all, or is only employing two or three, sees his way to taking a job that would employ ten men, and making £1 a week clear profit, he may bid for them. There will only be, at most, two or three shillings a week to set against the gain. He, therefore, might become an effective competitor for labour in the market. But if the business is one that it is difficult to enter without the expenditure of large capital and the lapse of considerable time, the established employers will be shielded for a considerable period against competition from fresh employers, who have not the choice between normal and abnormal profit in the business, but only between the normal profit and none at all. This seems to be the true economic justification of collective bargaining; for, if the hands are sure of their case, they can, by the threat of a strike, place before the established employer the alternative that would face him if he were thinking of entering the trade, namely, the payment of the economic wage of 28s., or ceasing to conduct the business at all.

But while discovering the economic justification of collective bargaining we have also unveiled the theoretical possibility of its being an economically destructive force; for the established employer is not, after all, in the position of the man who is thinking of entering the industry. His capital is not free for other alternatives, and it is conceivable that a powerful organisation may compel him to make such terms as would have precluded him from entering the industry and will preclude others from doing so. This course, if successfully maintained and persisted in, would ruin the industry. Hence, it would appear that the action of Trade Unions in demanding a rise or resisting a fall of wages is justified only when the ideal economic position coincides with their demands. And by the ideal economic position

I mean the position that would be determined by the marginal economic worth of every man if they all moved freely to the positions in which that worth was highest, depleting the less remunerative trades and so raising the marginal significance of labour in them and replenishing the more remunerative trades and so bringing down their marginal rewards to equality with those of the others. This being so, it is conceivable that an arbitrator or even a government official might be able to form a closer estimate of the actual economic position than would be arrived at by a combination of employers and a combination of employed trying their strength one against the other. On the other hand, it would be exceedingly dangerous to assume that this would be so, and only so far as it was so could the award be really effective; for, though it is conceivable that an external authority might determine that all persons employed in a certain industry should be paid at a certain rate, it would be impossible to enforce the employment of a given number of men at that rate. Men might turn to other employments, or employers might take on fewer hands, if the award did not correspond with the economic facts of the situation.

A number of questions arise in connection with the enforcement, whether by Unions or by the State, of a standard or minimum wage. If no one is to be employed in a certain industry at less than 28s. a week, then no one who is not deemed worth 28s. a week will be employed in that industry at all, and the ranks of the unemployed may be swelled. The unwillingness of employers to take on any but young men, and the cruel hardship suffered by men who have passed their full strength, because they cannot find employment at the standard wage and the employers are forbidden by the Unions to pay them anything less, is, with apparent justice, attributed to this cause. And all proposals for establishing a rigid minimum wage should take careful note of this. You cannot make a man worth a given wage by saying that he shall not be offered and shall not take any less. You rob him of such earnings as he could make and the community of such results as his labour could produce, and this sterilising of his powers of production seems to have no compensation. The Trade Unionists, as a body, appear to be convinced that allowing a man who is not worth the full wage to accept a lower remuneration would have a detrimental effect on their interests, but it is difficult to see any general principle on which this apprehension can be based; and possibly it may rest in part on that most natural, but socially most pernicious, conception, that we have spoken of elsewhere as the lump-of-labour theory.[1] The necessity of making some provision for their own members when out of work must act as a check upon powerful Trade Unions which might otherwise be tempted to maintain a wage which would involve extensive unemployment. Any proposal that relieves or tends to relieve those who have a powerful voice in fixing the rate of wages from this burden, so as to give the higher wage to those who are employed and throw the care for the unemployment it causes upon other shoulders, should be watched with the utmost jealousy.

And this brings us to our last series of remarks on the subject of Trade Unionism. If, and in so far as, the Trade Unions seek to limit their numbers, or to limit the output, and so to maintain their wage, they are seeking to establish themselves as privileged members of society, and are acting unsocially. And if, and in so far as, they successfully resist an access to their numbers which would reduce their marginal significance while increasing that of other groups (by hypothesis now lower than theirs), they are again acting unsocially, though naturally. Lastly, the justification of a strike must be that there are not a sufficient body of persons able and willing to do the work demanded at the wage offered. If the employers can find competent workers who will accept the wage they offer, that is an indication that, should the claims of the strikers be met, these others, able and willing to do the work on certain terms, would be driven to alternatives less eligible to themselves. And this, again, is establishing and maintaining a position of privilege to the detriment of the unprivileged workers. We are driven, therefore, to the hard saying that the hatred of the blackleg, however natural, has no social justification, and if ever a Union has to invoke

[1] Page 354.

public odium to assist it in defeating the blackleg, it seems to shew that its position is economically unsound. It is, of course, possible that the blacklegs, being inferior workmen, may really be less than worth their wage, so that permanent employment of them would be economically ruinous to the employer. In such cases the show of carrying on the business may be mere bluff, intended to demoralise the Unionists by a pretended independence of them. But, if the blacklegs are really doing the work, they are demonstrating that the Unionist claim is for a position of privilege and is anti-social. Acts of personal cruelty and spite in this connection are always formally condemned; but, under the impression (a mistaken one as I have tried to shew) that such acts are done in a good cause and are directed against men who are "traitors" not only to their own mates but to humanity, they are sometimes judged leniently or altogether condoned. If it is true that acts of cruelty and tyranny are largely practised, as is hotly asserted and as hotly denied, no one can be more interested in their extirpation than the leaders of the Trade Unions themselves.

CHAPTER III

CONCLUSION

SUMMARY.—*Unearned revenues of some kinds may be appropriated to public purposes, and exceptionally high private revenue of all kinds may be taxed, to a degree that cannot be theoretically determined beforehand, without detriment to the springs of industrial efficiency. A man's share in such public revenue may be independent of his economic worth. So far men may be required to give according to their means, and may receive according to their needs. But the economic forces tend to give every man what he is worth to others, neither less nor more. The economic problem of poverty, therefore, regarded as a part of the social problem, but not the whole of it, is the problem of making the "underpaid" worth more so that they will receive more under the pressure of the economic forces. This may be attempted by developing their powers, physical and mental, and by impartially securing access to opportunities. The consequent abolition or reduction of privilege may cut down many of the mighty from their seats, and exalt the humble. Preparing for the Kingdom.*

In a brief concluding chapter we may attempt to draw together the conclusions that are warranted by the whole course of our inquiry, so far as they bear upon the question of securing a less uneven distribution of wealth. Every one is shocked by the co-existence of luxurious wealth and hopeless poverty side by side. The time is gone for a fatalistic acquiescence. The warning that if we try to mend things we shall only make them worse is losing its terror. On the other hand the heyday of Utopias, in which both the conditions of life and human nature itself were to be completely revolutionised, seems to be passed. Few people are now either so certain that they will succeed or as much afraid of trying as they were even a few years ago. Increased intellectual caution and increased practical boldness seem to characterise the present in contrast with a very recent past. But theory may still be useful, partly in pointing out the most hopeful lines for experiment and yet more in enabling us to understand and profit by its results. It is true that an appalling sense of helplessness must often overwhelm the student as he contemplates the magnitude of the problems and the uncertainty and feebleness of the methods by which the attempt is being made to solve them; but a note of hopefulness can generally be heard from those who are most closely engaged in the actual battle, and who, one would think, have best reason to despair. To us, too, in all social matters hope is a "paramount duty," but so is a determination not to feed ourselves and others on illusions.

Setting aside more ambitious and revolutionary schemes, and taking it that the economic pressures, which urge every man to place himself under the conditions in which he will be useful to others, will remain the great moving forces of the industrial world, we ask how the general level of success in gaining a steady foothold in that industrial world may be raised, and how failure, rising from lack of opportunity, lack of capacity, or accident, may be robbed of its sting. The successful have always acknowledged some kind of obligation to the unsuccessful. Theoretically, no man need starve in our country, but until lately the public as distinct from the private provision for the defeated and unsuccessful has been consciously and intentionally grudging and reprobating. It has been thought that, dread of want being the great stimulus to effort, the natural or social penalties of failure may indeed be mitigated to some extent, but must not be allowed to become other than terrible. A marked change is coming over our feelings in this respect. It is already difficult to recover the attitude of mind in which it was seriously believed that the prospect of a workhouse, little short of penal in its regulations would create an energy and thrift which the prospect of an old age pension would hamstring.

But in what sense need there be any failures at all? What proportion of the failures are due to lack of opportunity? And how far need the success of one be accompanied not only by the relative but by the absolute failure of another? This is the problem to which we are now addressing ourselves, and there is a widely spread and still spreading conviction that the actual human material that comes into existence year by year is capable of indefinitely better development than it now receives, with indefinitely better results. We have seen reason to believe that some of the contemplated methods of amelioration are illusory, but the awakened spirit of humanity will not accept defeat. If our investigations have been in any degree enlightening, they will be forgiven for being sobering.

The central thesis of this book is that, so far as the economic forces work without friction, they secure to every one the equivalent of his industrial significance at the point of the industrial organism at which he is placed. The full and comprehending acceptance of this principle would at once dispel a number of hopes and banish a number of fears and scruples. It used to be maintained, for instance, that if the workers of the country had allotments, or if cheap baths and wash-houses were provided for them at the expense of the municipality, or if in any other way their condition were improved, their wages would automatically fall. Naturally it is true that if such improved conditions were extended to persons within a certain area, and were not available elsewhere, there would be a tendency to migrate to that area, and so to overstock the local markets of labour and reduce the wages there; but this would not be because the workers were better off, but because there were more of them without proportional increase in the other factors of industry. Again, we may set aside at a stroke the fear that old age pensions, for example, will lower the rate of wages by creating a set of persons who " can afford to work cheap." If men get what they are worth, and if the worth of a man who has 5s. a week safe is as high as that of one who has nothing, then he will receive as much. It may of course be true that he was receiving more than he earned because the payment was not wholly economic, and that when the obligation to keep the man's head above water is assumed by the State it is dropped by the individual. But that is another matter. And so far as any friction caused by imperfect markets and imperfect mobility has to be overcome, the man who has something to fall back upon will be better able to exact the payment for his full economic worth than the man who has nothing.

On the other hand the idea that life can be improved by a simple decree that higher wages shall be paid, in other words the hope of social regeneration by the enactment of a minimum wage, appears to be illusory. We have noted again and again that you cannot make a man worth so much a week by saying that he shall receive it, and that the economic forces will never induce any one to give a man more for his work than that work is worth to the giver. The only circumstances under which the enforcement of a minimum wage can be theoretically defended are when there is reason to believe that the economic conditions really justify a higher wage, but that friction and lethargy prevent the economic forces acting; or when the creation of a certain amount of unemployment is deliberately contemplated under the idea that it will be easier to deal with than a mass of employment at starvation wages. We start, then, from the thesis that if there are great bodies of persons in every country receiving starvation wages, it must be either because the economic forces cannot overcome certain frictions, or because the persons in question, under existing circumstances, are not industrially worth any more than they are receiving. If so, it is no use denouncing some one else for not giving them more than they are worth. We must either overcome the industrial frictions, or make them worth more where they are, or place them somewhere where they will be worth more. The steady tendency of present movements is to concentrate on the attempt to make them worth more. The cry for feeding school children, which defies all the wisdom of our fathers, justifies itself by pleading that ill-nourished children will be worth nothing, and, therefore, will get nothing, in the industrial world. This is only carrying a step further the principle that was acknowledged long ago in the State aid of education, and finally in the full acceptance of the national responsibility for the education of the people. But many are bitterly disappointed with the results of compulsory education and sceptical as to the value of our present methods, and are trying to conceive of a system of true education, at once industrial and human, that shall be a great instrument for training, sorting, and directing the faculties and developing the characters of the community, so as to make every talent available for the highest and most urgently needed function which it is capable of performing, and making every normally efficient man and woman worth enough at the margin to be able to command the means of a human life.

The "population question" in the old sense no longer troubles us. We have no fear of "population overtaking the means of subsistence" in the abstract. But it may well be that labour exchanges and emigration offices may have to be organised on an international scale to secure the due balance and distribution of efforts; and the growing belief that it is our collective duty to take charge in some way or other both of the children and of the unemployed directs many minds to speculate on the possible rise of the stupendous problem of the regulation of population in the not distant future. Only experience, however, can decide whether better conditions of life and a fuller sharing by the State of the responsibilities of the parent will really tend to stimulate, in any unmanageable degree, the multiplication of a helpless population. There are many reasons, to say the least, for gravely questioning it.

Meanwhile, we can already trace in the Allotments and Small Holdings Acts the feeble beginnings of a movement to open fresh opportunities, and to force, against the obstruction of prejudice or class jealousy, fresh channels through which the economic forces may beneficently flow.

The means for all these developments must be secured by a frank recognition of the claims of the unsuccessful and unfortunate upon the successful and the fortunate. The tax on "unearned increment" is an initial claim of the community on the unearned income which is perpetually flowing into private hands. And the super tax even on earned incomes, if they are sufficiently high, is an acknowledgment of the principle that success, as such, has its special duties. Our general principle will not incline us to fear that if success is "robbed of its reward," to a certain extent, it will cease to be attractive, and men will be too much discouraged to care to exert themselves. On the contrary, we have seen reason to believe[1] that the more highly a man is paid, the less work he is likely to wish to do for pay, so that in theory cumulative taxation should make men of exceptional ability and success more rather than less industrious. And surely we may hope (or at the very least we may "dream a dream of good" and be the better for it) that the time will come when a rich and successful man takes a pride in thinking that his direct public usefulness automatically increases with his growing command of resources for his private purposes.

We have already spoken of the fund, let us hope the growing fund, of public spirit which devotes administrative talent to the communal service.

But we, the privileged, must remember that if we are in earnest we are endeavouring to curtail or to abolish privilege. We are throwing open the preserves, and in proportion as we succeed in our endeavours, we and our children will have to take chances in a world that has no special care for us. We can contemplate the prospect without dismay if we believe that the lowest places in a regenerated industrial society will be places that can be filled with dignity and satisfaction, and will yield the conditions of a truly human life. So and only so can we accept without either terror or self-reproach a competitive system. We can only regard the highest success as an object of honourable ambition, if the failure to attain success does not involve the exclusion from all that makes life worth living.

And, finally, how are we individually to "prepare for the Kingdom"? By learning to find our chief delights in the things which all may share and which are the solace, not of our class, but of our humanity. By learning to rejoice in the common weal, and to respect and enjoy the communal property. By learning to feel that "keeping up appearances" is a sorry substitute for grasping realities which would cost the same sum. And above all by understanding that the

[1] See page 77.

relatively wealthy and successful man, by unconsciously shewing what the things for which he most cares really are, directs the ambitions and moulds the aspirations of those who have less power of realising their ideals than he has himself.

As the wealthy are called upon to bear more and more of the public burdens, as the privileged see their preserves invaded, as equality of opportunities more and more prevails, and men rank according to their worth, not according to their antecedents, there will be bitterness and indignation wherever the value of humanity has not come to be felt as higher than that of position. The triumph of a material democracy, without the corresponding spread of the democratic spirit, would cause acute distress and sense of wrong in the face of phenomena which would be hailed with heartfelt thankfulness were the democratic spirit penetratingly present.

THE END

Printed by R. & R. CLARK LIMITED, *Edinburgh.*

BY THE SAME AUTHOR

THE ALPHABET OF ECONOMIC SCIENCE. (1888.) 2s. 6d.

AN ESSAY ON THE CO-ORDINATION OF THE LAWS OF DISTRIBUTION. (1894.) 5s. (See note on page 373 of this volume.)

MACMILLAN AND CO., Ltd., LONDON.

WORKS ON POLITICAL ECONOMY

In Three Volumes. Medium 8vo. 21s. net each.

DICTIONARY OF POLITICAL ECONOMY

EDITED BY SIR R. H. INGLIS PALGRAVE.

Vol. I.—A to E.   Vol. II.—F to M.
Vol. III.—N to Z (With Corrections and New Appendix, 1908).

Appendix to Vol. III. separately, 2s. 6d. net.

PRINCIPLES OF ECONOMICS. By Professor ALFRED MARSHALL, M.A. 8vo. Vol. I. 12s. 6d. net.

ELEMENTS OF THE ECONOMICS OF INDUSTRY. By Professor ALFRED MARSHALL, M.A. Crown 8vo. 3s. 6d.

NATIONAL INDUSTRIES AND INTERNATIONAL TRADE. By Professor ALFRED MARSHALL, M.A. 8vo. [*In the Press.*

PUBLIC FINANCE. By Professor C. F. BASTABLE, M.A., LL.D. 8vo. 12s. 6d. net.

THE THEORY OF INTERNATIONAL TRADE WITH SOME OF ITS APPLICATIONS TO ECONOMIC POLICY. By Professor C. F. BASTABLE, M.A., LL.D. Crown 8vo. 3s. 6d. net.

THE PRINCIPLES OF POLITICAL ECONOMY. By Professor HENRY SIDGWICK. 8vo. 14s. net.

THE ECONOMIC ANNALS OF THE NINETEENTH CENTURY. By Professor WILLIAM SMART. Part I. 1801-1820. 8vo. [*In the Press.*

THE DISTRIBUTION OF INCOME. By Professor WILLIAM SMART. Extra Crown 8vo. 5s. net.

THE RETURN TO PROTECTION. By Professor WILLIAM SMART. Crown 8vo. 3s. 6d. net.

MACMILLAN AND CO., LTD., LONDON.

ImTheStory.com

Personalized Classic Books in many genre's

Unique gift for kids, partners, friends, colleagues

Customize:

- Character Names
- Upload your own front/back cover images (optional)
- Inscribe a personal message/dedication on the inside page (optional)

Customize many titles Including
- Alice in Wonderland
- Romeo and Juliet
- The Wizard of Oz
- A Christmas Carol
- Dracula
- Dr. Jekyll & Mr. Hyde
- And more...

CPSIA information can be obtained at www.ICGtesting.com
Printed in the USA
LVOW10s1128110316

478694LV00051B/967/P